DATE DUE

DEMCO 38-297

TAKING IT LIKE A MAN

WHITE MASCULINITY,
MASOCHISM, AND
CONTEMPORARY
AMERICAN CULTURE

DAVID SAVRAN

PRINCETON UNIVERSITY PRESS

PRINCETON, NEW JERSEY

5/98

\# 37567432

Library of Congress Cataloging-in-Publication Data

Savran, David, 1950–
Taking it like a man : white masculinity, masochism,
and contemporary American culture / David Savran.
p.   cm.
Includes bibliographical references and index.
ISBN 0-691-01637-2 (cloth : alk. paper).
ISBN 0-691-05876-8 (pbk. : alk. paper)
1. White men—United States.   2. Masculinity—United States.
3. Men in popular culture—United States.   4. Men in
literature.   5. Masochism—United States.   6. Reverse
discrimination—United States.   I. Title.
HQ1090.3.S28   1998
305.31′0973—dc21   97-39856

This book has been composed in Times Roman

The lost paradises are the only true ones not because, in retrospect, the past joy seems more beautiful than it really was, but because remembrance alone provides the joy without the anxiety over its passing and thus gives it an otherwise impossible duration. Time loses its power when remembrance redeems the past.

Still, this defeat of time is artistic and spurious; remembrance is no real weapon unless it is translated into historical action. Then, the struggle against time becomes a decisive moment in the struggle against domination. . . .

—Herbert Marcuse, *Eros and Civilization*

CONTENTS

ACKNOWLEDGMENTS

DURING the five years I have spent working on this book, I have received tremendous encouragement and help from a great many people. I first want to thank my tireless research assistants, Ed Brockenbrough, Rhett Landrum, Sianne Ngai, Lloyd Pratt, and Jesse Wennik; as well as the participants in the Lesbian/Gay Seminar and the Psychoanalysis and Culture Seminar at Harvard's Center for Literary and Cultural Studies, especially Michael Bronski, Carolyn Dean, Lisa Duggan, Barbara Freeman, and Phillip Brian Harper. My gratitude to the Rockefeller Foundation for a residency at the Bellagio Study and Conference Center where I had the decidedly peculiar pleasure of waking every morning in one of the most beautiful settings on earth to write about William Burroughs's tortured prose. My appreciation to the other residents during my 1995 stay, especially Herb Kutchins and Helene Keyssar, and to my friends Ken Aptekar, Michèle Dominy, David Hult, Saul Olyan, Gwendolyn Parker, Joseph Roach, John Rouse, and Ralph Wushke. I also want to thank A. Deborah Malmud at Princeton University Press, the Press's readers—Sue-Ellen Case, Susan Jeffords, and W. B. Worthen—for their incisive feedback, and Lauren Lepow for her peerless editing.

At Brown University many colleagues and students have been enormously generous and helpful over the years. I want in particular to thank my colleagues Nancy Armstrong, Mary Ann Doane, Coppélia Kahn, Neil Lazarus, Ellen Rooney, Philip Rosen, Paula Vogel, and Elizabeth Weed; and students and former students Melanie Breen, Mark Cohen, Peter Cohen, Mark Cooper, Steven Evans, Loren Noveck, Susan Schmeiser, Bradford Simpson, and Todd Ziegler. My gratitude to the participants in the 1996 Senior Seminar in Sexuality and Society and the members of my class on Masculinity and Cultural Production, especially Terry Costello, Jane Fronek, Jed Herman, Courtney Kemp, Marshall Miller, Kerry Quinn, and Austin Winsberg.

Portions of this book have been previously published in some form. Part of chapter 5 appeared in *Theatre Journal* 47 (1995) and a part of chapter 3 in *differences: A Journal of Feminist Cultural Studies* 8, no. 2 (1996).

I want to thank Keith Mayerson for his brilliant play *A Child Is Being Beaten*, which, when I directed it in 1988, first spurred me on to read Freud's essay of the same title and to recognize my fascination with masochistic fantasies and practices. My appreciation to Ronn Smith for his keen editorial skills and tremendous support over the years. Finally, my thanks to Scott Teagarden who, more than anyone else, has helped turn pain into pleasure.

TAKING IT LIKE A MAN

INTRODUCTION

> We don't like what is going on now, and we do know we don't have
> any future. As social power decreases faster and faster, state power
> increases faster and faster. And we see ourselves, if you will pardon
> the expression, as the new niggers.
>
> *(Tom Metzgar, leader of the White Aryan Resistance [1995])*

> So there was a new breed of adventurers, urban adventurers who
> drifted out at night looking for action with a black man's code to
> fit their facts. The hipster had absorbed the existentialist synapses
> of the Negro, and for practical purposes could be considered a
> white Negro.
>
> *(Norman Mailer, "The White Negro" [1957])*

MUCH TO THE chagrin of U.S. pundits and politicians, the 1995
bombing of the Alfred P. Murrah Federal Building in Oklahoma
City turned out to be the act not of fervid Libyan or Iraqi terrorists
but of true-blue, all-American patriots. The arrests of Timothy McVeigh and
Terry Nichols on charges of planting a homemade explosive device that killed
168 people (on the second anniversary of the siege of the Branch Davidians at
Waco) threw a lurid spotlight on the so-called Patriot movement, a loose alliance of right-wing, antifederalist religious and constitutional fundamentalists.
According to observers, the movement may number as many as five million
followers and ranges from the almost respectable John Birch Society to the
armed militias now found in all fifty states, from the extreme Christian evangelical Right to avowed white supremacist and anti-Semitic groups like the
White Aryan Resistance, the Ku Klux Klan, and the Southern White Knights.[1]
Despite their sometimes contradictory social and political agendas, these
groups invariably deplore the sprawling, corporatist state as well as federal
restrictions (especially gun control and affirmative action) on what they claim
to be inalienable rights. They are populated overwhelmingly by white, heterosexual, working- and lower-middle-class men who believe themselves to be
the victims of the scant economic and social progress made in the United
States over the past thirty years by African Americans, women, and other racial, ethnic, and sexual minorities. Trading places, rhetorically at least, with
the people they loathe, they imagine themselves (through a kind of psychic
prestidigitation) the new persecuted majority or, in the words of one zealot,
"the new niggers."[2]

While Timothy McVeigh and Terry Nichols are awaiting trial (and I am
writing these words), the U.S. press teems with stories about the so-called

white male backlash of which the Patriot movement is only the most glaring example. Affirmative action is under fire both locally and nationally on many fronts, from the grotesquely misnamed California Civil Rights Initiative (Proposition 209) to the Clinton White House.[3] Patrick Buchanan garners electoral victories and credibility in the media by his appeal to racists and disaffected antifederalists. Immigrants, both legal and illegal, are harassed and beaten.[4] Welfare is under attack. Assorted conspiracy theorists, antitax protesters, and apocalyptic millennialists hole up in Idaho, Montana, or Texas awaiting either the end of the world or the FBI. And although these different phenomena are not routinely considered by the press to be symptoms of the white male backlash, I believe they all represent an attempt on the part of white men to recoup the losses they have allegedly suffered at the hands of those women and persons of color who, in fact, have had to pay for the economic and social prosperity that white men have historically enjoyed. The very diversity of these phenomena announces the ascendancy of a new and powerful figure in U.S. culture: the white male as victim.

Some thirty-eight years before the Oklahoma City bombing, however, Norman Mailer described a very different kind of oppressed white male whom he styled "the white Negro." In a groundbreaking and trenchant cultural critique, Mailer analyzed a new figure on the U.S. cultural stage: the hipster, "the American existentialist," the new "frontiersman in the Wild West of American night life."[5] For Mailer, the hipster—whom he assumes to be both male and white—rebels against a society that guarantees "a slow death by conformity," and, abjuring his race and class privilege, voluntarily takes up a "Negro" positionality.[6] Like the psychopath, he is "a rebel without a cause, an agitator without a slogan," a creature devoted to the "immediate satisfaction" of his every desire.[7] Yet unlike the contemporary White Aryan Resister, who longs nostalgically for a homogeneous America that never existed, the hipster is hailed as the man of the future who, Mailer notes intriguingly, "is equally a candidate for the most reactionary and most radical of movements."[8] If Mailer is correct on that score, it is because the hipster serves historically as the godfather of both the political and social revolutionaries of the 1960s and the partisans of the Patriot movement.

Taking It Like a Man is an analysis of this contradiction, an attempt to understand the peculiarly bifurcated evolution of the white hipster and why, in particular, his "most radical" promise has been extinguished. It constructs a genealogy of the fantasy of the white male as victim, beginning with his appearance on the U.S. cultural scene in the 1950s and ending with his transformation into a number of disparate but related figures (both fictional and nonfictional) who have of late assumed rather high profiles in U.S. culture: Rambo, Iron John, Forrest Gump, and Timothy McVeigh. It is an attempt to explain why, some forty years after the Beats, in Allen Ginsberg's words, first assailed "Moloch" as the deity presiding over a land "whose blood is running money" and "whose breast is a cannibal dynamo,"[9] Ginsberg peddles for the Gap, William Burroughs hawks for Nike, and "hip" has become "the orthodoxy of Information Age capitalism."[10] It argues that a marginalized and dissident masculinity of the 1950s has become increasingly central and hegemonic in U.S. culture. It documents the transformation of the discontented white hipster (and, later, the rebellious hippie or political radical) into several variations upon the theme of the white male as victim: the angry white male, the sensitive male, the male searching for the Wild Man within, the white supremacist, the spiritual male.

The turning point in this book's narrative is surely what is so often called the end of the '60s: the splintering and collapse of the New Left, the victory of Richard Nixon's "silent majority," and the ascendancy of identity politics and various cultural nationalisms (most notably Women's Liberation, Black Power, and the gay and lesbian liberation movement). On the cultural front, this turning point coincided with the popularity of Dennis Hopper's *Easy Rider* (1969), the rise of so-called blaxploitation films, and the Charles Manson murders of 1969, which, not unlike the Oklahoma City bombing, revealed the homicidal potential of paranoid white men and bore out Mailer's portrait of the hipster as psychopath. And although the savageries of Manson's "family" may have stoked the popular imagination, the fantasy of the white male as victim surely crystallized most sharply in the person of Allan Bakke, an ex-marine and Vietnam veteran, who in 1974 brought a lawsuit against the University of California for twice denying him admission to its medical school at Davis. Insisting that the university's quota system for racial minorities violated his constitutional rights, Bakke styled himself a victim of discrimination. Four years later the Supreme Court supported his claim, and the white male as victim became an increasingly visible and belligerent figure on the U.S. cultural stage. In analyzing these events and cultural texts, this book is suggesting neither that racism and nativism are recent inventions nor that they do not have long, tortuous, and violent histories in the United States. Rather, it argues that a new masculinity became hegemonic in the 1970s because it represents an attempt by white men to respond to and regroup in the face of particular social and economic challenges: the reemergence of the feminist movement; the limited success of the civil rights movement in redressing gross historical inequities through affirmative action legislation; the rise of the lesbian and gay rights movements; the failure of America's most disastrous imperialistic adventure, the Vietnam War; and, perhaps most important, the end of the post–World War II economic boom and the resultant and steady decline in the income of white working- and lower-middle-class men.

In constructing a genealogy of the white male as victim, *Taking It Like a Man* argues that with the erosion of the modernist divide between mass and elite culture, with the development of niche marketing, with the unprecedented monopolization of the media and a decentralization of U.S. culture (the collapse of the studio system, the proliferation of cable TV stations, the end of Top 40 radio, the Internet explosion),[11] what began as a minor and adversarial social and literary movement has developed into the new orthodoxy of post–Cold War America. As a result, the nature of the cultural texts I survey necessarily shifts, from the relatively specialized and marginalized works of the Beats (mainly Burroughs, Ginsberg, and Kerouac) and the experiments of The Living Theatre to the rise of movie stars (and masculine icons) like Sam Shepard, Sylvester Stallone, Michael Douglas, and Tom Hanks. And although I examine a great diversity of documents here, all of them can be understood (in one way or another) as performance texts. In the plays and films, the visuality and materiality of performers are obviously crucial for the production of gendered and racialized identities.[12] But even the narrative fictions, poems, and other social texts analyzed in this book are sites in which and through which masculinities are regulated, iterated, and performed. Moreover, all the texts analyzed in this book are situational; they function as cultural (and commercial) transactions, as enunciatory acts through which a speaker or writer addresses a real or imagined audience, performs certain specific tasks, and takes up an implied (and often contradictory) gendered and racialized identity.

Taking It Like a Man focuses on this diversity of fictions as well as what are ostensibly nonfictional texts—essays, biographies, autobiographies, legal decisions, and reportage—neither to assert an equivalency between literature and the discourses of civil society, nor to dissolve the distinctions between these different kinds of texts. Rather, I hope to demonstrate that social, political, and economic initiatives are always constructed as narratives and that cultural texts simultaneously shape, consolidate, and reflect diverse subjectivities and social practices. For Raymond Williams is certainly correct to note the totalizing effects of media culture, that under late capitalism "cultural work and activity" by no means represent, "in any ordinary sense, a superstructure." Rather, "they are among the basic processes of the [social and economic] formation itself and, further, [are] related to a much wider area of reality than the abstractions of 'social' and 'economic' experience."[13] Literary and cultural texts, in other words, because of their high entertainment value and their success in engineering consent ("that was real!"), are decisive for the ongoing production of hegemony, which, in Williams's celebrated formulation,

> sees the relations of domination and subordination, in their forms as practical consciousness, as in effect a saturation of the whole process of living—not only of political and economic activity, nor only of manifest social activity, but of the whole substance of lived identities and relationships. . . . Hegemony is then not only the articulate upper level of "ideology," nor are its forms of control only those ordinarily seen as "manipulation" or "indoctrination." It is a whole body of practices and expectations, over the whole of living: our senses and assignments of energy, our

shaping perceptions of ourselves and our world. It is a lived system of meaning and values—constitutive and constituting—which as they are experienced as practices appear as reciprocally confirming. . . . It is, that is to say, in the strongest sense a "culture," but a culture which has also to be seen as the lived dominance and subordination of particular classes.[14]

As Williams suggests, hegemony represents "a lived system" in which values are constantly being reproduced and contested. It is a site of struggle in which both popular and elite cultural texts do not function merely as passive reflections of some allegedly preexistent, autonomous social reality. Rather, they actively participate in the production of "the whole substance of lived identities and relationships." They also engage in an ongoing debate on the future of political culture, on the configuration of personal and collective identities, and on the constitution of the nation. Indeed, fictional texts, I believe, are particularly important for the production of hegemony, representing sites at which a wide range of ideologies and values can be visualized, reaffirmed, and challenged.

For the purposes of this book, the central structural inquality in U.S. society is taken to be the difference between masculinity and femininity. And the primary focus of my analysis is the cultural construction of men—the primary but by no means exclusive exemplars of masculinity—as a dominant class. Yet having made this assertion, I want immediately to qualify it in four ways: first, by noting that masculinity and femininity do not represent a simple binary opposition. Rather, as Eve Sedgwick notes (drawing on the work of Sandra Bem), they are orthogonal to each other, "in different, perpendicular dimensions, and therefore . . . independently variable."[15] As many cultural productions suggest, a subject may be coded as being both masculine and feminine at the same time. Moreover, the proliferation of more subtle and insinuatingly judgmental adjectives for characterizing gender—*effeminate, macho, femme, butch,* etc.—complicates the assignment of any gendered identity. The spectacularized male, for example, that features so prominently in many action films of the 1980s and 1990s is feminized insofar as he is constructed as an object of the cinematic gaze, yet, as a rule, he aggressively resists an effeminizing logic (with its suggestions of sexual deviance). Masculinity is thus, like femininity, a complex and unstable concept, "a vexed term," in the words of the editors of a recent anthology, "variously inflected, multiply defined, not limited to straightforward descriptions of maleness."[16] Or as Freud tersely puts it, "the concepts 'masculine' and 'feminine' . . . are among the most confused that appear in science."[17]

Second, masculinity and femininity are always embodied characteristics and, as such, are continually being constructed in relation to other visible (and invisible) categories that are taken to define the subject—especially race, social class, and sexual orientation. It is a central thesis of this book that racial difference, in particular, is a powerful force for the production of any gendered identification and that the latter, in fact, remains incomprehensible unless understood, like Mailer's (white) hipster, as an implicitly racialized term. But a racialized category is not simply to be added to gender. For gender is always articulated *through* race, through possibilities opened up by particular racial identities. And class and sexual orientation are arguably just as crucial. Thus, for example, working-class masculinities since World War II, although sharing many characteristics with those of the professional-managerial class, have also been historically distinct (and this difference is particularly important in a society in which class distinctions generally tend to be ignored). Moreover, the production of gender is deeply bound up with what Judith Butler calls the "heterosexual matrix," the "grid of cultural intelligibility through which bodies, genders, and desires are naturalized," a grid whose intelligibility is based in the practices and ideologies of compulsory heterosexuality.[18] Both normative and dissident masculinities cannot be understood, then, unless analyzed in relation to the dynamics and regularizing force of the heterosexual matrix.

Three, masculinity and femininity are always historically contingent, always in the process of being reimagined and redefined according to changing material conditions. And despite the continuing existence of bodies styled male and female, despite the long history of the identification of phallicism with masculinity, there is no transhistorical essence of masculinity or femininity. Even the phallus—and patriarchy, of which it is a prop—is a historical construction, a fiction of sorts, which retains its power only insofar as it denies its own historicity. Moreover, I would like to suggest that a gendered identity, on account of its contingency, is of all identifications the one most subject to intensive social pressures, the most anxiety-ridden, the most consistently lubricated in social, political, and economic negotiations, and thus the most sensitive barometer of culture.

And this assertion brings me to point four: gender is always an imaginary identification. It is based not on an allegedly universal sexual dimorphism but on fantasy. For as feminist biologists have demonstrated, sexual dimorphism is itself not a "fact of nature" but a historical and social construction.[19] As such, gender is always, as Judith Butler has rather famously observed, *performative* and stabilized through repetition. "Gender," in her words, is "acquired" and always "assumed in relation to ideals that are never quite inhabited by anyone."[20] An imitation of an imitation, it "is always a doing, though not a doing by a subject who might be said to preexist the deed."[21] Rather, because the subject is constituted by the very act of performing gender, it is not necessary that "the construction of 'men' will accrue exclusively to the bodies of males or that 'women' will interpret only female bodies."[22] Yet gender, as she emphasizes, is not volitional but coercive. It is not something that one chooses innocently, as one chooses a shirt from one's closet, but "a regulatory ideal whose materialization is compelled, and this materialization takes place (or fails to take place) through certain highly regulated practices."[23]

I aim in this book both to denominate the highly regulated performances and practices of white masculinity and to analyze the cultural texts in which they are embedded. Because of my dedication to questions of historicity, I am particularly concerned—unlike Butler—to investigate the conditions of performance: the multiple social positionalities of the performer (rather than his or her intentions), the discursive strategies put into play by the performance, and the reception of said performance.[24] I aim, in short, to write a materialist history of the performance of white masculinities.

From Erotic Flagellation to Masochism

Why masochism? Why does a condition that was first labeled a psychosexual pathology at the end of the nineteenth century become the privileged instrument for an analysis of white masculinities at the end of the twentieth? Given the protracted history of the identification of masochism with femininity—and sadism with masculinity—this privileging seems perhaps, at best, counterintuitive; at worst, positively perverse. Yet this book consistently attempts to demonstrate that modern white masculinities are deeply contradictory, eroticizing submission and victimization while trying to retain a certain aggressively virile edge, offering subjects positions that have been marked historically as being both masculine and feminine, white and black. In analyzing these subjectivities, I have found the tools of psychoanalysis indispensible, drawing in particular on Freud and a number of more recent theorists who have revised the Freudian paradigms, especially Leo Bersani, Gilles Deleuze, Theodor Reik, and Kaja Silverman. The work of these latter has in many ways enabled my own, despite my serious concerns about its ability to grapple with and answer what for me are in essence historical questions. Of all these theorists, Silverman is certainly the most sensitive to questions of cultural application, attempting explicitly to historicize her analyses through the concept (borrowed from Louis Althusser) of "the dominant fiction," which is to say, the "ideological 'reality'" of a particular era that she takes to be historically produced. This fiction is maintained, she argues, through a system of "*collective* belief," through an elaboration of fantasy that represents "in some ultimate sense reality for the subject . . . because it articulates . . . our symbolic positionality, and the *mise-en-scène* of our desire."[25] And while I find her emphasis on the structure of fantasy crucial for an analysis of gendered differences, the unremittingly universalizing tendencies of psychoanalysis—at least as she uses it—and her disdain for "economic determinism" make it impossible for her to speculate on causality, to sustain an analysis of modes of production, or to offer any systematic periodization.[26] Thus, for example, her analysis of the deployment of racial categories in the work of T. E. Lawrence is based far more on details of Lawrence's biography than on the structure and history of British imperialism.[27] Similarly, her concept of "historical trauma" (based on Freud's notion of "war trauma"), used to explicate the crisis of post–World War II masculinity, disallows a consideration that the crisis might have material as well as psychological causes.[28] She does not make note, for instance, of the massive shifts in the employment of women following the war, or the development of consumer capitalism, or the rapid growth of the professional-managerial class. Rather than illuminate the complex workings of social process, her concept of "historical trauma" becomes a substitute for an engagement with a set of unprecedented social and economic redistributions.

In its analysis of masochistic masculinities, *Taking It Like a Man* is an attempt to press psychoanalysis into service for a historical project. It endeavors to explain, as Abigail Solomon-Godeau puts it, "the circumstances and determinations that at different historical moments promote one fantasy of masculinity over another."[29] For psychoanalysis, which was developed as the "science" of fantasy, desire, and sexual difference, still provides, I believe, the most compelling tools for an analysis of any and all gendered identifications, based as they are on fantasy, desire, and disavowal. And while I continually deploy the categories of psychoanalysis in this book, I hope at the same time to use them with some awareness of the fact that they are historical constructions, and to reveal their complicity with a particular history of the subject. Before turning to Freud, by far the most important and influential theorist of masochism, I want to provide a brief history of masochism—and its antecedent, erotic flagellation—and to link that history with the rise of the bourgeois subject. I hope thereby to demonstrate that masochism is not the perversion that late-nineteenth-century sexologists considered it to be. Nor is it the form of false consciousness it was—and is—widely imagined to be, whether by the antipornography feminists of the 1980s, or by certain well-intentioned liberals today. It is, rather, part of the very structure of male subjectivity as it was consolidated in western Europe during the early modern period.

Richard von Krafft-Ebing coined the word *masochism* in 1886, basing it on the surname of Leopold von Sacher-Masoch, whose 1870 novel, *Venus in Furs*, furnished Krafft-Ebing with a model for masochistic sexual practices. In his encyclopedic *Psychopathia Sexualis*, he categorized masochism as one of the many "perversions" (or nonprocreative sexualities) and used it to signify the condition of a person who exacts sexual pleasure from pain, humiliation, and abuse. He regarded it as a congenital condition, developed out of a "hereditarily tainted individuality," and he diagnosed varying degrees of the "perversion," ranging from "the most repulsive and monstrous to the silliest."[30] Most important, he regarded it not as a prelude to genital sexual intercourse but as an end in itself, a self-contained erotic formula.

For Krafft-Ebing, as for most theorists of sexuality both before and after Freud, masochism is classified in relation to its ostensible "opposite," sadism, which Krafft-Ebing describes as "the experience of sexual pleasurable sensations (including orgasm) produced by acts of cruelty."[31] In his *Psychopathia*, he defines masochism as

> a peculiar perversion of the psychical *vita sexualis* in which the individual affected, in sexual feeling and thought, is controlled by the idea of being completely and unconditionally subject to the will of a person of the opposite sex; of being treated by this person as by a master, humiliated and abused. This idea is colored by lustful feeling; the masochist lives in fancies, in which he creates situations of this kind and often attempts to realize them.[32]

According to Krafft-Ebing (and Freud after him), this "perversion" is first and foremost a psychological disturbance that is characterized by its ability to transform humiliation, abuse, and pain into sexual pleasure. Second, masochism always partakes of a dualistic sexual economy in which passive and active agents are clearly differentiated. In comparison with Freud, Krafft-Ebing sees both categories as relatively fixed and envisions little likelihood of slippage or role reversal. Rather, he underscores the imputedly binary structure of sadomasochism by inscribing it within compulsory heterosexuality. Third, according to Krafft-Ebing, masochism is understood to be preeminently a fantasmatic process that may, but need not, lead to an acting out. His stress on the fantasmatic, moreover, implies that masochism is always already narrativized by the subject, replete with a scenario and dramatis personae. As later theorists have noted, it is thus incontestably the most dramatic and theatrical of the "perversions"—in its reliance upon suspense, upon the development of a plot to an inexorable *jouissance* (or peripeteia), and in its necessarily performative mode.[33] To invert Laura Mulvey's celebrated declaration: masochism demands a story.[34]

Yet Krafft-Ebing's *Psychopathia*, for all its exhaustive systematization, is merely one in a long history of texts that analyze the transformation of physical pain into sexual pleasure. In 1629, a German physician, Johann Heinrich Meibom, wrote the first treatise devoted to a study of practices that, through a kind of sexual alchemy, perform this transformation. Meibom's slim volume, *De Flagrorum Usu in Re Veneria & Lumborum Renumque Officio* (On the use of rods in venereal matters and in the office of the loins and reins), at once became an authoritative text and was widely cited for two hundred years. In his treatise, Meibom attempts both to prove that flagellation acts as an incentive to erection and to elucidate the anatomical intricacies of the process. Surveying various historical and literary accounts (from contemporary and classical sources), he maintains "that there are Persons who are stimulated to *Venery by Strokes of Rods, and worked up into a Flame of Lust by Blows*; and that the *Part*, which distinguishes us to be *Men*, should be raised by the Charm of invigorating Lashes."[35] In Meibom's treatise, erotic flagellation is less an end in itself (as it becomes for Krafft-Ebing) than an incitement to erection and further sexual adventure.

Meibom then attempts to answer the question that has preoccupied all theorists of masochism since: how is it that "Pain" is experienced by the flagellant as "Pleasure"? To answer, Meibom appeals not to psychology but to a mechanistic model of male sexual arousal (Meibom's text attests to the hegemony of the pre-Enlightenment one-sex model in which female is understood as being merely a variation on a primary male anatomy).[36] He explains that semen is produced near the kidneys and that it descends, when heated and excited, to the testicles. Because in some men, however, the vesicles remain inexplicably cold, these poor creatures require flagellation of the lower back and buttocks to revitalize the semen.

> It is no wonder that such shameless Wretches, Victims of a detested Appetite, . . . have sought a Remedy by FLOGGING. For 'tis very probable, that the refrigerated Parts grow warm by such Stripes, . . . from the Pain of the *flogg'd* Parts, . . . 'till the Heat is communicated to the Organs of Generation, and the perverse and frenzical Appetite is satisfied, and Nature, tho' unwilling drawn beyond the Stretch of her common Power, to the Commission of such an abominable Crime.[37]

Although Meibom argues that flogging is necessary for the attainment of erection in certain "Wretches," his treatise testifies to the status, even in the mid-seventeenth century, of erotic flagellation as "an abominable Crime," the product of a "perverse and frenzical Appetite" that has the effect (as it will for so many later theorists) of feminizing the male subject, consigning him to the domain of impotence, passivity, and submission. Furthermore, although other seventeenth-century accounts of flagellation, both historical and pornographic, attest to women's "perverse" enjoyment of the sport, Meibom's irreducibly male paradigm completely ignores it.

The second major treatise on flagellation was published in 1700, the Abbé Boileau's *Historia Flagellantium, de recto e perverso flagrorum usu apud Christiano* (The history of the flagellants, and of the correct and perverse use of rods among Christians). In this rather more extensive volume, the Abbé speaks out against the use of the rod, arguing that the obsessive self-flagellation (or performance of "*Disciplines*") observed in the contemporary church was a recent invention, "unknown in the happy periods of the primitive Church" and contrary to the will of God. Providing a flagellatory typology, he distinguishes between flogging "the bare back or shoulders," which he calls the "*upper*" discipline, and "the posteriors," which he names "the *lower* discipline."[38] Drawing on Meibom's anatomical studies, he finds "the lower discipline" particularly vexing and hazardous, the prime exemple of the "perverse use of rods" noted in the title of his book. And because he too uses the one-sex model, he never explicitly analyzes the delight experienced by the many female flagellants in his volume (as is so often the case in discourses on sex and sexuality, female pleasure is erased). The 1777 English edition, whose translation and annotation are attributed to John Lois Delolme, is filled with references to and descriptions of flagellatory practices that date back to antiquity. And although both writer and annotator dignify their discourse with countless literary illustrations (from the works of La Fontaine, Cervantes, Molière, Fielding, and many others), they condemn erotic flagellation both as an end in itself and as a stimulant to genital intercourse.

In 1788 François-Amedée Doppet published the next major scientific work on flagellation, the *Aphrodisiaque externe, ou Traité du fouet et de ses effets sur le physique de l'amour* (Exterior aphrodisiac, or treatise on the whip and its effects on the physics of love). Unlike the Abbé Boileau, Doppet was more concerned with pedagogical than ecclesiastical flagellation, forcefully recommending that flogging the naked buttocks of children be curtailed because it functions, dangerously and prematurely, as a sexual stimulant. He takes issue with Meibom's anatomy, opining that "the lower discipline" is erotically stimulating not because of seminal vesicles in the back but because of the proximity between buttocks and genitals. Doppet decries the whipping of children because the "interest in the buttocks often leads to children whipping each other, to fondling and masturbation." Furthermore, noting a strikingly homosexual complexion to the flagellation of children, he believes that some teachers' "sodomitic inclinations" lead them "positively [to] enjoy whipping their pupils on the buttocks."[39]

The nineteenth century witnessed the gradual transformation of sex into sexuality, erotic flagellation into masochism.[40] As David Halperin points out (elaborating on Foucault), the modern notion of sexuality—as opposed to sex—is predicated on two assumptions: first, upon "the eighteenth-century discovery and definition of sexuality as the total ensemble of physiological and psychological mechanisms governing the individual's genital functions," and second, upon "the nineteenth-century interpretation of sexuality as a singular 'instinct' or 'drive,' a force that shapes our conscious life according to its own unassailable logic and thereby determines, at least in part, that character and personality of each of us." By the time of Krafft-Ebing and Freud, sexuality had been linked to a metaphysics of depth in which it was defined as *the truth*, the foundation of identity, the "inmost part" of the human subject. As Halperin emphasizes, "Sexuality holds the key to unlocking the deepest mysteries of the human personality: it lies at the center of the hermeneutics of the self."[41] The extraordinary proliferation of sexological texts increasingly situated flagellation among other so-called perversions that describe and prescribe particular "hermeneutics of the self" (Krafft-Ebing clearly marks the culmination of this taxonomic fervor).[42] Although most writers followed the lead of Meibom and Doppet, they underscored the imputed perversity of flagellation by their adoption of a new familial ideology intent on eradicating all sexual practices except heterosexual genital intercourse between married partners. Their emphasis on reproduction, coupled with their increasing psychologization of the subject, marks, in fact, the most important distinction between the discourses of erotic flagellation and masochism. As nineteenth-century physicians brought the sexuality of children under particularly close scrutiny, they inevitably linked the flogging of children to masturbatory practices. William Acton, for example, insists that "whipping children [i.e., boys] on the nates . . . has a great influence in exciting ejaculation." As the case of Jean-Jacques Rousseau so eloquently demonstrates, flogging is the "first incitement to masturbation," which, he warns, is extremely hazardous, leading inevitably to the failure of a boy's health and the dimming of his "intellectual powers."[43] Foucault points out, however, that this concerted and notorious campaign against masturbation in Europe and America was less committed to actually suspending the practice than to using "these tenuous pleasures as a *prop*" by which to vindicate an entire medico-sexual field of discourse and an elaborate system of surveillance.[44] The categorization, pathologization, and criminalization of nonreproductive sexual practices gave the nineteenth-century state apparatus an unparalleled level of control over the sexuality of both children and adults and, as a result, over the propagation of the labor force during a period of unprecedented industrial and imperial expansion.

A résumé of treatises from Meibom to Krafft-Ebing, written between the heyday of mercantile capitalism and the height of the industrial revolution, testifies both to the widespread observance of erotic flagellation and to the deeply problematic and vexing status of this practice. Dating back to the mid-seventeenth century, the application of rods to incite erection or produce sexual pleasure was seen as being deeply contradictory, dangerous, and "perverse," that is, "turned away from the right way or from what is right or good (*OED*). And while some writers, like the Abbé Boileau, attempt scrupulously (as the title of his treatise suggests) to differentiate the "correct" from the "perverse," the distinction becomes in his text more and more inadvertently problematized. In attempting to distinguish the dangers of "the lower discipline" from the relative decorousness of the "upper," the text testifies ironically to the inextricable linkage between the two in the history of flagellation and to the fact that the "perverse" is always inscribed within its presumed opposite, the "correct." The former constantly threatens and taunts the latter, but it can never be expunged from the field of sexual discourse because its erasure would destroy the very meaning and moral force of the "correct." In his rereading of Freud's theory of perversion, Jonathan Dollimore emphasizes the constitutive role of the perverse in constructing normative models of sexuality. He notes that culture always "exists in a relationship of difference with the alien, which is also a relationship of fundamental, antagonistic, discursive dependence."[45] In matters of sex and sexuality—at least since the seventeenth century—European culture has positioned the alien simultaneously in the margins of the dominant social formation (in liminal subcultures and dissident subjects), at the geographical periphery (in "the New World" or "the Orient"), and within the human subject. While the two former figurations are linked to some of the most murderous chapters in Western history, the last has proven the more scandalous ontologically: the recognition, far more frequently disavowed than professed, that the other is sited ineluctably within the self. The Abbé Boileau may not like or countenance erotic flagellation, but he can no more do without it than the saint can the "pervert."

Connected to this radical interdependence of the "correct" and the "perverse" is perhaps the most extraordinary feature of both the early treatises on erotic flagellation and more recent discourses on masochism. In even the most narrowly moralistic, sanctimonious, or medicalizing of them, in the descriptions of even the most pious flagellations by the most ascetic of flagellants, the pain of the whip is obsessively ghosted by sexual pleasure. And it is at this point that I would like to offer a redefinition of terms and argue that the decisive link between erotic flagellation and masochism is the *undecidability of pleasure and pain*, the relentless and tortuous reinscription of the one within the other. Furthermore, this undecidability not only characterizes sexual practices, it also colors the discourses of both erotic flagellation and masochism. Is it the sheer joy of classification, the thrill of calculating inventory, that incites the Abbé Boileau to record voluminous and often frightful incidents of flagellation, or James Glass Bertram to write 532 pages filled with lurid descriptions of the use of the rod?[46] Or is there not, embedded within their disgust and their obsessive catalogs of this "mania," a rapt fascination with the very practices they abhor?[47] Furthermore, sexual pleasure is ubiquitous in the pages of these texts: either as that which flagellation seeks to curb or as the inadvertent and unwanted by-product of the whip. The Abbé may recount numerous chronicles of whipping used as a remedy for "lustful ardour," but in so many of these instances the exact nature of the cure—as well as whether the rod inflicts pain or pleasure—remains tantalizingly ambivalent. He cites, for example, the case of Saint Bernardin who was once approached by the "Wife of a Citizen" wishing to "have [her] will" with him. In seeming acquiescence, he asked her to "strip off her clothes," but rather than grant her "will," he proceeded to whip her "vigorously," not leaving off "fustigating her, till her lustful ardour was extinguished." The good Abbé then assures the reader of the efficacy of the cure, averring that "[s]he loved the holy Man the better for that afterwards."[48] But what exactly is this better love? Has her desire been expunged or satisfied?

Delolme's extensive and divagating annotations (which are approximately as long as the Abbé's discourse) are even more equivocating than the main text and testify to an even greater permeability in the boundary between pleasure and pain. Delolme seems to take particular delight in his predecessor's many examples of erotic flagellations and often appends examples of his own, like the flogging of Heloise by Abelard whose "sweetness surpassed that of the sweetest perfumes."[49] Elsewhere, he confounds punishment and illicit desire etymologically, quibbling over the Abbé's reading of a Latin text by noting that "the word *flagrum*; which indeed signifies a whip, ... also signifies a lustful passion."[50] Perhaps the most extraordinary example of the admixture of pleasure and pain, however, is to be found in Delolme's castigatory zeal toward the author of the *Historia*. In the last chapter, the Abbé remarks that self-flagellation is complicated by injunctions against "religious persons ... inspect[ing] any part of their naked bodies." The pious author wonders at this: "How can Nuns avoid, in those instants, having at least a glance of those excellent beauties ..."—at which point Delolme intervenes with a startling note: "*Ho, ho, Monsieur l'Abbe!* How come you to be so well acquainted with beauties of the kind you mention here?"[51] Discerning lascivious motivation in the forbidden, narcissistic "glance" of a nun, the Abbé is attacked for his own proscribed glance. Apprehended for his prurient peep, he is forced to submit to Delolme's voyeuristic gaze. Delolme's eye, meanwhile, overseeing and denouncing the stolen glances of both nun and Abbé, confirms the historical alignment of voyeurism with sadism. In an instant, the text's protocol is reversed, and the annotator who delightedly espies the lecherous cleric demonstrates the very mastery—and the violence of the masculinized gaze that signals mastery—which qualifies him as author, authority, and sadist.

With almost eighty years intervening between text and commentary, between the reverent and authoritative Abbé and the impudent Delolme, *The History of the Flagellants* is a compounded text, a text turned against itself, a provocative and—dare I say it?—deeply masochistic discourse. Delolme may dispute with the good Abbé, laugh at him, ridicule his hypocrisies, omit sections he deems extraneous, and correct his imputed faults. He even acknowledges the Oedipal relationship with his discursive progenitor ("There prevails, as may have been perceived, a kind of competition between my Author and me, who shall tell the best story").[52] Yet despite his status as a resourceful and adroit annotator, as the overwriter of his master's discourse, Delolme's pen must in the end submit to his "Author"'s and let the Abbé literally have the last word. Delolme even absents his name from the title page, on which he is referenced only by his dissimilarity to the Abbé Boileau: he is the one "who is *not* a Doctor of the Sorbonne" (my emphasis). This incompletely Oedipalized double text (competing for the love and admiration of the reader) thereby attests to perhaps the most important characteristic of masochistic discourse—its self-division, its partition into an authoritative discourse and a servile, if sometimes resentful and impertinent, commentary. Yet in the end, each is held in thrall to the other, as the "correct" is to the "perverse," as pleasure is to pain. Each acts as a mirror in which the other misrecognizes its self—the one as master, the other as slave. For despite the attempt of this double discourse to establish a fixed and stable organization, the relationship between the two parts is constantly destabilized. As such, it reveals the fact that since the seventeenth century, both erotic flagellation and masochism may be seen to function discursively as *deconstructive tropes*, problematizing and calling into question the very binary oppositions they attempt so fervidly to install: masculinity and femininity, the "correct" and the "perverse," master and slave. Within this perversely compounded text, the Abbé's discourse exerts its priority, the annotation its belatedness. The one silently taunts the other with its authority while the other impertinently teases its rival/model. But in the end, which text, in this attempt to explicate the most contradictory of the perversions, is in command here? Which is the active partner, which the passive; which the controlling, which the acquiescent; which the rebellious, which the submissive; which the masculinized, which the feminized? Which takes more pleasure in its (other's) pain?

MASOCHISM AND BOURGEOIS SUBJECTIVITY

Perhaps Doppet and the nineteenth-century sexologists were not completely mistaken. Perhaps there is a connection between the flogging of children and erotic flagellation. In his *Three Essays on the Theory of Sexuality* (1905), Freud also suggests they are causally linked and, invoking the case of Rousseau, characterizes "the painful stimulation of the skin of the buttocks" as "one of the erotogenic roots of the *passive* instinct of cruelty (masochism)."[53] Since flogging in childhood constantly reappears in the etiologies of masochism, perhaps the two practices are connected, both ontogenetically and culturally. Just as the beaten child may grow up to be a masochist, so may the culture of flagellation develop into a culture of masochism. Perhaps the flagellant is the shadow lurking behind the bourgeois subject as it is being consolidated in diaries, fictions, and philosophical tracts. And perhaps sparing the rod does not so much spoil the child as prepare it to take its own self-regulating place in a self-disciplining society.

Up through the period when Meibom composed his *De Flagrorum Usu*, flogging was the standard method in Europe of punishing unruly children. In early modern England, both in homes and schools, across the boundaries of social class, the birch rod—as administered by parents, servants, nurses, tutors, or teachers—became the conventional instrument of retribution. Both boys and girls were expected to be unremittingly deferential to their elders and were beaten routinely for a great range of offenses: disobedience, obstinacy, laziness, a missed stitch, a flubbed Latin conjugation. And the punishments varied enormously in severity, from a gentle hand slap to prolonged, violent whippings that sometimes resulted in the death of the child. For the determined castigator, the child's hand, mouth, face, and buttocks (either naked or clothed) were fair game. In addition to the birch rod, a ferula—a wooden slat with a large rounded end and a hole in its middle—could be used to raise a large and painful blister. Lawrence Stone notes that in the grammar schools (which drew a far greater number of boys than they had during the late Middle Ages) the standard method of administering the rod required one active and two passive participants: a boy would be beaten "with a birch" by his master "on the naked buttocks while bent over and horsed on the back of another boy."[54] Even in universities, young men were regularly submitted to public whippings, floggings over a barrel, or detention in the stocks. Contemporary evidence suggests that John Aubrey's recollections of violent disciplinary procedures are not as extravagant as they might seem:

> The Gentry and the Citizens . . . were as severe to their children as their schoolmaster; and their Schoolmasters, as masters of the House of correction. The child perfectly loathed the sight of his parents, as the slave his Torturor. Gentleman of 30 or 40 years old, fitt for any employment in the common wealth, were to stand like great mutes and fools bare headed before their Parents; and the Daughters (grown woemen) were to stand at the Cupboards side during the whole time of the proud mothers visit. . . . Fathers and mothers slash't their daughters . . . when they were perfect woemen.[55]

During this same period, however, some illustrious voices were being raised in opposition to physical punishment and the slavish obeisance it produced. The most eminent European and English humanists (including Erasmus, Sir Thomas More, and Thomas Elyot) were unanimously averse to the routine use of the rod and, like Roger Ascham, insisted that "young children were sooner allured by love than driven by beating, to attain good learning."[56] This humanistic crusade, however, only infrequently resulted in real educational reform, and most schoolmasters found flogging far more expedient than cajolery for teaching Latin conjugations.

At the end of the seventeenth century, however, in a decisive historical shift, a concerted and widespread campaign developed to mitigate the violence of corporal punishment. Anonymous pamphleteers condemned flogging in schools while John Aubrey denounced "the ordinary schoolmaster's tyrannicall beating and dispiriting of children [from] which many tender ingeniose children doe never recover again."[57] John Locke, meanwhile, enunciated and popularized this new educational philosophy. His best-selling volume *Some Thoughts Concerning Education* of 1693 had an enormous impact on the rearing of children, was immediately translated into French, and was reprinted twenty-four times before 1800.[58] Locke's compelling summons to reform marks far more than the triumph of humanistic compassion. More important, its popularity is symptomatic of a new attitude toward education. Finally, after two hundred years of terrorized children, the "repressive ardour" (in Philippe Ariès's estimation) of a hierarchical and authoritarian disciplinary system began to "cool . . . down," to be superseded by a much more discreet, subtle, and insidious means of control.[59]

In a piquant historical coincidence, at the same time that the philosophers were calling for restraint in the use of the rod, another discourse began to flourish in England in which the same instrument was figured as a vehicle for sexual pleasure. During the Restoration a spate of pornographic texts were published, including three books in English translation from the original French (*The School of Venus* [1680], *Tullia and Octavia* [1684], and *Venus in the Cloister* [1692]), which feature, amongst other delights, scenes of flagellation used, as Meibom had described, to promote erection.[60] *The School of Venus*, for example, tells of women who, as a prelude to copulation, beat men with rods "until they see their yards growing erect."[61] Simultaneously, such books appeared as *Whipping Tom Brought to Light, and exposed to View* (1681), which details the adventures of an itinerant flagellator who would seize "upon such as he can conveniently light on, and turning them up, . . . make . . . their Butt ends cry Spanko."[62] Although pornographic texts had previously circulated in England (principally the works of Petronius, the Roman poets and satirists, and Aretino), the Restoration became the golden age of English pornography. Despite heavy government censorship, much of the pornography (like the infamous play, *Sodom; or the Quintessence of Debauchery*, attributed to the earl of Rochester) scathingly satirized the reputedly effeminate court of Charles II. In fact, the sudden proliferation of texts suggests that rather than suppressing obscenity, the very act of prohibition (as is so often the case under the bourgeois regime) worked instead to *produce* this impressive body of transgressive texts, texts that, in effect, take up the restrictive principles of Puritan morality (its obsessive concern with chastity and self-restraint) only to invert them. Why else would "a significant number," in Roger Thompson's words, "of writers, readers and owners of disreputable works [come] from devoutly Puritan backgrounds"?[63] Restoration pornography seems proof positive that the Puritan apprehension of sex, its tendency to represent sex as disgusting, produced its own reverse discourse. And what better way to celebrate the squalor of the body than to take delight in the very punishments used to discipline and purify this filthy clog?

The Restoration stage, meanwhile, became yet another platform for the production of sexually explicit scenes not only of seduction and cuckoldry but also of some exotic and violent varieties of (mostly) heterosexualized sex. Toward the end of Charles II's reign, however, two plays were performed that for the first time incontestably link beating with sexual pleasure. Thomas Shadwell's satire *The Virtuoso* (1676) features an irascible and ridiculous older man, Snarl, who pays a visit to his suggestively named whore:

> SNARL: Ah poor little rogue. In sadness, I'll bite thee by the lip, i'faith I will. Thou has incens'st me strangely; thou has fir'd my blood; I can bear it no longer, i'faith I cannot. Where are the instruments of our pleasure? Nay, prithee do not frown; by the mass, thou shalt do't now.
>
> MRS. FIGGUP: I wonder that should please you so much that pleases me so little.
>
> SNARL: I was so us'd to't at Westminster School I could never leave it off since.
>
> MRS. FIGGUP: Well, look under the carpet then if I must.
>
> SNARL: Very well, my dear rogue. But dost hear, thou art too gentle. Do not spare thy pains. I love castigation mightily. So here's good provision. *Pulls the carpet; three or four great rods fall down.*[64]

Shadwell explicitly figures Snarl's disagreeable and cruel nature as an analogy of his sexual practices, which are imagined, as if in anticipation of Doppet, as the result of the beatings he received as a child at Westminster School (during the Restoration, its master, Dr. Busby, was renowned for his disciplinary "severity").[65] *The Virtuoso* thus offers a genetic theory—much like Doppet's and Freud's—to explain the "love" of "castigation" and thereby imagines the flagellatory scene as an attempt to turn childhood pain into adult pleasure, to reconfigure the trauma of flogging as *jouissance*.

The most notorious literary representation of the erotics of flagellation, however, comes from Thomas Otway's tragedy *Venice Preserved* (1682). In two elaborate scenes, a corrupt Venetian senator, Antonio, goes to visit his whore, Aquilina, to be beaten, whipped, kicked like a dog, and verbally abused. However, because Aquilina's very real detestation of her client serves only to intensify his sexual pleasure, she—unhappily—has little choice but to play along.

> ANTONIO: Do kick, kick on, now I am under the table, kick again—kick harder—harder yet, bough waugh waugh, waugh, bough—'odd, I'll have a snap at thy shins—bough waugh waugh, waugh, bough—'odd she kicks bravely.—
>
> AQUILINA: Nay then I'll go another way to work with you; and I think here's an instrument fit for the purpose. *(Fetches a whip and bell.)* What, bit your mistress, sirrah! Out, out of doors, you dog, to kennel and be hanged—bite your mistress by the legs, you rogue?— *She whips him.*[66]

After two acts of dexterous and impassioned blank verse, the first Nicky-Nacky scene (so-called because of Antonio's pet name for his mistress) explodes with stuttering prose. Radically disrupting the tragic momentum—and decorum—of *Venice Preserved*, it introduces an unusually scandalous and lascivious tone, even by the standards of Restoration comedy. Except for the pornographic volumes of the period, the Nicky-Nacky scenes provide the most detailed and complex representation in Restoration literature of the transformation of pain, contempt, and loathing into sexual pleasure (the emphasis on Antonio's humiliation and his role-playing makes the scenes seem far closer to

Krafft-Ebing than to Meibom). Although these scenes were very popular when the play was first performed, they have made critics since the seventeenth century distinctly queasy and, in fact, were cut from performances early in the play's stage history—well before 1718, possibly even in the 1690s—and were not acted again until 1895.[67] Yet they remain the most remarkable and provocative representations of erotic flagellation before Sade.

Contemporary with *Venice Preserved*, Locke's *Some Thoughts Concerning Education*, marks an important moment in the development of pedagogical theory. Unlike other seventeenth-century educational writings, Locke's was not designed as a handbook to help parents and teachers cram more and more information into children. Rather, he was concerned with pedagogy in the broadest sense, intent on demonstrating how to produce a child fit to take his or her place in the expanding middle class, which is to say, healthy, honest, industrious, strong, respectful, and moral. As a result, Locke's focus is not on disciplinary minutiae but on "the *process* for the formation of character, of *habits* . . . of mind and body."[68] Locke is particularly concerned with teaching self-regulation since, in his view, that faculty is the very foundation of education and, by extension, civilization itself. To that end, Locke strongly and repeatedly urges that flogging be forsworn, except in cases of "*Obstinacy* or *Rebellion*," since "Beating, by constant Observation, is found to do little good."[69] He repudiates the rod because it

> contributes not at all to the Mastery of our Natural Propensity to indulge Corporal and present Pleasure, and to avoid Pain at any rate; but rather encourages it; and thereby strengthens that in us, which is the Root from whence spring all Vitious Actions, and the Irregularities of Life. For what other Motive, but of sensual Pleasure and Pain, does a Child act by, who drudges at his Book against his inclination, or abstains from eating unwholsome Fruit, that he takes Pleasure in, only out of Fear of *whiping*?[70]

Focused on the opposition between nature and culture, Locke contrasts "Natural Propensity" with learned behavior. Scorning the former, he insists that it is the very "Business" of education not to oblige nature, but "to root out and destroy" a child's "Natural Propensity" to indulge pleasure and avoid pain. In other words, enculturation for Locke is predicated upon the transformation of "Pain" into "Pleasure." Locke repeatedly emphasizes the importance of this process, that "the great Principle and Foundation of all Vertue and Worth, is placed in this, That a Man is able to *deny himself* his own Desires. . . ." The very basis of humanistic education, therefore, must be to inculcate self-denial, to teach a child to be "obedient to Discipline," to forswear immediate gratification, and to withstand present pain in expectation of a less sensuous and more intangible reward, of narcissistically "find[ing] a Pleasure in being esteemed" by others.[71]

Within the Lockean scheme, then, the old order of flogging is replaced by a new, psychologized approach to education based not on physical threats but on a much subtler species of inducements and deterrents. Locke disparages the traditional system of punishment in favor of holding up for the child the promises of "*Esteem* and *Disgrace*," which he calls "the most powerful Incentives to the Mind." Furthermore, he urges these be bestowed "not as particular Rewards and Punishments," but that they be internalized by the child as positive and negative ideals. The disdain or honor of others brings one "into a State of Disgrace or Commendation," a "State" that one effectively colonizes and inhabits, as one does the social class into which one is born.[72]

Locke's theory of education bears witness to the radical reconceptualization of the middle-class subject during the late seventeenth century, that is, to "the growing ideal of a human agent who is able to remake himself by methodical and disciplined action."[73] It attests to a reconfiguration of the family and the increasing obsolescence of the "stern, repressive father" who was "incompatible with the new model of the family as emotional center for the nurturing of children and the new model of the individual as an autonomous self."[74] Simultaneously, it testifies to the breakdown of the system of discipline that had been inherited from the late Middle Ages. More strikingly than other texts of the period, Locke's treatise unwittingly exploits the polyvalence of the word "discipline," derived from the Latin *disciplina*, meaning instruction of disciples. The oldest English usage of the word, however, has little to do with pedagogy. As Delolme explains in *The History of the Flagellants*: "The word *Discipline* originally signified in general, the censures and corrections which persons who were guilty of Sins, received from their Superiors; and when *Flagellation* was to be a part of those corrections, it was expressly mentioned; and they called such Discipline."[75] The *OED* confirms the fact that the earliest usage of the word in English, dating from 1225, is monastic and that it signifies "[c]orrection; chastisement; punishment inflicted by way of correction and training; in religious use, the mortification of the flesh by penance." This usage antedates the more conventional meaning of "mental and moral training" by more than two hundred years. So when Locke called upon parents and teachers in 1693 to make "the Mind" of children "obedient to Discipline," the original meaning of *discipline* would have been by no means obliterated (by 1622 the word had also come to denote the instrument of discipline, the whip or scourge). Rather, this referential equivocation testifies to the status of Locke's *Thoughts* as a palimpsest in which a history of physical punishment is overwritten by a theory of psychological inducement, and in which the flogged disciple is replaced by a self-regulating subject. Yet beneath the new text, the earlier disciplinary injunction is still legible. Far more definitively than earlier treatises on education, Locke's volume attests to the fact that under the bourgeois pedagogical and epistemological regime, the subject takes on the responsibility for disciplining him- or herself, for a severe and uncompromising self-regulation.

This new subject is so clearly the one described by Foucault, emerging historically in the transition between the older coercive order and a new regime whose

> methods, which made possible the meticulous control of the operations of the body, which assured the constant subjection of its forces and imposed upon them a relation of docility-utility, might be called "disciplines." Many disciplinary methods had long been in existence—in monasteries, armies, workshops. But in the course of the seventeenth and eighteenth centuries the disciplines became general formulas of domination.[76]

In the years following the Restoration, these "general formulas of domination" became decisive in both propelling and consolidating economic change in an England that was being converted from a "semi-feudal into a semi-modern state."[77] With the abolition of feudal tenures, a capitalist agrarian economy quickly developed, forcing the younger sons of aristocrats, who received "their patrimony in the form of a capital sum, not in land," to pursue "a career . . . [in] the expanding professions and the civil service." At the same time, the Navigation Act of 1660 facilitated England's growth as an imperial power by allowing for the expansion of foreign trade. Although until 1640 cloth was virtually the only English export, by the end of the century its exportation had been nearly overtaken by "re-exports of non-European commodities, or exports to India and America." As a result, by 1700, there was "a rapid expansion of the cheap consumer-goods industries" as industrial development was actively promoted by Parliament and the courts.[78] This sudden and rapid expansion of the English economy and, in particular, the real initiation of industrialization demanded the production of a different kind of subject, a more efficient, diligent, and ambitious worker who was able to regulate and deny his or her own desires and to redirect them toward utilitarian ends. After the success of Locke's volume on education, "every advertisement" for private schools would boast "that the school will instill those virtues—sobriety, obedience, industry, thrift, benevolence and compassion—that educationalists regarded as the virtues of a successful social man" and, more important, businessman.[79]

The Lockean subject, founded on self-discipline and self-denial, is, I believe, startlingly analogous to the one charted by Freud in "The Economic Problem in Masochism" (1924) and there designated the "moral masochist." For Freud, moral masochism results from a kind of hypertrophy of the super-ego that retains the harsh features of the introjected parents, "namely, their power, their severity, their tendency to watch over and to punish." This "harsh, cruel and inexorable" superego then tyrannizes the ego, which "reacts with feelings of anxiety (pangs of conscience) to the perception that it has failed to perform the behest of its ideal."[80] In this resexualization of the Oedipus complex, the ego of the moral masochist "begins to enjoy and indeed to provoke the super-ego's severity" by "seek[ing] punishment, whether from the super-ego within or from the parental authorities without."[81] To satisfy this desire, the moral masochist—this irreducibly divided subject—will deliberately but unconsciously "do something inexpedient, act against his own interests," and thereby provoke the inevitable and sought-for punishment. Freud emphasizes that while the moral masochist is likely to perceive the sadism of his superego "acutely" and "consciously," he remains quite oblivious to "the masochistic impulse of the ego" that, because it "remains hidden from the person[,] must be inferred from his behaviour."[82] Moreover, Freud distinguishes moral masochism from the two other forms of masochism, the erotogenic and the feminine, because it is both unconscious and "loosened [in] its connection with what we recognize to be sexuality."[83]

Most theorists of masochism agree that moral masochism is the most widespread of the so-called perversions. In *Three Essays*, Freud remarks that sadism and masochism are "the most common and the most significant of all the perversions."[84] Thirty-five years later, Theodor Reik, in a boldly universalizing move, would insist that "traces of moral masochism will be found in the tendencies and behavior of every one of us." Discerning its mark in countless cultural institutions, he calls it "a significant factor in the life of social, national and religious bodies."[85] Following a very different line of argumentation, Leo Bersani universalizes masochism without loosening its connection to sexuality. By defining sexuality as a force that disturbs "the organization of the self," that, indeed, "is intolerable to the structured self," he claims that sexuality must of necessity be "ontologically grounded in masochism."[86] Kaja Silverman, meanwhile, asserts that masochism is crucial to an understanding of the modern subject's articulation because "conventional subjectivity . . . closely adjoins moral masochism."[87]

Rather than posit some universalized, transhistorical psychological mechanism to explain this ubiquity, however, I am arguing that the male moral masochist (together with the discourses in which he is represented and theorized) is a historical production. Living a relentless and cruel self-division, he is the new being mapped by Locke whose superego becomes increasingly tyrannical against the ego, who "gains control through disengagement," through the "transposition of first-person experience into an objectified, impersonal mode."[88] This subject—also designated the liberal humanist subject—is founded on the confounding of pleasure and pain, on the need to subdue one's "Natural Propensity to indulge . . . Pleasure, and to avoid Pain."[89] Gradually emerging in the West during the sixteenth and seventeenth centuries, coincidentally with the development of mercantile capitalism, the breakdown of absolutism, and the emergence of liberal democracy, he is (mis)recognized as the autonomous author of meaning and action and enunciated in new and highly personalized literary forms like the diary and autobiography. Lawrence Stone observes that there are two fundamental aspects to this newly individualized subject: "firstly, a growing introspection and interest in the individual personality; and secondly, a demand for personal autonomy and a corresponding respect for the individual's right to privacy, to self-expression, and to the free exercise of his will within limits set by the need for social cohesion."[90] This ostensibly free, male individual is posited as the basic social unit, his sovereignty founded upon the inviolability of private property and the unrestricted market. His privacy, meanwhile, is guaranteed by the fact that the bourgeois settlement constructs public and private, and the political and the domestic, in strict opposition to each other. (While fifteenth- and sixteenth-century great houses "had been constructed of interlocking suites of rooms," late-seventeenth-century architecture "allocated space to corridors, which now allowed access without intruding upon privacy.")[91] Stone argues that the "affective individualism," as he calls it, that produces this newly privatized subject is closely connected to the personal ideology of Puritanism, with its "overpowering sense of sin and the preoccupation with individual salvation." Further, he emphasizes the causal connection between the call to self-regulation and bourgeois individualism: "The interest in the self sprang from the urgent need to discipline the self."[92]

Yet, as Locke's text acknowledges, the self-disciplining male subject is predicated not on unlimited license or "Natural Propensity" but on *denial*. To become healthy, industrious, and moral, he must "deny" himself "the Satisfaction of his own Desires."[93] Aspiring to freedom and reason, he must, to prosper, disavow the knowledge that his independence requires submission to an economic system in which he remains a cog, and a despotic superego that has internalized the Law, the Father, and the Word. Furthermore, Locke's treatise demonstrates incontrovertibly that male subjectivity is founded on *violence*, on "root[ing] out and destroy[ing]" the subject's "natural" indulgence.[94] Constantly impugning his desires, this new bourgeois must tirelessly police himself and his desires while calling this submission "freedom." He must work rigorously to confound pleasure and pain, and to welcome the severity of punishment. He must always be ready to discipline, that is, to scourge himself for his shortcomings and irresponsibilities, and, if he is to win esteem (from either the superego or others), never allow the introjected rod to fall from his grip.

In *The Tremulous Private Body*, Francis Barker connects the self-disciplining subject to the emergence of a new kind of censorship in seventeenth-century England. Reading Milton's *Areopagitica*, he notes that the new censorship, rather than relying on prepublication prohibition (preemption), is "deterrent" in its operation, threatening the subject with punishment "if the offending book comes out, while she or he remains 'free' to publish it." Barker emphasizes that this represents an innovative method of control and that "[f]ar from the 'untaught and irreligious gadding rout' . . . which a pre-emptive censorship must assume the people to be," the new settlement presupposes "a remarkable degree of that *self-discipline* which . . . is to become the linchpin of a move articulated by the text from the unmediated and overt violence of the older settlement to a more indirectly ideological control implanted in the new subjectivity." In other words, the consolidation of bourgeois subjectivity testifies to the shift from physical coercion to ideology. No longer need the state apparatus, like a strict parent or tutor, stand always attentive with a "discipline," ready to whip its charge for disobedience. Ideological control ensures that "the state succeeds in penetrating to the very heart of the subject, or more accurately, in pre-constituting that subject as one which is already internally disciplined, censored, and thus an effective support of the emergent pattern of domination."[95]

It is far more than the force of convention which dictates that the Lockean subject be denominated with a masculine pronoun. For although Locke himself recommends similar methods for the rearing of boys and girls, he acknowledges that his "Discourse . . . will not so perfectly suit the Education of *Daughters*."[96] For this new self is first and foremost a *masculinized* subject, one being readied to perform in the public, commercial, and political spheres. His articulation, however, does not represent a mere refinement of an earlier paradigm. Rather, Lockean discourse bears witness to a wholesale reconfiguration of gendered norms that will culminate in the eighteenth century with the consolidation of the two-sex model, the "companionate marriage,"[97] and a presumptively democratic body politic founded on the inviolability of the legal contract and the enfranchisement of property-owning men. On the one hand, this reconfiguration leads to a relative masculinization of the male subject in relation to his former "'effeminized' status . . . under absolutism."[98] On the other hand, the demands made of this subject to submit to self-discipline, to the relentless and exacting authority of the superego, have the effect of, if not exactly feminizing him, at least modeling his ego's submission upon a feminine ideal. As eighteenth-century fictions from Steele to Austen demonstrate, this newly sovereign subject becomes a prototype for the middle-class man of business and sensibility, the man able to wield a not so gentle authority (over both himself and others) and simultaneously to elicit the sentimental responses associated with female subjectivity.

Yet the foundation for the new male subject had been laid over the course of the preceding century. As the birch rod was gradually delivered from its severe and obligatory service to children's buttocks, it was left increasingly at the disposal of the fantasmatic. And the discourses in which it is figured, from Locke to Otway, testify at once to a process of *sublimation* and *desublimation*. In the first instance, flagellation is purified and exalted, introjected by the subject and placed at the disposal of an industrious civility. Translated into self-discipline, it forms the basis for a new theory of pedagogy, a putatively benevolent educational system, and a rational and utilitarian culture. In the second instance, flagellation is eroticized, rendered "detested," debased, and irrational, and made the subject of intensive scrutiny and fascination. The business of finding sexual "Delight in the Midst of Torment," as figured in plays and pornographic fictions, emerges as both a classifiable sexual practice and a "perversion."[99] The overtly masochistic subject, Senator Antonio, groveling to be spit upon, kicked, and used like a dog, is merely the pathologized double of Locke's model student who has "root[ed] out and destroy[ed]" his "Natural Propensity to indulge . . . Pleasure, and to avoid Pain."[100] For both figures, the difference between pleasure and pain has been rendered undecidable, a symptom of what Freud would later analyze as masochistic self-division. Since bourgeois subjectivity remains predicated upon this internal rupture, is it any wonder that masochism, since the seventeenth century, has become the most universalized and ubiquitous of the perversions?

THE FREUDIAN SYNTAX

Because masochism is a historical production, one so bound up with the development, on the one hand, of capitalism and, on the other, of sexuality as a particular medical and juridical regime, the sexological accounts must hold pride of place in any attempt to use masochism as a heuristic tool. And among the sexological accounts, Freud's is unquestionably the most important, providing the basis for all subsequent analyses of masochistic subjectivities and practices. For Freud, however, masochism represents not a solution but a problem, a daunting challenge to psychoanalysis, a phenomenon "so hard to clear up."[101] Although in *Three Essays* he admits his inability to put forward a "satisfactory explanation of this perversion," two later texts continue the attempt, " 'A Child Is Being Beaten' " (1919), and "The Economic Problem in Masochism" (1924).[102] If " 'A Child Is Being Beaten' " is remarkable for providing the most detailed explication of masochistic fantasies, "The Economic Problem" is crucial for its setting forth Freud's influential typology of three different kinds of masochism: erotogenic, feminine, and moral. In reading these texts, I am principally concerned with analyzing how, in Freud's account, the masochistic scenario splits the subject and disrupts normative gender identifications, with an eye to understanding the psychic—and cultural—work performed by masochistic fantasies.

Freud's attempt to account for the ontogenesis of masochism was greatly facilitated by his theorization of the death drive in *Beyond the Pleasure Principle* (1920). Freud there conceives the death drive in contradistinction to eros, or the pleasure principle, and defines it as that instinct within each organism which attempts to destroy or annihilate it. Recognizing the potentially devastating power of the death drive, Freud claims that the libido is responsible for neutralizing it, for rendering this destructive instinct harmless.[103] The libido accomplishes this by directing the death drive "towards objects of the outer world" where a portion of it will function as "the instinct of destruction, of mastery, the will to power." This is the portion that "is placed directly in the service of the sexual function" and becomes "true sadism." But there is another portion of the death drive that is not displaced outward but "remains within the organism and is 'bound' there libidinally." This forms the basis for what in "The Economic Problem" he calls an "original erotogenic masochism," a lust for pain, which, Freud asserts, underlies the other two forms and, being a *primary* mechanism, does not represent (as he suggests in earlier essays) a derivation of sadism.[104] Kaja Silverman notes that the death drive thus functions to reproduce a primary masochism by compelling the subject "to repeat experiences of an overwhelming and incapacitating sort—experiences which render the subject hyperbolically passive."[105]

The passivity and incapacitation that incidentally mark the erotogenic masochist become greatly accentuated in what Freud refers to as feminine masochism. Although Freud maintains that feminine masochism is "the form most accessible to observation" and the "least mysterious," his analysis is based on a curious contradiction. Although he describes it as "an expression of feminine nature," his objects of study (at least in this essay) are not women at all but men who fantasize "of being pinioned, bound, beaten painfully, whipped, in some way mishandled, forced to obey unconditionally, defiled, degraded." Freud emphasizes that in feminine masochism "the [male] subject is placed in a situation characteristic of womanhood, *i.e.* . . . is being castrated, is playing the passive part in coitus, or is giving birth."[106] As Silverman points out, "feminine masochism is a specifically *male* pathology, so named because it positions its sufferer as a woman," Only in men is Freud able to discern feminine masochism because in women it remains virtually invisible. "It is an accepted—indeed a requisite—element of 'normal' female subjectivity, providing a crucial mechanism for eroticizing lack and subordination."[107]

For Freud, there are several crucial characteristics of feminine masochism. First, it remains (like Krafft-Ebing's concept of masochism) essentially a fantasmatic mode that may or may not lead to enactment. Freud emphasizes that even "the real situations" the masochist conceives, scripts, and executes are "only a kind of make-believe performance of the phantasies." In other words, even "the real" here is an imitation, a performance of a fantasy that by definition can never be fully present to the fantasizing subject. Like a theatrical performance based on a written script, the actors are only standing in for imagined subjects whose presence is perpetually deferred, who are neither "in" the script nor "on" the stage. Second, feminine masochism is always tied to a failure of Oedipalization that demands a (re)infantilization of the subject: "the masochist wants to be treated like a little, helpless, dependent child." Third, as in moral masochism, there is always an association of guilt. The masochist wants to be treated "like a naughty child." Noting this "feeling of guilt," Freud explains that it is "assumed that the subject has committed some crime . . . which is to be expiated by his undergoing the pain and torture."[108]

"'A Child Is Being Beaten'" is Freud's most extensive and provocative investigation of the "perversion" he was five years later to designate feminine masochism. Unlike "The Economic Problem in Masochism," "'A Child Is Being Beaten'" is a far more speculative and strangely inconclusive text that attempts explicitly to relate adult beating fantasies to the operation of the Oedipus complex. The essay is based on six case studies, four female and two male, in all of which Freud notices a similar three-phase structure of fantasy in which the first and third phases are conscious and the second (except in the case of one male subject), unconscious. What is most remarkable about the six cases is first, that the female and male fantasies are not, as Freud expected, opposite and symmetrical; second, that they consistently undermine normative concepts of sexual difference; third, that they are marked by a powerful, if repressed, homosexual content; and fourth, that they pivot around the relationship between father and child and therefore are crucial to an understanding of the superego's production and the process by which the father (and all he represents) is introjected by the subject.

Because the four female fantasies are more heavily censored and thus more obliquely transgressive than the two male fantasies, they function more clearly to illuminate feminine masochism's disruption of normative sex and gender roles. The female fantasies center on the child's desire for her father and the impossibility of representing that desire. The first, quasi-sadistic phase of the fantasy is represented by the phrase, "My father is beating the child whom I hate." Freud understands this to be a product of "the child's jealousy" but notes that the gratification is neither clearly sexual nor sadistic, simply "the stuff from which both will later come." The second and unconscious phase (which Freud admits is "a construction of analysis") is the pivotal one, enunciated by the phrase, "I am being beaten by my father." It is accompanied, Freud notes, "by a high degree of pleasure" and is "of an unmistakably masochistic character." Here the active is changed into the passive voice and the guilty *desire* for the father transformed into *punishment* by the father.

> This being beaten is now a meeting-place between the sense of guilt and sexual love. *It is not only a punishment for the forbidden genital relation, but also a regressive substitute for it*, and from this latter source it derives the libidinal excitation which is from this time forward attached to it, and which finds its outlet in onanistic acts. Here for the first time we have the essence of masochism.[109]

So for Freud, "the essence" of feminine masochism lies in the displacement of libidinal excitation from the forbidden genital relation with the father to the beating imagined by the subject for her prohibited desire. The Freudian syntax thus shuffles cause and effect, producing punishment as the payment for desire and shifting the libidinal cathexis. It describes an economic transaction, a relation of exchange and expenditure in which the masochistic subject's initial erotic investment is repaid with a kind of foreign currency that the subject immediately converts into the local erotic coinage.

The third and most complex phase of the fantasy is an imitation of the first phase and is illustrated by a somewhat more complex scenario: "Some boys are being beaten. I am probably looking on." Unlike the second phase, this describes a tripartite relation that includes female spectator, beater, and the punished boys. According to Freud, the one doing the beating represents the persistence of the father "in the shape of a teacher or some other person of authority." By so identifying this agent as the father, Freud deciphers the fantasy and makes it almost identical with phase one: "My father is beating the other child; he loves only me." Freud explains that the second part of the formulation ("he loves only me") has undergone repression, which is why the fantasy appears in a sadistic guise. He insists, however, that the spectatorial subject's pleasure is masochistic precisely because of her cross-sex identification with the boys being beaten, who are, after all, "nothing more than substitutes for the child itself." As in the second phase, the masochistic gratification has simultaneously "taken over the libidinal cathexis of the repressed portion" as well as "the sense of guilt which is attached to its content."[110] In other words, the sexual pleasure that the female subject experiences through the imagined beating of herself (as a group of boys) represents a displacement and fulfillment of her repressed desire. The subject thus appears twice in phase three, as both the strangely passive spectator in the fantasy and the guilty male subjects being punished by the father for their love for him.

Freud's elaborate paradigm of feminine masochism finally produces a female subject who is radically divided, both spectator and victim, producer of desire and recipient of punishment, sexually aroused and desperately guilty. Yet the third phase is even more scandalous than this self-division suggests because of the subject's identification with the beaten boys. Freud notes that in turning away "from their incestuous love for their father," the female subjects "spur their 'masculinity complex'" and "from that time forward only want to be boys." One might expect that the masochistic syntax would accentuate the conventionally feminized subject position and render the female masochist doubly passive. Yet Freud insists that this female fantasmatic masculinizes the subject and incites her desire to be a boy. "The heroes were always young men," Freud notes, and women did not "come into these creations at all."[111] However, the boys in the fantasy are by no means normative male subjects. On the contrary, in being punished by the father for their love for him (as in phase two), they are defined exclusively by their (repressed) homosexual desire. The female subject is thus reconfigured as a male homosexual. As Silverman notes,

although this homosexual cathexis makes it "transgressive for a man to occupy" that subject position, the latter becomes "almost unthinkable for a
woman, since it implies an identification with male homosexuality."[112] According to Freud's analysis, normative constructions of both gender and sexuality are thus severely disrupted by the masochistic scenario. The female
subject is rendered both homosexual and heterosexual, masculinized and
feminized, her passivity at once affirmed and contradicted by its projection
onto a male homosexual subject.

The male fantasies that Freud analyzes exhibit both an analogous homosexual investment and a subversion of conventionally gendered subject positions. And they do so more explicitly than the female fantasies because they
are less radically censored. Like the latter, the male fantasies progress through
three phases: "I am being loved by my father." "I am being beaten by my
father." "I am being beaten by my mother." Freud explains that in the male
scenario, masochistic desire is produced not by the operation of the positive
Oedipus complex but by the negative one, "the inverted attitude," that is, by
the boy's identification with the mother (rather than the father) and thus with
the mother's desire for the father.[113] Freud emphasizes that, as in the female
fantasies, the libidinal significance of masochism is directly linked to the
guilty transformation of desire for the father into the desire to be punished by
the father (for the original desire). Thus "being beaten . . . stands for being
loved (in a genital sense), though this has been debased to a lower [i.e., anal]
level owing to regression." Even more markedly than the female fantasy, the
male one is "passive from the very beginning, and is derived from a feminine
attitude towards his father."[114] The masochistic male subject's gender identification is thus severely disrupted, and he is invariably rendered "feminine"
and "passive" in Freud's account. Like his female counterpart, although in a
less elaborate way, the male masochist inadvertently problematizes the
gendered positions that Freud, in so many of his other texts, is intent on natu-
ralizing and promoting.

Yet perhaps the most significant component of the male fantasy, the passage
from unconscious to conscious, from phase two to phase three, is its heterosexualization. As Freud elsewhere notes, "the wish to be beaten by the father . . .
is closely connected with the other wish, to have some passive (feminine)
sexual relations with him."[115] Although the subject makes no attempt to disguise the fantasy's masochistic content, he carefully "evades his homosexuality by repressing and remodeling his unconscious fantasy." Thus in phase
three, a mother who is endowed "with masculine attributes and characteristics"
is abruptly substituted for the father, and the fantasy, so heterosexualized,
becomes tolerable for the subject. As Freud emphasizes, "a feminine [i.e.,
passive] attitude" is adopted in the last phase "without a homosexual object-
choice."[116] Unlike the female fantasy, which in its third phase makes a conclu-

sive identification with a male homosexual subject position, the male fantasy pivots around the repression of homosexual desire. Yet, in both cases, male homosexual desire is decisive in the masochistic scenario. In the one, it is the effect of repression; in the other, its cause.

The crucial positioning of male homosexuality—and its disavowal—in Freud's theorization of feminine masochism is validated by many discourses and practices in the long histories of both erotic flagellation and masochism. From the image of the seventeenth-century schoolboy being horsed—elevated on the back of another boy in order to be flogged—to contemporary gay sadomasochistic pornographic fictions (like *Drummer* magazine or the stories of John Preston, Aaron Travis, and Pat Califia), relations between men, and particularly between sons and their real or imagined fathers, enjoy a privileged status in theories and accounts of flagellatory and masochistic practices. For masochism, as the (necessary) failure and resexualization of the Oedipus complex, represents no more nor less than a scandalous eroticization of patriarchal relations, a desire for the father that is transformed into a desire to submit to the cruelty of the father's will and all he represents (an ambivalence neatly played out in the compounded text of the Abbé Boileau and Delolme). Masochism functions, in short, as a mode of cultural reproduction that simultaneously reveals and conceals (through the mechanism of disavowal) the homoeroticism that undergirds patriarchy and male homosocial relations. It is little wonder that Doppet is terrified lest the whipping of boys inflame "sodomitic inclinations"[117] or that a late-seventeenth-century German physician should write: "I have known a very learned man . . . who, whenever in school or elsewhere he sees a boy punished, unbreeched and beaten, and hears his cries, at once ejaculates semen copiously without any tension or erection of the penis but with such mental confusion that he could almost swoon. . . ."[118] And although Krafft-Ebing attempts to heterosexualize both sadism and masochism, his *Psychopathia* repeatedly attests (like "'A Child Is Being Beaten'") to a strikingly homosexual component in both male and female masochistic fantasies.

The classic sexological texts are, of course, decisive in the history of sexual inversion that imagines the homosexual male subject to be the victim of womanly desires. The Freudian masochistic paradigm, in particular, with its inevitable homosexual cathexes, necessarily posits a linkage conjoining male masochism, homoerotic desire, and femininity. And despite the many well-founded objections to that linkage (and in particular to the connection between male homosexuality and femininity), it often plays itself out in masochistic fictions. Sometimes the identification is acknowledged, and, as in Allen Ginsberg's "Kaddish" or Tony Kushner's *Angels in America*, the male subject, with only minimal resistance, takes up a feminized (and homosexualized) positionality. Yet as "'A Child Is Being Beaten'" and countless contemporary cultural texts suggest, feminine identification, especially on the part of a self-identified heterosexualized male, is made under great duress or in an extremely circuitous way—and more often than not disavowed. In its use of the Freudian paradigms, *Taking It Like a Man* aims to analyze both the diversity of feminine identifications made by white male subjects and the historical changes in these patterns of identification since the 1950s. Constructing a cultural history, it charts the ascendancy of feminine masochism and so-called Christian masochism during the 1950s and 1960s respectively and the gradual supersession of these paradigms during the 1970s by what Freud calls reflexive sadomasochism, a condition in which the ego is ingeniously split between a sadistic (or masculinized) half and a masochistic (or feminized) half so that the subject, torturing himself, can prove himself a man.[119] It also attempts to interrogate the relationship between ostensibly heterosexual and ostensibly homosexual white masculinities in U.S. culture, arguing that they are far more alike than they might at first appear to be. Reacting in remarkably similar ways to anxieties over what they fantasize to be an encroaching feminization of the male subject (and of U.S. culture), they are sometimes almost indistinguishable.

Yet it is clear from the discourses of the white male as victim (and even from the work of the sexologists) that far more is at stake in male masochism than an imagined feminization of the male subject. The historical linkage between Mailer's "white Negro" and Metzgar's "new nigger," along with the widespread and compulsive performance of white male victimization in recent cultural texts, suggests that the contemporary white male subject is not only feminized by a masochistic identification but implicitly blackened as well. And this operation, too, has its roots in classic sexological theory. Consider, for example, Krafft-Ebing's "Case 57": a white, ostensibly heterosexual male, who always attains erection while reading *Uncle Tom's Cabin.* "Particularly exciting for me," he explains, "was the thought of a man being hitched to a wagon in which another man sat with a whip, driving and whipping him."[120] In other words, "Case 57" inadvertently reveals the outrageous truth that for a white male subject living in a pervasively racist and misogynist culture, a black positionality can function analogously to a feminine one insofar as both represent positions of abjection. This is not by any means to equate femininity and blackness as social and political constructions but rather to suggest how the masochistic fantasmatic is able to pose an implicit equivalence between them. Indeed, this slippage between sexual and racial differences is one reason why masochistic fantasy has such enormous psychic power and is able to accomplish such an extraordinary amount of cultural work. It allows the white male subject to take up the position of victim, to feminize and/or blacken himself fantasmatically, and to disavow the homosexual cathexes that are crucial to the process of (patriarchal) cultural reproduction, all the while asserting his unimpeachable virility.

Taking It Like a Man

Among all the analyses that attempt to diagnose and, in some cases, cure that masochistic subjectivity which I am designating a historical production, perhaps the most provocative—and the one closest to my own project—is that of Herbert Marcuse. The most Americanized of the Frankfurt School philosophers (he was the only one to remain in the United States after World War II), Marcuse was a stalwart critic of the technological rationality of industrial capitalism as it emerged triumphant from the war. More committed, as Fredric Jameson notes, to "[t]he Utopian idea" than most of his colleagues, he sought to keep "alive the possibility of a world qualitatively distinct from this one" by imagining the union of "the philosophical and the artistic impulses. . . ."[121] His books, *Eros and Civilization* (1955) and *One-Dimensional Man* (1964), had a tremendous impact on the social, political, and sexual radicals of the 1960s, and he succeeded, during the heyday of McCarthyism and the Cold War, in almost single-handedly reinvigorating a dialectical Marxism that "had all but disappeared from the American landscape in the 1950s."[122]

In *Eros and Civilization*, Marcuse's radical rereading of Freud, he militates for the liberation of Eros in the face of the widespread repression of the libido under late capitalism. Arguing that industrialized society both represses sexuality and enforces its strict genitalization, he notes unhappily that "the libido becomes concentrated in one part of the body, leaving most of the rest free for use as the instrument of labor."[123] Setting forth a philosophy of "radical hedonism,"[124] Marcuse prefers pleasure to labor, the "reactivation of all erotogenic zones" to a rigorous genitalization, and the liberation of Eros (or nonrepressive desublimation, as he calls it) to sexual repression (201). As a result, he looks forward to a utopian future when rationality and eroticism are no longer antithetical, when, "[w]ith the transformation [of] sexuality into Eros, the life instincts evolve their sensuous order, while reason becomes sensuous, . . . protecting and enriching the life instincts" (49, 223). And the key to this utopian order is the liberation of memory, which represents the truth of the unconscious, the means by which both Eros and the traces of the "polymorphous-perverse" are recalled: "The psychoanalytic liberation of memory explodes the rationality of the repressed individual" (19, 49). For the "truth value" of memory lies in its ability "to preserve promises and potentialities which are betrayed and even outlawed by the mature, civilized individual, but which had once been fulfilled in his dim past and which are never entirely forgotten"[125] (18–19).

Despite Marcuse's utopianism, most of *Eros and Civilization* is devoted not to the production of a formula for the liberation of Eros (which, after all, is posited for some unspecified futurity) but to an analysis of the repressive order of late capitalism. And the social (and psychic) mechanism crucial for the stifling of Eros Marcuse calls surplus-repression. Unlike basic repression ("the 'modifications' of the instincts necessary for the perpetuation of the human race"), surplus-repression signifies "the restrictions necessitated by" particular forms of "social domination" (35). And despite the fact that "all civilization" represents "organized domination," surplus-repression has been greatly intensified under the increasingly regulated social conditions of late capitalism (34). Surplus-repression is thus first and foremost a *historical* formulation, the result of the subject's internalization of a specific pattern of domination. As such, it also represents Marcuse's attempt to historicize Freud, to recapture the "historical substance" that haunts "[t]he 'unhistorical' character of the Freudian" concept of repression (34–35). It is crucial to Marcuse's project (and to my own) of reading Freud with and against Marx, of transforming, as Paul Robinson notes, Freud's "unhistorical perceptions—the notion, for example, that civilization was always and inevitably repressive—into historical ones, thereby enabling Marcuse to correlate psychoanalytic theory with the presuppositions of Marxism."[126]

Surplus-repression is implicitly analogized by Marcuse to Marx's concept of surplus-value, which, in the latter's words, designates "the difference between the value of the product and the value of the elements consumed in the formation of the product, in other words the means of production and the labour-power."[127] Surplus-value, in short, is that which is extracted from the worker through exploitation under the capitalist mode of production. For the owner of the means of production, it represents profit, while for the laborer, it is the signpost of misery. Marcuse notes that although "basic repression and surplus-repression have been inextricably intertwined," the latter represents a restriction on sexuality and freedom, a system of "additional controls" (additional to "those indispensible for civilized human association") that arises "from the specific institutions of domination" (38, 37). Surplus-repression is thus the guarantor of the subject's submission to an oppressive social and economic order and an attempt on Marcuse's part to theorize a way out of Freud's unhappy conclusion "that a non-repressive civilization is impossible" (17). Most intriguingly, surplus-repression is virtually synonymous with what Freud designates as moral masochism. For it is predicated on the superego's introjection of "a number of societal and cultural influences . . . until it coagulates into the powerful representative of established morality and 'what people call the "higher" things in human life.'" Marcuse emphasizes (echoing Freud) that "the 'external restrictions' which first the parents and then other societal agencies have imposed upon the individual are 'introjected' into the ego and become its 'conscience'; henceforth, the sense of guilt—the need for punishment generated by the transgressions or by the wish to transgress these restrictions . . . —permeates the mental life" (32). The "individual," in other words, is haunted by the need to submit to the exigencies of parents and "other societal agencies." By introjecting the forces of oppression, by learning to enforce its own repression, by developing a "sense of guilt," the individual becomes a subject who now delights in his or her own subjugation. For as Marcuse repeatedly insists,

> repression is a historical phenomenon. The effective subjugation of the instincts to repressive controls is imposed not by nature but by man. The primal father, as the archetype of domination, initiates the chain reaction of enslavement, rebellion, and reinforced domination which marks the history of civilization. But ever since the first, prehistoric restoration of domination following the first rebellion, repression from without has been supported by repression from within: the unfree individual introjects his masters and their commands into his own mental apparatus. The struggle against freedom reproduces itself in the psyche of man, as the self-repression of the repressed individual, and his self-repression in turn sustains his masters and their institutions. (16)

Although Marcuse notes the crucial position of the father for the production of surplus-repression, he endeavors to minimize the effects of the Oedipus complex, which, he insists, "is certainly not the central cause of the discontents in civilization" (204). For Marcuse is intent on loosening the development of the superego (and the guilty conscience) from Oedipus and so demonstrating the social and economic causes of surplus-repression. As a result, Robinson is certainly correct to note that Marcuse effectively allegorizes the narrative of the primal horde insofar as the concept of surplus-repression transforms "Freud's primal father into the capitalist entrepreneur, and the band of brothers into the European proletariat."[128] Moreover, Marcuse carefully distinguishes between the utopian liberation of Eros that would be "the result of a societal transformation" and the "release of constrained sexuality" within an oppressive society. For this temporary "release" will always appear under the guise of "socially sanctioned masochism,"[129] or false consciousness, "manifest[ing] itself in the hideous forms so well known in the history of civilization; in the sadistic and masochistic orgies of desperate masses . . . " (202). What is perhaps most dangerous about the society of late capitalism (as Marcuse understands it) is its genius at self-perpetuation by (re)producing subjects who, through the operation of surplus-repression, both eroticize and seek out their subjection.

If, following Marcuse, I am correct to suggest that the masochistic male subject is both a function of the rise of capitalism and a necessary cog in the process that reproduces patriarchal, heterosexualized relations, he can neither be wished away nor transformed (pace Marcuse) by the liberation of Eros. He cannot, through an act of individual will, reinvent himself or fight his way out. He cannot cure himself and the culture he represents by discovering his inner child or beating drums. Rather, he proves an intractable subject for all those systems designed for personal transformation, from psychoanalysis to meditation to twelve-step programs. He proves the extraordinary resilience of an oppressive cultural hegemony and of white men in retaining their enormous economic, political, and social power. As a result, this book takes issue with those poststructuralist theorists for whom the disintegration of the liberal humanist subject offers radically subversive possibilities.[130] Kaja Silverman, for example, sees masochism (because it betrays the "phallic standard") as one of several "'deviant' masculinities" that "represent a tacit challenge not only to conventional male subjectivity, but to the whole of our 'world'—that they call sexual difference into question, and beyond that, 'reality' itself."[131] But this book attempts to demonstrate that masochism functions precisely as a kind of decoy and that the cultural texts constructing masochistic masculinities characteristically conclude with an almost magical restitution of phallic power.

Taking It Like a Man is written in two parts, each composed of three chapters. The first part constructs a broad historical narrative (from Mailer's "white Negro" to Timothy McVeigh) that maps the production of both normative and deviant white masculinities in relation to the primary social, political, and economic struggles of the past fifty years. Providing a relatively comprehensive overview of U.S. culture, its three chapters focus respectively on the 1950s, the '60s and early '70s, and the mid-'70s to the mid-'90s. The three chapters constituting the second part of the book deal with specific historical and theoretical problems that complicate the portrait of white masculinity I draw in chapter 3: the emergence of gay machismo at the end of the '70s, the resurgence of nationalism during the '80s and its relation to the surprising commercial success of Tony Kushner's *Angels in America*, and the resurgence of a spiritualized white masculinity in the '90s. Despite my attempt at a comprehensive analysis, I have found it necessary even in part 1 to cover the enormous range of U.S. cultural production selectively. I have chosen to focus on particular texts because I believe them to be both representative and crucial for the reproduction of social norms. There is no question but that relatively elite cultural forms, like theater, reach much smaller audiences than *Rambo*, but this does not mean that they too do not actively participate in the production of hegemony. Throughout part 1, I have deliberately mixed genres not to minimize the differences between and among media and the audiences to which they are addressed but to demonstrate how, within in a given culture, hegemony necessarily works itself out on many different levels.

Despite the avowedly bipartite form of this book, it also argues that a crucial historical shift takes place during the 1970s. As a result, although the first two chapters chart the gradual ascendancy of the new, more feminized and blackened white masculinity associated with the Beats and the hippies, the last four, by focusing on the backlash against the progressive movements of the '60s, analyze the development and transformation of these new masculinities and their role in the crusade against continuing progressive social change in the United States. The first two foreground what at the time were considered alternative cultural productions; the last four, what pass as mainstream. The final three chapters, in addition, analyze and evaluate those strategies—sexual liberation, nationalism, and religion—that have become increasingly popular and widespread in this country since the '60s as ways of imagining a solution to the "problem" of masochism, which is to say, of conceiving a white masculinity less destructive (and self-destructive) than its antecedents.

To close, a word about the title. I have always found the expression "taking it like a man" a curious one in part because it seems to reveal inadvertently so many of the contradictions connected with a masculine identification. It seems tacitly to acknowledge that masculinity is a function not of social or cultural mastery but of the act of being subjected, abused, even tortured. It implies that masculinity is not an achieved state but a process, a trial through which one passes. But at the same time, this phrase ironically suggests the precariousness and fragility—even, perhaps, the femininity—of a gender identity that must be fought for again and again and again. For finally, when one takes it like a man, what is "it" that one takes? And why does the act of taking "it" seem to make it impossible for the one doing the taking, whoever that might be, to *be* a man? Why does this little word, "like," with the annoyingly imitative relationship that it denotes, always get in the way? Why can the one doing the taking only take it *like* a man?

PART I

Chapter One

THE DIVIDED SELF

> "Possession" they call it. . . . As if I was usually there but subject to goof now and again. . . . *Wrong! I am never here.* . . . Never that is *fully* in possession [. . .]. I am always somewhere *Outside* giving orders and *Inside* this straight jacket of jelly.[. . .] (Ellipses, except those in brackets, appear in the source.)
>
> *(William S. Burroughs,* Naked Lunch *[1959])*

> To become new men, these children of the future seem to feel, they must not only become more Black than White but more female than male.
>
> *(Leslie A. Fiedler, "The New Mutants" [1965])*

UNTIL William Burroughs discovered the splendors of Tangier in the mid-1950s, Mexico was his exilic homeland. After a difficult year in New Orleans (memorably fictionalized by Jack Kerouac in *On the Road* [1957]) during which he was arrested for the possession of marijuana, heroin, and sundry firearms, he removed his family to Mexico City in October 1949. Rum, tequila, and boys were cheap, drugs easily obtainable (although not the benzedrine inhalers of which his common-law wife, Joan Vollmer, was so fond), young men walked the streets arm in arm, the clap could be treated for two dollars, and the police were expendable. "In Mexico," the thirty-five-year-old Burroughs wrote to Allen Ginsberg, "it is often cheaper and safer to shoot a cop than to argue with him."[1] Vollmer, meanwhile, relishing her expatriate status, confided to Ginsberg that she would "rather be on the outside looking in, than on the inside looking out."[2] The two-hundred-dollar monthly allowance Burroughs collected from his family (the heirs of the Burroughs adding machine fortune) and the seventy-five a month he was allotted care of the G.I. Bill went much further in Mexico than they had in Louisiana (though never far enough). Yet as *Queer*, his fictionalized account of the time, suggests, this most eccentric of the Beats was far from content. His journey to South America in search of the miracle hallucinogen, yage, with Lewis Marker (the Eugene Allerton of *Queer*) whose lover he aspired to be, was a fiasco. When he returned to Mexico City, he discovered that Vollmer's health had deteriorated, and he wrote despondently to Kerouac that Mexico is "an Oriental country that reflects 2000 years of disease and poverty and degradation and stupidity and slavery and brutality and psychic and physical terrorism."[3]

In September 1951 Burroughs was, as usual, broke, and so he decided to sell one of his guns, a .380 automatic. On the afternoon of the sixth, Burroughs, accompanied by Vollmer and a suitcase full of guns, went to the apartment of a friend who had located a prospective buyer. While waiting for the buyer to arrive, and inspired and inspirited by much gin-and-*limonada* and talk, Burroughs and Vollmer decided to stage a little performance for their friends. Burroughs describes it to Ted Morgan, his biographer:

> Let's see, Joan was sitting in a chair, I was sitting in another chair across the room about six feet away, there was a table, there was a sofa. The gun was in a suitcase and I took it out, and it was loaded, and I was aiming it. I said to Joan, "I guess it's about time for our William Tell act." She took her highball glass and balanced it on top of her head. Why I did it, I don't know, something took over. It was an utterly and completely insane thing to do. . . . I fired one shot, aiming at the glass.[4]

He missed, shooting Vollmer in the head and killing her.

As Burroughs explains it, the capricious murder of his wife was a turning point in several respects. And although he has never written about it at any length, he confesses in the introduction to *Queer*: "I am forced to the appalling conclusion that I would never have become a writer but for Joan's death, and to a realization of the extent to which this event has motivated and formulated my writing."[5] Despite its "appalling" nature, however, Burroughs's mythologization of Vollmer's death as the origin of writing has gained a good deal of currency, having been repeated in Ted Morgan's biography and used as the basis for David Cronenberg's free cinematic adaptation of *Naked Lunch* (1992). Although *Junky* (1953), written before Vollmer's death, employs a "straightforward narrative method," Burroughs is apparently suggesting that he considers both that book and that method hardly to be writing at all.[6] *Queer*, as well, begun in 1952, also employs a traditional narrative. Yet *Junky* gets written out of Burroughs's account—it antedates the beginning of writing— and *Queer* remains a footnote (Burroughs was unable to get it published in the 1950s and later suppressed it until 1985).

Burroughs did not become a real writer, as he understands it, until 1954 when he began diligently to transcribe his so-called routines, the flamboyant, parodistic verbal performances (or riffs or collages) that would pour undiluted into his first real novel, *Naked Lunch*. Reading his letters penned during the writing of *Naked Lunch*, one notices an extraordinary transformation. He does indeed become a writer, insofar as his understanding of the relationship between subjectivity and textuality changes radically. Inspired by the routines, which he dubs "completely spontaneous, . . . fragmentary, inaccurate," he is able for the first time to write his incoherence as a subject, his doubleness, his difference from himself.[7] And it is precisely this self-difference that is thematized in his narrativization of the murder. His assertion to Morgan that "something took over" is echoed in his introduction to *Queer* in which he notes (immediately following the lines cited above): "I live with the constant threat of possession, and a constant need to escape from possession, from Control. So the death of Joan brought me in contact with the invader, the Ugly Spirit, and maneuvered me into a lifelong struggle, in which I have had no choice except to write my way out."[8] For Burroughs, the subject is always in the process of being (dis)possessed by a foreign agent, by (an)other who bears a double relationship to the self, being sited both within and without the subject (this process is repeatedly and obsessively dissected in his fiction). And subjectivity is always multiple, divided, fragmentary. To some extent, Burroughs nervously attempts to arrest the proliferation of doubles by conceptualizing this multiplicity as a "[d]ualism," which, he insists, "is the whole basis of this planet," and which is reflected in "the human body" itself, split into "two halves."[9] Like most binarisms, this one reproduces a gendered opposition, and in Burroughs's notoriously misogynist Manichaeanism, women are the source and symptom of evil, of the "Ugly Spirit": "I think they were a basic mistake, and the whole dualistic universe evolved from this error."[10] So although Burroughs insists that both "the death" and (apparently) the life "of Joan" brought him into "contact with the invader," with an "error," "the invader" is imagined as a "basic" fact of the universe. And the murder not only failed to stem this "error" but also—and more horrifyingly—revealed the power and the inescapability of "error."

Yet the murder of Joan Vollmer, if not quite the primal scene of writing that Burroughs suggests, nonetheless instantiates both a particular kind of masculinity and a particular way of representing (and to some extent, treating) women that have become increasingly prevalent in U.S. culture during the Cold War. For Burroughs, outlaw, junky, homosexual, despite his personal eccentricities and the peculiarities of his novels—of all the Beats his writing is indisputably the most difficult and idiosyncratic—seems to me strangely emblematic of a crucial shift in the construction of white masculinities that begins to take place in the immediate post–World War II years. Or rather, both Burroughs's writing and his self-fashioning as a writer are indicative and predictive of major cultural transformations that, although clearly delineated in the beat subculture of the late 1940s and 1950s, become widespread in the United States only in succeeding decades. Before proceeding, however, to an analysis of these changes and to an evaluation of the role of the Beats in effecting them, I want to revisit the scene of the crime, for it seems to me that the murder of Joan Vollmer—and Burroughs's interpretation of it—are uncannily suggestive of the desires, obsessions, fears, and anxieties that characterize these new male subjectivities.

In a 1965 interview, Burroughs indignantly disavows the very narrative of Vollmer's death that he would later reconstruct for his biographer (and that was circulating widely at the time). Insisting that the William Tell incident is no more than an "[a]bsurd and false" rumor, he explains that Mexico in the early 1950s was a deeply violent culture: "If you walked into a bar, there would be at least 15 people in there who were carrying guns."[11] In other words, Mexico, in Burroughs's fantasies, in some way replicates a frontier society that had largely disappeared in the United States by the 1950s. And despite his anxiety over the level of violence, he is also strangely drawn to a land and a culture that remain "sinister and gloomy and chaotic with the special chaos of a dream."[12] The Mexico of his fantasy allows Burroughs to carry a gun and perform a machismo that is in short supply (or at least more precarious) in his native country. And according to Eddie Woods, one of the witnesses to Vollmer's murder, Burroughs was indeed goaded on by a desire to perform: "I don't know how the conversation got around to it, but Burroughs said, 'Joanie, let me show the boys what a great shot old Bill is.'"[13] According to Woods, the William Tell act is thus set up as a spectacle for "the boys," as a performance of a particular kind of masculine bravado for the delectation of other men. Unlike the legendary William Tell, a fierce opponent of political and social tyranny forced to shoot an apple off the head of his son, Burroughs has no political cause and elects merely to display his marksmanship and courage using his wife. Vollmer, meanwhile, is rendered passive, contingent, Medusa-like within the performance—an object at once to be seen and avoided, a target at which to aim and not aim. Moreover, as friends of Burroughs's and Vollmer's suggested at the time, the murder may in part have been a suicide. Ginsberg commented on Vollmer's suicidal recklessness as a driver in a letter to Neal Cassady, while Carolyn Cassady later wrote: "Allen's comments made us wonder if there had been some desperation in Joan that might have played a part. She could easily have willed—consciously or unconsciously—this fate and moved her head. . . ."[14]

In some respects, the William Tell act and Vollmer's stance within the scene emblematize the position of women in the oppositional culture of the 1950s. In all of the discourses by the Beat writers or about them, the protagonist is always male. Invariably, he is enrapt in a number of intense, passionate homo-social bonds that are often difficult—or impossible—to distinguish from homosexual bonds. Women, when they appear at all in these narratives, function as girlfriends, whores, wives, mothers—figures defined almost exclusively by their relationship to men. Often they are completely erased. In both *Junky* and *Queer*, Burroughs goes to considerable lengths to expunge Vollmer from the narrative. In *Junky*, she is not mentioned until almost two-thirds of the way through the novel. In *Queer*, she is simply not there. Less than a year after the murder, as he was revising *Junky* for publication and anxious about the queer content of his confessional narrative, Burroughs decided to insert references to his wife "here and there," despite the fact that she has no apparent impact on the plot and is never characterized.[15] Yet as Burroughs himself later suggests, her presence/absence is decisive to his autobiographical narratives of those years. What I want to emphasize here is less her ontological instability in the text, her status as a kind of vengeful ghost haunting both novels, than the *violence* that attends her erasure, a violence condensed in Burroughs's repeated and chilling disavowal: "she has no bearing on the story whatever."[16] This assertion is the sign not only of Vollmer's crucial importance to the narrative but also of her function in the complex psychic processes that the novels enact. For Joan Vollmer exists not simply as a suicide or as an erased—and murdered—woman, but also as *an introjected subject*, as that figure who has possessed the writer and who takes up lodging within the melancholic self.[17] According to the logic of identification, the male subject, as Burroughs so clearly suggests, both identifies with and is possessed by a feminized other, an "invader." But insofar as he also self-identifies as a man, he must continually do battle with the femininity that has invaded him and inheres within. For as a subject, he is always split into a masculine—and sadistic—half that delights in displaying his prowess and his marksmanship, and a feminine—and masochistic—half that delights in being used as a target. His (impossible) project, as man and as writer, is to master the femininity that constantly gets in his way, the femininity at which he aims and does not aim, to write his way "out."

THE NEW BOHEMIANS

Both the Beat writers and the beat subculture of the late 1940s and 1950s took up an avowedly oppositional stance during what is surely the most repressive period in modern U.S. history, the era that witnessed the apogee of the postwar economic boom, the Cold War, and McCarthyism. Together with several closely related groups—hipsters, beatniks, and juvenile delinquents—they consciously, if confusedly, rebelled against and critiqued the deeply conservative official culture that emerged at the end of World War II, a culture that was consolidated very rapidly as hostilities in Europe and Japan were winding down and remained more or less intact, I believe, until the early 1960s (and the rise of the the civil rights movement and New Left).[18] The Truman administration made it very clear that the United States, having emerged from the war with its infrastructure relatively unscathed (it was the only major industrialized nation to do so), was determined to secure leadership of the world economy. In March 1945, undersecretary of state William C. Clayton bluntly declared to Congress, "We've got to export three times as much as we exported just before the war if we want to keep our industry running at somewhere near capacity."[19] Truman, putting greater stress than had the Roosevelt administration on economic expansionism and rolling back a number of New Deal programs, knew that American prosperity was dependent on the nation's securing the domination of markets worldwide. To that end, he announced the Truman Doctrine in 1947, opposing capitalist "free enterprise" to communist "planning," insisting that markets be kept open to American goods, and, in a move that would be repeated countless times over the next forty years, sent economic aid and military advisers to a so-called developing nation in the throes of a civil war (this time, Greece) to prop up a repressive right-wing government against leftist insurgents.[20] Inspired by the doctrine of containment, the Truman administration pursued a vigorous anti-Soviet policy, instituted the Marshall Plan to rebuild and stabilize capitalism in western Europe, fortified its economic and political domination of Latin America, and doubled its holdings of oil in the Middle East.

The economic boom that followed the Truman Doctrine effected a dramatic increase in U.S. production and exports, and a doubling of median family income between 1945 and 1973.[21] Yet the cost of economic success was daunting. After the disruptions of the Great Depression and the war, the postwar years bore witness to a return to conservative social and political values and to strictly enforced gender roles.[22] McCarthyism aimed to police the body politic and the body sexual by demonizing and scapegoating alleged communists and homosexuals. Its effectiveness, however, lay in its ability less to harass, purge, destroy the careers of, or drive to suicide avowed communists and homosexuals than to intimidate and terrorize the already anticommunist and homophobic majority. Perhaps the most successful police action in U.S. history, McCarthyism, together with the dramatic demographic changes enabled by the boom, oversaw the virtual destruction of the Left and traditional working-class communities. Because, during the 1950s, "suburbs grew six times faster than cities," the old urban coalitions quickly disintegrated. Moreover, the United States was becoming an increasingly mobile culture, and between the end of the war and 1960 "the number of cars in the country increased by 133 percent."[23] As Paul Buhle notes, "[s]uburbanization and automobilization taking the younger people especially from the ethnic ghettoes, fragmented old solidarities and rechanneled aspirations."[24]

The postwar hegemony exerted some of its greatest power, however, not in the public sphere but precisely on those privatized lives to which so many retreated. The nuclear family, in particular, newly isolated in the suburbs from the extended family, became a crucial site for the consolidation and reproduction of normative subjects. Morris Zelditch, a postwar sociologist, offers an especially vivid portrait of 1950s domestic bliss:

> Father helps mother with the dishes. He sets the table. He makes formula for the baby. Mother can supplement the income of the family by working outside. Nevertheless, the American male, by definition, *must* "provide" for his family. He is *responsible* for the support of his wife and children. His primary area of performance is the occupational role, in which his status fundamentally inheres; and his *primary* function in the family is to supply an "income," to be the "breadwinner." There is simply something wrong with the American adult male who doesn't have a "job."

American women, on the other hand, tend to hold jobs *before* they are married and to quit when "the day" comes; or to continue in jobs of a lower status than their husbands. And not only is the mother the focus of emotional support for the American middle-class child, but much more exclusively so than in most societies. . . . The cult of the warm, giving "Mom" stands in contrast to the "capable," "competent," "go-getting" male. The more expressive type of male, as a matter of fact, is regarded as "effeminate," and has too much fat on the inner side of his thigh.[25]

In conceptualizing this (unmistakably middle-class) nuclear family as a self-contained unit, Cold War domesticity aimed at enforcing submission to a wide variety of social and cultural norms.[26] Most important in this process was the policing of gender roles, which, as the above citation suggests, were rigorously defined in terms of both their labor power and emotional profile. Moreover, those who deviated from these norms, such as the "expressive" male, were pathologized and, in this case at least, literally stigmatized by their dissidence (by being made to bear the incriminating bodily signifier, "too much fat").

Yet what is perhaps most important about the normative masculinity of the 1950s is that it represents a retreat from the more independent- and entrepreneurial-minded masculinities that preceded it. Zelditch is correct to note the primacy of the "occupational role," but the nature of that role changed considerably during the postwar years. For it is no accident that the Allied victory in 1945 coincidentally "brought Fordism," as David Harvey notes, "to maturity as a fully-fledged and distinctive regime of accumulation." With its use of mass-production and assembly-line technology, Fordism rationalized the workplace and helped to consolidate corporate power, guaranteeing "a new system of the reproduction of labour power, a new politics of labour control and management, a new aesthetics and psychology. . . ."[27] The consolidation of the Fordist regime in the United States worked to stabilize both blue-collar and white-collar labor forces and promoted the mass consumption of automobiles, refrigerators, dishwashers, and televisions. It also oversaw the rise of the "organization man" who was expected to subordinate his personal ambitions for the good of the corporation and develop those interpersonal skills that were becoming an increasingly important part of the business world. As Robert Corber explains, "men were discouraged from competing aggressively with one another and were expected to submit to corporate structures in exchange for obtaining a secure place in the organizational hierarchy." Unlike the self-reliant entrepreneur of the nineteenth and early twentieth centuries, the "organization man" was expected to cultivate "respect for authority, loyalty to one's superiors, and an ability to get along with others—all qualities traditionally associated with femininity."[28] At the same time, men's roles in the domestic sphere were changing. Despite the importance of their occupational status, husbands were expected to make an increasing investment in their families and in the rearing of children. "The American man," Arthur

Schlesinger observed in 1959, "is found as never before as a substitute for wife and mother—changing diapers, washing dishes, cooking meals and performing a whole series of what were once considered female duties." The reconfiguration of workplace and home, in other words, signaled a feminization and domestication of normative, white, middle-class masculinity. Not surprisingly, this feminization was perceived by many as being the sign of a male identity crisis. "What has happened to the American male?" Schlesinger complains, "[t]oday men are more and more conscious of maleness not as a fact but as a problem."[29]

In some respects, the rebel males of the 1950s, whether beats, beatniks, or hipsters, were the symptoms of this crisis, offering both a solution to this "problem" and a significant challenge to the rigors of normative masculinity. Sociologists, politicians, and commentators tirelessly warned of the threat posed to the well-being and (imaginary) coherence of the body politic by these rebel males. J. Edgar Hoover was appalled by the explosion of teenage crime and considered "'the juvenile jungle' alongside communism as a threat to American freedom."[30] As beat apologist John Clellon Holmes noted, "the beat generation" protested the inflexibility of social norms and "the conformity of our national life" by an "affirmation of individuality"—in other words, by an attempt to resuscitate the entrepreneurial and fiercely individualistic masculinities of the pre–World War II period.[31] Responding to the triumph of Fordism in the workplace and, in the aftermath of Hiroshima, to both the loss of faith (in religion, nationalism, science, progress) and the apparent precariousness of Enlightenment epistemologies, the beats embarked on a quest. "What the hipster is looking for," Holmes argues, "in his 'coolness' (withdrawal) or 'flipness' (ecstasy) is, after all, a feeling of somewhereness, not just another diversion."[32] Alienated from elite and mass culture alike, from Rodgers and Hammerstein and Tennessee Williams as much as Elvis Presley and I Love Lucy, the hipster withdrew into an urban subculture that offered him or her both community and anonymity as well as a set of alternatives to the nuclear family. Sociologist Ned Polsky, in his 1960 study of Greenwich Village beats, notes that the beat, unlike the normative working man/husband/father, goes to great lengths to avoid work (as "a matter of conviction"), believing "that voluntary poverty is an intellectual gain."[33] And for most beats, poverty was, if not exactly voluntary, at least a novelty, insofar as two-thirds of them, according to Polsky, came from middle- or upper-class families. Yet Polsky judges these disaffected bourgeois "keen critics of the society in which they have grown up" for whom the "anti-work ideology" is "a sign of disaffiliation from particular, mutable realities."[34] Like many of his contemporaries, Polsky notes that the beat's rebellion represents a studied rejection of American political culture: "They are not apolitical but consciously and deliberately antipolitical. . . . They totally 'resign' from society in so far as this is possible, not least of all from its politics, and reject extreme political sects with no less vigor than they reject major parties."[35] Yet as Polsky implies, the resigned, disaffected, anti-political beat on a search for somewhereness makes a somewhat unlikely hero, practicing as he does, as Holmes puts it, "a kind of passive resistance to the Square society in which he lives."[36] Unlike the normative working man/husband/father, he imagines himself a *victim* of American culture: "To be beat is to be at the bottom of your personality, looking up."[37]

Arguably the most influential (and controversial) analysis of the male beat as victim is Norman Mailer's "The White Negro," originally published in *Dissent* in 1957. In this essay, Mailer describes the hipster (his preferred designation) as "the American existentialist."[38] Mailer reveals a certain ambivalence toward the hipster, whom he regards simultaneously as one who offers a "life-giving answer" to a pathological society (sickened by "atomic war" and "conformity"), and as a pathologized figure himself, a psychopath (2). According to Mailer (quoting the work of psychologist Robert Lindner), the hipster, like the psychopath, is "a rebel without a cause, an agitator without a slogan, a revolutionary without a program: in other words, his rebelliousness is aimed to achieve goals satisfactory to himself alone . . . " (7). An infantilized and potentially violent subject, the psychopathic hipster is on a quest for Eros or, as Mailer puts it, "an orgasm more apocalyptic than the one that preceded it" (9). This "frontiersman in the Wild West of American night life," hopped up on jazz, marijuana, and mysticism, is overwhelmed by a "burning consciousness of the present" and consumed by a "language of energy" (3, 5, 11).

In his portrait of the hipster, Mailer is describing for the first time what thirty years later would be widely recognized as the postmodernist subject, the fragmented, decentered, ephemeral subject of late capitalism. This "new kind of personality" (which could well "become the central expression of human nature before the twentieth century is over") is intensively and exclusively presentist in his orientation. For him the only "truths" are the "isolated truths of what each oberver feels at each instant of his existence" (7, 14). Unable to comprehend his relation to history or to the nation, the "perpetually ambivalent" hipster immerses himself in the moment, making and unmaking himself in each instant (14). Most tellingly, this "psychic outlaw" is incapable of recognizing the extent to which he is rendered a schizophrenic subject, oblivious (like the Burroughs of the introduction to *Queer*) to the "conservative power which controls him from without and within" (15, 16). A rebel who has introjected the very forces against which he is rebelling, the hipster is at once a victim of the repressive and conformist society of which he is a part and a potentially violent, if directionless, opponent of that society.

According to Mailer, it is this double positionality of the hipster as victim and aggressor—along with the obvious attraction to jazz, marijuana, and "the language of Hip"—that qualifies him as a "white Negro" (4). Mailer notes that the hipster has been coupled (heterosexually, of course) to the Negro by means of a "wedding" in which "it was the Negro who brought the cultural dowry" (4). In Mailer's narrative of cultural miscegenation, the heavily mythologized "Negro" (in whom all class-based and gendered differences are erased) plays the part of a seductive bride, bringing to the marriage both an unusually vital culture and an attitude toward and way of managing white hegemony that inspires identifiation on the part of the hipster. This feminization of "the Negro" is echoed by a romanticization wherein he (for he retains his masculine identity despite his feminine positionality) is imagined to embody all those characteristics that Mailer seems to desire. On the one hand, he is rendered (quite correctly) the victim of racist violence, excluded from the comforts and securities promised by Zelditch's middle-class domestic idyll. On the other hand, he is also identified with the body and with authenticity; he understands "in the cells of his existence that life [is] war" and so keeps "for his survival the art of the primitive." With jazz, in particular, "he gave voice . . . to his rage, and infinite variations of joy, lust, languor, growl, cramp, pinch, scream and despair of his orgasm" (4). In Mailer's fantasy, "the Negro" (and especially his music) embody an ecstatic, orgasmic, and utopian wholeness and plenitude that have been lost in white, bourgeois American culture. He represents a more basic, "primitive," and, indeed, salubrious subjectivity. Unlike the hipster, he apparently is not a psychopath insofar as he is reacting to real rather than at least partially imagined persecution. Moreover, he has invented a unique, ironic language, a language of "cunning" and "abstract ambiguous alternatives in which" to speak "from the danger of . . . oppression" (10). Anticipating Henry Louis Gates's concept of Signification (a metadiscourse that critiques "the nature of [white] meaning itself" and "luxuriates in the inclusion of the free play of . . . associative rhetorical and semantic relations"), the language of Hip is "different in kind from white slang" and is rooted in and authenticated by experience.[39]

Despite the hipster's "wedding" to "the Negro," the hipster (who, in Mailer's formulation, *must* be white) remains strangely dematerialized even in Mailer's relatively sympathetic account. For he is of necessity a pale imitation of a subject to which he can never do justice (in at least two senses). Since the language of Hip "cannot really be taught," the hipster is imagined as a kind of fake, as one who mimics an original whose experiences and subjectivity remain fundamentally incommunicable (10). In his "primitive" authenticity, "the Negro" is produced simultaneously as feminized (he represents nature as opposed to culture, body as opposed to mind) and as hypermasculinized, which is to say that he becomes, in James Baldwin's words, a "walking phallic symbol," embodying (an)other masculinity, a masculinity so powerful and phallicized that it can be imagined only as other.[40] (In Mailer's fantasy, "the Negro" brings a revolutionary "sexual impetus" that "may rebound against the anti-sexual foundation of every organized power in America" [16].) In relation to the schizophrenic masculinity of "the Negro," the imitative masculinity of the hipster is both stabilized and destabilized. On the one hand, he is imagined as the indisputably masculine partner in the marriage. On the other hand, he is placed in the impossible position, within a heterosexualized economy at least, of both desiring and identifying with his partner. (Heterosexualization—and Oedipalization, for that matter—are predicated on the incommensurability of desire and identification. As a man, one is supposed to desire women and identify with other men.) The white hipster, in other words, plays the part of a husband who scandalously desires to be *like* his wife, who longs to dress in her clothes and co-opt her experience.

I would like to propose that the portrait Mailer offers of the white, transvestite, male hipster wishing he were black demonstrates in fact a remarkably acute (if unconscious) understanding both of the beat's self-representation and of his cultural reception during the 1950s.[41] For if nothing else, the fascination with and notoriety of the beat testifies to an extraordinary amount of anxiety circulating around the production of white masculinity during the domestic revival. ("Why," Baldwin asks, "malign the sorely menaced sexuality of Negroes in order to justify the white man's own sexual panic?")[42] Unlike Zelditch's normative "breadwinner," the beat is coded as being both masculine and feminine. He is frontiersman, adventurer, and rebel, as well as decadent, fake, and psychopath. He is at once a Natty Bumppo of the atomic age, wedded to a black Chingachgook, and a female impersonator. Indeed, Mailer analogizes the very word "beat" to "flip," which he characterizes as a loss "of control," the revelation of "the buried weaker more feminine part of your nature" (12–13). So to be beat is by definition to betray the feminine within. Moreover, as in so many discourses of the period, the disruption of gendered norms is inextricably linked to a sexual pathology. For not only are "many hipsters . . . bisexual," according to Mailer, but homosexuality is also cited as one of the unmistakable signs of the "violent" psychic regression of the psychopath or hipster (12, 8).

In addition to disclosing anxieties associated with normative masculine identities, the construction of the hipster also reveals fears circulating around the struggle of African Americans for equity in a deeply racist society. Although the Supreme Court's 1954 ruling in *Brown v. Board of Education* struck down the "separate but equal" doctrine and mandated the desegregation of public schools, the process was delayed by the intransigency of most southern states and the indisposition of Eisenhower to take action. In 1955 and 1956, meanwhile, the Montgomery bus boycott applied further pressure to the principle of segregation and laid the groundwork for the civil rights struggles of the 1960s.[43] So when "The White Negro" was published, there was both tremendous racial tension in the United States and a sense of waiting. (Violence finally erupted in September 1957 when Arkansas governor Orval

Faubus called out the National Guard to prevent nine African-American children from attending a formerly segregated school in Little Rock.) From its discourse on race, "The White Negro" is clearly a product of this moment of suspense, and Mailer seems aware of the direness of the situation and its very high stakes. On the one hand, Mailer's "so antique a vision," in Baldwin's words, his romanticization of "the Negro," represents yet another rehearsal of racist tropes and, to that extent, Ned Polsky makes an important point when he notes that most white beats "accept the Negro only for his 'Negro-ness' (as bringer of marihuana and jazz, etc.) and thus practice an inverted form of 'keeping the nigger in his place.'"[44] On the other hand, looking more broadly at the role of Hip in American political culture, Mailer recognizes that "the organic growth of Hip depends on whether the Negro emerges as a dominating force in American life." For he maintains—ominously—that "the Negro"'s knowledge of "the ugliness and danger of life" will grant him, if he can "win his equality," a "potential superiority." And this superiority, Mailer argues (looking ahead to the backlash against the civil rights movement that would begin in the 1970s), inspires a "fear" that "has become the underground drama of domestic politics, . . . for the Negro's equality would tear a profound shift into the psychology, the sexuality, and the moral imagination of every White alive" (16). In other words, Mailer divines quite correctly that white Americans are terrified lest "the Negro" attain equality insofar as racial equality is unimaginable in the United States. Rather, even an approximation of equality would signal the defeat of white Americans because it would destroy those economic, social, and political privileges and perquisites that historically have signified whiteness in America.

The figure of the white rebel male is, I believe, so important historically because of its condensation of fears circulating around questions of masculinity, male sexuality, race, and social class. Unlike the normative middle-class working man/husband/father, the hipster is a hybridized subject, a product of cultural miscegenation, a cross-dresser, neither completely white nor black, masculine nor feminine, heterosexual nor homosexual, working-class nor bourgeois. Rather, as I will demonstrate, his oscillation between these different positionalities produces him as a schizophrenic, self-defeating—and masochistic—subject. Embracing blackness, femininity, homosexuality, and poverty to declare himself white, masculine, heterosexual, and a man of independent means, he is unable, however, to stabilize any of these positions. In his confusion and multiplicity, he is the first exemplar of the postmodern subject who by the mid-1970s will become hegemonic in U.S. culture. And he stands as the immediate precursor of the rebels *with a cause*, from New Leftists to Black Panthers, radical feminists to gay liberationists, the ones who saw to it, in Mailer's words, that the McCarthyite "time of conformity" would be replaced during the 1960s by a "time of violence, new hysteria, confusion and rebellion" (16).

THE BEATS AS CULTURAL PRODUCERS

The chance meeting of William Burroughs, Allen Ginsberg, and Jack Kerouac in a New York City apartment during the waning months of World War II was a pivotal moment in the histories of American literature and culture. (Burroughs was thirty at the time, Ginsberg eighteen, and Kerouac twenty-two.) Although none of the three would be able to secure publication for his work until the 1950s, the three began to produce a body of literature that, despite its many and varied precursors, in some ways marks a significant break with earlier American fiction and poetry, especially with the modernism of Hemingway, Fitzgerald, Eliot, and Faulkner. More clearly than their contemporaries, they "shattered the conformity of the Eisenhower era and dramatically rekindled vital themes in the broad tradition of American dissent."[45] As writers and cultural icons, they became instrumental (like Johnny [Marlon Brando] and his motorcycle gang in *The Wild One* [1953]) in inspiring a generation of young, white Americans to rebel against the conformity bred by the domestic revival, a generation who, as Paul George and Jerold Starr note, "slouched around in T-shirts and jeans, wore long sideburns, took drugs, 'dug' bebop, and talked like the original hipsters."[46] In the late 1950s and 1960s, these disaffected youth "represented a new social category created by a number of factors, including the need to delay the assimilation of the 'baby boom' cohorts into the economy, the growing reliance of private industry on universities for low-wage, high-skill labor (graduate students) for research and development, larger federal subsidies to higher education, . . . a credential inflation in the job market, and rising status competition in the expanding middle class."[47]

In *Naked Angels*, one of the first and most influential book-length studies of the significance of the literary subculture, John Tytell notes that Burroughs, Ginsberg, and Kerouac (along with a number of other writers) managed, despite the lack of a platform or manifesto, to cohere as a "literary group."[48] As he emphasizes, they consciously produced themselves as part of an oppositional social and cultural formation, styling themselves urban "outcasts, exiles within a hostile culture, freaky progenitors of new attitudes toward sanity and ethics, rejected artists writing anonymously for themselves."[49] All three figures were charged at one time or another with criminal offenses; all used drugs; all responded to jazz; all valued spontaneity, happenstance, the accidental; all, in different ways, shunned (and were shunned by) the literary establishment. Despite their suspicion of literary traditions, they are clearly the heirs of several: the American transcendentalists, especially Thoreau, Melville, and Whitman; the French symbolists, Baudelaire and Rimbaud; the first avant-garde, especially the dadaists and surrealists; Ezra Pound, Hart Crane, and the leftist poets of the 1930s; Artaud, Céline, Genet, and Henry Miller. Yet they were also instrumental in undermining the opposition between elite and mass culture—

this clearly links their writing to the conventions of postmodernism—and their works owe as much to pulp fiction, detective novels, the blues, folk songs, comic books, science fiction, film noir, true confessions magazines, and various American oral traditions as they do to their literary predecessors. "The side streets and bars of New York City," Andrew Jamison and Ron Eyerman write, "with their ethnic subcultures and small-time criminals, kept the Beats in touch with another America" and consolidated their belief that "poetry should not only deal with the everyday experience of common people but should also speak their language."[50] Moreover, they were fortunate to be producing during an extraordinary efflorescence in the publishing industry. For the production of *Howl and Other Poems* (1956) by a small press like City Lights and the appearance of numerous mass-distribution magazines and newpapers that featured the writing of the Beats could not have occurred without the development after the war of "new printing technology" that "greatly reduc[ed] the labor and cost involved in self-publishing."[51] At the same time, the inexpensive paperback editions of Kerouac and Burroughs that flooded bookstores in the late 1950s and 1960s would not have been possible without what one historian notes to have been "the mightiest outpouring of mass market books of every kind that had ever been seen in publishing history."[52] Unlike many other writers and intellectuals, the Beats "did not resist . . . attention from the mass media," instead actively seeking them out and using them to further their interests.[53]

Among all the ostensibly revolutionary projects of the Beats, perhaps none is more important than their subversion of the differences between the public and the private spheres. The bourgeois settlement, especially under the terms of the postwar domestic revival, works to effect the strict separation of the private from the public, the domestic from the political, the sexual from the commercial. The home is conceptualized as "a secure private nest removed from the dangers of the outside world," while the nuclear family offers "a psychological fortress" to keep out the fears and anxieties of the atomic age (in fact, of course, these exclusions never finally hold and must be compulsively reasserted).[54] The writing of the Beats, however, unlike most modernist American fiction, emphatically challenges these norms by taking an avowedly confessional stance. All of the Beats intermix fiction and autobiography, writing their subjectivities and personal histories simultaneously with their fictional narratives. Ginsberg notes that "[j]ust as Kerouac's entire body of work is 'The Vanity of Kerouac,' . . . or 'Visions of Kerouac,' so, Burroughs has actually got one giant visionary scope for his novel. Both of these are autobiographies of the psychological or spiritual history, . . . visionary panoramas."[55] All three have produced bodies of diverse texts that publicize—and exalt—those humiliating secrets (especially sexual and pharmacological secrets) that are supposed to remain hidden away in the private sphere (in Kerouac's words, writing should be no more nor less than "UNINTERRUPTED AND UNREVISED FULL

CONFESSIONS ABOUT WHAT ACTUALLY HAPPENED IN REAL LIFE," and all of his novels can be read as romans à clef).[56] By so defying the prohibitions of Cold War culture and turning "stigma into a blessing, shame into defiance," they helped to establish "the pattern for the black, youth, women's and gay revolutions" of the following decade, which would similarly produce varieties of what Foucault calls reverse discourse.[57] Moreover, the autobiographical nature of their so-called fictional texts is complicated by their countless essays and interviews (including those, like Odier's *The Job*, that freely mix opinion with fictional texts), and the appearance in recent years of several volumes of journals, memoirs, and letters.[58] Indeed, no writers before them seem to have textualized their activities as thoroughly and obsessively as the Beats or to have as self-consciously mythologized themselves and their activities. For the Beats, the self is understood to be less the immutable ground of being than a performance, a construction that must continually be reimagined and reiterated. Ginsberg is certainly correct, then, when he agrees with an interviewer that his work, like that of his friends, constitutes a "spiritual autobiography" of the invented self, and that between and among Burroughs, Kerouac, and himself, "with all the interconnected letters, it's quite continuous tissue, continuous fabric."[59] This obsessive textualization of the interconnected self, along with the focus that it throws onto what Kerouac calls the "unspeakable visions of the individual," also connects the Beats with the project of the historical avantgarde (especially dada and surrealism), which, in Peter Bürger's celebrated phrase, aimed "to reintegrate art in the praxis of life."[60] Like their avant-gardist precursors, the Beats rejected the aestheticist separation of the self-contained artifact from "the praxis of life" and attempted to turn their lives into works of art that would be, if not coterminous with their texts, at least indissolubly linked to them.

   The personal and literary interconnections among the male Beat writers and the virtual impossibility of separating fictional from nonfictional texts, autobiography from novel, make the Beats a particularly rich source for studying the structures of gendered subjectivities. Their writing practices, in addition to revealing the necessarily fictive, indeed fantasmatic, nature of all autobiography, obliquely but powerfully illuminate the social geography of Cold War America. For despite what Polsky correctly diagnoses in their work as an "oversimplified anti-academicism and anti-historicism," despite their conscious attempts to break with tradition, to focus on the personal and the private, and to expunge historical and political context, their discourses consistently reproduce and reconfigure the male body, male homosociality, and the idea of America in revealing and sometimes startling ways.[61] Moreover, their ability to disclose what is perhaps best described as the unconscious of Cold War America is directly linked to their self-fashioning as an oppositional force in U.S. culture, an oppositional hegemony that, I believe, remains mortgaged to the very structures it would dismantle. On the one hand, this linkage testifies to the seemingly boundless potential of the "hegemonic function," to borrow Raymond Williams's turn of phrase, "to control or transform or even incorporate" both alternative and oppositional formations.[62] It also emphatically supports Sacvan Bercovitch's contention that despite appearances to the contrary, so many "major writers" of American literature "were not subversive at all," or "were radical in a representative way that *reaffirmed* the culture, rather than undermining it." The success of the Beats attests to the remarkable power of the cultural dominant in the United States since World War II (and in postmodern culture more generally) to contain revolutionary forces, to adopt "utopia for its own purposes."[63] On the other hand, this process of co-optation should not blind one to the fact that "works of art," in Williams's words, often serve as "especially important sources of . . . complex evidence" as to the structure of "the hegemonic" not only "in its active and formative but also its transformational processes."[64]

Among the Beat writers, Jack Kerouac is usually singled out as the most representative (he also most emphatically bears out Mailer's assertions about the hipster as "white Negro"). Good-looking, an athlete and football player, an observant Catholic, the most conservative both literarily and politically, the most compulsively heterosexual, Kerouac was always the least threatening of the Beats for the cultural establishment. And the publication of *On the Road* in 1957 represents perhaps the most important single event in their popularization. Written in three weeks in April 1950 in New York City on a roll of teletype paper (about events that occurred between 1946 and 1950), *On the Road* received a mixed reception upon its publication. The daily *New York Times* called it "an authentic work of art" and "the most beautifully executed, the clearest and the most important utterance yet made by the generation Kerouac himself named years ago as 'beat,' and whose principal avatar he is."[65] The Sunday *Times*, on the other hand, was less enthusiastic, describing it as "a road . . . that leads nowhere," while Kerouac's more academic critics were appalled by both the book itself and its popularity.[66] In a notorious critique of "The Know-Nothing Bohemians," then-leftist Norman Podhoretz attacks the Beats, and Kerouac in particular, for anti-intellectualism, worship of the primitive and instinctual, clichéd and vague writing, and a bleary, infantile radicalism that disinclines them from rebelling against "anything so sociological and historical as the middle class or capitalism or even respectability."[67] Leslie Fiedler, meanwhile, more preoccupied with the self-mythologization of the Beats, complains that their texts are "fake adolescent books," and that Kerouac has been marketed as "a fantasy figure capable of moving the imagination of rebellious kids with educations and literary aspirations, as his more *lumpen* opposite numbers, Elvis Presley, Marlon Brando, and James Dean, were moving their less literate and ambitious contemporaries."[68] For both Podhoretz and Fiedler, in other words, the Beats constitute a *fraudulent* rebellion that not only is incapable of producing any real social change but functions as a displacement of what could be an effective oppositional political movement. They render real discontent harmless and benign. Like the "white Negro," they are substitutes, imitations, phonies.

In some respects, the critiques of Podhoretz and Fiedler, despite their elitism and homophobia, represent an accurate reading of the Beats as a force for social change. For the Beats were distinguished from earlier American rebels and bohemians, whether Wobblies, social activists of the Progressive Era, suffragists, or Old Leftists, by their lack of an avowedly political project and agenda (to some extent, Ginsberg, who began to get involved with radical politics in 1960 and went to his first demonstration three years later, is the one exception).[69] There is no question but that the Beats' inability to foment anything other than a vague cultural revolution is itself historically determined. For with the Beats and their kin, the other rebel males, a radical movement took shape in the United States for the first time that was intent on producing not political or social change but *cultural* transformation. As Burroughs describes it, "[t]he Beat movement was a worldwide literary, cultural and sociological manifestation, rather than a political one." And unquestionably, in many respects, this oppositional hegemony, or, in Burroughs's words, "cultural protest against conventional dress and behavior," challenged many of the values of the domestic revival.[70] But it was predicated, as Burroughs suggests, on the exclusion of the political from the "literary, cultural and sociological." In Laslo Benedek's *The Wild One*, one of the first Hollywood films to foreground these rebel males, the motorcycle gang that invades a small California town profoundly shakes up the community. Their cynicism, aggressivity, disrespect, and lack of regard for private property clearly oppose small-town values ("None of these outlaw outfits ever want to do anything but foul things up for everybody else," remarks one of the townsfolk). Moreover, the tough, angry gang members, in their black-leather jackets with skulls-and-crossbones, challenge the "square," bureaucratized, ineffectual masculinity of the petty bourgeois shopkeepers and policemen. But the opposition is articulated primarily in terms of *style*. The gang (like rustlers in a 1950s western) are vaguely criminalized, they dress and speak differently, and their motorcycles scare the townspeople. But the exact nature of their rebellion is never articulated. "Hey, Johnny," a "square" asks, "what are you rebelling against?"—to which Johnny peevishly replies, "Whaddya got?" Although clearly malcontents, the gang have no coherent program—they are apparently against everything—and their rebellion is coded as an Oedipal conflict rather than a political project. Moreover, the film is careful to retain certain traditional narrative features. Unlike much of the work produced by the Beats, it by no means rejects either heterosexual romance or traditional plot structure. As in so many classic Hollywood films, the focus remains on the erotic entanglement between Johnny and Cathy, the local policeman's daughter, who, like so many female characters in diverse cultural productions of the 1950s, is constructed as the primary domesticating force within the fiction, the one who would cure the hero of his rebelliousness.[71] Johnny may abjure her at the end of the film, but his involvement with her functions, at least to some extent, to woo him away from his all-male gang and to prepare for an as yet deferred taming of this wild one.

Although there are important differences between *The Wild One* and *On the Road*, both focus on a specific kind of rebel male, the man on the move, the one who refuses to be tied down ("you don't go any one special place," Johnny explains, "that's cornball style—you just go"). So, too, both Sal Paradise, the narrator of *On the Road*, and his buddy, Dean Moriarty (a.k.a. Neal Cassady), are dedicated to continuous movement. Restless, insatiable, and "mad," they "burn, burn, burn like fabulous yellow roman candles" and are "desirous of everything at the same time. . . ."[72] Tellingly, Sal links this insatiability repeatedly to the history and constitution of the nation. Dean's "'criminality'" is no mere individual aberration but "a wild yea-saying overburst of American joy; it was Western, the west wind, an ode from the Plains, something new, long prophesied, long a-coming . . . " (11). So Dean (like Johnny) takes his place alongside other heroes of American westerns whose promise he fulfills, and Kerouac, as it were, reimagines the cowboy, now riding a Cadillac rather than a palomino. In their search for "everything" they obsessively push against the edges of the United States, bouncing back and forth between New York and San Francisco, feeling trapped within the borders. Moreover, it is no accident that their final and climactic journey takes them across the border, to Mexico where, immersed in Indian culture (and oblivious to the social and political oppression that the Indians suffer), they are finally able to share in "the essential strain of the basic primitive, wailing humanity" for which they so desperately yearn (229). For the apprehension of this primitive and authentic "humanity" represents a return to the origin, to the "great, grave Indians" who are "the source of mankind and the fathers of it" (230). And if the novel is a quest narrative, focused on the fruitless search for Dean's father, these other "fathers" function as a displacement of the original lost father, simultaneously fulfilling desire and leaving it unsatisfied and insatiable (the penultimate clause of the novel's long final sentence still mourns "the father we never found" [254]). Insofar as the (founding) father is also associated with the nation, the journey to Mexico and back simultaneously represents a (re)discovery of America, or rather, of the liminal status of these two figures and, more generally, of the culture of which they are a part. For the narrative of *On the Road* finds Dean and Sal riding a fantasy of a utopian nation in which America stands at once for an (unfulfilled) promise, for "joy," for (un)imaginable possibilities, and for the stultifyingly banal reality of postwar daily life, for "the gloom" from which "a new beat generation" was slowly "rising" (46). Repeatedly, the writing of the Beats enacts this contradictory understanding of America as a land of infinite possibility and crushing repression. As Joan Vollmer noted to Ginsberg, there is only an impossible choice for the disaffected or dissident subject. One can elect to be "on the outside looking in" or "on the inside looking out." For wherever they go, the Beats bring this fantasy of the nation with them and remain burning and insatiable, on a quest for America, for the source, for the father, neither fully citizens of this utopian nation nor fully dispossessed.

This ambivalent understanding of the nation (and of the national subject) is the direct result of the contradictory class positionality of Burroughs, Ginsberg, Kerouac, and most of the other Beat writers. Although from diverse backgrounds (upper-class for Burroughs, middle-class for Ginsberg, and working-class for Kerouac), all three matriculated at Ivy League universities and retained (or accrued) a good deal of what today is called upward mobility. Because they held salaried jobs only infrequently, preferring to self-identify and live as (itinerant) writers during the 1950s, they became, by default, men of independent means, an aristocracy manqué, while receiving few of the dollars or perquisites usually attending upper-class association. Moreover, the Beats were producing their most groundbreaking and celebrated work during one of the most tortuous moments in U.S. history, during the Cold War, the Korean War, and the height of McCarthyism. Bruce Cook is correct to note that they "turned the idea of America inside out," offering "dirt" for "cleanliness," "sloth" for "industry," and "a morality with principles but no rules" for the "American Protestant ethic."[73] But in turning the nation inside out, rebelling against conformity, they reproduced merely a variation upon the dominant ideology. Prizing freedom above equality, they resuscitated a quirky version of individualism that, oscillating between libertarianism and anarchism, exalts the will and privatized passions of the individual at the expense of the community, the state, and the public sphere. Their writing practices may have helped to undermine the distinction between the private and the public (and to anticipate the feminist motto that the personal is the political), but they did so by politicizing the personal realm, not by challenging the constitution of the public sphere or attempting a meaningful intervention into it. As Dan Georgakas argues, the Beats, "[b]ased on a highly individualistic anarchism, . . . denounced capitalist Moloch without the slightest hope for a Marxism whose authoritarianism was frequently assailed."[74] (Ginsberg links the Beats not with Marxism at all but with "the traditional bohemian-Anarchist-West-Coast-Wobbly-Chicago-American Populist tradition.")[75] Unlike communism, or more progressive forms of liberalism, "[a]narchism is no mass movement, has no stable class base, lacks unified theory, posits uncertain tactics, and has no long-term organizations."[76] Pitted against the rule of law and the sovereignty and territoriality of the modern state, it is "directed towards the vindication of 'natural society,' i.e. a self-regulated society of individuals and freely-formed groups."[77] In short, the anarchist sympathies and strategies of the Beats (and the beatniks and hipsters) truly made them rebels without a cause.

The rejection of community, the public sphere, and the organized Left on the part of what purports to be an oppositional social formation represents—ironically and regrettably—one of the signal triumphs of McCarthyism and the conservative hegemony of the postwar years. For these latter targeted mass-movement politics *tout court*, attacking organized labor as well as alleged communists and homosexuals. Immediately after World War II, the Truman administration aimed to weaken the labor movement, which had acquired a good deal of power during the 1930s. As William Chafe notes, "by 1948 hopes for a progressive liberal/labor alliance had foundered on the issue of communism." And although trade unionism remained an important force, "labor leaders accepted corporate domination of industrial management, jettisoning demands to restructure control over the workplace."[78] Congress, meanwhile, passed the Taft-Hartley Act in 1947, one of the most repressive labor laws in U.S. history. The law crippled organized labor by granting the president "the right to obtain injunctions forcing strikers to return to work," banning "contributions from union dues to political candidates," giving "states the power to pass 'right-to-work' laws, outlawing the closed shop," and requiring "union officials to sign non-Communist affidavits."[79] And to a large extent the Taft-Hartley Act succeeded. Although, as Chafe notes, the United States "in 1956 crossed the line from an industrial to a 'post-industrial' state, with white-collar workers outnumbering blue-collar workers for the first time," this shift further weakened organized labor. Hoping to distance themselves from a blue-collar ethos, many of the new white-collar workers were reluctant to unionize, and "between 1945 and 1960, the unionized portion of the country's nonagricultural workers fell by 14 percent" while organized labor itself "became more and more conservative."[80] These developments, together with an acrimonious series of exchanges on the part of communists and former communists during the 1950s over the legacy of Stalinism, decimated what remained of the Left and the Communist Party, in particular. The latter, Paul Buhle notes, "staggered through the fifties somnambulently, a ghost rattling phrases from the past, while its best talent increasingly found themselves a place in non-ideological movements pointing to the future, or simply resigned to living their private lives."[81]

Thus during the 1950s neither a well-organized and effective Left nor a meaningful working-class community existed to which the Beats could turn for support and solidarity. Even in San Francisco, which, as Kenneth Rexroth notes, had strong links to the Wobblies and the radical labor movement in the 1930s and early 1940s, the radical tradition had for the most part been dissipated.[82] And while a pacifist and antistatist anarchism enjoyed "a mild revival" in the Bay Area after World War II, it was largely unconnected with the tradition of the Old Left.[83] As a result, the rebellion against the norms of the Cold War and the domestic revival almost of necessity assumed an individualist, anticommunitarian, and antistatist character. Or rather, the desire to produce change that, during the 1930s, had been directed into a variety of different social and political movements, had little choice during the 1950s but to be channeled in nonpolitical—or even antipolitical—directions. Culture replaced the political arena as the primary site of struggle. Anticipating many of the new social movements of the 1960s, the Beats backed away from dealing with issues of economic distribution and social class and turned their attention instead to civil society, to privatized practices and identities, and to questions of cultural production.

At this point I want to turn once more to the idea of the Beat as "white Negro" because I think it, too, is crucial to an understanding of the Beats' turn away from political culture during the 1950s. Among Beat literary productions, the classic account of cross-race identification is surely *On the Road*. Throughout the narrative, Sal Paradise promiscuously identifies with many of the men—never the women—whom he and Dean Moriarty encounter in their travels. Yet what is perhaps most remarkable is that this process of identification so often crosses racial lines. Just as Remi Boncoeur "pick[s] up" the "one greatest laugh in all this world" from "a Negro called Mr. Snow," so does Sal, suddenly and without explanation, desire to "climb in" to the skin of "an old Negro" whom he sees "plodding along" to "find out just what he's poor-ass pondering . . . " (52, 94). Elsewhere, while traveling with his Chicana girlfriend, Terry, and her family and working as a cotton-picker, he romantically primitivizes himself, becoming "a man of the earth." And the Okies staying in the camp collude with him; they "thought I was a Mexican. . . . " "And in a way," Sal adds, "I am" (82). Working and living with Mexicans, quite literally mimicking them, and loving Terry effect a psychic transformation in Sal so that in him (as in Mailer's "white Negro") the difference between identification and desire is eroded. "[I]n a way," he becomes that which he desires.

Sal's most revealing (and notorious) fantasy of cross-race identification, however, occurs while he ambles through

the Denver colored section, wishing I were a Negro, feeling that the best the white world had offered was not enough ecstasy for me, not enough life, joy, kicks, darkness, music, not enough night. . . . I wished I were a Denver Mexican, or even a poor overworked Jap, anything but what I was so drearily, a "white man" disillusioned. All my life I'd had white ambitions. . . . I passed the dark porches of Mexican and Negro homes; soft voices were there, occasionally the dusky knee of some mysterious sensual gal; and dark faces of the men behind rose arbors. . . . I was only myself, Sal Paradise, sad, strolling in this violent dark, this unbearably sweet night, wishing I could exchange worlds with the happy, true-hearted, ecstatic Negroes of America. (148–49)

With its melancholic romanticization of otherness, Sal's desire completely—and horrifyingly—ignores the economic and social realities of African-American urban ghettos in the 1950s.[84] Or rather, those realities are transformed, inverted, if you will, so that they become the "ecstatic" symptom (and ruins) of a lost utopia. In his fantasy, whiteness signifies disillusionment, sobriety, alienation, while blackness (or, more exactly, nonwhiteness) signifies not only ecstasy, life, joy, softness, the mysterious and sensual, but also a figurative darkness, "enough night." But just as important as this racial polarization is the contrast of the solitary white man with the vibrant life of a community from which he feels excluded. For all of the figures that he discerns along the street belong to social groups with communal histories, and it is precisely that sense of community and history that the atomized, alienated, white man so desperately desires, and whose evocation makes the night both "violent" and "unbearably sweet."

The cross-race identification that runs through the work of Kerouac and the other Beats is, I believe, a symptom of a melancholic process whereby the subject attempts to incorporate that which he has lost. According to Freud, both mourning and melancholia represent "the reaction to the loss of a loved person, or to the loss of some abstraction. . . ."[85] The difference between the two consists in the fact that "melancholia is in some way related to an unconscious loss," unlike "mourning, in which there is nothing unconscious about" it.[86] In both cases, however, the experience of loss compels the subject's ego, as Judith Butler explains, "to incorporate that other into the very structure of the ego, taking on attributes of the other and 'sustaining' the other through magical acts of imitation." But because the melancholic (unlike the mourner) refuses to relinquish the love-object, "internalization becomes a strategy of magically resuscitating the lost object, not only because the loss is painful, but because the ambivalence felt toward the object requires that the object be retained until the differences are settled."[87] It is precisely this act of sustenance that is reenacted repeatedly in *On the Road*, in Sal's obsessive and profoundly ambivalent identification with Mexicans, Japanese, and the "ecstatic Negroes of America." Unable to face the loss of joy, of a sense of belonging—and unconscious of the fact that he has even lost them—the "disillusioned" and melancholic white male subject attempts to become black himself. This act of impersonation represents a fantasmatic recovery of that which he has lost, of that otherness which he so desperately desires, and which is instantiated as a sense of community, ecstasy, the body, sensuality, sexuality, the primitive, the authentic, the paternal (the narrative is impelled from the beginning by Dean's search for his father). This logic of melancholic identification also informs those sequences in *On the Road* that are about jazz. For jazz, as an improvisatory art form, functions for the "white Negro" as a way of experiencing spontaneity, which is to say, of being completely immersed in the moment. Going to a jazz club allows the white subject, like Dean, his eyes fixed firmly on those of a tenor saxophonist, to go into a "trance" (through a magical act of imitation and introjection), to become "a madman who not only understood but cared and wanted to understand more and much more than there was . . . " (163). At the same time, the very nature of jazz functions as a model for literary production itself. Like Sal (a " 'white man' disillusioned"), Kerouac champions the technique of spontaneous prose in an attempt to unleash an "undisturbed flow from the mind of personal secret idea-words, *blowing* (as per jazz musician) on subject. . . ." By so abdicating consciousness, and writing in a "semi-trance," the writer, like Dean, is able to declare a victory over repression—and hence whiteness—by recording "what conscious art would censor."[88] In his fantasies, in the very act of writing, the writer becomes other than and to himself.

The process of melancholic cross-race identification is crucial to the production of the Beat as an irreducibly split subject. Freud emphasizes the psychic violence of melancholia, that the logic of identification guarantees that "the loss of the object [becomes] transformed into a loss in the ego, and the conflict between the ego and the loved person [or object] transformed into a cleavage between the criticizing faculty of the ego and the ego as altered by the identification."[89] In other words, the lost object is reconstructed within the ego as a "criticizing faculty," and the resentment and anger originally directed at the object—or rather, at the loss of the object—are reversed and visited against the self. As a result, the introjected object and the ego (as it were) cohabit the self, with the former taking its revenge on the latter. Freud emphasizes that in this process "hate is expended upon this new substitute-object [the ego], railing at it, depreciating it, making it suffer and deriving sadistic gratification from its suffering. The self-torments of melancholiacs, which are without doubt pleasurable, signify . . . a gratification of sadistic tendencies and of hate, both of which relate to an object and in this way have both been turned round upon the self."[90] In splitting the ego into a sadistic half and a masochistic half, melancholia produces a subject that is crippled by self-reproach and self-hatred. Unable to resolve the schism, it simultaneously longs for and hates that which it has lost. In the suburbanized, bureaucratized, commodity culture of postwar America, so much has been lost, and the Beat, more acutely and more consciously perhaps than his orthodox brethren, lives this loss and knows himself "disillusioned" and split, both white and black, self and other. Narrated by a restless melancholic, *On the Road* seems a particularly sensitive barometer of this loss (it is little wonder that it has become the emblematic Beat novel).

Yet Kerouac's masochism and his obsession with disillusionment are by no means unique. Adolescent agonies motivated by loss and the search for the father are similarly dramatized in Nicholas Ray's *Rebel without a Cause* (1955), widely regarded as "the touchstone for generational strife in the 1950s."[91] Both Jim (James Dean) and Plato (Sal Mineo) conspicuously lack fathers who embody the masculine ideal of the 1950s—Jim's wears an apron and lacks the "guts to knock mom cold," while Plato's is simply absent. Longing for a masculinity with which to identify (and in Plato's case, the film suggests, to desire), the two flirt recklessly with disaster, Jim by agreeing to a suicidal game of chicken with his nemesis (and double), Buzz, and Plato by his suicidal last stand at the deserted planetarium. And while the latter site clearly symbolizes the anxieties of the nuclear age, it is the abandoned mansion to which the teenagers retreat with Judy (Natalie Wood) that most clearly represents the house of postwar culture. With its broken windows, decaying facade, and rubble-strewn hallways, the mansion represents both a lost magnificence and a lost domestic (and utopian) space and becomes the site at which the three perversely play house. Yet as subjects produced by and mimicking perpetually dysfunctional Oedipal triangles, all three remain irreducibly split, the casualties of parents unable to play normative gender roles and a culture that barely knows what it has lost.

The split subjects of *Rebel without a Cause* and *On the Road* are also unmistakably the obverse of the doubled subjects that proliferate in the film (in the persons of Jim/Buzz and Jim/Plato) and throughout Kerouac's novels (in the persons of Jack Kerouac/Sal Paradise, Sal Paradise/Dean Moriarty, Dean Moriarty/Neal Cassady, Neal Cassady/Cody Pomeray, Cody Pomeray/Dean Moriarty, etc.). Each is produced as the double of the other, or rather, as the embodiment and token of that which the subject has lost and so desires. For he can never forgive his double for the promise (the paradise, as it were) that the latter both embodies and forecloses. And as he assaults his other, he always thinks:

> Every one of these things I said was a knife at myself. Everything I had ever secretly held against my brother was coming out: how ugly I was and what filth I was discovering in the depths of my own impure psychologies. (176)

For the melancholic white rebel, the (mis)recognition of the (br)other is simultaneously a (mis)recognition of the self. The one takes a sadistic revenge on the other while the other masochistically enjoys his own suffering. Unable to understand what has been lost, he turns the "knife" back against himself, suddenly discovering in the self the ugliness and filth that properly belong not to the self at all but which, through a magical resuscitation, inexorably take up residence within the " 'white man' disillusioned."

THE FEMINIZATION OF AMERICAN LITERATURE

Despite its being peopled by a multitude of eccentrics, homosexuals, and misfits, the canon of American literature was singularly ill-disposed toward the Beats. During the late 1950s and early 1960s, both the New Critics and the more politically engaged New York intellectuals (especially the *Partisan Review* crowd) were extremely reluctant to claim the Beats as anything more than spoilers. Moreover, their high level of visibility, success in using the mass media, unabashed populism, interest in drugs and Asian religions, and unapologetic homosexuality (at least on the part of Ginsberg and Burroughs) militated strongly against their inclusion as part of an elite tradition of American literature. Although I do not want to underestimate the force of these dissensions from cultural norms, I would like to suggest that the real scandal of the Beats was their production of an unprecedented kind of masculinity and with it a novel—and rather queer—redefinition of male homosociality.

A key to understanding this new masculinity is, I believe, an essay by Leslie Fiedler that offers an intriguing portrait of the Beats and their relationship to the canons of American literature. Elaborating upon his critique of the Beats in *Waiting for the End*, Fiedler in 1965 published a broader and more freewheeling attack on them in the *Partisan Review* entitled "The New Mutants." As in his earlier text, Fiedler berates the "new irrationalists," as he calls them, and other producers of "post-Modernist literature" for familiar reasons: their inattention to history, their "rejection of the notion of cultural continuity and progress," and their disengagement from "Humanism" and "the cult of reason" that stretches majestically from Socrates to Marx and Freud.[92] Taking a position similar to Mailer's (but bitterly condemnatory), he writes that these "new barbarian[s]"—who, like Mailer's hipster, *must* be white—prefer "porno-esthetics" to art and refuse "whiteness," which for them is "a stigma and symbol of shame," in favor of "Negro jazz" and various non-European artifacts and religions (513–15). But the most original and, I think, startling of Fiedler's claims is that the Beats and their followers are responsible for the feminization both of male subjectivity and, more ominously, of American literature and culture. Unlike the (male) humanist, they attempt "to assimilate into themselves . . . that otherness, that sum total of rejected psychic elements which the middle-class heirs of the Renaissance have identified with 'woman.' To become new men, these children of the future seem to feel, they must not only become more Black than White but more female than male" (516). Believing the increasing mechanization of the workplace to be the cause of a crisis in the production of masculinity, Fiedler sees these men as victims of a kind of false consciousness that has "shaken their faith in their primary masculine function" and "in their ability to achieve the conquest (as the traditional metaphor has it) of women" (516). Insisting that these "new men" are no longer able to conquer women or "deal . . . out death by hand," he sees them as being frightened, passive, and castrated (516) and cites part of a poem by Brother Antoninus (William Everson) as proof:

> "*Annul in me my manhood, Lord, and make*
> *Me woman sexed and weak . . .*
> *Make me then*
> *Girl-hearted, virgin-souled, woman-docile, maiden-meek . . .*"
> *(519, emphasis and ellipses in Fiedler's text)*

Turning to other examples of "post-heroic" literature (in which he includes the works of Bellow, Ginsberg, Albee, Salinger, and Corso, and of which he dubs Burroughs "the chief prophet"), Fiedler argues that the much-touted production of the antihero represents simultaneously a "conversion" of the male "into the non- or anti-male" (517). Moreover, as in so many discourses of the period that elide gender deviance with sexual deviance (and pathologize both!), Fiedler associates this feminization with impotence and homosexuality. The critiques of bourgeois domesticity in the works of these writers he reads as no more than a derisible attempt to foist "a neo-Whitmanian gaggle of giggling *camerados*" upon an unsuspecting public (519). Most distressingly, he finds that this "radical metamorphosis of the Western male" represents an objectification of the male who now is given the role "*of being beautiful and being loved*" (519). With his long hair, "high heels," and "jeans tight over the buttocks," the new man has retreated "from masculine aggressiveness to female allure" because even if "basically heterosexual," he has unconsciously been corrupted by the homosexually invented "style called 'camp'" (520).

In Fiedler's polemic, the "new [white] man," both as writer and as social actor, represents both the defeat of an active, phallicized masculinity and the victory of the enemy: women, Negroes, and homosexuals. He regards this victory as an extremely dangerous situation with far-reaching implications, for the reconceptualization of the white male as *victim* (or "occasion of maximum violence") has serious repercussions in the public sphere (521). Buoyed by the achievements of the civil rights movement, the new man now practices a "nonviolent or passive resistance" toward which Fiedler betrays a certain ambivalence but which he seems to regard as a kind of phony political activism that offers "the possibility of heroism without aggression, effective action without guilt," leaving "us" to confront not real political issues but "homey female questions" like "*Did Mario Savio really bite that cop in the leg as he sagged limply toward the ground?*" (521–22, emphasis in original). Doubtless betraying the guilt of his own apostasy, Fiedler, the former Old Leftist, is quite correct to note that old-style political heroism ill accords with the increasing personalization of New Leftist politics during the 1960s.[93] But for him this feminization of the public sphere marks a dangerous development. Perhaps the most revealing moment in the essay in terms of Fiedler's own anxieties, however, is an attack on drug use, which, predictably, he also regards as a feminization: "What could be more womanly . . . than permitting the penetration of the body by a foreign object which not only stirs delight but even (possibly) creates new life?" (522). This rhetorical question betrays the real scandal of the white male's feminization: *he desires to be penetrated* by drugs, femininity, blackness, or a penis, and thus to have his precious "body-fluids" contaminated (as in the 1963 film *Dr. Strangelove*, to which Fielder refers [524]).[94] Like a cross between the body politic in a McCarthyite fantasy and a hapless human specimen in a sci-fi movie, he is all too likely to be impregnated by a gaggle of dangerous and alien beings. In Fiedler's feverish imagination, women represent that alien being and are constructed, on the one hand, as being porous and passive, and on the other, as representing a sexual "threat" that has the power to castrate all but the most vigilant and heroic of men (517). Faced with a foe at once submissive and imperious, the male must protect his (imaginary) bodily integrity at all costs, lest he be seduced to the side of the enemy, unmanned, invaded.

Despite Fiedler's assertions, the feminization of the new mutant represents less a complete break with than a paranoid variation upon normative Cold War masculinities. Although the working man/husband/father is masculinized by his (over)investment in the "occupational role," he is also feminized situationally, by his acquiescence, in the workplace, in the interests of the corporation and, in the domestic sphere, to the role of helpmate. The Beat, on the other hand, is masculinized by virtue of his resuscitation of the entrepreneurial and maverick self, yet simultaneously feminized both by his sexual dissidence and by the practice of writing itself, that is, by his association with the cultural and artistic sphere. An early poem of Allen Ginsberg's makes the equation explicit:

When I sit before a paper
   writing my mind turns
in a kind of feminine
   madness of chatter. . . .[95]

In Ginsberg's imagination, the act of composition necessitates a revolution (literally, a turning around) of the mind, a momentary possession of the subject by the feminine and by those modes of enunciation that have long been associated with femininity: madness and chatter, which is to say, speech unrestrained by the conscious and censorious self. Yet Ginsberg's feminizing and pathologizing fantasies were echoed by his critics. One early reviewer suggests that "the poet's revulsion" in *Howl and Other Poems* (1957) "is expressed with the single-minded frenzy of a raving madwoman."[96]

Ginsberg's assertion that writing necessitates a turning to femininity and madness is a remarkably candid and revealing confession. It is also, I believe, a key to understanding how the Beats negotiated the treacherous binarism of sexual difference during an era in which both gender and sexual deviance were, to say the least, subject to extraordinary negative pressure. In what passes for American literature, the Beats were the first explicitly to embrace a feminized position—but only on condition that they could beat a hasty and horrified retreat from it. Time and again, their poems and fictional texts—as well as their own narrative self-fashionings—enact an obsessive oscillation between feminized and masculinized positionalities, between victim and street tough, martyr and tyrant, aesthete and proletarian. Moreover, it is my

belief that this oscillation is the result of the incessant intrapsychic performance of sadomasochism (in which the writer switches back and forth between submissive and dominant roles). Not only do Burroughs, Ginsberg,
and (more reluctantly) Kerouac take up feminine positions as writers, but
their texts, as I will demonstrate, incessantly, if surreptitiously, perform the
kind of masochistic fantasies that Freud identifies with what he calls feminine
masochism, in which the subject is "pinioned, bound, beaten, . . . forced to
obey unconditionally, defiled, degraded," treated like "a naughty child," and,
more generally, "placed in a situation characteristic of womanhood," which is
to say, castrated.[97] In other words, it is the playing out of the masochistic
fantasmatic that is responsible for turning men into women and feminizing
American literature.

A sense of the psychic sadomasochism of the Beats is reinforced by a reading of Robert Lindner's portrait of the psychopath in *Rebel without a Cause*
. . . (the book that Norman Mailer cites in "The White Negro") which vaguely
inspired the 1955 film that starred James Dean and was published in the
same year Burroughs, Ginsberg, and Kerouac first met. A former prison psychologist, Lindner represents the implicitly male psychopath as the distinctive
subject of modern Western society (replete with the "abomination of un-
planned cities and mushroom industrial centers").[98] Yet according to Lindner,
the psychopath, unlike the correctly socialized subject, is driven to satisfy "his
immediate wishes and desires" at the expense of society.[99] Fixated at an infantile level of emotional development, the psychopath is unable to delay
gratification and remains perennially frustrated and aggressive. Like Freud's
masochist, he or she suffers a disorder in the relationship between superego
and ego that is connected to an unsuccessful resolution of the Oedipus complex. While the masochist must endure a hypertrophy of the superego that
reactivates the Oedipus complex and resexualizes morality, the psychopath is
the victim of "an abrupt cessation of psychosexual development *before* the
successful resolution of the Oedipus situation."[100] In both cases, the relationship with the father is decisive for the production of deviance. The masochist,
because he or she seeks the (forbidden) love of the father, experiences a sense
of profound guilt, while the psychopath suffers "a profound hatred of the father."[101] In both cases, however, because the subject is beset by incestuous
fantasies that he believes must be punished, the superego becomes sadistic and
the ego masochistic:

> "I have sinned against my father and I must be punished" is the unverbalized theme
> of psychopathic conduct: and for this reason they very often commit crimes free from
> acquisitional motives. . . . That such activities constitute a species of "neurotic gain"
> is also to be considered. The fact of punishment sought, received and accepted does
> not complete the tale: there is in addition a narcissistic "yield" which derives directly
> from the punitive act. . . .[102]

Like the masochist, the psychopath derives pleasure from being punished for real or imagined crimes; he or she takes narcissistic delight in playing the role of victim, in taking up a feminized position. And in a later essay, Lindner extends his theory by introducing what he calls "Mass Man," a "mechanized, robotized caricature of humanity," which, he insists, is the psychopath *in excelsis.*"[103] Neatly (and falsely) collapsing the collectivity into the commodity (and denouncing both), "Mass Man" represents a new masochistic and feminized subject with a damaged ego, a "slave in mind and body, whose life signifies no more than an instrument of his masters' power. . . ."[104] Drawing on a long tradition that associates both the commodity and mass culture with femininity, this "virulent epidemic" signals no more nor less than a feminization of "the race of man."[105] And for Lindner, the psychopath's status as a gender deviant is confirmed by his observation that psychopathology is accompanied—as it is compulsively in Cold War fantasies—by sexual deviance. "Where," in the psychopath, "there is a sympathetic attachment toward another human," Lindner notes, "it is frequently homoerotic or perverse in some other sense."[106]

The paragon of this new, feminized, perverse subjectivity, Allen Ginsberg is surely the most explicitly masochistic of all the Beats, in his embrace, as poet and chronicler of a generation, of the role of victim and prophet, in his confession that he has "always approached love affairs with a sort of self contradictory, conscious masochism," in a sense of personal shame (in which he seems to take a certain delight) that runs through his many texts, and most baldly in his notoriously masochistic poem "Please Master" (1968, although an elaboration upon a 1954 journal entry).[107] Yet he is by no means unique. Burroughs even more flamboyantly, if more covertly and tortuously, writes texts in which pleasure is indistinguishable from pain, ecstasy from death. Moreover, his own disavowal of the sadism that informs his work and his professed lack of personal interest in sexual sadism cannot disguise what one critic aptly recognizes to be the "deeply sadomasochistic" nature of his fictions.[108] And although Kerouac may appear the least obviously masochistic (and most obviously heterosexual) of the three, his melancholic penchant for gloom and his conflicted delight in the "filth" of his "impure psychologies" suggest that he, too, writes—and is written by—a profoundly masochistic discourse.

The intrasubjective dynamics of the individual Beat writers (and of what I am tempted to call a distinctive Beat fantasmatic) cannot, however, be fully understood without an analysis of their intersubjective relations. For during the late 1940s and 1950s, Burroughs, Ginsberg, Kerouac, and Cassady were exploring tangled and shifting homosocialities that not only challenge the normative male bonds of the domestic revival but also dramatize a deep-seated disturbance in the relations between son and father, the subject and the Law, and the writer and the society in which he must reluctantly participate. Despite the fact that the first two figures were ostensibly homosexual and the latter two ostensibly heterosexual, the complexity and intensity of their bonds attests to the difficulty in separating the homosexual from the homosocial. Catharine Stimpson is certainly correct to note the Beats' ascription of "sublimity" to "male friendship." Yet if they were indeed "writing a legend of male love more rugged and American than *The Symposium*," its very Americanness as well as its (post)modernity stem in part from the fact that their appropriation of the Platonic and Whitmanesque legends represents more an intensification than a perversion of the norms of postwar male culture.[109]

Certainly, the liaisons among the four were complicated, to say the least. Never one to kiss and *not* tell, Ginsberg explains that he "made it with Kerouac quite often," that he and Burroughs "made it a lot over many years," and that he also conducted a passionate (if difficult) affair with Cassady that is memorialized in his letters, journals, and poetry: "Neal Cassady was my animal: he brought me to my knees / and taught me the love of his cock and the secrets of his mind. . . ."[110] Although both Kerouac and Cassady were bisexual, the former was apparently much more conflicted about his homosexual liaisons. According to Gerald Nicosia, Kerouac

> fought all his life against the label *queer*. It wasn't just a matter of defending his masculinity; for when drunk he often boasted of the men who had "blown" him, invited other men to do so, or challenged men to let him fuck them. But he believed in man's role as the head of the family, as the ruggedly honest, stoically suffering breadwinner who "took no shit from anyone," the role personified by his father, as well as countless film heroes from Jean Gabin to Gary Cooper. The "queer" stance—sniffling, sardonic, dissembling—seemed the very opposite of this.[111]

As the most traditionally minded of the Beats, Kerouac shared this (some would say, homophobic) position with Ginsberg and Burroughs, all of whom carefully distinguish between two kinds of homosexual, between, in Ginsberg's words, the "populist, humanist, quasi-heterosexual, Whitmanic, bohemian, free-love, homosexual" and the "privileged, exaggeratedly effeminate, gossipy, moneyed, money-style-clothing-conscious, near-hysterical queen."[112] As Ginsberg suggests, the differences between the "homosexual" and the "queen" are marked by both gender and class. The former is a masculine, universalized proletarian, while the latter remains a feminized, minoritized, campy bourgeois. For Burroughs as well, there is a clear distinction between the "strong, manly, noble" homosexuals (or "queers") and the dehumanized "fags" who "jerk around like puppets on invisible strings, galvanized into hideous activity that is the negation of everything living and spontaneous."[113] Like Lindner's "Mass Man," the queen and the fag represent the triumph of consumerism, deception, theatricality, and femininity—and the utter commodification of the human subject. Evoking considerable castration anxiety in all of these writers, they—like women—threaten to destroy the male subject unless they are rigorously subjugated ("I'll see him castrated before I'll be called a Fag," Burroughs notes in reference to Carl Solomon's suggestion that *Queer* be retitled *Fag*).[114] And homosexual practices are tolerable, and even alluring, as long as they reinforce the subject's phallic identification and his status as social rebel, as long as the "Fag" within remains under wraps.

Although there is no evidence that Kerouac and Cassady had genital contact with each other, their relationship bears witness to the familiar pattern of a male homosociality so intense that its homoerotic component must continually be disavowed and displaced. Both *On the Road* and *Visions of Cody* (1972, written 1951–52) attest to the difficulty in separating identification from desire insofar as they document Kerouac's obsessive identification with—and love for—the "great hero," the "Arbiter of what I think," who has penetrated his very essence: "Cody and I have the same soul. . . ."[115] Both novels document a loss of boundaries to the extent that the personal narrative of one subject is so often appropriated by the other that it is hard to know where the one leaves off and the other begins ("Our fates are very mixed and intermuddled, wild!" [348]). Kerouac explains that he even "got the idea for the spontaneous style of *On the Road* from seeing how good old Neal Cassady wrote his letters to [him], all first person, fast, mad, confessional. . . ."[116] But, as numerous texts affirm, the two friends shared more than souls and writing practices. Cassady also offered his wives to Kerouac, constructing a classic erotic triangle in which, through the exchange of women, men both cement their bonds and displace their homoerotic desires.[117] Freely trading LuAnne and Carolyn, "Neal had always encouraged [Kerouac] to enjoy his women, and had asked to share Jack's women as well."[118] In *Visions of Cody*, Kerouac fictionalizes the incident with LuAnne by describing how the two men share Joanna ("'Gee, what an honor to have two men at the same time, Cody and Jack'" [341]).[119] And in *On the Road*, when Sal confesses that Dean "wanted me to work Marylou," the motivation behind the exchange is taken for granted: "I didn't ask him why because I knew he wanted to see what Marylou was like with another man" (108). Sal's knowledge allows Dean, in Sal's fantasy, to "see" his wife having sex with his friend. Yet one wonders: how does the play of identification and desire work in this fantasy? And more important, whom does Sal "see"? (It is *his* fantasy, after all.) With whom does he identify? And how is it that Sal imagines he is granted this private, telepathic knowledge of his friend's desires?

The profound anxiety surrounding homosexual identities and practices that this tortuous linkage of fantasies suggests is also betrayed in a passage in *On the Road* in which Sal confesses: "Several times I went to San Fran with my gun and when a queer approached me in a bar john I took out the gun and said, 'Eh? Eh? What's that you say?'" Pulling out his pistol (rather than the other weapon that the queer doubtlessly would have preferred), Sal scares away the frightened pervert. Yet he immediately acknowledges that his motivation (unlike Dean's) remains mysterious: "I've never understood why I did that. . . ." Ascribing his actions to "the loneliness of San Francisco and the fact that I had a gun," Sal, face to face with the queer, suddenly finds himself inflamed: "I had to show it to someone" (62). Writing gun when he means cock, the subject must prove that he "has" the phallus while compulsively disavowing his desires. Yet in the end, he remains, like Cody, an "Oedipus who sees all and sees nothing . . . " (83).

In *Visions of Cody*, meanwhile, Jack describes Cody fucking a "real pansy" (in a scene cut from *On the Road*) with considerable ambivalence. He is horrified by the "pansy" because the latter is impossible to decipher: "you just couldn't tell what he was, sadist or masochist and from which end and with whip, dress, or oyster pie . . . " (357). The "slambanging big sodomies" with Cody that follow may have "made [Jack] sick," but he remains fascinated, sitting "in the castrated toilet listening and peeking" at these "Arabian pleasures" (358). In Kerouac (as in countless fictions of the 1950s), the homosexual is elided with the "dopefiend," the "mugger," and the "Communist" (those who "look away from each other's eyes") as a criminalized danger both to the state and to the sovereignty of the male subject (261). Homosexual desires become the sign of almost unbearable castration anxiety; homosexual practices, of a hidden and exoticized knowledge that must constantly be seen and not seen; and homosexual identities, of undecidability, of the loss of a fixed gendered and sexual identity. Cody Pomeray and Jack Duluoz freely admit that they love each other (it "makes me [Jack] feel good"), but the latter is careful to distinguish between his "ethereal" "feeling for Cody"—"like for a character in a book"—and his "sexy, malevolent, manlike" passion for Cody's wife (330, 340). In other words, the homosocial is distinguished from the heterosocial (with its malevolent virility) by virtue of its literariness: its relation to a tradition of distinctively American literature (reaching back to Irving, Thoreau, and Whitman) in which men honorably love other men and to Cody's role as ghost (or actor) in a literary collaboration in which Jack plays the medium (or ventriloquist). Even here, however, the disconsolately playful Jack Duluoz is unable to keep literature free of a homosexual taint:

> FAGS ANONYMOUS especially me and the lit
> ones (this does not mean
> literary, it means lit
> with a match).

> (255)

Ever a genius at disavowal, Jack, by his very disclaimer, serves to underscore the candor of his free association that links homosexuality, addiction, the (writing) self, literature, and the condition of being inflamed. Like Ginsberg, he embraces the feminized position of the writer and the homosexuality to which it points only on condition that he can repudiate both at will, the first, through the virility of his spontaneous prose (with its privileged relation to Logos), and the second, through the compulsive reportage of his heterosexual adventures.

Perhaps the most extravagant homoerotic fantasy in Beat writing is found, not in Burroughs or Ginsberg, but in Jack Duluoz's ecstatic apparition in *Visions of Cody* of his "Nietzschean hero" in drag:

> He loves to mimic women and wishes he was a sweet young cunt of sixteen so he could feel himself squishy and nice and squirm all over when some man had to look and all he had to do was sit and feel the soft shape of his or her ass in a silk dress and that squishy all over feeling, and he'd like to spend all day over a hot stove and finger himself and feel the rub of his dress on his ass and wait for hubby who has one sixteen inches long. (338, 296)

In Jack's feverish imagination, Cody, in an intriguing variation upon the sexological model of inversion (a man's soul in a woman's body), takes up both male and female positions. And as is so frequently the case in Kerouac, women are represented synechdochically by that "squishy" part that stands in for the whole and is the sign of their abjected and commodified status as an object of masculine desire. Yet Cody, oscillating between the roles of desiring subject and object of desire, is produced as a narcissistically complete subject, the one who, by virtue of both having and being a cunt, both "is" and "has" the phallus. Even in this rhapsody of genderfuck, however, Cody's status as object is entirely dependent upon a heterosexualized and specularized economy of desire in which the compulsion "to look" on the part of "some man" (who could that be?) turns him/her into a permutation of the normative bourgeoise who, liking "to spend" (in more ways than one) her days over a "hot stove," prepares herself to be penetrated by her hypermasculinized "hubby." At the same time, one must recall that this is, after all, Jack's fantasy and that while feminizing Cody, Jack, as is his wont, attempts to reinforce the phallic identification of the unidentified "hubby" whose excitement ("sixteen inches long") for Cody's cunt is as excessive as Jack's fear, waiting in the "castrated toilet," "listening [to] and peeking" at the "big sodomies" taking place in the other room.

Of all the discourses that document the vexed relationship between the homosocial and the homosexual among the Beats, none is more revealing of the psychic mechanisms at work than the texts exchanged between Allen Ginsberg and Neal Cassady. The two met in New York in 1947 and began to have an affair (despite Cassady's hyperactive heterosexuality) that is tenderly and powerfully commemorated in Ginsberg's 1956 poem "Many Loves," which, in its slightly antique diction, suggests both Whitman and the Song of Solomon. In the poem, Cassady is fashioned as the poet's "animal," a man strong as iron (a metaphor repeated three times) and yet "gentle," "sweet," and "kind." In addition to his raw, physical power and beauty, Cassady appeals to the poet in part because of his heterosexuality ("his belly a thousand girls kissed in Colorado. . . ."), because, being "angel & greek & athlete & hero and brother and boy of my dreams," he is so radically different from the queer or fag constructed in other contemporary narratives. Cassady and Ginsberg begin a relationship ("*of manly attachment*," as the epigraph from Whitman puts it) that is clearly based on a play of dominance and submission and in which Cassady's heterosexualized masculinity is preserved by his becoming Ginsberg's "master," the one who "brought me to my knees. . . ." The poet, in contrast, is constructed as the feminized worshiper, the incurably desiring subject, the one who (although they "owned each other bodies and souls") can never finally possess his master and remains a prisoner of his "dreams of insatiety & lone love." So begins the "love match that continues in my imagination to this day a full decade."[120]

When Cassady left New York for Denver, the two began a correspondence that even more clearly reveals the sadomasochistic foundation of a relationship that, I believe, is not exceptional among the Beats but rather typifies their associations. Over the course of two or three years, Cassady and Ginsberg more or less end their love affair (Cassady was splitting up with LuAnne and wooing Carolyn Robinson at the time) while clarifying and preserving an intense homosocial bond in which "masochistic abnegation" is incessantly and unpredictably combined with "hero-worship."[121] Yet the positions produced in the letters (unlike those in "Many Loves") are not fixed, and the two men wantonly shift back and forth between submissive and dominant roles. Cassady constructs himself (much as he is constructed in Kerouac's fiction) as his friend's "other self," the one who both desperately needs Ginsberg's love and support and yet distances himself sexually from the poet ("I, somehow, dislike pricks & men & before you, had consciously forced myself to be homosexual" [7, 11]). Admittedly confused and no longer forcing himself to be homosexual (since it now comes naturally?), Cassady hopes that his love will help heterosexualize the young poet, transforming the latter's desire into identification. Yet, ironically, Cassady can never bring to completion both his therapeutic project and his own desires: "as you become more straight through me, or otherwise, you will need me less, and, also secondarily, because I know as that happens I shall need you more" (9). Caught in a classic double bind, Cassady can only lose—either he succeeds in his therapy, in which case he loses Ginsberg, or else he fails, in which case he will be forced to reject the poet's love. Feeling "a nerotic [*sic*] negative almost compulsive need" of Ginsberg, hoping and not hoping that his heterosexualization works, Cassady seems to derive a distinct pleasure from abasing and feminizing himself ("I feel as if I were a woman about to lose her man" [9]). Like his literary associates, he switches back and forth in his discourse between dominant and submissive roles, alternately subjugating his "other self" (both Ginsberg and the feminine within), sabotaging his own affair, and relishing his subjection.

Even more undisguisedly than his comrade-in-arms, Ginsberg acknowledges that his own "love is one compounded of hostility & submission" (27). Lovelorn and terrified, he admits in one 1947 letter that he "will do anything" to retain Cassady's love: "I mean to bend my mind that knows it can destroy you to any base sordid level of adoration and masochistic abnegation that you desire or taunt me with" (28). Asserting, like Freud's feminine masochist, that he is "worthless" and "only a child," he is wracked with (pleasurable) torment that he believes he has earned: "my guilt makes me mad" (28–29). To expiate it, he turns to his lover whom he invites to "inflict any punishment . . . you want" (28). Ever resentful and desirous of Cassady (and his own obeisance), Ginsberg knows—more consciously than Cassady or Kerouac—the contradictions bred by masochistic desire: "I blame you yet I still ask for the whip" (28). For the masochist, like Lindner's psychopath, suffers from a disturbance of the ego in which he alternates between feeling omnipotent and impotent, masculinized and feminized, phallicized and castrated. And Ginsberg, asserting that he has a unique gift, a "spiritual genius," and, in the next breath, that he is "not worthy," both resists and embraces his punishment: "I was impure and pure, too pure to be drowned in vomit" (28–29). Yet ever the litterateur, Ginsberg recognizes the power of his own fantasy—and how like Kerouac this is—to produce the myth of Neal Cassady ("[y]ou know . . . that you have no existence outside of me") at the same time that he begs his lover to give him substance, "to save" him from himself (29).

Although this letter is, in many ways, extraordinarily revealing of the structure of both the poet's subjectivity and Beat homosociality, Ginsberg is unwilling completely to avow his own insights. Or rather, the very articulation of his contradictory position serves finally to unmake him as a subject: "I don't know what I am when I speak like this but it is near my true speech" (28). For in speaking the truth, the male masochist discovers that his position is well-nigh uninhabitable and that his sense of masculine self-sufficiency is radically threatened. Most important, the masochist (like Lindner's psychopath) is a casualty of Oedipus, and all his relationships with other men are turned into a search for the father whom he has misserved. For Dean Moriarty is hardly the only figure in these many narratives who is pursuing a lost father. In writing to Ginsberg, Neal Cassady styles himself "a prodigal, sickened son who has wronged his father" and takes the poet for the father-substitute whom he can worship, fear, hate, and love: "you are my father" (38). And tellingly, Cassady's Oedipal fantasy works to feminize himself and masculinize Ginsberg, even in comparison with Kerouac ("you show more of these supposedly virile, masculine, enigma problems than does . . . even, especially, Jack" [38]). And although Cassady later withdraws his imputation ("your not my father. I have none. I felt the need for one lately & artifically picked you"), his disavowal betrays the facts that the selection of the father-substitute is always arbitrary and that the "need" for the father can never be completely desexualized (48).

In Kaja Silverman's elaboration of Freud, she notes how the contradictory demands of the Oedipal narrative are decisive for the production of the male masochist. These demands, in turn, ensure that the ego is always ready to take pleasure in the pain exercised upon it by the superego and that the superego is always "susceptible to sexualization." They guarantee, in short, that there will always be a linkage between male masochism and male homoerotic desire. Although, she explains, "the relationship of the male ego to the super-ego would seem to grow out of, and 'ideally' undo, the romance between father and son," there is a "fundamental impossibility about the position in which the male subject is held." For in analyzing the constitution of the superego, she recognizes that there are always two "mutually exclusive imperatives" operating for the male subject: "'You *ought to be* like this (like your father)' and 'You *may not be* like this (like your father)—that is, you may not do all that he does; some things are his prerogative.'" The first imperative, she points out, issues from the ego-ideal, "whose function is to promote similitude between itself and the ego." The second is formed "through the internalization of the father as Law, gaze, voice-on-high" and is "irreducibly masculine, at least within the present social order." In relation to this second, oppressive "paternal function," "the ego is always-already guilty . . . by virtue of Oedipal desire." And it is precisely "through moral masochism" that the male subject is able to play out his contradictory relationship to the father, to ensure that his ego will be "beaten/loved by the father," beaten because guilty of love.[122] Thus Neal Cassady, Allen Ginsberg, and Jack Kerouac, because irremediably guilty of desiring (and wanting to be) the heroic, phallicized father, seek out punishment to atone for their guilt and derive gratification from receiving it. Cassady, in other words, craves Ginsberg precisely because he (mis)recognizes him as his father. And Ginsberg, meanwhile, is elsewhere even more candid about his sexual fantasies, "[r]ecalling [his] incestuous relation with [his] brother in fantasy & partial fact; and also with father."[123] Both must be punished, of course, for desiring the father-substitute: feminized, tortured, and treated like the guilty children they imagine themselves to be.

If Cassady and Kerouac epitomize the moral masochist who, Silverman observes, "remains oblivious to the passion for self-destruction that burns ferociously within," then Ginsberg takes up the position of the feminine masochist for whom the beating fantasy is "available to consciousness, albeit not necessarily to rational scrutiny."[124] Throughout his work, Ginsberg plays out a fantasy in which he momentarily abnegates a masculine position (by fancying himself a child and asking "for the whip") and identifies with his mother (most obviously in "Kaddish," in which he commemorates "my halflife and my own as hers").[125] Or rather, through the act of writing he consciously and willingly takes on a feminine role in order both to assail it and to purge himself of it, to root out the treacherous femininity within.

It is little wonder, then, that Leslie Fiedler would attack these "new mutants" for their desire to be penetrated, feminized, and humiliated and for their role in demasculinizing American literature. He failed to recognize, however, that they mark not the exception but the rule; that they instantiate a wholesale reconfiguration of masculine gender roles in the commodity culture that triumphed after World War II and that required a certain feminization of male subjectivity (albeit in very different ways depending on one's class position). He also failed to notice what happens to real women in this process and that the treatment of wives, whores, and girlfriends (with "sexy, malevolent, manlike" passion) often physicalized the psychic violence that tends to be romanticized in the masochistic fantasies of the Beats.

The persistent marginalization of the women connected with the Beats hardly hints at the level of physical and psychological abuse that was often visited upon them. Unlike the bourgeois housewife/mother, they were rarely afforded the comforts or economic security that could offer at least some compensation for their subservience. In a letter discussing Kerouac's 1950 marriage to Joan Haverty, Ginsberg paints a portrait of the bride that makes her identical with the exemplary bourgeoise: "she can't compare with Jack in largeness of spirit and so I don't know what she can give him except stability of sex life, housekeeping, and silent, probably sympathetic company while he's sitting around, and children" (81). Like the wife of the organization man, Haverty is to remain silent and subordinate, putting out for her husband and taking care of children. In his reply, Cassady characterizes both Kerouac's and his own marriages as "a combination of willful blindness, a perverted sense of wanting to help the girl and just plain what the hell" (89). He knows that a time will come when Kerouac, as he had done, "breaks under the complete awareness of one females demands and his inability to meet them, besides which he'll tire of staying on her level, she would, but can't, get on his" (90). Constructing women as a temptation that blinds, "breaks," and castrates men, and marriage as a perversion, a caprice, Cassady represents heterosexuality as a kind of farce that produces only frustration and failure. *On the Road*, as well, betrays a great deal of anxiety on the part of men confronted with resistant women. Sal and Dean discover "the sweetest woman in the world" in the person of the wife of "a colored guy called Walter" who never utters "a harsh word" or "a complaint," who, in fact, "never said a word" (168). This "*real woman*" will let "her old man . . . come in any hour of the night with anybody and have talks in the kitchen and drink the beer and leave any old time" (168). Acquiescent and silent, she is completely different from the other wives, Lee Ann, who—like Medusa—harbors "hate in her eyes," and Marylou, whom Dean is convinced is "a whore" and "a pathological liar" (53, 136). If, as Sal insists, "love is a duel," then the (sexually) active woman's mutinous speech and murderous gaze represent the threat of castration, the power to inflict a fatal wound. And as both the writings and the biographies of the Beats suggest, she must be either rigorously subjugated or, better yet, abandoned (85).

Carolyn Cassady's memoir of her life with the Beats, *Off the Road*, tells a rather different story. In Carolyn's account, Neal is a violent, if charismatic, figure who lacks "the warm physical attraction" she ascribes to Kerouac, and whose sexual performances give Carolyn more pain than pleasure.[126] (Like her husband, she too is given to acting out masochistic scenarios, insisting, despite Neal's violence, that he is "the only man for me," and "feeling sick with self-disgust" after verbally attacking him for his irresponsibility [126, 77].)[127] In Carolyn's account, Neal is totally undependable, an "animal raging in lust," the bestower of as much misery as happiness who twice breaks his hand as a result of beating up his first wife: "LuAnne . . . I hit her . . . stupid broad" (19, 88). Carolyn, moreover, clearly recognizes that Neal's male friends are far more important to him than his family, and she angrily confronts him when he wants to leave with Kerouac on a jaunt that would later be commemorated in *On the Road*:

> "What about *me*? What have I been doing? Can you even imagine what it's been like for me? [. . .] How could you lie about loving me . . . use me . . . make me bear your child? All you do is take advantage of people . . . You'd just walk out with all our money?" (76; ellipses, except the first, appear in the original.)

And even Burroughs, never exactly a supporter of women's rights, wholly confirms Carolyn's accusations: "Neal is, of course, the very soul of this voyage into pure, abstract, meaningless motion. He is The Mover, compulsive, dedicated, ready to sacrifice family, friends, even his very car itself to the necessity of moving from one place to another. Wife and child may starve, friends exist only to exploit for gas money . . . Neal must move" (ellipsis appears in the original).[128]

Unable to remain the silent, acquiescent wife any longer, Carolyn Cassady (echoed by Burroughs) suggests that the male homosociality celebrated in the work of the Beats exacts a terrible price from the women with whom they lived. The Beats may have (with considerable ambivalence) feminized both American literature and their own subjectivities, yet they did so—ironically— by subjugating real women and constructing a mythology of male friendship in which the relations of dominance and submission, mastery and servitude, that were characteristically played out in the sphere of Cold War domesticity were displaced and reconfigured so that they could be performed between men. It is appropriate, therefore, that the last words of Carolyn's memoir be given not to her own feelings but to the suggestion of an ex-girlfriend of Neal's, Diana Hansen, that Neal's ashes be buried in Jack Kerouac's grave (the two died within a year and a half of each other): "maybe I'll get a plaque—something about Neal being buried in Jack's heart" (428). For in the self-mythologization of the Beats, Neal, the alter (super)ego, is indeed produced as the lover Kerouac never dared to love, the father whom he never could find, the always fictional subject who is produced by Kerouac and yet who colonizes him completely, the one who makes the heart of his other self "BEAT—the root, the soul of Beatific" (161).

THE BODY POLITIC

In his move from visionary to political activist to progressive quietist, Allen Ginsberg of all the Beats best personifies the cultural changes that have taken place in the United States since the early 1950s. Catapulted to celebrity by his reading of "Howl" at San Francisco's Six Gallery in 1955, he has attracted, as Paul Breslin observes, "the largest readership of any poet who also commands the respect of literary critics."[129] Confessional poet and self-styled prophet, he owes as much to assorted urban idiolects and the cadence of bebop as he does to his avowed mentors, Whitman and Blake. And the publication of *Howl and Other Poems* one year before *On the Road* was a crucial event in the popularization of the Beats as outlaws and rebels. Not only did the collection (with its frank avowal of freaky, violent, queer sex) profane the canons of postwar poetry, but it also provoked a legal scandal, being, along with *Naked Lunch* (1959), one of the last books to be banned in the United States.

For Ginsberg, as for Kerouac and Burroughs, writing is less an imaginative or psychic activity than an intensively physical practice. The very title of "Howl" suggests that the poem is a transcription of an ululating voice overwhelmed by passion and barely capable of rational argument. Its "incantatory syntax," as Breslin notes, "draws attention to the poem as speech rather than as an object of contemplation."[130] And Ginsberg, like many of the first avantgardists (especially the dadaists and surrealists), often attempts to deny the textuality of speech, insisting on its status as Logos—as a pure, mystical presence. Linking poetry to the body from which it issues, "just like sexual impulses," the former is "a rhythmic articulation of feeling." "It's a feeling that begins somewhere in the pit of the stomach and rises up forward in the breast and then comes out through the mouth and ears, and comes forth a croon or a groan or a sigh." Poetry, in other words, is written by the body and is a reminder of that imaginary wholeness which the subject must forfeit upon entering the Symbolic (it starts as "a definite body rhythm that has no definite words").[131] Yet corporeality plays itself out in Ginsberg on the level of content as well as form, and many of his most celebrated poems, including "Howl" and "Kaddish," foreground a profoundly materialized body. For it is through the discursive construction (and deconstruction) of the body that femininity, whiteness, and politics enter Ginsberg's volatile poetic structures. Referring to the opening line of "Howl," Breslin is certainly correct to observe that the "effect of Ginsberg's language is to sexualize the concept of 'mind,' making it more bodily and instinctive, while simultaneously spiritualizing the body. . . ."[132] In other words, there is an incessant double movement in Ginsberg, both a materialization and a dematerialization, that renders the abstract corporeal and the corporeal abstract. Thus, for example, the "bared . . . brains" and the "windows of the skull" at the beginning of "Howl" function both literally and figuratively, signifying a subjectivity that is at once mutilated and offered to the inquisitive eye of the reader.[133]

Ginsberg's tendency simultaneously to materialize and dematerialize is the sign of a profound ambivalence toward a body that is implicitly masculine and white despite the poet's refusal to specify the gender or race of "the best minds of [his] generation" (who are, like Mailer's "white Negro," set in opposition against "the negro streets" through which they pass [126]). And throughout "Howl," the white male body of the "angelheaded hipster" is insistently figured as a site of violence and martydom. For the poet's "generation" is nothing if not a generation of victims, "destroyed" both by inexorable historical forces, an oppressive society whose god is Moloch, and by their own "great suicidal dramas"—whether eating "fire in paint hotels," chaining "themselves to subways," being pierced "with a sword," or cutting "their wrists" (126–29). Indeed, the entire first part of the poem is a catalog of victims (including many of Ginsberg's friends) who are ravaged by greed, cruelty, and despair and who, like Reik's emblematic masochist, are constantly "being shown and so to speak put on display."[134] And throughout the poem, material violence is coded as being the other side of a psychic and emotional violence done to subjects who are (to borrow Breslin's term) unmistakably spiritualized. Moreover, most of the violence involves activities guaranteed to provoke anxiety in critics like Leslie Fiedler: the penetration or perforation of the body and the ingestion of foreign substances. Yet this characteristic mode of (self-)destruction also functions in the poem as a metaphor for the permeability of the subject when it is faced with the horrors of Moloch: "Moloch who entered my soul early!" In other words, the "best minds," having introjected the god, attempt to exorcise him by allowing themselves masochistically to be penetrated, adulterated, maddened, befouled—in short, feminized—by various sharp metallic objects, drugs, poisons, and cocks. Grisly variations upon the subjects of postwar commodity culture, they are sickened and destroyed by that which they compulsively and helplessly consume.

In part 2 of "Howl," Moloch is constructed as the force that produces victims, an ancient Middle Eastern deity to whom children were sacrificed, who, in Ginsberg's revision, is transformed into the oppressive god of a dehumanized, industrialized, urban society. Unlike its victims, who are fragile and porous, Moloch is associated with the mineral kingdom, with "cement and aluminum," "machinery," "smokestacks," "sexless hydrogen," "oil and stone." In this updated version of a modernist protest against the fruits of industrial capitalism, Moloch is also produced as an embodiment of the public sphere: "jailhouse and Congress," "the vast stone of war," "skyscrapers," and "factories" (131). Unequivocally masculinized in relation to his maddened, perverse, all-too-corporeal victims, Moloch is much like the aliens in *Invasion of the Body Snatchers* (1956) who exterminate and inhabit their prey. Yet as Breslin emphasizes, "Howl" enacts a deep ambivalence toward this process:

> One might conclude that Ginsberg himself thinks it is a misfortune to be crazy, lonely, and homosexual; he would rather be sane, surrounded by friends, and heterosexual, but Moloch has twisted him. . . . Or one might conclude, with equal warrant from the poem, that to be crazy, lonely, and homosexual is . . . a medal of honor, the sign of one's solitary resistance to Moloch within a subjugated culture.

This ambivalence, the fact that "Ginsberg wants it both ways," that the "granite cocks!" of Moloch are both horrifyingly and ecstatically tumescent, is, I believe, a key to the poem's success and popularity (132).[135] Like the other works of the Beats, and like cinematic representations of rebel males during the '50s, "Howl" is unequivocally critical of commodity culture, yet the rebellion against it is figured as being as ambivalent, confused, and ineffectual as the subjects who instigate it. Resistance may be heroic, but it is also perverse and fruitless, the sign of irremediable corruption. In other words, rebellion is figured as proof of the simultaneous masculinization and feminization of the male subject, "shaking with shame" and excitement, in whom the Oedipal struggle between paternal authority and childish impertinence is endlessly played out (130).

For Ginsberg, rebellion is an extremely vexed process, being the sign of his interpellation into both masculine and feminine positions: his father's vocation (as poet and representative of the Law) and his mother's aberrance (as madwoman and communist). For as "Kaddish" makes clear, radical politics (or resistance to Moloch) appears on the scene thanks to the "Communist beauty" and "holy mother" whom the poet has introjected and whose life he both narrates and relives (223). Moreover, it is precisely this ambivalent taking up of a feminine position, of the role of victim, that produces the materiality of the subject.[136] For if the paternal, like Moloch, is severe, granitic, and finally abstract, then the maternal is corporeal. Ginsberg, by rewriting the long historical association of the feminine with the material as well as the specific and pervasive anxiety during the postwar years about "Momism" (the stifling, overbearing mother who feminizes or homosexualizes her son), imagines his mother as absolute—which is to say, disgusting—flesh.[137] In "Kaddish," he represents her body as that of the unwilling consumer, compulsively disgorging what it has ingested: "red vomit," "diarrhea water," "urine," and "black feces" (218). At the same time, her flesh is figured as being like a book on which countless narratives of cutting and penetration can be read, with her "scars of operations, pancreas, belly wounds, abortions, appendix, stitching of incisions pulling down in the fat like hideous thick zippers" (219). Much like the catalog of victims in "Howl," and much like the poet himself, Naomi Ginsberg is literally revolting—a nauseating rebel, victim of Moloch and resistant subject.

Throughout Ginsberg's work this ambivalent identification with femininity and with radical politics plays itself out as a desire for masochistic self-abnegation, a desire to be penetrated both physically and metaphysically, and so, as if by magic, to be transubstantiated or, in effect, remasculinized. Like the "best minds" of his generation "who let themselves be fucked in the ass by saintly motorcyclists, and screamed with joy," the poet in "Please Master" beseeches an unnamed male divinity: "please master order me down on the floor, / please master tell me to lick your thick shaft . . . " (128, 494). Begging to be fucked "till it hurts" and he yelps "with terror delight," he asks to be treated "like a girl" (495). Yet as always with Ginsberg, being subjugated by an omnipotent master is not only a form of self-abasement; it also makes the subject "thy vehicle," an instrument or medium for that phallicism which the subject so pathetically lacks (495). It authorizes him to share in the power, mastery, and authority that otherwise elude him. Moreover, because materialization in Ginsberg is always linked to dematerialization, "Please Master" can also be read as a kind of theological disquisition. As James Breslin puts it, using an uncannily appropriate metaphor, "materiality functions . . . as a kind of whip, flagellating Ginsberg into vision."[138] And as Ginsberg himself suggests: "There's a mysticism in being screwed and accepting the new lord divine coming into your bowels—'Please Master.' "[139] Thus in "Magic Psalm" (1960) he grovels before a particularly cruel divinity: "invade my body with the sex of God, choke up my nostrils with corruption's infinite caress" (255). Fearful yet desirous of what sounds suspiciously like Moloch himself, the poet longs to be driven "crazy," to be "disgrace[d] . . . in the eye of the earth" (256). He prays that the "Softmouth Vagina . . . enters my brain from above" to await its fulfillment (as described in "The Reply" [1960] to "Magic Psalm"): "a vast Being" who ensures that "The universe turns inside out to devour me!" (255–57). For it is through humiliation, madness, and consumption that the poet may "taste the shit of Being at last," "that the vast Ray of Futurity" may "enter my mouth to sound Thy Creation Forever" (256). In other words, being fucked by Moloch (as by those "saintly motorcyclists"), one shares in the divine in the only way that one can, learning to ventriloquize for Moloch, to channel his phallicism, to be remasculinized, and so to exalt "Thy Creation."

The masochistic fantasies (that are repeatedly enacted in Ginsberg's early poetry) of becoming a vehicle for a cruel and earth-shattering divinity are insistently linked to his radical politics. Indeed, in many respects the writer of these texts seems to epitomize what Kaja Silverman calls the Christian masochist, the one who pits him- or herself "against the society in which he or she lives" and becomes "a rebel, or even a revolutionary of sorts." As she emphasizes, this figure, by attempting to remake him- or herself after "the suffering Christ, the very picture of earthly divestiture and loss," inevitably harbors "a strong heterocosmic impulse—the desire to remake the world in another image altogether, to forge a different cultural order."[140] In other words, with Ginsberg (as with other Christian masochists) the desire to change the world is indissolubly linked to the subject's self-abasement. He ecstatically fashions himself a martyr in the hope that he can destroy Moloch. Yet, ironically, the effect of this masochistic self-fashioning is finally to depoliticize the social so that rebellion is understood not as a culturally specific practice but as part of a universal process of becoming. As Paul Breslin puts it, "Ginsberg seems at times to think that the problem is the unredeemed condition of the world rather than any particular social evil."[141] And the poet himself has repeatedly distanced himself from a class-based social analysis and refused to ally himself with an avowedly leftist political party. In a 1966 interview this exemplar of American anarchism explains that he "didn't ever feel that there was any answer in dogmatic Leninism-Marxism." And although he clearly believes that the "general idea of revolution against American idiocy is good," he insists that "the dogmatism that follows is a big drag."[142]

Given Ginsberg's "general idea of revolution" and his insistent metaphysicalization of the political, it is little wonder, then, that "Howl" became such a sensation in the late 1950s and that he has since emerged as such a popular and iconic figure. By seeming to attack material social conditions while in fact subordinating them to a theological design, Ginsberg is able to protest a demonstrably oppressive regime while secretly (and masochistically) acceding to its cruelties. And by taking this oppression upon himself, by becoming the victim and vehicle of Moloch, he fashions himself the spokesperson of an anguished generation and simultaneously the emblematic male masochist (as described so compellingly by Silverman): "he acts out in an insistent and exaggerated way the basic conditions of cultural subjectivity, conditions that are normally disavowed; he loudly proclaims that his meaning comes to him from the Other, prostrates himself before the gaze even as he solicits it, exhibits his castration for all to see, and revels in the sacrificial basis of the social contract."[143]

Unlike the other Beats, Ginsberg seems very well aware of the masochistic foundation of his fantasies, so much so that his basic project could be described as an attempt to get *beyond* masochism. Thus he has turned repeatedly to Asian religions (both Hinduism and Buddhism) as a way of answering those people whose faces are "twisted by rejection," and of overcoming "hatred of self," which he sees (with some justification) as the "internalization of that rejection." Seeking to substitute "the shining self" for the masochistic self, he looks to Bhakti yoga as a means of transcendence. He explains, "[T]he only way to drag up, from the depths of this depression, to drag up your soul to its proper bliss, and understanding, is to give yourself, completely, to your heart's desire," to "get on your knees" and "sing and chant prayers and mantras, till you reach a state of ecstasy and understanding, and the bliss overflows out of your body."[144] (Bhakti yoga is a devotional movement that focuses on an intense emotional attachment between a devotee and his or her personal deity.)[145] In other words, with its emphasis on adoration, Bhakti provides the theological basis for both "Please Master" and "Magic Psalm" and, in Ginsberg's hands, becomes a way of eroticizing—and rendering ecstatic—servitude and abjection in the hope that they will lead to a definitive dematerialization of the subject, or "sense of cosmic consciousness."[146] But by imagining "the drone of creation adoring its Slayer," these poems do not, I believe, so much go beyond masochism as trace the logic of masochistic self-abnegation as far as it can go—short of the material extinction of the subject (257).

As my analysis suggests (although I will take up this question again in chapter 6), I doubt whether Ginsberg's "*only* way out" is a way out at all.[147] It seems to me, rather, that his appropriation of Hindu spirituality ironically serves his Christian masochism all too well. Moreover, his celebration of religious mysticism is insistently linked to his habit of conceptualizing the political as a subset of the theological, as a problem of consciousness rather than of material social conditions. Thus, for example, "the whole cold war," he maintains, "is the imposition of a vast mental barrier on everybody, . . . a shutting off of the perception of desire," rather than, say, a political and economic struggle.[148] Despite this compulsion to dematerialize, however, Ginsberg never completely forsakes a knowledge of the power of social institutions that comes to him through the body, through his feminine identification and his ongoing battle with Moloch. Thus, he suggests: "Somebody has got to sit in the British Museum again like Marx and figure out a new system; a new blueprint. Another century has gone, technology has changed everything completely, so it's time for a new utopian system. Burroughs is almost working on it."[149] Tossing the ball to William Burroughs, Ginsberg asserts the power of literature to effect real social change while tacitly acknowledging his own failure to conceptualize "a new system." And although Burroughs has yet to displace Marx as a political philosopher, Ginsberg is certainly correct to note that this most willfully perverse of the Beats, the one with his finger on the pulse of late capitalism in a particularly delirious way, is indeed working up a utopian system. Almost.

The Self as Text

If Allen Ginsberg is the most forthright of all the Beats (and the least prone to obsessive disavowal), then William Burroughs is certainly the most cunning, contradictory, and difficult to pin down. His writing may be, as Ginsberg suggests, deeply utopian, but it also works to complicate the concept of the political associated with the Cold War consensus in peculiar ways. Burroughs himself, meanwhile, whether writing as William S. Burroughs or as William Lee, has constructed a fictive self much more self-consciously than his associates. Or rather, unlike Ginsberg and Kerouac, who employ confessional narratives both to decipher a disarticulated self and to make it (appear to) cohere, Burroughs clearly delights in his own plurality and belatedness, his promiscuous textuality as the subject of/in his own writing. As The Invisible Man explains in *Nova Express* (1964), " 'These colorless sheets are what flesh is made from—Becomes flesh when it has color and writing—That is Word And Image write the message that is you on colorless sheets determine all flesh' " (*NE*, 30).[150] Rather than being stable and unified, the self is a volume of fleshly transparencies on which are written the contradictory words, images, and narratives that produce the "message that is you," the optical (and textual) illusion called the subject. And Burroughs—unapologetic junky, homosexual, murderer, expatriate, and scion of a wealthy family—practices a writing that may, like that of his associates, compound autobiography with fiction but also works to unseat that arch-falsification (as he calls it), *"The IS of Identity"* that "always carries the implication of that and nothing else, and . . . the assignment of permanent condition" (*TJ*, 200). Recoiling from stability, unity, and permanence, Burroughs has proven that, as hit man, he has better aim when contemplating humanist subjectivity than when targeting a glass on his wife's head.

The most elusive of the Beats, Burroughs has also proven the most controversial. Both his biography and his fiction have elicited strong responses from government censors, distraught and delighted readers, and a wide variety of literary critics. Indeed, judging from the Modern Language Association's bibliography of scholarship, Burroughs, of all the Beats, has amassed, if not the greatest literary prestige, then at least the greatest amount of literary criticism.[151] Kerouac may have his admirers and detractors, but they rarely write with the passion and polemical force of Burroughs's critics. Given the pulverization of narrative in Burroughs's fiction, and his outspoken and extremely idiosyncratic notions about culture, politics, and society, Burroughs often functions as a kind of Rorschach test for critics. (Leslie Fiedler, as I have indicated above, is especially revealing on that score.) A continuing source of dismay is the absence of clear signals of meaning in a body of fiction that, at first glance, is so flamboyantly misogynist, racist, homophobic, and anti-Semitic. During the 1960s, the debate about his work centered on the imputed morality or immorality of his writing, with the implicit, unanswered question always being: is Burroughs a particularly deft satirist or simply a journalist from hell?[152] (Burroughs himself has often taken cover behind the shield of the moralist, opining in the 1974 *The Job*, for example, that he is "perhaps too much" the "great moralist" [*TJ*, 50].) With the subsequent triumph of poststructuralism and postmodernism in the academy, questions of morality have recently been subordinated to more formal investigations that problematize

Burroughs's linkages not to Jonathan Swift but to Nietzsche, Barthes, and Derrida.[153] While I do not want to dismiss these questions, it seems to me that Burroughs's first six novels, not despite but because of their eccentricities, provide a particularly fascinating barometer of postwar American culture, and, in particular, of unconscious attitudes toward the production of gendered subjectivities and bodies, toward social and political institutions, and toward questions of commodity production and exchange. Moreover, I find that, as with the other Beats, Burroughs's self-mythologization must be considered another of his texts. For Burroughs, as the most explicitly deconstructionist of the Beats, deliberately blurs the lines between and among different kinds of discourses. Thus *The Job* intermixes (one might even say, confuses) interview and fiction, while this and other interviews, essays, and prefaces often quote his novels verbatim. His letters to Ginsberg, meanwhile, contain so many pieces of what will become *Naked Lunch* that he finally confesses, "Maybe the real novel is letters to you" (*L*, 217). Even more distinctly than Kerouac or Ginsberg, Burroughs understands his subjectivity and his practices to be a collection of texts, and "[h]uman bodies," in Cary Nelson's estimation, to be "the accumulated residue of speech."[154]

Given Burroughs's revulsion toward coherent identities, it should hardly be surprising that his texts (especially *Naked Lunch* and the cut-up [see below for an explanation of this technique] trilogy, *The Soft Machine* [1961], *The Ticket That Exploded* [1962; revised 1967], and *Nova Express*) are paradigmatic examples of heteroglossia: a text compounded of several tongues, which is to say, of competing, simultaneous discourses. All of these novels are based on Burroughs's so-called routines, which he first developed in the 1940s but which he did not begin to transcribe until he was writing *Queer* (they saturate *Naked Lunch* and the cut-up trilogy). These extravagant, improvised, parodistic performances became increasingly important for Burroughs during the 1950s and are crucial, as I have indicated at the beginning of this chapter, to his becoming what he calls a writer. In a 1954 letter to Ginsberg, he insists, however, that his routines need a "receiver." Without one, "routine turns back on me . . . and tears me apart, grows more and more insane (literal growth like cancer) and impossible, and fragmentary like beserk pin-ball machine and I am screaming: 'Stop it! Stop it!'" (*L*, 201). In other words, unless a routine is part of a concrete exchange, it becomes an instrument of self-destruction, splitting the subject into an active, performing, masculinized self and a passive, feminized self that is operated upon. Despite its association with need, however, the routine is also explicitly theorized as a displacement of desire: "Whenever I encounter the impasse of unrequited affection my only recourse is in routines," which are "[r]eally meant for the loved one" (*L*, 204). In other words, the routine may be therapeutic for Burroughs but is still—like desire— always linked to failure because without a "loved one" to receive it, it leads to psychosis. Yet if the subject is loved, he has no need of the routine. The routine, therefore, signifies both the presence and absence of the "loved one." And without it, "my life is a chronic nightmare" (*L*, 201). So the choice for Burroughs is between a receiverless routine and no routine at all, between psychosis and nightmare, with the prospect of requited affection ever more and more attenuated.

For Burroughs, the routine—that is, writing—becomes the emblem of his inevitable defeat as a subject, linking what otherwise pass as polar oppositions: the psyche with the flesh, writer with reader, text with desire, and the masculine with the feminine part of the self. And in all these cases, the relationship between the two terms is always unstable and perilous. The one needs the other and yet must repudiate it. The performing self (or writer) requires a receiver despite the fact that the receiver (or reader) can never be adequate to the task. The submissive part of the self needs the dominant part, but only if the former is guaranteed to be able to regain control. This spectacle of failure, moreover, is exacerbated by the undecidability of the status of the text (and of artistic production more generally) vis-à-vis what Bürger would call "the praxis of life." For the routine, Burroughs insists, unlike other art forms, "is not *completely symbolic*, that is, it is subject to shlup over into 'real' action at any time (like cutting off finger joint and so forth)" (*L*, 216). The routine, in undermining the distinction between writing and "'real' action," is thus the sign of the materiality of the text, of its status as a form of (avant-gardist) life-praxis. It is also symptomatic of the constant instability of the figurative and the literal in Burroughs, of the fact that his texts are always about the literalization of the figurative, the transposition of the conditional into the actual, the word become flesh, and the flesh become word.

Finally, the routine, as Burroughs suggests by the association with his own amputation, with poultry shears, of the end of his little finger, is also linked to castration. His amputation (done in 1939 out of unrequited love for a friend, Jack Anderson) is the subject of an early short story, "The Finger," in which it is figured as a masochistic rite de passage, a kind of mirror stage in reverse in which the subject regresses from the Symbolic to the Imaginary.[155] For in Burroughs's narrative, told (appropriately enough) in the third person, his perennial alter ego, Bill Lee, holds the shears and looks "in the mirror" while "composing his face into the supercilious mask of an eighteenth-century dandy." The masquerading adult (who, as a dandy, is both masculinized and feminized) secures his own gaze in the mirror and, taking "a deep breath," presses "the handle quick and hard." Feeling only a "deep pity for the finger joint," he is suddenly reinfantilized, speaking "in a broken child's voice." Yet this castration, this performance of the role of victim, this regression from haughty adult to wounded child, is eagerly embraced: "Waves of euphoria swept through him as he walked down the street." Dismemberment, like the routine, thus becomes the emblem of the male subject's victimization and of his masochistic delight in being castrated, which, ironically, is performed precisely to prove his courage, to prove that he (unlike his unnerved, "whiny, shrill, almost hysterical" psychiatrist) can take it like man (*I*, 15).

Desire, too, like the routine, is always figured in Burroughs as the sign of castration, of the subject's inevitable isolation and failure. Of all his novels, *Queer* most explicitly and coherently analyzes the dynamics of desire, the "unrequited affection" that leads to the production of writing (and the writer). Throughout the text (again narrated in the third person), desire is conceptualized as an "aching pain," a "frenzied search," "desperately rummaging through bodies and rooms and closets" (*Q*, 25, 84). Perpetually unfulfilled, perpetually (un)closeted, desire possesses Bill Lee, constantly threatening to obliterate him or corrode the boundaries of his flesh. For it is desire that produces the "imaginary hand" which caresses Allerton (Lee's love-object) with "ectoplasmic fingers" and "phantom thumbs," desire that makes his body "pull towards Allerton, an amoeboid protoplasmic projection, straining with a blind worm hunger to enter the other's body, to breathe with his lungs, see with his eyes" (*Q*, 25, 36). As happens obsessively in Burroughs, desire can never be dissevered from identification. Rather, always contravening the heterosexualizing and Oedipal imperatives that try to disjoin the two, it produces a subject who longs to *become* the other (this is doubtlessly part of what makes Burroughs's writing so queer). Moreover, because desire is always experienced through the body, through a relentless incarnation that literalizes emotion, it can never be fulfilled (insofar as human protoplasm resists amalgamation). And this impossibility of fulfillment—which is the very substance of desire—is always experienced as a kind of castration, in which the "part of himself" that "tentatively stretched out towards the other had been severed," leaving the desiring subject "looking at the bleeding stump in shock and disbelief" (*Q*, 58).

Subjectivity in Burroughs (along with routine, writing, and desire) is always predicated upon castration. And the moment of castration (or of the recognition of castration), in turn, is always the turning point in a masochistic narrative in which the male subject willingly takes up a feminized positionality or rather, proudly exhibits his castrated status, on condition that he can repudiate both at will, that castration becomes mutatis mutandis the badge of his masculinity and power as writer and desiring subject. This pattern, moreover, is played out in his writing in numerous registers. Stylistically, for example, although Burroughs has recourse to many different narrative voices, his novels tend to be dominated by two: a flat-footed, deadpan, matter-of-fact voice and the voice of a hard-boiled detective. The first tends to construct short, simple, declarative sentences and scorn subordinate clauses. Although it has little time for elaborate descriptions, it sometimes reaches for (and finds) *le mot juste* or appropriates more specialized vocabularies (usually drawn from medicine, science, pseudoscience, or pornography). And like the voice of much '50s pornographic fiction, it denominates, simply but vividly describing the contortions and interpenetrations of flesh. This is the voice of the "factualist" who insists that he is "concerned with *facts*," and only facts, "on all levels of experience" since they "exist on infinite levels" (*L*, 68, 71). The second voice (heard, for example, at the beginning of *Naked Lunch*) is much like the narrative voice in the fiction of Raymond Chandler or Dashiell Hammett or a voiceover in film noir. Like the first voice (on which it is really a variation), it eschews complex sentences and subordinate clauses but uses a richer and more slangy and idiosyncratic vocabulary that tends to be drawn from the criminal/junkie/police/ private eye/G-man/spy underworld. It is the voice of the consummate insider. Unlike the first, it takes the reader for his intimate (sometimes even his "loved one") and always bears a privileged relationship to discourses of power; it is a voice in the know.

Yet what seems to me most important about these two voices in Burroughs's fiction is that they are so adamantly masculine. Even when describing the most baroque feats of queer sex, even when at their most gorgeously or perversely erotic, they remain tough and declarative, never venturing off into the purple prose or the detailed descriptions of emotional states associated with fags or fruits. This masculinization is clearly related to the difference that I have detailed above, in Burroughs's writings, between the queer and the fag and his willing identification with the former and revulsion from the latter. But even more important, it betrays the fact that it is not the homosexualization of the male subject that is scorned in Burroughs, but his feminization. As a result, his homophobia should really be seen as a species of misogyny, or gynophobia. Like so much official discourse of the period (and like Ginsberg's poetry), this is a misogyny that cannot help but associate the flesh with femininity. For flesh in Burroughs is always subject to periodic changes; it is always in process, always growing, decaying, shrinking, its organs being tranformed, combined, and/or dissolved:

> In his place of total darkness mouth and eyes are one organ that leaps forward to snap with transparent teeth . . . but no organ is constant as regards either function or position . . . sex organs sprout anywhere . . . rectums open, defecate and close . . . the entire organism changes color and consistency in split-second adjustments. . . . (*NL*, 9)

The remarkable mobility of sex organs suggests that the body-in-pieces (the castrated body) in Burroughs is always fetishized, always produced as an object of desire—and revulsion—that stands in for the absent phallus. This is why bodies are relentlessly specularized and made the subject of violence (like the little finger joint), why they are composed of disarticulated pieces that, because they have a life of their own (like the talking asshole in *Naked Lunch*), are sometimes able even to kill off the body of which they are a part. Moreover, the body-in-pieces is always porous, always ejecting or being penetrated by a myriad of tumescent objects and bodily fluids and hence undermining the distinction between inside and outside. Like the bodies of Naomi Ginsberg or the "American Housewife" in *Naked Lunch* ("opening a box of Lux" with her "intestines . . . all constipated"), it functions as a demonic parody of the postwar consumer, taking in and expelling commodities rapidly and compulsively (*NL*, 124).

Yet Burroughs, unlike Ginsberg (who always reaches for transcendence), makes no attempt to rise above the flesh. Indeed, no writer of the period is as obsessed with bodies, fluids, organs, consumption and excretion, and the mechanics of sex and reproduction. The consummate materialist, Burroughs creates prose that both luxuriates in and is revolted by the flesh. Yet it is precisely this obsessive production of the flesh that, as it were, requires the masculinization of the narrative voice. For Burroughs's texts always stage a war between content and style, between a feminized body in the text and a masculinized voice of authority that ceaselessly attempts to subjugate and master the body (lest male subjectivity and discourse be fatally feminized). Moreover, as I have suggested, the cultural specificity of the masculine voice is relatively unambiguous. For in postwar American culture, the hard-boiled detective, as C.L.R. James keenly observes, represents "the individual seeking individuality in a mechanized, socialized society, where his life is ordered and restricted at every turn, where there is no certainty of employment, far less of being able to rise by energy and ability or going West as in the old days."[156] In opposition to the organization man, the detective (who, as Corber notes, "is a descendent of the gangster") represents a "form of male identity" that functions "as an antidote to . . . disaffection." Identifying with the detective, much like becoming a beat or hipster, is thus an act of rebellion against cultural norms that takes the form of "a desire to return to an earlier stage of capitalism where the entrepreneurial spirit flourished."[157] Not only does it allow the (re)masculinization of both the writer and the male reader, it also authorizes a fantasmatic (and nostalgic) return to a moment in which, it is imagined, the male subject has far more freedom and prerogatives than in postwar consumer culture.

Burroughs's texts, both fictional and nonfictional, are the site of a relentless battle between the present and the past, between a feminized, commodity culture and a fantasy of rugged masculinity that is associated, if not explicitly with the old American West (although it sometimes is), then at least with the kind of entrepreneurial enterprise that Burroughs's grandfather and namesake exercised when founding the first corporation to manufacture the recording adding machine. This is a battle that is constantly being rewaged between the flesh and the voice, the literal and the figurative, in which there is and can be no resolution because subjectivity itself is irrevocably split between the masculine and the feminine, the dominant and the submissive. As Nelson notes, "[o]ur perceptions duplicate the male-female doubleness of our social and sexual roles, and our experience is a complementary alternation of pleasure and pain."[158] In Burroughs's texts this doubleness ensures that the male subject is always divided between a masculinized and sadistic superego and a feminized

and masochistic ego: "The body is two halves stuck together like a mold—
That is, it consists of *two* organisms" (*TE*, 159). As with Ginsberg, the subject's masochistic self-division is derived, as Freud explains, from the working
out of the negative Oedipus complex in which the male subject identifies with
the mother and maintains "a feminine attitude towards the father" that necessarily betrays the subject's "*incestuous attachment*" to him. But because the
subject is unable to avow this attachment, he turns to masochistic fantasy that
becomes, then, "a direct expression of the sense of guilt, to which the love for
the father is now subordinated."[159] The male subject, in other words, is split
into two by his desire and guilt, with the sadistic superego making the masochistic ego suffer for its love. In Burroughs, the two principles struggle eternally against each other much as, on the level of social organization, "[t]he war
between the sexes split the planet into armed camps right down the middle"
(*SM*, 157). Moreover, the dynamics of self-division are themselves always in
process, always subject to change. Often, the self (as in the Introduction to
Queer) is imagined as having multiple personalities or being possessed by its
other ("[s]ometimes an entity jumps in the body" [*NL*, 221]). And Burroughs's
fiction teems with flesh that has been invaded or is being devoured or comman-
deered by an alien life form:

> Every man has inside himself a parasitic being who is acting not at all to his advan-
> tage. Why do you spill things? Why do you drop something? You have the equipment
> there not to drop something. Why isn't that capacity being used? Something is pre-
> venting it. And you come down to some sort of basic dualism. There isn't one person
> out there, but two. Acting against each other.[160]

Male subjectivity, founded on self-division, is doomed to failure. "Something"
is always at work that prevents "[e]very man"'s "equipment" from functioning
as it should.

Given both Burroughs's predispositions and the rigid bifurcation of gender
roles under the terms of the domestic revival, it is perhaps not surprising that
gender is a crucial category for the playing out of dramas of self-division and
possession. Sex reassignment in Burroughs's fiction happens frequently and
unpredictably. Thus Carl, when spread with the Commandante's jelly, "could
feel his body draining into the woman mold. His genitals dissolving, tits swelling . . . " (*SM*, 109). Or Johnny, prancing in "a jockstrap of undifferentiated
tissue," experiences a "penis [rising] out of the jock and dissolv[ing] in pink
light back to a clitoris, balls retract into cunt with a fluid plop" (*SM*, 73). It
seems to me, however, that these transformations are about as close as one can
get to what I am tempted to call natural process in Burroughs. For is it not the
very nature of the castrated body-in-process (the body-in-pieces) to obscure
gender differences, or rather, to demonstrate the impermanence and fantasmatic nature of any gender identification? ("Male and female castrated he
them" *NL*, 40.) Robin Lydenberg is correct when she observes that "women

play little if any role in Burroughs' utopian fictions," insofar as un-ambiguously female characters are virtually nonexistent in Burroughs's writing. But then again, so are unambiguously male characters. Rather, it seems to me that, in accord with the laws of masochistic subjectivity, all identities in Burroughs are subject to what Silverman refers to as a heteropathic identification that, rather than "constituting the self at the expense of the other who is in effect 'swallowed,' . . . subscribes to an exteriorizing logic, and locates the self at the site of the other." The obsessive feminization of male bodies and subjectivities in Burroughs is thus the mechanism by which "one lives, suffers, and experiences pleasure through the other."[161] This claim is not meant to palliate the misogynist thrust of Burroughs's fiction. (On the contrary, the latter, it seems to me, can be seen almost to rehabilitate the pre-Enlightenment one-sex model in which female anatomy is understood as being merely a variation upon and inferior derivation from a primary male anatomy.)[162] This claim is intended, rather, to demonstrate that there is always a heteropathic logic at work behind Neal Oxenhandler's observation that Burroughs's "characters are simultaneously men and women, simultaneously masochistic and sadistic, simultaneously anal and oral, simultaneously dependent and autarchic, and so on."[163] The structure of Burroughs's fictions (and of his fantasies) guarantees, however, that this alleged simultaneity plays itself out not in a static opposition but in a ceaseless and vertiginous oscillation between masculine and feminine positionalities.

According to Ted Morgan, this careening back and forth between opposing gender roles is by no means restricted to Burroughs's writing (and I cite the following example not as an originary narrative but rather as a particularly vivid example of Burroughs's predisposition toward fluid gender identification). During Ginsberg's affair with Burroughs in 1953, the poet (much to his dismay) discovered that his lover habitually enacted a rather startling transformation while having sex:

> This reserved, sardonic, masculine man became a gushing, ecstatic, passionate woman. . . . He seemed to melt completely, to take on a different identity, . . . to become some recognizable female type, a St. Louis dowager perhaps. His distinction and reticence gave way to a mushily romantic, vulnerably whimpering female persona, as if he was able to contain within himself the personalities of both sexes.[164]

Although it is impossible, given Morgan's methods, to know the exact source of the misogynist overtones in the quoted passage (the contempt for those characteristics that are coded feminine), it seems clear that (homo)sexual practices for Burroughs are a privileged arena in which male subjects both work out their gender identifications and purge themselves of a femininity that is both monstrous and irresistibly seductive. Burroughs himself can always return, more or less safely, to the "reserved, sardonic, masculine man" he is at the beginning of the narrative. As such, he is much like Carl whose gender

reassignment surgery serves as the precondition for a vicarious remasculinization, for his submersion in an eerily utopian (and endlessly tumescent) social
scape dominated by "two vast penis figures" and countless fetishized "living
penis urns," and ruled by "The Living God Cock" (*SM*, 111–16).

Despite Burroughs's focus on the mechanics of (male) subjectivity and on
a panoply of sexual practices, his fictions always take place in what are recognizable, if idiosyncratic, human societies. Moreover, the grisly nature of their
populations should not disguise the fact that his cut-up novels (like most science fiction, of which they are a variation) represent visions that are haphaz-
ardly and unpredictably utopian and dystopian. If there is a key to understanding social organization in Burroughs's fiction, it is the concept of control. For
in many ways, his imagined communities (Benedict Anderson's celebrated
formulation of the nation seems a particularly apt description) are all paranoid
fantasies in which power is centralized, exercised from the top down, held in
place by an apparatus of terror, and inflicted directly on the bodies and minds
of subjects.[165] Thus, for example, he describes the "Mayan control system"
with its mysterious rotating "instruments" used to "control units of thought"
and its "horrible punishments meted out to anyone who dared challenge or
even think of challenging the controllers" (*SM*, 94–95). Or in *Naked Lunch*, he
invents the malevolent Dr. Benway, "a manipulator and coordinator of symbol
systems, an expert on all phases of interrogation, brainwashing and control"
(*NL*, 21). Benway, it turns out, is the executant of a kind of sadomasochistic
terrorist state in which the repressive state apparatus ("concentration camps,
mass arrest") has been largely superseded by a more subtle and well-oiled
ideological state apparatus that cunningly engineers consent (*NL*, 21). An expert at psychological warfare, he knows how to make his victims torment
themselves, saving the state the expense of further torture:

> prolonged mistreatment, short of physical violence, gives rise, when skillfully ap-
> plied, to anxiety and a feeling of special guilt. . . . The subject must not realize that
> the mistreatment is a deliberate attack of an anti-human enemy on his personal iden-
> tity. He must be made to feel that he deserves *any* treatment he receives because
> there is something (never specified) horribly wrong with him. (*NL*, 21)

The "anti-human" control system, in other words, turns the subject into a
masochist whose identity is shattered and who scourges himself with his
own "special guilt." And although Benway knows that "the threat of torture is
useful to induce in the subject the appropriate feeling of helplessness and gratitude to the interrogator for withholding it," he still has available "several
forms of disciplinary procedure" as well as instruments of "sexual humiliation" (*NL*, 24, 27). Benway's police, meanwhile, manage to obliterate the
concept of private space insofar as they have "pass keys to every room in the
city" and are always accompanied by a "mentalist" who is able to read the
subject's mind (*NL*, 23).

In its sophisticated use of psychological warfare, Benway's terrorist police state is a clearly recognizable (per)version of the national security state that emerged in the United States in the late 1940s, and Benway himself can be seen as a particularly sadistic variation upon rabid anticommunists like Richard Nixon or Joseph McCarthy. Although the persecution of political dissidence started in the United States long before World War II, the Truman Loyalty Order of 1947 authorized the government to launch a campaign against every organization and "group or combination of persons" deemed "totalitarian, Fascist, Communist or subversive." Not only membership, but even "*sympathetic association*" could get one dismissed from government service.[166] Eisenhower's Security Program of 1953 went even further in its refusal to allow the accused to answer his or her accusers or to appeal judgment. Moreover, Eisenhower expanded the campaign so as to include several new categories of proscribed practices (of all of which Burroughs and his associates would have been found guilty): "[a]ny criminal, infamous, dishonest, immoral, or notoriously disgraceful conduct, habitual use of intoxicants to excess, drug addiction, or sexual perversion."[167] As many historians have emphasized, the most important aspect of these programs was (as *Naked Lunch* suggests and as I have noted earlier in this chapter) less to root out actual communists and perverts than to exercise control over the noncommunist and heterosexual majority. In this context, Burroughs's agents of control can be seen to represent a parody of the security state that reveals the subtle (and not so subtle) psychological mechanisms reaching into the very depths of the human subject to guarantee his or her acquiescence.

At the same time, the proliferation of secret agents belonging to an array of ominous organizations whose operations and goals are never clearly defined (Factualists, Divisionists, Liquifactionists, etc.) reads as an ingenious transformation of both the organization man and the government agent. For Burroughs recognizes that the development of a state apparatus based on surveillance and psychological control (in which the necessity of partisan allegiance is coupled with a suspicion of subversive association) tends to make any identity suspect. As a result, the agent in Burroughs never knows finally to whom he has pledged allegiance: "I am a secret agent and don't know who I work for" (*SM*, 31). Because the subject gets his "instructions from street signs, newspapers, and pieces of conversation"—because, in other words, he is the paradigmatic subject of commodity culture and is beset by so many "[c]ontradictory commands"—he is "disorient[ed]" and no longer knows who employs him ("[y]ou can never be sure of anyone in the industry" [*SM*, 31; *TJ*, 41; *NL*, 146]).[168] Or as Clem Snide puts it: "I am a Private Ass Hole—I will take on any job any identity any body—I will do anything difficult dangerous or downright dirty for a price . . ." (*SM*, 71). Given the conflicting economic demands placed on the male subject, he is split in so many different ways that he is always, to some extent, working against his own interests. The subject, as a result, is always elsewhere: "*I am never here.* . . . Never that is *fully* in possession . . . I am always somewhere *Outside* giving orders and *Inside* this straight jacket of jelly" (*NL*, 221).

The heteropathically identified subject of Borroughs's fiction is recognizably the double agent, as described by Peter Sloterdijk, who cannot help but work against him- or herself because of the contradictory demands imposed by incompatible identities and allegiances. According to Sloterdijk, this "present-day servant of the system" is necessarily schizoid:

> By day, colonizer, at night, colonized; by occupation, valorizer and administrator, during leisure time, valorized and administered; officially a cynical functionary, privately a sensitive soul; . . . outwardly a follower of the reality principle, inwardly a subject oriented toward pleasure; functionally an agent of capital, intentionally a democrat; . . . objectively a strategist of destruction, subjectively a pacifist; basically someone who triggers catastrophes, in one's own view, innocence personified.

The subject of late capitalism (a.k.a. Clem Snide, Bill Lee, or any one of Burroughs's countless "Private Ass Hole"s) is always the double or triple agent who has been bought off so many times that he or she no longer knows for whom he or she is working:

> On which side do our loyalties lie? Are we agents of the state and of institutions? Or agents of enlightenment? Or agents of monopoly capital? Or agents of our own vital interests that secretly cooperate in constantly changing double binds with the state, institutions, enlightenment, counterenlightenment, monopoly capital, socialism, etc. . . . ? What is self-interest in someone who no longer knows where his "self" is?[169]

Barely cognizant of one's multiple identities, the agent remains unaware of the masochistic structure of his or her subjectivity that makes a virtue of self-division and eroticizes submission.

Burroughs's politics, however, are far more complicated and vexed than this brief analysis suggests. His writings, like those of the other Beats, indisputably represent a reaction against and critique of the norms of postwar culture. They take aim in particular at all manifestations of control systems, both statist and nonstatist institutions that serve as relays for what Burroughs conceives to be a kind of worldwide authoritarianism in which the Cold War is a phony war that functions above all to maintain "the establishment of the West and in Russia" (*TJ*, 67). And while his politics amount to little more than a sophisticated conspiracy theory, he never specifies the exact control center, although he knows, for example, that "they" are "behind Watergate and Nixon" (*TJ*, 20). (And Nixon is by no means the only chief executive to have abdicated power. The president in *Naked Lunch*, who is a junky, "has sacrificed all control, and is dependent as an unborn child" [*NL*, 67]). In *The Job*, Burroughs appropriates a vaguely (new) leftist rhetoric that inveighs against the CIA, the mass media, the military, the nation, the police, nuclear weapons, the containment of communism, and the national security state. Describing America as a "nightmare" and "the source of such emotional plagues as drug hysteria, racism, Bible belt morality," and the "Protestant capitalistic ethic," he also suggests that "America may well be the hope of the world" because in the United States "dissent has a better chance of effecting basic changes" (TJ, 78).

Despite Burroughs's attempt in *The Job* to support what in the early 1970s was generally regarded as a progressive agenda, his rhetoric betrays certain contradictions. Thus, for example, his assertion that "the quality of the human stock is declining disastrously" owing to "overpopulation" suggests, if not support of, then at least sympathy for a theory of eugenics that would ill accord with his anxieties about control systems (TJ, 78). He also maintains that the assassination of Robert Kennedy "was arranged by the far right, and that the arrangers are now taking this opportunity to pass anti-gun laws and disarm the nation for the fascist takeover" (TJ, 83). In fact, the right to bear arms was as much a conservative cause célèbre in the 1970s as in the 1990s, and it is therefore extremely unlikely that "the far right" would have conspired "to pass anti-gun laws."[170] In such moments, one hears a premonition of the modern-day militia movement as well as an echo of the William Burroughs of twenty-five years before who doesn't "figure to take any shit off anybody" and notes proudly, "Shooting is my principal pastime" (L, 39, 27). And while Burroughs's political views certainly became more progressive by the 1970s, I believe that he never really discarded his paranoid anarcho-libertarianism of the late '40s and '50s and that this position in fact explains the antistatism that deeply infuses *Naked Lunch* and the cut-up trilogy.

In his discourse of the late 1940s, Burroughs's politics are driven (much as they are during the 1970s) by his opposition to all systems of control ("the only *possible* ethic is to do what one *wants* to do" [L, 42]). Yet unlike his stance of later years, Burroughs (growing marijuana and exploiting cheap farm labor—an adventurous entrepreneur, like his grandfather) specifically targets both the liberal establishment and the then-burgeoning welfare state. (In the Employment Act of 1946, Congress declared it the "responsibility of the Federal Government" to "coordinate and utilize all its plans, functions, and resources for the purpose" of promoting "maximum employment, production, and purchasing power.")[171] In a series of letters in 1949 and 1950, he insists that to "dictate to a man what he can do and can't do with his own property is *Un-American Socialism*," that the " 'Welfare' State" is an "obscenity," and that "law-making bodies" in the United States are "stupid and hysterical" (L, 44, 57). "What ever happened," he asks, "to our glorious Frontier heritage of minding ones [sic] own business? The Frontiersman has shrunk to a wretched, interfering, Liberal bureaucrat" (L, 61). And liberals, he believes, are primarily responsible for destroying the entrepreneurial self insofar as they are "weaklings" who support "the most damnable tyranny, a snivelling, mealy-mouthed tyranny of bureaucrats, social workers, psychiatrists and Union officials" (*L*, 51, 61). Here, Burroughs's anti-institutionalism tends (as it would continue to do) to erase the distinctions between and among very different kinds of social institutions, all of which, he believes, represent an assault on individualism, and on the "freedom of the individual" (*TJ*, 60). And he recommends to the doubtlessly horrified Ginsberg that the latter study Westbrook Pegler (the "only" newspaper columnist "who possesses a grain of integrity"), who was, in fact, the most conservative columnist of the era, a vehement anticommunist libertarian who attacked the Supreme Court, the wealthy, and the U.S. tax system (*L*, 57).

Burroughs's obsession with the victimization of the individual male subject at the hands of a meddling, interfering government provides a clear connection between the casualty of control systems (the "white Negro" of the 1950s) and the figure of the white male as victim that has become so prominent in U.S. culture since the mid-1970s. (Allan Bakke's 1974 suit against the University of California for twice denying him entrance to its medical school at Davis, which I analyze in detail in chapter 3, was arguably the pivotal moment in this narrative.) In Burroughs, more clearly than in the work of any other rebel male of the 1950s, white men are imagined to be not the powerful and wealthy constituency they were—and are—but the victims of nameless bureaucrats, controllers, and racialized others. As one of Bill Lee's chance acquaintances puts it in *Junky*:

> "The same people are in both narcotics and Communism. Right now they control most of America. I'm a seaman. I've been shipping out for twenty years. Who gets the jobs over there in the NMU Hall? American white men like you and me? No. Dagos and Spiks and Niggers. Why? Because the union controls shipping, and Communists control the union." (*J*, 71)

So drugs are linked to communism, which is linked to the persecution of the American everyman, "white men like you and me." While it is perhaps tempting to dismiss these paranoid ravings as a parodic routine on Burroughs's part, they conform all too closely to his own beliefs and tie into what was even then a hundred-year history of nativist activism. Moreover, as he confessed to Ginsberg two years after *Junky* was published: "Neither in life nor in writing can I achieve complete sincerity . . . *except* in parody," (*L*, 272).

It seems to me that the one constant in Burroughs's politics—his scorn for all control systems, bureaucracies, and institutions that threaten individual "freedom"—is founded on an attempt to secure the masculine sovereignty of the political subject. Ever the champion of a frontier ethic, Burroughs decries what he sees as the feminization of politics (and, more generally, of the public sphere under commodity culture) and the castration of the subject. During the early 1950s, he locates the primary threat to masculinity in the welfare state. Twenty years later, he finds it in the national security state. In both instances, however, he opposes himself to the collective, to conformity, and to what the young Richard Nixon decried as "increased federal control over the lives of people."[172] By setting himself so firmly against a feminized, liberal hegemony in the United States, with its advocacy of reformism, regulation of the marketplace, and the organization of workers and consumers, he takes up an allegedly masculine, radical position that is simultaneously leftist and rightist (in 1952 he suggested that "an old-fashioned, bomb-throwing terrorist movement might he amusing," while in 1974 he saw the "total destruction of existing institutions" as "the only alternative to a nuclear war" [L, 145; TJ, 108]). Like so many of the new leftists his fiction inspired, he has no sympathy for an organized political opposition, particularly one that views the working class as a revolutionary agent. Like so many on the radical Right, he inveighs (even in the 1970s) against gun control, government interference, communism, overpopulation, and feminism.

Yet what is perhaps most revealing about Burroughs's obsession with control systems (and the victimization of the individual male subject that they produce) is his profound ambivalence toward them. On the one hand, control systems are clearly coded as a feminizing and collectivizing force that imperils the imaginary coherence of the male subject. This becomes explicit in Burroughs's construction of "the dream" (by which he means the "disturbing factor of spontaneous, unpredictable life") as the opposite of "a control system." According to his formulation, "[t]he non-dream program," a.k.a. the control system, "is specifically directed against the male principle. It is above all antisexual and anti-male" (TJ, 102; L, 268). In other words, control systems represent a kind of antimasculine conspiracy, that, like "the whole anti-sex orientation of our society, . . . is basically manipulated by female interests" (TJ, 118). On the other hand, this same chain of associations also has the effect of masculinizing control systems. For the latter are, above all else, the primary agents in the social sphere for the production of phallic power. Like Benway's project of "Total Demoralization," they castrate male subjects by turning them into masochists who engineer their own destruction (NL, 21). Like Benway himself, they take a certain sadistic pleasure in tormenting their victims. Moreover, science in Burroughs's discourse (as in the culture at large) is always associated with masculinity and power. This (perhaps inadvertent) masculinization of control systems has the added effect of eroticizing them, of making seductive both the sadistic exercise of power and the masochistic submission to it. And, in fact, it seems to me that it is precisely this eroticization that accounts for the widely shared belief in the sadomasochistic nature of Burroughs's fictions.[173] For Burroughs, who seems to identify far more readily with the victim than with the agent of control, is clearly as attracted as he is repelled by control systems. Hence he suggests that "[c]itizens who want to be utterly humiliated and degraded—so many people do, nowadays . . . offer themselves up for passive homosexual intercourse," which, in Burroughs, is the sign of both submission and ecstasy, of the "unendurable delight" of those men (like Burroughs himself, according to Ginsberg) who "can't keep from ejaculat[ing] when you screw" them (*NL*, 118, 78, 28).[174] Is it any wonder then that the agent of control, being both alluring and repulsive, masculine and feminine, sadist and masochist, can cohere no better than his victim, that "Benway's face" is "subject at any moment to unspeakable cleavage" (*NL*, 28)? Or that there is really "only one main character" in his fiction (because Benway, Carl, and Lee "are, of course, one person") who is relentlessly constructed and deconstructed (*L*, 375)? Or that pleasure in Burroughs is always ghosted by pain, that hanging is linked both to death and to orgasm, that the utopian is always inscribed within the dystopian, that his "sado-masochist visa to Sodom" never expires, or that "we see God through our assholes in the flash bulb of orgasm" (*L*, 411; *NL*, 229)?

JUNK

Every subject and every thing in Burroughs reproduces a doubleness that is inextricably linked both with the sadomasochistic structure of subjectivity—which is to say, desire—and with the commodity form. While the first connection is played out seemingly everywhere in Burroughs's writing, the second is explicitly theorized in the introduction to *Naked Lunch*, which reads almost like a burlesque of the first chapter of Marx's *Capital*. In this text, Burroughs theorizes junk as "the ideal product . . . the ultimate merchandise," which is to say, as a parody of the commodity that exposes both the commodity's structure and the social mystifications it produces (*NL*, xi). For like the commodity, junk has both use value and exchange value. The former is realized "in consumption," or as Burroughs puts it, "addiction," and the latter, in the dynamics of the marketplace, or in Burroughs's phrase, the "pyramid of junk" that is "built on basic principles of monopoly" (*NL*, x).[175] For Burroughs realizes that the power of junk, like that of the commodity, comes from the fact that it is addictive: "The more junk you use the less you have and the more you have the more you use" (*NL*, xi). Since both can never finally satiate the needs they arouse, the "dope fiend," like the loyal and idolatrous consumer, "is a man in total need" (*NL*, xi). In other words, junk is the *ideal* commodity because it produces only the desire for more ("I never had enough junk—no one ever does" [*NL*, xiii]). Moreover, like the commodity, which acquires a "phantom-like objectivity" because of "the different concrete forms of labour" that disappear into it, junk "feed[s] on peoples of the world" (*NL*, x).[176] For just as the commodity ends up standing, as it were, "on its head," so does junk ironically end up consuming the consumer: "The junk merchant does not sell his product to the consumer, he sells the consumer to the product" (*NL*, xi).[177] And in this respect, junk acquires a fetishistic character that is much like the fetishism of commodities, insofar as a "definite social relation between men themselves . . . assumes here . . . the fantastic form of a relation between things."[178] This is the mystery of junk, that, being an object of such intense (and unsatisfiable) desire, it ends up objectifying the user. In other words, the "junk merchant," through the process of distribution and consumption, establishes a kind of sadomasochistic relationship with "the client" in which the latter is "degrade[d] and simplifie[d]" (NL, xi). And so "The Algebra of Need" that keeps the "pyramid of junk" in place (inadvertently) exposes the fact that capitalism (by its very nature) and the commodity form (by virtue of its structure) turn the consumer into a slave who remains totally in thrall to the commodity: "You would lie, cheat, inform on your friends, steal, do *anything* to satisfy total need" (NL, xi). And junk, the most seductive and feminized of commodities, exerts an irresistible fascination for the desiring subject, being the source of need and revulsion simultaneously. Like capitalism, it is the ultimate control system and the one on which, for Burroughs at least, all others are modeled. Ruthlessly exposing the workings of consumer culture, junk reveals the lie behind the commodity's promise of bliss.

WRITING

Perhaps the most intriguing expression of Burroughs's deep-seated ambivalence toward control systems—and this is something he shares with Ginsberg and Kerouac—is his understanding of writing as a material practice. For all three figures, writing is conceptualized as a kind of routine to which the subject must submit, and all three early in their careers developed methods to ensure their subjugation to the word. As I noted at the beginning of this chapter, Burroughs's letters to Ginsberg attest to his emergence as a writer beginning around 1955 as a result of his ability to devise ways by which to write not just his own incoherence but also his subjection, that is, his submission to multiple control systems. This is why he started transcribing his routines and using the techniques of the cut-up (made with a typewriter and scissors, whereby passages are cut in together "at random") and the fold-in (whereby two passages are folded together also at random) to produce new meaning, new texts, and "new connections between images" (TJ, 28; PR, 25). Like Ginsberg and Kerouac, Burroughs found it necessary to discover a method that wrests writing from the conscious control of the writer, that allows him "simply" to "transcribe Lee's impressions," that is, the vision and being of the other ("[t]he only way I can write narrative is to get right outside my body and experience it" [L, 251, 375]). As a result, he insists that the manuscript which would become Naked Lunch, because it has produced "[c]hanges" in his "psyche" that are "profound and basic," "supersedes, in fact makes obso-

THE DIVIDED SELF 101

lete, anything" he has "written hitherto" (*L*, 376, 339). Yet, at the same time, Burroughs notes with a certain pride, "[w]riting now causes me an almost unbearable pain" (*L*, 286). "Parentheses pounce on me and tear me apart. I have no control over what I write, which is as it should be" (*L*, 289). In other words, becoming a writer means learning a masochistic submission to the practice of writing, to the cut-up that tears apart the subject of writing, and to the fold-in, which "fit[s] together a composite being" made of "the two halves of our bodies" (*SM*, 90).

Burroughs's belief in the servitude of the writer is echoed by Ginsberg, who values most highly the spontaneous, the unconscious, and the sudden juxtaposition of dissimilar things whose meanings are not "necessarily *know[n]*" to the poet "in the moment of composition," but that "comes to mean something later."[179] This is why Ginsberg, too, found it necessary to use various devices, like drugs, that would allow the unconscious to write itself ("I did get the idea of how interesting it could be . . . if you commit yourself irrevocably to accepting the traces of your mind during the composition").[180] And for Kerouac, as well, spontaneous prose means allowing one's self to be led "to the edges of language where the babble of the subconscious begins."[181] It means making one's self "[s]ubmissive to everything . . . [i]n tranced fixation," "[c]omposing wild, undisciplined, pure, coming in from under. . . ."[182] Moreover, the spontaneous method ensures that writing for Kerouac, as for Burroughs, will be torturous, because "the best writing is always the most painful," much like a "fire ordeal" one has "to get through . . . 'to prove your innocence' or just die in it 'guilty', . . ."[183]

Producing their key texts during the efflorescence of postwar consumer culture, and desperately attempting to assert their dissension and independence, the Beats conceptualized writing as a site of struggle between domination and submission, an arena in which the seductive force of the national security state (a.k.a. the control system) confronts the rebellion of the lone, privatized male subject. The latter, when faced with this masculinized authority, both fears and desires to comply, dreading his victimization and the requisite feminization that goes along with compliance, yet longing to share in the state's power and prestige. As a result, Burroughs, Ginsberg, and Kerouac—the emblematic bourgeois rebels without a cause—are constantly oscillating between feminine and masculine positionalities, writing and unwriting their submission. Burroughs, in particular, is deeply aware of the normalizing and disciplinary functions of discourse, and he points out that "[t]he word," as exercised, for example, by the press, "is one of the most powerful instruments of control" (*TJ*, 33). Yet he wishes to sabotage this control, less by producing an autonomous, resistant discourse than through a subversive repetition of the discourse of power. "Now if you start cutting these up and rearranging them you are breaking down the control system" (*TJ*, 33). But if the cut-up functions, as Burroughs alleges, to subvert systems of domination, it does so only by enlisting the writing subject's submission to the word. Intriguingly, Burroughs even acknowledges this contradiction in a letter to Ginsberg in which he confesses that the dream, which he otherwise regards as the antithesis of the control system, is itself a form of control: "There is nothing stronger than the dream, because dreams are forms of THE LAW" (L, 397). Burroughs, in other words, aligns even resistance with "THE LAW" and all that it stands for—the word, the father, writing, and control. He is thereby forced to admit his failure (and the failure of all bourgeois rebels?), forced to admit that—as a man—he can resist the power of the word, the law, and the state only by submitting to it ("To speak is to lie—To live is to collaborate" [NE, 14]). And his texts, like those of Kerouac and Ginsberg, are deeply imbued with the desire to surrender, to take up ecstatically a feminized position, and, in the next instant, to flee in horror or, better yet, to disavow and kill off the offending part of the self. Is it any wonder that Burroughs, in writing to Ginsberg about Joan Vollmer's death, should attempt to vindicate himself by imagining the murder to have been a form of suicide? Isn't that the excuse that men who assault women always use: they had it coming; they asked for it; it's "as if the brain *drew* the bullet toward it" (L, 263)?

In the years immediately following World War II, as the Cold War and the domestic revival were being consolidated, many American men were unable or unwilling to accede to both the demands of the national security state and the dominant models of white, middle-class masculinity. And during this era, a whole "beat generation" attempted a highly individualized rebellion against whiteness, against commodity culture, against masculinity. And so they attacked Moloch, or (in Kerouac's words) the "sinister new kind of efficiency" that "appeared in America," or endeavored (in Burroughs's phrase) "to make people aware of the true criminality of our times" (PR, 49).[184] But in imagining themselves victims of "America," they could not help but be seduced by the insurrectionary vision of the artist as cowboy, rebel, entrepreneur. And so they used writing to try to negotiate a way out, imagining that writing contained and expressed all they so desperately desired: both rebellion and submission, masculinity and femininity, blackness and whiteness. Perhaps this obsession with writing helps to explain the crucial role of fictional texts—and fictionalized real lives—in producing a beat culture that rather than overturn hegemonic social values gave them an ecstatic spin. For as glorious and painful as the act of writing was for the Beats, it never led them fully to recognize that, as atomized and divided subjects, they had internalized the very systems of control against which they were fighting (in addition to social structures they were not explicitly contesting: racism, misogyny, and homophobia). Perhaps the most poignant disavowal of this failure, and the one most predictive of the collapse of the '60s rebellion to which the Beats were godfathers, is Burroughs's assertion that because "life is literally a dream," because it represents at once the control system and its antithesis, "political action fails." And trying one more time to free himself from domination, he reinvents the aestheticist solution: "the whole existing system can be *dreamed away* if we get enough people dreaming . . . " (*L*, 398). For Burroughs, as for so many rebel males of the 1950s, political activism is suppressed in favor of retreat to an imaginary world in which control, the flesh, and the word are simply dreamed away. Which means that in the darkness and horror of Cold War culture, the end of writing—both its goal and its ruination—is utopia.

Chapter Two

REVOLUTION AS PERFORMANCE

> [O]ne of the most remarkable aspects of the counter culture is its
> cultivation of a feminine softness among its males. It is the occa-
> sion of endless satire on the part of its critics, but the style is clearly
> a deliberate effort on the part of the young to undercut the crude and
> compulsive he-manliness of American political life.
>
> *(Theodore Roszak,* The Making of a Counter Culture *[1969])*

> The first time I put on the black silk panties I got a hardon right
> away. I felt humiliated in the garter belt. It felt good. I became a
> prisoner in the high heeled shoes. I had hot and cold flashes. I was
> delirious. I wanted to bow down and be stepped on. I put on the
> black uniform of the slave and I was so unbalanced by the sensation
> of submission that I wanted, needed, to feel Madame's domination
> to balance me out.
>
> *(Julian Beck,* The Life of the Theatre *[1972])*

SPEEDING on their Harleys across the painted deserts of the Southwest
in Dennis Hopper's *Easy Rider* (1969), Captain America (Peter Fonda)
and Billy (Dennis Hopper) are Americans on the move—and the unmistakable heirs of *The Wild One* and *On the Road*. Drug dealers, potheads,
hippies, free spirits, they, like so many of the generation they represent, rebel
against the conservatism of the cultural orthodoxies of the domestic revival by
taking to the road on their motorcycles, making up their own laws, and impro-
vising their lives. Owning only what they can carry (and carrying a large stash
of bills earned from a cocaine deal at the beginning of the film), they go where
they want when they want. Mobile and independent, they challenge the settled
domesticity of both the ruling bourgeoisie and the hippie commune to which
they pay a visit. Unlike their contemporaries commuting to work in blue-collar
shirts or three-piece suits, they are decked out in a kind of masquerade, Captain
America in a black leather jacket with a large American flag sewn on the back,
and Billy in a Buffalo Bill–style buckskin jacket and cowboy hat.

Easy Rider, written by Fonda, Hopper, and Terry Southern, and made for a
mere $375,000, marked an auspicious directorial debut for Hopper. It garnered
good (if sometimes grudging) reviews and became a tremendous popular
success, grossing an estimated $60 million worldwide and signaling "a new
wave of iconoclasm, or at least independence, in [U.S.] film production."[1] The

press singled it out as "the first feature film to capture successfully the conflict between the new hippy, 'tribal,' drug-oriented generation and their opposite numbers in the straight world."[2] And whether describing plot, characterization, cinematography, or acting, virtually all the critics peppered their reviews liberally with the words "honest," "vital," and "real" or their near synonyms. For they hailed the film as a barometer of U.S. culture: "Its importance is not as a work of art but as a cultural document that expresses—more by instinct than design—many of the feelings of today's youth. The film is so phenomenally popular because it is so completely in tune with its college and teenage audience—the movie-makers and the movie-goers share identical fantasies and anxieties."[3] Seeing the film as a portrait of youth culture and the nation (and unaware of its subsequent role in constructing and consolidating that culture), critics used it as an opportunity to speculate on a myriad of issues, including violence, drugs, the state of film acting, and race relations. Despite the omission of considerations of gender in most reviews of the film, I believe that a key to its popularity was its success in consolidating an image of a new kind of masculinity, one understood as being more theatricalized, innocent, vulnerable, and ultimately tragic than its predecessors. For Captain America and Billy are repeatedly brutalized in the course of the film, thrown in jail, beaten with lead pipes, and finally killed. Why did this violence prove so compelling for young moviegoers in 1969? How is it connected to widespread "fantasies and anxieties" about certain gendered and racialized identifications? Why do the "people who conceived this film and the people who applaud it," as one critic puts it, "take a certain masochistic satisfaction in casting themselves as martyrs, as poor innocents slaughtered by the barbarians"?[4] And why, finally, does the fantasy of martyrdom—Christian or otherwise—animate so many fictions associated with both the counterculture and the New Left during the 1960s?

To begin to answer these questions, let me consider what I believe to be the film's pivotal sequence (and the first, in fact, to be filmed).[5] Immediately after the the brutal murder of their friend George Hanson (Jack Nicholson, in the role that catapulted him to stardom), Captain America and Billy reach what from the beginning of the film had been their destination, New Orleans and Mardi Gras. Not only is this sequence the only part of the film that takes place in an urban setting, but it is also set off from the rest of the movie by its use (particularly during the LSD scene) of experimental techniques—handheld camera, graphic editing, very quick cuts, and extradiegetic sound—in a film that for the most part obediently follows the conventions of Hollywood narrative cinema. The sequence opens with Captain America and Billy eating fancy food in a fancy restaurant, spending their easily earned cash, becoming tourists and consumers for the first time. As they eat, the Electric Prunes' "Kyrie Eleison" fills the sound track, establishing the strong religious, and specifically Christian, tone that will dominate the entire sequence. The film cuts to

Madame Tinkertoy's whorehouse where the men go to fulfill George's dream. The brothel, however, is first identified not by its whores but by the paintings and other artifacts that fill what looks like a cross between a nineteenth-century mansion and a tarted-up church. Tacky pornographic paintings rub shoulders with a fake Leonardo and a fake El Greco, while rococo decorations, statuary, and empty bookcases frame Madame Tinkertoy's stable of girls. For the first time in the film, the past intrudes on the present—but in the form of a fragmented, discontinuous history, somebody else's history—while Captain America, characteristically disconnected and aloof, in the process of being converted into something of a Christ figure by the juxtaposition of montage and music, flashes forward for a split second and imagines his forthcoming passion and death by fire.

After Madame Tinkertoy brings in the two women that the men have purchased (Captain America's is tellingly named Mary [Toni Basil]), the four venture outside where, in what looks like grainy documentary footage (it was shot in 16mm), they watch floats, revelers, and masked figures, both black and white, pass through the narrow, garishly lit streets of the French Quarter, while the singing of three black jazz musicians, playing guitar and tambourine, provides the sound track. The film suddenly cuts to daytime, while the four continue their carousal and end up in St. Louis Cemetery No. 1, New Orleans's most famous cemetery, where they drop acid. The remainder of the sequence represents (using an array of avant-gardist cinematic techniques) what can be described only as a real bum trip. Quick cuts make for a fast, irregular rhythm, while the figures in the brief shots are alternately paralyzed or frenetic. Images of flames, flowers, tombs, and crucifixes abound. Unexplained persons hover and menace. Fragmentary diegetic dialogue is superimposed against an extradiegetic text, a reading of the Nicene Creed and the "Hail Mary" by a woman who, in one shot, is discovered standing in the cemetery. Mary undresses in the narrow space between two large tombs, the two couples play erotically, deliriously, and threateningly, while Captain America lies in the arms of a statue of the Virgin Mary (as Queen of Heaven) and murmurs: "I hate you so much. You never think about me. Why did you leave like that? . . . I love you, oh God, I love you. And you're such a fool mother and I hate you so much."

The trip in *Easy Rider*, because of its privileged position narratologically and cinematically, seems both a crystallization of the film's main themes and a way of making (more or less) explicit the characters' underlying anxieties. LSD thereby functions in the film—as it does in so much '60s discourse—as a mechanism of derepression, a kind of truth serum, or, in drug-guru Timothy Leary's words, "a powerful releaser of energy as yet not fully understood."[6] As represented in the film, sex (and, indeed, all human contact) under LSD becomes both ecstatic and terrible as the subject is forced to confront repressed desires and fears as well as the personal history that has produced them (Captain America's confession is the only information given in the film about the past or family of any character). And the contents of the bum trip could not be more different from the drug-cult mysticism exemplified by Leary's statement that the "goals of an LSD session," for the heterosexual male, at least, "are to discover and make love with God, . . . yourself, and . . . a woman."[7] Instead, the trip functions to intensify the sense of profound alienation (decried by countless countercultural chroniclers) that is allegedly endemic to an industrialized, technocratic, militarist society. It reveals that these new men and women of the counterculture are *victims*—victims of a drug that dispossesses them of their rational defenses, of desires over which they have no control, of their gendered identifications, and of a traumatic family history.

Yet the setting for this pivotal sequence is, in many ways, as important as the trip itself. For New Orleans, and Mardi Gras in particular, serve as the emblematic sign of American carnival, of that "release," as Joseph Roach explains (drawing on Bakhtin), "from the oppression of official culture, a suspension of its laws, an exhilarating inversion of its authority, a momentary state of topsy-turvydom, in which the common people become powerful and the powerful people become ridiculous."[8] And in that way, the city and its festival become figures for the counterculture and its aspirations, the site at which systems of authority, both secular and religious, are challenged and inverted, in which the outcasts are sainted and the low exalted. It is hardly coincidental, then, that New Orleans and Mardi Gras would become during the late '60s and early '70s a preferred destination for hordes of "long-haired, perspiring hippies," who, in the view of "[m]any locals," represented "the biggest threat since Reconstruction."[9] With their theatricalized appearance, celebratory spirit, and challenge to gendered norms—and, as the above quotation implies, to racialized norms as well—hippies embody the spirit of Mardi Gras. Yet they also represent its antithesis insofar as their "whole way of life," in particular their mystical bent and disdain for commodity culture, fly "in the face of the alcohol-flavored commercialism of Bourbon Street."[10] In that sense, Captain America and Billy represent simultaneously the embodiment and repudiation of Mardi Gras.

And the St. Louis Cemetery No. 1, site of the acid trip, represents a particularly suggestive setting in the film, both architecturally and symbolically. The oldest cemetery in New Orleans (dating back to the early eighteenth century), it attests to the increasing segregation of the dead under Enlightenment urban planning, the compulsion that "the dead," as Roach elegantly puts it, "withdraw from the spaces of the living."[11] With its rows of multiform and diverse graves and its mazelike alleys, its elaborate and well-kept tombs abutting crumbled ruins, the cemetery becomes a veritable city of the dead that both separates and intermixes the rich and the poor, "grow[ing] on the margins [of the city] to define the social distinction of the fictive center."[12] This sense of the cemetery as a kind of ghost town is particularly true in New Orleans where, because of the high water table, graves must be built above ground and are often fashioned as miniature houses. Unlike the real city at its gates, St. Louis No. 1 represents both an integrated space (it includes, for example, the grave of Homer Plessy of *Plessy v. Ferguson* fame) and a religious one, in which every dwelling is a kind of church. It functions, in short, as the place of memory and loss, heaven and earth, body and soul, human and divine, past and present, black and white, salvation and damnation.

In *Easy Rider*, Hopper exploits the cemetery both visually and symbolically for its contradictory evocations. Upon the characters' arrival, it functions as a utopian figuration (like LSD itself in the discourses of prodrug activists), a miniature city that represents a haven from the chaos of Mardi Gras. But once the foursome drop acid, the sinister potential of the cemetery is realized. In several extreme low angle shots, the large tombs look like walled-up apartments, while the four characters, squeezed between the houses of the dead, appear to be suffocating. And Mary's disrobing is coded as an act more of desperation than liberation. Moreover, the ubiquitous religiosity of the site (a crucifix at every turn) serves less as a reassurance or concrete manifestation of faith than as the sign of the characters' lack of faith. The Nicene Creed ("I believe in God, creator of heaven and earth . . .") functions to underline their blasphemous intrusion upon holy ground. And most scandalously, they transform the house of the spirit into a temple of the flesh. "I want you to be beautiful," Billy mutters, while Karen (Karen Black) cries, "No, no." The city of the dead becomes the occasion for sex and death: "I'm dying," Karen cries, neatly evoking the early modern conflation of the two, "I'm gonna die. I'm dead." Meanwhile, Captain America, lying in the arms of the Queen of Heaven, reproaches her/Mary/his mother for their death/abandonment of him: "I hate you/I love you." The cemetery, in short, is reimagined as a crossroads at which the utopian ineluctably and unpredictably changes into the dystopian, and vice versa.

In *Easy Rider*, LSD in the city of the dead functions as a kind of magical elixir that, willy-nilly, transforms things into their opposites. The whore becomes a Virgin awaiting the Annunciation ("please help me conceive a child," Karen cries), while Captain America, cradled in his mother's arms, is rendered infantilized and helpless, a masochistic child guiltily acting out his subjection to a cruel femininity, his desire, in Freud's words, to be "treated like a little, helpless, dependent child."[13] The prominence of this faux Pietà, in which he is transformed into a simulacrum of the dead Christ, also bears witness to the ascendancy both in the counterculture and (more ambivalently) in the New Left of what Kaja Silverman describes as the Christian masochist, the religious martyr, the suffering victim placed on display for the pleasure of a cruel and implacable God. As she explains, "[w]hat is being beaten" in the Christian masochistic fantasy "is not so much the body as the 'flesh,' and beyond that sin itself, and the whole fallen world."[14] For the Christian masochist "seeks to remake him or herself according to the model of the suffering Christ, the very picture of earthly divestiture and loss. Insofar as such an identification implies the complete and utter negation of all phallic values, Christian masochism has radically emasculating implications. . . ."[15] And both Captain America and Billy, preferring Mardi Gras and LSD to sex, are dephallicized by their failure to have sex with women who are being paid, after all, to shore up their hetero- sexuality ("What's the matter," a worried Mary asks Captain America, "don't you like me?"). Throughout *Easy Rider* and countless other '60s fictions associated with the counterculture, the white male subject is reimagined as an emasculated martyr, a longhaired freak, a simulacrum of Christ who mortifies his flesh, suffers, and dies for the sins of the world. It is little wonder, then, that the film's pivotal sequence, identifying Captain America—and the nation for which he is named—with the suffering Christ, should be the preamble to his fiery death.

THE VARIETIES OF YOUTH CULTURE

The youth culture of the 1960s was an extravagantly heterogeneous venture, composed of disparate political and social groups with diverse and often con- tradictory goals, ideologies, and strategies. And while it is relatively easy to distinguish among them, it is much more difficult to establish a taxonomy that charts their interrelationships. Most historians, following contemporary com- mentators like Theodore Roszak, tend to oppose "the mind-blown bohemian- ism of the beats and hippies" to "the hard-headed political activism of the student New Left."[16] And although this polarization, which is predicated on a distinction between the private and public spheres, is in some ways justified, it tends to obscure the position of those groups that were most intent on dis- rupting the separation of private from public and which, subsequently, have had the greatest impact on U.S. political culture: the civil rights and Black Power movements, on the one hand, and groups like the Yippies and the Women's Liberation movement committed to both cultural and political revo- lution, on the other. But any taxonomic project must begin with an examina- tion of the setting in which youth culture developed, the post–World War II economic and baby booms.

An era of unprecedented growth, the years between 1945 and the early 1970s saw the gross national product and average family income more than double while unemployment steadily declined, reaching 4 percent during the 1960s.[17] Concurrently, the birthrate soared among all classes as children were being reimagined as "a 'defense—an impregnable bulwark' against the terrors of the age"—the hydrogen bomb, the Korean War, and most of all, commu- nism.[18] During the '50s and '60s, the professional, managerial, and technical sectors of the labor force were expanding so quickly that by the early 1970s the

United States had become "the only country to employ more people in services than in the production of tangible goods."[19] This shift from an industrial to a service economy had a profound impact on the baby boomers who were just beginning to come of age, and "[b]etween 1960 and 1966 the number of students enrolled in college more than doubled, topping 7.3 million."[20] Delaying marriage and entry into the full-time labor market, students thus became an increasingly large and recognizable class, living in dormitories or rental housing in relative poverty and rarely involved in local community institutions or struggles that preceded their arrival. It is among this class of youth, both black and white, that the oppositional political movements and cultures of the '60s began to develop.

Historians are agreed that all the oppositional cultures of the 1960s, despite their diversity, have their roots in the civil rights movement's crusades for racial equality. Although desegregation was first mandated in the United States with the landmark *Brown v. Board of Education* ruling of 1954, it was not until the end of the decade that schools in the South began to dismantle the "separate but equal" system. Shortly thereafter, in the event that perhaps most vividly marks the beginning of the '60s, four black college students sat down in February 1960 at a segregated lunch counter at a Woolworth's in Greensboro, North Carolina, to challenge the legacy of Jim Crow. By the end of the week, 1,600 other students joined them in protest. During the next two years, despite the violent opposition of local police, the Ku Klux Klan, and other white supremacist groups, "an estimated 70,000 people participated in over 100 nonviolent protests from Florida to Virginia, from Maryland to Arkansas."[21] Under the leadership of Martin Luther King, Jr., and others, the Congress for Racial Equality and the Student Non-Violent Coordinating Committee (SNCC) were founded to speed desegregation efforts that, during the early 1960s, relied primarily on confrontation and passive resistance. During the summer of 1961, the SNCC-sponsored Freedom Rides, peopled mainly by middle-class college students, both black and white, worked to desegregate public accommodations in the South. These actions combined with the Mississippi Freedom Summer of 1964 (during which three protesters were murdered) led to the passage of the Civil Rights Act of 1964, the Voting Rights Act of 1965, and the Housing Act of 1968, which were decisive blows to institutionalized racism in the United States, outlawing discrimination in employment, labor unions, and all places of public accommodation, strengthening voting rights, and demanding that school desegregation proceed with "all deliberate speed."[22] As James F. Scott points out, however, desegregation during the '50s and '60s was not simply an expression of goodwill by the white majority but was inextricably tied to the exigencies of the postwar boom. "The urgency of an economy that required expansion of its capacity to mass consume to match its productive output made local efforts to change black-white relations too unpredictable. Mass production and mass consumption are mutually supportive; and a segregated society excludes segments of the population, especially blacks, from the 'mainstream' as effective consumers or producers."[23]

When, in 1962, the Students for a Democratic Society (SDS), the most prominent progressive political organization of the decade and one composed in its early years principally of middle-class whites, issued its major document, the Port Huron Statement, it clearly drew on the principles and methods that had propelled SNCC. More than any other text, the Port Huron Statement set the agenda for the New Left, putting its emphasis, in Stanley Aronowitz's estimation, on *process* and signaling "an almost religious return to *experience* and a converse retreat from the abstractions of the red politics of yesterday."[24] Inspired by "the Southern struggle against racial bigotry," and reacting as much against traditional Marxist categories and rhetoric as against the Cold War and "the idolatrous worship of things by man," the Port Huron Statement called for "a participatory democracy" based on equality, nonviolence, and community and revolution from the bottom up.[25] It attempted to break decisively with the legacy of American radicalism, and indeed, as Paul Buhle points out, its principles were hardly radical at all "by the standards of the Old Left": "It spoke for human relationships over the fragmentation blessed by the various existing social systems; it called for more freedom for the young (specifically on campus); it condemned the Cold War restriction of political debate even as it condemned existing Communism; and it urged a democratic, peaceful approach to world problems."[26] The humanistic rhetoric and somewhat naive idealism of the Port Huron Statement did not, however, long dominate SDS. The increasing deployment of American troops and matériel in Southeast Asia came more and more to preoccupy SDS and other leftist organizations (like the Berkeley Free Speech Movement), and by 1965 the New Left coalesced as a loose confederation of political and social movements linked by their radical opposition to the Vietnam War. The escalation of U.S. involvement in Vietnam profoundly changed the nature of SDS, radicalizing, in Buhle's words, "the student revolt at a dizzying rate while simultaneously investing it with profound public responsibilities for organizing opposition to the war."[27] Coincidentally, a new generation of activists "from lower-middle-class and working-class families" became involved who "wore their hair longer, smoked pot, and were clearly more anti-intellectual, alienated, and anarchistic."[28] Increasingly, SDS turned its attention to global concerns, transforming universities into centers of resistance to both the Vietnam War and the draft and provoking increasingly militant confrontations with university and civil authorities.

By the mid-1960s, as the New Left was becoming more aggressive, civil rights leaders began to reconsider the movement's nonviolent strategies. A loving community of black and white had failed to coalesce, and tensions increased between "bossy" white organizers and many blacks in the movement, "especially those from lower-class backgrounds."[29] The race riots in

Harlem in 1964 and Watts the next year "revealed a greater depth of frustration and rage among the black urban underclass than had been realized."[30] The 1965 assassination of Malcolm X, the U.S. publication of Frantz Fanon's anti-colonialist manifesto, *The Wretched of the Earth*, and a steady flow of news stories from an Africa undergoing rapid decolonization impelled a number of black leaders to consider the similarities between race relations in the United States and the structures of colonialism. The next year, Stokely Carmichael gained control of SNCC on a "Black Power" platform that rejected the integrationist and assimilationist aspirations of King and the NAACP and expelled whites from the organization. During the summer of 1967, the impoverished, largely black ghettos of many major American cities erupted in riots. The most devastating, in Detroit, left 43 persons dead and 7,200 arrested. H. Rap Brown described the riots as a "dress rehearsal for revolution."[31] Carmichael, meanwhile, recognizing the structural impediments to racial equality, called for a radical—and worldwide—redistribution of economic and political power:

> Ultimately, the economic foundations of this country must be shaken if black people are to control their lives. The colonies of the United States—and this includes the black ghettoes within its borders, north and south—must be liberated. For a century, this nation has been like an octopus of exploitation, its tentacles stretching from Mississippi and Harlem to South America, the Middle East, southern Africa, and Vietnam. . . .[32]

And Carmichael's radical analysis was supported by many other black leaders. Drawing on Fanon and other anticolonial writers, Robert Blauner, one of the leading exponents of the internal colonialist model, described racist oppression in the United States as being like colonialism insofar as it is coercive, "constrains, transforms, or destroys indigenous values," is "administered by representatives of the dominant group," and is supported ideologically by racism.[33] Moreover, in Blauner's formulation, internal colonialism demands a black nationalist solution which insists that the "social problems of the Black community will ultimately be solved only by people and organizations from that community." And echoing Fanon, Blauner argued that "some violence is almost inevitable in the decolonization process."[34]

Despite their dissimilarities, the Black Power movement was allied, in rhetoric at least, with SDS during the mid- to late '60s by its attention to American imperialism worldwide and its acknowledgment that only revolutionary change could shake the "economic foundations" and "liberate" the oppressed. And by 1968, virtually all of the radical political movements looked for inspiration to Third World revolutionaries like Mao Ze-dong, Fidel Castro, and Che Guevara. For as Fredric Jameson notes, the New Left must be understood as a part of "the great movement of decolonization" under way during the 1960s. And he emphasizes that the "First World 60s owed much to Third-Worldism in terms of politicocultural models, as in a symbolic Maoism, and, moreover, found its mission in resistance to wars aimed precisely at stemming the new revolutionary forces in the Third World."[35]

But by 1969 the fragile coalition that had constituted the New Left had come apart. The Black Panthers (founded in 1966) committed themselves to anticapitalist rebellion, combining, in Todd Gitlin's words, "the anarchist impulse" with a "Third World mystique, the aura of violence, and the thrust for revolutionary efficiency."[36] Despite (or, perhaps, because of) the Panthers' success in mobilizing black urban communities, their relationship with white radicals was uneasy and conflicted. The latter, meanwhile, had splintered into an array of often antagonistic groups, including the neo-Maoist Progressive Labor Party, the Revolutionary Youth Movement, the Yippies (or the "Youth International Party"), the Women's Liberation movement, the Gay Liberation Front, and the Weathermen. As James Weinstein points out, each of these factions conceived of itself as "the one true or key revolutionary agent" and thereby rejected both the valorization of local struggles and the broad-based consensus ("participatory democracy") that had been founding principles of the New Left.[37] Identity politics, in other words, had been born. Despite the continuation of the Vietnam War and of severe racial and economic oppression at home, the New Left, which had never developed a national strategy to influence electoral politics, had come, in Buhle's words, "to a crashing halt" by 1971, ending what had been the only genuinely popular revolutionary political movement in the United States since the Great Depression.[38]

Despite its failure to effect lasting radical social and economic change, the polyglot New Left transformed both American progressive politics and certain cultural norms. Perhaps its most important contribution—and one that undoubtedly led to its decline and disintegration—was its rejection of a politics of class struggle and its embrace, as Jameson puts it (echoing Herbert Marcuse), of "new 'subjects of history' of a nonclass type (blacks, students, Third World peoples)."[39] Poverty, rediscovered by SDS in the early 1960s, came to supersede questions of class, and for the duration of the decade, an alliance between the impoverished urban and rural classes, the student activists and blue-collar workers, never materialized. On the contrary, the white working class remained, for the most part, among the most vehement opponents of both SDS and the Black Power movement. Buhle notes the contradictory implications of the New Left's eschewal of class politics, observing that the lack of "analytical (or ideological) roots in socialized labor, and in racial and ethnic community life" significantly attenuated the efficacy of the New Left's program but, by the same token, unleashed "a powerful utopianism based, like the Civil Rights movement, on the American radical tradition" that stretched from Thoreau to Debs to W.E.B. Du Bois. Faced with the truculence of legislators and judges, the young revolutionaries promoted a politics of protest, intervention, and direct action; faced with the bureaucratic hierarchy, they advocated the dismantlement of "all authority structures in a society of anarchic freedom and abundance"; faced with the dominion of the nuclear family and the sober norms that had dominated postwar America, they offered cultural revolution.[40]

Despite its singularity during the '60s, the New Left cannot be understood without reference to the social movement with which it enjoyed a deeply ambivalent and conflicted relationship: the counterculture. Inspired by rebels without a cause and the wild ones of the 1950s, by the growing popularity of folk music, rock 'n' roll, and marijuana, and most of all by the free-form lifestyles of the beats, with their devotion to "principled poverty" and their "taste for sexual libertinism," a new and oppositional youth culture began to coalesce in the early 1960s.[41] And the story of this counterculture is largely the story of the hippie, who, even more than the student radical or Black Panther, dominated the reportage of intergenerational struggle in the United States from 1966 on. In many respects, Leonard Wolf is correct to identify hippies as "second-generation beats" and to find the most notable differences between them to be matters of style. While beat was "dark, silent, moody, lonely, sad— and its music was jazz," hippie was "bright, vivacious, ecstatic, crowd-loving, joyful—and its music [was] rock."[42] Like the beats, they had a profound disdain for commodity culture, for a technocratic, militarist, and corporate society, and for the social and sexual norms of the postwar domestic revival. And, like the beats, they turned to Zen Buddhism and other (mainly Asian) varieties of religious mysticism for inspiration. As Peter Berg puts it, "[w]hen I read *Howl*, I knew I didn't have anything to lose. That's what did it."[43] Unlike the beats, however, most hippies prized community, sometimes practicing "a kind of Utopian communism in which lodging, food, and clothes were provided free to those in need."[44] Like so many American utopians (going back to the Second Great Awakening of the early nineteenth century), they looked not to a technologized future but to a fantasy of a pastoral, primordial, preindustrial society in which "respect for nature, personal craftsmanship, and cooperative and sharing relationships" were combined with "greater personal autonomy and self-expression."[45] Most famously, perhaps, many preached a philosophy based on love—loving "yourself" and "the whole universe"—in the expectation that this love could change the world.[46]

During the 1960s, members of this "scandalously subversive" subculture were alternately reviled and idolized by large groups of Americans.[47] On the one hand, most civil and military authorities considered hippies a "threat to common decency," and some (like the mayor of Cambridge, Massachusetts) went so far as to judge them "obviously mentally deranged."[48] On the other hand, countless youth, both in the United States and elsewhere in the First World, believed them to constitute a social and cultural vanguard and saw them as harbingers of a new age of peace and love. By 1966, as (hetero)sexual liberation surged in the wake of widespread distribution of "the Pill," as LSD became the drug of choice, as Bob Dylan went electric, and the Beatles and the Jefferson Airplane supplanted Peter, Paul and Mary and the Beach Boys, the counterculture blossomed in San Francisco's Haight-Ashbury and New York's East Village and quickly spread to other major cities and university towns, dedicated to sex, drugs, and rock 'n' roll. Rejecting political organizations (whether of the Right or the Left) and committed to the creation of a new, ostensibly free subject in a new, ostensibly loving society—in short, to a revolution in consciousness—the counterculture carved out alternative communal spaces and produced an art and culture that were derisive of bourgeois conventions, deeply utopian, and often weirdly mystical. Rock, in particular, celebrated this revolution in consciousness, commandeering the airwaves and the record players of millions of teenagers, "spread[ing] the hippie way of life," as a *Ramparts* exposé put it, "like a psychedelic plague."[49] When the Jefferson Airplane sang its anthem for a new race of men and women, the voices of Grace Slick and Marty Balin wailing in an ecstatic counterpoint, a whole generation listened:

> We are all outlaws in the eyes of America
> In order to survive we steal cheat lie forge fuck hide and deal. . . .

But the song insists, "We can be together."[50] Stressing their status as outlaws and delinquents, they sang of community and a new world struggling to be born.

One of the most important characteristics of the counterculture, as "We Can Be Together" suggests, is its tendency to invert the norms of so called straight society. Where the dominant culture prizes rationality, logic, the rule of law, sobriety, technological advancement, wealth, and occupational stability, the counterculture celebrates the irrational, emotional, lawless, psychedelic, preindustrial, impoverished, and transient. Where the dominant culture endeavors to purge the public sphere of the private and the sexual, the counterculture desires (to paraphrase the Beatles) to do it in the road. But, as a number of critics pointed out, this pattern of transgression, rather than destroy hegemonic structures, may have ended up ironically reinforcing hierarchical social configurations and the inequitable distributions of power and wealth that accompany them. As the *New York Times* put it, "many hippie attitudes represent only a slight and rather engaging distortion of the Protestant Ethic that they purport to reject."[51] Perhaps the most telling example of this distortion is the contradictory positionality of the hippie relative to consumerism. On the one hand, conspicuous consumption is unanimously disdained: "We've got so many things we could all puke."[52] And as a result, most hippies attempt not to participate in the production of commodities. "Rather than making 'good' use of their time, they 'waste' it."[53] On the other hand, the hippie economy functions as a curious parody of commodity culture. For the very ability of hippies to "waste" time so profligately necessitates a society of plenty in which their labor power represents a surplus and expendable value. Patronizing "free stores" while being only minimally involved in the production of commodities themselves, they epitomize the shift, under late capitalism, from relations of production to those of consumption and, indeed, to the wholesale erasure of those material relations of production that were, in fact, undergoing a radical transformation with the consolidation of the international division of labor. For during the late 1960s and 1970s, the growth of multinational corporations was moving an ever-increasing part of the proletariat of the First World to the Third World, to the very societies that the hippies so revered and exoticized. As a result, dropping out of industrial society—the refusal to produce—ironically ends up becoming inadvertently complicit with the colonialist (and neocolonialist) projects that the counterculture, the New Left, and the black nationalists so decried. Only in a culture of plenty can the refusal to produce be so easily accommodated.

And there were other ways, as well, in which hippie subcultures complied unwittingly with hegemonic structures. During the mid-'60s, for example, the counterculture continued to enforce the separation of culture from politics that had characterized the postwar settlement. Until the end of the decade, most self-identified hippies carefully maintained their distance from the New Left, which they believed to be as embroiled in an illusory and dangerous game as the dominant culture (in Timothy Leary's words: "Don't vote. Don't politic. Don't petition. You can't do *anything* about America politically").[54] Rather than working toward political change, many, impelled by a deep nostalgia for a mythologized preindustrial society, urged retirement to a self-contained, romanticized, agrarian world.

By 1967, however, when the Summer of Love coincided with a summer of race riots and a newly intensified wave of antiwar protests, the New Left and the counterculture, despite certain irreducible differences, became less polarized. The former, as Gitlin explains, was dedicated "with discipline, organization, commitment to results *out there*," while the latter was devoted to the "idea of living life to the fullest, *right here*, for oneself, or for the part of the universe embodied in oneself, or for the community of the enlightened who were capable of loving one another. . . ."[55] The former was committed to the Marxist principle that material circumstances produce consciousness, while the latter espoused a belief in a nearly autonomous consciousness that, if "expanded" (whether by sex, drugs, rock 'n' roll, or mystical enlightenment) could change the world. Despite these stark differences, the late '60s sometimes bore witness to an improvised, albeit uneasy, alliance of the antiwar Left and the counterculture that was pledged to revolutionary social and cultural change. For not all New Leftists disdained hippie culture. As Todd Gitlin notes, some on the left, "mostly PL [Progressive Labor] types," resisted the "siren songs of the counterculture" by "lash[ing] themselves to the mast of

Puritanism." "Drugs, they thought, were bourgeois self-indulgences, distractions from discipline. But many more radicals—especially in Berkeley—were stunned by the wonders of marijuana and LSD. Even if they feared that the Haight-Ashbury stood for an unsupportable 'flower-child innocence,' that drugs 'divorced the will from political action,' the force of acid itself could not be denied, or forgotten, or assimilated."[56] Moreover, few activists could reject the idea of cultural revolution and the idea that "there was a direct line from the expressive politics of the New Left to the counterculture's let-it-all-hang-out way of life."[57]

And unquestionably by the end of 1968, the year of the Tet Offensive and the disastrous Chicago Democratic National Convention, many in the counterculture had been politicized in a way they could not have foreseen just a year before. Among radical groups, the anarchic Yippies seemed most clearly to embody this impossible union, in their attempt at fashioning a carnivalesque revolution and instituting what Abbie Hoffman described as a "revolutionary action-theater." Calling for the "blending of pot and politics," he imagined the Yippies as "a cross-fertilization of the hippie and New Left philosophies."[58] And in many respects, Hoffman's "theater" was a crucial event for the antiwar Left—a model of total revolution, a hybrid of radical politics and aesthetics that made (and continues to make, when practiced by groups like Queer Nation) the more orthodox (and ascetic) Left a bit uneasy. This hybrid plainly epitomizes the Althusserian reconceptualization of politics and culture during the 1960s that authorized the ideological "superstructure" to be pried (almost) loose from the economic "base." Jameson sees this reconceptualization as a pivotal theoretical shift and identifies it with Althusser's notion of the "'semi-autonomy' of the levels of social life" that would license "a repudiation of old-fashioned class and party politics of a 'totalizing' kind." In so reconfiguring the association between politics and culture, the Yippies, like the Black Panthers, coincidentally aligned themselves with an American brand of Maoism ("richest of all the great new ideologies of the '60s"), in which "the new binary opposite to the term 'bourgeois' [is] no longer . . . 'proletarian' but rather 'revolutionary,' and the new qualifications for political judgements" are made "in terms of personal life."[59] Jerry Rubin neatly summarized this populist cultural revolution in his equation, "Our lifestyle—acid, long hair, rock music, sex—is the revolution."[60] By so undermining the opposition between politics and lifestyle, between public and private revolution, the Yippies and their fellow travelers in the politicized counterculture helped, in Jameson's view, to open "a whole new political space, a space . . . articulated by the slogan 'the personal is the political,'" which, during the 1970s, would be colonized most conspicuously by the Women's Liberation movement and the Gay Liberation Front, and would thereby transform American political culture.[61]

But the relationship between the counterculture and the New Left, for all its difficulties, was in some respects much less strained and vexed than that between the counterculture and black activists. For one fact that passes unnoticed in most reportage is that the hippie, almost without exception, is white. A *Time* exposé does note that the "Negro, a model of cool to the beats, is a rare figure in the hippie scene."[62] And a number of assertions by hippies point to palpable political and ideological tensions between members of the hippie subculture and black activists, whether civil rights workers or Black Power advocates. Thus, Jack Newfield reports: "'Civil rights is a game for squares,' one hippie told me. 'Why should I demonstrate to get the spades all the things I'm rejecting?'"[63] An essay in *Ebony*, meanwhile, quotes one hippie as saying, ". . . most Negroes are just like white folks . . . or trying to be[. . . .] Either they're imitating sick white Americans or else they're getting caught up in the race war bag . . . that's the same thing" (ellipses, except the third, appear in the source).[64] In other words, for many white hippies, racial struggle in the United States was understood as a bourgeois project in which African Americans were trying merely to become imitation middle-class whites. The assertion of this unnamed white hippie betrays his or her ignorance of the fact that most black radicals were attempting less to secure equality than to change fundamentally the distributions of power and wealth in the United States, to destroy "the basic institutions of this society."[65] It also betrays an implicit romanticization of African Americans, who are imagined, unless "caught up in the race war bag," as being less "sick" than the white bourgeoisie.

On the other side, many African Americans were "irritate[d]," as Hans Toch describes it, "that pampered hippies," most of them from middle-class backgrounds, "have the audacity to proclaim themselves the most persecuted minority in America." And he proceeds to explain that "[t]housands of persons who daily experience persecution and indignities find bitter irony in the monumental debates and apologies following battles between park commissioners and practitioners of 'acid rock'. . . ." He notes that the "hippie's status as a privileged, rather than a victimized, member of society is clear to the real victims." Seeing hippies as spoiled children, as a dissident fraction of the dominant class, he recognizes the difference between voluntary, temporary poverty and real indigence, between an antibourgeois poseur and one committed to the struggle against social and economic oppression: "The hippie's temporary self-exile into the gutter can be an unconvincing performance to a ghetto audience. 'The hippies really bug us,' one young Negro explained to a reporter, 'because we know they can come down here and play their games for a while and escape.' 'After the hippies go back to their middle-class homes,' declared another Negro observer, 'we'll still be here.'"[66] Yet inner-city African Americans were not unique in voicing their anxiety over the implicit racism of the counterculture. Many young middle-class blacks also suffered a kind of schizophrenia from the antipathy between hippies and an increasingly militant black politics. Thus Gwendolyn Parker, for example, notes that while she was at Harvard College, her "hippie life and [her] black revolutionary life were like two opposing legs," rarely "traveling in the same direction."[67]

Yet what is perhaps most remarkable about the hostility between hippies and African Americans is that the former's disdain for racially based political and economic struggles did not inhibit them from a romantic identification with black Americans and other persons of color. On the one hand, *Ebony* is certainly correct to note that for hippies, unlike beats, "their spiritual hero is not the Negro but the American Indian or the Oriental mystic."[68] And many hippies (unlike Mailer's "white Negro") identified with Native Americans—or rather, their exoticized fantasy of Native Americans—those whom Ron Thelin (owner of Haight-Ashbury's Psychedelic Shop) calls "traditional Indians," who follow

> the Great Spirit's way, which happens to be the way of this continent; it happens to be the way of God; it's harmonious with nature, reverent toward nature. . . . A consciousness that was whole, that had a sense of history [. . .] they were here first. The white man has just marched over them and pushed them, and they live on; and yet they do not hate people; they are able to laugh; they are able to teach us. They are really wise[. . . .] (The first ellipsis appears in the source.)[69]

For Thelin, like many other hippies, the genocidal history of North American conquest gives the surviving Native Americans possession of a secret knowledge and makes them the source of an imagined authenticity and psychic wholeness lacked by European or African Americans.

On the other hand, the romanticization of Native Americans in no way inhibited many countercultural partisans from claiming a black positionality and taking over housing and other public spaces that had previously been occupied by African Americans, in both San Francisco and New York. During the 1950s, many African Americans moved into Haight-Ashbury, which became "a tolerant and multiracial neighborhood" before the hippie invasion of the mid-'60s.[70] Moreover, Bill Graham's Fillmore Auditorium, the most important and celebrated venue in San Francisco for countercultural rock, "previously had presented mostly black performers."[71] In New York's East Village, meanwhile, the influx of hippies led to "soar[ing]" rents as many of the neighborhood's "polyglot population of Puerto Ricans, Negroes, Jews, Italians and Slavs—most of them desperately impoverished"—were displaced.[72] So on both coasts, the hippies literally colonized what had been black public spaces. Moreover, much countercultural discourse betrays a profound ambivalence toward what was during the '60s the largest racial minority in the United States.

This ambivalence is intriguingly repeated in some sociological texts of the late '60s that are sympathetic to the counterculture, the new white Negroes. In a 1968 study, for example, John Lofland, attempting to theorize students as representing a new social class, describes what Starr labels "the 'niggarization' of youth," whom Lofland sees as occupying a social niche analogous to that of African Americans.[73] Lofland argues that the territorial segregation of students in cities like Ann Arbor, Michigan, produces "ghettos" in which students share the "failings attributed to ghetto dwellers throughout American history":

> One hears it commented that "they" are boisterous, they have no respect for property, they work irregularly and drive recklessly. They throw garbage out of their windows, and break bottles in the streets and on the sidewalks. . . . They gamble all night, fail to pay shopkeepers and landlords, shoplift, and engage in riotous drinking sprees. . . . They let their dwellings run down, living like "animals," crowded six and seven together in small apartments.[74]

Lofland is certainly correct to observe the sensationalistic and pathologizing rhetoric of anticountercultural exposés that characteristically describe the typical hippie enclave as an "urban slum" and revel in the lurid details of alleged hippie depravity.[75] He is also correct to note the exoticization of ghetto dwellers in these texts and that "these revelations contain a mixture of horror and fascination with 'people who live that way.' "[76] But at the same time, the widespread "niggarization" of youth finally has the effect, if not exactly of erasing, then of yet again displacing African Americans, whose oppression is imagined as being less severe than that of a new, even more oppressed group. More distressingly, these discourses almost without exception tend to neglect two crucial differences between students and African Americans. First, they ignore the fact that youth is a stage of development and that students tend to pass in and out of student ghettos rather quickly. Second, they fail to acknowledge that white students do not have a long history of racism and economic and political oppression with which to contend.

Nonetheless, both pro- and anticountercultural discourses of the '60s seem bent on reproducing a fantasy in which the hippie both takes up and disavows a black positionality, both identifying romantically with African Americans as an oppressed community and asserting an incommensurability between what they believe to be the black struggle for the "sick" perquisites of bourgeois culture and the hippie struggle for peace, love, and enlightenment. This contradiction is dramatized by one unnamed hippie's rhetorical question, "How can a Negro drop out? . . . He's there, at bedrock, all the time," which betrays his or her fantasy of an African American less as a social being than as an abstracted symbol that represents the authentic "bedrock" of the self, the universalized truth of the (oppressed) subject.[77] This fantasy (much akin to Mailer's fantasy of the *black* Negro) is also played out in Peter Berg's conceptualization of the "blues life." According to Berg, a former member of the San Francisco Mime Troupe and "a white Snick nigger," in Abbie Hoffman's words,[78] the "blues life" dictates that if you want to do anything, you have to lose your left arm. You have to pay a lot of dues . . . to live full out—full out, not far out—as you can[. . . .] The only people that can do it are oppressed . . . the hard-kick seekers who laid down the patterns of extreme beauty for this civilization . . . like the blues singers and John Dillinger, Willie Sutton and Billie Holiday.[79] (Ellipses, except the second, appear in the source.)

For Berg, "the blues life" is defined by an authenticity that is the product of oppression "without recourse," a condition that he also calls "hard kicks."

It's a way of extending yourself [so that] something spectacular and beautiful can be available to you. But you gotta reach through linoleum to get it—that's the thing. You gotta push past the crap of recognition. . . . It's called Life. I'd rather shiver when it rains than not.[80]

In Berg's fantasy, "the blues life" designates a condition of reaching through the floor, pushing past the shit, or shivering in the rain, a voluntary and masochistic abasement that—through the power of mystical prestidigitation (recalling the effect of LSD in the city of the dead)—becomes the sign of "extreme beauty." It is a pure state of victimization, of castration ("you have to lose your left arm"), an embrace of oppression that is identified specifically with African Americans, with "blues singers" and outlaws. Thus, for Berg, "black people" are only a white fantasy: "they are the black mirror. We see our dark image in black people."[81] By gazing at and identifying with this "dark image" of the self, the white subject is able vicariously to (mis)recognize him-or herself as black, to recolonize the ghettos, to eroticize subjection, all the while knowing (at least unconsciously) that he or she remains the white, middle-class master.

This widespread fantasy of victimization, this simultaneous identification and disavowal of that identification with African Americans on the part of young white men and women of the counterculture, leads me to conclude that although the backlash against the civil rights and Black Power movements first grabbed the headlines in 1976 with the Supreme Court's notorious *Bakke* decision (see chapter 3), it in fact commenced much earlier. Undeniably, there is a long history of racist violence in post–Civil War America, reaching back to Reconstruction, on the part of avowed white supremacists like the Ku Klux Klan (and, later, the American Nazi Party), which became greatly exacerbated in the wake of *Brown v. Board of Education* during the late '50s and early '60s.[82] But these explicitly racist organizations by no means had a monopoly on racist activism during the '60s. The overwhelmingly white counterculture may have been manifestly dedicated to peace and love, to many traditionally liberal social values, and to a battle against the destructive effects of industrial capitalism, imperialism, and commodity culture. But this dedication also concealed a disdain for antiracist struggle coupled with an exoticization of the cultures and plights of African Americans and other persons of color. This, in part, accounts for the overwhelming importance of '60s rock, which, borrowed in large measure from the blues and other African-American musical forms, became for whites a means of realizing, in the words of Charles Reich, one of the counterculture's leading apologists, that "their own identity was also oppressed and denied."[83] Reich freely admits that "[w]hite youth, in searching for a culture of their own, have in large measure looked to black culture as a model" and that it was "the blacks, and not youth, who first developed a radical view of America and an alternative culture and life-style."[84] Blues-inflected rock in particular allowed "the new generation" to practice a kind of musical blackface and, by mimicking "the intense sexuality of the blues and the yearnings and mysteries of black soul," to discover "white 'soul,'" this generation's being as an oppressed class.[85] For the counterculture was in thrall to the idea of victimization, and time and again its partisans reveled masochistically in describing themselves, in Abbie Hoffman's impudent up-dating of Norman Mailer's phrase, as "the white niggers."[86] To sustain this image of oppression, they needed an economic, social, and political elite in the United States against which to fight. On the one hand, they needed a conservative, "straight" culture in relation to which they could obsessively restage their abasement. On the other hand, they simultaneously needed an abjected community of African Americans in which they could see reflected their own "dark image."

THE FEMINIZATION OF WHITE MASCULINITY

As Theodore Roszak suggests, the counterculture was distinguished in part from so-called straight culture by its disruption of normative gender roles, especially for men: "one of the most remarkable aspects of the counter culture is its cultivation of a feminine softness among its males."[87] And both pro- and anticountercultural discourses repeatedly emphasize the feminization of hippie men in relation to the norms of the domestic revival. "If a man wore beads, he was of course saying 'no' to his father's Countess Mara necktie" and was "adorning himself for his own pleasure." Not only did hippie men don fem-inized adornments like beads and brightly colored clothes, but they also began to assume theatricalized costume, "to appear as pirates, as bedouins, as troop-ers in armies long since dispersed and forgotten," or as holy men, "boys dressed in white sheets, carrying gnarled sticks."[88] Masculine self-presenta-tion, in other words, became both more feminized (at least by the conventions of postwar culture) and more explicitly performative.

As Roszak notes, this new "style" had a certain subversive edge and "is clearly a deliberate effort on the part of the young to undercut the crude and compulsive he-manliness of American political life."[89] For during the '60s, normative masculine identity (at least for the notorious "over 30" generation) continued to be organized, as it had been during the '50s, around a conflict between the desire for occupational stability and fatherhood and the nostalgia for an old-fashioned, entrepreneurial masculinity. A man's primary responsibility was to the family he administered, a family that would contain the potential hazards of both male and female sexuality and ensure the proper domestication of potentially rebellious offspring. But, at the same time, this responsibility could never be completely reconciled with widespread fantasies of a more active and "he-manly" masculinity that led the normative male subject "to tackle jobs, override obstacles, attack problems, overcome difficulties, and always seize the offensive. He will take on any task that can be presented to him in a competitive framework, and his most important positive reinforcement is victory."[90] Men, in other words, continued to imagine themselves (and be imagined) as entrepreneurs, go-getters, daredevils. The extroverted and regressive masculine heroics of John Wayne (whose movie *The Green Berets* [1968] was one of the few films about Vietnam made during the war) continued to stoke the popular imagination. For most members of what Richard Nixon dubbed "the silent majority" (working-class or middle-class men and women who supported the Vietnam War and "law and order"), the real man was supposed to be independent, adventurous, competitive, morally upright, and, like Wayne, wholly predictable, a "figure whose meaning seems absolutely fixed."[91] And the normative Cold War male subject, despite being seated behind a desk—or rather, because of that fact—imagined himself imperialistically at the frontier, or on a battlefield, struggling against clearly recognizable enemies, dedicated to a noble mission.[92]

For most countercultural youth, however, this aggressive masculinity was an embarrassment. "The breed of hombre generally portrayed by John Wayne is already an anachronism," George Leonard declared, adding that "if the narrow-gauge male is not laughed out of existence, he may, literally, *die* out."[93] The new masculinity broke most obviously with the old in terms of fashion, which in a consumer society represents a particularly important mark of cultural difference. Long hair, beads and other adornments, bell-bottoms, colorful and exotic clothing were now the norm among countercultural men. Many young women, meanwhile, dispensed with dresses and skirts, as well as traditional feminine undergarments (burning their bras, as the press liked to put it), and began to wear more conventionally masculine attire, jeans and workshirts, for example. But for most countercultural apologists, these changes in fashion were symptomatic of a more fundamental change in attitude toward gendered differences. Countless writers noted that the new masculinity is not, like the old, structured around fears and anxieties. "There is no masculinity or femininity hang-up," Reich observes. "A boy does not feel he has to dress in a certain way or 'he will not be a man'; he is not that anxious or concerned about his own masculinity."[94] Leonard notes the "clear message" being sent "to all who will listen: 'We are no longer afraid to display what *you* may call "feminine." We are willing to reveal that we have feelings, weaknesses, tenderness—that we are human.' "[95] Men, in other words, were reimagined as androgynous beings who could be "both assertive *and* yielding, independent *and* dependent, job- *and* people-oriented, strong *and* gentle, in short, both 'masculine' *and* 'feminine.' "[96]

The concept of androgyny mobilized in countercultural discourse, this both/and formulation, simultaneously subverts and reinforces the binary system of gender. For at the heart of the idea of androgyny (at least as it was articulated during the late '60s, early '70s) is a fundamental equivocation over whether gendered differences are historical constructions or the state of nature. Does the fact that "human beings" are "naturally androgynous" demonstrate the constructedness of a bipolar system of gender or the immutability and universality of sexual difference?[97] Is gender a social institution that is arbitrarily imposed (although for clearly discernible political ends), or is it the ostensibly natural expression of an ostensibly universal sexual dimorphism? By trying to have it both ways, the discourse of (male) androgyny both reifies and destabilizes sexual difference. As such, it is strikingly analogous to the discourse of radical feminism (to which it was an analogy and a response), which, in the years before Gayle Rubin's groundbreaking essay "The Traffic in Women: Notes Toward a Political Economy of Sex" (1975), also equivocated over the relationship between biology and history, between the question of sexual difference and the ubiquitous institutionalization of gender-based oppression.[98] (Unlike the discourse of radical feminism, however, the discourse of androgyny remained decidedly ambivalent toward the struggle against male supremacy. For although dedicated to a new age and a new consciousness, social critics like Reich and Leonard are more intent on agitating for "a common humanity" than on redressing the history of patriarchal oppression.[99] As a result, their militancy must be seen as representing a kind of depoliticized feminism that takes the sting, for men at least, out of Shulamith Firestone's declaration that the "goal of feminist revolution must be . . . not just the elimination of male *privilege* but of the sex *distinction* itself: genital differences between human beings would no longer matter culturally.")[100] For the prophets of the new masculinity, sexual difference is an unfortunate fact of nature to which androgyny offers an antidote, the possibility of a utopian transcendence. For androgyny, or rather, "the growth of a full and androgynous flexibility," is understood in their discourses as representing less an easily attainable achieved state than the goal of personal development.[101] And it is invariably associated with that fantasy of psychic unity which provides the solution to the Marxian problem of alienation and which, as a result, remained the most precious of commodities for countercultural apologists: "a wholeness of self, as against the schizophrenia" of industrial capitalist culture.[102]

As the reemergence of feminism at the end of the '60s began to have a profound impact on social attitudes among the young, the feminization of men identified with the counterculture (which is to say, young white men) became widely recognized and debated. For the rise of feminism and the publicity generated by the women's movement guaranteed that the assignment of gender roles would become an important political issue. "Between 1970 and 1972," Nancy Woloch reports, "every national network and major publication devoted time and space to the women's movement, making the new vocabulary of feminism—'sexism,' 'male chauvinism,' 'sisterhood,' 'sexual object'—a part of common parlance."[103] And this new feminist vocabulary was linked to an important liberalization in attitude toward gendered differences, especially on the part of the young. Daniel Yankelevich reports that by 1971 only 35 percent of all college students were inclined to reject social changes leading to "less differences between the sexes."[104] And Jerold Starr argues that a wholesale "dedifferentiation of sex roles" took place among the young by the early '70s, and he sees this dedifferentiation as the result of increased technological development in the United States, noting that "the more primitive the economy, the greater the differentiation."[105] He maintains that the "greatly increased independence of the high technology American economy from the superior average strength of the male has created the possibility of a division of labor significantly free of gender differentiation." And he emphasizes that "the greatly expanded, high prestige human service occupations have role requirements (e.g., sensitivity, nurturance, understanding, gentleness) which have been traditionally defined as feminine in character."[106] The "dedifferentiation of sex roles"—and the reemergence of feminism, for that matter—are thus for Starr an inevitable result of the transition from an industrial to a service economy.

Although I believe that Starr is correct to link sexual dedifferentiation to deindustrialization, I would like to suggest that the much-vaunted feminization of men in some respects represents a misrecognition. Yes, men increasingly adorned themselves in traditionally feminine ways. But the new, countercultural masculinity represents a much more deeply contradictory identity than either its supporters or its detractors acknowledge. John Wayne may be an anachronism, but the relatively androgynous new (white) male by no means signals a repudiation of traditionally masculine goals. Nor does he embody, as his defenders argue, a less anxious or fearful subjectivity. On the contrary, his gender identification testifies, I believe, to a reconsolidation of the characteristics and fantasies associated with a residual, entrepreneurial masculinity combined with an avowal of certain qualities traditionally associated with femininity. Leonard, for example, argues that the new masculinity represents a reaction against the organization man, and he insists that "the man of the future will be a hunter, an adventurer, a researcher—not a cog in a social machine."[107] Like many other countercultural apologists, he justifies his claims for the new male and the new "retribalized" age by referencing the practices of "primitive tribes" who "make little distinction between the ideal qualities of male and female."[108] The neoprimordial young man, victorious in the Oedipal struggle against his bureaucratized father, will, in other words, mark the fantasmatic return of an earlier stage of capitalism and the entrepreneurial masculinity to which it was historically linked.[109] At the same time, in learning behavior that "would make a John Wayne character wince," he becomes one of the new "manly males" who are yet able to "reveal their emotions, . . . become sensitive to others," and "weep openly if that is what they feel like doing."[110] He is the representative, in short, of a more radically schizoid male subjectivity, "both 'masculine' *and* 'feminine,'" in which "both these 'sides'" practice a kind of guerrilla warfare one against the other, in which the masculine part of the self, feeling increasingly threatened and vulnerable, subjugates its other (within the self).[111]

The new, seemingly androgynous, countercultural masculinity is constructed in innumerable cultural texts. Among films of the late '60s, *Butch Cassidy and the Sundance Kid* (1969), directed by George Roy Hill with a screenplay by William Goldman, is important in part for redefining the western and adapting it to the taste of a new generation of moviegoers. An "enormous popular success," the film replaces the tough, John Wayne–like masculinities of the old western with softer, more comic and affable heroes.[112] Unlike most earlier westerns, it aims "to woo and soften up its audience" by presenting deeply sympathetic protagonists.[113] Its basic aim, in Vincent Canby's words, is to provide a portrait of "men of the mythic American West who have outlived their day."[114] Based on a true story and deeply romanticizing the old entrepreneurial masculinities, the film uses sepia stills and a mock–silent movie accompanying the opening credits to underscore its nostalgic, pseudo-documentary character. The narrative, moreover, clearly exploits an analogy between hippies and its two outlaw-(anti)heroes. With his long, blond hair and moustache, and quietly diffident persona, the Sundance Kid (Robert Redford) much resembles the ubiquitous image of the hippie. Butch Cassidy (Paul Newman), meanwhile, is constructed as being both "a soft touch" and, in the eyes of his favorite whore, Agnes (Cloris Leachman), "the only real man I've ever met." And both are figured—like hippies—as highly individualistic (and wayward) men, desperados, living happy-go-lucky lives according to their own surprisingly nonviolent morality (Butch never kills a man until near the end of the film), "doing what comes naturally," in the words of one critic.[115] Moreover, like so many hippies, they bear a parasitic relationship to capitalism, refusing to produce goods in favor of "liberating" the wealth of others. And sharing Etta Place (Katharine Ross), Sundance's girlfriend, between them in a Sedgwickian (and clearly post–sexual revolution) triangle that cements their homosocial bond, they are figured as comrades-in-arms, brothers, almost a desexualized version of Bonnie and Clyde (according to most critics, *Butch*

Cassidy bestows "somewhat slavish nods" to that influential 1967 film in both content and style).[116] Yet the old West, like the West of *Easy Rider*, no longer has room for entrepreneurial (anti)heroes, and so Butch, Sundance, and Etta head to a romanticized, premodern Bolivia where they become the "Banditos Yanquis," imperialistic robbers who, unable to speak Spanish, must read from a crib sheet in order to pull a heist. Yet the two men are clearly cast as the most sympathetic characters in the film, the "free" ones (in the words of the movie's hit song, "Raindrops Keep Falling on My Head") who sacrifice themselves, much like the protagonists of *Easy Rider*, to the principle of freedom, to "doing what comes naturally." When they are finally massacred by what seems to be half the Bolivian army, the freeze-frame in which they come out shooting (and die) slowly fades to a sepia print, underscoring the film's nostalgia both for the old West and for the old-fashioned, entrepreneurial masculinities—but now with "a soft touch"—that they embody.

Both *Butch Cassidy and the Sundance Kid* and the testimony of many young men identified with the counterculture make it clear that the new, "retribalized" masculinity by no means marks a repudiation of those masochistic heroics associated with older masculinities. On the contrary, the new masculinity of the 1960s—much like that of the beats—is predicated upon a masochistic self-abasement that requires a feminized part of the ego to submit to a masculinized part. On the one hand, Butch and Sundance joyously (and obsessively) continue their thievery to prove their heroism, to prove that masculine strength can triumph over their visibly aging bodies. Among the counterculture, on the other hand, this pattern of masochistic submission is rendered particularly clear in relation to drug use. Thus, for example, one young speed freak (sounding like a drugged-out version of Butch Cassidy) boasts that "[o]ver the years I've shot more junk, stuck more spikes in my arm than any man I know." And he proudly announces that "I been in a couple down-to-the-death dope contests," but "I lived through it all so far."[117] And Ernest Dernburg, quoted as a kind of expert witness in an article deeply critical of the drug culture, analyzes what he considers to be the sadomasochistic dynamics of drug use:

> "Drugs like methamphetamine [speed] make these young people think they are gods, supermen who can have and handle anything they want. . . . The whole time, the kids think they are in control of their needles; this illusion gives them a sense of mastery over both their depression and anxiety, emotional states which in fact they cannot control. . . . the externalizing process . . . leads the 'hoodies' into competition to see how much dope they can take, who's man enough to do himself the most harm."[118]

Drugs, in other words, are used both to regulate a free play of (psychic) dominance and submission and to signal a perversely heroic masculinity.

Although an antidrug polemic, Dernburg's argument is curiously echoed by the discourses of prodrug activists. Thus Patrick Gleeson explains that although he's "afraid" of taking STP, afraid that "there'll be the revelation of something that I'm not willing to accept," he insists that he will brave it out.[119] Moreover, his description of the effects of LSD suggests that it does indeed produce a kind of masochistic self-abnegation: "Every time you take acid you undergo the destruction of the ego and even the body as you know [it]. . . . Your ego really dies."[120] And even Timothy Leary underscores the ego-destroying properties of the LSD experience, which for him is all about "[m]erging, yielding, flowing, union, communion."[121] For if nothing else, LSD, like a divine mandate, hijacks the subject and enforces submission. Pulverizing subjectivity, "it requires a lot of courage. . . ."[122]

For Dernburg, drug use is a symptom of what Freud called reflexive sado-masochism, in which the ego is split between a sadistic part and a masochistic part and in which the "desire to torture has turned into self-torture and self-punishment. . . ."[123] The hapless male subject proves his courage by a reckless and suicidal game of chicken. By competing ruthlessly both with himself and with his peers, by making his flesh submit helplessly to the cruelty of his will, he attempts to prove that he alone can take it like a man. For Gleeson and Leary, on the other hand, LSD is symptomatic of Christian masochism, of what Kaja Silverman calls the "heterocosmic impulse—the desire to remake the world in another image altogether, to forge a different cultural order."[124] The Christian masochist thus attempts to model him- or herself after the suffering Christ who, through the sacrifice of "the ego," and "even the body," redeems the fallen world. Leary, in particular, repeatedly emphasizes that "the LSD experience is a confrontation with new forms of wisdom and energy that dwarf and humiliate man's mind." And he insists, "I consider my work basically religious, because it has as its goal the systematic expansion of consciousness and the discovery of energies within, which men call 'divine.'"[125] Seeking to transform both the self and the world, Leary relishes the humiliation that LSD produces because it is the surest path to and sign of salvation. Leary's confession also suggests that the term "Christian masochism" is something of a misnomer when applied to '60s culture. For although a number of countercultural figures (like Captain America) are clearly constructed in relation to Christ, most (like Leary) identify themselves with secularized or decidedly non-Christian (often Buddhist or Hindu) prophets and martyrs.

Undeniably, the meaning and politics of drug use during the '60s remained a flashpoint of controversy. But at the risk of echoing polemicists like Dernburg, I would like to suggest that its ubiquity among the counterculture is symptomatic of the consolidation of a more overtly masochistic subjectivity among men identified with the counterculture than among white men identified with the "straight" world. Unlike their fathers, many young rebels of the 1960s endeavored not only to change the world but if necessary to sacrifice themselves (in certain ways, at least) to effect this change. Refusing a secular-ized, commodified society, they longed for a culture in which meaning was immanent, in which the "divine," the revolutionary, or the utopian was imme-diately apprehensible. Unlike the male beats who characteristically took up a feminine (masochistic) positionality only on the condition that they could beat a hasty and panicked retreat from it, the male hippie casts himself in the role of Christian (or pseudo-Christian) masochist, becoming, like Captain Amer-ica, a messianic simulacrum ready to sacrifice himself to produce a radically different and better world that he can only dimly envision.

Moreover, although the new man, as Christian masochist, in some respects takes up a feminized positionality, this process by no means requires a phallic divestiture. On the contrary, the imitation of Christ is most frequently de-ployed to reinforce the subject's imagined phallic—and heterosexualized—authority. Thus Leary, for example, as a self-proclaimed "charismatic public figure," brags of his astonishing sexual power:

> Every woman has built into her cells and tissues the longing for a hero, sage-mythic male, to open up and share her own divinity. . . . Any charismatic person who is conscious of his own mythic potency awakens this basic hunger in women. . . .[126]

In Leary's discourse, the "sage-mythic male" functions to dominate and "open up" eagerly submissive women, displacing onto them his own disavowed desires to be mastered and humiliated by the divine power of acid. And as in so much countercultural discourse, women are imagined as the (passive) bodies on which Christlike men, charismatic and suffering, restage their domination. (And it is important to recall here that Leary did not always have such a glorious impact on women. His first wife, Marianne, committed suicide in 1957.)[127]

Even more distinctly than Leary, Jim Morrison of the Doors constructed himself (and was constructed) as both Christian masochist and phallic super-man. Arguably the most charismatic male American lead singer of the era, he kept the Doors uninvolved with the radical politics that preoccupied most other serious U.S. rock groups during the mid- to late '60s. Instead, he wrote songs that became the "anthems for a generation turning inward, away from politics" (it is little wonder, then, that their popularity should have been re-kindled in the 1980s with the release of Oliver Stone's film *The Doors* [1989]).[128] Unlike the music of their politicized brethren, the Doors' insists, as Joan Didion notes, "that love is sex and sex is death and therein lies salva-tion."[129] And curiously, their concerts lacked the otherwise ubiquitous multitudes of screaming teenagers, being populated rather by those who "sat in rapt attention, . . . as if in homage to some primitive ritual."[130] Morrison, meanwhile, who was described by the *New York Times* as "the most potent sex symbol to come along in our popular culture since Jimmy Dean and Elvis

Presley," fashioned himself as a kind of sadomasochistic deity, a dark god of (in his own words) "sex," "chaos," and "movement without meaning."[131] But for most observers, the decisive element of Morrison's power was surely that one body part, characteristically concealed in black vinyl pants, which synechdochically stood in for the whole. Or as one of his female admirers, Sherry, puts it:

> "Listen, any man who cuts himself down to just one part of the whole and nothing but, the way Jim does, becomes a lot *bigger* than the whole, he's finally *made* himself whole where the rest of us who pretend that there's a lot more to us than just *that*, we stay split up and down and sideways."[132]

By becoming the object of Sherry's fervid gaze, by sacrificing himself to "*that*," to a discreetly nameless part, Morrison reconstructs himself—unlike the rest of "us"—as an (unimaginably) whole subject. But he transforms himself into the one who unmistakably "is" the phallus only by enduring a kind of castration, "cut[ting] himself down," becoming a spectacularized object of desire. And in so doing, he takes up what can be described only as a feminine positionality. Yet Sherry's rhetoric betrays her understanding that this being who "is" the phallus also "has," if not it, then at least a respectable simulacrum of it. As a result, Morrison is placed in the contradictory position of both "being" and "having" the phallus, of being simultaneously feminized and hypermasculinized, of being at once an image of the suffering Christ who dies for "us" and of the plenipotent deity. Disrupting sexual difference, this catalyst of derepression becomes the "flag" of "a country where they've sloughed off all restraints and nicenesses and do anything with body and mind they feel like, the never-never land of the polymorphous-perversers."[133]

Yet the public phallicization of this '60s masculine icon remains strikingly at odds with his private self. Or rather, Morrison's private self is revealed to have been obsessed with a drama whose rather sensational content is only hinted at by his contradictory public posture. For it is clear from Sherry's testimony that Morrison was far more conflicted about his phallicism than he would admit:

> "He wanted dirty talk from me, it excited him. 'Act like a bitch in heat, that's all you are.' 'You have to beg me for it, say please.' . . . The sadomasochistic games. Always spanking me. 'You've been a bad girl, haven't you. You want to be punished. Come on, cry[. . .]. Answer me. Say yes, say yes, sir.' . . . He wanted mostly to be the passive one. . . . I had to do things to him. He was mostly impotent[. . . .] Sometimes when it didn't work, no matter how I tried, he'd turn violent. Very. Choke me and beat me[. . . .] Twice I think I was very close to getting killed, had to run. . . . Remember what he wrote about seeking to break the spell of passivity with actions cruel and awkward. He knew what he was talking about[. . . .] I never had a full response and it would drive him wild, he thought I was holding out on him on

purpose, he'd squeeze my windpipe hard. . . . The brute and the baby. His oscillation between the two. A lot of roughing up, then the sudden collapse, whimpering, 'I need somebody to love me, please take care of me, please don't leave me.'"[134] (Ellipses, except those in brackets, appear in the source.)

According to Sherry's testimony, Morrison repeatedly acts out both his assumption of the divine prerogative ("the brute") and his submission to the divinity of the other ("the baby"). Oscillating compulsively between these two positions, he debases himself, or rather, uses Sherry to debase himself. But most important, his masochism does not rule out his violent (and potentially lethal) abuse of women. Like William Burroughs, he acts out his hatred and fear of femininity both by scourging the (imagined) feminine part of the self and by "roughing up" women who happen to be in the wrong place at the wrong time. And as with Burroughs, this sadomasochistic performance represents not a traditional, scripted S/M scene between two consenting parties but sexual violence. There is no contract here, no safe word. Rather, it represents a kind of pure acting out, a violent and unpredictable improvisation that literally imperils Sherry's life and signals a slippage between his writing and his sexual practices. A woman lights Jim Morrison's fire at her own risk.

Jim Morrison and Timothy Leary unquestionably represent extreme versions of countercultural masculinity. But I would like to suggest that their iconic status during the mid- to late '60s is symptomatic of the extent to which the ostensibly new masculinity represents a variation upon the old. For the violence of their rhetoric—and their practices—suggests that there was far more fear and anxiety around gender identifications than countercultural apologists were willing to admit. For the male Christian masochist, flagellating both the (feminized) self and the (feminized) other, in some respects represents a novel recombination of both the masochistic masculinity of the beats and the stern masculinity of the domestic revival. The fantasy of the "sage-mythic male," the wise and imperturbably autocratic guru (yet another omniscient Western subject in Eastern drag) was as much a permutation of the authoritarian father of the domestic revival as the feminine ideal, the bounteous Earth Mother (another intermediary between "nature" and "culture"), was of the organized, caring housewife. As in the commune that Billy and Captain America visit in *Easy Rider*, the hippie woman was expected to be, if not exactly barefoot and pregnant, at least dutiful, submissive, and nurturing. "A woman's job," Lenore Kandel notes, "is feeding her man, taking care of those about her," and "radiating the feeling of warmth."[135] At the same time, she was often cast in the role of breadwinner, taking a job in the "straight" world, for example, when she and "her man" needed money, and so securing a measure of, if not exactly economic independence, at least economic clout that her mother probably lacked. Joan Didion calls this "the woman's trip" and observes, "Whenever I hear about the woman's trip, which is often, I think a lot about

nothin'-says-lovin'-like-something-from-the-oven and the Feminine Mystique and how it is possible for people to be the unconscious instruments of
values they would strenuously reject on a conscious level."[136] It is little wonder, then, that as more and more women became conscious of their oppression,
the women's movement grew in large part out of (and against) the counterculture, for the latter, despite its protests to the contrary, did little to transform
oppressive gender structures. By 1966 a revitalized feminist movement was
beginning to offer a radical critique of sexism and all that it sanctioned, calling,
in Kate Millett's words, for "freedom and full human status" for "the female
sex," for a "re-examination of traits categorized into 'masculine' and 'feminine,'" and for an end to sexual violence, "the patriarchal proprietary
family," and "enforced perverse heterosexuality."[137]

As a generation of hippies and activists rebelled against the mores and politics of their parents' generation, sexual liberation surged, becoming part of an
"over-arching transcending" rebellion: "Orgasm was the permanent revolution, ... or was it that The Revolution was orgasm writ large?"[138] And the
press teemed with stories about hippie sexuality: "All manners of sexual practice are tried. There are no rules about sex, only the noted hippie maxim: 'If it
feels good, I'll do it.'"[139] But ironically, sexual liberation turned out in certain
ways to be as conservative as the sexual ethos of the domestic revival. As in
Butch Cassidy and the Sundance Kid, in most circles it meant strictly heterosexual liberation. For if the new man was anxious about his masculine identification, he was terrified of transgressing heterosexual boundaries. As Kandel
observes, "the men are being threatened, and have to go through all sorts of
funny trips. Hostility to homosexuality; proofs of virility."[140] And Sandra Butler asks: "I think the biggest fears . . . like men don't want to be feminine. Why
not, you know? [. . .] so what if men hug and things like this, why be afraid of
homosexuality?" (the first ellipsis appears in the source).[141] Both of these discourses testify to a slippage between feminization and homosexuality. For
during the 1960s, gender deviance and sexual deviance remained inextricably
linked in both the hip and "straight" imaginations (although there is a long
history of this linkage in Western culture, it was not in fact fully consolidated
until the emergence of a theory of sexual inversion at the end of the nineteenth
century in which male homosexuality was imagined to be essentially a form of
gender deviance: a woman's soul trapped in a man's body).[142] As a result, the
feminized white male was constantly struggling with anxiety over his sexual
identity and was constantly having to prove his heterosexuality. Moreover, the
discourses of sexual liberation and (male) androgyny either fail to consider
homosexuality or else regard it as a form of false consciousness, a symptom of
repression that will be remedied when an individual is liberated. Thus Timothy
Leary promotes LSD as a "specific *cure* for homosexuality" that he (like many
psychologists of the 1960s) believes results from "freaky, dislocating childhood experiences" and can be successfully remedied.[143]

The homophobia of the feminized, white male hippie is complicated further by his perception in the "straight" world. Thus Dan Wakefield notes in an essay on *Easy Rider* that among "the crew-cut superpatriot set," hippies are frequently elided with political and sexual dissidents as "Hippie-Commie-Queer-Pervert-Fags." (Could Wakefield's own vexation with sexual dissidents be signaled by the fact that he nervously needs three words to describe them?) In any case, he admits that, because of his long hair, he "was sneeringly called a hippie by strangers," and both his "manhood" and "patriotism were questioned on streets and in stores."[144] For among "the silent majority," the counterculture was widely (and usually incorrectly) linked to political and sexual deviance, and in both popular and more esoteric discourses, hippies and homosexuals remained pathologized and criminalized. Opposition to the Vietnam War and "flower power" were characteristically perceived as cowardly and politically subversive, despite the fact that hippie radicalism rarely went further than a generalized and toothless pacifism. And the ubiquity of illegal psychotropic drugs made all hippies outlaws in the eyes of the "superpatriot set." Countless newspaper and magazine stories, meanwhile, dwelled luridly on alleged hippie epidemics of hepatitis and sexually transmitted diseases.[145] And most intriguingly, the psychological analyses of hippies often uncannily echoed the psychopathologizing rhetoric used against homosexuals: "[m]ost of them come from emotionally inconsistent backgrounds, fatherless homes in which the mothers were often depressed and resented the unwanted children they had to support."[146] Like those texts that discover the ontogenesis of male homosexuality in the distant father and overprotective mother, this rhetoric suggests that both the hippie and the homosexual represent a failure of Oedipalization.[147] The absent father disallows his son an appropriate paternal identification while the maladjusted mother either alienates her son (the hippie) or smothers him (the homosexual). In either case, the mother is held responsible for perverting her child.[148]

And despite the New Left's commendable concern with broad cultural issues in addition to political ones, the vast majority of political radicals did not question the structures of heteronormativity. In his history/memoir, *The Sixties*, Todd Gitlin provides a complex portrait of SDS, emphasizing the importance of what he calls a "transpersonal libido" operating in the movement, a "circle of energy" that was "intellectual and moral, political and sexual at once."[149] And *The Sixties* testifies to the fact that radical politics and an autocratic masculinity were as inseparable in the student movement as they had been in the Old Left. SDS was steeped in patriarchy and machismo. Its primary actors were almost exclusively heterosexual men, the cowboys of the New Left, among whom were passed sexual appurtenances—women—who remained strictly subordinate to the male activists and constituted the "cement" that held SDS together. Gitlin quotes approvingly one woman's only "half-ironic" quip of 1962, that "[t]he movement hangs together on the head of a penis," and in retrospect concedes "the homoerotic implication of male bonding" among the student activists (which at the time was altogether disavowed).[150] As in the counterculture, women were often disadvantaged by being stripped of "the defenses available in bourgeois social relations," while most gay men and lesbians found it as necessary to conceal their homosexuality from their comrades-in-arms as from their families.[151] In a 1969 article in the *Berkeley Tribe*, Konstantin Berlandt vividly documents the homophobia of the National Students Association, as emblematized by one woman delegate who, although "pretty radical" in most areas, confessed to Berlandt, "I saw one man with his arm around another's leg and I freaked."[152]

The fictional scene that perhaps most viscerally captures the contradictory construction of the "Hippie-Commie-Queer-Pervert-Fag" is the sequence in *Easy Rider* in which Billy, Captain America, and George stumble into a luncheonette in rural Louisiana. As soon as the three enter, they are greeted by the sneers of the Sheriff and the Deputy sitting at a booth:

> SHERIFF: What the hell is that? Troublemakers?
> DEPUTY: You name it, I'll throw rocks at it, Sheriff.

To these two middle-aged white men, the hippies represent an unknown other that challenges their systems of classification, and they spend the rest of the scene hurling assorted insults at "it" half under their breath. (The fact that Hopper recruited local men and women and asked them to improvise their lines gives the scene a particularly chilling veracity.)[153]

> DEPUTY: Check that girl with the long hair. . . . I think she's cute.
> SHERIFF: Isn't she, though? Guess we put 'em in a woman's cell, don't ya reckon?

The mock desire of the two men, however, for the feminized and criminalized hippies collides unexpectedly against the real desire of six young women seated in another booth: "I like his hair going down his head," one says, while another comments, "and I like his eyes." For the dramatic tension in the scene is based in large part on the conflict between the hostility of the men and the desire of the women. For the latter, the hippies are attractive precisely because of their feminization. Billy's long hair and necklace ("the teeth about his neck") make him an object of heterosexual desire. The Sheriff, Deputy, and a group of men at another booth, meanwhile, practice other slurs:

> MAN ONE: They look like a bunch of refugees from a gorilla love-in.
> MAN TWO: You could mate him up with one of those black wenches out there—and that's about as low as they come.
> MAN THREE: Man, they're green. . . .
> DEPUTY: I thought most jails were built for humanity and that won't quite qualify. . . . I saw two of them one time, they were just kissing away—two males, just think of it.

To the men and women of this small, rural community (and for many other Americans), hippies represent a challenge to gendered and racialized norms, a locus of cultural and taxonomic contradiction. To the men, they are a source of fascination, characterized variously as women, animals, green creatures (naïfs—or perhaps space aliens?), sexual partners for black women, and homosexuals. Being simultaneously feminized, heterosexualized, and homosexualized, they occupy a subhuman, "colored" positionality. To the women, they represent an exoticized and alluring masculinity, one that is refreshingly foreign and iconoclastic. The three outcasts, meanwhile, the locus of such intense anxiety and desire, attribute the antipathy of the natives to the latter's fear of what the three represent: "freedom." "They see a free individual," George says, "it's gonna scare 'em." For George, freedom means being plucked from the bosom of the nuclear family. It means traveling where and when one chooses, being able to consume what one wants. Forsaking his bourgeois comforts for a different kind of (upward) mobility, he becomes, like the hippies with whom he travels, a kind of expatriate, or "internal émigré," "living on our shores but beyond our society."[154] At the same time, he and his confreres stake a claim to an authentic Americanness insofar as the film clearly opposes the three heroes against the bigoted, small-minded Southerners and identifies the former with the traditional (bourgeois) American values of independence and tolerance. For the struggle more generally between the "superpatriot set" and the hippies is a struggle over which masculinity is the truly American masculinity: the bellicose or the pacifist, the nakedly imperialist or the gently commandeering, that which destroys or that which exoticizes cultural and racial otherness. It is also a struggle over the meaning of mobility—geographical, ideological, and psychic. Sometimes, like Butch Cassidy, the Sundance Kid, and Etta Place, the hippies must literally exile themselves (preferably to a Third World or premodern culture) in order to stake a claim to what are imagined to be traditional American values. For Americans are not only "the most mobile people on the face of the earth" but also the ones whose national identity has historically been predicated most upon immigration, migration, conquest, Manifest Destiny.[155] Perhaps the most scandalous contribution of the counterculture to the nation was its identification of America with a white masculinity that is relatively feminized, for sure, but even more important, unstable, unfixed, unhinged—a plural, heterogeneous (and sometimes lunatic) masculinity in which male subjects are encouraged to try on in passing different, more feminized, more "colored" positionalities. Perhaps that is the freedom which so disgusts the men and so fascinates the women in the luncheonette, along with Captain America's audacity in having a U.S. flag sewn on the back of his jacket: his implicit claim that this "girl with the long hair" and two day's worth of stubble, this "refugee from a gorilla love-in," is the authentic representative of the nation. As Ron Thelin, one of the leading entrepreneurs of Haight-Ashbury, puts it, speaking for his generation more than he knew, "[w]e are the real Americans."[156]

EROS AND CIVILIZATION

The youth culture of the 1960s represents the threshold between modernism and what, in most circles, passes for postmodernism. On the one hand, it is clearly an extension and reinvention of the historical avant-garde, and, on the other, it signals the increasing obsolescence of the (modernist) divide between elite and mass culture, between the artisanal and the mechanically reproduced. The songs of Bob Dylan, the Beatles, and the Doors, to name only the most obvious, drew explicitly on diverse classical and popular forms and made a claim to what was for pop a new kind of musical and lyrical seriousness. Even the Beach Boys started recording art-rock. Popular film, theater, and fiction, meanwhile, embraced increasingly esoteric content (under the influence of European existentialism) or formerly taboo subjects (like sex, drugs, and madness). Simultaneously, mass cultural forms started to deploy various avant-gardist techniques (fragmentation, montage, dissonance, chance) to an unprecedented degree while retaining their mass appeal. And developments in what had been the field of high culture, most notably pop art, dramatized the process of commodity production and foregrounded the commodity status of the work of art far less guiltily than did most modernist productions, for which the commodity status of art remained deeply unnerving. Reacting against the universalizing tendencies of high modernism (from abstract expressionism to the international style), and its dedication to seriousness, abstraction, and elegance, the new artists (from Andy Warhol to the Rolling Stones, from Kurt Vonnegut to The Living Theatre) delighted in extending the range of art, in juxtaposing the exalted and the abject, the sacred and the profane, in being vernacular and relevant, and in rudely transgressing bourgeois norms.

Those new cultural producers who attempted to fashion a radical art, meanwhile, reached back (either knowingly or unwittingly) to various marginalized modernisms, especially dada and surrealism, both to appropriate their radical methods and to adjust them to the exigencies of a rapidly deindustrializing society. Despite the diversity of this neo–avant-garde, it was loosely united by the attempt, to borrow Peter Bürger's phrase, "to reintegrate art in the praxis of life," to break down the separation between life and art, politics and aesthetics.[157] Youth culture followed the lead of surrealism (as Walter Benjamin characterizes it), intending, like "an inspiring dream wave," to integrate "everything with which it came into contact" and to push "the 'poetic life' to the utmost limits of possibility."[158] Like the surrealist project, that of youth culture aimed at the "loosening of the self by intoxication" and the exaltation of the dream ("dream loosens individuality like a bad tooth," to quote Benjamin's startling metaphor).[159] The new art delighted in all those characteristics that postwar bourgeois culture disdained: the garish, illogical, oneiric, arbitrary, histrionic, obscene, and sacred. And although giddily plundering the past for styles it fancied, the new art (as exemplified by *Easy Rider*) characteristically represented, in Fredric Jameson's estimation, a "weakening of historicity," both politically and personally, "both in [the] relationship to public History and in the new forms of . . . private temporality."[160] Many of the young artists of the late '60s disowned traditional Western art. And few of them would have endorsed Robert Motherwell's 1951 declaration: "Every intelligent painter carries the whole culture of modern painting in his head. It is his real subject, of which everything he paints is both an homage and a *critique*."[161] Refusing both the dedication to tradition and the self-reflexiveness of high modernism, the new, mass-produced art took its place among the other commodities that littered the U.S. cultural landscape.

Although many of the new cultural producers set the pattern for postmodernism by embracing and exploiting consumerist culture, much of the new art (like much modernist art) remained deeply conflicted about the commodity status of the work of art. For many in the counterculture, the most prized characteristics remained the authentic, spontaneous, and natural. Just as they tended to refuse the competitive, militarist foundations of the U.S. economy, so did they reject, in Reich's words, "streets made hideous with neon and commercialism, servile conformity, . . . the ruin of nature by bulldozers and pollution, . . . the coarse materialism of most values."[162] Looking back nostalgically to a time before industrial capitalism, many young artists attempted to resuscitate a lost sense of entrepreneurship and artisanal production. For them, craftsmanship and art were antithetical to mass production. Nature was the presiding goddess. And with an eye ever on nature, many in the counterculture turned to premodern societies and the ideological and religious systems associated with them, from Zen Buddhism and other Asian religions to the cultural and spiritual ways of Native Americans. Trying to exempt themselves from mass production, they preferred making, growing, and processing their own merchandise and often set up collectives to market and distribute their homemade and homegrown goods.

Although these two tendencies—the postmodern and the premodern— would seem to be incompatible, I believe that the youth culture of the '60s was in fact unique in its attempt, if not to integrate them, then at least to elide their contradictions. Poised at the moment of worldwide decolonization, youth culture constantly enacted its conflicted relationship with the powerful, rich, and seductive metropolitan centers of the First World (of which it was, after all, a product) and a Third World—undergoing increasing industrialization and exploitation, both by its former colonizers and by its nationalist bourgeoisie—to which it was powerfully drawn. Enjoying the benefits of affluence, it looked longingly to those traditional cultures that, in fact, as Jameson notes, were disappearing as the "older village structure and precapitalist forms of agriculture" were being "systematically destroyed."[163] For the '60s were the moment when the enlargement of capitalism on a global scale simultaneously produced an immense freeing or unbinding of social energies, a prodigious release of untheorized new forces: the ethnic forces of black and "minority," or Third World, movements everywhere, regionalisms, the development of new and militant bearers of "surplus consciousness" in the student and women's movements, as well as in a host of struggles of other kinds.[164]

More vividly than other U.S. social groups of the '60s, youth culture embodied the irresolvable antagonism between the increasing globalization of capital and an unprecedented "unbinding of social energies." Its artistic productions, in turn, allegorized the conflicts between the First and Third Worlds by turning them into a struggle between culture and nature, between consumerism and the nostalgic longing for a "retribalized" society. On the level of production, this tended to play itself out in the conflict between (as Reich puts it) "the freedom and economy of mass production" and "touches of the handmade," and on the psychic level, by the opposition between the "divided or schizophrenic being" of the First World and the desire for an "utter *wholeness*" of being associated with preindustrial societies.[165]

As many critics noted, rock may have been the most popular and influential art form during the late '60s, "the deepest means of communication and expression" that negotiated the incompatibility of the postmodern with the preindustrial by attempting to unite "a mass culture" with "a genuine folk culture."[166] But I would like to suggest that if rock was the most popular form, performance was the most emblematic. First, performance, at least in its '60s forms, most facilitates the accomplishment of the neo–avant-gardist dream, the transformation of art into life, and life into art. For unlike rock, performance embraces all media and all forms of expression and, indeed, retains a privileged relationship to "the praxis of life" (it is important to bear in mind that rock concerts in the late '60s were increasingly coming to resemble performance theater). Second, as '60s performance was usually theorized, its aim is to make not an object or commodity but rather an action and a subject. Performance thus attempts to short-circuit the process of commodity production and to restore what Benjamin would describe as the aura to the subject, a sense of that "uniqueness" which "is never entirely separated from [the work of art's] ritual function."[167] Third, and most important, performance dovetailed with the new politics of participatory democracy in a powerful and compelling way. As countless '60s activists suggested (and proved), mass-movement politics is always a kind of performance. And as countless theater innovators demonstrated, performance is a profoundly political act.

In order to become the emblematic art of the '60s, performance had to break forcibly with the literary theater of the domestic revival that preceded it. Rejecting the poetic (sur)realism of Tennessee Williams as surely as the well-made drama of Arthur Miller, the new performance theater was influenced by greatly diverse sources: dada and futurist performance, the action painting of the abstract expressionists, the interdisciplinary experiments at Black Mountain College, the so-called theater of the absurd, the newly translated theories of Antonin Artaud and Bertolt Brecht, happenings, Zen Buddhism, the *I Ching*, and the experiments of the Polish director Jerzy Grotowski. The new performance theater flatly rejected the mimetic basis for art, insisting that performance was about being, not imitating. An elaboration of Artaud's theater of cruelty, it "is not," as Jacques Derrida notes, "a *representation*. It is life itself, in the extent to which life is unrepresentable."[168] And it attempted to redefine the actor as one who is no longer the recycler of another's words but an original creator. In summarizing Grotowski's position, the critic Ludwik Flaszen neatly sums up the aspirations of the new performance theater: "The performance is not an illusionist copy of reality. . . . Performance itself is reality; a literal, tangible event. It does not exist outside its own substance. The actor does not play, does not imitate, or pretend. He is himself; he makes a public confession; his inner process is a genuine process, not the work of a deft performer."[169] Unlike a play based on a previously written text, performance is not an imitation but life itself. And the actor is no longer an interpreter of other's words but an acrobat of the soul, a creator who makes visible his "inner process," who turns himself inside out.

Although indebted to diverse practices and philosophies, the new performance theater found its primary intellectual bulwark in the Freudian revisionism of Norman O. Brown, Paul Goodman, Rollo May, and, most important of all, Herbert Marcuse. Marcuse's *Eros and Civilization* had a tremendous impact when first published in 1955 and more than any other theoretical text provided a philosophical and psychoanalytical anchor not only for the artistic revolutions of the '60s but also for the politics of liberation. An idiosyncratic mixture of Freud and Marx, *Eros and Civilization* represents, as Jameson notes, an "ironic reversal" of Freud's position in *Civilization and Its Discontents*. Where Freud "posited an irreversible and unavoidable interdependency between progress in the evolution of society and unhappiness in the repressed psyche of individual man," Marcuse regards social progress and material prosperity as the sign of "increasing manipulation and the most sophisticated forms of thought-control. . . ."[170] *Eros and Civilization* provides both an analysis of repressive, postindustrial society and a prescription for change, for the liberation of Eros, for ways of using "the social wealth for shaping man's world in accordance with the Life Instincts, in the concerted struggle against the purveyors of Death."[171] For Marcuse, like most of his Frankfurt School colleagues, bases his theory of culture on the Marxian concept (developed in the *Economic and Philosophic Manuscripts of 1844*) of the alienation that necessarily attends capitalist modes of production and represents, for Marcuse, the "negation of the pleasure principle" (45). But "phantasy" (which he equates with "imagination") functions as a sort of cure for alienation, a mode of remembrance by which the repressed subject is able to apprehend "the structure and the tendencies of the psyche prior to its organization by the reality [principle]" (142). By thus (unconsciously) preserving "the 'memory' of the subhistorical past, . . . imagination envisions the reconciliation of the individual with the whole, of desire with realization, of happiness with reason" (142–43). And if the imagination is the key to memory, to *de*repression, then art is the key to the imagination; it is that which provides (in Theodor Adorno's words) "the 'image of man as a free subject'" (144). Following Adorno (although tempering his disdain for mass culture), Marcuse sees the "archetypal content" of the "genuine work of art" as the liberation of fantasy, "the negation of unfreedom" (144). For Marcuse, like Adorno, "genuine" art is always oppositional, and it "survives only where it cancels itself," where it provides an intuition of that which is *not*, which is to say, of utopia (145). It is through art, in other words, that the one who, as Jameson puts it, "has lost the experience of the negative in all its forms"—the consumer, marooned in a culture of assent and abundance—is able to recall and commemorate that negative principle which "alone" is "ultimately fructifying from a cultural as well as an individual point of view."[172] It is little wonder, then, that Marcuse (echoing Adorno again) singles out for praise the "surrealistic and atonal" art that "saves its substance by denying its traditional form," that most explicitly unleashes the power of fantasy (145). In surrealism especially, Marcuse (correctly, given the historical alliance of the French surrealists with the Communist Party in the 1920s) sees "[a]rt allied . . . with the revolution" as a symptom of the Great Refusal (149). For as he acknowledges, quoting André Breton: "Imagination alone tells me what *can be*" (149). And it is through the utopian force of imagination (and memory) that he attempts to reclaim the stigmatized "images of Orpheus and Narcissus"—both of them, intriguingly, purveyors of nonreproductive sexualities (homosexuality and narcissism, respectively)—as symbols of the Great Refusal who "will release the powers of Eros now bound in the repressed and petrified forms of man and nature" (164).

Whether consciously or unconsciously, U.S. performance theater of the 1960s is heavily indebted to Marcuse's theory of derepression and his understanding of art's ability to reawaken, inflame, and (to some extent) satisfy utopian desires. Moreover, his advocacy of fantasy, imagination, and the negative, as well as his championing of surrealism, had a profound impact on those theater practitioners who were attempting to fashion a revolutionary theatrical praxis that rejected syllogistic dramatic forms and traditional modes of production. As C.W.E. Bigsby points out, the new performance theater

> sought to liberate the instincts, to destroy repression and revert to that stage of erotic and sensual spontaneity which is characteristic of childhood in the individual, and primitive and largely pre-literate physicality in the race. . . . Its adherents were not concerned with delineating the moral burdens implied by necessary sublimations but

with liberating the individual and art from social and mimetic constraints. For them the theatre was no longer to be a part of that system which placed the mind over the body, the reality over the pleasure principle. It was to be a revolutionary force returning man to a prelapsarian state of grace. It was not to be a reflection of life; it was to be life itself.[173]

Like the postmodern/premodern culture that it ecstatically announced, performance theater is rigorously presentist in its orientation. It is a theater of action and life, for which the past exists only in the form of allegedly universal archetypes or antique stories that prod and illuminate the present. Historicity is only a fiction, a quaint tale that bears no meaningful relation to the present moment. Or as Julian Beck, cofounder of The Living Theatre, puts it, "[c]linging . . . to the past is necrophilia."[174] What matters instead is performance's bid to transform life, to raise consciousness, to liberate the individual (and the collective), and to release the powers of Eros. For this theater is posited on the belief that an essential, authentic self lies stifled by the forces of repression, just waiting for liberation or, in Beck's words, a "breakthrough into the present."[175] Attempting to position itself "outside the money system," outside commodity culture, it longs to re-create a primordial and holy rite, "a congregation led by priests, a choral ecstasy of reading and response, dance, seeking transcendence, a way out and up, the vertical thrust, seeking a state of awareness that surpasses mere conscious being and brings you closer to God."[176] It strives to eradicate all forms of mediation, to dissolve the "difference between actor and spectator," to "break down the walls," in the hope of passing beyond representation, to "life itself."[177] And following Marcuse, it sees imagination as the key: "The work of the artist as the creation of solutions thru exercise of the imagination."[178]

As has been widely recognized, the project of '60s performance theater did not succeed, or rather, it could have succeeded only by bringing to an end theater as it had been defined historically for 2,500 years. For as Herbert Blau observes, "[t]here is nothing more illusory in performance than the illusion of the unmediated. It is a very powerful illusion in the theater, but it *is* theater, and it is *theater*, the truth of illusion, which haunts *all* performance, whether or not it occurs in the theater."[179] For by disavowing its fictionality, the "truth of illusion," theater denies its very being. And the trigger for this disavowal, at least among the twentieth-century theatrical avant-gardes, has been the vexed relationship between speech and writing. For although Beck insists that "[l]anguage is the key," he writes sympathetically of Artaud's contempt for theater as a form of re-presentation (or branch of literature) and its reliance on previously written texts. For Artaud wanted above all else to break with metaphysics, to overthrow the reign of logocentrism in order to create "a new physical language, based upon signs and no longer upon words."[180] Echoing "our mentor," Artaud, Beck argues that "all writing must be left behind, the printed word, the library forgotten."[181] Yet as Derrida points out, Artaud's critique of logocentrism is itself subject to deconstruction insofar as even Artaud is forced (tragically) to admit that in the end "all these gropings, researches, and shocks will culminate nevertheless in a work *written down. . . ."*[182]

For Julian Beck, the problem of language centers on the question of verse in the theater, the verbal form that gave The Living Theatre its "greatest difficulties": "nothing in the theatre can get closer to life than verse and nothing further away. . . ."[183] The problem with verse lies in its simultaneous immediacy and distance from speech and life. On the one hand, its "piercing phrases . . . illuminate your life forever, the whole staggering jumble of harmony of all things poetry. . . ."[184] On the other hand, the admittedly artful (or artificial) quality of verse presents a serious challenge to actors, especially all those American "Method" actors who were trained during the 1950s to perform psychologically realistic plays. For Beck, the difficulty with verse drama lies in the impossibility of inhabiting it fully and so using it to produce (the illusion of) life. For "when divorced from the body, from movement, from action, from the confrontation which means this life here and now," it "becomes like dead tissue, the severed head of a beautiful woman, disgusting."[185] Like the mark of original sin, verse is the sign of schism between "the body" and "this life," that which inadvertently reveals the scandalous truth that the body, action, and life are derived and secondary relative to text. Yet at the same time, verse also represents no more than "dead tissue"; it is both seductive and "disgusting," like "the severed head of a beautiful woman." For Beck's metaphor betrays his belief that the relationship between language and the body is a violent one. And performance represents a disfiguration, that which reveals the truth of the castrated, dismembered subject. Verse itself, with its "piercing phrases," may be a masculine force (in relation to the fragile body), but it also kills, decapitating the weak, objectified, feminized, yet "beautiful" flesh.

Why, I wonder, is Julian Beck's metaphor so startling and so apt? What is the source of the violence that so brutally dismembers the objectified body of the performer? What does this violence reveal about the process that genders performing bodies? And what, finally, does this violence suggest about the function of performance theater during a decade when revolution itself was understood to be a performance?

PERFORMANCE AS REVOLUTION

The Living Theatre was founded in 1948 by Judith Malina and Julian Beck, who together oversaw its operations until Beck's death in 1985. During its first twenty-five years, The Living Theatre was arguably the most controversial, innovative, and influential experimental theater company in the United States.

Developing a poetic theater during the 1950s (its inaugural production was of verse drama by Brecht, Lorca, Stein, and Paul Goodman in 1951), it moved on to the hyperrealism of Jack Gelber's *The Connection* (1959) and Kenneth Brown's *The Brig* (1963), and thence to a series of strikingly original, collaborative pieces in the '60s and '70s that worked to change the definition of theater for a generation of actors, directors, and critics. Indeed, John Tytell's recent evaluation of it as "the most radical, uncompromising, and experimental group in American theatrical history" is not an overstatement.[186] And it had a profound impact not only on the most important experimental theater to follow (the Open Theatre, Richard Foreman, Robert Wilson, the Performance Group, Mabou Mines, the Wooster Group) but also on many of the new Off-Off-Broadway playwrights of the '60s (Sam Shepard, Megan Terry, Lanford Wilson, Maria Irene Fornes). Margaret Croyden, meanwhile, writing during the group's heyday, deemed it "[t]he most important American counterculture group to develop an answer to the questions posed by Artaud and the happening."[187] And more than any other theater company (or "counterculture group"), The Living Theatre, with its fervid supporters and detractors, served as a focal point for struggles taking place in radical political and artistic culture in the United States.

During the 1950s, reacting against the prevailing realism of the American commercial theater, The Living Theatre concentrated on the verse dramas that presented such a challenge not only for Malina and Beck but also for actors unfamiliar with the demands of a poetic theater. In some respects, however, their breakthrough came with *The Connection* and *The Brig*, which, played in real time in a performance style that deliberately blurred the line between illusion and reality, brought a new level of verisimilitude to the American theater. In *The Connection*, a play about heroin addicts, the presence of real jazz musicians on stage "encouraged the actors to avoid roles or posturing."[188] Moreover, according to Larry Rivers, at least some of the time "there was real heroin in the capsules handed out to anxious actors waiting onstage, some of whom shot up in front of the audience."[189] Perhaps the company's most influential works, however, were the pieces they produced in exile during the mid-'60s. For when they were evicted in 1964 from their New York theater by the Internal Revenue Service for nonpayment of $28,000 in back taxes, they decamped to Europe. There they became increasingly dissatisfied with the knowledge that even *The Connection* and *The Brig* were finally fictions, and they began to try conclusively to break down the distinction between illusion and reality, art and life. Working collaboratively, they developed three pieces in which they attempted to fulfill the avant-gardist dream: *Mysteries and Smaller Pieces* (1965), *Frankenstein* (1966), and *Paradise Now* (1968). In addition, they presented adaptations of Genet's *The Maids* (1965) and the Sophocles/Hölderlin/Brecht *Antigone* (1967) before making a controversial and stormy tour of the United States in 1968–69.[190]

Meeting in 1943, both Malina and Beck considered themselves political and artistic radicals, committed to various pacifist and anarchist causes and captivated by the European avant-garde. Malina had always been fascinated with theater, studying with Erwin Piscator in 1945, while Beck was drawn to painting, and they began to see as much New York theater (and as much of each other) as they could. Despite Beck's homosexual inclinations, they were married in 1948 and became acquainted with a number of important cultural figures who strongly influenced their developing aesthetic and political sense, including Jackson Pollock, Paul Goodman, and William Carlos Williams. And during the 1950s, as Malina's journal documents, they became involved in the downtown (homosexual) art scene and friendly with many of the leading (homosexual) writers, painters, musicians, and their assorted hangers-on.[191] They also became increasingly active politically, protesting U.S. foreign policy, and in 1955 Malina was arrested at an antinuclear demonstration and briefly locked up in the Criminal Psychiatric Observation Ward at Bellevue Hospital (the first of a long series of political incarcerations). Attempting to combine political with aesthetic radicalism, they launched a series of mass-movement demonstrations including the General Strike for Peace in 1962, which, "[f]rom the beginning" they saw "as a theatrical activity."[192] When, the following year, the IRS tried to darken the theater, the company used "the lights of television cameras . . . to illuminate the stage" and performed *The Brig* "as an anarchist direct action, an act of civil disobedience."[193] Tried for income tax evasion and inciting a riot, they were found guilty on seven counts, the judge ruling (patronizingly) that they were " 'misguided but sincere people who were unable to adjust to living in a complex society.' "[194] Fleeing to Europe, the company started work on *Mysteries*; in this work, for the first time, the actors practiced what Malina calls "nonfictional acting, in which [they] played themselves, not characters in roles."[195] And while in exile, they put together those pieces on which their subsequent fame—and notoriety—would rest.

Of all The Living Theatre's productions, the one that most vividly dramatizes Marcuse's theory of a repressive and (self-)destructive culture is *The Brig*, which Pierre Biner also dubs their "most dazzling act of rebellion against Establishment theatre."[196] The representation of a society become prison-house, it "came closest," as Bigsby notes, "to realising their enthusiasm for Artaud" by dramatizing the demonic Artaud, the Artaud who warns that "[w]e are not free" and that "the theater has been created to teach us that first of all."[197] A performance of total unfreedom directed by Judith Malina, *The Brig*, as Beck maintains, "is the Theatre of Cruelty."[198] The product of Brown's three years in a Marine Corps base in Japan, it is a play virtually without action or dialogue, or rather, one in which all of the action and dialogue are controlled by the guards who themselves are subject to a strict protocol, and in which the prisoners are absolutely forbidden to take any initiative. The brig is governed by an elaborate set of regulations (printed in the playtext and reproduced in the original programs) that bid the prisoners, identically costumed with shaved heads, to stand at attention at all times when not performing a task and forbid them to speak to each other. Running from place to place, they may not cross the white lines that are drawn on the floor in front of every entrance and exit without asking permission of the guards, sadistic and absolute authorities who wield "an eight-inch billy club" that they do not hesitate to use on the prisoners (a.k.a. the actors!) for the slightest infraction of the rules.[199]

The play's action consists entirely of the brig's daily rituals during which the prisoners perform meaningless tasks and are routinely brutalized by the guards, usually by being punched violently in the stomach. According to Brown, the prisoners (and the guards) constitute a single-sex and multiracial lot that "*make[s] up a cross-section of American society*," and the text goes to great lengths to deindividualize and depsychologize all the characters, who are distinguished only by the tasks they perform and their position on one or the other side of the master/slave dialectic (48). The only interruption in the repetitive and mechanical terrorization takes place in the play's penultimate scene when Prisoner Six suddenly freaks out, "*emit[ting] a terrifying scream and fall[ing] to his knees*" (72). Crying, "[L]et me out of this madhouse," he is attacked by the guards, with whom he "*fights savagely*" until he is finally subdued and straitjacketed and, having reclaimed his name ("My name is not Six. It's James Turner"), is carried out of the brig on a stretcher babbling incoherently (72–73).

The published text of *The Brig*, which all but dispenses with character psychology and traditional plot structure, is significant less for its literary qualities (or lack of them) than its status as a blueprint for a performance designed as a kind of homeopathic ritual in which the theater is rendered, in Malina's words, "so violent that no man who experienced it would ever stomach violence again."[200] "[A] place of horrible extremes of discipline and order," the brig occupies the entire stage and, for Malina and Beck, represents "the image of the world as a whole and, by analogy, of such microcosms as the school, the family, the factory, the state."[201] I would like to suggest that the "world" which Malina and Beck descry is a gendered "world," and that the play also functions as a "microcosm" of unfree—which is to say, normative—masculinity, in which masculinity is contained by and consolidated in the sadomasochistic dynamics of guard and prisoner. For *The Brig* functions to dramatize the self-division that Marcuse analyzes in *Eros and Civiliation*: "the superego [secures its development under the reality principle] by directing the ego against its id, turning part of the destruction instincts against a part of the personality—by destroying, 'splitting' the unity of the personality as a whole; thus it works in the service of the antagonist of the life instinct" (53). The master/slave dialectic in the play works not only to dramatize this "splitting" but also to make it clear that because the production of unfree masculinity is such a violent phenomenon (in the service of the death instinct), masculinity in a repressive society is, by definition, an overproduction that must be obsessively, feverishly reiterated.

Both the playtext and Malina's production are structured around multiple, interlocking acts of submission in which (under the guidance of Artaud, her "madman muse") the distinctions between play violence and real violence, rehearsal and performance, the military and the theatrical, are vertiginously called into question (86). For it was clear to Malina from the beginning that the play was to be as much an ordeal for the company as for the audience. She recognizes that "the villain" of the piece is, as it were, out there: "The Immovable Structure" (reminiscent of Burroughs's control systems), whether prison, school, factory, family, government, or "The World As It Is" (83). But at the same time, she insists that the company simultaneously discover "the villain" within by reproducing this structure throughout the process of rehearsal and performance. For both the demands of Brown's scenario and the fact that they are reproduced in the form of a written playtext also represent an "Immovable Structure" to which she and the company must bow: "We know that the price of discipline is the rigor of authority, the wages of order is submission. We know that the only real call to order is the needs of the work of art. Any other authority is usurped" (91). Submitting herself to the authority of the work of art and echoing the "cruelly demanding perfectionism" of the brig regulations, she draws up a rigorous "rehearsal discipline" to regulate every aspect of the rehearsal process, silence the actors when they are not on stage, and specify penalties for lateness, absence, misconduct, failure to pass clothing inspections, etc., as well as to demand the same absolute precision in performance that *The Guidebook for Marines* mandates (92). The object is to produce the same sense of anomie, the same "terrible loneliness of separation," the same authoritarian, sadomasochistic dynamic in rehearsal that represents the very substance of the play (95). It is, in short, to draw a "Magic Circle" of victimization fully around the theater, inside of which the victim consents to give over his or her power: "the belief of the victim in the power of Authority makes what is unreal real" (102). And Malina's diaries make it clear that she had long been fascinated with the masochistic character not only of industrialized society but also of her own desires: "are the passions that make us sick no more nor less than addictions to the desired one?"[202]

Although it might seem that the schemes of Brown and Malina (and the marines, for that matter) produce a system of stable binary oppositions, Malina's process suggests that this is not at all the case. For it is clear that only after studying *The Guidebook for Marines* repeatedly (as the prisoners in the play must study it repeatedly), and by submitting to the exigencies of the playtext, is she able to set herself up as a surrogate for a textual authority and a military authority that is properly nowhere to be found, or rather, whose imputed origin represents only one node in an endless chain of command. And the very endlessness of the chain produces the unnerving revelation that no one "has" the phallus because every authority (including the prison guards) must in turn submit to a higher authority. Phallicism is thus imagined as a perpetual deferral, subject to an endless series of displacements. The script, the director, the prison guard can take up a phallic positionality only provisionally. This provisionality, moreover, is dramatized by Malina's insistence that the actors trade parts: "The roles were being rotated, so that the actor playing, say, prisoner No. 5 one night would play a guard the night after."[203] So given the logic of displacement, one might never know until the last moment which role one was to play. One might not recognize until one was being punched in the stomach that one didn't "have" the phallus after all. Or even then, one might never know who or what one was.

For the gender definition of the prisoners is produced in extremely compli-cated and contradictory ways. On the one hand, each one is insistently infantil-ized and feminized by the guards who call him "boy" and accuse him of "little-girl tricks" (50). On the other hand, until Prisoner Six cracks, they repeatedly demonstrate that they can take whatever the guards can dish out. Malina sug-gests, provocatively, that it is precisely the primary act of violence in the play—being punched in the stomach—that most clearly subverts the distinc-tion between illusion and reality and dramatizes (and complicates) the play of dominance and submission. According to Malina, the prisoner (a.k.a. actor) first prepares himself; he "*hardens* himself both muscularly and psychologi-cally" the moment before impact (98). But when the blow comes, he "has lost his total rigidity because now he can save himself only with resiliency," which, she notes, "is a feminine (*ergo*; cowardly) attribute." Submitting his body to the (phallic) rhythm of tumescence and detumescence, the prisoner allows himself to be feminized, to be "vulnerable and tender" only "swiftly and su-perficially." For the moment of impact is "the vulnerable moment at its cli-max," after which "the mind," suddenly remasculinizing itself, "flicks back from its instant of unconsciousness," which is to say, its instant of femininity (99). As the prisoner recovers, he "now enacts the will taking over." He feels "a sense of achievement" as he recovers: "he has regained his manhood." "Each blow is a total demolition, each recovery a total restructure. After the blow the prisoner stands erect and proud, having, if not overcome, at least survived. Even if it hurts him" (100). The prisoner proves his masculinity only by letting it go momentarily, by surrendering to an unconscious femininity, and allowing himself to be hurt. Ever the Christian (or pseudo-Christian) mas-ochist, he identifies himself for an instant with the suffering martyr in order to redeem the world. And Malina makes it clear that this process unleashes the heterocosmic impulse in both prisoner and spectator. For the spectator identifies with the prisoner only because of the latter's momentary feminiza-tion by the blow: "the contraction of his body is repeated *inside* the body of the spectator" (98). "If the Moment of Impact has made us feel viscerally, then the Moment of Recovery should move us to revolutionary action for our fallen brother" (100). Identifying with the prisoner's miraculous remasculinization, the spectator discovers a revolutionary potency. Malina's statement thus makes explicit what is implied in many political tracts of the 1960s: revolution, regardless of the gender or race of the one making it, represents a profoundly masculinizing activity. But it is one, crucially, that is predicated on a prior feminization. Only by temporarily relinquishing the phallus can the revolutionary make him- or herself an imitation of Christ and claim a revolutionary potency. Only by making him- or herself "vulnerable and tender" is the martyr given the moral authority (and sympathy) to win hearts and minds for the revolution.

For whether practiced by The Living Theatre or the Yippies, the avantgardist dream—the reintegration of art into the praxis of life—became during the '60s the primary formula for cultural revolution, for that attempt to produce political change by forging a change in consciousness, or what Beck calls "transcendence-which-is-revolution."[204] It also represents an attempt to reassert and stabilize the masculine identity of those men (and women) who, trying to distinguish themselves from their bureaucratized fathers, are intent on producing a radical political culture. It represents a revolt against not only bourgeois values and morals but also the more feminized identification of the organization man. And this project holds true throughout both the New Left and the politicized counterculture. The Yippies, for example, remained intent on demonstrating their political toughness, individuality, and impertinence in relation, on the one hand, to all persons in uniform ("just another extension of machine living"), and on the other, to those effete participants in "the fag-ridden peace movement."[205] For despite the very different histories and strategies of The Living Theatre and Abbie Hoffman, the latter's concept of revolutionary praxis serves as both an extension and a farcical (mis)reading of Malina and Beck in which the deadly earnestness of the latter two is transformed into a kind of sly, utopian laughter (and Malina notes that "Abbie's book [*Revolution for the Hell of It*] is beautiful").[206] Pinning Hoffman down is difficult, not only because he keeps his tongue so decidedly in cheek, but also because he so patently distrusts words (as opposed to actions), which, he insists, "are the absolute in horseshit."[207] Frankly admitting that "so much of what we [Yippies] do is theater," he declares that he is "more interested in art than politics," that is, if it is a "revolutionary art."[208] And like Malina and Beck, he often references Artaud who, by his reckoning, "is alive at the walls of the Pentagon, bursting the seams of conventional protest, injecting new blood into the peace movement."[209] But Hoffman's Artaudian protest also suffers severe castration anxiety. Despite the manic exuberance of his politics and his prose, he imagines all men as being terrified for the safety of their "peckers" in the continuing struggle between the cops and the Yippies (which for him is a real-life version of hide-and-seek or capture the flag). Cops are so obsessed with a particular "image of masculinity" that they call Hoffman and his cronies "'scum-bags' and 'fairies'" who "ain't got no pecker, just a little piece of flesh."[210] And despite Hoffman's idiosyncratic—and often brilliant—critique of business-as-usual, his political discourse is as profoundly masculinist as that of his opponents. Perusing his rehearsal of revolution, one is likely to believe that the primary struggle in U.S. political culture during the late '60s is over who "has" the phallus and who "has" only the "little piece of flesh." For revolutionary potency in Hoffman is always defined in phallic terms:

> Fidel lets the gun drop to the ground, slaps his thighs and stands erect. He is like a mighty penis coming to life, and when he is tall and straight, the crowd immediately is transformed.
>
>   "Now the Revolution begins."[211]

Even if one credits Hoffman with more than a little irony here, revolution remains a profoundly masculinizing occupation. According to his heterosexualized allegory, the phallic leader disavows his castration by strutting his stuff while the (feminized) audience trembles in delight, preparing themselves to be penetrated by the charismatic political actor.

Malina and Beck may be less aggressively masculinist than Hoffman, but their concept of revolution also insists on a phallicized idea of revolutionary praxis. Moreover, their texts are noteworthy in part for demonstrating how in the discourse of revolution-as-performance the distinctions between body and soul, and art and life, get gendered. For the revolutionist, the schism between the body, on the one hand, and soul, on the other, echoes the distinction between a feminized art and a masculinized praxis of life. Malina notes, in connection with *The Brig*, that although the (feminized) "body of the prisoner is totally captive," the (masculinized) "soul of the prisoner is potentially totally free" (101). And Beck invokes precisely the same binary opposition, considering the body an empty, "passive element" that must be filled, and "the soul," its "freedom."[212] The body submits, but the soul resists. Yet it is also clear that theater, as a form, remains allied to femininity. As art and as a technics of the body, it represents a feminized practice (and acting has long been regarded as a feminized occupation) that avant-gardism would subsume into a masculinized praxis of life, into revolution. For as Malina notes, the "trip between these two points," between body and soul, captivity and freedom, "is the crucial experience" of *The Brig* (101). Revolution-as-performance, in other words, denotes not a single practice but a union of opposites; it represents an enactment of countless subjections (whether to text, character, director, etc., or to a repressive political, economic, and social system) at the same time that it constantly dramatizes the limitless potential for what is imagined to be total freedom. Whether in the theater or on the streets, performance is imagined as a privileged arena for playing out the dialectic of unfreedom and liberation, art and revolution, femininity and masculinity. The performer-as-revolutionist, moreover, split between body and soul, is the site at which the violence implicit in this dialectic becomes recognizable. Malina and Beck may be committed to "violentless (non-coercive) human relations," but their concept of performance does a definite violence to the performing subject, much the way Beck's poetic texts (figuratively) decapitate the beautiful body of the actor, or Grotowski's actor uses a role "as if it were a surgeon's scalpel, to dissect himself."[213] And Hoffman may be dedicated to an aestheticized politics, but he, too, implicitly recognizes that examples of "revolutionary art," like "the Vietcong attacking the U.S. Embassy in Saigon," are always predicated on violence.[214] Performance-as-revolution, in short, always represents the ascendancy of a cruel and transcendent masculinity.

Toujours L'Esclave a Singé Le Maître

Part manifesto, part autobiography, Julian Beck's *The Life of the Theatre* is also an anatomization of the violently split performer-as-revolutionist. Beginning with the rather Marcusean declaration "I am a slave," it meditates on subjection (a.k.a. the universal brig) in a more earnestly confessional way than most other countercultural manifestos.[215] At its most incisive, it analyzes the process by which social slavery or, in Marcuse's terms, "surplus-repression," is produced. The latter is a crucial category for Marcuse, who defines it as "the restrictions necessitated by social domination" and opposes it to "(basic) *repression*," whose roots are in the "primal horde" and whose reproduction is contingent upon the presumptively universal character of the Oedipus complex (35, 61). Surplus-repression, on the other hand, is linked to "a specific sociohistorical organization of reality," to a patently oppressive system of culture (34). Yet like basic repression, it results from the internalization of this oppressive system: "The struggle against freedom reproduces itself in the psyche of man, as the self-repression of the repressed individual, and his self-repression in turn sustains his masters and their institutions" (16). Domination is so effective and dangerous because the slave introjects the forces and structure of oppression so that "the sense of guilt . . . permeates . . . mental life," making the slave seek out punishment (32). It succeeds, in short, by permeating conscience "with the death instinct" and so producing a race of masochists who eroticize submission: "the individual lives his repression 'freely' as his own life: he desires what he is supposed to desire; his gratifications are profitable to him and to others . . ." (53, 46). Or as Beck puts it: "For me the bourgeoisie is always there, always, confronting me, because I am it, . . . and I sing of it to itself. Because I am singing my way out with a knife" (88).

Despite the obviously heartfelt character of Beck's volume, it serves more as an anthology of '60s Artaudian performance and social theory than as an inflammatory guidebook for the resourceful revolutionary (as Hoffman's *Revolution for the Hell of It* does). With its (albeit ambivalent) scorn for bourgeois theater and culture, and its celebration of community, madness, anarchism, and sexual liberation, it calls rather predictably for the performer, "in a state of trance," to "play the Theatre of the Revolution" (62–63). But perhaps the most intriguing sections of the book (and the ones most illuminating politically) are those in which Beck analyzes his own masochism, his own eroticized identification with a class of slaves, and attempts contradictorily both to make revolutionary claims for that identification and to undo it. His memories of the rehearsals for *The Maids* provide a particularly piquant commentary on the pleasures of submission:

> The first time I put on the black silk panties I got a hardon right away. I felt humiliated in the garter belt. It felt good. I became a prisoner in the high heeled shoes. I had hot and cold flashes. I was delirious. I wanted to bow down and be stepped on. I put on the black uniform of the slave and I was so unbalanced by the sensation of submission that I wanted, needed, to feel Madame's domination to balance me out. (144–45).

For Beck, cross-dressing is linked to submission, masochism, and ecstasy. And his hard-on represents a particularly sensitive reaction to Genet's text, which is rather famous, to put it mildly, for its eroticization of submission. He goes on to quote Malina's gloss:

> "It is a play about man in the position of the lady's maid." Judith. "It is a play about the class structure. The torture. It is a play about the revolt of the oppressed classes and it is also about their inability to consummate that revolt. They can never stop imitating and wanting to imitate in fact, wanting to be Madame." *"Toujours l'esclave a singé le maître."* Proudhon. (145)

For as Malina recognizes, *The Maids* (like most of Genet's plays) dramatizes both the desire for revolt and the allure of imitating the master, the erotic force of the old order that the revolutionaries find finally too seductive (and too powerful) to destroy. It thereby reminds the reader that imitation is the sincerest—and most deadly—form of flattery.

Despite being the product of a culture that virtually equates gender deviance with sexual deviance, Beck is less concerned with the homosexualizing potential of cross-dressing than with its erotic and masochistic power. For as *A Life in the Theatre* suggests, Beck's masochistic identity remains far more stable than his sexual orientation. He takes pains not to disavow his homosexuality but to see it as an element of what Marcuse (after Freud) calls the "polymorphous-perverse" (49). "I have licked every part of a man and woman," he announces joyously, but "the masochist . . . is my name, my nature and pattern" (33, 193). And good Freudian that he is, Beck links masochism both to the mechanics of Oedipus (to "people . . . trying to recover . . . the alienated love" of "generations of mechanized, cold, alienated fathers") and to "the homosexual syndrome" (145). On the one hand, Beck regards masochism as a revolutionizing force. Ever the Christian masochist, he equates it with "altruistic love" (145). Masochism is "part of my revolt"; it is a mechanism "for feeling something, even if it is pain." For as *The Brig* makes clear, it allows for an identification "with the whole slave class and with (its) suffering." And this, in turn, "evokes altruistic feelings" and "leads to revolutionary action" (146). But, on the other hand, what disturbs—and excites—him is the erotic charge he gets out of submission insofar as he fears that it betrays not the woman or the queer within but the counterrevolutionary.

Despite Beck's ambivalence about his own masochistic desires, his text is emblematic of those discourses from the late '60s that, although committed to sexual liberation (including lesbian and gay liberation) are deeply disquieted by sadomasochism. For liberationists like Beck, sadomasochism represents an insoluble problem. At one moment it may exemplify the sexual cosmopolitanism and open-mindedness that these champions of the "polymorphous-perverse" pride themselves upon. But at the next, both sadomasochistic fantasies and practices, understood as the eroticization of the master/slave dialectic, may be regarded as epitomizing the false consciousness that characterizes not only capitalist modes of production but any social relation based on domination. (Despite frequently echoing Marcuse, Beck differs markedly from Marcuse on this issue. For the latter attempts—quite progressively—to distinguish between "the hideous forms" of "*suppressed* sexuality," including "the sadistic and masochistic orgies of desperate masses" and consensual S/M [202]. He is careful to point out that "the function of sadism is not the same in a free libidinal relation and in the activities of SS Troops" [203]. He is also, given the orthodoxies of 1950s politics and clinical psychology, almost startlingly antihomophobic in his promulgation of "a fuller Eros" against "the repressive order of procreative sexuality" [171].) Beck does not distinguish between private and social forms of sadomasochism, and for him, the "fundamental revolution of culture" depends on "the work of freeing ourselves from our enslavement to our masochistic-sadistic character" (194). "Our work is to awaken everyone to their revolutionary potential, to show that there is another position that breaks with Masochism" (227). Beck's understanding of masochism as false consciousness neatly dovetails historically with the concerns of many feminist activists of the 1970s who, like Beck, regard female masochism as a particularly insidious and intractable form of false consciousness (see chapter 4). His most extreme statements, "[t]he penis is a bludgeon" and "[f]ucking . . . is a process of pain, domination and submission, . . . of master and slave," eerily anticipate the pronouncements of Andrea Dworkin or Catharine MacKinnon (191).[216]

In many respects, *A Life in the Theatre* and The Living Theatre's work of the '60s and '70s can be seen as an—unsuccessful—attempt at a liberation from the exigencies of masochism. Its one work that most pointedly dramatizes this theorization (and which, according to Tytell, corresponds exactly with Malina's personal initiation into S/M practices) is *The Legacy of Cain*, first performed in Brazil in 1970 with a title borrowed from one of the novels of Leopold von Sacher-Masoch, whose ideas about sexuality the group discussed while in rehearsal.[217] This short play is structured around a series of actions (spoken by a narrator and enacted by a pair of actors), each of which illustrates a different aspect of the master/slave dialectic (money, love, property, the state, war, and death), attempting to show, as Tytell notes, that "the essential masochism of the people supported the sadism of the leaders . . . whose power came from the support of those whom they oppressed."[218] The play culminates in Action 8: The Rite of Bondage, in which

> *each actor playing a Master opens a small black bag . . . and takes out his special equipment for tying up his slave. . . . When all the Masters have bound all the slaves, the Masters proceed to bind one another until only Death remains.*
> *The binding, during which both participants sing, is an act of seduction and compliance, both performers playing out both the pain and the erotic pleasure of the relationship.*[219]

Conflating desire and repulsion, pleasure and pain, Action 8 represents a literal *nouement*, or tying up, which awaits its *dénouement*, or untying. And, in typical Living Theatre style, the audience must initiate the resolution by going up to the actors and unbinding them, setting them free. (According to Tytell, the actors sometimes waited for as long as twenty minutes for the audience to take action.)[220]

The Legacy of Cain may dramatize the slave's pleasures and the interconnections between different forms of domination, but The Living Theatre's solution to the problem of enslavement (which, as Marcuse notes, is not synonymous with consensual S/M) represents the kind of "merely" theatrical solution that the group elsewhere disdains. First, the action guarantees that the audience is able clearly and immediately to recognize enslavement as such, and, second, the (traditional) relationship that the piece sets up between performers and spectators allows the latter to perform a simple task to end it. *The Legacy of Cain* may be valid as an allegory of the enslavement of Brazilian peasants, but it is still dependent on an individualist and voluntarist concept of agency in which the oppressed are suddenly and magically empowered to liberate others. Simultaneously, the play seems to suggest—against Marx— that a revolution in consciousness (or a change of perspective) will produce a political uprising. And while it would undoubtedly represent an oversimplification for a late capitalist audience, it also, I believe, significantly undervalues the psychological power of neocolonialism to produce particular kinds of (unconscious) desires. For despite the attempt of both Malina and Beck in all their work to address the relation between conscious and unconscious, the piece ultimately frees the oppressed only by erasing the unconscious and disavowing masochistic pleasure.

In its complex—and reductive—theorization of masochism as a form of false consciousness, The Living Theatre is very much in step with the politics of sexual liberation of the late '60s (which, after all, it had no small part in popularizing, especially during its '68–'69 U.S. tour). At the same time, *The Legacy of Cain* and *The Life of the Theatre* also suggest how profoundly problematic and troubling the relationship between the master/slave dialectic and masochism remained for would-be sexual liberationists. For by conceptualizing the social in terms of the sexual, domination in terms of masochism, these activists almost inevitably reinforce the binary opposition between the private and public spheres (associated with bourgeois ideologies) in which the private is granted an epistemological—and strategic—primacy. For despite the attempt by Beck and countless other political activists to conceptualize revolutionary agency as collective agency, the linking of the master/slave dialectic to masochism suggests finally (and fatally?) that the sexualized private sphere is the privileged site for an emancipatory politic. And liberation becomes the result not of a cooperative initiative but of individual agency. One *wills* oneself beyond masochism. After (somehow) having become illuminated, one rises from one's seat, approaches a performer, and loosens the ties that bind.

At the same time, the focus on a politics of consciousness leads to a crisis around questions of determination. Beck writes, for example, that in the struggles between races and classes, "[t]he whites will eventually be coerced," by means of "revolution from below," into comprehending "the misery and splendor of the exploited people in the street." He then adds, "They [the whites] must make an interior revolution" (70–71). But what is the relationship between the uprising in the street and "interior revolution"? How is the revolution in consciousness to take place? Is it predicated upon political and social revolution "from below," upon a radical change in relations of production? Or has it fortuitously preceded the revolution? Is it accomplished by dint of force, or of ideology? How is it related to the class consciousness of the "people in the street"? Do the latter come as the bearers of a ready-made revolutionary class consciousness? Or must they, too, have been enlightened at some point? In the writings of Beck and Malina, these questions remain unanswered. And even for Marcuse, issues of determination remain strangely vague. On the one hand, he argues that social being produces consciousness, reasoning that the "transformation of the libido would be the result of a societal transformation that released the free play of individual needs and faculties" (202). On the other hand, he also suggests that social transformation can be the result of "freely developing individual needs" that will facilitate the "emergence of a non-repressive reality principle" (201). Yet how can individual needs possibly be "freely developing" in a profoundly repressive society?

Neither Marcuse nor Beck specifies how revolution is to take place. They only know, despite the cries of "paradise now!" that it hasn't happened yet.

Moreover, these impasses around questions of agency and determination were by no means resolved by those movements, Women's Liberation and Gay and Lesbian Liberation, that most notably picked up and developed the rhetoric of sexual liberation during the early 1970s. Nor were they resolved elsewhere in the politicized counterculture, which for the most part remained notoriously unconcerned with pedagogy. This is particularly true of the Yippies who, preferring to levitate the Pentagon than to educate the proletariat, tended to substitute dramatic irony for persuasion. And even The Living Theatre, which was much more sensitive to pedagogical issues, found direct confrontation a more provocative (and theatrical) strategy than reasoned argumentation or coalition building. But the politicized counterculture's almost total refusal to become involved in electoral politics should not be considered solely their failing, for it was motivated in large part by the lack of choice offered by the two-party system and the enormous increase during the late '60s in state-sponsored violence. Moreover, the often violent and illegal campaigns of disinformation and sabotage waged by U.S. internal security forces were remarkably successful in discrediting both the New Left and the Black Power movement. As a result of these tactics, the forces of corporate capitalism were able in the end to strengthen their hold over the political process and virtually to obviate the possibility of forging a genuinely democratic public sphere.

At the same time, the politicized counterculture never succeeded in forming alliances, on the one hand, with the professional-managerial class or, on the other, with what, during the '30s, '40s, and '50s, had been the most progressive agents of change in the United States: the white working class (particularly organized labor) and the black underclass. On the contrary, it consistently antagonized an increasingly conservative and indignant white working class and jeered its culture. For as Marcuse emphasizes, the working class was forced by the "stabilizing and integrating power of advanced capitalism . . . to integrate itself into the bourgeois-democratic process, and to concentrate on economic demands, thereby inhibiting rather than promoting the growth of a radical political consciousness."[221] At the same time, the counterculture's nearly obsessive habit of proclaiming its partisans, in Abbie Hoffman's words, "the new niggers," rendered it incapable after 1968 of doing much more than aping black militancy.[222] Mutual distrust and revolution by mimicry do not facilitate coalition politics. The politicized counterculture may have produced a powerful and seductive program for change, but its most revolutionary political projects were almost without exception forestalled by the forces of reaction. "For it is precisely," Marcuse notes, "the objective, historical function of the democratic system of corporate capitalism to use the Law and Order of bourgeois liberalism as a counterrevolutionary force, thus imposing upon the radical opposition the necessity of direct action and uncivil disobedience, while confronting the opposition with its vastly superior strength."[223] As a result, the counterculture's most lasting contributions, in the end, turned out to have been its production of an alternative consciousness (later designated New Age) that proved all too easily co-opted by commodity culture and a revolutionary art that never managed its own reintegration into the praxis of life.

REVOLUTIONARY SUICIDE

Narratives of the 1960s always seem to end in tragedy: the election of Richard Nixon, the assassination of Martin Luther King, Jr., the bombing of Cambodia, the murders at Kent State and Jackson State, the disintegration and fragmentation of the New Left, the collapse of mass-movement politics, the rise of identity politics, the Weathermen, Charles Manson. Or as Captain America put it while sitting with Billy around what would end up being their last campfire, "We blew it." And the action and discourse of both the heroes of *Easy Rider* testify to the fact that the politicized counterculture, for all its talk of androgyny and sexual liberation, did little to change the structure of white masculinity. As Robin Morgan notes, "Hip Culture and the so-called Sexual Revolution" have "functioned toward women's freedom as did the Reconstruction toward former slaves—reinstitut[ing] oppression by another name."[224] Yet again analogizing the experience of African Americans and imagining a new oppressed class, Morgan argues that both "the male-dominated peace movement" and "the 'straight' male-dominated Left" constitute a "counterfeit" Left that represents a "cracked-glass-mirror reflection of the Amerikan Nightmare."[225] Merely reflecting the thoroughgoing misogyny and sexism of bourgeois culture, the masculinist Left perpetuates a system of oppression in relation to which women constitute an authentically revolutionary agency, "the real Left."[226] ("Goodbye," Morgan says, "to [Abbie Hoffman's] hypocritical double standard that reeks through all the tattered charm.")[227] And many radical feminists of the late '60s and early '70s proved their revolutionary credentials by producing trenchant critiques of different kinds of patriarchal social structures, by attacking the psychology of feminine submission, and by working to dismantle institutionalized sexism.

Morgan is correct to accuse the politicized counterculture of reinventing oppressive masculinities despite its avowed opposition to the strictures and orthodoxies of bourgeois culture. The new, countercultural, white masculinity, as epitomized by the Christian (or pseudo-Christian) masochist, does indeed place the male subject, or rather, his flesh and blood, at the center of the revolutionary project. Through a process of self-abnegation, this (pale) imitation of Christ attempts, as Kaja Silverman notes, to mortify the flesh "and beyond that sin itself, and the whole fallen world."[228] Whether in the person of Captain America, Butch Cassidy, Jim Morrison, Abbie Hoffman, or Julian Beck, his is the body to which violence is done, the one that is arrested, spat upon, and shot, that is dismembered (castrated) and consumed, that dies so that others may live. And despite Morgan's well-grounded critique of the centrality of the suffering white male subject in the countercultural fantasmatic, I would like to suggest that of all (masochistic) masculinities, the Christian masochist has proven historically to be potentially the most productive and progressive. For unlike the feminine masochist or reflexive sadomasochist, the male Christian masochist is dedicated unashamedly to producing a radically different world and is prepared, indeed eager, to sacrifice himself if that is the price that must be paid. Granted, the Christian masochist is made terribly anxious by the possibility of his feminization and attempts eagerly and compulsively to remasculinize himself after momentarily allowing himself to be made "vulnerable and tender." Granted, the Christian masochist also falls prey to the most reactionary of positions, and Morgan is correct to note that Charles Manson, with his paranoid fear that it "was now [the black man's] turn to take over the reins of power" in the United States, and his messianic delusions, represents "the logical"—and psychotic—"extreme of the normal American male's fantasy."[229]

But not all Christian masochists are psychopaths. And perhaps the most provocative project for producing a Christian (or pseudo-Christian) masochistic subject dedicated to revolutionary activism is that of Huey Newton, founder and leader of the Black Panther Party. In the introduction to his 1973 autobiography, *Revolutionary Suicide*, he sets forth the differences between what he calls "reactionary suicide" and its "revolutionary" likeness. Noting that the suicide rate for black men had doubled during the 1960s, he defines "reactionary suicide" as "the reaction of a man who takes his own life in response to social conditions that overwhelm him and condemn him to helplessness." A "spiritual death," it designates the total victory of surplus-repression—and racism—and is the mark of those who "have ceased to fight the forms of oppression that drink their blood."[230] "Revolutionary suicide," in contrast, marks the antithesis of "a death wish" and represents the "strong desire to live with hope and human dignity":

> it is better to oppose the forces that would drive me to self-murder than to endure them. Although I risk the likelihood of death, there is at least the possibility, if not the probability, of changing intolerable conditions.[231]

Revolutionary suicide, in other words, is a profoundly utopian project. Founded on a recognition of the intolerability of the present moment, it designates a commitment to struggle, resistance, and revolution. And most intriguingly, the one killed off in revolutionary suicide is less the activist's own body than the old bourgeois ego that prizes individual success and happiness above the well-being of the collective. For revolutionary suicide dissolves the bourgeois ego in favor of "[t]he people of the world," who, Newton feels assured, "will prevail, seize power, seize the means of production, wipe out racism, capitalism, reactionary intercommunalism. . . ." As such, it represents a kind of desubjectification wherein the individual (Christian masochistic) subject is sacrificed both to the collective and to "the survival of the entire world." (It also betrays a more than passing likeness to the experience of desubjectification dramatized in the LSD sequence in *Easy Rider* and noted by various drug gurus.) Newton recognizes that "all historical revolutionary movements" have acted "in the same way," and he aligns himself with both the bourgeois revolutions of the eighteenth century and the Third World national liberation struggles of the 1960s.[232] Drawing inspiration from Bakunin, Castro, Che Guevara, and Mao Ze-dong, he insists that the revolutionary "must always be prepared to face death" and "see his death and his life as one piece."[233]

For Huey Newton, the way beyond masochism lies not, as it does for most of the politicized counterculture, in an allegedly subversive repetition of masochistic subjection. Unlike Julian Beck, he does not delight in playing the slave (or aping the master), but in dedicating himself to "[t]he people of the world." Moreover, despite the Black Panthers' cultural nationalism and Newton's recognition that "white radicals . . . are not faced," as black ones are, "with genocide," his revolutionary program is startlingly universalizing in its thrust.[234] For he acknowledges that "intolerable conditions" affect "Black and white alike" and that both racial groups are consequently "ill in the same way."[235] Yet the cure he proposes is very different from that proposed by The Living Theatre or the Yippies. For next to revolutionary suicide, revolution-as-performance seems most distinctive for being *merely* performance, which is to say, a fiction, a simulacrum. And revolutionary suicide is not the same as the pacifistic, homeopathic remedy that hopes to extirpate violence by miming it. Rather, it aims to accomplish what needs be done at whatever price—short, that is, of intensifying the subjugation of other oppressed groups. For in one of the most remarkable documents of the era, Newton in 1970 signaled his support for both Women's Liberation and Gay Liberation. Acknowledging that opposition to these movements stems from personal "insecurities"—the fear that "we might be homosexual" or that "she might castrate us"—he argues that "[w]e must gain security in ourselves and therefore have respect and feelings for all oppressed people."[236] And although his prose evinces palpable anxiety (especially around homosexuality's relationship to "the decadence of capitalism"), he unequivocally supports individual rights, insisting both that "we recognize the woman's right to be free" and that "a person should have the freedom to use his body in whatever way he wants." Bearing witness to the emergence of identity politics in the United States as a potent political force, he calls for the "full participation of the gay liberation movement and the women's liberation movement" in Black Panther activities, going so far as to suggest that "maybe a homosexual could be the most revolutionary" of activ-

ists.[237] Despite his doubly tentative claim ("maybe," "could"), Newton recognizes the importance of diverse liberation movements and endorses "a
working coalition" with other potentially revolutionary agents.[238] Moreover,
his politics of inclusion is decidedly ambivalent toward heterosexualized,
masculine authority. On the one hand, his use of masculine pronouns (and
the rather notoriously patriarchal disposition of the Black Panthers) suggests
that revolutionary agency is a specifically masculine prerogative.[239] On the
other hand, his universalizing rhetoric also suggests that revolutionary suicide
dissolves the specifically masculine identity of the revolutionary agent, substi-
tuting a collective humanity for the individual subject. To that extent, his
utopian vision is much in line with Fanon's call for a new, anticapitalist humanism that breaks with the old, degraded European humanism by seeking to
install "a new man."[240] For despite a commitment to "[t]he people of the
world," '60s radicalism—at least until the rebirth of feminism—tended to remain indentured, however uncomfortably or guiltily, to a phallicized concept
of revolutionary agency.

Just before he becomes the victim of a reactionary suicide in *Easy Rider*,
George Hanson, sitting around the last campfire, sets forth his philosophy of
the desire for "freedom" that inspirits both American liberalism and a revolutionary politic.

> [T]alkin' about it and bein' it, that's two different things. I mean, it's real hard to
> be free when you are bought and sold in the marketplace. Of course, don't ever
> tell anybody that they're not free 'cause then they're gonna get real busy killing
> and maiming to prove to you that they are. They gonna talk to you and talk to you
> and talk to you about individual freedom. But they see a free individual, it's gonna
> scare 'em.

A veritable explosion of state-sponsored violence at the end of the '60s proved
the veracity of George's statement, demonstrating that these countercultural
heroes do indeed occasion a tremendous anxiety on the part of the unfree
majority. Not only does George virtually write his own obituary here, but he
also pronounces an epitaph for the '60s, describing the forces of reaction that
were just then beginning to descend en masse to crush youth culture's rebellion, to drive it to a kind of reactionary suicide. Yet *Easy Rider*, a part of the
commodity culture it critiques, also suggests that the violent revenge of the
unfree was motivated in part by what turned out in the end to have been largely
unfounded fears of gender deviance and sexual deviance. For despite the
rhetoric of sexual liberation and androgyny, the counterculture for the most
part remained as mortgaged to traditional gender roles as the bourgeois
culture it opposed. It thereby attests to the persistence of Cold War orthodoxies, at least in regard to gender and sexuality, well into, and beyond, the
'60s. *Easy Rider*, meanwhile, in its fixation on the tragedy of the individual,

white, rebel male, can only barely imagine the idea of revolutionary suicide. But perhaps that impossible—and utopian—imagining is precisely the political unconscious of the LSD scene in the St. Louis Cemetery: the simultaneous representation of an unrepresentable desubjectification and act of mourning for the fact that, under the aegis of the National Guard and the FBI, revolutionary suicide is itself in the process of being killed off. For those who remember the revolution that almost happened and mourn the loss, the victory of the corporate state remains bitter. George, on the other hand, was lucky. He never knew what hit him.

Chapter Three

THE SADOMASOCHIST IN THE CLOSET

> Public heroes, of course, have been a touchy subject ever since Viet-
> nam, and "macho" has been a dirty word for so long it seems safe to
> use only for selling cologne. Now here, suddenly, we have an epic
> vision of strong silent men doing manly things for many reasons—
> and damned if it's not exhilarating to men and women alike.
>
> *(David Ansen with Katrine Ames, review of*
> The Right Stuff, Newsweek *[1983])*

> We're the same, you and me.
>
> *(Neo-Nazi Nick [Frederic Forrest] to D-FENS*
> *[Michael Douglas], in* Falling Down *[1992])*

PHILIP KAUFMAN'S 1983 film *The Right Stuff* is an oddly ambivalent representation, both adventure film and satire, celebration and critique of the "macho" American male so giddily cited by the *Newsweek* critics and of the increasingly commodified and mediatized culture that emerged after World War II.[1] Based on Tom Wolfe's 1979 novel, it featured Sam Shepard as Chuck Yeager who, in 1947, became the first pilot to break the sound barrier. The film was something of a coup for Shepard, providing him not only with the one role with which he has been most closely identified (and one that plays to his strengths as an actor), but also with his only Academy Award nomination. It is also virtually schizophrenic structurally. The first part is the story of the strong, silent loner, Chuck Yeager, cowboy and test pilot—the pilot is clearly set up as a technologized version of the cowboy—who repeatedly risks his life to help bring America into the space age. Its climax is Yeager's harrowing flight in the X-1 (he is suffering broken ribs from a spill he took while riding the day before) into the wild, blue yonder beyond Mach 1. The film is held together by Sam Shepard's rendering, in one critic's estimation, of "a Mr. Cool performance so consciously 'mythic' that it seems a parody of something."[2] The second part focuses on the seven Mercury astronauts, Yeager's heirs, presenting them as amiably arrogant exemplars of space age derring-do who willingly sell themselves, their wives, and their families to the media. The first part of the film is invested in fortifying the image of Yeager as a true-blue hero, as a "gallant, gum-chewing individualist," while the second casts an affectionately cynical eye on those who followed somewhat more ostentatiously in his footsteps.[3]

About midway through the film, in a sequence that connects the two parts, two recruiters from Washington (Harry Shearer and Jeff Goldblum) drive up to Pancho's slightly antiquated wild West saloon outside Edwards Air Force Base to shop around for astronauts for the fledgling space program. Looking like a cross between typical '50s G-men and Tweedledum and Tweedledee (Goldblum is tall and skinny, Shearer short and compact), dressed in identical black suits and ties, they get out of their car and approach the bar. Suddenly each, glancing at the other, realizes he has donned the other's jacket, and, in a stock comic routine, the two switch jackets. (The sequence is filmed in one long take, in medium shot, as if to ensure there will be no identification of these comic foils with the more empathic pilot-heroes.) As they trade clothes, they talk about their unsuspecting quarry:

RECRUITER 2 (Goldblum): Who's they?
RECRUITER 1 (Shearer): The best test pilots in the world.
RECRUITER 2: Here?
RECRUITER 1: Yeah, they got some kind of a little brotherhood. They keep thinking they got the right stuff.
RECRUITER 2: What kind of stuff? Heroism? Bravery? Wait a minute, there aren't any snakes around here, are there?
RECRUITER 1: Yeah, in the bushes. Heroism and bravery are part of it, but there seems to be more to it.
RECRUITER 2: What do they say it means?
RECRUITER 1: They don't say anything. That's part of the thing. They don't talk about it.

In this conversation, which casually explicates the title of the film, two comic doubles, one in the know, the other ignorant, try to define "the right stuff." It is not simply heroism or bravery—"there seems to be more to it," an unspoken (and perhaps unspeakable) supplement that is never articulated but that, judging from the evidence of the film, seems to have something to do with arrogance, swagger, and an obsessive flirtation with death. This tacit something "more" not only contrasts implicitly with Recruiter 2's fear of snakes and Recruiter 1's nonchalance about them, it also sets the pilots apart from these organization men. Whatever "the right stuff" is, it is a mysterious phenomenon, like the fantasized snake in the bushes—or the ever-elusive phallus of which this poisonous snake is so clearly a displacement. Most important, "the right stuff" is so awesome it stymies discourse as surely as it does the comprehension of the uninitiated.

This chapter will explore and name that something "more" which is embodied so strikingly by Sam Shepard as Chuck Yeager in *The Right Stuff* and by countless other white male celluloid heroes, from Sylvester Stallone to Michael Douglas, who have emerged since the mid-1970s. It will examine the recuperation of "macho" during the '70s and '80s that the authors of the

Newsweek review of the film find so "damned" exhilarating and the suggestive link they draw between Shepard and Yeager: "Kaufman saw, correctly, the mythic core—deeply private, mysteriously self-contained—that this counter-culture artist shares with the military ace."[4] How does this masculinized "mythic core," as embodied by Shepard, relate to the new white masculinity? Why do the reviewers feel moved to invoke the counterculture when describing one of its paradigms? What relation does it have to the ambivalently feminized masculinities of the 1960s? How does it relate to Sam Shepard's identity as an artist and to the construction of male subjectivity in his plays? Why is it that a film set during the height of the Cold War (1947–63) resonated so deeply with 1980s fantasies about the (re)construction of an imperialist masculinity? And finally, how does the masculinity of Shepard et al. connect to other recently recuperated white masculinities, from that produced by the self-consciously "mythic" men's movement, to that associated with the paramilitary Patriot movement?

I hope, in answering these questions, to demonstrate that *The Right Stuff*, with all its ambivalence regarding heroism and "more," exemplifies a newly dominant style of masculinity—in effect, a new cultural fantasmatic—that emerged in the mid-1970s, after the Vietnam War, and continues to the present day, one whose iconic figures include not just Sam Shepard as Chuck Yeager but also the playwright's male protagonists of the '70s and '80s. This is the new masculinity that takes Sylvester Stallone's John J. Rambo as its preferred icon and whose bible is Robert Bly's best-selling guidebook on how to become a real man, *Iron John*. It is a masculinity that is based both in a "little brotherhood" of men (like the Mercury astronauts) and in an inexorably divided self (allegorized by Recruiter 1 and Recruiter 2). Moreover, this masculinity is not solely the property of fictional characters. As embodied by Timothy McVeigh and Patrick Buchanan, it is the identity to which partisans of the Patriot movement aspire. In its relentless flirtation with pain, injury, and death, it goes beyond heroism and bravery to a kind of self-torture. As a result, it attests, I believe, to the emergence of a particular kind of masochistic male subjectivity—dubbed reflexive sadomasochism by Freud—which has become hegemonic in American culture over the course of the past twenty years.

POSTMODERNISM AND THE NEW NARCISSIST

If U.S. society of the late 1960s was organized around a generational split between the counterculture and so-called straight culture, then the 1970s saw this rupture turn into radical fragmentation. For if nothing else, the '70s was a decade of crisis. Politically, it witnessed the loss of the Vietnam War, Watergate, and the Iran hostage crisis. Three presidents—Nixon, Ford, and Carter—were brought down in disgrace. Economically, it marked the end of the postwar boom and the beginning of a serious crisis in Western capitalism. During the difficult transition from an industrial to a postindustrial (or service) economy, U.S. imports exceeded exports for the first time since World War II, and by 1972, as William Chafe notes, "the United States experienced a $10 billion balance of payments deficit, threatening the credibility of the American gold reserve and the dollar."[5] During the '70s, the price of gold rose from $35 to $800 an ounce, and oil imports ballooned from $4 billion to $90 billion. Industrial productivity remained virtually stagnant, while inflation soared and the U.S. standard of living fell to fifth in the world.[6] As union membership dwindled and real income declined by 2 percent in each year between 1973 and 1981, confidence in the economy plummeted. In a 1979 poll, "55 percent of all Americans believed that 'next year will be worse than this year.'"[7]

The economic crises of the mid-1970s coincided with a weakening of the Fordist mode of production, which had been firmly in place in the United States since the early 1950s and which, in Simon Clarke's words, denotes "the mass production of homogeneous products, using the rigid technology of the assembly line with dedicated machines and standardized (Taylorist) work routines."[8] For beginning in the late 1960s, "new strategies" of accumulation, as Michael Rustin notes, began to be

> developed by capital, both intellectually and in political practice. These included the internationalization of its operations, transferring "Fordist" forms of production to less developed countries, while maintaining crucial command and research functions in the metropolises; the imposition of more stringent market disciplines on capital and labour, through the international "de-regulation" of trade, movements of capital, and labour; the internal "marketization" of operations within large firms, through the institution of management by local profit-centres; the development of new technologies and forms of production and marketing; . . . and a dispersal and reduction of the scale of production to elude the countervailing cultures and institutions of organized labour.[9]

Since their emergence, these new (post-Fordist) strategies have tended not to displace Fordism but, as Neil Lazarus argues, to be "integrated with Fordist production in the core capitalist economies" and with "Fordist and other forms of production in the peripheral economies of the capitalist world-system."[10] This hybridized late capitalist economy that began to take shape during the 1970s was stabilized during the next decade (in the United States at least) by the economic policies of the Reagan administration. Changes in the tax code, an explosion of military spending, a massive increase in the federal deficit, and a wholesale deregulation of industry reinforced class divisions and produced a swift and unprecedented upward redistribution of wealth.[11]

As has been widely noted, the emergence and stabilization of late capitalism coincided with the development of postmodernism as the dominant cultural mode throughout most of the First World. Although I feel that the innovative characteristics of postmodernist culture have been vastly overstated (virtually all of them can be found in various minority modernisms, like dada or surrealism), postmodernism does represent at the least a subtle change in attitude toward modernity. Deeply suspicious of Enlightenment epistemologies, preferring surface to depth and signifier to signified, postmodernism has no use for the critique of the commodity (or of industrialization) that was so crucial to modernism. Rather, as Fredric Jameson notes, postmodernism delights in the utopian vistas opened up by consumerism and represents "the consumption of sheer commodification as a process."[12] Postmodernism in the West has borne witness to the end of the divide between elite and mass culture and, as Jameson emphasizes, a significant "weakening of historicity, both in our relationship to public History and in the new forms of our private temporality. . . ."[13] For the 1970s oversaw the development of whole genres—the nostalgia film, postmodernist architecture, punk rock—that cannibalize styles of the past while refusing to credit the kind of narratives that have (historically) been understood to constitute history. Instead, pastiche—defined as "blank parody," "a neutral practice of . . . mimicry"—has come to substitute for historicity in, for example, a host of nostalgia films from *American Graffiti* (1973) to *Back to the Future* (1985) to *The Brady Bunch Movie* (1994).[14] As Jameson argues, "'intertextuality'" has come to function "as a deliberate, built-in feature of the aesthetic effect and as the operator of a new connotation of 'pastness' and pseudohistorical depth, in which the history of aesthetic styles displaces 'real' history."[15] And as all of the films cited above suggest, postmodernist cultural productions characteristically provide an aroma of history without encouraging the consumer to confront the economic, political, and social struggles that define a particular historical moment. Although postmodernism—and, I would like to add, that variety of theory which celebrates postmodernism—unquestionably owes a great deal to the utopian projects associated with the New Left and the counterculture, Jameson is certainly correct when he notes that it also represents "the substitute for the sixties and the compensation for their political failure. . . ."[16] It thereby testifies to the collapse of both mass-movement politics and a critique of capitalism in the early '70s and signals a kind of depoliticized rebellion (or, more correctly, pseudorebellion) that would become more and more characteristic of U.S. cultural productions during the '80s and '90s.

The development of postmodernism coincides with the triumph of mass-mediated culture—the collapse of the old studio system and the rise of independent film, the proliferation of cable TV stations and satellite dishes, the end of Top 40 radio, and the Internet explosion—and testifies to a wholesale decentralization (and some would say, democratization) of U.S. culture. This decentralization—along with the emergence of niche marketing—is clearly tied to the rise of identity politics during the late '60s and early '70s and signals not only the end of the polar opposition between the counterculture and straight culture but also the proliferation of disparate (and often opposing) cultures and audiences. In the 1970s, for example, the ascendancy of disco, with its roots in Motown and rhythm and blues, coincided both with the development of a more easy-listening, adult rock and the rise of punk and new wave music, which, unlike disco, revisited white rock 'n' roll of the '50s and '60s with a new, angry, and often anarchist edge. (And punk's particular style of rebellion—subversive repetition—would become the dominant mode of transgression in the West under the regime of postmodernism.) In theater, the rapid growth of regional companies in the United States during the 1970s led to a similar fragmentation of theater audiences. In New York, the period bore witness, on the one hand, to the increasing obsolescence of Broadway as a forum for serious drama and, on the other, to the institutionalization of the avantgarde (in the case, for example, of The Wooster Group, Robert Wilson, and Mabou Mines). At the same time, it testified to the mainstreaming of a number of playwrights (like Sam Shepard, David Mamet, and Lanford Wilson) who started Off-Off-Broadway, earned respectability in the regional theaters, and went on to win Pulitzer Prizes. The film industry was correspondingly transformed during the 1970s by the development of cable and video technologies and the increasing demand that studios (most of which had been taken over by conglomerates during the '60s) make blockbuster movies. As Timothy Corrigan notes, the blockbusters, aiming to "attract not just a large market but *all* markets," became "the central imperative in an industry that sought the promise of massive profit from large financial investment."[17] But demographics worked against this desired consolidation of markets as a dramatic shift in moviegoing audiences from city to suburb encouraged the development of multiple-screen theaters, which, Margie Burns observes, are "less like 'movie palaces'" and more like the "the fast-food operations located next to them in suburban shopping malls."[18] As a result of these changes, "the center of movie viewing has shifted away," Corrigan avers, "from the screen and become dispersed in the hands of" a fragmented audience "with more (real and remote) control than possibly ever before."[19] So despite the studios' fever for blockbusters, Hollywood almost by default ended up producing increasing specialized products for increasingly specialized audiences.

For many social theorists of the late 1970s, the political disasters of the 1970s coupled with the triumph of mass-mediated culture became symptomatic of a precipitous moral decline in the United States and an ominous disintegration of American civil society. Birthrates plummeted during the decade (reaching an all-time low), divorce rates climbed dizzyingly, and the "number of individuals living in 'single households' skyrocketed from 10.9 percent in 1964 to 23 percent in 1980."[20] Perhaps the most influential volume to address this alleged social crisis was Christopher Lasch's best-seller, whose subtitle betrays its basic attitude toward the era, *The Culture of Narcissism: American Life in an Age of Diminishing Expectations*. For Lasch, the United States suffers a "crisis in confidence" as a result of "[d]efeat in Vietnam, economic stagnation, and the impending exhaustion of natural resources. . . ."[21] Surveying American culture, he correctly describes the displacement of history by "nostalgia," the triumph of consumerism and bureaucracy, the spectacularization of politics, the loss of faith in science, the intellectual bankruptcy of traditional liberalism, the decline of the nuclear family, and the "political crisis of capitalism" (23, 18). As the most vociferous critic of the so-called me generation, he charges that "[a]fter the political turmoil of the sixties, Americans have retreated to purely personal preoccupations" (29). And he ascribes this social and moral crisis to the logic of "competitive individualism, which in its decadence has carried the logic of individualism to the extreme of a war of all against all, the pursuit of happiness to the dead end of a narcissistic preoccupation with the self" (21). In opposition to this logic, he offers a literally reactionary solution: "I see the past as a political and psychological treasury from which we draw the reserves . . . that we need to cope with the future" (25). Taking a position that veers unpredictably between a cranky neoconservativism and a quasi-Marxism, he is particularly critical of the "fashionable" and "pernicious" "[c]ultural radicalism" left over from the '60s that has ironically ended up reinforcing the status quo and producing a "new narcissist" who is "haunted not by guilt but by anxiety" and turns not to religion or politics for help but to ineffectual therapies of all kinds (21–22). In his view, the self-besotted narcissist has become the emblematic new (and pathologized) social type who "lives in a state of restless, perpetually unsatisfied desire" and "depends on others to validate his self-esteem" (23, 38).

In attacking the alleged decadence of commodity culture and the new narcissist who inhabits it, Lasch is clearly critiquing what can be described only as a feminization of both U.S. culture and its newly emblematic subject. For it is more than the force of convention that dictates his use of the masculine pronoun throughout the book. Lasch is made particularly uncomfortable by the new narcissist in part because "he" has become the exemplification of what has been marked historically as a distinctively feminine (and infantile) disorder. The narcissist (who, in his formulation, is implicitly male and middle- to upper-class), with his endless capacity for "self-absorption," represents a sharply divided subject characterized by his "dependence on the vicarious warmth provided by others combined with a fear of dependence, a sense of inner emptiness, boundless repressed rage, and unsatisfied oral cravings" (61, 74). "Outwardly bland, submissive, and sociable," he seethes "with an inner anger for which a dense, overpopulated, bureaucratic society can devise few legitimate outlets" (40). And Lasch pointedly sets this schizoid subject against the unequivocally masculinized "rugged individualist" whom he holds up (despite some misgivings) as a relatively salutary counterexample (38). For Lasch, for whom the "conquest of nature and the search for new frontiers have given way to the search for self-fulfillment," the authoritative, imperial self has been lamentably superseded by a narcissist forever gazing longingly in the mirror at his own likeness (61). And feminism, in his view, tends to exacerbate the problems that men face. For although he recognizes that women are justified in attacking "masculine privilege," he sees feminism primarily as a form of "sexual recrimination" that "makes women more shrewish than ever in their daily encounters with men" (335–36).

Lasch, in short, regards the new, male narcissist as the latest casualty of the U.S. culture wars and, like so many of his contemporaries, clearly positions him as a victim. But for Lasch the most serious problem confronting those (like himself) who would cure the new narcissist is the latter's apparent enjoyment of his predicament. For the narcissist is also a masochist, and the terms of Lasch's discussion almost exactly replicate Freud's analysis of moral masochism. Lasch complains that an unparalled "growth of bureaucracy" regrettably

> erodes all forms of patriarchal authority and thus weakens the social superego, formerly represented by fathers, teachers, and preachers. The decline of institutionalized authority in an ostensibly permissive society does not, however, lead to a "decline of the superego" in individuals. It encourages instead the development of a harsh, punitive superego that derives most of its psychic energy, in the absence of authoritative social prohibitions, from the destructive, aggressive impulses within the id. Unconscious, irrational elements in the superego come to dominate its operation. As authority figures in modern society lose their "credibility," the superego in individuals increasingly derives from the child's primitive fantasies about his parents—fantasies charged with sadistic rage—rather than from internalized ego ideals formed by later experience with loved and respected models of social conduct. (40–41)

The (male) narcissist, in other words, is the product of an unfortunate weakening of "patriarchal authority" in a feminized culture (306). Because he no longer has "loved and respected" figures to emulate, he retreats to fantasy and develops a "sadistic superego" (derived from the id) that assaults his now masochistic ego (41n). A hapless victim of the "social changes" wrought by "[t]he new permissiveness," he testifies to the strengthening of "the alliance" between the "superego and Thanatos—that 'pure culture of the death instinct,' as Freud called it, which directs against the ego a torrent of fierce, unrelenting criticism" (306).

Lasch's analysis of a specifically masculine malaise that pits a sadistic part of the self against a masochistic part of the self is an important diagnostic portrait of the subject of late capitalism. However, despite his claim that this figure marks a new development, Lasch is in fact reviving a theory of a self-destructive, victimized masculinity that bears a striking resemblance to Robert Lindner's analysis some thirty-five years earlier of the psychopath, a.k.a. the rebel without a cause. And I would like to suggest that the supposedly new postmodernist subject no more signals a new species of man than postmodernism itself does a break with the tenets of modernism. The only thing truly new about the new narcissist (or new sadomasochist—take your pick) is that he represents a now *dominant* figure on the U.S. cultural scene, no longer relegated to the margins. And in that sense, *The Culture of Narcissism* testifies to the triumph of the countercultural model of masculinity. Yet the book also makes it clear that this model represents—for Lasch and many other social critics—not a solution but a problem. For so many of the arbiters of culture during the 1980s, the feminized, internally divided, masochistic male subject is something of an embarrassment. And it is precisely this new-old masculinity that the men's movement would attempt to correct.

THE WILD MAN WITHIN

In 1981, two years after *The Culture of Narcissism* was published, the poet and onetime antiwar activist Robert Bly began leading weekend retreats for men in which, by sharing diverse rituals, they would, he hoped, be able to get in touch with what he calls "the deep masculine."[22] Over the course of the decade he gradually expanded both his philosophy of the gendered subject (drawn from Jung, Joseph Campbell, various pop psychologists, and, to a lesser extent, Freud) and his workshop techniques (inspired by consciousness-raising groups of the 1960s, twelve-step programs, various religious and tribal rituals, and the "masculinity therapy" of the 1970s).[23] Bly acquired a small, albeit devout, following until 1990 when he was featured in a widely broadcast (and rebroadcast) PBS show with Bill Moyers, "A Gathering of Men," which catapulted him—and the movement of which he has been dubbed the "patron saint"—into the mainstream.[24] Since then the men's movement (as it has been dubbed by the media) has provided the most visible and widely publicized focal point for the discourses of masculinity in America. A myriad of articles has appeared in the popular press about the movement, while Robert Bly has basked in the glow of his phenomenally best-selling manifesto, *Iron John* (1990), which made the *New York Times* hardcover best-seller list for sixty-two weeks. This book details his "mythopoetic" formulation of masculinity and has lucratively revived what had been a flagging literary career. The workshops for men, meanwhile, conducted by Bly, his followers, and imitators, have proven fantastically successful, netting their organizers up to twenty thousand dollars per weekend. (One writer estimates that as of 1991 more than a hundred thousand American men had participated in at least one workshop.)[25]

In recent years, the men's movement has provoked widespread adulation and criticism and is, I believe, a particularly telling barometer of those pressures and anxieties circulating not just around normative notions of masculinity but also around questions of sexuality and racial difference. Its defenders laud it for rescuing the American male, making him more sensitive, assertive, and spiritual, while its detractors attack it for its alleged misogyny, racism, and homophobia. Yet even defining the movement is more problematic than it at first appears. As Bly himself admits, what passes for the men's movement represents in fact several discrete movements (with unusually flexible and permeable boundaries) that could be roughly divided as follows: (1) the "mythopoetic" sect (under Bly's aegis) committed to a renewal of "spiritual values" (15); (2) the right-wing, overtly antifeminist camp; (3) the profeminist; (4) the gay men's movement; and (5) the African-American men's movement.[26] Despite this diversity, Bly's wing has received far more attention in the press than any other, not just because of Bly's showmanship and success with the mass media, but also because of the social and economic clout wielded by its followers: white, middle- and upper-middle-class, heterosexual men in their thirties and forties (the popular press repeatedly stresses the overwhelmingly white constituency). If I focus primarily on the "mythopoetic" wing, it is precisely because of its dominant position with respect to the men's movement as a whole.

Its bible, Bly's *Iron John*, is an extraordinarily disordered and eclectic text, part sociology, part anthropology, part pop psychology, part self-help manual, part holy writ. Indiscriminately combining fairy tales with New Age spiritualism, Native American myths with a shamelessly superficial and inaccurate cultural critique, it has such an improvisatory quality and is so deeply conflicted and overgeneralized that it is often very difficult to pin down ideologically. (One writer describes it as "Bly's everything-but-the-kitchen-sink interpretation of a Grimm's fairy tale.")[27] It is also filled with gross historical, sociological, and anthropological errors, often citing theories that were discredited a generation ago.[28] The gist is as follows: according to Bly—a biological essentialist if there ever was one—the women's movement of the late '60s and '70s reversed traditional gender roles by producing what he labels "the 'soft male'": "a nice boy who pleases not only his mother but also the young woman he is living with" (2). In rhetoric remarkably evocative of that decrying the smothering "Momism" of the 1950s, Bly deplores the state of those feckless men whose power has been sapped (almost vampirically) by "strong women who positively radiate energy" (3).[29] Since the onset of the Industrial Revolution, Bly argues, the "love unit most damaged . . . has been the father-son bond," whose health he (much like Lasch) believes decisive for the production of a strong, healthy male. Unless a son makes "a clean break from the mother," he will always end up as a heterosexualized wimp, "afraid" of his own masculinity (19, 25). As a cure for this social disease of gender inversion (which retains more than a whiff of the opprobrium traditionally attached to "sexual inversion"), Bly urges a recuperation of "the deep masculine," the primitive and "true radiant energy" that all men "*instinctive[ly]*" know and possess, the "Wild Man" whom the purportedly effeminizing culture of late capitalism has locked away in a cage (8). For several hundred dollars, a man can join Bly on a weekend retreat to unlock the "Wild Man," don a mask, crawl around like an animal, recite myths, volunteer personal confessions, endure the heat of a Native American sweatbox, and beat drums until he is exhausted.[30]

In its rigorous polarization of the masculine and the feminine, in its longing for the production of an ostensibly whole and full human subject (possessed of "Zeus energy," 22), in its imperialistic and indiscriminate appropriation of myths and Jungian archetypes, in its fetishization and exoticization of premodern and Third World cultures, in its unabashed quest for "spiritual values," and in its obsession with communitarian rituals, Bly's "mythopoesis" bears an almost uncanny resemblance to the countercultural yearnings of the '60s and early '70s. However, *Iron John* is by no means simply a recycling of '60s utopianism. For one thing, unlike most of the texts of the counterculture, the bible of the new masculinity cannot maintain the political as a meaningful category. For Bly, for example, the story of "[r]ebellious students at Columbia University" who during the 1960s "took over the president's office looking for evidence of CIA involvement with the university" is legible only as a parable about the remoteness of sons from fathers (which is to say, from "all male figures of authority" [21–22]). Yet Bly's reading of this event is symptomatic of his tendency relentlessly to collapse the political into the psychological and the familial. In so doing, Bly's text not only obviates political action but also stands as a sorry testament to the collapse of mass-movement politics in America since the end of the Vietnam War. It also attests to the habit, especially widespread among those neoconservatives who came to power the same year that Bly initiated his weekend retreats, of reading '60s militancy not as political activism but as a kind of regrettable national adolescence. Rather than being an aberration, however, *Iron John* is in fact emblematic of the strategies of self-help literature, which, despite its debt to the counterculture, characteristically imagines social and political problems to be entirely the responsibility of maladjusted individuals and understands "revolutionaries and activists of all kinds" as being little more than "the new tyrants and the new oppressors."[31]

Bly's followers passionately defend his program and maintain that the men's movement has made them more open emotionally and taught them more gentle ways in which to be assertive. "We tried to be kind to women, and they don't love us for it," one man notes; "We got weak, and we need to be strong again." Another claims, "I've read how we've been robbed of our masculinity and conditioned to be passive, but drumming makes me feel rejuvenated. . . ."[32] Don Shewey believes that Bly has found in mythology "richer, deeper, [and] more complex images of masculinity than those in today's pop culture," and that Bly's method helps men recognize and deal with previously unacknowledged feelings, especially grief.[33] Bly's detractors, meanwhile, insist that the men's movement is primarily a reaction against the women's movement and represents an attempt to recoup and reconsolidate the masculine prerogatives that have been threatened by feminist critiques and the limited economic achievements of women in certain spheres. Susan Faludi argues that "[t]he true subject of Bly's weekends, after all, is not love and sex, but power—how to wrest it from women and how to mobilize it for men."[34] Taking an even longer historical view, Suzanne Gordon observes, "You cannot equate the systematic domination of women for centuries, . . . the violence against women, the restrictions of women's talents and options . . . with any amount of pain and suffering and confusion that modern men may feel." Even Jackson Katz, the leader of Real Men, an avowedly profeminist wing of the men's movement, feels that Bly's emphasis on "how men are oppressed" effaces the extraordinary level of "violence against women" in American culture.[35] Tellingly, Carol Bly provides a particularly trenchant critique of her ex-husband's recent exploits. Deeming the movement "frightening," she rightly draws attention to its deeply nostalgic and quasi-fascistic rhetoric, its "attraction to an old Germanic war mythology and . . . paranoiac appeal to 'recapture what we have lost.' "[36]

Susan Faludi's reading of the men's movement as part of the antifeminist backlash is difficult to refute. Although the movement tends to see itself as a "parallel development" rather than a "reactionary response," and although Bly himself attempts to distinguish between his wing and the "antifeminist" one, *Iron John* unequivocally suggests that feminism is primarily responsible for producing the problems that the men's movement seeks to alleviate, and it repeatedly positions men as the victims of feminism.[37] Not only does *Iron John* undertake a relentless tirade against the supposed dominion of mothers, but it also specifically accuses "the separatist wing of the feminist movement" of laboring "to breed fierceness out of men" (46).[38] Yet the attacks on mothers and on feminism per se are only a small part of the ideological machinery that the book mobilizes in its attempted reconstruction of masculinity. The more closely one examines the workings of the text, the more one notices that the apparently stabilized and hierarchical gender roles it attempts to institute are, in fact, profoundly contradictory. Masculinity in *Iron John* is by no means singular and integral. It is not simply the "Wild Man energy" that Bly insists "leads to forceful action undertaken . . . with resolve" (8). Rather, it is endlessly conflicted, wounded, riven by pain, doubt, and darkness, always set in a deeply ambivalent relationship to the categories of nature and culture, inside and outside, male and female. And despite Bly's plea that his book "does not constitute a challenge to the women's movement," its cultural positioning is impossible to ascertain without an examination of the history of masculine reactions to the women's movement over the past twenty years (x).

In the mid-1970s, most of the popular literature about and for men attempted to capitalize on the success of "women's liberation" and, like Warren

Farrell's *The Liberated Man* (1975), suggested that men could avoid the "emotional constipation" that accompanies the "masculine mystique" by allowing themselves to become more vulnerable, communicative, and expressive.[39] By the end of the decade, however, as R. W. Connell points out, men's liberation had gradually turned into "a defense of men's interests against women's." Increasingly, men banded together to form " 'men's rights' groups ... to oppose women in divorce and custody cases."[40] During the Reagan years, as antifeminist lobbying became more and more acceptable, attacks on women and feminism became an increasingly conspicuous part of male activism. This recent wave of antifeminism, however, long predates Reagan and can in fact, as Faludi documents, be traced back to the very beginning of the 1970s.[41]

At the height of the feminist insurgence, conservative critic George Gilder published *Sexual Suicide* (1973), an avowedly antifeminist polemic that stages a withering attack on what Gilder perceives to be the primary ambition of feminism: "the abolition of biological differences between men and women."[42] For Gilder, this abolition, together with its attendant horrors—promiscuity, gender confusion, and, above all, homosexuality—leads inexorably to sexual suicide, to the loss of that "procreative energy" which alone will "carry a community into the future" (8). The violent rhetoric of *Sexual Suicide*, together with its overt misogyny and homophobia, contrasts stridently with Bly's meditative manifesto (which frequently goes out of its way to attempt to appease feminists and, at least once, to propitiate the hapless gay man who stumbles upon it). Thus Gilder insists unapologetically that "[t]he feminist program ... usually consists of taking jobs and money away from men, while granting in return such uncoveted benefits as the right to cry" (13). Yet minus the cynicism and vitriol, *Sexual Suicide* remains an unambiguous precursor of *Iron John*, the founder of a particular mode of discourse that imagines men to be the victims of feminism, and that became increasingly popular during the neoconservative 1980s and 1990s. Like Bly, Gilder observes essential and irreducible biological differences between men and women and maintains that the oppression of women has been grossly overestimated because "[w]omen, in fact, possess enormous power over men" (14). Like Bly, Gilder insists that "[m]en can be creatively human only when they are confidently male and overcome their sexual insecurity by action" (18). Like Bly, Gilder bases his analysis in an imperialistic cross-culturalism that appeals to the "Zulu" more frequently than the European, and indulges in a wholesale romanticization of premodern cultures, especially hunting societies, finding in them the most immediate expression of "male sexual rhythms" (16, 84). Like Bly, Gilder sees the Industrial Revolution as "perhaps the most cataclysmic event in history" (84) and despairs at the state of contemporary culture:

> The man discovers that manhood affords few distinctive roles except in the decreasingly respected military. . . . It is increasingly difficult for him to hunt or fight or otherwise assert himself in an aggressive, male way. Most jobs reward obedience, regularity, and carefulness more than physical strength or individual initiative. If he attempts to create rituals and institutions like the ones used by similarly beleaguered men in primitive societies, he finds them open to women. (104)

Yet what is perhaps most startling about *Sexual Suicide* (and this, too, makes it remarkably similar to *Iron John*) is its failure, despite its repeated attempts, to produce anything resembling a stable, integral, and full male subject, one based on presence (as opposed to absence), on hardness (as opposed to flaccidity). Rather, masculinity is continually figured as a *lack*, and the phallus as an elusive and mysterious commodity. Gilder complains of the impossibility of a self-composed masculinity because

> unlike femininity, relaxed masculinity is at bottom empty, a limp nullity. While the female body is full of internal potentiality, the male is internally barren (from the Old French *bar*, meaning man). Manhood at the most basic level can be validated and expressed only in action. (18)

For Bly, as well, the essentialized masculine self, the "Wild Man," does not simply inhere (even in a dormant state) within the male subject. Rather, it remains tantalizingly "outside the human psyche," like the perennially displaced phallus, striven for yet never achieved, an exemplum passed mystically from father to son (36). Yet even patrilineality is a murky and perilous pathway for the "Wild Man" to travel insofar as Oedipalization is a hazardous process. For all fathers perforce have a "dark side" (and Bly invokes Darth Vader here) that restrains them from being "good all the way . . . " and gives them a certain cruel power to ward off the son's challenge (117). As a result, "true masculinity," as Fred Pfeil emphasizes, can be attained only by the man who confronts and heals "the wound of the father's rejection and/or damage. . . ."[43] Yet Bly, like Gilder, builds his project on disavowal, on the hope and fantasy that the son will, despite the perils of Oedipus, magically inherit his father's "Wild Man energy" and be capable of "forceful action" (8).

Despite the figuration of masculinity as an imaginary production, as a lack that can be filled only by some unspecified "action," neither Gilder nor Bly goes so far as to maintain that it is *merely* performative, merely one role amid many equally valid possibilities. On the contrary, both argue that there remains an essence of masculinity, a mythic potency discerned in the rigors of a (patriarchal) biology that would draw an absolute equation between penis and phallus. Gilder grounds his ontology in the collapse of male subjectivity into a grotesquely reductionistic view of male sexuality ("[m]en have only one sex organ and one sex act: erection and ejaculation" [17]), while Bly, more coyly and allegorically, sublimates his phallicism, proposing that man is in essence a "life-giving," hirsute hunter (woe betide those races with little or no body hair) who must always be prepared to lift his trusty "sword to cut his adult soul away from his mother-bound soul" (3, 165). To universalize this longed-for phallic male, both obsessively cite litanies of patriarchal myths and rifle through the histories of various premodern cultures. Yet both are finally unable to stabilize masculinity because both are fatally ambivalent about its position vis-à-vis that most powerful and overdetermined of social constructions, the opposition between "nature" and "culture."

Both *Sexual Suicide* and *Iron John* begin with a thesis that reverses the traditional polar opposition between masculinity and femininity, the very one that monopolized American culture during the domestic revival that followed World War II. In dominant representations of gender from the '40s well into the '60s, femininity was squarely positioned on the side of "nature," sexuality, and irrationality, whereas masculinity was equated with "culture," intellect, and reason. According to the logic of Cold War culture, it was the task of men to control, domesticate, and rationalize women and their dark sexuality, to ensure that "feminine" would forever remain a synonym for "submissive."[44] But by the early 1970s the balance began to shift, as the women's movement began to challenge men's domination of the workplace and the appalling disparity in wages between men and women.[45] As men began to feel increasingly threatened economically, masculinist discourse began to reposition them so that they too could lay claim to the state of "nature," to a raw physical and sexual power that purportedly antedates cultural apparatuses. Thus, according to Gilder (whose volume so clearly documents the change from the paternalism of the domestic revival to a post-60s antifeminism), modern culture is little more than a trap for "[w]omen [to] domesticate and civilize male power," a vehicle of repression that "prohibits, constricts or feminizes [a man's] purely male activities" (23, 104). Bly, as well, consistently imagines women as the driving force of an enculturation that serves only to rob the male subject of his "Wild Man" energy: "A mother's job is, after all, to civilize the boy . . ." (11). As a corollary to this, *Iron John* repeatedly associates with masculinity those very characteristics that were linked in Cold War culture to femininity, in effect reconstructing masculinity (and what irony there is in this move) on the very terrain of femininity. According to Bly's "mythopoesis," the "Wild Man" is "wet, moist, foresty, ignorant, [and] leafy . . ." (232), while "the deep masculine" is a place of shadows and silence, a dark continent of sexuality and power into which a man must descend, "protected by the *instinctive* one who's underwater" and sustained by "the *nourishing* dark" (8, 6).

Yet neither *Sexual Suicide* nor *Iron John* is content simply to invert the binary opposition between "nature" and "culture," to long nostalgically (and almost fascistically) for a premodern age—the good old days of feudalism— when men ruled with merry, brute strength. On the contrary, the two texts consistently contradict their avowed plans and inadvertently betray that old-fashioned misogyny which sees women as deceitful, dangerous, and in need of domestication. Thus Bly will one moment evoke the civilizing force of women and the next cite approvingly a New Guinea maxim that a "boy cannot change into a man without the active intervention of the older men," unlike a girl who "changes into a woman on her own," that is, through the inexorability of her "nature" and sexuality (86–87). Unlike *Sexual Suicide*, which seems oblivious to its voluminous inconsistencies, *Iron John* ceaselessly attempts to negotiate contradictions by forcing male subjectivity to inhere both inside and outside civilization, by making men the guardians of "nature" and "culture," sexuality and rationality simultaneously. It accomplishes this sleight of hand by making conflict the very basis for subjectivity and culture, that is, by installing Manichaean dualisms everywhere—both in society at large and within the individual subject. "[W]e know each man has a woman inside him, and each woman has a man inside her" (98). In Bly's fantasy, the subject is necessarily split into male and female, light and dark, strong and weak, good and evil. The resolution that Bly proposes for this schizophrenia is stunning in its obfuscation: "To live between we stretch out our arms and push the opposites as far apart as we can, and then live in the resonating space between them" (175). Even Bly's pseudopoetry is incapable of disguising the fact that male subjectivity in *Iron John* is invariably turned against itself and exists in a constant state of war with itself—it is little wonder that the "inner warrior" is in many ways *the* crucial archetypal figure for Bly. For as Pfeil notes, Bly's concept of masculinity is "defined by its perpetual oedipal oscillations between rebellion, submission, and emotional pain. . . ."[46] And it is the "inner warrior" that is the principal player in this series of oscillations, repeatedly vanquishing that which the male subject imagines to be the feminine, wounded, traitorous part of the self.

In its dramatization of the male subject at war with himself, *Iron John* suggests that the new man validates himself less by turning against women—although he does that often enough—than by turning against himself, by producing himself as the ground on which irreducibly opposing forces collide and do battle. This is the subject of what Freud called reflexive sadomasochism, a particular mode in which the individual subject is split into a sadistic half and a masochistic half (a mode that I will explicate below). Beginning in the 1970s, reflexive sadomasochism became, I believe, an increasingly powerful mechanism for the production not just of male subjectivity but of a culture and economy whose jurisdiction over both the First World and the Third (after the American debacle in Vietnam) was to become ever more precarious. In this situation, the relatively stable masculinity of the domestic revival was thrown into crisis. No longer having others on whom to inflict his power and his pain with impunity, the male subject began to turn against himself and to prove his mettle by gritting his teeth and taking his punishment like a man.

THE AUTEUR AS ACTOR

No living American playwright has been mythologized to the degree that Sam Shepard has. Variously styled as "counterculture artist," "matinee idol," "cowboy laureate," and "American fantasy," Shepard has become a commanding masculine icon whose notorious reclusiveness serves only to redouble the popular fascination with the man characteristically described by his academic devotees not just as "interesting and exciting" but as "the dominant American playwright of his generation" (an assessment with which many of his critics agree).[47] Following his first one-act, prophetically entitled *Cowboys* (1964), with a string of antinaturalistic and wildly inventive (if sometimes reckless and obscure) plays, he was already being hailed by the end of the decade as "the leading *avant-garde* playwright of his generation."[48] Notorious for refusing to rewrite his first drafts, he practiced, like Kerouac, a kind of spontaneous prose, thereby reinforcing the widely disseminated image of himself as cowboy and natural genius.[49] During the 1970s—arguably the second stage of his career—he turned toward a more rigorous and self-consciously American (and mythic) mode of writing to amass wider acclaim and greater respectability. With *Curse of the Starving Class* and *Buried Child* (both 1978), Shepard for the first time exploited the one form that remains emblematic of modern American drama, the three-act family tragedy, and unequivocally staked a claim to the mantle of O'Neill, Williams, and Miller. While both plays have been invaluable to those academic critics anxious to secure him a place in the canon, *Buried Child* also secured his reputation with the middlebrow theatergoing audience by winning the 1979 Pulitzer Prize (this was the first time a play received the prize without playing on Broadway).

Yet Shepard's real celebrity, which I would call the third phase of his career, started in the early 1980s and is a complex phenomenon, owing at least as much to his film acting as to his writing. On the day he won the Pulitzer Prize, he was shooting his second film, *Resurrection* (1980), for which he received star billing and excellent reviews. Named one of the ten sexiest men in America that year by *Playgirl* magazine, he was quickly on his way to becoming a bona fide movie star. Even his wife O-Lan wrote him a "filthy fan letter."[50] In 1982 he began a much-publicized relationship with his *Frances* costar, Jessica Lange (which continues to this day), and the release of *The Right Stuff* the next year seemed to confirm his near-legendary status. His apotheosis was complete by 1985 when he graced the cover of *Newsweek* and the accompanying essay proclaimed his multiple talents: "It's as if . . . F. Scott Fitzgerald had added to his standing as the great novelist of the jazz age an additional career as Hollywood's golden leading man."[51] During this period, Shepard has written fewer and fewer plays, and those he has written are, to my mind, far less distinctive than his earlier work and regrettably derivative, almost self-parodies (*A Lie of the Mind* [1985], in particular, reads and plays like "Sam Shepard's Greatest Hits.") Rather, it seems that most of his energy has gone into his acting and to the cultivation of the mystique of a *bricoleur* of genius: "avid horseman, instinctive musician, and amateur landscape architect," in one writer's description, or in another's, even more tellingly, "actor, playwright, man-in-love."[52]

The Sam Shepard of the early interviews (through the mid- to late 1970s) is charming, reflective, a bit innocent and starstruck, a real aficionado of theater, and only perfunctorily anti-intellectual. In recent interviews, however, Shepard projects a very different image. In part, it is marked by a jaded nonchalance, a more overt anti-intellectualism, and the playwright's considerable skill at using straight-shooting rhetoric (talking like a cowboy). Yet what is unique about this image is the tension between these characteristics—invariably coded as ruggedly masculine, individualistic, distinctively American, and, if not exactly working-class, at least hostile to domestic, bourgeois values—and the deep sense of personal angst that runs through his discourse. One moment he will attack Method acting as "neurotic" and "self-indulgent" while in the next complain of "a profound sense of emptiness," "aloneness," and "disconnectedness" that allegedly underlies consciousness.[53] Moreover, in his view, even masculinity is not immune from anxiety and doubt. Fresh from his brooding performance in *The Right Stuff*, Shepard spoke balefully about masculinity and violence to the *New York Times*:

> [T]here's something about American violence that to me is very touching. In full force it's very ugly, but there's also something very moving about it, because it has to do with humiliation. There's some hidden, deeply rooted thing in the Anglo male American that has to do with inferiority, that has to do with not being a man, and always, continually having to act out some idea of manhood that invariably is violent. This sense of failure runs very deep. . . .[54]

For the Shepard of this melancholy confession—and how similar this is to the woeful musings of Robert Bly—white (i.e., "Anglo") masculinity is neither an innate instinct nor a quality that the male subject possesses spontaneously. Rather, it is performative, like a masquerade that must unceasingly be reiterated, "act[ed] out." Founded not on presence, but on absence, masculinity compensates for "inferiority," "humiliation," and "failure," commodities to which it is ineluctably linked in Shepard's economy of desire. Like the ever-elusive phallus, masculinity is never possessed by the male subject (the one who has the humble penis in compensation) but is always pretended to. For Shepard, this perpetually deferred masculinity produces a sense of profound anxiety and is connected both discursively and behaviorally to violence, to a violence toward which, moreover, Shepard maintains an astonishing ambivalence. In his estimation, it is simultaneously "ugly" and "touching," ruthless and strangely sweet, an agent of destruction and an object of nostalgic fascination.

Like Robert Bly, Shepard remains deeply ambivalent about those violent qualities traditionally associated with an active masculinity. Yet unlike Bly, who tirelessly asserts irreducible biological differences, Shepard seems reluctant to presume the existence of a purportedly male essence. The "sense of failure" that "runs so very deep[ly]" seems almost to call into question the transhistorical foundation upon which Bly seeks so desperately to construct his ontology. So too with Shepard's will to mythologize. Like Bly, Shepard insists on the primacy of myth as that which "connects you and me to our personal families" and "to the generations of races of people" and of "tribes." But unlike Bly, Shepard insists that in modern culture, "[m]yth in its truest form has been demolished," that "[a]ll we have is fantasies about it," that this link to the past has been irremediably sundered (this skepticism has by no means restrained him from obsessively cultivating a cowboy mystique and shamelessly romanticizing the old West).[55] Despite these crucial differences, Shepard's representations of gender and his documentations of masculine anxiety began in the early 1970s, at the apogee of women's liberation, to crystallize around an ideology and an iconic male subject that display an uncanny similarity to those circulating through *Sexual Suicide* and *Iron John*. As initiated by Shepard's three-year sojourn in England (1971–74), this work marks a significant break with his early plays. Unlike his preceding works, these new plays, *The Tooth of Crime* (1972), *Action* (1974), and, most conspicuously, *Suicide in B-Flat* (1976), appropriate traditional comic techniques and styles in order to figure male subjectivity as anything but comic, which is to say, as relentlessly wounded, split, suicidal, and painfully turned back upon itself. As such, these are the first of Shepard's plays to focus explicitly on the production of a masculine mystique, and, in that sense, they quite literally set the stage for his own self-mythologization during the next decade.

Who is the fragmented and disorderly male subject who lords over his work of this period and whose violent and murderous instincts are characteristically turned against himself—masochistically, suicidally? Who is this fractured hero driven to distraction, pleasurably tortured by his multiple selves, the one who, like Kosmo in *Mad Dog Blues*, "has a sadomasochist hid in his closet"?[56]

KILLER'S HEAD

Suicide in B-Flat, first performed at Yale Rep in 1976, has been read as one of Shepard's most "tantalizing," "inventive," and "enigmatic" plays.[57] It is also invariably interpreted as being about the artist (often with a capital *A*) and, as a result, an unusually self-reflexive play.[58] Like *The Tooth of Crime* and *Geography of a Horse Dreamer* (1974), it is regarded both as documentation of the process of artistic production and as an interrogation—and indictment—of the commodity status of the work of art. While I do not dispute this designation, I believe that the play, which has a structure that seems unusually close to free association, offers far more than a portrait of the artist as a vaguely anonymous jazz musician. Rather, I see it as an analysis, or psychoanalysis, if you will, of what for Shepard, and for the culture of which he is a part, is the primal scene of masculinity.

Structurally, *Suicide* looks like an absurdist episode of *Dragnet*. It brings two detectives, Pablo and Louis, to the scene of a murder, complete with the outline of a man's sprawled body drawn on the floor, and then documents their reconstructions of the killer's motives and their interrogation of witnesses. The play ends with the ostensible reenactment of the crime and the apprehension of the murderer. Yet this summary omits the most original aspect of Shepard's play. Unlike most whodunits, *Suicide* pivots around the simultaneous presence and absence of the man who (if we are to believe the play's title) is simultaneously murderer and victim. About halfway through the play, Niles, the jazz musician, enters, both visible and invisible to the others in the room, both dead and not dead, both suicide and killer who blew off someone else's face. At the appearance of this doubled subject clearly on a quest for something, the dramatic action is itself doubled and turned back upon itself as Niles (together with his accomplice Paullette, playing Virgil to his Dante) reenacts the suicide/murder. Past is superimposed onto present, mortem onto postmortem. Unlike the traditional crime drama (or the so-called well-made play, for that matter), which moves toward the disclosure of a past that conclusively settles and stabilizes the present, Niles's crime remains to the last undecidable. Is he a suicide, murderer, or victim of a frame-up? Is he dead or on the lam? Is the body present or absent, self or other?

Shepard's deconstruction of the formal tenets and parameters of the whodunit are redoubled by a deep perturbation in the play's production of subjectivity. All of the characters are unremittingly destabilized. The two detectives are clearly farcical doubles (variously dubbed "bogus Bogarts" and "daffy dicks") not only of each other but also of Niles, whose death they unwittingly reenact.[59] Petrone and Laureen, Niles's musician friends, are also produced as symbiotic extensions of Niles, characters uniquely capable of telling his story, inhabiting his space, playing his music, reading his mind. Niles, meanwhile, the perennially dead/not dead hero, is quite unlike the unitary subject that dominates liberal humanist cultural productions. Rather, he is radically fragmented, a collection of disparate selves (musician, murderer, suicide, cowboy, tuxedoed swell, among others) each of which he longs to kill off. "They're crowding me up," Niles exclaims. "They've gotten out of control. They've taken me over and there's no room left for me."[60] At the same time, Niles's status as a jazz musician gives him a privileged relationship to African-American culture. And although Niles's race is never specified in the text—which means he is assumed to be white—his presence/absence in the stage space is signified by a white outline painted on the dark stage floor. And he is constructed, like so many of Shepard's musician-hipster-heroes (and like so many white males as victims), as an imitation black man, a '70s counterpart to the "white Negro."

The production of these doubles in the play is insistently linked to a level of psychic violence that cannot easily be accommodated by the conventions of parodic comedy. At the same time, it evokes a broad range of affect, among both characters and spectators, ranging from those sentiments that characteristically circulate in thrillers (fear, pain, anxiety, and rage) to a kind of farcical giddiness. Even the play's starting point, the titular suicide, is far more than simply an initiating plot device. Rather, it seems so clearly the symptom of an intense emotional violence that is virtually ubiquitous in the play but whose foundation is never fully illuminated. One way of interpreting the suicide is as a pure realization of that most controversial of all the Freudian drives, the death instinct, which "rushes" the organism "forward so as to reach the final aim of life as swiftly as possible."[61] As initially formulated in 1920 in *Beyond the Pleasure Principle*, the death instinct in many ways functions as a linchpin to the Freudian system. Set in opposition to the life instinct (or eros), it "is held to represent the fundamental tendency of every living being to return to the inorganic state" and is characterized by Freud as the cardinal instinct, indeed, as the "factor which determines the actual *principle* of all instinct."[62] By means of this formulation, Freud for the first time was able not only to explicate the logic of masochism (a "perversion" for which he formerly could find "no satisfactory explanation"), but also to theorize an original erotogenic masochism that is not dependent on an inversion of the aggressive instinct.[63] In "The Economic Problem in Masochism" (1924) Freud consequently redefined masochism as a conjuncture of the death instinct with the libido, which is to say, as that part of the death instinct that "remains within the organism and is 'bound' there libidinally."[64]

In this context, *Suicide in B-Flat*, with its rush toward self-destruction and its doubled characters, seems a remarkably clear and conclusive playing out of masochistic fantasy. As Freud and his successors have pointed out, masochism is defined by a particular narrativization of the self. According to Laura Mulvey's celebrated formulation, "[s]adism demands a story, depends on making something happen, forcing a change in another person, a battle of will and strength, victory/defeat, all occurring in a linear time with a beginning and end."[65] So too with masochism. Indeed, masochism, of all the so-called perversions, is the one most dependent on fantasy and on a fully enunciated (if partly unconscious) scenario through which humiliation and pain are transformed into pleasure. In "'A Child Is Being Beaten,'" Freud analyzes masochistic scenarios in order to elaborate on the process by which repressed desire produces masochistic fantasy. Theodor Reik, meanwhile, in the most encyclopedic of the psychoanalytical works on masochism, details scores of fantasies and scenarios. Reik maintains that "[m]asochistic practices are but an acting out of preceding phantasies, daydreams that are transferred into reality." For Reik, the masochistic subject works like a dramatist, producing a highly ritualized and symbolic "scene" that "corresponds . . . to the staging of a drama."[66] This scene (or ritual) depends for its effectiveness on endless reiteration: "A change or disturbance of this masochistic ritual diminishes its lust-value."[67] Reik emphasizes that this scene, this drama, furthermore, is always on display, always being performed for a real or implied audience, always accompanied (not unlike the Brechtian scene) by a gesture of showing, of demonstrating. And although "[t]he demonstrative feature is essential to . . . masochism," the audience may be a willing participant in the drama or even the masochistic subject himself.[68] Reik observes that "[f]requently young men—rarely women—practice self-flagellation before a mirror."[69] Moreover, this scene (like the setting for *Suicide in B-Flat*) retains "a certain theatrical flavor" and the self-conscious "character of a performance."[70] Furthermore, the fantasies documented by Reik suggest that the emblematic masochistic drama, like a whodunit, is always predicated upon the prolongation of suspense, and that "masochistic tension vacillates more strongly than any other sexual tension between the pleasurable and the anxious."[71]

The formulation of the masochistic subject by Freud and his successors is always marked (as I have detailed in chapter 1) by a rupture within subjectivity itself. In moral masochism, the split occurs between ego and superego. Because the superego becomes "harsh, cruel and inexorable against the ego which is in its charge," the moral masochist seeks punishment, "whether from the super-ego within or from parental authorities without."[72] The so-called feminine masochist, on the other hand, is positioned "in a situation characteristic of womanhood": "degraded," "bound," "forced to obey unconditionally." The feminine masochist assumes guilt for having "committed some crime . . . which is to be expiated by his undergoing pain and torture."[73] (Significantly, Freud observes feminine masochism almost exclusively in men because, as Kaja Silverman points out, "it is an accepted—indeed a requisite—element of 'normal' female subjectivity.")[74]

In both of Freud's formulations, and in masochistic fantasy and performance, subjectivity is necessarily split into two parts. As he explains: "the most remarkable feature of this perversion is that its active and passive forms are habitually found to occur together in the same individual. . . . A sadist is always at the same time a masochist. . . ."[75] So in any and every masochistic subject, there is a sadistic part that fantasizes the infliction of pain and identifies with the real or imagined tormentor and a properly masochistic part that delights in its other's humiliation. Yet even this binary structure is, to my mind, insufficient to explain the complexity of masochistic subjectivity. As Reik points out, the bipolarity is always supplemented by a third term, a spectator, whether real or imagined, whose voyeuristic delight in the masochist's pleasurable pain redoubles it. Moreover, as Reik emphasizes, because the spectatorial position is always to some extent introjected, the masochist is always, as it were, performing in front of a mirror for his or her own exquisitely cruel pleasure.[76] If Reik is correct, then, there are three parts to the masochistic subject: sadist, masochist, spectator; one desiring to hurt, the second to be hurt, the third to watch the spectacle, each delighting to be simultaneously self, other, and destabilizing third term.

As an enactment of both masochistic fantasy and subjectivity, *Suicide in B-Flat* conforms almost uncannily well to the psychoanalytical paradigms. Formally, Shepard not only mobilizes the exemplary masochistic structure, the whodunit, the literary form that most arouses anxiety in the reader or spectator, but also finds a way of prolonging the suspense even beyond the play's end. By refusing finally to elucidate the mystery, which is to say, identify the victim, he leaves the reader or spectator in a state of frustrated and pleasurable unknowing that is by no means incompatible with the play's overriding comic tone (Reik emphasizes that masochistic performance "seldom becomes a matter of 'deadly earnest,'" as sadism often does).[77] Furthermore, Shepard is constantly taunting the reader or spectator, providing, by means of the various conflicting explanations of the crime, both a way of solving the case and the proof of its impossibility. And as is so often the case in masochistic practices that depend on ritualistic reiteration, the play's action clearly suggests a ceremony or, more exactly, a series of sacrificial performances in which identities are ritualistically both assumed and cast off. Paullette even labels the act of casting off a "ritual" (221).

Yet it is on the level of subjectivity that *Suicide in B-Flat* most strikingly conforms to the masochistic model. The apparent suicide, Niles, is clearly split in three, into an active and murderous self, a passive and suffering one, and a spectatorial self who observes and meditates upon the scene. Niles's fissured identity is introduced even before his entrance in the two biographies of Niles that Louis and Pablo construct. Both narratives focus on Niles the irascible genius who suffers (like so many other Shepard heroes) from a serious case of *dispossession*. In both fantasies, the jazz musician is radically alienated from his own body. According to Louis, Niles hears his own voice "like it belongs to another body. . . . He hears the crack of his own flesh" (196). In Pablo's more melodramatic narrative, Niles's "music was driving him mad" and he began to feel "possessed . . . by his own gift." "His own voracious hunger for sound became like a demon. Another body within him that lashed out without warning. That took hold of him and swept him away. Each time with more and more violence until his weaker side began to collapse" (203). According to Pablo, Niles's "weaker side" was destroyed by another body within, the active, sadistic, demonic part of the self. And late in the play, this process of destruction is literally enacted as Niles takes on two roles, the cowboy and the millionaire (by donning two costumes, "a kid's cowboy outfit" and "black tails") in order to kill off these two selves (212, 221).

Yet Niles is by no means the only masochistic subject here. Pablo and Louis, almost indistinguishable doubles (reminiscent of *The Right Stuff*'s two Recruiters), are themselves bound by a masochistic logic, unwittingly—and ridiculously—obstructing each other's efforts. "I know you've been trying to sabotage this project right from the start," Pablo warns his sidekick. "There's something in you that wants to destroy me" (198). Moreover, the suicidal circumstance that they have come to investigate becomes strangely conta- gious, or rather (like Reik's masochistic scene), subject to endless repetition and variation. Early in the play Louis "*suddenly*" and inexplicably "*puts the butcher knife up to his own neck as though about to kill himself.*" Then, Dr. Strangelove–like, he "*starts to struggle with one hand against the hand that's holding the knife against his neck,*" and he continues to struggle as the action goes on around him (203). This contagion points to a desperate sympathetic identification and even confusion between victim and detective that the farci- cal business by no means mitigates. When Niles's selves are shot, first with an arrow, then with a bullet, Louis and Pablo, respectively, are the ones who are hit, who feel the pain. "IT MAKES NO DIFFERENCE," Pablo exclaims, "WHETHER OR NOT WE WERE DESTROYED FROM WITHIN OR WITHOUT!" unable to separate inside from outside, suicide within from killer without (223). And when Niles finally turns himself in, the relationship between criminal and detective, inside and outside, self and other, becomes completely, finally, radically destabilized: "Are you inside me or outside me?" Niles asks his doubles,

> Am I buzzing away at your membranes? Your brain waves? Driving you beserk? . . . Or am I just like you? Just exactly like you? So exactly like you that we're exactly the same. So exactly that we're not even apart. Not even separate. Not even two things but just one. Only one. Indivisible.

When Niles finishes this speech, Pablo and Louis come up on either side of him and handcuff him "*so that all three are locked to each other,*" slave to master, master to slave, indissolubly linked in a logic of interchangeability, of absolute identification (229).

In its search for the killer within the self, for doubles that are at once radi- cally different and self-identical, *Suicide in B-Flat* stages the dynamics of masochistic desire *en abîme*, vertiginously rewriting the economy of self and other. The final image in the play is an image of masochistic desire fulfilled: the one in thrall to the other, to that upon which it depends for its identity, the criminal bound—emotionally, physically, violently—to the police. Working backward from this moment of completion, I believe that this master-slave dialectic is finally revealed to be the key to the construction of the categories of self and other in this play. In so doing it provides what is the master narra- tive not just of *Suicide in B-Flat* but of so many of Shepard's dramatic works: the self comes to believe that it has lost its true being because the latter has been hijacked by an other, outside the self. Separated from its inner essence,

feeling bereft, it is ineluctably drawn to this other that, it believes, both contains and is its true being. Desiring to assimilate this being, it shackles itself to
its other. Yet because it is unable to become or reincorporate its other, it can
only in the end reiterate its tragic enslavement ad infinitum (like the eagle and
the cat clawing each other to death in the final lines of *Curse of the Starving
Class*).[78] Moreover, as *Suicide* demonstrates, within this master-slave dialectic
the positions of self and other are always symmetrical and reversible. For
which subject, in the play's final tableau, is really the slave? Are not the police
as enslaved to the criminal as the criminal is to the police? Does not the one
find its identity, its very being, through its utter submission to the other? Yet
as *Suicide in B-Flat* makes clear (and as Hegel's master/slave dialectic confirms), this desire for the other is also the very ground of what is called self-
consciousness. As Judith Butler explains, "[s]elf-consciousness seeks a reflection of its own identity through the Other, but finds instead the enslaving and
engulfing potential of the Other."[79] Seeking itself, seeking its misplaced identity (remember the face blown off of the victim?), the subject tracks down the
other only to find that it is always already enthralled to the other, humiliated
and consumed by its double that is finally revealed to be sited catastrophically
both within and without the self.

THE VIOLENCE OF DESIRE

I began my analysis of the masculine mystique in Shepard by citing an interview in which he notes (as Niles might if he were more analytically inclined)
that because "humiliation," "inferiority," and "failure" are so "deeply rooted"
in the American male, the latter must "invariably" "act out" a "violent" "idea
of manhood." In other words, male subjectivity in Shepard is founded—masochistically—on a split between a passive and humiliated self and an active and
violent self. Desire then circulates between the two, with the self longing for
its other, which may be located either inside or outside the self—it makes little
difference which. The desire to submit or be submitted to that links the passive
to the active, one part to another part of the self, Niles to the police, the police
to Niles, is, I believe, the primary libidinal mode in Shepard's work (and in so
many recent cultural productions). Significantly, however, it is usually marked
less by eroticism than by *violence*, by a longing to dominate and consume the
other. For is not the violence that circulates between self and other the very
mark of desire, the sign by which desire becomes visible? And does not this
closed system—joining self with other, humiliation with exultation, pain with
pleasure—precisely describe the masochistic economy of desire?

A glance at *Suicide in B-Flat, The Tooth of Crime, Action,* or *True West* will
reveal that this masochistic logic produces both a distinctively masculinized
subject and an unmistakably masculine network of social relations. Shepard's

feminist critics have often pointed out that this network ensures that women in his plays almost without exception will assume peripheral roles: "men have their showdowns or face the proverbial abyss while women are absorbed in simple activities and simplistic thoughts."[80] Like the writings of the leaders of the men's movement, and like the plays of David Mamet, John Patrick Shanley, and many other playwrights, Shepard's works privilege the male bond as a kind of transcendental connection (like the "little brotherhood" denominated in *The Right Stuff*), while the writer himself observes in one interview, "It always seemed to me that there was more mystery to relationships between men. . . ."[81] Almost all of his plays attest to a level of intensity and "mystery" in male bonding that is rarely evident in relations between men and women (*Fool for Love* is perhaps the exception that proves the rule). This intensity leads Florence Falk, with some justification, to note that Shepard's masculine world is "essentially homoerotic," a claim contested by Alan Shepard who, noting how accusations of homosexuality function in Shepard's plays, asserts that, on the contrary, "Shepard's territory is not principally homoerotic but homophobic."[82]

Amending both Falk and Alan Shepard, I want to argue that Sam Shepard's writing produces a "brotherhood" that—like the culture of which it is a part— is *both* homoerotic *and* homophobic (and this too brings Shepard's masculinism perilously close to that of Bly and the men's movement). As Eve Kosofsky Sedgwick has pointed out, within a homophobic, patriarchal culture the range of male bonds is far less continuous than the range of female bonds. A clear demarcation separates male homosociality from male homosexuality, a demarcation, moreover, that is rigorously policed so as to insure that "'men-promoting-the-interests-of-men'" will not be confused with "'men-loving-men.'"[83] Within a patriarchal culture, the more intense male homosocial desire becomes, the more intensely male homosexual desire becomes stigmatized and proscribed. As Sedgwick emphasizes, this pattern has proven crucial at least since the early modern period for the maintenance of relations between men: "The importance . . . of the category 'homosexual' . . . comes not necessarily from its regulatory relation to a nascent or already-constituted minority of homosexual people or desire, but from its potential for giving whoever wields it a structuring definitional leverage over the whole range of male bonds that shape the social constitution."[84] For Sedgwick, the vigilant policing of the male bond ensures that desire between men will rarely be directly expressed in (what passes for heterosexual) discourse. Rather, by means of an erotic triangle, male desire is mediated through the body of a woman whom two men profess to love. As she observes, in this triangle, "the bond that links the two rivals is as intense and potent as the bond that links either of the two rivals to the beloved."[85]

Although none of Shepard's plays is focused squarely on an erotic triangle (*Fool for Love* is perhaps the closest to the Sedgwickian pattern), relations between men still unmistakably bear the mark of triangulation. The female object of desire may be absent or relegated to the background (as in *Forensic and the Navigators*), but Shepard's men are almost invariably locked into a system of intense competition less for power, glory, and the girl than for the distinction of being the toughest, most ornery, most angst-ridden, most rugged individual in the (true) West. The male subject in Shepard, especially in his plays of the 1970s, is articulated primarily through his relationships with other men, who invariably figure as both his alter egos and rivals, both other and same (Sedgwick emphasizes "that the bonds of 'rivalry' and 'love,' differently as they are experienced, are equally powerful and in many senses equivalent").[86] And his associations with them are as conflicted and unstable as the logic of identification and rivalry would suggest. The deep perturbation that is produced by this masochistic economy guarantees that the relation between self and other, double and rival, desire and hatred, will always be volatile. Rivalry drives a wedge between self and other, asserting at once absolute difference and absolute identification.

One effect of this volatility is the constant displacement of homoeroticism throughout Shepard's work (and this feature has been crucial, I believe, in producing Shepard as the emblematic American playwright of his era). On the one hand, as I have argued, there is an extraordinary overvaluation of and overinvestment in the male bond. On the other, this bond is also relentlessly subject to the brutal injunction against homosexual desire that organizes both Shepard's playwriting and, more generally, post–World War II American culture (the 1960s counterculture no less than the domestic revival before it).[87] As a result, the male bond is never explicitly or uncomplicatedly eroticized. Rather, it is always the site of intense anxiety, and the homoeroticism that perpetually threatens it is constantly being dislocated, evacuated of affect, or, more ominously, made discernible primarily as violence between men. In *The Tooth of Crime*, it figures in the deadly game of rivalry that Hoss and Crow play out, a dance of death and desire that ends with Crow's appropriation of Hoss's life, title, and girlfriend. (Crow twice humiliates Hoss by accusing him of being a "fag," and, if one is to believe Crow's vehement command, by forcing Hoss down to his knees in a state of abjection and sexual slavery: "Just get down on my thing boy! Just get down! Get on down!")[88] In *Suicide in B-Flat*, on the other hand, as male desire is more characteristically reconfigured as a fiercely competitive rivalry among all the men, its erotic dimension is almost entirely silenced and suppressed. Two of the more puzzling and obscure transactions in the play, however, unmistakably bear its imprint: Petrone's nearly inexplicable decision to sit on Pablo's lap, followed by Pablo's nearly inexplicable decision to sit on Louis's lap (these actions also point to the ineluctably contagious, even infectious, nature of male desire [200, 208]).

The volatility of male desires in Shepard and the extraordinary level of anxiety that they evoke guarantee that the masochistic scenario will be routinely heterosexualized, which is to say, submitted to the binary logic of gender. For as Freud's analysis suggests, the logic of masochism is gendered, and within a patriarchal culture, the active/passive binarism tends to be reinscribed within a masculine/feminine one. As a result of this reinscription, masculine desire in Shepard habitually produces violence against women or against another part of the male self that is obligatorily feminized. In a recent interview, Shepard specifies the connections among violence, the divided self, and the production of gender.

> You know, in yourself, that the female part of one's self as a man is, for the most part, battered and beaten up and kicked to shit just like some women in relationships. That men themselves batter their own female part to their own detriment.[89]

In *Suicide*, the two parts of Niles that are "battered" and killed off, the cowboy and the millionaire, the selves in the *"kid's cowboy outfit"* and in the *"black tails,"* are respectively infantilized and feminized in relation to the cool jazz musician who first appears *"dressed in a crumpled black suit"* and who is romanticized every bit as much as the black musicians in *On the Road* of whom he is, in some ways, a pale imitation (212, 221, 208). And while there is no explicit brutalizing of women in this play (as there is in *A Lie of the Mind*), the violence of desire still leaves its traces in the recurrent scream of a woman that punctuates the play. Listening in the dead silence, Pablo and Louis (mistakenly) think they hear the sound of "a woman screaming," "like a woman being tortured" (199). Shortly thereafter, the *"high shrill scream of a woman"* inexplicably sounds—a scream that, Shepard indicates, "should be delivered like a musical note," which is to say, aestheticized, made into an object for (masculine) consumption (200). And when Laureen enters, she for no apparent reason *"screams on a high note and continues the scream until she's crossed to center stage"* (205).

Despite these mysterious traces of sexual violence, gender roles in *Suicide in B-Flat* attest to a curious reversal that often occurs in masochistic texts. While Pablo and Louis, as "dicks," are unmistakably masculinized (they talk tough and act tough), the rest of the characters have much more unstable gender identifications (and even Pablo and Louis are feminized to some degree by virtue of their masochistic desires). The two female characters, Laureen and Paullette, appear as feminine (the former *"dressed in a bathrobe,"* the latter *"in a skimpy dress"*) but enact strangely masculinized roles (205, 208). Laureen, the player of a string bass, a low and resonant (i.e., masculine) instrument, seems almost indistinguishable from her colleague Petrone, while Paullette, despite her apparel, seems to the wear the pants in relation to Niles. Throughout the play she acts as his guide and chaperone. She is the one in the know, the one who protects and warns a hero who is, as I have indicated, feminized to an unusual degree, constantly battering and destroying his surrogate selves.

The particular mode of battering the self described here Freud called reflexive sadomasochism, and he described it as mediating between sadism and masochism proper. In "Instincts and Their Vicissitudes," he observes that "a primary masochism . . . seems not to be met with," and he argues instead that masochism represents a "reversal" of sadism (and the transformation of an active into a passive aim: "sadism turned round upon the subject's own ego"). But because this turning round is a "process," it includes an intermediate (or reflexive) stage in which the "object" of sadistic violence "is given up and replaced" not by an "extraneous person" but "by the subject's self." Unlike sadism or masochism proper, reflexive sadomasochism has the effect of splitting the subject's ego between a sadistic (or masculinized) half and a masochistic (or feminized) half. So the reflexive sadomasochist, rather than humiliate and master others, turns this impulse back upon him- or herself: "the desire to torture has turned into self-torture and self-punishment."[90] As Kaja Silverman points out, the reflexive sadomasochist differs from the feminine masochist (who "manifests a single-minded determination to inhabit the passive role") because of a "dual identificatory relation" to the sadomasochistic fantasy.[91] Both aggressor and victim, active and passive, masculinized and feminized, the reflexive sadomasochist always plays both roles, using the reflexive position simultaneously to eroticize and to disavow both domination and submission. And it is reflexive sadomasochism, I believe, that forms the "structuring action" of the new white male fantasmatic, producing the man whose violent instincts are turned not only against others but also against the self.[92] This is the figure who is ubiquitous in U.S. culture, whose likenesses populate the Patriot movement and who, since the mid-1970s, has come to dominate both mass and elite cultural representations (although, as *Suicide* suggests, it appears much more obliquely and esoterically in what remains of elite culture). Moreover, the reflexive sadomasochist also clearly marks a development of— and, in a strange way, a cure for—Lasch's new narcissist. For the main distinction between the two consists of the fact that the narcissist's sadistic superego becomes transferred to a part of the reflexive sadomasochist's ego. This displacement produces a male subject who is less guilty (because less tortured by his superego) and more seemingly tough because his sadism is directed at another part of the self.

Suicide in B-Flat, as an exercise in the self-torture of the fragmented subject, in the production of a seditious other within the self that may be punished and subjugated, represents a virtual textbook case of reflexive sadomasochism. And what of Shepard's other plays of the 1970s, *The Tooth of Crime*, *Action*, and *True West*? Are they not as well beholden to the logic of reflexive sadomasochism? Consider another fatal narrative, Shooter's story in *Action* about "a guy" who "began to fear his own body" until he was finally killed by it: "One day it just had enough and killed him." And then there is Jeep's self-torture in the play's final speech, as he describes his entrapment, his "stalking

[him]self" in a "*cell*" that he both remembers and creates anew as he speaks his lines: "I'd just crash against the wall. I'd just smash my head in. . . ."[93] (In both cases, the speaking subject is serendipitously masculinized at the expense of the subject represented in the utterance, who is figured as a fragile and feminized body.) Or consider the chorus of men in *The Tooth of Crime*. "I saw my face in yours," they sing, "I took you for myself / I took you by mistake—for me."[94] And then, they might have added (to oblige the logic of reflexive desire and simultaneously summarize the play's plot), I killed you, which is to say, I killed me. Theodor Reik provides an elegant distillation of the brutal (and brutalizing) logic of reflexive sadomasochism: "*As I do to you, so do I to me.*"[95]

In so many of Shepard's plays, reflexive sadomasochism functions as a kind of fantasmatic machine that relentlessly reproduces a tough male subject who proves his toughness by subjugating and battering his (feminized) other. Silverman emphasizes that "because it does not demand the renunciation of activity," reflexive sadomasochism "is ideally suited for negotiating the contradictions inherent in masculinity. The male subject can indulge his appetite for pain without at the same time calling into question . . . his virility. . . ."[96] Niles, Crow, Shooter, Jeep, and Austin prove their masculinity (and their ability to contain a mutinous self) by staging a battle with an other who is simultaneously figured as a part of the self. If Niles's masochism is the most flamboyant and fully dramatized of the five, perhaps that is the result of his being an artist, a jazz musician, the one most acutely in danger of being feminized, the one most insecure about his masculinity. "Does he make his women walk in ditches because he's so short?" Niles asks anxiously about his infantilized cowboy self. "Does he wear elevator cowboy boots?" (217). Reflexive sadomasochism allows Niles not only to subjugate but also, and more importantly, to disavow the tainted, artistic, feminized parts of the self by killing them off. It permits each of these Shepard protagonists to prove his manhood, to verify his strength and courage, to prove that he has the right stuff, by kicking his other "to shit."

BACKLASH

Pressing psychoanalysis into service for a historical project, I want now to examine the social, political, and economic struggles that I believe have determined the structure of the post-'60s white male fantasmatic. For reflexive sadomasochism—the linchpin, I am arguing, to a new American white masculinity—is far more than an idiosyncratic libidinal logic that Shepard happened upon in the early 1970s. Rather, it seems to me that it has been produced in response to five historical events: the reemergence of the feminist movement; the loss of the Vietnam War; the limited success of the civil rights movement in effecting a redress of gross historical inequities through affirmative action legislation; the rise of the lesbian and gay movements; and, perhaps most important, the end of the post–World War II economic boom and a resultant and steady decline in the income of white working- and lower-middle-class men.

During the late 1960s and early 1970s—the decisive moment in all five historical narratives—American women remained the targets of systematic economic discrimination. Women's wages actually declined between the late '50s and the early '70s, while "women workers continued to congregate at the lowest rungs of the economic ladder. . . ."[97] Even in the elite professions, a woman earned only forty-eight cents for every dollar earned by a man.[98] Women continued to be grossly underrepresented in government and in the public sphere. However, with the rebirth of the women's movement in the late 1960s, with calls for "self-determination" and "self-enrichment,"[99] with the consolidation of women's political groups ranging from reformist to separatist to Marxist, women came increasingly to acknowledge and deplore their subjugation under the terms of the domestic revival. With or without young children, they became increasingly committed not only to pursuing careers but also to working in traditionally masculine disciplines (the number of women entering law schools, for example, during the 1970s soared by 500 percent).[100] And American men began to feel sorely threatened, their economic privilege jeopardized for the first time. During the 1980s, as men's real wages shrank dramatically, they became increasingly anxious about gender roles. Many became enraged at what they perceived—incorrectly—to be women's sensational economic and social success, and "sexual violence against women," ranging from sexual harrassment, to domestic violence, to rape, saw "a spectacular rise."[101]

Just as American men were trying to manage these changes, they were also having to cope with the United States' first defeat on the battlefield in a notoriously unpopular war that more American men and women than ever before protested and resisted. The result of Cold War policies that mandated the containment of purported communist expansionism, the Vietnam War was an extraordinary drain on resources and finally necessitated the commitment of 540,000 American soldiers to a country that most Americans had never even heard of before the war began. In concert with other American imperialist exploits in Iran, the Dominican Republic, Chile, and El Salvador, it was a crucial step in the consolidation of the national security state after World War II and the permanent militarization of the U.S. economy. The cost of this intervention was, however, by any standard, appalling. An estimated three million Vietnamese were killed during the war, half of them civilians, while the countryside was devastated by carpet bombing and defoliation. On the American side, 55,000 lives were squandered, along with over $160 billion.[102] To some extent, the very magnitude of this disaster served to mask the devastating impact of the economic policies that had been pursued during war years. On the home front, the transition from an industrial to a service economy was proving difficult and costly. Spiraling inflation, soaring oil prices, and rising unemployment put an end to the post–World War II boom. In the early 1970s, the American standard of living fell to fifth in the world, while in 1974 alone the gross national product was off over 5 percent. The next year inflation reached 11 percent, and unemployment rose (from 4 percent in the 1960s) to almost 9 percent. Over the course of the next decade, the real discretionary income of the average worker was to fall 18 percent, while America was to become more and more obviously a two-tiered society (the postwar boom to some extent camouflaged class differences).[103] Whether one attributes the national trauma of the mid- to late 1970s to the failure in Vietnam or to an impasse of American capitalism, or to both, one thing is clear: disillusionment, mistrust, and guilt came to constitute the dominant disposition in a nation whose days of unparalleled prosperity and unlimited growth were numbered.

Yet this narrative of economic and social crisis remains fatally incomplete without noting the impact of the struggle of African Americans for equality. As has been widely acknowledged, the civil rights legislation of the 1960s marked a significant blow to institutionalized racism, outlawing discrimination in employment, labor unions, and all places of public accommodation, strengthening voting rights, and demanding that school desegregation proceed with "all deliberate speed." And during the 1960s, African Americans did make some significant gains. Black enrollment in colleges doubled during the decade, and the "proportion of black families earning more than $10,000 a year (in constant dollars) leaped from 13 percent in 1960 to 31 percent in 1971 (it had been 3 percent in 1947)."[104] But legislation alone could not transmute the long and violent history of racism and economic inequality in the United States. During the 1960s, the income of African Americans was still only 61 percent that of white Americans.[105] At the beginning of the next decade blacks owned less than 1 percent of America's businesses. Between 1945 and 1970 the ratio of black to white family income grew by only 4 percent. And the ratio of black unemployment to white actually increased between 1948 and 1965 (from 1.6 to 2.1).[106]

The remarkable level of prosperity of white men relative to women and African Americans by no means prevented them from later identifying themselves as the victims of the slender and precarious gains made by these groups. As the economy contracted during the mid-1970s and unemployment rates rose for both whites and blacks, the white response to the progress of black Americans began to shift.[107] The landmark case was the lawsuit that Allan Bakke, an ex-marine and Vietnam veteran, brought in 1974 against the University of California for twice denying him admission to its medical school at Davis. Insisting that the university's quota system for racial minorities violated his constitutional rights, Bakke styled himself a victim of discrimination. Four years later the Supreme Court, in an equivocal ruling that in some respects has proven more significant symbolically than for its practical effects, supported his claim, striking down quotas while upholding the principle of affirmative action. Liberals decried the decision. In his dissent, Thurgood Marshall pointed to an ignominious history of oppression, insisting that the "experience of Negroes in America is not merely the history of slavery alone, but also that a whole people were marked inferior by the law. And that mark has endured."[108] Jesse Jackson called the decision a "devastating blow to our civil rights struggle" and saw it—prophetically—as "consistent with the country's shift to the right, a shift in mood from redemption to punishment."[109]

Yet the *Bakke* decision was so widely debated and publicized (it made the cover of both *Time* and *Newsweek*) in part because it served as a sign of the emergence of a backlash against civil rights and affirmative action during a period of economic retrenchment, a sign of the desire for the "punishment" of African Americans for having purportedly compromised the white standard of living. Conservatives applauded the blow to what they—in an audacious attempt to equate the grievances of white males with the legacies of slavery— called "reverse racism," which, Robert Allen points out, "attempts to make racial minorities scapegoats for the problems that have been fostered by the inherent social irresponsibility of the corporations and banks that dominate" the U.S. economy.[110] Turning a blind eye to history (and anticipating the total amnesia that would characterize conservative discourse of the 1980s), one irate correspondent speciously blamed "minority fetishism" for a decline in American competitiveness and "law enforcement," for the decay of American cities, and for the deterioration of the public school system.[111] Yet as Allen emphasizes, these accusations end up blaming those who historically have been the victims of racist violence, and ignore the "institutional racism" that is maintained by the "'normal' operation of the institutional and capitalist market mechanisms."[112]

The severe recession of the mid-1970s and the end of the post–World War II economic boom had dire consequences for the United States. Not only did they stall the move toward social justice, but they also produced a backlash against feminism, affirmative action, and lesbian and gay civil rights. Moreover, they became imbricated with a sense of profound anxiety over the loss of the Vietnam War, and more generally over the United States' role as an imperial power. These signal changes, I am arguing, eventually produced a wholesale reconfiguration of white American masculinity, a reconfiguration that has proven a protracted and complex process. Just as the Vietnam War divided the country, so did it initially produce two competing versions of masculinity. As chapter 2 argues, during the late '60s, normative masculine identity continued to be organized around occupational stability and fatherhood, and the real man was supposed to be independent, adventurous, and morally upright. Yet among those young enough to protest the Vietnam War, "macho," as the writers of the *Newsweek* review of *The Right Stuff* point out, became virtually "a dirty word." It is precisely among this group, generally identified with the counterculture, that a new concept of masculinity began to take hold. For the Sam Shepard of *Suicide in B-Flat* and *The Right Stuff*, for the Robert Bly in search of "the deep masculine," the heroics of John Wayne were embarrassingly out of place. In reacting against this clamorous, confident virility, with its clearly defined boundaries and its relentless pursuit of enemies, Shepard and his generation reimagined the white male subject as if to solve the following problems: how can masculinity be reinvented to go beyond the polarizing logic of Cold War politics? How can it authenticate itself in a world grown increasingly suspicious of direct military intervention and the violent subjugation of native populations? How can it respond to the demands of feminism without forfeiting its male prerogative? How can it adjust to irrevocable economic decline? And perhaps most important, how can it be compatible with the fantasy of the white male as victim?

As the various European empires dissolved, as the older mode of colonial domination by foreign armies (as exemplified by the Vietnam War) was gradually dismantled, a neocolonialism emerged to consolidate an international division of labor (with the Third World serving as the First World's proletariat) along with a "free" market guaranteed not to disrupt the distribution of wealth both within a given nation and worldwide.[113] In the wake of African independence, after the fall of Saigon, as the World Bank and the International Monetary Fund replaced the colonial armies, as hegemony came to substitute for military might, and subtle coercion supplanted brute force, a new masculinity began to take shape in America that was no longer contingent either upon the production of enemies *out there* or upon nakedly imperialistic forays abroad. Having a new set of cultural conflicts to negotiate, it became more independent, more pliable, more apparently responsive to the demands of local populations and to the challenges posed by various rebellions (like the feminist insurgency). Yet at the same time, as the last vestiges of traditional societies were being penetrated by market forces, as the "older village structures and precapitalist forms of agriculture" in the Third World were being "systematically destroyed," as "nature" was increasingly being sacrificed to "culture," European-American men were becoming increasingly domesticated and bureaucratized.[114] For the professional, managerial, and technical sectors of the U.S. labor force had expanded so quickly that by the early 1970s the United States had become "the only country to employ more people in services than in the production of tangible goods."[115] Under these circumstances, it became all the more urgent that the masculine fantasmatic be reconstructed to bear the unmistakable traces of a robust, independent, and entrepreneurial masculinity. The new fantasmatic of the 1970s, therefore, features not the gallant commander leading his regiment to glory for traditional American (that is, imperialistic) principles but the lone guerrilla, making his way through the dark jungle, picking off enemy soldiers, on a dangerous and mysterious mission; or the test pilot described by Tom Wolfe, fascinatedly peering into the abyss:

> the idea here . . . seemed to be that a man should have the ability to go up in a hurtling piece of machinery and put his hide on the line and then have the moxie, the reflexes, the experience, the coolness, to pull it back in the last yawning moment—and then go up again *the next day*, and the next day, and every next day, even if the series should prove infinite.

No matter what pain he might experience, or what morbid medical condition he might develop from his Icarus-like exploits, "he shows not the slightest concern . . . that the condition might be permanent and affect him in whatever life awaits him outside the arena of the right stuff."[116] He learns to master his frail body, to make it submit absolutely and repeatedly to the cruelty of his will. Not only does reflexive sadomasochism provide the ideal mechanism to turn this new hero's pain into pleasure, but it also allows him to adjust to the exigencies of living in a (post)feminist and post-*Bakke* culture. It authorizes him to be both wild and domestic, to cultivate a "feminine" part of the self (or at least to endure his feminized flesh), and at the same time to subjugate it violently, and to take on the roles simultaneously of humanitarian and of casualty of feminism and affirmative action. It allows him to play the part of victim and yet be a man.

And this is where the men's movement comes in again. For what is perhaps most remarkable about Robert Bly's rhetoric of "the deep masculine" is its stress on a primordial and untouchable inwardness, its ability to produce a pure and fantasmatic virility that will accord with polite social norms while leaving unsullied "the Wild Man" within. As I have noted above, this fantasmatic, like Shepard's, is founded not on a unitary or self-identical subject but on a divided subject, on a masculine self within that inevitably works a violence upon a feminized, acculturated other. Furthermore, this fantasmatic (despite appeals to the contrary) is unequivocally heterosexualized and racialized. I have already detailed the distress and violence that circulate around the homosocial/homosexual boundary in Shepard's work. In some ways the men's movement betrays an even greater anxiety in relation to this same boundary (Connell emphasizes the all-male constituency, noting that the movement is "a mirror-image of the separatist feminism of the late 1970s").[117] Bly does not even broach the possibility of male homosexuality in the main text of *Iron John*. Yet he dares maintain in the preface that although "[m]ost of the language in this book speaks to heterosexual" men, it "does not exclude homosexual men," and that the underlying "mythology . . . does not make a big distinction" between the two (x). (Proceeding from bad faith to gross historical inaccuracies, he then notes: "It wasn't until the eighteenth century that people ever used the term homosexual; before that time gay men were understood simply as a part of the large community of men" [x]).[118] In fact, however, even a cursory reading of the text will reveal that the mythologies invoked are unremittingly hetero-sexual. Indeed, the Grimm fairy tale on which the book is based is very clearly an expression of that most emblematic of patriarchal narratives (as detailed by Teresa de Lauretis) in which a masculine hero goes on a quest, overcomes formidable obstacles, and finally wins a distinctively feminine prize (here, "the King's daughter" [258]).[119] Moreover, the thoroughgoing biological essential-ism disallows the facile substitution of one sex for the other. There is no room in *Iron John* for erotic desire between men because his mythology is abso-lutely incapable of accommodating it. Furthermore, the testimony of partici-pants at Bly's weekend retreats indicates that male bonding can occur only under the auspices of fear, under the cover of a deep-seated homophobia which ensures that men-sustaining-men will never be mistaken for men-loving-men. Even Don Shewey, in his defense of gay men in the men's movement, admits to the underlying homophobia. He quotes an observation made by Michael Meade (one of Bly's right-hand men), "Well, you know, the brothers are very homophobic," and notes that in Bly's presence, "when gay topics come up, he tends to change the subject quickly."[120] Both in *Iron John* and in the move-ment, male homosexuals represent what Judith Butler describes as "a domain of abject beings, those who are not yet 'subjects,' but who form the constitu-tive outside to the domain of the subject," a dangerous and perverse identity that must be silenced, disavowed, or displaced.[121] If nothing else, the men's movement (like Shepard's plays) confirms the homophobic cultural logic that the more closely bonds between men are drawn, the more crucial becomes the injunction against becoming, in the words of a weekend participant, one of those gay "vampires."[122] Furthermore, despite the participation of a few Afri-can-American men in the movement, Bly's "mythopoetics" remains a "white mythology," firmly rooted in imperialistic fantasies.[123] One of the most reveal-ing moments in *Iron John*, in regard to both the racialization of "the Wild Man" and his masochistic proclivities, is the story of an African initiation ritual (Bly describes this as "[o]ne of the best stories [he's] heard") in which a boy, after having fasted for three days, sits in a circle with a group of older men. "One of the older men takes up a knife, opens a vein in his own arm, and lets a little of his blood flow into a gourd or bowl." And so around the circle. "When the bowl arrives at the young man, he is invited to take" a drink. Bly comments that in this way, the boy not only learns to take "nourishment" from men, "he also learns that the knife can be used for many purposes besides wounding others" (15). In other words, he learns that the knife can always be turned against the self and that the act of self-mutilation is the purest and most absolute expression of virility. Fortuitously, this writing of masculinity upon the male body does not require willing partners. Give the man a weapon, let him slice up his own flesh, let him prove himself a warrior. And all the better that this lesson should be taught the white American male by African bodies, by black bodies who, in Bly's imperialist fantasy, approximate "the deep masculine" far more effectively than does the Western subject, marooned as he is in a feminized culture. And yet, does not the *desire to be the other*, to appropriate his cultural apparatus, at the same time betray a barely concealed *terror of the other*? Does not this narrative, and the masochistic logic that drives it, represent the last stand of the embattled white male imagining himself (in the words of Tom Metzgar of the White Aryan Resistance), a "new nigger," now grown enraged and paranoid at seeing his economic power challenged not only by women but also by those dark-skinned others, whether in the Third World or within America's inner cities?[124]

THE SPECTACLE OF MASCULINITY

Like Sam Shepard, Sylvester Stallone is a mystique-wrapped figure who has been styled both actor and auteur. He has impersonated as well as scripted or coscripted two of the most popular movie heroes of all time, Rocky Balboa and John J. Rambo. With the sensational success of the two series during the 1980s, he became the highest-paid actor in movie history (up until that time). In the Rambo series, in particular, with its endless action sequences and jingoistic homilies, he was able virtually to abjure spoken language (never, as is also true of Shepard, his strong point as an actor) and hone his muscle-bound image to glistening perfection. All three films—*First Blood* (1982), directed by Ted Kotcheff; *Rambo: First Blood Part II* (1985), directed by George P. Cosmatos; and *Rambo III* (1988), directed by Peter Macdonald—were cowritten by Stallone and are based on (or based on characters from) David Morrell's 1972 novel, *First Blood*. The first was the big hit of the fall 1982 season, while the success of the sequel was legendary. It earned $32 million its first week (at the time, the third strongest opening in history), and for months held America in the grip of what *Time* magazine called "Rambomania."[125] The third, in contrast, the least successful (and interesting) of the three, was "something of a disaster with the 'untimely' Russian withdrawal from Afghanistan."[126] Nonetheless, with its celebration of macho individualism (unlike the buddy movies that followed) and its nearly fascistic politics, the Rambo trilogy seemed to tap into the zeitgeist of the decade brilliantly.

While at first glance it may appear that Rambo, as a working-class hero, is far removed from the more elitest productions of Robert Bly and Sam Shepard, it is my contention that the films not only provide a privileged perspective on post-Vietnam American culture but also evince a hegemonic masculinity uncannily similar to the one that circulates in the works of Stallone's more literary brethren. In a sense, the three films literally flesh out the masochistic fantasies that underlie the work of Bly and Shepard, in particular, and of post-Vietnam machismo more generally. Susan Jeffords is certainly correct to note that the Rambo films are paradigmatic of a historical shift, occurring at the beginning of the Reagan era, which, after the demasculinizing '70s, bore witness to a resurgence of hard, masculine bodies on the screen that "reestablished the boundaries not only of the individual masculine figure but of the nation as a whole."[127] Yet for all their bravado and hardness, the three Rambo movies figure masculinity not as an unconflicted and pure phallicism but as a contradictory, mysterious, and even strangely feminine business, one constantly under siege, not just from enemies without, but, even more ominously, from the enemy within. And here I must differ with Jeffords who, in her fine analysis of the first two films, emphasizes "the devictimization of the white male" that they undertake.[128] And while, certainly, all three (especially *Rambo*) go to great lengths to enforce that devictimization, it is, in my view, a much more deeply conflicted and compromised enterprise.

The three films clearly attempt, by replaying the Vietnam War (the first in the forests of the Pacific Northwest, the second in Vietnam itself, and the third in Afghanistan), to reclaim the victimized white male (and Vietnam veteran) as hero. John J. Rambo (Sylvester Stallone) is a former Green Beret and Congressional Medal of Honor winner who in *First Blood*, mistaken for a drifter and leftover hippie, is arrested by a small-town police chief, Teasle (Brian Dennehy), only to escape from jail and blockade himself in the forest. The American flag sewn onto his army fatigue jacket signals his cultural undecidability—both hippie and patriot—thereby blurring the line between the two identities and signaling an important link between the new man of the '80s and his countercultural predecessor. Battered, bloody, and practicing a kind of makeshift guerrilla warfare, he maims most of the local police force and the National Guard sent out after him (the fact that he refrains from actually killing anyone only demonstrates his extraordinary prowess and control). In the final sequence, confronted by his former Green Beret commander, Trautman (Richard Crenna), he gives a tearful, self-pitying speech and surrenders himself to the authorities. The sequel finds him several years later in a prison camp from which he is rescued by Trautman to perform a top-secret mission, searching for prisoners of war allegedly still held captive in Vietnam. Parachuted into the jungle and assisted by a Eurasian woman, Co Bao (Debra Paget), he locates a small cadre and frees a prisoner but is betrayed by a government thug named Murdock (Charles Napier) who was supposed to have rescued him. After being captured and brutally tortured by a sadistic Soviet commander, and after the death of Co Bao, he single-handedly fights his way back to the base camp in Thailand with all the POWs, slaughtering scores of Vietnamese and Soviet soldiers along the way, only to corner the cowardly Murdock and contemptuously spare his life. *Rambo III*, meanwhile, takes Rambo from a Buddhist monastery in Thailand (to which he has retreated after the carnage of *Rambo*) to the mountains of Afghanistan, where he joins the mujahideen, rescues his friend, Trautman, from another sadistic Soviet commander, and slaughters hundreds of Soviet troops.

Despite the obvious connections among the films, they feature, in fact, what can be described only as two different Rambos. Although the title character of *Rambo* and *Rambo III* is recognizably the same, he "shift[s] dramatically," in Jeffords's words, between *First Blood* and *Rambo*, becoming more conventionally heroic and imperialistic in the sequel (his fury is more other-directed, and he is more clearly an actor in an imperial arena).[129] I believe, however, that it is useful to read them together, insofar as characteristics that remain latent in one Rambo inevitably become overt in the other (and in this sense, they are oddly reminiscent of Pablo and Louis in *Suicide in B-Flat*). They both find themselves the victims of treacherous American authorities, and they share a compulsion to venture forth on solitary and extremely dangerous enterprises. Like Yeager in *The Right Stuff*, they display a courage that frequently slides over into an almost suicidal recklessness. Moreover, both characters move in almost exclusively male communities (Co Bao is the only even halfway substantial female role in all three films), and both hold most dear their compatriots who fought in Vietnam and were abandoned by a callous and ungrateful government. Both heroes use their body as their primary weapon, and both repeatedly display an almost preternatural ability to withstand physical pain. Perhaps most important, however, the hypermasculine Rambo of all three films is consistently transformed into a spectacle to be consumed. When he is forced to shower in the police station at the beginning of *First Blood*, his perfect physique is unveiled, marred only by the scars he wears from Vietnam. And even when prodded during the succeeding interrogation, he is unwilling (or unable) to take up the position of the speaking subject—he negotiates not with words but with his body. His rippling flesh thereby attests to the remarkable popularity in mainstream cinema during the 1980s of white men as spectacularized objects of desire.

In all three films, however, the process of making Rambo a spectacle produces intriguing side effects. On the one hand, his enormous strength, self-confidence, and resilience clearly mark him as a phallic male, as the one, indeed the only one in the trilogy, who "has" the phallus. On the other hand, his masculinity and his muscles are so constantly and extravagantly on parade that he simultaneously undergoes what can be described only as a feminization. David Denby notes in his review of *Rambo* that "the camera seems to have developed a peculiar, not to say pathological, interest in Sylvester Stallone's body"—an interest that is coded as "pathological" because in Hollywood narrative cinema it is associated with the female, not the male, body (Lacan observes that both "virile display" and the "exaggeration of masculinity" appear as "feminine").[130] As Laura Mulvey famously points out, the cinematic apparatus (along with a masculinized spectatorial gaze) "play[s] on [the audience's] voyeuristic phantasy" by turning a woman into "an objectified other," an object of scopophiliac desire.[131] What makes *Rambo* so "peculiar" (if not to say queer), is that Stallone's perpetually oiled body is subject to precisely the same objectification. Just before Rambo is to leave for Vietnam, the camera catches him in preparation for his mission. The sequence begins with a shot of his tanned and rippling right shoulder that is filmed in such extreme close-up that the flesh seems more cinematic hallucination than recognizable musculature. The camera then slowly tracks down his bulging biceps and forearm to his hand and comes to rest on his knife, his lethal weapon, which is submitted to an almost microscopic scrutiny. What is so remarkable about this sequence, and, indeed, about *Rambo*'s repeated spectacularization of Stallone's body, is that it insistently figures Rambo—with his knife—as a fetish object, as "a perfect product, whose body, stylised and fragmented by close-ups, is . . . the recipient of the spectator's look."[132] Rambo is not only the one who "has" the phallus, he is also the one who "is" the phallus, the one whose body, under electric-shock torture in *Rambo*, is subject to precisely the rhythm of tumescence and detumescence that characterizes a phallic economy. As a result of his dual identification, Rambo cannot be said simply and unassumingly to embody masculinity. He *performs* it or, rather, reveals that it is always already a performance, not just for the audience but also for his own narcissistic pleasure. He thereby becomes, in the words of Barbara Creed, "an anthropomorphised phallus, a phallus with muscles," a "simulacr[um] of an exaggerated masculinity."[133] His rippling flesh thereby attests to the fact that at least this white male as victim is constructed as a spectacularized object of desire, and that during the 1980s the "white male body," as Jeffords notes, "became increasingly a vehicle of display—of musculature, of beauty, of physical feats, and of a gritty toughness."[134]

The dual identification of Rambo (as both hypermasculine and feminized, as both "having" and "being" the phallus) seems to me to be crucial to an understanding of both the fantasies of the white male as victim and the contradictory positions he repeatedly occupies in all three films. Rambo is not simply the passive object of the spectator's gaze but the producer of a near fatal gaze (especially in *Rambo*), his deep, droopy brown eyes always alert, omniscient, watching, whether through the jungle foliage or the floorboards of a Vietnamese hut. Moreover, like the masculine ideal in both *Iron John* and *Sexual Suicide*, he is allied far more compellingly with "nature" than with "culture." Refusing to participate in commodity culture, he prefers his own self-made, primitive tunic in *First Blood* to police garb and then, in town, giddily destroys the signs of consumerism, the Dairy Queen and the gas station. In *Rambo* (in a clearly racist construction) he is said to be "of Indian-German descent." On the one hand, he is shown to be instinctual and autochthonous, literally of the earth (one of the most extraordinary moments in *Rambo* occurs when he magically materializes out of the mud, as though out of the earth itself, to kill a Soviet soldier). And in the three films he seems to be more "Indian" than "German," more animal than human, a creature relying on reflexes and brute strength more than intellect. Furthermore, both his retreat into the forest and his expedition to Vietnam are clearly coded as a move back to an ostensibly primeval state whose alignment with "nature" is inevitably underscored by his discarding of clothing. On the other hand, his "German"—which is to say, Aryan—half makes him cunning and ingenious, uniquely capable of taking what lies at hand and turning it into a deadly weapon. And it is this half that seems to ally him with the sky (one of the most memorable sequences in *First Blood* is his descent from the wall of a cliff to the canyon below, and in *Rambo* and *Rambo III* his escape in stolen Soviet helicopters). Moreover, it is his "German" half that distinguishes him racially from the Vietnamese and the Afghans, in contrast to whom he seems a luminous giant on an imperialistic spree. A high-tech simulacrum of the White Aryan Resister, holed up in the woods or off rescuing his comrades betrayed by cowardly federal authorities, he is simultaneously an Aryan and a "new nigger."

Yet what is perhaps most striking about John J. ("what you choose to call hell, he calls home") Rambo is his rigorous submission to a sadomasochistic economy of desire. His simultaneous identifications with the masculine and the feminine, with "nature" and "culture," ensure that he will always be at war with himself. "You're always going to be tearing away at yourself until you come to terms with what you are," Trautman warns him in *Rambo III*. In all three films his derring-do seems to be driven by a mechanism very close to the death instinct.[135] In *First Blood*, in particular, Rambo ("a man who's been trained to ignore pain") brings disaster upon himself by refusing to hearken to the law, or rather, by willfully setting himself up as an alternative authority (much like the armed militias, the Montana Freemen, or David Koresh and the Branch Davidians), motivated not by heroic principles but by a belated sense of grief over his dead comrades. "You did everything to make this private war happen," Trautman rebukes him in the final scene. Furthermore, in all three films Rambo undergoes an extraordinary sequence of ordeals. He is stripped, tortured, beaten, bombed, shot at, electrocuted, overrun with rats, and suspended in pig shit. In *First Blood*, he sutures his own wounded arm, while in *Rambo III* he performs surgery on himself, removing an enemy projectile from his side and cauterizing the wound with gunpowder. These ordeals, I would argue, must be seen as being self-willed, as being the product of his need to prove his masculinity the only way he can, by allowing his sadistic, masculinized half to kick his masochistic, feminized flesh "to shit" (Pauline Kael remarks that "like Rocky, Rambo always has to have bigger guys in his movies . . . to beat him up").[136] And intriguingly, Rambo's ordeals are echoed by Stallone's own masochistic proclivities. According to a *Newsweek* profile,

Stallone has developed a real hankering for pain: "'If I don't break a few ribs,' he says [of his film fighting], 'I think it's bad luck.'" And when shaving, he "refuses to use shaving cream, or even water, preferring, he says with a laugh, 'to gross out my girlfriend . . . by coming downstairs every morning looking like someone used my face for a dart board.'" Even his muscles function as a signifier of pain, of an arduous five-hour daily workout that "sometimes brings his body fat to such dangerously low levels that 'I'm so woozy, I can't remember my own phone number.'"[137] So both the star Stallone and the character Rambo prove the efficacy of reflexive sadomasochism as a libidinal logic that produces a heroic male subject who proves his toughness by subjugating and battering a feminized other, an other that has mysteriously taken up residence within the self. Kaja Silverman emphasizes that "because it does not," unlike other kinds of masochism, "demand the renunciation of activity," reflexive sadomasochism "is ideally suited for negotiating the contradictions inherent in masculinity. The male subject can indulge his appetite for pain without at the same time calling into question . . . his virility."[138]

Stallone's extraordinarily successful film career has been built on two principles: his taste for spectacles, which, according to *Newsweek*, "biannually transform . . . a body beautiful into a human blood blister," and his ability to produce two lucrative series of films.[139] For despite the fact that Rocky (especially in the first three films) and Rambo have very different antagonists and that Rocky ends up rich and famous (unlike the more demonstratively victimized Rambo), both sets of films rely on the same libidinal logic. It seems especially apt that sadomasochism has proven the perfect engine for Stallone's Rocky and Rambo series because the sadomasochistic scenario will allow no resolution—only sequels—since the battle with the self by definition can never be resolved. (Furthermore, given the Rambo trilogy's eschewal of a heterosexualized teleology, marriage never appears as an option.) Because masculinity is figured in his films as not a presence but a lack, as not a stable state of being but a performance, he must continually restage his inner struggle, challenging himself anew, since it is only in the instant of triumph that he can become (narcissistically) fully present to himself. His heroically scarred body thereby serves, ironically, as a reminder that he does not finally "have" the phallus, and that his desire can be fulfilled only through a sadomasochistic reiteration which commemorates ad infinitum both his limitless desire for pain and his perpetual victory over pain. At the same time and more disturbingly, the obsessively sadomasochistic bent of Stallone's Rambo is linked inextricably to his reactionary politics (so deeply appreciated by the Reaganite Right during the '80s and the partisans of the Patriot movement who, like Rambo, feel betrayed by the federal government).[140] By aiming destruction not only at others but also at the self, by becoming a self-righteous near-martyr, a target of the "evil Empire," Rambo gains moral authority and turns his own imperialistic violence into what passes, in some quarters at least, for justice.

Even more suggestively, however, the Rambo series attests to an indissoluble link in contemporary culture between the spectacularized male subject and the masochistic economy of desire. For within a homophobic culture, the spectacle of the male body is a perilous and anxiety-producing commodity, all too easily coded (as in Kael's review of *Rambo*) as homoerotic.[141] *First Blood* and *Rambo* attempt to disavow the homoeroticism implicit in Rambo's status as an object of the masculinized gaze in two ways. First, *First Blood* (like most action movies) evokes male homosexuality not as sexual deviance, as love between men (a very slippery and dangerous category in this tale of passionate male bonding), but as gender deviance, as a kind of feminization ("Afraid of the bogeyman, goddamn pansy?" one policeman taunts another). Within this framework, Rambo's hypermasculine strength, accoutrements, and tools would appear to inoculate him against being the object of a homoerotic gaze. For he is clearly phallicized in relation to the flabby Teasle, the ineffectual police deputies, and the inept National Guardsmen (one of these domesticated "weekend warriors" whines that he cannot help dig up the collapsed mine shaft because he has to be back at the drugstore). Second, and most important, Rambo's masochism, his insistent self-production as a victim of torture, works to protect him from being an object of male desire. As Jeffords notes (drawing on the work of Steve Neale), "the chief mechanism in mainstream cinema for deferring eroticism in the heterosexual male body is through establishing that body as an object of violence, so that erotic desire can be displaced as sadomasochism."[142] Any delight that the male spectator might derive from watching Rambo's rippling flesh is mitigated by the fact that that same flesh is insistently brutalized and turned into a spectacle of pain which the spectator might be expected, if not to avert his eyes from, at least to wince at. Ironically, however, this process serves only to extend the sadomasochistic economy and make the spectator complicit in the sadomasochistic transaction. If Rambo is produced as both spectacularized object and desiring subject (and if, as Janet Bergstrom maintains, the cinematic apparatus always produces both desire and identification), then a part of the spectator will inevitably take on a sadistic role, enjoying the spectacle of the body in pain, while another part will take on a masochistic role, identifying with the victim.[143] In the extraordinary proliferation of films during the 1980s in which men are figured as objects of scopophiliac desire (from the Rambo, *Lethal Weapon*, and *Terminator* series to *The Right Stuff*), sadomasochism functions to facilitate the male spectator's disavowal of a homoerotic investment. But does this disavowal work? Does the spectacle of the male body in pain actually foreclose desire? Are not sadomasochism and homoeroticism always mutually imbricated in a patriarchal culture that cannot accept the truth (to which the Rambo trilogy so obviously attests) that its investment in male homosociality is far stronger than its investment in the heterosexual bond? And cannot pain also be understood as the inevitable price of looking, the price a man must pay for desiring another man? In this context, it seems singularly appropriate that John J. Rambo's name should echo that of his homonymic forebear, Arthur (*A Season in Hell*) Rimbaud.[144]

The homosocial and homophobic bravado of the new masculinity suggests that in some ways it represents a continuation of the masculinity that was normalized during the height of the domestic revival, with its violent crusades against alleged communists and homosexuals. Bly longs nostalgically for the good old days of the Cold War, noting that "[t]he Fifties male had a clear vision of what a man was" (although quibbling with "the isolation and one-sidedness of his vision" [2]). Moreover, both *The Right Stuff* and the Rambo trilogy reexamine and replay crucial battles of the Cold War in order to consolidate the delusion, so dear to Reagan's heart, that the American empire remains triumphant and invulnerable. Both look longingly at the past and refigure a war that, as Michael Rogin explains, "was fought mainly with symbols and surrogates," as a spectacle for mass consumption.[145] Both reconstruct masculinity in the ruins of Cold War culture, turning the "macho" man into a spectacle in the hope that his self-inflicted pain will redeem that heroism which a cynical culture finds both embarrassing and irresistibly alluring.

I have already set forth a number of reasons why I believe reflexive sadomasochism has become the distinctive feature of the new, post-Vietnam white male as victim. Yet there is another register in which this figuration plays itself out that must be investigated. For coincidental with the ascendancy of the sadomasochist has been both the rise of poststructuralism in the U.S. academy and the embrace by many poststructuralist theorists of the idea that the disintegration of the liberal humanist subject offers radically subversive possibilities.[146] Several contemporary theorists of sexuality, in developing this thesis, regard male masochism, in particular, as posing an irresistible threat to the imaginary coherence of the unitary subject. Kaja Silverman sees masochism (because it betrays the "phallic standard") as one of several "'deviant' masculinities" that "represent a tacit challenge not only to conventional male subjectivity, but to the whole of our 'world.'" And although she recognizes that the reflexive position can all too easily operate "at the behest of a terrifying psychic imperialism," she argues forcefully that these dissident masculinities "call sexual difference into question, and beyond that, 'reality' itself."[147] Leo Bersani, meanwhile, in *The Freudian Body* (1986), insists rather notoriously that sexuality (which for him is "ontologically grounded in masochism") is inherently destabilizing and "intolerable to the structured self." And although Bersani has qualified these claims in *Homos* (1995), he argues in the earlier work that sexual excitement inevitably produces radical possibilities by "shattering" and disturbing the desiring subject.[148]

While I agree with Silverman and Bersani that male sadomasochism splits the male subject (or rather, reveals the rift that is always already constitutive of subjectivity), I do not agree that reflexive sadomasochism, at least as it circulates in contemporary American culture, offers a radical challenge to the "structured self," let alone to "the whole of our 'world.'" Rather, I see the insistent bifurcation of the male subject (in Bly, Shepard, Stallone, and elsewhere) as a way (contradictorily) of preserving and even consolidating his imaginary coherence. In an essay analyzing the "vital function" of "masochistic activities" within "the narcissistic sector of the personality," Robert Stolorow argues that both masochism and sadism often function "to repair . . . damaged self-repesentation." Rather than endangering the coherence of the subject, they prove particularly useful in times of psychic—and, I would like to add, social and economic—crisis because they can operate "to restore and maintain the structural cohesiveness, temporal stability and positive affective colouring of a precarious or crumbling self-representation." Reflexive sadomasochism, in particular, with its self-contained, narcissistic system of gratification, would seem particularly adept at reconstructing an independent, autonomous, masculine subject and "re-establishing a sense of existing as a bounded entity, a cohesive self."[149] For does not the reflexive sadomasochist's illusory autonomy make him an ingenious revision of the voluntarist subject—self-contained, individualistic, and beholden to no one? Furthermore, as *Rambo* makes clear, spectacularization and feminization by no means demand phallic divestiture.

Moreover, Bly's and Shepard's analogous positionings of the male subject on the side of self-division, grief, and lack hardly disguise what seems so clearly an attempt to reclaim a vigorous, if masochistic, male subject for a postfeminist culture in which "'macho' has [become] a dirty word." As Reik argues, masochism does not always require the repudiation of power or will. Drawing on Freud's observation that "[a] sadist is always at the same time a masochist," he emphasizes both the fluidity of these identifications and the instability of the sadomasochistic contract.[150] For he recognizes that masochism by no means entails a complete renunciation of power. Rather, the masochist gains a certain authority by proving that he or she can take whatever is being dished out. Thus, "by a peculiar detour," he or she "attempts to maintain his ego, to enforce his will. . . . The lambskin he wears hides a wolf." Like the "yielding" of Rambo, the masochist's "yielding includes defiance," and "his submissiveness[,] opposition."[151] Judith Butler, pointedly responding to Silverman, speculates, "I would question whether the strategies of male masochism and 'feminization' . . . couldn't also be construed as a subtle strategy of the phallus, a ruse of power—that's to say that 'divestiture' could be a strategy of phallic self-aggrandizement."[152] And, as Paul Smith notes, the narrativization of male masochism in cultural texts represents a "way for the male subject to temporarily . . . subvert the phallic law" while "guaranteeing" that he remain "the origin of the production of meanings."[153] If one accepts these arguments, then the work of Silverman and Bersani takes on a rather different cultural significance. For the insistent substitution by these theorists of psychoanalysis for history, which renders them incapable of analyzing the material forces that have foregrounded the masochistic white male subject at this particular historical moment, must itself be read historically. In their work, that incapacity is coupled with scant attention to the fact that their exemplary masochistic male subjects are almost always demonstratively or implicitly white. Yet they consider neither the history of white masculinity (in the United States or elsewhere) nor the fact that its meaning has changed radically since the 1960s. I would like to suggest that their admittedly ambivalent celebration of male masochism represents as much a symptom as it does a critique of the increasing naturalization in U.S. culture of narratives and images of the white male as victim. It demonstrates that theory is as subject to the exigencies of history as the texts it purports to decode.

THE WHITE MALE AS VICTIM

As constructed in the work of Shepard, Stallone, and Bly, the white male as victim may take "a peculiar detour" to pleasure, but he has not seen his economic and political authority significantly decline. One recent survey compares the racial and sexual distribution of senior corporate executives between 1979 and 1989. It finds that in those ten years the proportion of African Americans had increased from 0.2 to 0.6 percent, of Latinos from 0.1 to 0.4 percent, and of women from 0.5 to 3 percent of the total.[154] Yet many white American men now consider themselves an oppressed group, the victims of discrimination, intolerance, and "reverse racism." "The white male," one protests, "is the most persecuted person in the United States."[155] "European males," one African-American man is quoted as saying, "have always had the propensity to say 'I feel threatened' while holding a gun to somebody else's head."[156] And the mainstream press has remained tellingly ambivalent on the subjects of the white male as victim and "reverse racism," both critiquing and disseminating these mythologies. On the one hand, it sometimes appears eager to debunk the claim the "the white male [is] truly an endangered species" or an oppressed class.[157] On the other hand, it has, especially since the 1994 election, made white male victimization a major political issue, reporting characteristically that "[s]ome of the white male pique is no doubt justified" insofar as "some white men surely have seen minorities and women of lesser competence pass them by."[158] Only after the Oklahoma City bombing did the press even begin to consider that there might be a relationship between the mythology of the white male as victim and the growth of the paramilitary Right.[159]

Most important, the press has significantly underreported the massive upward redistribution of wealth in the United States since the late 1970s. For senior corporate executives may remain overwhelmingly white and male, but they do not swell the ranks of the White Aryan Resistance. Working- and lower-middle-class white men, on the other hand, the ones most involved with the Patriot movement, have seen their incomes stagnate or fall over the past twenty years (despite the slight overall rise in income of white households). The transition from an industrial to a service economy has proven far more painful than the prophets of technology, mass consumerism, and the "free" market expected.[160] During the 1970s, spiraling inflation, soaring oil prices, and rising unemployment put an end to the post–World War II boom. During the next decade, as Faludi points out, "the 'traditional' man's real wages shrank dramatically (a 22 percent free-fall in households where white men were the sole breadwinners)."[161] Yet these wages were being channeled from working-class white men not to African Americans but to the very rich (who are overwhelmingly white). Moreover, the largest peacetime military buildup in history, as well as changes in the tax structure, have had a far greater impact on the decline in male earning power than the entrance of women into formerly masculine professions. Economic inequality has been on the rise since the 1970s, and by 1995 the United States had become "the most economically stratified of industrial nations" in which the wealthiest 1 percent of households "owns nearly 40 percent of the nation's wealth."[162] Those households in the bottom three-fifths have seen their incomes steadily decline. As Chip Berlet and Matthew Lyons emphasize, however, "the Patriot movement diverts attention away from actual systems of power by the use of scapegoating and by reducing complex reasons for social and economic conditions to simple formulaic conspiracies."[163]

A wide range of American cultural productions since the mid-1970s have insistently reenacted the contradictory spectacle of white men proclaiming themselves victims while simultaneously menacing—or blowing away— somebody else. Sam Shepard's plays of the 1970s are filled with images of self-torture used to consolidate the sense of the white American male as victim, from Hoss's excruciating defeat by his alter ego, to Jeep's humiliation at his own hands, to Niles's pseudosuicide. Like Iron John, Rambo, the Russian-roulette addicted Nick (Christopher Walken) in *The Deer Hunter* (1978), or the suicidal Martin Riggs (Mel Gibson) in *Lethal Weapon* (1987), these heroes remonstrate against a culture made uneasy by traditional machismo by proclaiming themselves victims, by turning violence upon themselves and so demonstrating their implacable toughness, their ability to savor their self-inflicted wounds. Of all these celluloid heroes, perhaps the most emblematic is Michael Douglas, who regressed from countercultural paragon—the collegiate, idealistic liberal in *The Streets of San Francisco* (ABC, 1972–77) and producer of *One Flew over the Cuckoo's Nest* (1971) and the antinuclear film *The China Syndrome* (1979)—to the persecuted, molested, and belligerent victims of *Fatal Attraction* (1987), *Falling Down*, *Basic Instinct* (both 1992), and *Disclosure* (1995). As J. Hoberman notes, "Douglas's stardom depends on his capacity to project simultaneous strength and weakness. He is the victim as hero—a bellicose masochist, aggressive yet powerless, totally domineering while battered by forces beyond his control. . . ."[164] As is obvious from the conduct of all of these put-upon warriors, a penchant for pain by no means rules out the possibility of turning violence against others, especially women or feminized and racialized others who happen to get in the way.

Of all of Douglas's recent films, *Falling Down* most clearly foregrounds the white male as victim, although by no means unambiguously. For surely Pfeil is correct to note that it is "a rampage film that comes wrapped in its own critique."[165] The film's reluctant vigilante hero, D-FENS (Douglas), so named for the vanity license plate of the car that he abandons in a freeway traffic jam at the film's opening, is unequivocally presented as a victim of persons of color (a Korean shopkeeper, Latino gang members) and of his hystericized ex-wife, Beth (Barbara Hershey). Yet at the same time, the pivotal scene in the movie, his encounter with the super-Patriot, neo-Nazi Nick (Frederic Forrest) in the back room of the latter's army surplus store, is disquietingly ambivalent. Decrying "pussies," "niggers," and "faggots" in an excruciatingly homophobic/ homoerotic scene, Nick attempts, in what is arguably the key line in the scene (and the film), to woo the man whom he regards as his double: "We're the same, you and me." D-FENS, meanwhile, terrified by the possibility that Nick might be right, tries desperately to assert his difference: "I'm an American, you're a sick asshole!"[166] But in the end, the film proves unable to distinguish definitively between them insofar as it simultaneously invites and denies "a view of white straight men as pathogenic fascist monsters whose sense of rights is based on their entitlement to exploit and conquer others even unto death."[167]

Yet D-FENS's attempt to lay claim to a solidly American identity is crucial to the film's attempt (much like that of *First Blood* and *Iron John*) to produce white men as exemplars of the nation and critics of commodity culture. D-FENS is clearly constructed as a spoiled leftover from the '50s, in his alienation from consumerism and his attempt to blame minorities for his destabilized masculinity and personal failings as worker, son, husband, and father. His costume identifies him as almost a caricature of a '50s worker—crew cut, black horn-rimmed glasses, white short-sleeve shirt, necktie, and briefcase packed with his lunch—and he represents an unwelcome intrusion from the past into the very paradigm of postmodernist culture, Los Angeles. A bad consumer, moreover, he fails time after time to negotiate purchases successfully. Outraged over the price of a can of coke (eighty-five cents), he flies into a rage at the Korean shopkeeper, crying, "I'm just standing up for my rights as a consumer!" Driven to a violent rampage at a Whammy Burger because of the unavailability of breakfast, he shoots up the place and tells the manager, "The customer is always right!" Profoundly alienated from commodity culture and the city that is patently falling down before him—and proceeding on a journey that is no less than an unguided tour of the other—he wants only to "go home,"

longing for a time before the commodity, before colonization, before boundaries had been dissolved and categories blurred. Yet curiously, all the while
decrying the alleged victories of the other, D-FENS (like Bly, Shepard, Stallone, and his brethren in the Patriot movement) attempts in fact to take the
place of the other in order to restore his lost dignity. The only character with
whom he seems to identify is a lone African-American man picketing a bank
with a sign reading "ECONOMICALLY UNVIABLE." Moreover, D-FENS relentlessly appropriates the weapons of those racialized others he defeats (the base-
ball bat, butterfly knife, and machine guns). Yet the purloined water pistol of
his daughter is finally no match for the real bullet that kills him and sends him
over the Venice pier, beyond the edge of the nation to which he so desperately
struggles to lay claim. A tragic (and deeply masochistic) version of a patriot—
and Nick's true blood brother—he is destroyed by a society that has passed
him by.[168]

Falling Down may be a work of fiction, but recent events, from the Oklahoma City bombing to renewed attacks on affirmative action, have demonstrated the unpredictability and potentially dire consequences of this newly
hegemonic masculinity. For as the scene between Nick and D-FENS suggests,
the partisans of the White Aryan Resistance or the Michigan Militia embody
not a qualitatively different kind of masculinity from that enacted in the films
of Douglas and Stallone but an enterprising, malignant—and, since Oklahoma
City, suddenly demonized—variation upon the latter. Consider, for example,
the all too real Timothy McVeigh whose masculinity, like that of his fictional
brethren, is radically unstable. Described by one of his former army buddies as
being "so gullible, so vulnerable, . . . so unbalanced about being tough," he is
the same volatile figure who is remembered by a gun collector as being a
"polite" and friendly guy who "doesn't interrupt" and yet obsessively speeds
while clenching his phallic signifier:

> "He drove like a wild man," the gun collector said. "He never drove under the speed
> limit; he drove over it. And he always carried that big pistol."[169]

Or consider Pat Buchanan, whose autobiography, peppered with innumerable
accounts of bloody fistfights in school, exults in his ability to withstand
abusive treatment from his tyrannical father (much given to the use of "the
'strap'") and friends and enemies alike: "To show emotion and feeling
was considered an unmanly thing to do; we were to be stoic about pain."[170]
For all these would-be saviors of the white race, reflexive sadomasochism
is profoundly imbricated with their deeply conflicted senses of power and
victimization.

Yet even as this new white masculinity is endlessly examined and dissected
in the press and in mass culture, its underlying logic is rarely acknowledged.
Concealed under a veneer of righteous indignation, willfulness, anger, grief, or
guilt, and repudiated by the would-be heroic male subject, reflexive sadomas-

ochism has become the primary libidinal logic of the white male as victim. And in that sense, to the extent that it remains an open secret—seen and yet not seen, decisive and yet disavowed—it may be said to occupy a *closet*, a site of repression, a private space that is at the same time pivotal for the production of public practices and subjects. Kosmo is hardly the only Shepard hero with "a sadomasochist hid in his closet." Perhaps it is time now to "out" these other heroes, to "out" Robert Bly, Sylvester Stallone, Michael Douglas, Timothy McVeigh, and the culture they instantiate, and to admit that what these white men *really* want, what gives them the greatest thrill, is pain.

PART II

Chapter Four

QUEER MASCULINITIES

> Though [*Cruising*] is now preceded by a statement that the story is not meant to be an "indictment" or "representative" portrait of the homosexual world, it does succeed in creating a new homosexual stereotype: not the limp-wristed, effeminate pansy of old, but a menacing, macho muscleman who pursues sex with surly ferocity and barely suppressed violence.
>
> *(David Ansen, in* Newsweek, *February 18, 1980)*

TWO LEATHERMEN: one, a psychopath and killer, the other, his unsuspecting trick. They meet at an S/M club in the meatpacking district of New York's West Village and go to a grotty hotel room. In the next scene, the trick emerges from the bathroom in a black jockstrap (while in the room the closet door is—literally—wide open!). He lightly tweaks his nipples and goes over to a suitcase (in which his assorted sex toys, including a dildo, lie) to take a hit of amyl nitrite. Happily for the camera (for this is no mere written fiction), a mirror hangs on the wall above his suitcase, which not only allows his ministrations to be overseen but also permits the figure of the killer to be descried, standing in his leather and reflecting sunglasses in a corner of the hotel room. As the trick slowly crosses to him, the camera closes in voyeuristically on the image of the two men in the mirror as the microphone picks up the sound of scrunching leather, and these two unmistakably male bodies kiss. The trick then drops to his knees and unzips his friend. Cut to two pairs of naked legs clad in black boots. On the floor wrestling magazines lie scattered. The trick sits on the edge of the bed as the killer slowly and deliberately grinds his boot into the other's foot. The trick obligingly caresses his friend's hard leather. The killer sinks to the bed, and slowly both pairs of boots rise off the floor as the scene discreetly fades out. Cut to the next morning: the trick is hog-tied and brutally and repeatedly knifed.

Despite—or, perhaps, because of—the absence of genital contact in this sequence (although fellatio is clearly implied by the timely edit), it has all the trappings of a paradigmatic S/M scene. Two spectacularized male bodies engage in a relationship of dominance and submission. The master (who, as bad luck would have it, also happens to be the killer) stands inscrutable, commanding, shrouded in leather, his eyes shielded from his slave's (and the camera's) gaze. He waits to be serviced by his nearly naked ministrant who, although unequivocally male (and pumped up), becomes, in his sleekly oiled demeanor, oddly feminized. The master waits silently; his slave services him. The one grinds his boot into the other's; the other responds with a grateful and loving caress. This insistent (re)production of master and slave, moreover, is reinforced by the power and directionality of the gaze. Because of the mirror's placement, the master, his own eyes hidden, is able to oversee his slave both directly and as reflected in the mirror. The slave, meanwhile, sees his own image, first in the mirror, then in the sunglasses of his master. As he draws near, (mis)recognizing the self in the mirror of the other, he seems compelled to avert his eyes, and he kneels in supplication. At the same time, however, that this master/slave dialectic is being stabilized, both participants are subjected to the gaze of a third, the camera, whose voyeuristic scrutiny of the scene constructs these binary oppositions, producing a couple that, although unambiguously homosexual, is governed by an economy not of sameness but of difference: dominant/submissive, veiled/denuded, masculine/feminine. And desire, that most restless—and yet, at least within the S/M scenario, strangely predictable—of forces, is produced in the disjunction between the terms of each of the binarisms.

Despite its usefulness as a paradigm, this soon-to-be fatal scenario does not describe a typical S/M fantasy since the overwhelming majority of S/M scenarios do not end in the death (or even injury) of one of the players. But unlike other S/M narratives, produced by and for a select group of initiates, this scene is part of a big-budget—and much-decried—film, *Cruising* (1980), written and directed by William Friedkin (who, despite having also made *The Boys in the Band* exactly ten years earlier, aggressively asserts his heterosexuality in all press reports about the film). Based on Gerald Walker's 1970 novel, *Cruising* is the story of the excursion of an ostensibly heterosexual undercover cop, Steve Burns (Al Pacino), into New York's gay S/M subculture in search of a "homo killer" on the loose. The first major studio release to feature explicit sex between men, it was the first to bring cameras—and presumably Al Pacino— into a gay male S/M sex club. It was the first emphatically to challenge the stereotype of gay man as "pansy."[1] It was the first to produce a homosexual serial killer. It was also the first to provoke a well-organized campaign of opposition by a lesbian and gay community that believed the film would provoke increased violence against lesbians and gay men (it followed Anita Bryant's crusade to repeal civil rights protection for lesbians and gay men in Dade County by only two years, and the assassination of Harvey Milk by one). The controversy began when Arthur Bell reported in the *Village Voice* that the film "promises to be the most oppressive, ugly, bigoted look at homosexuality ever presented on the screen."[2] He implored his readers to disrupt the shooting and the owners of gay clubs simply to tell Friedkin to "fuck off." A "steady string of riots" ensued in the Village, and gay rights groups demanded unsuccessfully that Mayor Koch's office withdraw its support of the film.[3] The National Gay Task Force called it "a gross distortion of the lives of gay men by portraying them as violent and sex-obsessed," while one of its spokesmen compared the filming in the West Village with "the Ku Klux Klan making a movie about the black community on 125th Street in Harlem."[4]

Despite, to say the least, its vexed status as a queer artifact, *Cruising* remains, I believe, a privileged site for the examination of the production of both queer and straight masculinities. It also works to expose so many of the anxieties circulating around sexuality and around various sexual practices and identities (S/M in particular) during the late '70s and early '80s. For although *Cruising*, not surprisingly, resuscitates theories of homosexuality as contagion that date back at least to the nineteenth century, it also—in what is arguably its most radical move—reveals the profound instability of the categories "heterosexual" and "homosexual." For as the film progresses, Steve Burns becomes increasingly absorbed by and obsessed with both the subculture and the sexuality he has been sent to investigate. Several scenes in S/M sex clubs end with his being picked up and provide no clue as to whether or not he follows through. At the same time, his relationship with his girlfriend, Nancy (Karen Allen), steadily deteriorates. While having sex with her (which, tellingly, gets increasingly violent) he involuntarily hears the dance music of the S/M clubs, and he later confesses to her, "What I'm doing is affecting me." And as the film proceeds, it becomes more and more evident that Burns and the killer, Stuart Richards (Richard Cox), are being constructed as doubles: each weight lifting to keep in shape, staring at the other through windows, and dressed exactly alike in their highly eroticized, climactic confrontation. Most ominously, at the end of the film, when Burns's friend and neighbor, Ted Bailey (Don Scardino)—the film's one normative gay man (i.e., a friendly and nonpathologized writer who wears a *Christopher Street* T-shirt and is untempted by the leather scene)—is brutally murdered, it remains pointedly ambiguous whether the killer is Ted's irascible roommate/lover or the newly homosexualized and pathologized Burns himself.

In its undermining of the homo/hetero binarism, *Cruising* also subverts the distinction between the law and the queer bodies on which it is exercised. At the beginning of the film, one of the (straight) cops from the local precinct exacts a blow job from a drag queen/hustler as the equivalent of hush money. Later, when Burns entraps a hapless suspect, the police force's brutally homophobic interrogation squad is strangely supplemented by the film's most enigmatic character (whose presence is never explained): a menacing and burly black muscle man in a bulging jockstrap and cowboy hat who roughs up Burns and threatens the suspect (who is later commanded to strip and masturbate so the police can obtain a sperm sample!). Does the law, this sequence seems to ask, also indulge in S/M play? What goes on between cops when the doors are closed and the lights are low? From whose feverish—and racist—imagination does this creature emerge? The police? The writer/director? A post–civil rights and post-Stonewall America in which blackness represents both hypermasculinity and the principle that threatens the boundary between the homosocial and the homosexual? Yet if the interrogation scene represents the tragic dimension of (gay) American history, its farcical reiteration must surely be "uniform night" at the Cockpit, when the club is filled with hundreds of counterfeit cops, soldiers, and security guards, and from which the one real cop, Steve Burns, is summarily ejected because he is not wearing the right uniform. More clearly than any other sequence in the film, "uniform night" so flagrantly reveals (long before *Gender Trouble*) not only the necessarily performative nature of identities (sexual, gendered, and otherwise) but also the intense homoeroticism that is sublimated in what passes for normative male homosociality.

In its representation of gay subcultures, *Cruising* leaves little doubt that queer sex is a dangerous and thoroughly masculine affair. No "limp-wristed, effeminate pans[ies]" here (to quote *Newsweek*'s vivid prose), but leathermen pursuing "sex with surly ferocity and barely suppressed violence."[5] And, if nothing else, *Cruising* attests to a dramatic change during the 1970s in hegemonic representations of gay men—from sissies to leathermen. For the mid-1970s also bore witness to the emergence of the clone, the leatherman's first cousin, "a doped out, sexed-out, Marlboro man," who became "the leading social type within gay ghettos. . . ."[6] ("I want to be a macho man," sang the Village People in their 1978 disco hit.) Yet there is another side to this representational regime. Insistently throughout the film (despite the disclaimer that introduces it), S/M is, if not exactly normalized, at least taken for granted within the gay subculture.[7] (And interestingly, none of the protests against the film singled out its S/M content for condemnation or commented on the film's virtual collapse of male homosexuality into S/M.) Moreover, the film's linkage of S/M with homicide, coupled with its construction of the police and the S/M community as mirror images, produces contradictory—and deeply troubling—effects. Relentlessly, both in the film and in so much discourse surrounding it, S/M is both universalized and minoritized, rendered the "natural" and inevitable expression of an inherently violent male sexuality and at the same time a psychosexual disturbance of the few. So, on the one hand, both straight and gay masculinities, even the most apparently innocuous ones (like Ted Bailey's) are shown to be always already hostage to an S/M dynamic. There is nothing "beyond" S/M, insofar as it becomes (to paraphrase Leo Bersani) a tautology for sexuality *tout court*.[8] Even femininity is not immune when Nancy, at the end of the film, dons her boyfriend's leathers and joins him in the masquerade. On the other hand, S/M is also presented unmistakably as a kind of corruption, a sexual pathology that is the mysterious origin of a whole range of social and political disturbances plaguing American culture ("One day this whole city's going to explode," one cop tells another as they drive by the S/M clubs, and as ominous nondiegetic music plays. "You used to be able to play stickball on these streets. Now look at these guys. Christ, what's happening?"). The irreducibility of this contradiction ensures that throughout the film (and throughout the culture that it instantiates) S/M remains the source of deep anxiety. For the film is predicated on the notion that sexual violence and S/M are finally indistinguishable, that homicide is simply an extension of rough sex. This hypothesis is dramatized most vividly in the murder sequence that follows the scene in the hotel room described above. When the killer's hapless trick is tied hand and foot with his own leather straps, death becomes merely a prolongation of love-play, and murder figured as the logical and inevitable outcome of S/M. You play with fire, the film seems to warn, and you're going to get burned.

The contradictory position that *Cruising* takes in regard to both S/M and masculinity is by no means unique to this particular cultural artifact. It is in large part echoed by the writings of anti-S/M and antipornography feminists whose heyday corresponded exactly with the release of the film. According to these writers, S/M is *the* privileged instrument for the stabilization of heterosexual patriarchy, the false consciousness that eroticizes power and powerlessness and always reinforces oppressive gender roles: "Between a man and a woman, the conjunction of male sexual sadism and female masochism fully expresses the cultural definitions of what 'real' men and women are. . . ."[9] As such, it is always antithetical to "true sexual freedom," which "will be possible only when we break the connection between sex and power, when there is no power component in sexual interactions."[10] Equating masculinity with oppression, and penetrative sexuality with rape, anti-S/M discourse offers, to say the least, a rather monolithic view of a wide range of sexual practices. It insists that female masochism (whether lesbian or heterosexualized) is especially insidious because it epitomizes "self-loathing" and "internalized oppression."[11] And although it sometimes provides a provocative critique of the concept of consent, it refuses to problematize concepts like "self-determination" or the "internal power" of the self.[12] Focusing on questions of individual rights and "sexual liberation," and taking the autonomous, liberal subject for granted, it is deeply utopian in its thrust and, to that extent, is clearly an extension of the emancipatory politics of the 1960s (despite being far more puritanical than Marcuse's concept of a liberated Eros). Like so much emancipatory discourse, it is caught in the impossible space between asserting social determinism on the one hand, and claiming individual autonomy and free will on the other. Moreover, it refuses to recognize that the concept of internalized oppression continually implies the likelihood of one's somehow transcending or mastering the admittedly deeply oppressive system by which he or she is articulated as a sexed subject. It assumes that a line of demarcation can be clearly drawn between tyranny and liberation, between inside and outside, and works to reify these binary oppositions. Fatally mortgaged to bourgeois individualism, it insists (like so many twelve-step programs) that one can obtain a cure by an act of will (which looks to me far more like an act of repression or sublimation).[13]

Thanks to Madonna, Susie Bright, Judith Butler, Gayle Rubin (among many others), and the much greater level of visibility accorded so many forms of sexual dissidence, the feminist sex wars of the 1980s are over.[14] Yet the questions raised by *Cruising* and the anti-S/M feminists refuse to go away. S/M remains a site of continued contestation for the meaning of sex and gender. (Gayle Rubin argues persuasively that the rise of anti-S/M and anti-pornography feminism represents yet another of the periodic "sex scares" that have arisen in the United States during periods of repression, which is to say, in times of social, political, and economic instability.)[15] The attack by Jesse Helms and the religious Right over the inclusion of Robert Mapplethorpe's *X* portfolio in the *Perfect Moment* exhibition (1988–90) helped to consolidate what can be characterized (at the very least) as an anti-anti-S/M position among most of the self-styled Left. Nonetheless, Catharine MacKinnon retains her prestige, at least in the pages of the *New York Times*. Simultaneously—and in a particularly telling display of American culture's seemingly endless facility for cannibalizing what makes it most uneasy—S/M has since the late 1980s been hotly embraced by commodity culture. S/M-inspired fashions (including black leather, tattoos, uniforms, whips, body piercings, and various fetishes) continue to dominate fashion magazines (and even advertisements in the mainstream press). And although savaged by the press, Madonna's *Sex* (1992) remains the best-selling introduction to the mysteries of New York's fabled S/M club, the Vault. Yet the notoriety of *Cruising* and the prominence of figures like Mapplethorpe in defining this moment is indicative of the persistently volatile relationship in the cultural fantasmatic between S/M and male homosexuality. For although S/M is widely practiced in both lesbian and heterosexualized relationships, it remains particularly identified in mass culture with gay male sexualities. Thus Gayle Rubin notes that by the late 1970s, "leather/macho [had] replaced drag queen fluff as the dominant gay stereotype."[16] Since then, it has taken up the overdetermined position of being emblematic of the perverse as an entire class of persons and practices and, at the same time, of gay male sexuality in particular (in reviews of *Cruising*, for example, it is unclear whether the "subject matter" that even the so-called liberal press found "loathsome," "noisome," and "repulsive" was homosexuality, S/M, or both).[17]

The remainder of this chapter will analyze the deeply problematic and vexed relationships between and among masculinity, S/M, and homosexualities and, in so doing, attempt to answer the following questions: Why has S/M become so central to the production of gay male identities since the 1970s? Is there a link between the new masculinity of Robert Bly and Sylvester Stallone and these queer masculinities? How does the phallus function in a queer masculine fantasmatic? Can it be disarticulated from a male body? What is the relationship between the discourses of gay male S/M and those of lesbian S/M? Does gay male S/M represent a genuinely nonphallic sexuality (as Kaja Silverman argues), or is it yet another subterfuge? What does it mean to consider phallic sexuality in and of itself oppressive? Is it always so? Why, from *Cruising* to the queer pornography of Aaron Travis and Pat Califia, do these questions continue to haunt the American cultural imagination? Is there a way of answering these questions that does not fixate on problems of individual subjectivity? And finally, a question that animates part 2 of this book: What is "beyond" masochism?

THE PENIS AS FETISH

Within what passes for a queer community, no sexual practice has been more controversial, or has seen more extravagant claims made both for and against it, than S/M. At one extreme, Seymour Kleinberg, writing in 1978, attacks S/M in his analysis of a major change in the predominant mode of gay male self-production. For him, "effeminate camping" has been superseded by a new machismo, a "relentless pursuit of masculinity" and "power." Kleinberg argues that the appropriation by gay men of "the most oppressive images of sexual violence and dominance" (including "neo-Nazi adornments") functions to eroticize "the very values of straight society that have tyrannized" them. Like the anti-S/M feminists, he sees masochism in particular as a form of internalized oppression, as the emblazonment of "gay self-contempt, which in turn is exploited as an aphrodisiac."[18] For less polemical writers (at least around this issue) like Jeffrey Weeks and Dennis Altman, S/M represents "the extreme fringe of acceptable sexuality" and a "potential embarrassment . . . to the more 'respectable' [gay] movement."[19] Altman, in particular, remains deeply ambivalent about S/M. He refuses to believe that it is, as Kleinberg alleges, simply "an acting out of self-hatred," and recognizes that it is "almost certainly more complicated." Yet at the same time, he clearly associates it with cultural decadence, noting that it has been "most apparent at times and in places of moral and social upheaval, whether it is Rome during its decline, Berlin in the twenties, or New York today."[20] Despite their misgivings, however, Weeks and Altman are reluctant to condemn or minoritize S/M, and both suggest that S/M dynamics seem to inform all sexual relations to some extent. Moreover, both credit the subversive potential behind S/M's defiance of the reproductive mandate.

To members of the flourishing queer leather subculture, however, it all looks rather different. Pat Califia, Gayle Rubin, and other lesbian S/M activists have welcomed the increased visibility and importance that lesbian S/M enjoys in at least a part of the lesbian community. Having more or less successfully fought off attacks during the 1980s both from the Right (Jesse Helms et al.) and from anti-S/M feminists, they argue, in the words of Wickie Stamps, that it is "the S/M lesbians—female, queer and on the sexual fringes—who constantly remind us that what we are engaged in is a 'sexual' revolution."[21] Many of the women contributors to *Leatherfolk* (a 1991 collection of essays that in fact postdates by ten years the pioneering lesbian S/M anthology, *Coming to Power*) make similarly revolutionary claims for S/M practices. Tina Portillo deems S/M "the ultimate act of defiance," while Pat Califia believes that "the truly radical potential of S/M" lies in its ability to "challenge . . . the very meanings that we assign *all* sexual acts."[22]

Like their lesbian comrades-in-arms, most of the male contributors to *Leatherfolk* regard themselves as "continuing the unfinished sexual revolution" of the 1960s.[23] Mark Thompson, the editor of the collection, sees black leather "as a still daring symbol of cultural transgression," while Michael Bronski judges the "public image of the leather man (or woman) . . . an outright threat to the existing, although increasingly dysfunctional, system of gender arrangements and sexual repression under which we have all lived."[24] For master pornographer John Preston, "the great fuck-you of leather and S/M" attests to an "anarchistic" project whose "rules" are resolutely "anti-establishment."[25] Yet many of these same men view the increased popularity and visibility of S/M with cynicism and even alarm. Bronski is dismayed that leather has become a "lifestyle"—that most banal of euphemisms for *whom* or, in this case, *how* you fuck—which for him means "a movement away from S/M, away from the renegade and socially dangerous form of sexuality, toward one more acceptable and palatable to both the wider lesbian and gay community and the general (read: 'straight') culture."[26] Preston, too, is appalled that "[t]he world of S/M [has] been overtaken by sightseers," by those mesmerized by "the 'good' aspects of the 'leather life-style.'"[27] Mourning the fabled leather bars of the '50s and '60s, David Stein decries the loss of the "mystery" of S/M, the passing of the days—unlike now—"when tops outnumbered bottoms by ten to one," when a rigorous system of apprenticeship ruled, and when being "a master of bondage or flagellation" inspired a kind of universal "awe."[28] Nostalgic for the precommodified "'golden age' of the 1950s," these writers feel that the "truly *radical* potential" of S/M has been eviscerated.[29] At the same time, their texts consistently testify to the crucial importance of a discourse of professionalization that classifies and hierarchizes not only leathermen but also S/M communities, demarcating professionals (those accruing large sums of S/M subcultural capital) from mere amateurs (tourists, fashion victims, or voyeurs).

For leatherfolk, the potential radical subversion of subjectivities and cultural norms by queer S/M raises important and difficult questions. Moreover, any analysis is complicated by the necessity of drawing a distinction between gay male and lesbian S/M insofar as each has a different history and has been a partisan in different cultural struggles. Thus, for example, because gay male S/M has a much more indirect connection to the feminist movement than lesbian S/M, it has never been attacked with the fury visited on the latter in the early 1980s. It also does not have to address (and redress) a history of women as passive objects of (masculinized) desire the way that lesbian S/M does. Yet at the same time, it is important to see the points of agreement between them, insofar as these constitute what I believe is most intriguing (and perhaps even most progressive) about both movements. For if leatherfolk do indeed represent a sexual avant-garde, of what exactly are they in the forefront? What social and sexual ideologies are they advancing? I want to begin to answer these questions by looking at gay male S/M to consider the meaning of the historical shift in the status of the leather subculture as well as the relationship between S/M practices and discourses, on the one hand, and the production of queer masculinities, on the other.

Since S/M is the most explicitly fantasmatic of all sexualities, I cannot hope to position it culturally without an analysis of its fantasmatic content. Therefore, before directly addressing these questions, I propose to let one of the leading writers of S/M fiction, Steven Saylor (writing under the pseudonym Aaron Travis) provide an initiation to the delights and torments of leathersex. In particular, I want to analyze gay male S/M as a mode of social and psychic signification in which the penis functions (impossibly) as a fetish object.

The short story "Blue Light," originally published in *Malebox* in 1980, is an S/M classic by a writer whom John Preston has dubbed the chronicler of "the sexual exploits of an entire generation."[30] The most baroque of Travis's stories, it brings together the naturalistic and the fantasmatic with far more gothic exuberance than most S/M prose. Even Preston's own classic *Mister Benson* reads like a sober documentary in comparison with Travis's extravagant chronicle. Most important, "Blue Light," because it is so hallucinatory, serves to illustrate many of the thematics that are continually associated with masochistic subjectivities, texts, and practices: the deconstruction of the subject, the performative nature of identities (sexual and otherwise), the undecidability of pleasure and pain, the inexorability of castration, and the erotics of delay. The story is set in a picturesque and decaying part of Houston to which the narrator, Bill, an assured and experienced top with a Harley and a "studded leather armband for [his] left bicep," has fled from the anonymity of New York.[31] It focuses on Bill's one extraordinary sexual encounter with the mysterious and powerful Michael, who happens to own the house in which Bill has rented a room. From the very beginning, Michael is constructed as a mystery, "a nocturnal animal" (20). His room is a gothic dungeon, a shadowy, octagonal chamber with dark purple walls perched at the top of the house and equipped with vaguely medieval—and ominous—furnishings, ornaments, and symbols. "I don't know what he does up there," one of his women housemates bashfully declares (15).

Insistently coded as the unknown, Michael is from the first identified as the likely source of boundless pleasure and danger, a feminized object of fascination for both Bill and the reader. Michael is first glimpsed as he is working in the garden, and Bill is riveted by his long black hair, his stunning musculature, and his pale white skin, "like ivory" (16). Bill's narrative progressively fetishizes Michael, turning him into the one who unmistakably "is" the phallus, fragmenting his body into a catalog of discrete erotic components: his sleek hair, his dark brown eyes, "with long lashes and straight black eyebrows," his full, red lips, "pale cheeks," "square-muscled shoulders," legs like white marble pillars (18). And, of course, there's his big cock, with its privileged relationship to the phallus, which, as a synechdoche, nestled inside his "white nylon briefs," stands in for (to follow through with the logic of fetishization) the truth of at least *this* subject (18). Longing to "own," "possess," and "devour" Michael, Bill—the consummate top—spins masturbatory fantasies in which Michael is humiliated, abused, and made to bear the mark of castration, to be shorn of his lustrous black hair: "His naked skull would mark him as my slave" (19).

When Bill and Michael finally wend their way up to Michael's candlelit chamber, the eager top unexpectedly discovers that the windows have been replaced by mirrors (reminiscent, perhaps, of the mirror and mirrored sunglasses in *Cruising*) in whose endless reflections the room seems to have expanded "into infinity" (21). As a reader adept at discerning impending narrative peripeties may well have surmised by now, Bill is about to find himself radically disoriented and reversed within this vertiginous space as his identity and even his body are dismantled and reconstructed under Michael's expert tutelage. Having commanded Michael to fetch Bill's mysterious wooden locker, Bill unpacks his "toys" and readies his riding crop to service Michael's tender flesh (23). With a sudden flush of the supernatural, however, Michael takes command, incapacitating Bill and forcing him in silence to stare narcissistically at his own naked body in the mirrors, compelling him to submit to an extended and elaborate ritual wherein the hapless top, feeling "like an insect paralyzed in a spider's web," comes to (mis)recognize himself as a subjected being in the gaze of the other (25). Michael secures two chains, "made like dog chokers," and passes one over Bill's head and the other over his hard cock and balls (25). And as the sign of Bill's submission, the new top moves his new bottom's armband from his left to his right arm. "Against my will," Bill explains, "he had completely reversed our roles" (26). The omnipotent master then begins the torture and somatic transformation of his slave, literalizing the tropes of masochistic narrative.

Bill notices in the mirror that the chains begin to glow with "a ghostly blue light" as Michael fetches what appears to be a shimmering "hoop of glass tubing" which he lowers over Bill to strip him of his body hair, a move that produces a contradictory effect. On the one hand, considering the importance of hair as a fetish object, it represents a curious de-fetishization (or masculini-zation) of Bill, turning him from one who "is" the phallus to one who "has" it. On the other hand, it simultaneously serves to feminize him, to castrate him, to return him to a state of prepubescent hairlessness, to turn him into an object of desire both for his master and for himself, to turn self into other (26):

> It was as if I saw another man in the mirror. A hunky blond slave, totally hairless, his mouth hanging open like a dog's, his cock hard for his master.

In becoming a spectacle, "another man," Samson to Michael's Delilah, Bill fully accedes to the masochistic economy of desire that insists on the perfor-mative nature of identities. For as the narrative makes clear, the leatherman's sexual identity is finally revealed to be fictive, which is to say, strictly rela-tional and dependent upon the roles assigned the participants by a particular scenario (or a particularly despotic dungeonmaster). At the same time, the text suggests that in S/M the performance of identity, and of pain and pleasure, will always be a spectacle. (Theodor Reik notes that the masochist "can't do with-out a public," even if that public is only the masochistic subject him- or her-self.)[32] And although Michael's response is not documented, Bill (to say noth-ing of the one-handed reader) is "mesmerized" by his own hairless reflection in the mirror (27).

Yet the inexplicable shaving of Bill barely hints at what is to come. Michael grabs the chain around Bill's neck and pulls it so tightly that Bill fears he is being strangled. Suddenly, however, the choker drops freely and Bill feels himself "being lifted up—a sensation of weightlessness and vertigo" (28). Catching "a glimpse of something in one of the mirrors," he sees his body still "within the blue light field," while Michael, with "a look of contempt and total control," holds his severed head between his thighs (28). Dismembering Bill's body with a vengeance (as Bill's fetishizing narrative had formerly dismembered Michael's), Michael forces his slave's disembodied head to gratify its earlier wish to devour Michael's cock. With Michael fucking his face "for what seemed like hours," Bill—the victim of the conjunction of the literal with the metaphoric—experiences the "sensation of timelessness," "freed from [his] body," "beyond panic or pain" (29), that so many leathermen and -women report and that Pat Califia dubs the S/M orgasm: "the reaching of an emotional, psychological, or spiritual state of catharsis, ecstasy, or transcen-dence during an S/M scene without having a genital orgasm."[33] For Bill, this "disembodiment"—which represents yet another castration—also signals a loss of boundaries, a dissolution of that flimsy subjectivity which can no longer "tell where my throat ended and his thick shaft began" (30).

Yet the fantasmatic decapitation of Bill is only a prelude to the third, final and literal castration of this exceptionally versatile bottom. (According to Freud, the masochistic male subject is usually "placed in a situation character-istic of womanhood, *i.e.* they mean that he is being castrated, is playing the passive part in coitus, or is giving birth.")[34] Pulling the chain around Bill's genitals, Michael unmans Bill, holding aloft his "nine-inch shaft by the testicles" and leaving in its place a simulacrum of the mons veneris: "a smooth hairless swelling of flesh" (34). Michael then proceeds to do "the unthinkable" (34). First he pushes Bill's "disembodied cock" into Bill's "squatting ass," and then he slips his own "thick shaft" into the place that has "no opening" where Bill's genitals used to be (35). Wholly transformed, Bill is finally "emasculated," "mindless but hungry," "more a whore than a slave," "a creature of dark magic" (35). But because Michael warns Bill that when Bill ejaculates he will break the spell and remain forever in whatever anatomical disposition be happens to be in, Bill is forced to prolong the agonizing bliss as long as he can. (Reik observes that "[m]asochistic tension vacillates more strongly than any other sexual tension between the pleasurable and the anxious, and it tends to perpetuate this state.")[35] After several pages of transcendental fucking ("I felt my cockhead rubbing against his, deep inside my bowels"), Michael replaces Bill's head on his shoulders and decrees one final marathon cocksucking (35). Finally, as Bill tries agonizingly to postpone the inevitable, both men ejaculate just as Michael replaces Bill's genitals and renders the latter miraculously "whole" again (38). "Drained" and "exhausted," Bill departs Michael's chamber, and the following evening, shaken yet intact, he flees into the night (38).

Performative identities, dismemberment, castration, torturous delay, S/M orgasm, the impossible admixture of suffering and ecstasy: "Blue Light" has it all. A virtual master text of masochistic narrative, it insistently works, like the S/M scene, to prolong and thereby to intensify the pleasure of at least this reader who—playing bottom to Aaron Travis's top—both desires and fears the story's end. Moreover, the narrative exquisitely demonstrates what feminist and queer theorists have been saying all along: that male subjectivity is never self-identical or fully present to itself, that men never "have" the phallus, as much as they would like to make us believe it is equivalent to the humble penis. Normative masculine subjectivity, although founded on lack, must of course continually disavow its castration, its deficit. The male masochist, however, in Kaja Silverman's estimation, differs from the normative male subject on account of his acknowledgment of the fact of castration: "he acts out in an insistent and exaggerated way the basic conditions of cultural subjectivity, conditions that are normally disavowed; he loudly proclaims that his meaning comes to him from the Other, prostrates himself before the gaze even as he solicits it, exhibits his castration for all to see, and revels in the sacrificial basis of the social contract." For Silverman, the male masochist's conscious performance of lack, alterity, and specularity ensures his subversive status; it guarantees that "he radiates a negativity inimical to the social order."[36]

Yet it seems to me that "Blue Light," this quintessential masochistic text, does not in the end represent the abnegation of the phallus. On the contrary, I believe that it attests to the extraordinary inventiveness of phallic sexuality, to the ability of the masochistic male subject simultaneously to relinquish and to lay claim to the phallus. As Judith Butler suggests, the "phallic divestiture" that at least to some extent characterizes masochism may well be simply "a strategy of phallic self-aggrandizement" and not a definitive crossing over to what Silverman calls "the 'enemy terrain' of femininity."[37] If this is correct, then male masochism would represent a particularly "subtle strategy of the phallus, a ruse of power," working to consolidate rather than imperil masculinity.[38] Moreover, the evidence to support these claims is found not just in S/M fictions but also in presumptively nonfictional S/M texts (the insistent elaboration of fantasy in both suggests that a line of demarcation between them is untenable). So many of the discourses of gay male S/M are in fact deeply concerned with the effect of S/M practices and styles on the production of masculinities. From "Blue Light" to *The Leatherman's Handbook* to *Leatherfolk*, S/M texts suggest that S/M practices—and the fantasies that are enacted in them—function both psychically and socially rather differently from the way that Silverman suggests they do.

"Blue Light" would appear to be an ideal text for her, providing as it does a scenario in which multiple acts of castration are performed and in which male bodies are insistently fetishized and specularized. But the text inescapably suggests that the embrace of alterity works in the end to reinforce the delusion that the male subject "has" the phallus. Moreover, one can chart this delusion by following through with the logic of fetishism. In this story, as in so many gay male erotic texts, the penis itself, or, more precisely, the hard cock, is constructed (impossibly) as the preeminent fetishistic object, as displacement and sign of the ever-elusive phallus. And Leo Bersani is surely correct to see "love of the cock" as a "fundamental" characteristic of gay men.[39] No stranger to psychoanalytical theory, Larry Townsend, in *The Leatherman's Handbook II*, quotes and explicates Freud's definition of fetishism while adding a twist of his own. He suggests that if Freud visited the Mineshaft (a happy idea!), "he would revise his definition of fetish to include first and foremost the very object itself; i.e., the penis, the fully erect cock. . . ."[40] Townsend accurately notes that for Freud the fetish must be a "penis-substitute" and cannot designate "the very object itself." According to Freud, fetishism is a way of managing the truth of (female) castration. The male child must disavow the knowledge of his mother's castration (in order to disavow the possibility of his own castration) and so takes something else as a substitute (shoe, stocking, furpiece) for her absent penis. The fetish, functioning simultaneously as affirmation and denial, thus works as both "a token of triumph over the threat of castration and a safeguard against it. . . ."[41] So, in a strictly Freudian context, Townsend is correct: the penis cannot be a fetish.

Developing contradictions and ambivalences that are already at play in the Freudian texts, however, Lacan considerably refines and complicates Freud's formulation of fetishism. Most important, he attempts to distinguish between the penis and the phallus by conceiving of the former as biological (or Real) and the latter as a symbolic property, an effect of signification. As Kaja Silverman explains, "the male sexual organ can never be equivalent to the values designated by the phallus" as privileged signifier within the symbolic order.[42] This nonequivalence is decisive in Lacan despite the fact that the penis and the phallus do exist in a uniquely "intimate" relationship with each other in which the latter serves as the "image" of the former.[43] (And Silverman argues persuasively that there is far more slippage between the two terms in Lacan than he is inclined to admit.) Nonetheless, because the penis can at best—or worst—approximate the function of the Lacanian phallus, the fetishistic economies of Freud and Lacan are rather different.[44] Silverman attempts to distinguish between them by noting Lacan's own distinction between the "imaginary" and the "symbolic" phallus. The former, she explains, is the one "which comes into play in the Freudian account of castration," while the latter "is the one which no subject can ever be; it signifies that which must be sacrificed to language, that which has 'faded' away." The former designates the imaginary maternal phallus (signifier of "wholeness and sufficiency"), while the latter is the privileged and ubiquitous signifier of absence, of that which "every fully constituted subject has surrendered."[45]

This difference between the imaginary and the symbolic phallus seems to me to be indispensible to the theorizing of the (im)possibility of penis as fetish within (gay male S/M) discourse. First, in relation to the imaginary phallus: if the penis were to function as a fetish—which is to say, as a replacement for "the very object itself"—it would do so because it would substitute not merely (in Freud's words) for "any chance penis" but rather for the imaginary maternal phallus "that endows [the mother] with power and authority."[46] So within the fetishistic economy of desire, why could not "any chance penis" stand in for the maternal phallus as well as a shoe or a furpiece? Second, in relation to the symbolic phallus: no "chance penis" can ever be equivalent to the phallus that holds the symbolic order in place, the phallus that no subject can ever have or be. As Judith Butler explains:

> The phallus *symbolizes* the penis; and insofar as it symbolizes the penis, retains the penis as that which it symbolizes; it *is* not the penis. To be the object of symbolization is precisely not to be that which symbolizes. To the extent that the phallus symbolizes the penis, it is not that which it symbolizes. The more symbolization occurs, the less ontological connection there is between symbol and symbolized.[47]

As male subjectivity becomes increasingly predicated on the symbolization of the phallus, the penis becomes ever more subtilized and ever more the mark of the absence of the phallus, of that which has been lost. Even when all the veils are lifted, even when fully revealed (and perhaps especially when fully revealed), the penis can never signify the phallus. "Thus the erectile organ," Lacan explains, "comes to symbolize the place of *jouissance*, not in itself, or even in the form of the image, but as a part lacking in the desired image. . . ."[48] So within the fetishistic symbolic, could not the penis, like anything else that is not the phallus, possibly function as a substitute, as that which both displaces and signifies the phallus?

Considered in this context, "Blue Light," rather than repudiating the fetish, testifies to the fetishistic (im)possibilities of the penis itself. And given the economy of presence and absence, of having and losing, it is perhaps not surprising that it is precisely the act of castration that makes Bill aware of his own phallicism. While Michael is holding Bill's disembodied cock before his face, Bill meditates:

> [N]ow I saw it as my slaves had. Huge and pulsing, inches from my lips. And I knew why men had grovelled for it. Knew the power that made them crave it (36).

Relishing the intimacy between penis and phallus, Bill is spellbound by the majesty of his own disembodied penis, which, ironically, has become a veil for the phallus, that which preserves the authority of the phallus. And the act of castration, rather than humbling the subject, ironically serves further to mystify the penis, to accentuate its privileged relationship to "power."

The valorization of a distinctively phallic sexuality is redoubled by the restless circulation of desire in "Blue Light," which is in part the result of the complementarity of sadism and masochism (at least within the psychoanalytical scenario). Freud, like most of his followers, argues that the sadist and the masochist are absolutely dependent on each other. Moreover, he maintains that they represent unusually fluid and unstable points of interpellation, the one always ready to identify with or take the place of the other. Despite the fact that any given subject is likely to have more highly developed either "the active [sadistic] or the passive [masochistic] aspect," "a sadist," according to Freud, "is always at the same time a masochist."[49] (This intuition is borne out by the testimony of many leatherfolk who, like Larry Townsend, note that since the growth of the subculture during the 1970s "the majority [of leathermen] are switch-hitters, neither pure S nor pure M. . . .")[50] As a result, the S/M transaction involves a complex interplay of identification and desire in which top and bottom will always be mutually implicated in each other's pleasure and pain.[51] "Blue Light" attests to this interplay in two ways: first, in the reversal of roles on which the story's narrative structure pivots; and second, in the double interpellation to which both Michael and Bill submit. Michael, as both "primal force" and object of fetishistic fascination, occupies two contradictory positions (38). He is constructed as both "having" and "being" the phallus, the sign of both limitless power and limitless specularization. Bill, meanwhile, having leathersex with Michael, also occupies "two places at once" (33). Not only is he literally dismembered, he is also—on his own admission—both "[m]asochistic victim, and sadistic observer of [his] own humiliation . . ." (33). As a result, he is doubly Michael's doppelgänger. As specularized bottom, he too "is" the phallus. And as keeper of the sadistic gaze, he unmistakably "has" it. Moreover, it is precisely the interdependence of these two positions that produces Bill's extraordinary level of arousal, that renders him "crazy with excitement" (33). The experience of self-division allows Bill, on the one hand, to desire Michael, to worship him "like the primal force he [is]," and on the other, to identify with this "force" (38). In discovering the other reflected in the self ("It was as if I saw another man in the mirror"), he also espies "his" phallus in Michael, in Michael's cock that is also literally inside him, in the hole with "no opening" (27, 35). Fucked by the "perfect" cock, he (mis)recognizes Michael for the phallus he both "is" and "has" (28). The importance of both "being" and "having" the phallus suggests not only that S/M works tirelessly both to arouse and to allay castration anxiety but that this (im)possible position, in fact, describes the very ontology of S/M.

The fact that both narrative form and male sexual arousal inevitably proceed toward some kind of resolution or release, suggests, of course, that this contradictory and vertiginous bifurcation of subjectivity cannot be sustained. The sex climaxes in a "roar[ing]" double orgasm that—crucially—renders Bill "whole again" (38). Unsettled, but unequivocally remasculinized, he is carefully distinguished from Michael's sometime slave, Carl, the one who is not so lucky and whose penis Michael keeps in his dresser "wrapped in blue silk" (40). As a result, "Blue Light" arouses castration anxiety in order at least partially to allay it, to reassure both Bill and the reader who identifies with him that they are in the end intact. And while neither of them exactly "has" the phallus, they do at least have some access to the "power" that is insistently associated in the S/M narrative with phallic sexuality (36). Moreover, they are reassured to know that at least someone named Michael does "have" the phallus and that the possibility always exists of initiating an (albeit perilous) erotic transaction with him, or one of his ilk. The remasculinization of Bill also supports Robert Stolorow's contention that both masochism and sadism prove particularly useful in times of psychic crisis because they operate "to restore and maintain the structural cohesiveness, temporal stability and positive affective colouring of a precarious or crumbling self-representation." The cathartic machinery of "Blue Light" would seem particularly adept at salvaging the independent, autonomous, masculine subject and "re-establishing a sense of [his] existing as a bounded entity, a cohesive self."[52]

So many of the discourses of gay male S/M, like "Blue Light," are obsessed with the recuperation of an active and powerful masculinity (and this sets them clearly at odds with the thesis of *Male Subjectivity at the Margins*). The insistent masculinization of the S/M scene as a whole or of the top specifically—that is, the disavowal of his castration—may come as little surprise. Thus Michael Bronski credits S/M culture with "invent[ing] a new mode of masculinity, . . ." while Robert H. Hopcke describes S/M as a way for "gay men . . . to reclaim their primal connection to the rawness and power of the Masculine."[53] But S/M texts also and continually attempt to assert the masculinity of the bottom, indeed to endow the bottom with a privileged relationship to the masculine signifier. For Scott Tucker, to put his partner in bondage allows him to feel that his bottom's "beauty, youth, and manliness have been intensified and concentrated. . . ."[54] For Pat Califia, the (male) bottom in fist-fucking becomes "a new signifier for sexual potency and masculinity."[55] For George Stambolian's anonymous masochistic informant, submission is the way he "prove[s]" his "masculinity."[56] And for Larry Townsend, the masochist, "[b]y placing himself in the position of helplessness and subservience, . . . is proving he 'can take it like a man.'" "The heavier the punishment," Townsend observes, "the more this perception is reinforced."[57]

According to these testimonies, gay male S/M is a privileged arena for the male subject to manage his castration anxieties by playing them out—with a vengeance—and to master a femininity that, it is fantasized, adheres within the otherwise masculinized self. Indeed, S/M has become a privileged arena for gay men to negotiate the relationship between what are taken to be masculine and feminine attributes of the self. Moreover, the increased prominence and importance of S/M for gay men seems to me to be a direct result of the extraordinary level of anxiety around femininity that has been associated with male homosexuality. Although the feminized sodomite can be traced back to the consolidation of gendered subjectivities in the early modern period, the invert (whose specter lives on in much popular discourse) was constructed most notoriously by nineteenth-century sexology as a gender deviant, rather than a sexual deviant (a woman's soul trapped in a man's body). In the United States during the twentieth century, anxieties around gender definition (for both homosexual and heterosexualized subjects) became particularly widespread during two periods of social crisis: the domestic revival of the late '40s and '50s that oversaw a return, after the disruption of traditional gender roles in World War II, to more conservative ones; and the (post)feminist and post-Stonewall era that began in the mid-1970s and continues to the present, in which dissident gender and sexual identities remain the target not just of conservatives but also of anti-S/M feminists.[58] Given the continuing controversies over lesbian and gay civil rights (as epitomized by the disputes over lesbian and gay marriage and participation in the military), and the continued bashing of feminism, it seems unlikely that these cultural anxieties will be allayed in the near future. And S/M practices remain one of the most effective means for consolidating a gendered identity, of managing fantasmatically the feminine and the masculine within the self.

THE LESBIAN PHALLUS

Gay men are not, however, the only group to use S/M as a privileged mode of practice for negotiating gendered identities. For many lesbians, as well, S/M has become a vitally important arena in which to work out a relationship to masculinity, femininity, and, most important, power. Although one can no more consider lesbian sadomasochists part of a single community (with a single agenda) than one can leathermen, a great deal of lesbian S/M discourse is devoted to an analysis and attempted recuperation of the social, personal, and sexual power that is denied most women in a patriarchal and heterosexualized culture.[59] For the contributors to *Coming to Power*, S/M is principally (in Juicy Lucy's words) "about sexual power & specifically about lesbians becoming *more* powerful through their sexuality"; it is a "pathway to a more & more powerful self."[60] For Susan Farr and Kitt, S/M demonstrates that "power is not an invention of men," and that women can have "total control" over their bodies and pleasures.[61]

With their discourses of sex and power, many S/M lesbians are using S/M to claim the prerogatives of the phallus—to mime a masculinity that is already understood to be an imitation—and thereby to demonstrate that masculinity can be disengaged from a male body (and I am referring here less to a butch style of presentation than to a particular fantasmatic scenario). Although not explicitly addressing lesbian S/M, Judith Butler notes that "the displaceability of the phallus, its capacity to symbolize in relation to other body parts or other body-like things, opens the way for the lesbian phallus. . . ."[62] Critiquing those cultural feminists (including, prominently, anti-S/M feminists) who would attempt completely to banish the masculine (and whom Gayle Rubin dubs "femininists"), she argues that it is not a question of whether or not the phallus persists in lesbian sexuality, but of "*how* it persists, how it is constructed, and what happens to the 'privileged' status of the signifier within this form of constructed exchange."[63] She points out that rather than simply working to replicate "the scene of normative heterosexuality," the fiction of the lesbian phallus "signifies a desire that . . . is never fully free of the normative demands that condition its possibility and that it nevertheless seeks to subvert."[64] So for Butler, the lesbian phallus is a necessary fiction (at least within the psychoanalytical framework she employs) that both presumes and undermines the heterosexual matrix and thereby calls into question the very principle of gender dimorphism. It is a mode of "resignification" (like butch-femme) that "furthers a crisis in the sense of what it means to 'have' [the phallus] at all."[65]

Although few S/M lesbians avail themselves of deconstructive and psychoanalytical modes of analysis, it seems to me that Butler is, in fact, elucidating precisely what passes in the discourses of lesbian S/M. Like Butler, S/M lesbians argue not only that there is no way outside the heterosexual matrix, but also that there is no way outside the violent (and deeply oppressive) binary oppositions that structure subjectivity and culture: masculine/feminine, active/passive, top/bottom, and "having"/"being" the phallus. Unlike the anti-S/M feminists, they believe that "the connection between sex and power" will never be broken and that the best one can do is to attempt to rework this connection, to make sex and power signify in different ways, to disrupt the normative functioning of these binarisms. Is this not precisely what Wickie Stamps describes when she asserts that S/M lesbians, "instead of remaining victims to a . . . history of abuse," become "active agents in figuring out how, despite [or, more accurately, because of] emotional wounds, to reclaim themselves as sexual beings, . . ." or what Juicy Lucy characterizes as the "release & transform[ation]" of "pain & fear . . . "?[66]

Like these apologetic discourses, lesbian S/M fiction abrogates neither a personal and social history of pain, fear, and victimization, nor the prerogatives of phallic sexuality. In fact, much of it seems intent on recuperating a kind of feminized masculinity in which the phallus operates, to borrow Butler's term, as "a transferable phantasm" that structures sexual exchanges between female bodies.[67] In her S/M classic, "The Calyx of Isis" (1988), the story of an elaborate initiation rite, Pat Califia carefully preserves the lesbian signifier while pointedly complicating its referents. Not only do several of the characters have masculine or ambisexual names (Michael, Tyre, Alex, EZ), but Michael, in particular, is constructed as having a virtually undecidable sexual identity. Although Califia uses feminine pronouns to refer to Michael, the character is in every other way thoroughly masculinized. An ex-marine who wears "the dress-gray uniform of a West Point cadet," she sports a "blond moustache" and works as a chauffeur.[68] She also has a "cock" that is apparently subject to the rhythm of tumescence and detumescence, plus what so often goes along with it: the (masculine) experience of sexual desire as an unstoppable and irreversible force. "Get it up for me," Michael pleads, "and I won't be able to help myself. . . ."[69] Not until well into the climactic orgy, long after Michael has demonstrated the exquisite serviceability of her "hard-on," is it revealed to be a "strap-on."[70] Moreover, Califia deliberately uses a lexicon that is more frequently associated with gay male sexualities than lesbian ones. Characters "jerk off," have "circle jerks," and at least one relishes the role of "Daddy."[71] Most important, the characters in "The Calyx of Isis" continually demonstrate an active and aggressive sexuality that is more frequently associated with masculinity than with femininity. And not only the tops are masculinized; the bottom all too clearly proves that she too can take it like a man.

The masculinization of the lesbian subject extends even to the pronouns in Califia's story "Daddy," narrated from the points of view of both a lesbian Daddy and her lesbian son:

> When I'm Daddy, I want to get my dick into something hot and tight. I want to show that boy what his cock and his butt are for and fuck the come out of him. . . . Good daddies turn out boys who can be brave and strong as well as excellent cocksuckers.[72]

In this story, lesbians mime the masculine (which is itself, of course, always already an imitation) and appropriate both the privileges and the equipment that are usually associated with (gay) male sexualities. As Donna Minkowitz explains (to her presumptively lesbian readers), "looking for Daddy in another woman means explicitly acknowledging . . . something erotic—if only on a phantasmatic level—about a population we frequently hate and fear."[73] Analogous to the "release & transform[ation]" of "pain & fear . . ." that Juicy Lucy invokes to describe S/M, the lesbian impersonation of Daddy represents not only the assumption of the phallus (with its privileged relationship to the strap-on) but also an eroticization of patriarchy. For as the Califia citation makes clear, the father-son relationship is explicitly sexualized—and queered—in Daddy scenarios (in a way that clearly evokes Freud's notion of masochism as a resexualization of the Oedipus complex).[74] As happens relentlessly in S/M narratives, the abjected is negatived, and a source of pain is refigured as a site of pleasure. "For the majority of us," one Daddy explains, "a male figure conjures up some kind of abuse—emotional, sexual, or physical. For me, the word *Daddy* was a nightmare until I became one."[75] Becoming (or introjecting) the one she fears, the lesbian S/M subject lays claim to the pleasure and the power that have been denied her historically. Moreover, both "The Calyx of Isis" and "Daddy" testify yet again to the undecidable position of the S/M subject relative to the norms of gendered subjectivity. Like Bill and Michael in "Blue Light," and like the lesbian phallus, Califia's characters, moving between "having" and "being" the phallus, occupy both masculine and feminine positionalities and so take control over both their pleasures and their gendered identities.[76]

As I have noted above, S/M practices and narratives (whether lesbian, gay male, or even straight) function as privileged and safe sites for subjects to work out their relationship to masculinity and femininity. They allow consenting subjects control over the production and reproduction of these most important fantasmatic points of identification. They allow the assumption of both masculine and feminine subject positions and a fluid relationship to the phallus, thereby facilitating the subject's negotiation not just of castration anxieties but also of those insecurities and fears that come into play around questions of power and sex. Without fundamentally altering the social structures that produce oppression, they perform a kind of psychic alchemy, transforming the dross of abjection into gold, and offer a genuine, if limited, sense of empowerment to subjects who, in many cases, have been denied power as social actors. As such, S/M practices and narratives do indeed seem to function, as so many of its apologists maintain, as a kind of therapeutic tool for the subject, regardless of gender, to reimagine and mime a highly eroticized and ultimately benign masculinity that, for all its fierceness, remains bounteous, voluptuous, and kind.

THE MAINSTREAMING OF S/M

Given the radical differences between the histories of lesbians and gay men in the United States, the lesbian recuperation of masculinity through S/M has, I believe, very different implications from its gay male analogue. Most important, gay men as a class—and not only since Stonewall—have been a much more visible and powerful minority, with far more economic and cultural capital, than lesbians. Coincidentally, gay men have not seen, as lesbians have, their desires and sexuality consistently erased. On the contrary, as *Cruising* so vividly demonstrates, in many mass-mediated representations (both before and after AIDS), male homosexuality and promiscuity are virtually a tautology. At the same time, however, the insistent sexualization of gay men has often been accompanied by their feminization (according to which sexual deviance is reconceptualized as gender deviance). The gay macho style that developed during the 1970s to combat this feminization (the clone) owes much to S/M style, if not to the content of the S/M fantasmatic. So if lesbian S/M is in part a response to the desexualization of the lesbian, then gay male S/M is a sharp rebuke to the image of the queer man as pansy.

Much of the discourse by leathermen stresses S/M's remasculinizing force. Yet sometimes this process produces unexpected side effects, connecting S/M to masculinities that have, at best, problematic histories. Thus, for example, two of the contributors to *Leatherfolk* pointedly invoke Robert Bly's *Iron John*. Referring to Bly's description of various initiation rites, John Preston argues that "[w]hat Bly is talking about, . . . the S/M world can deliver."[77] Mark Thompson, meanwhile, much more indebted to New Age vernacular than Preston, adopts Bly's nomenclature of the "soft man" and presses into service both the jargon of authenticity and the metaphysics of depth to which Bly continually appeals, noting that what drives leathermen on is "a curiosity to know a deeper part of ourselves, that place where the source of our authentic power resides."[78] Given the historical positioning of Bly's work and of the men's movement, these moves strike me as being inauspicious.

Although Preston and Thompson seem unaware of the homophobia and misogyny that structure the men's movement, their observations about the masculinizing function of S/M, their nostalgia for a precommodified culture and an "authentic" self, and their barely concealed disdain both for "our feminine . . . selves" and for a (feminist) "movement . . . so focused on gender equality" as to forbid "*any* acting out of masculine roles" unmistakably connects their discourses with the misogynist and primitivist rhetoric of the men's movement.[79] And they are by no means unique. While not invoking Bly by name, Samuel M. Steward (a.k.a. Phil Andros) even more explicitly conjoins remasculinization, nostalgia, and antifeminism, noting that the "speed-up toward . . . matriarchy" (he even cites approvingly Philip Wylie's attack on "Momism"!) has made the "Hero" disappear from a "modern world" that has been despoiled by "automation." Dismayed at this prospect, Steward sees in S/M a "quest for the symbol of what [is] left of the world's masculinity."[80] For all three writers, leatherspace provides a privileged site for the construction of that which seems perilously close to hegemonic, straight masculinity: a marooned subjectivity, searching for power, for an "authentic," privatized self, always in the past, always elsewhere.

To conclude, however, that gay male S/M simply replicates the most oppressive features of straight masculinity is a gross oversimplification that merely parrots the most parochial anti-S/M positions. Indeed, the only way to adjudicate this question is to examine the different narratives in which S/M discourses and practices are embedded, and the effects they produce. It may well be, in fact, that the cultural positioning of gay male S/M is every bit as contradictory as its fantasmatic structure. As "Blue Light" suggests, the S/M fantasy both avows and disavows castration; it relinquishes the masculine prerogative in order to take it up again all the more imperiously. And the masculinity at stake in this process is itself contradictory, both transitive and intransitive, both specularizing and specularized, both "projected role" and "real essence."[81] Founded upon a homoeroticism that is embraced as feverishly by Preston, Thompson, and Steward as it is disavowed by Bly and his partisans, S/M provides a way for men to reclaim a pure—because wholly homosocial—masculinity.

Yet this same masculinity, which is tirelessly universalized by Bly and, to a lesser extent, by the discourses of both S/M and psychoanalysis, cannot be dissociated from specific social and economic developments. As it emerged during the 1950s, with its "intense masculine sexuality" propped up by black Harley-Davidsons, S/M masculinity reacted against the feminization not only of the gay man but also of the normative straight male subject in post–World War II culture, against his reconfiguration as "organization man," against his domestication in the roles of husband, father, and breadwinner.[82] (Who could be further from Ward Cleaver than a leatherman?) The development of a gay male S/M subculture during the 1950s was also in part a reaction against and a tacit critique of the valuation of homosexuality during the '50s and '60s as gender deviance. Having been stripped of their masculine identifications by a theory of sexual inversion that (like Simon LeVay's work today) attempts to position gay men, because they desire other men, on the terrain of femininity, leathermen were determined to prove they were real men and to reclaim the aggressive and brooding masculinity associated with the "wild ones" like Marlon Brando and James Dean. During the 1960s, with the proliferation of alternative youth cultures, these same S/M warriors became fierce partisans for the sexual revolution and, along with other lesbians and gay men, emerged as the preeminent figures in the so-called sexual avant-garde.

If Michael Bronski and others are correct, the mid-1970s marks a turning point in the fortunes of the S/M subculture. During this period, it not only grew exponentially but effected a wholesale change in "gay male iconography," moving it toward forms increasingly inflected by S/M styles and stereotypes.[83] By 1979, when William Friedkin started filming *Cruising* in New York, a large S/M subculture was at his disposal for use as a synechdoche for gay male culture in its entirety (this despite Friedkin's disclaimer that the part "is not meant to be representative of the whole").[84] Bronski argues persuasively that this "explosion" of S/M is the result of the growth and prosperity of the queer community after Stonewall, especially in the major urban centers, and of the recognition on the part of gay men and lesbians that they had "emotional and psychological power to govern [their] own lives."[85] So, as with lesbian S/M, gay male S/M performs (or authorizes leathermen to perform) the very real oppression that produces them as subjected beings, and, simultaneously, their relative economic and cultural empowerment as individuals (according to a 1993 survey, the average household income for self-identified lesbians is 25 percent higher and for self-identified gay men 40 percent higher than that of the average American household).[86]

At the same time, however, the essentialist discourse of "deep masculinity" links gay male S/M with the new masculinity and the reflexive sadomasochistic fantasies of Robert Bly and Sylvester Stallone. Although the cultural positioning of this masculinity and of queer leatherspace are completely different, I believe that normative and queer masculinities are more closely related than might at first appear and that the "explosion" of gay male S/M during the 1970s is also in part a response to the momentous social and economic changes that I outline in chapter 3. Although the roles in gay male S/M are usually clearly delineated (at least in each particular scene), there is, as I suggest above, a constant movement of identification and desire back and forth across the slash. Furthermore, S/M fictions like "Blue Light" clearly demonstrate the importance of the reflexive position in the S/M scenario insofar as Bill's assessment of his position, "[m]asochistic victim, and sadistic observer of my own humiliation," precisely describes the reflexive sadomasochist (33). Moreover, the emblematic S/M fantasy, whether dramatized in "Blue Light" or in *Mister Benson*, is uncannily similar to the structure of the Grimm fairy tale that inspires *Iron John* as well as to the scenarios of *First Blood* and *Rambo*.

In all of these texts, a male protagonist takes up the role of victim—usually with deep ambivalence—and struggles against a fierce opponent to prove his toughness, vigor, and masculinity. Whether he wins or loses seems to be almost immaterial. What matters is that he demonstrate that he can take it like a man. Moreover, despite the fact that the queer S/M community is by no means entirely composed of European-Americans (although among the 1,174 respondents to Larry Townsend's 1982 survey of leathermen only 2 percent were men of color), the fantasies that propel a considerable amount of S/M discourse are much like the white mythologies that *Iron John* and *Rambo* propound, in which racial difference is insistently exoticized and spectacularized.[87] Aaron Travis's "Crown of Thorns," for example, chronicles the insatiable appetite of its blond American narrator for an unmistakably orientalized Turk whose racial and cultural difference is decisive in producing him as an object of desire.[88] In "Blue Light," meanwhile, Bill's very first reaction to Michael is astonishment at the pallor of his skin, which (the inverse of the Turk's) marks him as a spectacle of whiteness. Although some S/M pornography has attempted to become less dependent upon these racist tropes, it unequivocally remains the product of an imperialist fantasmatic and often appeals (like most pornography and, more significant, like most American cultural productions) to racial and ethnic differences in constructing its erotic scenarios.

Yet there is one more crucial difference between the fantasies of Sylvester Stallone and those of Aaron Travis. Although the growth of the S/M subculture during the 1970s (which, according to most leatherfolk, really means the proliferation of bottoms) bears witness to the willingness of many gay men to masquerade as victim, "Blue Light"'s Bill is quite unlike John J. Rambo. Rambo may believe himself an individual casualty of the U.S. government's negligence, but the class that he stands for—straight, white men—has not, in fact, been oppressed historically relative to other groups. Therefore, Rambo's identification with the role of victim must finally be delusional—and paranoid. For gay men, however, as a class (and lesbians even more so), the role of victim is not a purely paranoid identification: they have repeatedly been exploited, harassed, bashed, and killed (either directly or, in the case of AIDS, by a conspicuous indifference). Thus a history of oppression has been decisive both for the constitution of gay men as subjects and for the production of their desires. The ascendancy of gay male S/M seems to me to be in part a tacit acknowledgment of that history and of the continued impossibility of distinguishing between those qualities that the anti-S/M feminists most desperately want to see disarticulated: abjection and desire, power and sex. The laws of (S/M) desire ensure that one will always, at least to some degree, both identify with and desire one's oppressor.

Yet for leathermen and -women (if one is to take them at their word), much more distinctly than for Rambo, the performance of victimization enables a mastery of subjection. Rather than reinforce submissiveness, the act of *choosing* humiliation, *performing* subjection, allegedly reactivates (at least a simulacrum of) individualized control and agency. Like the justificatory discourses of lesbian S/M, virtually all of the writings by gay leathermen also extol S/M's purported cathartic and therapeutic values, emphasizing that violence is both purged and mastered in S/M. Relentlessly, these discourses turn S/M into a vehicle of redemption, into an abrogation of the violent homophobia to which gay men and lesbians have been subjected. In this process, S/M is reconfigured as the most ecstatic, emancipatory, and revolutionary of sexual practices. It allows for an imaginary and privatized escape from and transcendence of a hateful and murderously homophobic culture.[89] Yet in taking up this position, S/M texts ironically become the mirror image of the anti-S/M discourses that they attempt to refute. Both take sexual practices to be the *key* to subjectivity, and both are obsessed with their utopian potential, with the possibility that a particular form of sexuality might finally prove salvational for the human subject (and the human species) and redeem a seemingly interminable history of oppression.

Despite the fact that for most leathermen, S/M performance does not automatically translate into progressive electoral or mass-movement politics (according to Townsend's survey, more leathermen in 1980 voted for Ronald Reagan than for Jimmy Carter), S/M subculture and "lifestyle" have become increasingly important in recent years for the articulation of what have become the new queer politics.[90] The latter, moving "beyond" the cultural nationalisms and identity politics of the 1970s, not only shares with S/M a performative concept of identity but also adopts the more aggressive, angry style that is often associated with the sexual practices of leatherfolk. John Preston's formula for S/M, "[l]eather [is] gay sexuality stripped of being nice. It offend[s]. It confront[s]," could easily be transposed to queer politics: "queer is gay politics stripped of being nice."[91] Like leathersex, it aims at outrage and confrontation (a contention I will take up in detail in the next chapter).[92] The strategies of ACT UP and Queer Nation may be much indebted to '60s activism, to the civil rights, Black Power, and antiwar movements as well as to the almost camp "revolutionary action-theatre" of the Yippies.[93] But at the same time, the ascendancy of both groups during the late '80s and early '90s coincides with the increasing "mainstreaming" (to borrow Bronski's word) of S/M and the increasing participation, at least since the 1987 March on Washington, of the queer S/M community in mass-movement politics.[94] Writing in 1991, leatherman Scott Tucker is "pleased to note the proliferation of Queer Nation groups nationwide," which he credits with registering "sexual and political dissent" and "raising fetishism to new heights of fashion" (but note the equal emphasis on activism and style).[95] Moreover, the new clone that emerged concurrently with ACT UP in the late 1980s, like the leatherman, uses his own body to play out his conflicted relationship to masculinity and femininity. With his tattoos, body piercings, black leather motorcycle jacket, and often outrageously camp accessories, he owes far more to S/M style than to his '70s plaid-shirted, mustachioed forebear.[96] The visibility of this new clone also testifies to the increasing commodification of S/M (and of queer style more generally), and the fact that the appropriation of queer fashions in the "gay '90s" does not necessarily lead to an endorsement of the political position of which it was initially a signifier. On the contrary, it seems that in mass culture queer fashion (particularly the much ballyhooed lesbian chic) has become not an incitement to, but a substitute for, a commitment to lesbian and gay civil rights.

Inscribed within contradictory histories, queer S/M remains a deeply conflicted phenomenon in American culture. On the one hand, it attests to the violent social and political oppression of lesbians and gay men and to the inevitability that desire (that most apparently individualized of drives) is always socially produced and always marked by a history of oppression. On the other hand, it also testifies to the relative economic and cultural empowerment of lesbians and gay men as a class (at least those who make up urban S/M subcultures and produce books like *Coming to Power* and *Leatherfolk*). It also bears witness to the vexed relation between the political and the sexual in American culture and the fact that queer identities at once disrupt the binary opposition between the public and the private and reinforce the belief that the private is the central determining feature, not just of subjectivity, but of the social as well. It thereby leads me to question how intensively privatized practices can be expected to lead either to legislative reform or to the sexual revolution of which many leatherfolk see themselves in the vanguard. How does the subversion of sexual norms produce progressive political change?

The importance of subversion as a political weapon is attested to almost everywhere in the discourses of dissident sexualities: in the popularity of Judith Butler's concept of resignification, in Wickie Stamps's notion of reclamation, or, for that matter, in almost any example of what passes these days for queer theory.[97] All of these discourses attest to the fact that subversion has become virtually an article of faith for the many poststructuralists and queer theorists intent on challenging hegemonic cultural constructions. Yet as Bersani argues, "resignification cannot destroy; it merely presents to the dominant culture spectacles of politically impotent disrespect."[98] For resignification will always to some extent reinscribe the very binarisms it hopes to deconstruct. Yet the ascendancy of these deconstructive politics (and of poststructuralism generally) in the academy in the mid-1980s has corresponded to a high level of interest, in both elite and popular culture, not only in S/M but in a wide range of dissident sexual practices and identities. It seems to me that this correspondence is far more than coincidental. And while there are many reasons for it (including the limited success, at least on college campuses, of the women's and lesbian and gay civil rights movements), I believe that both developments attest in part to the collapse of mass-movement politics, to the attenuation of anticapitalist struggle, and to a new conservative hegemony (at least in the United States and the United Kingdom) that emerged in the late 1970s. Obsessed with locating and valorizing sites of transgression and resistance, both poststructuralism and the discourses of sexual dissidence tend to imagine resistant political practices not in the collectivist terms of the 1960s (or the 1930s, for that matter) but in strictly individualistic terms. For both, resistance too often becomes a purely privatized affair, restricted to one's scholarship, one's teaching, one's bedroom, one's dungeon. And although these modes of critique do to some extent call into question the relationship between the political and the sexual, they still, I believe, conceptualize oppositional practice in individualistic terms. Moreover, in privileging the cultural realm they tend to ignore that sphere of activity which has historically been designated the political. As such, they inadvertently reveal the limitations of a politics of identity and "lifestyle." For what does the "power to govern our own lives" mean—beyond the "freedom" to consume—if it is not founded upon an ongoing social, economic, and political struggle for legitimation?[99]

Not only has that legitimation been withheld at both the federal and local levels (at least in the vast majority of cities and states in this country), but the constitutional right to privacy on which it is based has been summarily invalidated for gay men in *Bowers v. Hardwick*. Moreover, the continuing debate over lesbians and gay men in the military would seem to demonstrate—yet again—that queers do not warrant special protection under the Fourteenth Amendment. As individuals, David Geffen may be able to contribute large sums to various antihomophobic causes and David Mixner may have slept in the Lincoln bedroom, but these shows of power do not necessarily translate into political authority for lesbians and gay men as a class. It may well be that the "explosion" of gay male S/M, of the spectacularization of power(lessness), precisely enacts this disparity between the economic clout of many gay men and their political disenfranchisement. If so, then what does sexual liberation provide other than access to a "free" market of bodies and pleasures? How can it guarantee that the stigmatization of queers will go the way of the nineteenth-century crusade against masturbation, and consign those most violent of binary oppositions—public/private, male/female, homo/hetero—to the dustbin of history? Is it enough for leatherfolk to prove that so-called normal sexual practices are even more queer than their own?

Chapter Five

MAN AND NATION

> America, not just the nation, but an idea alive in the minds of people everywhere. As this new world takes shape, America stands at the center of a widening circle of freedom, today, tomorrow and into the next century.
>
> *(President George Bush, State of the Union Message,*
> *January 31, 1990)*

> We will be citizens.
>
> *(Prior Walter, in Tony Kushner's* Angels in America,
> Part Two: Perestroika *[1993])*

AT THE END of World War II, the United States staked both its identity as a nation and its plans for global economic dominance on its opposition to communism as an economic, political, and ideological system. However, in the early 1990s, the dissolution of the Soviet empire and the fall of communist parties from East Berlin to Moscow was greeted with something other than unalloyed jubilation. Behind the giddy triumphalism of George Bush's State of the Union Messages, one may detect the sense of a national identity crisis in the making. A reluctant president admitted in his 1992 address that "there's a mood among us. People are worried. There has been talk of decline."[1] To redress this "mood," and the possibility that the national security state might need to be dismantled, Bush (with the support of both Democrats and Republicans) accelerated the production of a new and threatening other: the terrorist or rogue state.[2] As a substitute for communism, terrorism is decried as an external and internal threat both to the state and to its near equivalent, U.S. business interests. John M. Deutch, the director of the Central Intelligence Agency (no doubt fearing for the life of the agency), predicted a "tremendous growth" in terrorism over the next ten to fifteen years and warned that this would have "immense impact on how we conduct our foreign policy, immense impact on how American businesses operate abroad." And because terrorism is a much more vague (and therefore expansive and useful) category than communism, it can include not only governments "inimical to democracy" but also transnational cooperatives of "drug traffickers, weapons smugglers, religious zealots and even business spies."[3] For like multinational capital—of which it represents both a perversion and a parody—terrorism threatens not just national security and national borders but the very idea of the nation as a sovereign political and economic entity. The difference between them is quite simply that the one promotes U.S. business (and, therefore, political) interests while the other is intent on sabotaging them.

In an attempt to underscore the power and malignancy of terrorism and to counter the dire threat of peace to military Keynesianism, Bush's reinvigorated national security state engineered deadly imperialist spectacles in Panama and Iraq. But these shows of force, in Paul Piccone's estimation, were not in themselves enough to shore up the "collective values and aspirations whose heterogeneity had hitherto been conveniently fused into a national *group* . . . by the external mediation of the threatening communist other."[4] A diffuse network of transnational terror could not produce the same relatively secure sense of national identity that the communist menace provided. What was needed was a compelling ideological fix, and in the early 1990s, Bush's vision of the United States as the "freest," "kindest," and "strongest nation on earth" provided the basis for a renewal of nationalist ideology.[5] Yet his speeches of the early 1990s did not merely recycle the shopworn rhetoric of freedom (that coincidentally celebrates the unrestricted international flow of capital). Wrapping himself in the sage's mantle, Bush noted in his 1992 address that "in the past 12 months, the world has known changes of almost biblical proportions."[6] And this address, like all his messages of the early '90s, overflows with an almost apocalyptic discourse of progress and transfiguration, repeatedly referencing "democracy's advance," "a new world order," and "a dramatic and deeply promising time in our history."[7] Attempting to revive U.S. nationalism and place the nation at the very center of history, they redefine "America" as "the beacon of freedom in a searching world."[8]

During this national identity crisis one theatrical event stands out. Since its first workshop production in 1990, Tony Kushner's *Angels in America: A Gay Fantasia on National Themes* has changed the face and scale of the American theater. Having amassed the Pulitzer Prize, two best-play Tonys, and other prestigious awards, it has proven, against all odds, that a play can tackle the most controversial subjects—including politics, religion, and sex—and yet be a hit. As a meditation on "national themes," *Angels* (more provocatively than any other recent cultural text) explicitly engages questions of national history, identity, and mission by reenvisioning both what has been and what could be. Moreover, the play insistently links the nationalist project to an anti-homophobic one by demonstrating the crucial importance of gay men in the construction of a national subject, polity, and literature. *Angels* queers the idea of America by reimagining the heavens and the earth, by producing hermaphroditic angels, an AIDS-stricken prophet, and a "flaming" God.[9] At the same time, *Angels* is centrally concerned with male masochism—which it understands as a problem—and its originality lies in part in its linkage of male masochism with U.S. political culture and the idea of America, and its attempt to promote a nationalist solution to this problem. This chapter, then, represents an examination of these disparate phenomena: the end-of-the-Cold-War identity crisis, the new (and old) nationalisms of the 1990s, the success of *Angels in America*, and its albeit ambivalent revival of the anti-S/M position that dominated much feminist and lesbian and gay discourse of the late '70s and '80s.

ANGELS IN AMERICA

Critics, pundits, and producers have placed Tony Kushner's *Angels in America: A Gay Fantasia on National Themes* in the unenviable position of having to rescue the American theater. The latter, by all accounts, is in a sorry state. It has attempted to maintain its elite cultural status despite the fact that the differences between "high" and "low" have become precarious. On Broadway, increasingly expensive productions survive more and more by mimicking mass culture, either in the form of mind-numbing spectacles featuring singing cats, falling chandeliers, and dancing dinnerware or in plays, like *The Heidi Chronicles* or *Prelude to a Kiss*, whose style and themes aspire to "quality" television. In regional theaters, meanwhile, subscriptions continue to decline and with them, the adventurousness of artistic directors. Given this dismal situation, *Angels in America* has almost single-handedly resuscitated a category of play that has become almost extinct: the serious Broadway drama that is neither a British import nor a revival.

Not within memory has a new American play been canonized by the press as rapidly as *Angels in America*.[10] Indeed, critics have been stumbling over each other in an adulatory stupor. John Lahr hails *Perestroika* as a "masterpiece" and notes that "[n]ot since Williams has a playwright announced his poetic vision with such authority on the Broadway stage."[11] Jack Kroll judges both parts "the broadest, deepest, most searching American play of our time,"[12] while Robert Brustein deems *Millennium Approaches* "the authoritative achievement of a radical dramatic artist with a fresh, clear voice."[13] In the gay press, meanwhile, the play is viewed as testifying to the fact that "Broadway now leads the way in the industry with its unapologetic portrayals of gay characters."[14] For both Frank Rich and John Clum, *Angels* is far more than just a successful play; it is the marker of a decisive historical shift in American theater. According to Rich, the play's success is in part the result of its ability to conduct "a searching and radical rethinking of the whole esthetic of American political drama."[15] For Clum, the play's appearance on Broadway "marks a turning point in the history of gay drama, the history of American drama, and of American literary culture."[16] In its reception, *Angels*—so deeply preoccupied with teleological process—is itself positioned as both the culmination of history and as that which rewrites the past.

Despite the enormity of the claims cited above, I am less interested in disputing them than in trying to understand why they are being made, why the play is both "radical" and popular. *Why* are these claims being made, and why are they being made *now*? Why is the play at once being universalized as a "turning point" in the American theater, and minoritized as the preeminent gay male artifact of the 1990s? These questions, in turn, lead me to another series that centers on notions of masculinity and sexuality: Why does a play about gay men in the age of Reagan and the age of AIDS amass such cultural capital? What makes these men and the problems over which they agonize so fascinating? Of what do their masculinities consist? Why are relationships between fathers and sons so decisive in the play? Why is the only sex in *Millennium* an S/M scene? And these questions, yet again, raise a different set of questions, this time about the idea of America: Why does a play that is so concerned with constituting and debating national mission and identity achieve such celebrity at the end of the Cold War? What is the play suggesting about both the nature of America and the disparate American histories to which it constantly alludes? What is the relationship between the queer sort of nationalism that the play seems to promote and the strategies and goals of Queer Nation, a group whose founding in 1990 only narrowly postdates the writing of the play? Finally, it seems to me, it is impossible to answer these questions by cordoning off the idea of the nation from constructions of sexuality and gender. One interrogates the structure of hegemonic masculinities in part by interrogating the history of the idea of America. One begins to imagine that which may lie beyond masochism by analyzing the constitution of the body politic.

Masochism, Internalized Oppression, and Normative Masculinity

The opposite of nearly everything you say about *Angels in America* will also hold true: *Angels* valorizes identity politics; it offers an antifoundationalist critique of identity politics. *Angels* mounts an attack against ideologies of individualism; it problematizes the idea of community. *Angels* submits liberalism to a trenchant examination; it finally opts for yet another version of American liberal pluralism. *Angels* launches a critique of the very mechanisms that produce pathologized and acquiescent female bodies; it represents yet another pathologization and silencing of women. A conscientious reader or spectator might well rebuke the play, as Belize does Louis: "you're ambivalent about everything."[17] *Angels*'s ambivalence, however, is not simply the result of Kushner's hedging his bets on the most controversial issues. Rather, it functions, I believe—quite independently of the intent of its author—as the play's political unconscious, playing itself out on many different levels: formal, ideological, characterological, and rhetorical (Frank Rich refers to this as Kushner's "refusal to adhere to any theatrical or political theory").[18] Yet the fact that ambivalence—or undecidability—is the watchword of this text (which is, after all, *two* plays) does not mean that all the questions it raises remain unresolved. On the contrary, I will argue that the play's undecidability is, in fact, always already resolved because the questions that appear to be ambivalent have in fact already been decided consciously or unconsciously by the text itself. Moreover, the relentless operation of normalizing reading practices works to reinforce these decisions. If I am correct, the play turns out (pace Frank Rich) to adhere all too well to a particular political theory.

Formally, *Angels* is a promiscuously complicated play that is very difficult to categorize generically. Clum's characterization of it as being "like a Shakespearean romance" is doubtlessly motivated by its rambling and episodic form, its interweaving of multiple plotlines, its mixture of realism and fantasy, its invocation of various theological and mythological narratives, as well as its success in evoking those characteristics that are usually associated with both comedy and tragedy.[19] Moreover, *Perestroika*'s luminous finale is remarkably suggestive of the beatific scenes that end Shakespeare's romances. There is no question, moreover, but that the play deliberately evokes the long history of Western dramatic literature and positions itself as heir to the traditions of Sophocles, Shakespeare, Brecht, and others. Consider, for example, its use of the blindness/insight binary opposition and the way that Prior Walter is carefully constructed (like the blind Prelapsarianov) as a kind of Teiresias, "going blind, as prophets do" (2: 56). This binarism, the paradigmatic emblem of the tragic subject (and mark of Teiresias, Oedipus, and Gloucester), deftly links cause and effect—because one is blind to truth, one loses one's sight— and is used to claim Prior's priority, his epistemologically privileged position in the text. Or consider the parallels often drawn in the press between Kushner's Roy Cohn and Shakespeare's Richard III.[20] Or Kushner's use of a fate motif, reminiscent of *Macbeth*, whereby Prior insists that Louis not return until the seemingly impossible comes to pass, until he sees Louis "black and blue" (2: 89). Or Kushner's rewriting of those momentous moral and political debates that riddle not just classical tragedy (*Antigone*, *Richard II*) but also the work of Brecht and his (mainly British) successors (Howard Brenton, David Hare, Caryl Churchill). Or the focus on the presence/absence of God that one finds not just in early modern tragedy but also in so-called absurdism (Beckett, Ionesco, Stoppard). Moreover, these characteristics tend to be balanced, on the one hand, by the play's insistent tendency to ironize and, on the other, by the familiar ingredients of romantic comedies (ill-matched paramours, repentant lovers, characters suddenly finding themselves in unfamiliar places, plus a lot of good jokes). Despite the ironic/comic tone, however, none of the interlaced couples survives the onslaught of chaos, disease, and revelation. Prior and Louis, Louis and Joe, Joe and Harper have all parted by the end of the play, and the romantic dyad (as primary social unit) is replaced in the final scene of *Perestroika* by a utopian concept of (erotic) affiliation and a new definition of family.

Angels in America thus produces itself as formally ambivalent, which is to say, heir to several different—and conflicting—dramatic traditions. This, I believe, explains in part why the play was instantly canonized by the press and why a broad range of critics have been able to accommodate the play to their conception of what a classic is. *Angels* is particularly adept in producing its precursors out of the most canonical and intellectually respectable of dramatic texts. And the irony here is that most of the precursors of this most American of texts belong not to the American realistic, narrative tradition at all but to various European traditions. And although one may see glimmers of Tennessee Williams's style in the play's poetry, eroticism, and its expansion of the conventions of realism, *Angels* also dramatizes both its belatedness to Williams and its ability (unlike Williams's early works) to be *out*. Prior's citation of Williams's most celebrated line, "I have always depended on the kindness of strangers," is met not with an appreciative and nostalgic sigh but with a rebuke: "Well that's a stupid thing to do" (2: 141). The successfully Oedipalized Kushner cleverly distances himself from his gay forebear and the playwright with whom he is most likely to be compared (and coincidentally offers sound advice to a gay man in a violently homophobic culture).

Given its conflicted relationship to the drama of the past, *Angels in America* not surprisingly adopts an ambivalent relationship to that most hardy and ubiquitous of dramatic forms, liberal tragedy. According to Raymond Williams, liberal tragedy (as originally codified by Ibsen) is centered on

> a man at the height of his powers and the limits of his strength, at once aspiring and being defeated, releasing and destroyed by his own energies. The structure is liberal in its emphasis on the surpassing individual, and tragic in its ultimate recognition of defeat or the limits of victory.[21]

In liberal tragedy, a usually male hero sets himself in opposition against a world "full of lies and compromises and dead positions, only to find, as he struggles against it, that as a man he belongs to this world, and has its destructive inheritance in himself."[22] Predicated on what Louis (and others) call "internalized oppression," liberal tragedy presupposes a limited porousness between the individual and the culture of which he is a part (1: 94). It assumes that the liberal subject introjects those qualities that are most injurious to his well-being and that threaten all that he holds most dear, his freedom and autonomy. In *Angels*, the paradigmatic liberal tragic hero is of course Roy Cohn, the one who has internalized a violently homophobic ideology and who, in one of the play's most memorable scenes, denies he is a homosexual insofar as he recognizes that this designation describes as much a political as it does a sexual identity:

> Homosexuals are not men who sleep with other men. Homosexuals are men who in fifteen years of trying cannot get a pissant antidiscrimination bill through City Council. Homosexuals are men who know nobody and who nobody knows. Who have zero clout. Does this sound like me, Henry? (1: 45)

Cohn's refusal to claim identity is presented as the source of his "tragedy," and he functions as the play's exemplum of that which must be superseded, the closeted gay man, the man who betrays his class. His adoptive son, meanwhile, Joe Pitt, is similarly insensitive (or blind, to use one of the play's dominant metaphors) to the contradiction between sexual position and ideology and, like his mentor, neatly takes up a liberal tragic position.

Yet both Roy and Joe remain something of a sideshow in *Angels*. Although the sources of, respectively, sardonic comedy and erotic fascination (for Louis, at least), they are not the spectator's or reader's primary point of identification. (One of *Angels*'s most intriguing and original moves is to relegate liberal tragedy to the margins of the text.) Rather, the other leading characters, Louis, Prior, Belize, Harper, and Hannah, are far more likely points of interpellation for the spectator or reader. And with all of these characters, questions of internalization become much more difficult and fraught. Since all of them fall into the category of oppressed persons (because of sexual orientation, HIV status, race, and/or gender) and most of them indulge in behavior that can be interpreted as self-destructive, they can be said to have internalized oppressive values. In this sense, Kushner has placed at the center of this play (if, in its attempted deconstruction of the difference between center and margin, it could be said even to possess a center) less a single character than a particular kind of psychosocial construct: internalized oppression. Yet the play finally remains ambivalent in regard to this construct and works aggressively to problematize it, insofar as it calls into question the separation between society and individual subject on which it must be based. For the concept of internalized oppression, whether mobilized by Louis or by anti-S/M feminists, both produces and undermines the binary oppositions between society and individual, outside and inside. Taking the autonomous subject as its starting point, it assumes that the oppressed subject could, presumably, at some point, work itself free of oppression. And this, it seems to me, is the most significant problem with the concept: less the idea that oppression is internalized than the likelihood that it might *not* be. For although it acknowledges the power by which one is interpellated as a subject, it also assumes that this same subject could be acculturated to a deeply hierarchical society and somehow, through an act of individual will, not internalize its values. Most important, it refuses to recognize that it is by one's submission to the cultural (and familial order) that one's desires are constituted. Loath to acknowledge that desire resists the conscious control of the individual subject, internalized oppression bestows both too much and not enough power on the unconscious and simultaneously refuses to recognize that one's desires are not always consonant with one's political beliefs.

Insistently, in *Angels in America*, in *Cruising*, in anti-S/M feminist tracts, and in so many different hegemonic discourses, internalized oppression gets collapsed into masochism. Because one is blind to oppression, the reasoning goes, one internalizes the hatred that originates from without and desires not to be loved but to be abused. In *Angels*, the relationship between internalized oppression and masochism is particularly complex and particularly revealing of the anxieties circulating around this formulation in American culture. Throughout *Angels in America*, subjectivity is produced by a masochistic desire for suffering. The self, wracked by guilt and remorse, eternally analyzing itself and finding itself wanting, seeks out the pain that it believes to be retribution for real or imagined sins. Most all of the characters fantasize being hurt, wounded, and destroyed, and seem to derive, if not pleasure, then at least a certain sense of security from their pain. (Kushner, significantly, sees S/M as "an enormously pervasive dynamic" that "plays through every aspect of life.")[23] Harper suffers from what her husband calls "emotional problems" and imagines a "man with a knife" waiting for her in the bedroom (1: 26, 24). She is the one who, as "a punishment," dreams that Joe "batter[s] away at me till all my joints come apart, like wax, and I fall into pieces." In her valium-induced fantasies, she sees herself dismembered by his violence, which functions, in turn, as a displacement for their jointly committed "sin": "It was wrong of me to marry you. I knew you . . . (*she stops herself*) . . . " (1: 37). Which is to say, she knew he was homosexual but married him anyway. For this (and doubtlessly other imagined sins as well) she suffers and, until the end of *Perestroika*, derives at least a measure of enjoyment from her suffering. As such, Harper not only embodies but sets the pattern for one of the dominant forms of masochism in the play, feminine masochism, in which the subject, in Freud's formulation, desires to be "pinioned, bound, beaten painfully, whipped, in some way mishandled, forced to obey unconditionally, defiled, degraded." Harper in particular (although she certainly has no monopoly on this desire in the play) "wants to be treated like a little, helpless, dependent child, but especially like a naughty child."[24] Thus she and Joe talk their baby talk and kiss their baby kisses.

The pivotal position of Joe, and specifically of Joe's repressed homosexual desires, in producing Harper's masochistic psychopathology is symptomatic of a crucial semantic figuration in the play. Throughout the text, masochistic desires and practices are connected relentlessly to repressed and/or mismanaged homosexualities (this clearly distinguishes it from the discourses of *Leatherfolk*). In other words, masochism becomes a marker of the maladjusted gay man. Thus the closeted Joe of *Millennium*, identifying with the biblical Jacob, imagines wrestling with an angel (who is "a beautiful man, with golden hair and wings") and prays to God "to crush me, break me up into little pieces," much the way that Harper imagines herself broken in pieces (1: 49). His bleeding ulcer is the sign of the battle between his "will" and his desire, the proof that he is literally devouring himself (1: 77). For Joe, desire is agonizing and phallicized: "it's like a nail, like a hot spike right through my chest." Simultaneously, however, his refusal to be impaled by desire turns him (perversely) into the one who threatens Harper and who torments himself with a different sharp object: "I'm the man with the knives" (1: 77). Given the play's association of repression with pain, it will come as little surprise that the other closeted gay Republican, Roy Cohn, is constructed as the paradigmatic masochist in the play. Roy is the one who not only proclaims that "[p]ain's . . . nothing, pain's life" but also boasts, "[w]hen they did my facelifts, I made the anesthesiologist use a local. They lifted up my whole face like a dinner napkin and I was wide awake to see it" (2: 27; the ellipsis appears in the source). He is the one who, stoned on morphine, asks to be taken, to be riven in two by Belize: "[d]eep and sincere but not too rough, just open me up to the end of me" (2: 76). Moreover, the erotogenic component of Roy's masochistic desires is rendered unmistakable in a passage from an early draft of *Perestroika*:

> ROY: I admire your bedside manner. I feel better already. Abuse me some more.
> BELIZE: You like abuse.
> ROY: Thrive on it.
> BELIZE: I'd never have figured you for a bottom.
> ROY: I'm not into fixed positions. In bed. In life, I'm a top. In bed . . .
> BELIZE: I don't want to know. (The ellipsis appears in the source.)[25]

What Belize doesn't want to know is that Roy's position in bed is the reverse of the one he plays in the political arena. Indeed, it is the secret of his sexuality or, rather, the sexual expression of his internalized oppression. His masochism, his desire for pain and humiliation, is the price he pays for refusing to be a homosexual.

Roy and Joe are also constructed as the play's only putative father-son unit. In *Millennium*, Roy selects Joe to be his tool, his creation, his disciple, because of the latter's ability to be "a good son to a father who pushes [him] farther than [he] would otherwise go." Just as Roy was once a good son, was faithful and "loved" (by "Walter Winchell, Edgar Hoover," and "Joe McCarthy most of all"), so he chooses Joe (who, tellingly, has the same name as Roy's adoptive father) to be his good son. "The father-son relationship is central to life," he philosophizes; "[w]omen are for birth, beginning, but the father is continuance." Held together by the bonds, indeed, the very shackles of love, the two jostle together in a cruelly loving relationship. "Sometimes a father's love," Roy explains, "has to be very, very hard, unfair even, cold to make his son grow strong in a world like this" (1: 56). Yet Joe adores his foster father ("I love you. Roy") as much for Roy's abuse as for his love. And Roy, playing the role of top, knows how to taunt him in a particularly hurtful way ("you're a sissy," he tells Joe [1: 107]). In this sadomasochistic economy of desire, love is perceptible only as pain: "It's OK that you hurt me because I love you, baby Joe. That's why I'm so rough on you" (1: 109). And this same cruel passion between father and son decisively undermines the distinction between the homosocial and homosexual, in the rough pas de deux between them at the end of *Millennium* (that contrasts with the more straightforwardly erotic dance of Prior and Louis in the next scene), filled with "*sudden violence*," in which Roy (who's "not into fixed positions") "*almost plead[s] to be hit*" (1: 110). In *Perestroika*, this homoeroticism is finally made explicit in Belize's fantasy that Joe is "Roy Cohn's buttboy" and in the soft kiss that Roy's ghost plants lovingly on Joe's lips (2: 94). (Kushner comments that "Roy's repressed, ardent desire for Joe" is related to Roy's understanding of homosexuality as "a form of tutelage, of transmission, of dominance and submission.")[26]

This sadomasochistic relationship between queer father and son functions virtually as a textbook case of what Freud calls moral masochism. Dramatizing the resexualization of the Oedipus complex with remarkable acuity, *Angels* evokes those fantasies of domination and submission that fuel the masochistic fantasmatic, both the sense of guilt and "the wish to be beaten by the father," which, Freud suggests, is "closely connected" with the wish "to have some passive (feminine) sexual relations with him." (This resexualization of Oedipus contrasts with Kushner's much more successful Oedipalization vis-à-vis the various dramatic traditions to which he is heir.) For the masochist, these desires will ensure not only the eroticization of the father son bond but also the effective transmission of the Law: "morality becomes sexualized afresh. . . . "[27] In the relationship between Roy and Joe (Pitt or McCarthy), the Law becomes a source of endless excitement and possibility, the very signature of the phallus: "the Law's a pliable, breathing, sweating . . . *organ* [. . .]" (1: 66; the first ellipsis appears in the source). A fetishized—and feminized—commodity, the Law is that which is passed on from father to son in their violent love trysts (Kushner recognizes that S/M is "inextricably wound up with issues of patriarchy").[28] And their access to the Law, to the Name of the Father, guarantees their efficacy as phallic actors: "Lawyers are . . . the High Priests of America[. . . .] We alone know how to use The Words" (2: 89; the first ellipsis appears in the source). With their privileged relation not just to speech but to the Word and the Law, with their impassioned and cruel homosociality, lawyers like Roy and Joe have the ability to transcend their position as subjected beings ("Make the law, or subject to it") and, indeed, become the very paradigms of an arrogantly phallic masculinity ("Reaganite heartless macho asshole lawyers," Louis exclaims [1: 108, 29]). Roy is an efficient actor on the political stage and, after all, "a heterosexual man" who just happens to "fuck . . . around with guys" (1: 46). Joe, meanwhile, is constructed as the normative American male, a mixture of "Hoss Cartwright" and "the Marlboro

Man," a "window-display Ken doll" who just happens to be queer (2: 94–95, 91, 68). Underscoring his Western pedigree, these appellations also suggest the crucial and continuing importance of the figure of the cowboy (the autonomous, free white man on the frontier, defender of the American imperialist project) in defining hegemonic masculinities. If *Angels in America* reveals the sadomasochism and homoeroticism that fuel these white, normative masculinities, it also exposes the violence that lies concealed behind manliness, charisma, and charm. Roy proudly takes responsibility for the murder of Ethel Rosenberg, while Joe confesses to being "the man with the knives" of whom his wife is terrified. Moreover, near the end of the play, at the culmination of a lovers' quarrel, Joe "*slugs Louis in the stomach, hard*" and then hits Louis "*repeatedly*" until he falls to the floor (2: 111).

The sadomasochistic transaction between Roy and Joe is both underlined and parodied in the other half of the split scene that runs parallel to Roy's lecture on correct filial deportment: the encounter between Louis and the Man in the Rambles in Central Park. The one unmistakable fuck scene in *Angels*, this sequence is also the most overtly sadomasochistic in the play (and, judging from the report of at least one reviewer, the one that produces the most anxiety in a Broadway audience).[29] The scene makes explicit what remains implicit in the dialogue between Roy and Joe:

> LOUIS: I want you to fuck me, hurt me, make me bleed.
> MAN: I want to.
> LOUIS: Yeah?
> MAN: I want to hurt you.
> LOUIS: Fuck me.
> MAN: Yeah?
> LOUIS: Hard.
> MAN: Yeah? You been a bad boy? (1: 54–55)

Wracked with guilt (for his desertion of Prior, among other things), Louis longs to be "punished" by yet a different surrogate daddy (1: 54). When the Man begins to fuck him and suspects that his condom has broken, Louis pleads, "Keep going. Infect Me. I don't care" ("I have no right not to suffer," he later confesses [1: 57; 2: 33]). In his suicidal nonchalance and desire to submit, Louis is constructed as yet another masochistic male subject. Unlike Roy and Joe, however, he is not the bearer of a hegemonic (would-be heterosexual) masculinity. Rather, with his campy excess, his wit, and his penchant for performance, Louis is cast in the role of normative white gay man. (Moreover, he is at the center of the play structurally, insofar as he connects all the other characters.) Suffering from the Jewish complaint ("Jews believe in Guilt"), Louis links "internalized oppression" with "masochism" in several ways (1: 25; 94). He is the one who, because of his fascination with and desire for that which he fears, gets involved with "the Marlboro Man." He is the one who, "losing [himself] in some ideological leather bar," later *"clings to Joe as [the latter] punches away"* at him (2: 36, 111).

Despite the similarities between Louis's desire for pain and the masochism of Roy and Joe, Louis is not closeted. He does not betray his class. On the contrary. Besides being the play's normative white gay man, he is also the normative white liberal, embodying all of the very considerable contradictions that go along with that position ("just another lost ineffectual leftie like me," Louis exclaims [2: 95]). Moreover, Louis, despite his fascination with Joe, is not held in thrall to the Law. Rather, he takes great pains to distinguish between "law" and "justice," the former being associated with "power" (and specifically with Reagan's smarmy henchmen), and the latter with abstract principles, with God, with the "expression of an ideal" (2: 110). Louis thus draws a distinction that the play is so intent upon upholding, between the Law—which is arbitrary and oppressive—and Justice—which is both an abstract idea and God himself, "an immensity, a confusing vastness" (1: 39). For the entire moral system of *Angels* pivots around this binarism, which is homologous to the oppositions between nature and culture, feminine and masculine. Unlike the Law, which is socially constructed, fallible, and feminized, Justice remains infallible, the emanation of nature and an unequivocally "male" God (2: 49). This same binarism also works to separate the bad (i.e., destructive) moral masochism of Roy and Joe, which subtends the feminized principle of the Law, from the strangely productive feminine masochism of Louis, with its strangely convoluted relationship to a masculinized God and the system of Justice of which he is the emblem. It separates conservatives and class traitors from well-intentioned liberals, and oppressive and violent masculinities from those deemed (and proven) more benign, which is to say, less injurious to oppressed classes.

Despite the important distinction that *Angels* draws between moral and feminine masochism, and between two different kinds of masculinity, it seems to me that masochism in the end serves more or less the same function for all of the masochistic characters. Perhaps the best way of gauging this is by looking for a moment at those characters who remain outside the sadomasochistic loop: Belize, Hannah, and, less unequivocally, Prior. Unlike the white (gay) men in the play, Belize, its only person of color, functions as an ideological point of reference, a kind of "moral bellwether," in the words of one critic.[30] Because his is the one point of view that is never submitted to a critique, he is, as David Román points out, "the political and ethical center of the plays." The purveyor of truth, "he carries the burden of race" and so seems to issue from what is unmistakably a "white imaginary" ("[t]his fetishization," Román notes, "of lesbian and gay people of color as a type of political catalyst is ubiquitous among the left"). He is also cast in the role of caretaker, a position long reserved for African Americans in "the white imaginary." But I would like to suggest that if, as Román argues, readers and spectators "never quite get

... a sense of his inner life or outer journey," this is in large part the result of his exclusion from the masochistic economy of desire that, I believe, is primarily responsible for bestowing on the characters in *Angels* the illusion of an "inner life."[31] Unlike the white men, Belize is not noticeably attracted to what disgusts him. Although intrigued by Roy, he refuses to play Roy's game of ritual abuse (except for one moment of anger in which he responds to Roy's violent racial slurs by calling him a "kike" [2: 61]). For Belize, the conflicts and questions that torture the other characters are rather distant. Yet at the same time, a certain penchant for performance (also long associated with African Americans) comes to substitute for his lack of an "inner life." His name (a stage name, in fact, and one usually reserved for women) commemorates not the Name of the Father but his status as a *"former drag queen"* (1: 3). To that extent, he is also positioned outside the Law (for him, "[j]ustice is simple"), as one whose identity is always performative, exoticized, and finally undecidable (is he really a former drag queen or, as he confesses to Louis, an "ex-ex"? [1: 100, 94]). Like Belize, Hannah is excluded from the sadomasochistic fantasmatic. Like him, she is a resourceful caretaker, besides being far more liberal than her "demographic profile" would suggest (2: 104). Prior, meanwhile, is also carefully constructed so as not to be a victim. And although he has "a war inside" him, he resists the self-destructive and suicidal fulminations to which the other characters fall prey as well as the Angel's attempts to turn him into an agent of "STASIS" (2: 23, 54). *"[D]efiantly"* dressed, *"corvine,"* and *"ragged,"* he poses a *"Biblical"* opposition to the other all-too-human subjects (2: 41). Moreover, Louis's groundless accusation that he's "just too much of a victim," too "[p]assive," too "[d]ependent," only serves to underscore his quite remarkable, even heroic, strength in the face of AIDS and the desertion of his lover (2: 84).

Unlike these three who refuse to be cast in the role of victim, Harper, Joe, Roy, and Louis are held in thrall to the masochistic fantasmatic. Unlike Belize and Prior, whose practice of drag suggests that they are relatively comfortable performing a certain femininity, all four have significant problems taking up gendered positions. Whether as gay men trying to shore up a precarious sense of masculinity or as a straight woman deeply insecure about her ability to attract her (gay) husband sexually, they all harbor a great deal of anxiety in regard to feminine identifications. As one sees in the fictions of Aaron Travis and Pat Califia, and in so many different cultural texts, masochism provides a privileged mechanism enabling the subject to negotiate a gendered identity. It provides a way of dealing with and mastering the feminine, or rather, what the subject fantasizes the feminine to be. Like drag, it allows one to *perform* and so manage femininity; it allows one to abnegate masculine privilege temporarily, to be able to take it up again all the better at the end of the performance. The predominance of this performative mode indicates that male homosexuality and fantasies about femininity continue to remain closely linked in hegemonic culture and that sexual deviance still tends to be coded as gender deviance.

Angels in America may be "ambivalent" about many issues, but there is at least one point on which it is unequivocal: the predominance of masochistic subjectivities and practices, and their linkage with the Law, demonstrate that masochism is finally understood (as it is in *Cruising*) to be a form of false consciousness, an internalization of oppression. Associated with the perpetuation of patriarchal structures, with "Reagan's children" (those "[s]elfish and greedy and loveless and blind" "criminal minds"), and with an irrevocably corrupted Law, it exemplifies all that is wrong with America (1: 74). And while the moral masochists (Joe and Roy) are clearly the most egregious of the lot, the feminine masochists (Harper and Louis), those who have been duped, remain part of the same problem. Yet in another way, the conceptualization of masochistic subjectivity in *Angels* marks a significant break with cultural productions like *Cruising* or "Blue Light." In an interview, Kushner attempts specifically to link masochism to a particular stage of economic development: "We subjects of capitalist societies have to talk about the ways in which we are constructed to eroticize and cathect pain, as well as the way pain is transformed into pleasure, and self-destruction into self-creation." Attempting to historicize the production of masochistic subjectivities and link them with the development of capitalism (much as I am trying to do in this book), Kushner asks a series of questions. In the remainder of this chapter I will call on *Angels in America*'s skill at addressing questions of national mission and identity to suggest some answers to those questions, "with which," Kushner slyly notes, "we've been torturing ourselves":

> What is the relationship between sexuality and power? And is sexuality merely an expression of power? . . . Is male sexuality always aggressive? What do we make of the phallus? . . . And how do we escape it? . . . There's the issue of reforming the personality to become a socialist subject, starting with the trash that capitalism has made of us. And people who are formed in the image of the individual ego . . . how do we remake that ego in a way that isn't masochistic? Is there a form of unmaking that isn't destructive?[32]

The Angel of History

Angels in America's title, its idea of utopia, and its model for a particular kind of ambivalence are derived in part from Benjamin's extraordinary meditation "Theses on the Philosophy of History," written shortly before his death in 1940. Composed during the first months of World War II, with fascism on its march across Europe, Benjamin's "Theses," in their darkness (and strange luminosity), attest not only to the seeming invincibility of Hitler but also to the impossible position of the European Left, "[s]tranded," as Terry Eagleton notes, "between social democracy and Stalinism."[33] In this essay, Benjamin sketches a discontinuous theory of history in which "the services of theology" are enlisted in the aid of reconceiving "historical materialism."[34] Opposing the universalizing strategies of bourgeois historicism with historical materialism's project of brushing "history against the grain" (257), he attempts a radical revision of Marxist historiography. Suturing the Jewish notion of messianic time (in which all history is given meaning retrospectively by the sudden and unexpected coming of the Messiah) to the Marxist concept of revolution, Benjamin reimagines proletariat revolution not as the culmination of a conflict between classes, or between traditional institutions and new forms of production, but as a "blast[ing] open" of "the continuum of history" (262). Unlike traditional Marxist (or idealist) historiographers, he rejects the idea of the present as a moment of "transition" and instead conceives it as *Jetztzeit*, "time filled by the presence of the now" (261), a moment in which "time stands still and has come to a stop" (262). Facing *Jetztzeit*, and opposing all forms of gradualism, Benjamin's historical materialism is bent not on imagining and inciting progressive change (or a movement toward socialism) but on "blast[ing] a specific era out of the homogeneous course of history" (263).

The centerpiece of Benjamin's essay is his explication of a painting by Paul Klee, which becomes a parable of history, of the time of the Now, in the face of catastrophe (which for him means all human history):

> A Klee painting named "Angelus Novus" shows an angel looking as though he is about to move away from something he is fixedly contemplating. His eyes are staring, his mouth is open, his wings are spread. This is how one pictures the angel of history. His face is turned toward the past. Where we perceive a chain of events, he sees one single catastrophe which keeps piling wreckage upon wreckage and hurls it in front of his feet. The angel would like to stay, awaken the dead, and make whole what has been smashed. But a storm is blowing from Paradise; it has got caught in his wings with such violence that the angel can no longer close them. This storm irresistibly propels him into the future to which his back is turned, while the pile of debris before him grows skyward. This storm is what we call progress. (257–58)

In Benjamin's allegory, with its irresolvable play of contradictions, the doggedly well-intentioned angel of history embodies both the inconceivability of progress and the excruciating condition of the Now. Poised (not unlike Benjamin himself in Europe in 1940) between the past, which is to say, "catastrophe," and an unknown and terrifying future, he is less a heavenly actor than a passive observer, "fixedly contemplating" that disaster which is the history of the world. His "Paradise," meanwhile, is not the site of a benign utopianism but a "storm" whose "violence" gets caught under his wings and propels him helplessly into an inconceivable future that stymies his gaze.

Benjamin's allegory of history is, in many respects, the primary generative fiction for *Angels in America*. Not only is its Angel clearly derived from Benjamin's text (although with gender reassignment surgery along the way— Kushner's Angel is "Hermaphroditically Equipped"), but so is its vision of Heaven, which has "*a deserted, derelict feel to it,*" with "*rubble . . . strewn everywhere*" (2: 48, 121). And the play's conceptualization of the past, of catastrophe, and of utopia is clearly inflected by Benjamin's "Theses" in the expectation that they will provide a link between historical materialism and theology. Moreover, rather than attempt to suppress the contradictions that inform Benjamin's materialist theology, Kushner expands them. As a result, the ideas of history, progress, and paradise that *Angels in America* invokes are irreducibly contradictory (often without appearing to be so). Just as Benjamin's notion of revolution is related dialectically to catastrophe, so are *Angels*'s concepts of deliverance and abjection, ecstasy and pain, utopia and dystopia, necessarily linked. Kushner's Angel (and her/his heaven) serve as a constant reminder both of catastrophe (AIDS, racism, homophobia, and the pathologization of queer and female bodies, to name only the play's most obvious examples) and of the perpetual possibility of millennium's approach, or, in the words of Ethel Rosenberg (unmistakably echoing Benjamin), that "[h]istory is about to crack wide open" (1: 112). And the concept of utopia/ dystopia to which s/he is linked guarantees that the vehicle of hope and redemption in *Angels*—the prophet who foresees a new age—will be the character who must endure the most agony, Prior Walter, suffering from AIDS and Louis's desertion.

Within the economy of utopia/dystopia that *Angels* installs, the greatest promise of the millennium is the possibility of life freed from the shackles of hatred, oppression, and disease. It is hardly surprising, therefore, that Roy Cohn is constructed as the embodiment and guarantor of dystopia. Not only is he the paradigm of bourgeois individualism—and Reaganism—at its most murderous, hypocritical, and malignant, but he is the one with the most terrifying vision of the "universe," which he apprehends "as a kind of sandstorm in outer space with winds of mega-hurricane velocity, but instead of grains of sand it's shards and splinters of glass" (1: 13). It is, however, a sign of the play's obsessively dialectical structure that Roy's vision of what sounds like hell should provide an uncanny echo of Benjamin's "storm blowing from Paradise." Yet even this dialectic, much like the play's ambivalences, is deceptive insofar as its habit of turning one pole of a binarism relentlessly into its opposite (rather than into a synthesis) describes a false dialectic. Prior, on the other hand, refusing the role of victim, becomes the sign of the unimaginable, of "[t]he Great Work" (2: 148). Yet as with Roy, so Prior's privileged position is a figure of contradiction, coupling not just blindness with prophecy but also history with an impossible future, an ancient lineage (embodied by Prior 1 and Prior 2) with the millennium yet to come, and AIDS with a "most inner part, entirely free of disease" (1: 34). Moreover, Prior's very name designates his temporal dislocation, the fact that he is at once too soon and belated, both that which anticipates and that which provides an epilogue (to the Walter family, if nothing else, since he seems to mark the end of the line). Prior Walter also serves as the queer commemoration of the Walter that came before—Walter Benjamin—whose revolutionary principles he both embodies and displaces insofar as he marks both the presence and absence of Walter Benjamin in this text.[35]

Throughout *Angels in America*, the utopia/dystopia coupling (wherein disaster becomes simultaneously the marker for and incitement to think Paradise) plays itself out through a host of binary oppositions: heaven/hell, forgiveness/retribution, communitarianism/individualism, spirit/flesh, pleasure/pain, beauty/decay, future/past, homosexuality/heterosexuality, rationalism/indeterminacy, migration/staying put, progress/stasis, life/death. Each of these functions not just as a set of conceptual poles in relation to which characters and themes are worked out and interpreted, but also as an *oxymoron*, a figure of undecidability whose contradictory being becomes an incitement to think the impossible—revolution. For it is precisely the conjunction of opposites that allows what Benjamin calls "the flow of thoughts" to be given a "shock" and so turned into "the sign of a Messianic cessation of happening" (262–63). The oxymoron, in other words, becomes the privileged trope by which the unimaginable allows itself to be imagined.

In Kushner's reading of Benjamin, the hermaphroditic Angel becomes the most crucial site for the elaboration of contradiction. Because her/his body is the one on which an impossible—and utopian—sexual conjunction is played out, s/he decisively undermines the distinction between the heterosexual and the homosexual. With her/his "eight vaginas" and "Bouquet of Phalli" (2: 48), s/he represents an absolute otherness, the impossible other that fulfills the longing for both the maternal and the paternal (or, in Lacanian terms, both demand and the Law). On the one hand, as the maternal "Other," s/he is constituted by "[d]emand ... as already possessing the 'privilege' of satisfying needs, that is to say, the power of depriving them of that alone by which they are satisfied."[36] On the other hand, "[a]s the law of symbolic functioning," s/he simultaneously represents the "Other embodied in the figure of the symbolic father," "not a person but a place, the locus of law, language and the symbolic."[37] The impossible conjunction of the maternal and the paternal, s/he provides Prior with sexual pleasure of celestial quality—and gives a new meaning to safe sex. At the same time, s/he also fills and completes subjectivity, being the embodiment of and receptacle for Prior's "Released Female Essence" (2: 48).

Although all of these characteristics suggest that the Angel is constructed as an extratemporal being, untouched by the ravages of passing time, s/he comes (quite literally for Prior) already culturally mediated. When s/he first appears at the end of *Millennium*, he exclaims, "*Very* Steven Spielberg" (1: 118). Although his campy ejaculation is clearly calculated as a laugh line, defusing and undercutting (with typical postmodernist cynicism) the deadly earnestness of the scene, it also betrays the fact that this miraculous apparition is in part the product of a culture industry and that any reading of her/him will be mediated by the success of Steven Spielberg and his ilk (in films like *Close Encounters of the Third Kind* and *E.T.*) in producing a particular vision of the miraculous (with lots of bright white light and music by John Williams). To that extent, the appearance of the Angel signals the degree to which utopia—and revolution!—have now become the product of commodity culture. Unlike earlier periods, when utopia tended to be imagined in terms of production (rather than consumption) and was sited in a preceding phase of capitalism (for example, in a preindustrial or agrarian society), late capitalism envisions utopia through the lens of the commodity and—not unlike Walter Benjamin at his most populist—projects it into a future and an elsewhere lit by that "*unearthly white light*" (1: 118) which represents, among other things, the illimitable allure of the commodity form.[38]

Although the construction of the Angel represses her/his historicity, the heaven s/he calls home is explicitly the product (and victim) of temporality. Heaven is a simulacrum of San Francisco on April 18, 1906, the day of the Great Earthquake. For it is on this day that God "[a]bandoned" his angels and their heaven "*[a]nd did not return*" (2: 51). Heaven thus appears frozen in time, "*deserted and derelict*," with "*rubble strewn everywhere*" (2: 121). The Council Room in Heaven, meanwhile, "*dimly lit by candles and a single great bulb*" (which periodically fails), is a monument to the past, specifically to the New Science of the seventeenth century and the Enlightenment project to which it is inextricably linked. The table in the Council Room is "*covered with antique and broken astronomical, astrological, mathematical and nautical objects of measurement and calculation. . . .*" At its center sits a "*bulky radio, a 1940s model in very poor repair*" (2: 128) on which the Angels are listening to the first reports of the Chernobyl disaster. Conflating different moments of the past and distinct (Western) histories, Heaven is a kind of museum, not the insignia of the Now, but of *before*, of an antique past, of the obsolete. Its decrepitude is also symptomatic of the Angels' fear that God will never return. More nightmare than utopia, marooned in history, Heaven commemorates disaster, despair, and stasis.

Because of its embeddedness in the past, the geography of Heaven is a key to the complex notion of temporality that governs *Angels in America*. Although the scheme does not become clear until *Perestroika*, there are two opposing concepts of time and history running through the play. First, there is the time of the Angels (and of Heaven), the time of dystopian "STASIS" (2: 54) as decreed by the absence of a God who, Prior insists, "isn't coming back" (2: 133). According to the Angel, this temporal paralysis is the direct result of the hyperactivity of human beings: "*YOU HAVE DRIVEN HIM AWAY!*" the Angel enjoins Prior, "YOU MUST STOP MOVING!" (2: 52), in the hope that immobility will once again prompt the return of God and the forward movement of time. Yet this concept of time as stasis is also linked to decay. In the Angel's threnody that ends the Council scene, s/he envisions the dissolution of "the Great Design, / The spiraling apart of the Work of Eternity" (2: 134). Directly opposed to this concept is human temporality, of which Prior, in contradistinction to the Angel, becomes the spokesperson. This time—which is also apparently the time of God—is the temporality connected with Enlightenment epistemologies; it is the time of "Progress," "Science," and "Forward Motion" (2: 132, 50). It is the time of "Change" (2: 13) so fervently desired by Comrade Prelapsarianov and the "neo-Hegelian positivist sense of constant historical progress towards happiness or perfection" so precious to Louis (1: 25). It is the promise fulfilled at the end of *Perestroika* when Louis, apprehending "the end of the Cold War," announces, "The whole world is changing!" (2: 145). Most important, the time of "progress, migration, motion" and "modernity" is also, in Prior's formulation, the time of "desire," because it is this last all-too-human characteristic that produces modernity (2: 132). Without desire (for change, utopia, the other), there could be no history.

Despite the fact that this binary opposition generates so much of the play's ideological framework, and that its two poles are at times indistinguishable, it seems to me that this is one question on which *Angels in America* is not ambivalent at all. Unlike the Benjamin of the "Theses on the Philosophy of History," for whom any concept of progress seems quite inconceivable, Kushner is devoted to rescuing Enlightenment epistemologies at a time when they are, to say the least, extremely unfashionable. On the one hand, *Angels in America* counters attacks from the pundits of the Right, wallowing in their post–Cold War triumphalism, for whom socialism, or "the coordination of men's activities through central direction," is the road to "serfdom."[39] For these neoconservatives, "[w]e already live in the millennial new age," we already stand at "the end of history," and, as a result, in Francis Fukuyama's words, "we cannot picture to ourselves a world that is *essentially* different from the present one, and at the same time better."[40] Obsessed with "free markets and private property," and trying desperately to maintain the imperialist status quo, they can imagine progress only as regression.[41] On the other hand, *Angels* also challenges the orthodoxies of those poststructuralists on the Left by whom the Marxian concept of history is often dismissed as hopelessly idealist, as "a contemptible attempt," in Aijaz Ahmad's words, to construct "grand narratives" and "totalizing (totalitarian?) knowledges."[42] In the face of these profound cynicisms, *Angels* unabashedly champions rationalism and progress. In the last words of *Perestroika*'s last act, Harper suggests that "[i]n this world, there is a kind of painful progress. Longing for what we've left behind, and dreaming ahead" (2: 144). The last words of the epilogue, meanwhile, are given to Prior, who envisions a future in which "[w]e," presumably gay men, lesbians, and persons with AIDS, "will be citizens." "*More Life*" (2: 148), he demands.

Kushner's difference with Benjamin—and the poststructuralists—over the possibility of progress and his championing of modernity (and the desire that produces it) suggest that the string of binary oppositions which are foundational to the play are perhaps less undecidable than I originally suggested. Meaning is produced, in part, because these oppositions are constructed as interlocking homologies, each an analogy for all the others. And despite the fact that each term of each opposition is strictly dependent on the other and, indeed, is produced by its other, these relations are by no means symmetrical. Binary oppositions are always hierarchical—especially when the fact of hierarchy is repressed. *Angels* is carefully constructed so that progress, communitarianism, rationalism, and so forth, will be read as being preferable to their alternatives: stasis, individualism, indeterminacy, and so forth ("the playwright has been able to find hope in his chronicle of the poisonous 1980s").[43] So at least as far as this string of interlocked binary oppositions is concerned, ambivalence turns out to be not especially ambivalent after all.

At the same time, what is one to make of other binarisms—most notably, the opposition between masculine and feminine—toward which the play seems to cultivate a certain studied ambivalence? On the one hand, it is clear that Kushner is making some effort to counter the long history of the marginalization and silencing of women in American culture generally, and in American theater in particular. Harper's hallucinations are crucial to the play's articulation of its central themes, including questions of exile and of the utopia/dystopia binarism. They also give her a privileged relationship to Prior, in whose fantasies she sometimes partakes and with whom she visits Heaven. Her unequivocal rejection of Joe and expropriation of his credit card at the end of the play, moreover, signal her repossession of her life and her progress from imaginary to real travel. Hannah, meanwhile, is constructed as an extremely independent and strong-willed woman who becomes part of the new extended family that is consolidated at the end of the play. Most intriguingly, the play's deliberate foregrounding of the silencing of the Mormon Mother and Daughter in the diorama is symptomatic of Kushner's desire to let women speak. On the other hand, *Angels* seems to replicate many of the structures that historically have produced female subjectivity as other. Harper may be crucial to the play's structure, but she is still pathologized, like so many of her antecedents on the American stage (from Mary Tyrone to Blanche DuBois to Honey in *Who's Afraid of Virginia Woolf?*). With her hallucinations and "emotional problems" (1: 27), she functions as a scapegoat for Joe, the displacement of his sexual problems. Moreover, her false confession that she's "going to have a baby" (1: 41) not only reinforces the link in the play between femininity and maternity but also literally hystericizes her. And Hannah, despite her strength, is defined almost entirely by her relationship to her real son and to Prior, her surrogate son. Like Belize, she is given the role of caretaker.

Most important, the celestial "sexual politics" (2: 49) of the play guarantees that the feminine remains other. After his visitation by the Angel, Prior explains that "God . . . is a man. Well, not a man, he's a flaming Hebrew letter, but a male flaming Hebrew letter" (2: 49). In comparison with this masculinized, Old Testament-style, "flaming"(!) patriarch, the Angels are decidedly hermaphroditic. Nonetheless, the play's stage directions use the feminine pronoun when designating the Angel, and s/he has been played by a woman in all of the play's various American premieres. As a result of this clearly delineated gendered difference, femininity is associated (in Heaven at least) with "STASIS" and collapse, while a divine masculinity is coded as being simultaneously deterministic and absent. In the play's pseudo-Platonic—and heterosexualized—metaphysics, the "orgasm" of the Angels produces (a feminized) "protomatter, which fuels the [masculinized] Engine of Creation" (2: 49). God, the mighty Engine, thus functions precisely like the cruel, sadomasochistic father whose unlimited power is derived from his absence and who delights in torturing his offspring. It is little wonder that Roy Cohn volunteers to represent him in a heavenly court: "[Y]ou're guilty as hell, no question, you have nothing to plead but not to worry, darling, I will make something up" (2: 139).

Moreover, the play's use of doubling reinforces this sense of the centrality of masculinity. Unlike Caryl Churchill's *Cloud 9* (surely the locus classicus of genderfuck), *Angels* uses cross-gender casting only for minor characters. And the movement across gendered difference works in one direction only. The actresses playing Hannah, Harper, and the Angel take on a number of male characters, while the male actors double only in masculine roles. (The closest the play comes to male-to-female drag is the scene in *Millennium* in which Prior is "*applying the face*" [1: 30]). As a result, it seems to me that *Angels*, unlike the work of Churchill or Split Britches (or Pat Califia, for that matter), does not denaturalize gender. Rather, masculinity is produced as a remarkably stable, if contradictory, essence that others can mime but which only a real (i.e., biological) male can embody. Thus yet another ambivalence turns out to be always already decided as much by the play's structure as by the force of habit, or the power of cultural hegemony. For unless a text vigorously and unambiguously challenges the hegemonic construction of gender, its normalizing force will be reaffirmed by the reading and theatergoing public. Moreover, it seems to me that the play's albeit guilty masculinism has been a powerful force behind its canonization. What is one to make of the remarkable ease with which *Angels in America* has been accommodated to that lineage of American drama (and literature) which focuses on masculine experience and agency and produces women as the premise for history, as the ground on which it is constructed? Are not women sacrificed—yet again—to the male citizenry of a (queer) nation?

As Eve Sedgwick and others have argued, both the American canon and the very principle of canonicity are centrally concerned with questions of male (homo)sexual definition and desire.[44] Thus the issues of homoeroticism, of the anxiety generated by the instability of the homosocial/homosexual boundary, of coding, of secrecy and disclosure, and of the problems around securing a sexual identity, remain pivotal for many of the writers who hold pride of place in the American canon, from Thoreau, Melville, Whitman, and James to Hart Crane, Tennessee Williams, and James Baldwin—in that sense, the American canon is always already queered. At the same time, however, unlike so much of the canon and, in particular, the canon of American drama, *Angels in America* foregrounds explicitly gay men. No more need the reader eager to queer the text read subversively between the lines, or transpose genders, as is so often done with the work of Williams, Inge, Albee, and many others. And while the backgrounding of women is hardly a prerequisite for the foregrounding of gay men, it certainly, at least in this case, facilitates the process, especially since questions of patriarchy and patrilineality are so decisive in this play for the articulation of male homosexual identities, subjectivities, and practices. In *Angels*, women are sacrificed to the construction of a gay American history.

Following Benjamin's prompting (and echoing his masculinism), Kushner attempts in *Angels* to "dissociate . . . himself" from those "cultural treasures" that the historical materialist "cannot contemplate without horror" because they have been part of the victory procession "in which the present rulers step over those who are lying prostrate." Brushing history "against the grain," the play demonstrates the crucial importance of (closeted) gay men in twentieth-century American politics—including, most prominently, Roy Cohn and his various surrogate fathers, J. Edgar Hoover and Joseph McCarthy (256–57). By so highlighting not just the (homo)eroticization of patriarchy but also the latter's indebtedness to a sadomasochistic economy of desire, it works to queer American politics and, most dramatically, those generals of the Cold War (and American imperialism) who were most assiduous in their persecution of political and sexual dissidents (and who are produced as the paradigms of false consciousness). Moreover, unlike the work of most of Kushner's predecessors on the American stage, *Angels* does not pathologize gay men. Or more exactly, gay men as a class are not pathologized. Rather, they are revealed to be pathologized circumstantially: first, by their construction (through a singularly horrific stroke of ill luck) as one of the "risk groups" for HIV; and second, by the fact that some remain closeted and repressed (Joe's ulcer is unmistakably the price of disavowal). So it is not homosexuality, per se, that is pathological, but its *denial*. Flagrantly uncloseted, the play provides a devastating critique of the closeted gay man in two medicalized bodies: Roy Cohn and Joe Pitt.

If *Angels in America* functions as a work of historical materialism (in Benjamin's sense), it does so by exposing the process by which the political (which ostensibly drives history) intersects with the personal and sexual (which ostensibly are no more than footnotes to history). Reagan's presidency and the neoconservative hegemony of the 1980s provide not just the background to the play's exploration of ostensibly personal (i.e., sexual, marital, medical) problems but the very ground on which desire is produced. For despite the trenchancy of its critique of neoconservativism, *Angels* also shows the strange attraction of Reagan's vision of America and the world, the sexiness, as it were, not just of imperialism, but of "a genuinely American political personality" that happens to be "[m]odeled on Ronald Wilson Reagan" (1: 63). Through Louis's desires, it demonstrates the allure of a particular brand of (masochistic) machismo perfected by the gleaming musculature of Sylvester Stallone's John J. Rambo and embodied more imperfectly by Joe Pitt: "The more appalling I find your politics the more I want to hump you" (2: 36). And if the Angel is indeed "a cosmic reactionary," it is in part because her/his position represents an analogue to the same utopian promises and hopes that Reagan so brilliantly and deceptively exploited (2: 55). Moreover, in this history play, questions of homosexual identity and desire are carefully juxtaposed against current legal debates about lesbians and gay men in the military and equal protection under the law. Louis attacks Joe for his participation in "an important bit of legal fag-bashing," a case that upholds the U.S. government's policy that it is not "unconstitutional to discriminate against homosexuals" (2: 110). And while the case that Louis cites may be fictional, the continuing refusal of the courts in the wake of *Bowers v. Hardwick* to consider lesbians and gay men a suspect class, and thus eligible for protection under the provisions of the Fourteenth Amendment, is anything but.[45] Unilaterally constructing gay men as a suspect class, *Angels* realizes Benjamin's suggestion that it is not "man or men but the struggling, oppressed class itself [that] is the depository of historical knowledge" (260). More decisively than any other recent cultural text, *Angels* queers America by placing this oppressed class at the very center of American history, by showing it to be not just the repository of a special kind of knowledge, but by recognizing the central role that it has had in the construction of a national subject, polity, and literature.

The American Religion

The United States is one of the few countries that became a political unit before it became a nation. After the Revolutionary War, it was consolidated as a political, commercial, and administrative entity (albeit an unusually diversified one), without, however, developing either a national culture or a consensus on what the defining qualities of the nation might be. Unlike other countries, it could not stake a claim to having a unique language. It shared English with its former colonizer, Great Britain, and with colonial states in North America. Moreover, during the first years of the republic, regional tensions ran high, principally between the North and the slave-owning South (they would, of course, continue until the Civil War—and long after). It was hoped, however, during what is called the National Period (1812–40), that a distinctive political system and various institutional policies—a national bank, protective tariffs, and a restriction on the rate of settlement in the West—would help forge the state into a nation. Given the expansionist character of both mercantile and industrial capitalisms (their ever-increasing need to secure raw materials and markets), the growing corporate sector, with its concern with continuity and inherited tradition, applied pressure on the idea of America. As one historian notes, "the advocates of corporate freedom . . . espoused what was later called a 'doctrine of institutions,' for they sought to objectify and institutionalize in some degree the subjective sense of national unity which came out of the War of 1812."[46] The Declaration of Independence and Constitution not only guaranteed the free American man certain inalienable rights but fostered personal characteristics that would well prepare an American subject for the rigors of capitalism: individualism, autonomy, self-reliance, industry. Unlike the old nations of Europe, with their inflexible class systems, the United States, in Crèvecoeur's words, had "no aristocratical families, no courts, no kings, no bishops, no ecclesiastical domination, no invisible power giving to a few a very visible one."[47] Offering unlimited economic opportunities to those white men willing to work, and linking property ownership to social equity, this "country of the Future," in Emerson's words, this "land of the laborer, of the democrat, of the philanthropist, of the believer, of the saint," staked its identity on the promise of unlimited prosperity and social concord.[48]

A state, however, is not synonymous with a nation. The latter, in Benedict Anderson's celebrated formulation, is "an imagined political community, . . . imagined as both inherently limited and sovereign."[49] And not until the 1830s and 1840s, with the success of Jacksonian democracy and the development of the ideology of Manifest Destiny, did a sense of an imagined community of Americans began to solidify, owing to a number of factors: the consolidation of industrialization in the Northeast, the proliferation of large newspapers and state banks, and a transportation revolution that linked the urban centers with both agricultural producers and markets abroad (market-oriented farm production was increasingly displacing subsistence farming).[50] Simultaneously, on many different fronts, a national culture was in the process of being constructed that would, in Frantz Fanon's words, make both "the totality of the nation a reality to each citizen" and "the history of the nation part of the personal experience of each. . . ."[51] The composition of American histories and the popularity of American writers (like Washington Irving, James Fenimore

Cooper, and William Cullen Bryant) in the years following the War of 1812 were crucial for producing the fantasy of a nation of boundless opportunity whose imaginative geography stretched from the quickly growing cities of the Northeast to the beckoning frontier. With the emergence of the "American Renaissance" in the 1830s and 1840s, the idea of America, or what Lauren Berlant designates as the "National Symbolic" ("the order of discursive practices" that interpellates subjects into "a collectively-held history"), finally crystallized "under widespread pressure to develop a set of symbolic national references whose possession would signify and realize the new political and social order."[52]

This new order demanded the production of a subject who would thrive in the increasingly competitive American marketplace. Reflecting on this period after the Civil War, Emerson explicates both the concept of modernity that animates this new subject and the individualism that provides his or her ideological core:

> There was a new consciousness. The former generations acted under the belief that a shining social prosperity was the beatitude of man, and sacrificed uniformly the citizen to the State. The modern mind believed that the nation existed for the individual, for the guardianship and education of every man. This idea, roughly written in revolutions and national movements, in the mind of the philosopher had far more precision; the individual is the world.[53]

For Emerson, and, indeed, for all those who endeavored to envision the nation, America is the land of the New, of the future; it is "the world's best hope" (to that extent, *Angels in America*'s vision of history as progress is perfectly attuned to this concept of the nation).[54] And the bourgeois state that administers it is constructed contradictorily as the guardian of the free, propertied, male subject, and as an apparatus that is put at his disposal. At the same time, Emerson's new concept of the nation and of individualism dutifully represses the state's relationship to an increasingly competitive and corporatized economy. In Klaus J. Hansen's words, "[t]he traditional, paternalistic conceptions of the state that had motivated the Federalists were gradually making way for the principle of laissez-faire, which exchanged the visible hand of government for the invisible hand of Adam Smith."[55] The growing power of the "free" market demanded the production of an increasingly self-motivated, self-governing, and masculinized individual for whom the relationship between body and soul, as Myra Jehlen points out, is reconceived as "a property relation." And the "self-possessive individualism" to which he is mortgaged implies not only "that the self and the body were ontologically separate," but also that "the empowerment of self-consciousness is a function of the division of the self."[56] As a result, it is perhaps not an overstatement to claim that the first American *national* subject, founded on self-division, was constituted as being, in his rigorous discipline of the self, always already masochistic, always already prepared (like Kushner's Roy Cohn) to turn the pain of subjection—to self, nation, capital, and, most ironically, to the idea of free-dom—into pleasure.

The production of a national subject and culture during the first half of the nineteenth century was thus a decisive step in aligning the state with the nation (at least in fantasy), and so ensuring both the stability of the body politic and its suitability for industrial capitalism (Anderson emphasizes that the bourgeoisie was the first class "to achieve solidarities on an essentially imagined basis").[57] It is far more than coincidence that the birth of modern America coincided with what is often called the Second Great Awakening (the First had culminated in the Revolutionary War). During these years, "the old paternalistic reform impulse directed toward social control yielded to a roman-tic reform movement impelled by millennialism, immediatism, and individu-alism." This movement, in turn, "made possible the creation of the modern American capitalist empire with its fundamental belief in religious, political, and economic pluralism."[58] For those made uneasy (for a variety of reasons) by the new individualism, this pluralism authorized the emergence of alternative social and religious sects, millennialist evangelical revivals as well as new communities like the Shakers, the Oneida Perfectionists, and, most promi-nently and successfully, the Mormons.[59] As Hansen emphasizes, "Mormonism was not merely one more variant of American Protestant pluralism but an articulate and sophisticated counterideology that attempted to establish a 'new heaven and a new earth. . . . '" Moreover, "both in its origins and doctrines," Mormonism "insisted on the peculiarly American nature of its fundamental values" and on the identity of America as the promised land. As Mormonism was being consolidated, it developed a deeply conflicted relationship to the new nation: on the one hand, its doctrines, scripture, and beliefs were so clearly a part of the widespread project of producing Ameria as both a unique and a uniquely privileged nation; on the other hand, it simultaneously repre-sented a profoundly "subversive" threat, not only to mainstream Prote-stantism, but also to the ideologies of individualism foundational to the Na-tional Symbolic.[60]

It perhaps comes as a surprise that Mormonism, at least as it was originally articulated in the 1820s and 1830s, maintains a very close relationship to the epistemology of *Angels in America*. Many of the explicitly hieratic qualities of the play—the characterization of prophecy, the sacred book, as well as the Angel her/himself—owe far more to Mormonism than to any other source. Even more important, the play's conceptualization of history, its millennial-ism, and its idea of America bring it startlingly close to the tenets of early Mormonism. Indeed, it is impossible to understand the concept of nation with which *Angels* is obsessed (and even the idea of queering the nation!) without understanding the constitution of Mormonism during the National Period. I will detail the similarities between the two, not to construct an elaborate homology, but to outline a particular ideological formation from the 1830s whose resuscitation, I believe, has been decisive for the play's success in the 1990s. Mormon mythology may be little known to those outside the Church of Jesus Christ of Latter-day Saints (as Mormonism is officially named), but it is crucial to the canonization of *Angels in America*.

Mormonism begins with a visitation, much like Prior's in the theatrical tour de force that ends *Millennium Approaches*. Joseph Smith, the founder of the religion, relates how in 1823 he was visited by an angel (much as the fictional Prior would be 160 years later) whose "feet did not touch the floor":

> He had on a loose robe of most exquisite whiteness. It was a whiteness beyond anything earthly I have ever seen. . . . [H]is whole person was glorious beyond description, and his countenance truly like lightning. The room was exceedingly light, but not so very bright as immediately around his person. . . . He called me by name, and said unto me that he was a messenger sent from the presence of God to me, and that his name was Moroni; that God had a work for me to do; and that my name should be had for good and evil among all nations, kindreds and tongues, or that it should be both good and evil spoken of among all people.

This masculine angel then tells Smith about a book (not unlike Prior's), "written upon gold plates, an account of the former inhabitants of this continent. . . . "[61] By his own account, Smith found the plates, translated them, and had them published in 1830 as *The Book of Mormon*. As Fawn Brodie points out, "the book can best be explained, not by Joseph's ignorance or his delusions, but by his responsiveness to the provincial opinions of his time."[62] So unmistakably a part of the "tremendous religious upswing" of the 1820s and 1830s, after "the relatively irreligious age of the revolution," *The Book of Mormon* recycles the ubiquitous millennialism of the era, the widespread search for a primitive Christianity, and the imperialist ideology (that is, Manifest Destiny) that facilitated the settling of the West and the near extermination of Native Americans.[63]

The Book of Mormon tells the story of Lehi, a Hebrew prophet, and his family, who fled Jerusalem, sailed to a new continent, and started a mighty civilization in the Americas that was visited by Christ after his resurrection (in A.D. 37, to be precise).[64] When this culture declined, a struggle erupted between the descendants of two of Lehi's sons, Nephi and Laman. The Nephites were the representatives of high civilization, while the Lamanites, who had turned to a nomadic life (and were, it is claimed, the ancestors of Native Americans), made war against their brethren. God punished them by darkening their skin: "they became a dark and loathsome, and a filthy people, full of idleness and all manner of abominations."[65] Mormon, one of the last Nephite prophets, wrote this history on gold plates and gave it to his son, Moroni, who buried them on a hillside near Palmyra, New York, "to allow their future discovery in preparation for the restoration of the Gospel in America."[66] Written in a pseudo–King James Bible, Old Testament–style prose, *The Book of Mormon* (which Mark Twain described as "chloroform in print") is only one of many volumes of the period to suggest that Native Americans are of Hebrew origin.[67] Moreover, its construction of race as a decisive category of difference and its unmistakable demonization of the "dark and loathsome" mutineers served to rationalize westward expansion (and, implicitly, to justify slavery as well). "It would seem," one apologist for American expansionism noted, "that the White race alone received the divine command, to subdue and replenish the earth! for it is the only race that has obeyed it—the only one that hunts out new and distant lands, and even a new world, to subdue and replenish."[68]

Providing Calvinism with its most radical challenge during the National Period, early Mormonism was deeply utopian in its thrust (and it remains so even today). Indeed, its concept of time is identical to the temporality for which *Angels in America* polemicizes. Like *Angels*, Mormonism understands time as evolution and progress (in that sense, it is more closely linked to Enlightenment epistemologies than romantic ones) and holds out the possibility of unlimited human growth: "As man is God once was: as God is man may become."[69] A part of a tremendous resurgence of interest in the millennium between 1828 and 1832, Mormonism went far beyond the ideology of progress implicit in Jacksonian democracy (just as *Angels*'s millennialism goes far beyond most contemporary ideologies of progress).[70] Understood in historical terms, this utopianism was in part a function of the relatively marginal economic status of Joseph Smith and his followers, subsistence farmers and struggling petits bourgeois, who remained "beyond the edge of successful, genteel society and the institutional Establishment of their time." For them, millennialism represented simultaneously the hopes and the sense of disillusionment of those "on the fringe of social and economic progress" in comparison with the rising tide of "self-made men of Jacksonian America." Tending "to be 'agin the government,'" these early Mormons were a persecuted minority and, in their westward journey to Zion, remained the subjects of widespread violence, beginning in 1832 when Smith was tarred and feathered in Ohio.[71] Much like twentieth-century lesbians and gay men—although most contemporary Mormons would be appalled by the comparison—Mormons were, throughout the 1830s and 1840s, attacked by mobs, arrested on false charges, imprisoned, and murdered. In 1838, the governor of Missouri decreed that they must be "exterminated" or expelled from the state. In 1844, Smith and his brother were assassinated by an angry mob.[72] As Smith had predicted, his name was indeed to be "had for good and evil among all nations."

The violent antipathy toward early Mormonism was in part the result of the fact that it presented a significant challenge to the principles of individualist social and economic organization. From the beginning, Mormonism was communitarian in nature and proposed a kind of ecclesiastical socialism in which "those entering the order were asked to 'consecrate' their property and belongings to the church. . . ." To each male would then be returned enough to sustain him and his family, while the remainder would be apportioned to "'every man who has need. . . .'" As Hansen emphasizes, this organization represents a repudiation of the principles of laissez-faire and an attempt "to restore a more traditional society in which the economy was regulated in behalf of the larger interests of the group. . . ."[73] This nostalgia for an earlier period of capitalism (the agrarianism of the early colonies) is echoed by Mormonism's conceptualization of the continent as the promised land. Believing the Garden of Eden to have been sited in America and assigning all antediluvian history to the Western Hemisphere, early Mormonism believes that the term "'New World' was in fact a misnomer because America was really the cradle of man and civilization."[74] So history is tied to theology (as with Benjamin), and the privileged character of the nation to its sacred past. At the same time, this essentially theological conceptualization of the nation bears witness to the "strong affinity," noted by Anderson, between "the nationalist imagining" and "religious imaginings."[75] As Timothy Brennan explains it, "nationalism largely extend[s] and modernize[s] (although [does] not replace) 'religious imaginings,' taking on religion's concern with death, continuity, and the desire for origins."[76] Like religion, the nation authorizes a reconfiguration of time and mortality, a "secular transformation of fatality into continuity, contingency into meaning."[77] Mormonism's spiritual geography was perfectly suited to this process, constructing America as both *arche* and *telos*, both origin and meaning of history. Moreover, as Hans Kohn has pointed out, modern nationalism has expropriated three crucial concepts from those same Old Testament mythologies that provide the basis for Mormonism: "the idea of a chosen people, the emphasis on a common stock of memory of the past and of hopes for the future, and finally national messianism."[78]

This conceptualization of America as the site of a blessed past and a millennial future represents a fulfillment of early-nineteenth-century ideas of the nation and—simultaneously—a repudiation of the ideologies of individualism and acquisitiveness that underwrite the Jacksonian marketplace. Yet, as Sacvan Bercovitch points out, this contradiction was at the heart of the nationalist project (and informed the work of those writers who would produce the "American Renaissance"). As the economy was being transformed "from agrarian to industrial capitalism," the primary "source of dissent was an indigenous residual culture," which, like Mormonism, was "variously identified with agrarianism, libertarian thought, and the tradition of civic humanism." These ideologies, "by conserving the myths of a bygone age" and dreaming "of human wholeness and social regeneration," then produced "the notion of an ideal America with a politically transformative potential." Like the writers of the "American Renaissance," Mormonism "adopted the culture's *controlling* metaphor—'America' as synonym for human possibility," and then turned it against hegemonic values. Both producing and fulfilling the nationalist dream, it "portray[ed] the American ideology, as all ideology yearns to be portrayed, in the transcendent colors of utopia."[79] A form of dissent that ultimately (and contradictorily) reinforced hegemonic values, Mormonism reconceived America as the promised land, the land of an already achieved utopia, and simultaneously as the land of promise, the site of the millennium yet to come.

The construction of America as the promised land, both for American nationalists, in general, and for Mormons, in particular, is indissolubly linked with the ideology of Manifest Destiny. As formulated during the National Period, Manifest Destiny is an expression of the belief, in the words of John L. O'Sullivan (who coined the term in 1845), that "our country is destined to be *the great nation* of futurity." Because "[w]e are the nation of human progress" and of "equality," no one can "set limits to our outward march."[80] Founded on an imperialism of the first-person plural pronoun, and believing territorial expansionism the analogue of progress, Manifest Destiny urges the settling of the West to construct an America that would span the continent. It was the cry of the Mormon pioneers who, after years of persecution, left their settlement in Nauvoo, Illinois, in 1846 and, under the leadership of Brigham Young, Smith's successor, began the trek to the Great Basin, which offered to them "the promise of a new world."[81] Like O'Sullivan, Young exploited biblical analogies and "compared the Mormon movement to the Exodus from Egypt under Moses." These analogies were "used to heighten the Saints' sense of leaving a place of persecution for a Promised Land and of being miraculously blessed and guided."[82] For Young and his followers, the Great Salt Lake became transubstantiated into the Dead Sea, Utah Lake into the Sea of Galilee, and their new city was the new Zion.[83]

The discourses of Manifest Destiny and Mormon expansionism provide a remarkably clear gauge of how the idea of America was gendered during the national period—and how it continues to be. O'Sullivan's perorations leave little doubt not only that the nation is a masculine construction (in relation both to the land and to other North American states) but also that Manifest Destiny represents an imperialist fulfillment of the heterosexual imperative. Meditating on the annexation of Texas, he avers that this new—and feminized—territory "is now ours. . . . Her star and her stripe may already be said to have taken their place in the glorious blazon of our common nationality; and the sweep of our eagle's wing already includes within its circuit the wide extent of her fair and fertile land." Urging the violent subjugation of other American states, which, like Texas, would "begin . . . to thrill" for union and eagerly await "consummation," O'Sullivan's rape fantasy constructs America as masculine, strong, and conquering in relationship not only to the feminized land but also to the "[i]mbecile and distracted" Mexico from which Texas had been pried. O'Sullivan's feverish imagination leaves little doubt that America, as promised land, is a masculinized citadel that promises refuge, salvation, and futurity. Or, as an early Mormon anthem puts it,

> We'll find the place which God for us prepared,
> Far away in the West,
> Where none shall come to hurt or make afraid
> There the Saints will be blessed.[84]

I recapitulate the history of Mormonism and its complex relationship both to the idea of the nation and to hegemonic ideological formations because I believe it is crucial to an understanding of how *Angels in America* has been culturally positioned. It seems to me that the play replicates both the situation and the project of early Mormonism with an uncanny accuracy and thereby documents the continued validity of both a particular fantasy of America (as masculinized promised land and land of promise) and a particular understanding of oppositional cultural practices. Like the projects of Joseph Smith and his followers, *Angels* has, from the beginning, on the levels of authorial intention and reception, been constructed as an oppositional, and sometimes radical, work. Structurally and ideologically, the play challenges the conventions of American realism and the tenets of Reaganism. Indeed, it offers by far the most explicit and trenchant critique of neoconservativism to have been produced on Broadway. It also provides the most thoroughgoing deconstruction in memory of a binarism absolutely crucial to liberalism, the opposition between public and private. *Angels* demonstrates conclusively not only the constructedness of the difference between the political and the sexual but also the murderous power of this distinction. Yet, at the same time, *not despite but because of these endeavors*, the play has been accommodated with stunning ease to the hegemonic ideology not just of the theatergoing public but of the democratic majority—an ideology that has become the *new* American religion: liberal pluralism.

The old-style American liberalisms, variously associated (reading from Left to Right) with trade unionism, reformism, and competitive individualism, tend to value freedom above all other qualities (the root word for liberalism is, after all, the Latin *liber*, meaning "free"). Taking the "free" individual subject as the fundamental social unit, it has long been associated with the principle of laissez-faire and the "free" market and is always reformist rather than revolutionary in its politics. At the same time, however, because liberalism, particularly in its American versions, has always paid at least lip service to equality (and democracy), certain irreducible contradictions have been bred in what did, after all, emerge during the seventeenth century as the ideological complement to (and justification of) mercantile capitalism. Historically, American liberalism has permitted dissent and fostered tolerance—within certain limits—and not only guaranteed that all men are created equal (women have long been excluded from the compact, as well as African-American slaves), but also essayed to provide equal opportunities for all. In fact, given the structure of American capitalism (with its imperialist ambitions), the incommensurability of its commitment to both freedom and equality has proven a disabling contradiction, one that liberalism has tried continually, and with little success, to negotiate. Like the masochistic subject that is its production and raison d'être, liberalism is hopelessly schizoid.

The liberal pluralism that has been consolidated in the United States since the decline of the New Left in the mid-1970s (but whose antecedents date back to the first stirrings of the nation) marks the adaptation of traditional liberalism to a post–welfare state economy. It pursues a policy of regressive taxation; its major constituent is the corporate sector—all others it labels "special interest groups" (I see no fundamental differences between the economic and foreign policies of Reagan/Bush and those of Clinton). Despite its corporatism, however, and its efficiency in redistributing the wealth upward, liberal pluralism speaks the language of tolerance (and this, to some extent, does distinguish it from at least hard-core Reaganism). Unable to support substantive changes in economic policy that might in fact produce a more equitable and less segregated society (on the bases of race and social class), it instead promotes a *rhetoric* of pluralism and moderation. Reformist in method, it endeavors to fine-tune the status quo while at the same time acknowledging (and often celebrating) the diversity of American culture. For the liberal pluralist, America is less a melting pot than a smorgasbord. He or she takes pride in the ability to *consume* cultural difference—now understood as a commodity, a source of boundless pleasure, an expression of an exoticized other. And yet, for him or her, access to and participation in so-called minority cultures is entirely consumerist. Like the new, passive racist characterized by Hazel Carby, the liberal pluralist uses "texts"—whether literary, musical, theatrical, or cinematic—as "a way of gaining knowledge of the 'other,' a knowledge that appears to replace the desire to challenge existing frameworks of segregation."[85]

Liberal pluralism thus does far more than tolerate dissent. It actively enlists its aid in reaffirming a fundamentally conservative hegemony. In doing so, it reconsolidates a fantasy of America that dates back to the early nineteenth century. Liberal pluralism demonstrates the dogged persistence of a *consensus politic that masquerades as dissensus*. It proves once again, in Bercovitch's words, that

> [t]he American way is to turn potential conflict into a quarrel about fusion or fragmentation. It is a fixed match, a debate with a foregone conclusion: you must have your fusion and feed on fragmentation too. And the formula for doing so has become

virtually a cultural reflex: you just alternate between harmony-in-diversity and diversity-in-harmony. It amounts to a hermeneutics of laissez-faire: all problems are obviated by the continual flow of the one into the many, and the many into the one. . . .[86]

According to Bercovitch, a kind of dissensus (of which liberal pluralism is the foremost contemporary example) has been the hallmark of the idea of America—and American literature—from the very beginning. (In *The Book of Mormon*, consensus as dissensus is represented in the almost Manichaean dialectic between the Nephites and the Lamanites, in "an opposition" that "must needs be . . . in all things," since "all things must needs be a compound in one.")[87] In this most American of ideologies, an almost incomparably wide range of opinions, beliefs, and cultural positions are finally absorbed into a fantasy of a utopian nation in which anything and everything is possible, in which the millennium is simultaneously at hand and indefinitely deferred. Moreover, the nation becomes the geographical representation of that utopia which is both everywhere and nowhere. For as Berlant explains, "the contradiction between the 'nowhere' of utopia and the 'everywhere' of the nation [is] dissolved by the American recasting of the 'political' into the terms of providential ideality, 'one nation under God.' "[88] This unity of the many in the one also provides the basis for what Jehlen refers to as "the American incarnation," which, she argues, "fused continent and civilization, nation and citizen, man and nature to constitute a universe where oppositions amounted to different versions each of which was the other's cathartic, so that their difference was itself transmuted into 'necessary' means to the emergence of the single and unchanging truth."[89] Under the sign of the "one," all contradictions are subsumed, all races and religions united, all politics theologized.

DISSENSUS AND THE FIELD OF CULTURAL PRODUCTION

It is my contention that *Angels*'s mobilization of a consensual politic (masquerading as *dis*sensual) is precisely the source not only of the play's ambivalence but also of its ability to be instantly recognized as a part of the canon of American literature. Regardless of Kushner's intentions, *Angels* can be, and has been, easily accommodated to a project whereby the theological is not only enlisted in the aid of the political and the historical but is constructed as a transcendent category into which the latter finally disappear. For all its commitment to a historical materialist method, for all its attention to political struggle and the dynamics of oppression, *Angels*, like the ideology of early Mormonism and other millennialist discourses, finally sets forth a liberal pluralist vision of America in which all, not in spite but because of their diversity, will be welcomed into the new Jerusalem. Like other apocalyptic discourses, from Joseph Smith's to Jerry Falwell's, the millennialism of *Angels* reassures an "audience that knows it has lost control over events," not by enabling it to "regain . . . control," but by letting it know "that history *is* nevertheless controlled by an underlying order and that it has a purpose that is nearing fulfillment." It thereby demonstrates that *"personal* pain," whether Prior's, or that of the reader or spectator, "is subsumed within the pattern of history."[90] Like Joseph Smith, Tony Kushner has proven himself unusually responsive to the opinions of his time and has successfully resuscitated a vision of America as both promised land and land of infinite promise. And he has done so at a crucial juncture in history, at the end of the Cold War, as the geopolitical order of forty-five years has collapsed.

Since the end of World War II, the identity of America has in large part been determined by its opposition to communism in general and to the Soviet empire in particular, despite the fact that American economic hegemony has always been the real goal behind American imperialism (whether colonialist or neocolonialist, via the Marshall Plan or the International Monetary Fund). During this period, most all of its many imperialist forays (in Korea, Vietnam, Grenada, Nicaragua) were justified as being part of a strategy to halt communist expansionism. With the fall of historical communism, however, the rationale for the largest arms buildup in history disappears, unless another threat can be produced. Although the United States has since the 1970s constructed a secondary antagonist in the form of an army of deadly "terrorists" (usually Islamic fundamentalists or representatives of disgruntled Arab states), the Gulf War of 1991 signaled the consolidation of international "terrorism" as the successor to the Soviet empire. Exploiting a patently racist symbology, the U.S. government has used this alleged threat to justify the continuation of the national security state and as an effective cover for imperialist ambitions in the so-called Third World.

Despite the successful mobilization of "terrorism" during the 1990s as a source of definition for the nation, the idea of America remains, I believe, in crisis (it seems to me that "terrorism," being less of a threat to individualism than communism, does not harness paranoia quite as effectively as does the idea of an evil empire). If nothing else, *Angels in America* attests both to the continuing anxiety over national definition and mission and to the importance of an ideological means of assuaging that anxiety. In *Angels*, a series of political dialectics (which are, yet again, false dialectics) remains the primary means for producing this ideological fix, for producing dissensus, a sense of "opposition in all things," of alternation between "harmony-in-diversity and diversity-in-harmony." The play is filled with political disputation—all of it between men, since women, unless in drag, are excluded from the political realm. Most is centered on Louis, the unmistakably ambivalent, ironic Jew, who invariably sets the level of discussion and determines the tenor of the argument. If with Belize he takes a comparatively rightist (and racist) stance, with Joe he takes an explicitly leftist (and antihomophobic) one. And while the play unquestionably problematizes his several positions, he ends up, with all his contradictions, becoming by default the spokesperson for liberal pluralism, with all *its* contradictions.

The pivotal scene that enunciates Louis's politics is his long discussion with Belize in *Millennium* that begins with his question, "Why has democracy succeeded in America?"—a question whose assumption is belied by the unparalleled political and economic power of American corporatism to buy elections, and from which Louis, as is his wont, almost immediately backs down (1: 89). (His rhetorical strategy throughout this scene is to stake out a position from which he immediately—and masochistically—draws a guilty retreat, thereby making Belize look like the aggressor.) Invoking "radical democracy" and "freedom" in one breath, and crying "[f]uck assimilation" in the next, he careens wildly between a liberal discourse of rights and a rhetoric of identity politics (1: 89–90). Alternating between universalizing and minoritizing concepts of identity, he manages at once to dismiss a politics of race (and insult Belize) and to assert its irreducibility. Yet the gist of Louis's argument (if constant vacillation could possibly be said to have a gist) is his disquisition about the nation:

> [T]his reaching out for a spiritual past in a country where no indigenous spirits exist—only the Indians, I mean Native American spirits and we killed them off so now, there are no gods here, no ghosts and spirits in America, there are no angels in America, no spiritual past, no racial past, there's only the political. . . . (1: 92)

For Louis, America hardly exists as a community at all (whether real or imagined). Rather, for this confused liberal, America is defined entirely by its relationship to the "political." With characteristic irony, Kushner chooses to present this crucial idea (which does, after all, give the play its title) in the negative, in the form of a statement that the rest of the play aggressively refutes. For if nothing else, *Angels in America*—like *The Book of Mormon*—demonstrates that there are angels in America, that America is in essence a utopian and theological construction, a nation with a divine mission (or, in Emersonian terms, the land of "a new consciousness"). Politics is by no means banished insofar as it provides a crucial way in which the nation is imagined. But it is subordinated to utopian fantasies of harmony in diversity, of one nation under a derelict God.

Moreover, this scene between Louis and Belize reproduces millennialism in miniature, in its very structure, in the pattern whereby the political is finally subsumed by utopian fantasies. After the spirited argument between Louis and Belize (if one can call a discussion in which one person refuses to stake out a coherent position an argument), their conflict is suddenly overrun by an outbreak of lyricism, by the intrusion, after so much talk about culture, of what passes for the natural world:

BELIZE: All day today it's felt like Thanksgiving. Soon, this . . . ruination will be blanketed white. You can smell it—can you smell it?

LOUIS: Smell what?

BELIZE: Softness, compliance, forgiveness, grace.

LOUIS: No [. . .]

BELIZE: I can't help you learn that. I can't help you, Louis. You're not my business.
   (He exits)
      (Louis puts his head in his hands, inadvertently touching his cut forehead.)

LOUIS: Ow FUCK! *(He stands slowly, looks toward where Belize exited)* Smell what?
   (He looks both ways to be sure no one is watching, then inhales deeply, and is surprised) Huh. Snow. (1:100; the first ellipsis appears in the source.)

Argumentation gives way not to a resolution (nothing has been settled) but to ostensible forces of nature: snow and smell. According to Belize, snow (an insignia of coldness and purity in the play) is linked to "[s]oftness, compliance, forgiveness, grace," in short, to the theological virtues. Like the ending of *Perestroika*, in which another dispute between Louis and Belize fades out behind Prior's benediction, this scene enacts a movement of transcendence whereby the political is not so much resolved as left trailing in the dust. In the American way, contradiction is less disentangled than immobilized. History gives way to a concept of cosmic evolution that is far closer to Joseph Smith than to Walter Benjamin.

In the person of Louis (who is, after all, constructed as the most empathic character in the play), with his unshakable faith in liberalism and the possibility of "radical democracy," *Angels in America* assures the (liberal) theatergoing public that a kind of liberal pluralism remains the best hope for change.[91] Revolution, in the Marxian sense, is rendered virtually unthinkable, oxymoronic. Amidst all the political disputation, there is no talk of social class. Oppression is understood in relation not to economics but to differences of race, gender, and sexual orientation. In short, *an identity politic comes to substitute for Marxist analysis*. There is no clear sense that the political and social problems with which the characters wrestle might be connected to a particular economic system (Comrade Prelapsarianov is, after all, a comic figure). And despite Kushner's avowed commitment to socialism, an alternative to capitalism, except in the form of an indefinitely deferred utopia, remains absent from the play's dialectic.[92] Revolution, even in Benjamin's sense of the term, is evacuated of its political content, functioning less as a Marxist hermeneutic tool than as a *trope*, a figure of speech (the oxymoron) that marks the place later to be occupied by a (liberal pluralist?) utopia. Because of the way in which the play imagines the millennium, *Angels* falls into line behind the utopianisms of Joseph Smith and the American Renaissance and becomes less a subversion of hegemonic culture than its reaffirmation. As Berlant observes, "the temporal and spatial ambiguity of 'utopia' has the effect of obscuring the implications of political activity and power relations in American civil life."[93] Like "our classic texts" (as characterized by Bercovitch), *Angels* has a way of conceptualizing utopia so that it may be adopted by "the dominant culture . . . for its purposes." "So molded, ritualized, and controlled," Bercovitch notes (and, I would like to add, stripped of its impulse for radical economic change), "utopianism has served . . . to diffuse or deflect dissent, or actually to transmute it into a vehicle of socialization."[94]

Yet *Angels in America*'s obsession with a utopia yet to come should not dissuade one from examining the play's understanding of the past, since (as Benjamin so well understood) utopia is always fantasized in relation to history. Earlier American utopianisms, whether those of Joseph Smith, Henry David Thoreau, or (for that matter) Ronald Reagan, tend to paint the future in the colors of an idealized past. Early Mormonism, like most of the utopianisms of the early nineteenth century, looked back both to a primordial America (an America that, in the case of Mormonism, provided the setting for the Garden of Eden), as well to an earlier stage of capitalist development. As Hansen emphasizes, by the time of Smith, "the old, cohesive village communities that had provided 'the entire range of social, economic, and political services' was [*sic*] at best a mere memory."[95] In reacting against an America that was rapidly becoming industrialized and urbanized, early Mormonism established its cooperative economic system as a way of reviving a fantasy of agrarian communitarianism. Like that of Joseph Smith, the avowedly conservative utopianism of Ronald Reagan looks back to an earlier phase of development, imagining— impossibly—that the supposed virtues of small-town America can somehow cure the ills that late capitalism has wrought.

Angels in America, by way of contrast, is much more suspicious of these fantasies, conceptualizing the past, particularly the post–World War II period, as a kind of nightmare, as a masochistic perversion of America (embodied, of course, by Roy Cohn). Inspired by Benjamin, it surveys history to discover catastrophe. The one specific moment in the past that the play invokes—and that thereby stands in for history—is April 18, 1906, the day of the Great San Francisco Earthquake. Like Mormonism, therefore, the play defines itself in relation to a moment that emblematizes an earlier stage of capitalism, specifically, in the case of *Angels*, the end of the period of monopoly capital that immediately preceeded the development of commodity culture. In exemplary postmodernist fashion, however, Kushner is far more suspicious of nostalgic longings than was Smith or Reagan, and his Heaven is a literal commemoration of disaster. But what is most important is the fact that on this day God abandoned his creatures and their world. In other words, even if the preceding centuries were a good deal less than perfect (the only characterization of premodern history that *Angels* offers comes in the woeful narratives of Prior's ancestors), that disaster which is the modern world appears to be the direct result of the absence of God (on this, too, the play is ambivalent). So it seems that despite a pervasive (if somewhat nebulous) antinostalgia, the play ends up grudgingly idealizing an earlier moment of economic development. In fact, it seems to me that this is precisely the function of one of the most enigmatic scenes in *Millennium*, the scene in Utah in which Hannah puts her house up for sale. Set at sunset, with a brilliantly illuminated sky, and offering a "view of heaven," of "the living city of heaven," it seems precisely to capitalize on the Mormon idea (derived from Manifest Destiny) of the American West as frontier, as Zion, as "vacant space" waiting to be claimed, rather than as the "bloody battlefield of conflict and conquest" it invariably was (1: 81).[96] And despite the fact that Sister Ella Chapter's disquisition on sin serves clearly to problematize the extreme conservativism of contemporary Mormon ethics, the scene still functions to provide a view of utopia, an image of another kind of world, one far removed, both geographically and culturally, from the two decaying urban metropolises represented in the play, New York and San Francisco.

The ambivalences that are so deeply inscribed in *Angels in America*, its conflicted relationship to various utopianisms, to the concept of America, to Marxism, Mormonism, and liberalism, function, I believe, to accommodate the play to what I see as a fundamentally conservative and paradigmatically American politics—dissensus, "the continual flow of the one into the many, and the many into the one," the "hermeneutics of laissez-faire." Yet it seems to me that the play's ambivalence (its way of being, in Eve Sedgwick's memorable phrase, "kinda subversive, kinda hegemonic")[97] is, finally, less a question of authorial intention or of normalizing reading practices than of the peculiar cultural and economic position of this play (and its writer) in relation to the theater, theater artists, and the theatergoing public in the United States. On the one hand, the Broadway and regional theaters remain in a uniquely marginal position in comparison with Hollywood. The subscription base for regional theaters continues to decrease, while more than half of Theatre Communications Group's sample theaters in their annual survey "played to smaller audiences in 1993 than they did five years ago." Moreover, in a move that bodes particularly ill for the future of theater, "workshops, staged readings and other developmental activities decreased drastically over the five years studied."[98] On the other hand, serious Broadway drama does not have the same cultural capital as other forms of literature. American playwrights, with one exception (Eugene O'Neill), do not win Nobel Prizes or become the figureheads of the literary world, the emblems of literature as an elite cultural practice, in the way that novelists like William Faulkner, Toni Morrison, or Thomas Pynchon do. Moreover, unlike poetry, with its dependence on small presses and a highly specialized and professionalized readership, theater is a manifestly commercial and public art. Mortgaged to a slew of others who must realize the playwright's text (and who, to the horror of some cultural elitists, even belong to trade unions), it has long been regarded as a bastard art. The relatively small public, meanwhile, that today attends professional theater in America is overwhelmingly middle-class and overwhelmingly liberal in its attitudes. Indeed, theater audiences are in large part distinguished from the audiences for film and television on account of their tolerance for works that are more challenging both formally and thematically than the great preponderance of major studio releases or prime-time miniseries. Moreover, since the 1988 controversies over NEA funding for exhibitions of Mapplethorpe and Serrano and the subsequent attempt by the endowment to revoke grants to the so-called NEA four (all of whom feature queer content in their work), theater, as a liberal form, has been distinguished from mass culture in large part by virtue of its queer content. In the 1990s, a play without a same-sex kiss may be entertainment, but it can hardly be considered a work of art. It now appears that the representation of (usually male) homosexual desire has become the privileged emblem of that endangered species, the serious Broadway drama. If theater is the queerest art, it is so in part because of its skill (at least at this historical moment) in universalizing homosexual subjectivities and producing them as being representative not of the perverse but of the normative, not of the subversive but of the national.

Because of its marginal position, both economically and culturally, theater is a privileged portion of what Pierre Bourdieu designates as the literary and artistic field. As he explains, this field is contained within a larger field of economic and political power, while, at the same time, "possessing a relative autonomy with respect to it, especially as regards its economic and political principles of hierarchization." It is this *relative autonomy* that gives the literary and artistic field both its high level of symbolic forms of capital and its low level of economic capital. In other words, despite its sometimes considerable cultural capital, it "occupies a *dominated position*" with respect to the field of economic and political power as whole.[99] And the individual cultural producer (or theater artist), insofar as he or she is a part of the bourgeoisie, represents a "dominated fraction of the dominant class."[100] The cultural producer is thus placed in an irreducibly contradictory position—and this has become particularly clear with the decline of patronage in the eighteenth century and the increasing dependence of the artist on the vicissitudes of the marketplace. On the one hand, he or she is licensed to challenge hegemonic values insofar as it is a particularly effective way of accruing cultural capital. On the other hand, the more effective his or her challenge, the less economic capital he or she is likely to amass. Because of theater's marginality in American culture, it seems to be held hostage to this double bind in a particularly unnerving way: the very disposition of the field guarantees that Broadway and regional theaters (unlike mass culture) are constantly in the process of trying to negotiate an impossible position.

What is perhaps most remarkable about *Angels in America* is that it has managed, against all odds, to amass significant levels of both cultural and economic capital. And while it by no means resolves the contradictions that are constitutive of theater's cultural positioning, its production history has become a measure of the seemingly impossible juncture of these two forms of success. Just as the play's structure copes with argumentation by transcending it, so does the play as cultural phenomenon seemingly transcend the opposition between cultural and economic capital, between the hegemonic and the counter-hegemonic. Moreover, it does so, I am arguing, by its skill in both reactivating a sense (derived from the early nineteenth century) of America as the utopian nation and mobilizing the principle of ambivalence—or, more exactly, dissensus—to produce a vision of a once and future pluralist culture. And although the text's contradictory positioning is to a large extent defined by the marginal cultural position of Broadway, it is also related specifically to Tony Kushner's own class position. Like Joseph Smith, Kushner represents a dominated—and dissident—fraction of the dominant class. As a white gay man, he is able to amass considerable economic and cultural capital despite the fact that the class of which he is a part remains relatively disempowered politically (according to a 1993 survey, the average household income for self-identified gay men is 40 percent higher than that of the average American household).[101] As an avowed leftist and intellectual, he is committed (as *Angels* demonstrates) to mounting a critique of hegemonic ideology. Yet as a member of the bourgeoisie and as the recipient of two Tony Awards, he is also committed—if only unconsciously—to the continuation of the system that has granted him no small measure of success. Bourdieu shrewdly describes this positionality:

> The dominated producers, for their part, in order to gain a foothold in the market, have to resort to subversive strategies which will eventually bring them the disavowed profits only if they succeed in overturning the hierarchy of the field without disturbing the principles on which the field is based. Thus their revolutions are only ever partial ones, which displace the censorships and transgress the conventions but do so in the name of the same underlying principles. This is why the strategy *par excellence* is the "return to the sources" which is the basis of all heretical subversion and all aesthetic revolutions. . . .[102]

For Kushner, this "return to the sources" entails not just the resuscitation of the idea of theater as a critical force in American culture but also the return to the concept of the American nation as it was first conceived, as the once and future utopia.

Both Bourdieu's account of subversion and accommodation (at least as it is articulated here) and Bercovitch's notion of consensus masquerading as dissensus represent rather fatalistic cultural narratives. Both assume that hegemonic ideology always already defuses and disables oppositional positions.

Both credit the seemingly endless ability of culture to absorb that which has the potential for disrupting or destroying it. Bercovitch, in particular, sees "our classic texts" as "making basic change seem virtually unthinkable, except as apocalypse." For him, "American ideology," with its endless powers of recuperation, seems invariably "to absorb the spirit of protest for social ends."[103] His theory, then, produces an "America" that will always represent a conservative hegemony, and "represses," in Donald Pease's words, "the social change an oppositional movement can produce."[104] This position, with its striking similarity to Foucault's widely influential theory of power as a self-contained field in which all "resistances" are finally "inscribed" within power "as an irreducible opposite,"[105] seems unquestionably to be a product of the political retrenchment that has taken place after the collapse of mass-movement politics in the early 1970s. It is also almost irresistible in the United States in the 1990s, when the revival of neither an effective political opposition nor mass-movement resistance seems at all likely. Yet for those very reasons, I think one must be wary of taking up a position that effectively forecloses the possibility of change. Just because Mormonism, the original American religion, was finally consolidated in the twentieth century as an extremely conservative ideology, despite its radical roots, it is not inevitable that all social movements must in the end serve the ideologies they were designed to oppose. To explore other possibilities of resistance, and of producing a subjectivity beyond masochism, I want to examine the emergence—and decline—of a new social movement that in theory at least offered the likelihood of both renewing radical change and reimagining the subject. I am speaking, of course, of a movement that coalesced a month before *Millennium Approaches* was given its first workshop production: Queer Nation.

QUEER NATIONALISM

In April 1990, members of ACT UP, the AIDS activist group, angered at the recent escalation of violence against lesbians and gay men as well as more generalized "visibility issues," met at the Lesbian and Gay Community Services Center in New York City.[106] Out of their impromptu meeting emerged a new movement, Queer Nation, which adopted a broader social and political agenda than that of ACT UP and was quickly consolidated in New York, San Francisco, Boston, and other major U.S. cities. Inspired by diverse sources, including ACT UP, the civil rights and Black Power movements, the post-Stonewall gay and lesbian liberation movement, the feminist movement, the countercultural action-theater of the Yippies, and the antiwar and nuclear freeze movements, Queer Nation represented one of the so-called new social movements. Unlike most pre-1960 forms of social and political activism in the United States, the new social movements serve primarily a middle-class rather than working-class constituency and are, in the main, less concerned with economic oppression than with social injustice. Turning their attention to civil society, they are dedicated to mobilizing around not just political issues but cultural ones as well, ranging from broad questions of enculturation and socialization to specific issues relating to the media, the construction of identity, and the effects of various discriminatory practices.[107]

Queer Nation, representing a heterogeneous and shifting constituency (like most new social movements), brought together a number of contradictory agendas without offering theoretical coherence. Ideologically, it was aggressively antiassimilationist and "nonestablishment."[108] Eschewing both political process and any hint of reformism in favor of direct confrontation, it staged militant and highly theatricalized actions (such as kiss-ins, zaps, and the occupation of heterosexualized spaces, like suburban shopping malls and straight bars) that, Henry Abelove points out, expressed "a felt need to create a wholly non-domestic site of excitement, outrage, and interest."[109] In the words of Allan Bérubé and Jeffrey Escoffier, "Queer Nation takes to the street wearing 'QUEER' stickers and badges on their jackets, fighting to keep queer turf safe from bashings." Like "queer urban street gangs," queer nationalists practiced a kind of guerrilla warfare against "straight" culture (which had the same highly negative ambience that "establishment" did for the New Left). The products of a mediatized and commodified culture, they (unlike their '60s forebears) did not reject consumerism but "embrace[d] the retrofuture/classic contemporary styles of postmodernism." Committed to a style that is "slick, quick, anarchistic, transgressive, [and] ironic," Queer Nation exemplified the new "politics of cultural subversion" (which became so popular both in the streets and in the academy during the 1980s), which invert or, more properly, *queer* the normative.[110] As described by Lauren Berlant and Elizabeth Freeman, "its tactics are to cross borders, to occupy spaces, and to mime the privileges of normality—in short, to simulate 'the national' with a camp inflection."[111]

Yet what was perhaps most remarkable about Queer Nation was its expropriation of the discourse of nationalism in an era when, at least for most self-identified leftists, nationalism was (and remains) deeply suspect. Rooted in a strong sense of communitarianism which insists that "whenever one of us is hurt we all suffer," Queer Nation affirmed, as Esther Kaplan explains, that "we are a *nation* of queers. . . ."[112] Like *Angels in America*, Queer Nation represented an attempt to queer America, to produce a counterhegemonic patriotism that militates for a redefinition of the nation and simultaneously for the recognition of the always already queer status of American culture (from Whitman to Madonna). Like *Angels*, it was tied not just to an end-of-the-Cold-War-induced national identity crisis but also to the various nationalist projects of the Reagan-Bush years: the ostentatious spectacles of nationhood (including, most prominently, the Statue of Liberty centennial and the 1984

Los Angeles Olympics), the controversies over flag burning and the Pledge of Allegiance, and the imperial muscle-flexing in Grenada, Panama, Libya, and Iraq. In the face of such extravagant—and murderous—spectacles of empire, Queer Nation and *Angels in America* offered a relatively benign nationalist counterexample.

As Bérubé and Escoffier point out, however, even the name Queer Nation is oxymoronic, asserting both difference and sameness. Insofar as "queer" designates a perverse or marginal positionality and "nation" an affirmation of commonality and centrality, Queer Nation necessarily combined "contradictory impulses."[113] Yet each part of the designation is itself contradictory. Historically, queer represents a stigmatizing term for lesbians and gay men that, like the pink triangle, has been reclaimed, inverted if you will, as a form of resignification. Its widespread usage during the 1990s among self-identified queers is indicative of at least an implicit rejection of the notion of "internalized oppression" that characterizes so much post-Stonewall discourse. Unlike many women and men who came of age politically during the 1970s (the heyday of lesbian and gay liberationist politics), queers recognize the difficulty in trying to distinguish between a stigmatized and a positively inflected identity. The disdain felt by some queers for the terms lesbian and gay—and for the ethos of the 1970s—is thus symptomatic of a generational split. Inevitably, in the discourse of many queers, lesbians and gay men are constructed as older, more *embourgeoisé*, and thus more conservative and assimilationist than queers.[114]

Yet queer is not only the symptom of generational and class-based conflicts, it also represents a different way of conceptualizing sexual identity and, more specifically, a means of destabilizing the binary oppositions homosexual/heterosexual, sex/gender, gay/lesbian, masculine/feminine, and male/female. As Eve Sedgwick observes, queer "can refer to the open mesh of possibilities, gaps, overlaps, dissonances and resonances, lapses and excesses of meaning when the constituent elements of anyone's gender, of anyone's sexuality aren't made (or *can't be* made) to signify monolithically."[115] Unlike lesbian and gay, it is an exorbitant signifier, designating a wide range of sexual and gender dissidents, including those (like leatherfolk, masturbators, or transgendered subjects) who may not be easily accommodated to the prevailing binary logic. Queer also enjoys the distinction of being—at least theoretically—gender-neutral so that it can describe both male- and female-sexed bodies. Queer, in other words, represents an attempt to problematize the older style of identity politics of the 1970s and the minoritizing discourses that are associated with lesbian feminism and gay liberation. To this extent, it is part of a new universalizing discourse that is able to include under its umbrella anyone willing to renounce the claims and prerogatives of heteronormativity. Not unlike the idea of America, it is a deeply utopian designation, opening up a vista of multiple, shifting, and gloriously polymorphous bodies and pleasures. Yet as so often happens in mass-movement politics, Queer Nation never completely realized these utopian hopes, and many queer nationalists complained that the organization and its functioning was dominated—yet again—by the persons, agendas, and styles of white gay men.[116] This fact, perhaps more than any other, was responsible for its virtual disappearance by the mid-1990s.

Like *Angels in America*, Queer Nation combined different—and contradictory—concepts of subjectivity, identity, and nationhood. Practicing a postmodernist identity politics that simultaneously asserts and destabilizes identity, it epitomized the turn in new social movements away from an economic and class-based—which is to say, Marxist—reading of oppression in favor of an ideological and cultural one. As Berlant and Freeman note, "Queer Nation's nationalist-style camp counterpolitics . . . shift[s] between a utopian politics of identity, difference, dispersion, and a specificity and a pluralist agenda in the liberal sense that imagines a 'gorgeous mosaic' of difference without a model."[117] Like *Angels*, its commitment to demarginalizing the queer subject meant in practice the privileging of white, gay men (women in the play tend to be pathologized and/or marginalized). Yet in this case the contradictions inherent in these cultural productions result, I believe, not just from the contradictory class positionality of the actors involved (a dominated fraction of the dominant class, to borrow Bourdieu's formulation), but from the specific situation of white gay men, many of whom, as individuals, possess a great deal of economic and cultural capital, but who, as a class, remain relatively disempowered politically.[118]

PERESTROIKA

Rather than dismiss Queer Nation and *Angels in America* (and the queer cultural moment of the early '90s that they instantiate) as being as reactionary as George Bush's State of the Union Messages and consequently of little use in imagining a progressive politics, I want to put pressure on the concept of queer nationalism implicit in these productions. For it is my belief that Queer Nation failed less because its theory of nationalism was faulty than because it was never able to actualize it. As Neil Lazarus notes, "mainstream scholars have characteristically deplored 'new' nationalisms wherever they have been mobilized, on the grounds that they foment revolution, or that they are totalitarian, or that they result only in an intensification of already existing social division."[119] They forget, as Benedict Anderson emphasizes, that "since World War II every successful revolution has defined itself in *national* terms."[120]

As Aijaz Ahmad points out, from the late 1940s until the late 1970s, "anticolonial nationalism—both in the form of nationalist ideologies . . . and in the form of revolutionary wars and post-revolutionary states of the socialist Left—was a constitutive element of the global configuration."[121] And nationalism in turn was often supported by a variety of First World activists and intellectuals (usually inspired by Fanon), as well as a broad range of cultural nationalists, especially (in the United States at least) black and Chicano nationalists. It was not, however, until the late '70s—coincidentally with the rise of poststructuralism—that First World literary and cultural theorists marshaled their forces against nationalism. Since then, the critique of anticolonial nationalism launched by Homi Bhabha, Gayatri Chakravorty Spivak, and Christopher Miller (among others) has been appropriated by and disseminated widely among the American poststructuralist elite.[122] Ahmad offers an acute reading of this development:

> The newly dominant position of poststructuralist ideology is the fundamental enabling condition for a literary theory which debunks nationalism not on the familiar Marxist ground that nationalism in the present century has frequently suppressed questions of gender and class and has itself been frequently complicit with all kinds of obscurantisms and revanchist positions, but in the patently postmodernist way of debunking *all* efforts to speak of origins, collectivities, determinate historical projects. The upshot, of course, is that critics working within the poststructuralist problematic no longer distinguish, in any foregrounded way, between the progressive and retrograde forms of nationalism with reference to particular histories, nor do they examine the even more vexed question of how progressive and retrograde elements may be (and often are) combined within particular nationalist trajectories; what gets debunked, rather, is nationalism *as such*, in more or less the same apocalyptic manner in which cultural nationalism was, only a few years earlier, declared the determinate answer to imperialism.[123]

It may be objected that the queer nationalism of both Queer Nation and *Angels in America* is, in essence, radically different from the anticolonial nationalisms about which Ahmad is writing. Not only did queer nationalism, from the outset, prove to be primarily a white, middle-class, male phenomenon (what Fanon would call a production of the national bourgeoisie), but its locus was not, as *Angels* demonstrates, the so-called Third World at all, but rather the imperial center. Queer nationalism militated for a nation very different from, say, the Algerian or Vietnamese nation insofar as it targeted only a portion of the populace. For the most minoritizing of nationalists, straights were emphatically excluded from the Queer Nation. Moreover, because the United States is only one of many states that shelters a queer minority, queer nationalism could have represented an internationalist nationalism (although, as Fanon points out, this hardly makes it unique: Arab nationalism, to name only one, is also internationalist).[124]

Yet it seems to me that this very incommensurability between the anticolonial nationalisms of the post–World War II period and queer nationalism could have proven more productive than disabling. Seen as a form of Fanonian national consciousness, queer nationalism offered (and still offers) a powerful tool for reimagining both America and its national subject. First, as *Angels* suggests, in America, queers—however minoritized or universalized one's definition—unquestionably represent a colonized population, one insistently pathologized, criminalized, and subjugated by the ubiquitous and violent claims of heteronormativity. Like the category "native," which, for Fanon, is brought into being and perpetuated by the "settler," the queer does not have an autonomous or presubjected being.[125] He or she is the construction of a system of oppression. To this extent, a queer nationalist like Prior Walter can never return to a nonexistent authentic self that preexists internalized oppression, but rather can only work toward constructing a different kind of subject which, according to Fanonian logic, can be produced only by a different kind of social and economic organization. For Fanon, that new subjectivity must first and foremost be a collective one based on the idea of "the people." *For it is only through this collective subject that internalized oppression can be overcome, that the masochism of the colonized can be extinguished.* According to Fanon, the struggle must be "to teach the masses that everything depends on them, . . . that the demiurge is the people themselves and the magic hands are finally only the hands of the people."[126] They must learn, in other words, that they need not submit to oppressive social, political, and economic forces. They must learn that there are ways of finding pleasure other than through the eroticization of subjection. They must learn "to terminate this neurotic situation," Fanon confesses, "in which I am compelled to choose an unhealthy, conflictual solution, fed on fantasies, hostile, inhuman in short." They must "rise above this absurd drama that others have staged round me, to reject the two terms [black and white, victim and victimizer] that are equally unacceptable, and, through one human being, to reach out for the universal."[127]

Like the ideologies of Queer Nation, *Angels in America*, and even early Mormonism (which, after all, had its roots in "Rousseau's concept of the collective personality of the 'people'"), Fanon's recognizes that the revolutionary overthrow of the regime of internalized oppression cannot take place without the complete participation of all who constitute the nation.[128] In these cultural productions, this means first redefining family and kinship. For queer nationalists, it entailed changing the designation "family" so that it was "inclusive" of all those one calls queer, those one chooses to call one's kin.[129] In the epilogue to *Perestroika*, in one of *Angels*'s most radical moves, family is redefined as the chosen and diverse few gathered to hear Prior's call to arms: "We will be citizens"—of a new nation that will abolish subjection (to the Law, to the Father), and that exists, as every nation does, only in fantasy (2: 148).

The construction of a queer minority that makes claims for citizenship and nationhood immediately evokes the history of black nationalism in the United States. During the late 1960s and early 1970s, many African Americans, disillusioned with both electoral politics and the civil rights movement, and inspired by anticolonialist wars (in Cuba, Algeria, Vietnam), came to believe that nationalist struggle provided the best chance for radical change. In their

1967 book, *Black Power*, Stokely Carmichael and Charles V. Hamilton explain that "black people in this country form a colony" which, because "it is not in the interest of the colonial power," cannot be liberated without a struggle. For them, "institutional racism" is synonymous with "colonialism," and, pointing to patterns of economic exploitation, they compare the United States to South Africa.[130] In their discourse, black nationalism functions to form a historical link connecting not only race with nation but also the subjugation of African Americans with the dynamics of a European imperialism that violently expropriated their ancestors as slaves from the African continent. Because of its diasporic character, it also represents, like queer nationalism, a form of internationalism. A history of forced migration, however, distinguishes black nationalism from queer nationalism, and the latter does not problematize the ideas of home, exile, and ancestry in the same way. For most black nationalists, the United States remains the once and future land of slavery. Unlike Queer Nation, which was intent on reclaiming (that is to say, queering) America, black nationalism characteristically finds the historical construction of America utterly irredeemable. To this extent, Belize's declaration that he "hate[s] America," that "[i]t's just big ideas, and stories, and people dying," serves to position him more closely to black than to queer nationalism (2: 96).

Yet, as *Angels in America* suggests, the question of America also remains vexed for queer nationalism. In *Angels*, the idea of America is inextricably bound up with questions of identity, migration, and progress. A queer identity, in particular, remains an elusive construction. As Eve Sedgwick's gloss on the word queer makes plain, sexuality, when understood as the primary determinant of identity, is highly unstable and polyvalent, more an "open mesh of possibilities" than a fixed structure of desire. Moreover, identity is always multiple, overdetermined, hybridized, which is to say, always being produced by a complex array of different (and contradictory) social and psychic factors. Kobena Mercer's elaboration of hybridity as the distinguishing mark of the work of certain black lesbian and gay artists also, I believe, describes more generally the production of identity in queer nationalist discourse and *Angels in America*. Rather than constructing a nation with inflexible borders, the latter inevitably (and ironically) "operates on the borderlines of race, class, gender, nationality, and sexuality, investigating the complex overdetermination of subjective experiences and desires as they are historically constituted in the ambivalent spaces in between."[131]

In *Angels*, identity is produced in the borderlands, these multidimensional sites that traverse and deconstruct the difference between center and margin, the normative and the perverse. Like the subjects who embody it, it is constantly on the move, constantly unmaking and remaking America. In so foregrounding the problematics of migration, both forced and voluntary ("some of us didn't exactly *choose* to migrate," notes Belize), the play insistently demonstrates the instability not just of the borders but also of the very idea of America (2: 55). The first scene constructs America as a land that was invaded and settled by diasporic peoples but which, perversely, cannot exist, which remains a site of absence. The eulogy that Rabbi Chemelwitz pronounces over Sarah Ironson constructs her as one "who crossed the ocean" and brought "to America the villages of Russia and Lithuania." But the nation to which she immigrated, "this strange place," is "the melting pot where nothing melted," a land that can never be home, never be more than a point of intersection for people on the move. "You do not live in America," he tells the assembled; "[n]o such place exists." Rather, all his listeners (and the scene deftly conflates assembled mourners and theater audience) have their feet in the "clay" of "ancient culture[s] and home[s]," in other histories. As if to remind his listeners that Jews, blacks, and Mormons are diasporic peoples, he declares (in Yiddish-ified English) that "every day of your lives the miles that voyage between that place and this one you cross. . . . In you that journey is." In other words, migration is the way that history is inscribed in the human subject, and the details of that migration produce not just identity but also the nation that isn't. The rabbi's final admonishment, "[y]ou can never make that crossing that she made, for such Great Voyages in this world do not any more exist," is set forth precisely to be refuted (1: 10–11). If nothing else, the play shows that "you" are always in the process of making a "Great Voyage," which is to say, that history and identity are always in process in the queer nation that does not yet exist. And at the very end of *Perestroika*, as if to underscore the pivotal status in the play of the struggle for national liberation, the final exchange of dialogue (that fades out under Prior's benediction) is the debate between Louis and Belize about the status of another national entity that does not yet exist: the state of Palestine.

The play's commitment to the idea of history as progress—and to Enlightenment epistemologies—has the effect of producing migration as the spatial analogue to the temporal concept of progress. "Migration" is figured as a form of "Forward Motion," which "shakes up Heaven" and violently disturbs the Angel, that "cosmic reactionary" (2: 50, 55). Linking migration and hybridity with progress, *Angels* imagines the queer nation as multiracial and multicultural, the future product of a ceaseless diaspora and crossing of identities and histories, a radical disruption of the relationship between master and slave. And its citizens, moving from one nation that does not yet exist to another, are always in exile, living their lives, like Americans, "in a state of perpetual landing."[132] This linkage between migration and progress has the effect not just of radically problematizing the idea of a fixed homeland but also of indefinitely deferring the production of the queer nation. In the process, the latter is reimagined (once again) as a utopian site, which, like Oscar Wilde's utopia, is "the one country at which Humanity is always landing. And when Humanity lands there, it looks out, and, seeing a better country, sets sail."[133] Faced with devastation, with the violence of heteronormativity, the queer nationalist is a perpetual exile who does not, unlike the black nationalist or Zionist, even have the fantasy of an ancestral homeland on which to fall back. Instead, the queer nationalist has what Fanon calls "a national culture"—including the American theater from Tennessee Williams and Edward Albee to Maria Irene Fornes and Tony Kushner—that can "rehabilitate" the nation and "serve as a justification for the hope of a future national culture."[134]

At the same time, the lack of a queer homeland in an America that does not exist speaks to the necessarily internationalist character of queer nationalism. Every nation is potentially a queer nation, less because every nation harbors a queer minority than because of the internationalist character of desire itself. Functioning as a kind of world language, and refusing to honor boundaries (both national and otherwise), desire cunningly and unpredictably undermines the distinction between the homosocial and the homosexual, producing subjects who finally defy even as they insist upon a sexual categorization. The queer nationalists produced by this contradictory process are both particularized and universalized by their desires. They are made, as Monique Wittig notes of Proust, "the axis of categorization from which to universalize," the perverts who prove the inadvertent lesson of Freud's theory of sexuality: that all desire is perverted. The nation they constitute "could be described," to quote Wittig again, "as being like Pascal's circle, whose center is everywhere and whose circumference is nowhere."[135] So imagined, the epilogue to *Perestroika* becomes the occasion for the deconstruction of the categories "queer," "nation," and "citizen," and for the calling into question of the boundaries implied by each designation. In so doing, it provides a possible model for an anti-imperialist struggle that, as Fanon emphasizes, must always proceed by way of the national. For "[i]t is at the heart of national consciousness that international consciousness lives and grows."[136] As history has demonstrated, it is only by means of the nation that a new definition of community and of the human subject has been produced.

As *Angels in America* suggests, for a queer nationalism to function as an internationalism, it must also ensure that "queer" denotes more than just a particularized, if universalized, form of sexual dissidence. It must also look to the construction of racialized, gendered, class-based, and (post)colonial positionalities. Yet I do not believe that Queer Nation would have succeeded if it had simply made "queer" a more inclusive or pluralist category. For queer nationalism to have become an internationalism, it would have had to go beyond the principles of identity politics as they have been constituted until now. Its most antiassimilationist proponents never recognized that Queer Nation was founded upon what remains a *strategic* essentialism, an essentialism that, although indispensible, in Gayatri Spivak's words, for defining "a scrupulously delineated 'political interest,'" is in the end "theoretically non-viable."[137] To be viable, in other words, queer nationalism must finally call into question the very categories of identity that have authorized its production in the first place. For as Wendy Brown notes, an identity politics, because of its tendency to reformulate exclusionary categories, tends to "resubordinate" a subject who is already "historically subjugated."[138] Moreover, analyzing the disintegration of the New Left during the late '60s, she argues that identity politics has proven to be "partly dependent upon the demise of a *critique* of capitalism and of bourgeois cultural and economic values." Rather than attempt to dismantle structures of power and privilege,

> identity politics may be partly configured by a peculiarly shaped and peculiarly disguised form of class resentment, a resentment which is displaced onto discourses of injustice rather than class, but a resentment, like all resentments, which retains the real or imagined holdings of its reviled subject as objects of desire. In other words, the enunciation of politicized identities through race, gender and sexuality may require—rather than incidentally produce—a limited identification through class, and may specifically abjure a critique of class power and class norms precisely insofar as these identities are established *vis-à-vis* a bourgeois norm of social acceptance, legal protection and relative material comfort.

Identity politics, in short, is "tethered to a formulation of justice which reinscribes a bourgeois (masculinist) ideal as its measure."[139] So however catholic or universalizing it may seem, it remains indentured to a voluntarist subject— stricken and paralyzed by resentment—as agent of history and, as a result, tends both to hypostatize a kind of bourgeois individualism and to protect capitalism from critique. It may attack the pieties of humanism, but it reifies a political subject uncomfortably similar to the one that has produced—and is produced by—a liberal pluralist politic. As Elisa Glick notes, identity politics "has valorized a politics of lifestyle—how we dress or get off—that fails to engage with institutionalized systems of domination."[140]

More important, as Brown suggests, the identity politics that has flourished in the United States since the late '60s, with a few exceptions (most notably, the Black Panthers, the Redstockings, and the Gay Liberation Front), has been if not downright hostile then at least indifferent to socialism. Like the new social movements to which it is linked, it has historically privileged a particular axis of identity while more often than not ignoring the relationship between the construction of identity categories and the functioning not only of American capitalism but, more important, of capitalism as a world system. Operating within a bourgeois *imaginaire*, it has only infrequently forged coalitions with working-class movements or addressed itself to the fact that the United States since 1980 has become "the most economically stratified of industrial nations."[141] Characteristically reformist rather than revolutionary in its strategies, it tends to reimagine the nation in liberal pluralist and ahistorical terms as a resplendent mosaic in which diversity is celebrated and consumed. Usually selecting culture as its primary target, it tends not to consider the material bases for cultural production. As a result, it inadvertently falls prey to the cultural logic that conceptualizes difference as a commodity rather than a political tool. This is the politics of "lifestyle," which, Rosemary Hennessy notes, obscures "social hierarchies by promoting individuality and self-expression but also a more porous conception of the self as a 'fashioned' identity."[142] As a mere glance at *Vanity Fair* or the "Styles" section of the *New York Times* will reveal, the marketing of queer culture—not least of all in the phenomenon of *Angels in America*—has increasingly come to resemble the commodification of black music (whether jazz, funk, disco, hip-hop, or rap), which at least since the 1960s has characteristically functioned as a *substitute* for an engagement with an antiracist politics. During the 1990s, controversies over lesbians and gay men in the military and the drive to repeal local statutes guaranteeing their equal protection have made lesbian and gay rights *the* civil rights issue in the United States. Yet the visibility of queer artifacts and the success of queer or queer-wannabe cultural productions (including *Angels*, Madonna, k.d. lang, and lesbian chic) have too frequently replaced a commitment to fighting either for equal protection under the law or for more radical kinds of political and social change. And although one of the most provocative aspects of Queer Nation was its all too postmodernist exploitation of corporate strategies—its construction of a flagrantly and defiantly queer consumer culture—it, like *Angels*, did not explicitly question the linkages between homophobia and economic exploitation.

One of the most problematic aspects of both Queer Nation and *Angels* is their ambivalence around the question of an alliance between a queer (inter)nationalism and other anti-imperialisms, in particular, the struggle—as attenuated as it may be at the present moment—against the system of global circulation for which national boundaries remain an impediment: capitalism. Comrade Prelapsarianov seems extremely skeptical of the idea that socialism might provide an answer both to imperialism and to the genocidal force of various bourgeois nationalisms (resuscitated most devastatingly in the former Soviet bloc). Searching for a "beautiful Theory," he would not agree with Ahmad that socialism is "the determinate name for [the] negation of capitalism's fundamental, systemic contradictions and cruelties . . ." (2: 14). For Ahmad emphasizes that socialism alone, by abolishing differences in economic class, remains "essentially universalist in character," insofar as its goal is the dissolution of all social classes and the international division of labor. Thus, "even as a transitional mode," it "cannot exist except on a transnational basis." At the same time, however, "the *struggle* for even the prospect of that transition presumes a national basis, in so far as the already existing structures of the nation-state are a fundamental reality of the very terrain on which actual class conflicts take place." A queer (inter)nationalism would have to agitate to overturn the existing bourgeois state apparatuses that have adjusted all too well to the exigencies of capital (even in the Third World). It would have to strive for a massive restructuring not just of the cultural relations that support a pluralist identity politics, but also of those international mechanisms, most notably the World Bank and the IMF, that work to deepen the international division of labor. For it is only "at the level of popular political forces, which are by the very nature of things in conflict with the state, that a nationalism can actually *become* an anti-imperialism."[143] Without popular and mass-movement resistance, transnational capital will only strengthen and extend the mechanisms of the bourgeois state.

One of the most intriguing proposals for restructuring was put forth by Mikhail Gorbachev in his 1987 book, *Perestroika*, which is also, by no mere coincidence, the title of part 2 of *Angels in America*. Gorbachev's project for restructuring (the literal meaning of "perestroika") was regrettably short-lived, having been precipitously smothered by an upsurge of consumerism and various deeply reactionary bourgeois nationalisms that led to the collapse of the Soviet Union. His book, however, written in one of those rare historical moments during which, to borrow Harper's phrase, a kind of "painful progress" seems possible, calls for a wide-ranging and fundamental reconfiguration not only of the Soviet economy but also of its politics, society, and culture (2: 144). A utopian manifesto, it does not look greedily at capitalism but envisions a different kind of socialism as the answer to the crises that engulfed the Soviet Union in the mid-1980s. Time and again, Gorbachev insists that perestroika does not signal a turn away from socialism, or from Leninism, but rather its fulfillment: "More socialism means more democracy, openness and collectivism in everyday life, more culture and humanism in production, social and personal relations among people, more dignity and self-respect for the individual."[144] Committed, like *Angels*, to reclaiming Enlightenment epistemologies, Gorbachev's *Perestroika* recognizes that "progress" remains "the product of the Revolution" and "the fruit of socialism."[145]

In their extremely disparate ways, Kushner's *Angels in America*, queer nationalism, Fanon's national liberation, and Gorbachev's perestroika all speak to the desirability of what Neil Lazarus refers to as "a 'new' humanism, predicated upon a formal repudiation of the degraded European form, and borne embryonically in the national liberation movement."[146] The deeply problematic nature of the old European (and American) humanism, with its championing of individualism, patriarchy, moral masochism, and the "free" market, and its inextricable connection with the imperialist project, seems all too obvious (it has, after all, served historically as the rationale for colonialism). But *Angels* suggests that humanism as an idea—no less than America as an idea—is by no means irredeemable (this seems to me to be crucial to its success). In his consideration of humanism, Ahmad usefully distinguishes between "the epistemological and the practical (i.e. political and ethical) issues involved" in the concept. He points out that while Marx clearly broke with a liberal humanist epistemology, "Marxism recoups its humanist energy" with regard to both the "constructedness of history (unauthored but humanly made) and the ethical life of the species-being (the struggle from necessity to freedom). . . . "[147] Understood in this sense, then, a Marxist humanist notion of freedom—from want, from necessity—differs radically from the liberal humanist idea of freedom, tied as it is to the exigencies of the capitalist marketplace. So, too, a Marxist humanist notion of universalism, which is linked to the transnational character of socialism as the answer to imperialism and the international division of labor it leaves in its bloody wake, must differ from George Bush's universalism that is connected both to the globalization of capital and to the universalist currency of the commodity form. Finally, a Marxist humanist egalitarianism, rooted in "the ethical life of the species-being," must differ both from a liberal humanism that promises equal opportunity but delivers only economic and social inequality, and a liberal pluralism that celebrates cultural difference but covertly reinforces the murderous subordination of margin to center, black to white, woman to man, queer to straight, master to slave, and the human subject to the unimpeded flow of capital. For only a Marxist humanism can, if not exactly abolish masochistic masculinity—and femininity—at least transform the material circumstances that produced both of them in the first place. The (inter)national crisis precipitated by the end of the Cold War thus represents an opportunity to imagine radical perestroika. By attempting this impossible project, *Angels in America* aims to reconceptualize and reclaim humanism, to think beyond internalized oppression, and to take up Fanon's challenge in the name of a queer internationalism:

> Let us consider the question of mankind. Let us reconsider the question of . . . all humanity, whose connections must be increased, whose channels must be diversified and whose messages must be re-humanized.[148]

Chapter Six

THE WILL TO BELIEVE

> We stand in witness . . . to a planet-wide mutation of mind which
> promises to liberate energies of will and resources of vision long
> maturing in the depths of our identity.
>
> *(Theodore Roszak, quoted in* Psychology Today *[1994])*
>
> Here's a guy who's got his act together. Here's somebody who's
> got it all figured out. Here's somebody who has the answer.
>
> *(Running man to title character in* Forrest Gump *[1994])*

I F ONE of the proposed solutions to the social and political crises that loom
at the end of the Cold War has been a revival of nationalism, then another
surely is the turn to spirituality. Indeed, the 1990s have witnessed the bur-
geoning of a multibillion-dollar industry of products and services that betray
what trendspotters call a "spiritual renaissance."[1] A multitude of books dealing
with spirituality have flooded the marketplace, from self-help manuals to accounts of near-death experiences, from New Age novels to catalogs of angels.
James Redfield's *The Celestine Prophecy,* Betty Eadie's *Embraced by the
Light*, Thomas Moore's *Care of the Soul: A Guidebook for Cultivating Depth
and Sacredness in Everyday Life*, and M. Scott Peck's *The Road Less Trav-
elled* have hovered on best-seller lists for years. In 1994 alone, books on spirituality accounted for one-quarter of the titles on the *New York Times* best-
seller list.[2] At the same time, millions of Americans have taken to supporting
an array of twelve-step programs, meditation centers, weekend retreats, and
countless other activities related to spiritual improvement. More people than
ever say that "they believe in such unexplained phenomena as mysticism,
miracles and celestial beings."[3] The recording of Gregorian chant by the Bene-
dictine monks of Santo Domingo de Silos (1994) has "mysteriously rocketed
to the top of the pop charts" and become one of the five most successful al-
bums of all time.[4] In short, "people in the merchandising business say spirituality is the buzzword of the Nineties."[5]

Some cultural observers argue that the 1990s may indeed be bearing witness
to what is sometimes described as the Third Great Awakening in U.S. history.[6]
However, this massive quest for spirituality, "unprecedented in modern
times," is quite different from its predecessors.[7] For as many commentators
have observed, this third Awakening is highly eclectic insofar as "its motive

power is not coming from mainstream institutionalized science, religion, or education."[8] Rather, the new spirituality seems to represent the soul (as it were) of the New Age movement. Although the resurgence of evangelical Christian sects in the United States is clearly a part of the new spirituality, most of the newly faithful are not associated with orthodox religious traditions. For one of its hallmarks is its (postmodernist) appropriation of characteristics and doctrine derived from a great diversity of both religious and nonreligious sources, including Asian philosophy and religion, meditation, the self-help movement, Jungian psychology, alternative medicines, pseudoscience (like astrology), quantum physics, environmentalism, computer technology, as well as from the more celebratory and communitarian aspects of various forms of identity politics, from African-American cultural nationalism to the men's movement. The new spirituality represents, in effect, a kind of secularized religion.

Commentators are divided on the causes and genealogy of the new spirituality. Some see it as an extension of the recovery movement's ascendancy at the end of the 1980s.[9] Others see it, because of its overwhelmingly middle-class constituency, as representing the soul-searching of thirtysomething and fortysomething yuppies whose materialism has failed to make them happy: "The money, the education, the success—it hasn't brought them anything—so it seems a lot of people are searching."[10] Some ascribe it to "millennial madness, a collective frisson at the year 2000 looming uncertainly ahead."[11] Others see it as marking the failure of rationalism, technology, and Enlightenment epistemologies.[12] Some regard it as an outgrowth of identity politics and environmentalism.[13] Others believe it a response to a "centre" that "no longer seems to be holding": " 'It's a very frightening time we're in,' says York University's [William Irwin] Thompson. 'Whether its Rwanda, Bosnia or the ozone hole over Antarctica expanding, we're moving towards a shared sense of planetary crisis. And people are turning to anything—everything.' "[14]

Despite the different diagnoses, however, most commentators agree that the new spirituality marks the somewhat belated triumph of the '60s counterculture. Theodore Roszak prognosticates: "We stand in witness . . . to a planet-wide mutation of mind which promises to liberate energies of will and re-sources of vision long maturing in the depths of our identity."[15] And Timothy Miller argues "that what was originally thought to be a passing fad of the 1960s has now matured into altogether new and well-secured communities of faith."[16] Sylvia Fraser, the author of the New Age best-seller, *The Book of Strange*, notes revealingly,

> "In the Sixties, the revolution was both sexual and spiritual. . . . But the spiritual revolution was tied to drugs and it crashed. So most people took the cheap, fast sexual route." Now after a decade of partying—and AIDS—the baby boomers, she says, "are going back to the other prong of the revolution."[17]

Fraser's observation is typical of new spiritualist social analysis insofar as it conveniently forgets what was in fact the third "prong" of the '60s revolution—politics. For among the vast majority of those youth associated with the counterculture, the attempt to produce political change (even if it meant only opposing the Vietnam War) was a crucial dimension of "the revolution." Yet in Fraser's account of the '60s—as in so many others—politics gets written out of the history. This amnesia is symptomatic of an aggressive antihistoricism among the new spiritualists, who are far more comfortable writing about allegedly universal myths and Jungian archetypes than about historical process, or for whom history counts only as a scattered series of discrete—and apocalyptic—events. Even Sam Keen, who is arguably the most politically aware of the gurus of the new masculine spirituality, remains fixated on an abstract "war system" that conveniently displaces both specific historical narratives of conquest and resistance and the inequitable distributions of wealth that are always linked to social crisis and struggle.[18] At the same time, this amnesia is indicative of a wholesale disillusionment with politics on the part of the overwhelmingly white, middle- and upper-middle-class constituency of the new spirituality (with the exception of a few tepid environmentalists and pacifists).[19] Indeed, this disillusionment remains an index precisely of the failure of electoral politics and the virtual disappearance during the 1990s both of a critique of capitalism and of mass-movement politics. The new spirituality thus represents the impossibility of imagining that the solutions to personal crisis could possibly be social or economic in character. As a result, I cannot agree with Fred Pfeil's characterization of New Age as "neither more nor less than the *lingua franca* of whatever alternative political culture is left in white America out beyond the groves of academe."[20] New Age and the new spirituality have nothing alternative about them and seem instead virtually to define hegemonic culture. For rather than dedicate themselves to producing social, political, and economic change, the partisans of the new spirituality desperately "search . . . for universal truth" by turning inward and ignoring the fact that today the only producer of universality (false as it is) is capitalism as a world system.[21] Keen, for example, argues that "the whole history of man" is not to be discovered in traditional fields of knowledge like history, sociology, or economics but is "contained in your psyche," under "the facade of your modern personality."[22] All "you" have to do is close your eyes and behold.

Spirituality has from the beginning been an important component of the men's movement, and its ideologies run the gamut from the explicitly non-Christian work of mainstream figures like Robert Bly, Sam Keen, Aaron Kipnis, Robert Moore, and Douglas Gillette to the avowedly antifeminist Christian evangelical Promise Keepers, who are dedicated to strengthening men's traditionally dominant role in the nuclear family, to honoring Jesus

Christ and his church, and "to practic[ing] spiritual, moral, ethical and sexual purity."[23] In this chapter, however, I will be focusing on the mainstream work because it remains the most influential and most emblematic. Aside from Bly, the mainstream extends from the relatively liberal, pacifist Keen to the indefatigably Jungian Moore and Gillette. Although Keen differs from the latter pair in his advocacy of a gentler, more humble masculinity, while Moore and Gillette are intent on reinvigorating ancient and aggressive archetypes, all these writers position themselves (in different ways) against feminism, or rather, against a caricature of feminism as a form of man-hatred drawn principally from the cultural feminism of the 1970s. Yet like the cultural feminists they attack, they reify and essentialize sexual difference and look back to mythology, legendary history, and non-Western cultures to provide an ahistorical essence of masculinity. All are intent on redeeming what Moore and Gillette call the "cosmic, life-engendering phallus," or what Keen describes as the "phallic principle that gives man dignity, . . . is worthy of worship," and allows him "to rise to the occasion, to answer the call of history."[24] And although Keen, to his credit, does critique homophobia and in several instances considers the experiences of gay men, Moore and Gillette completely erase gay men as well as the homoerotic component of so many of the myths and legends they invoke (and thereby produce sometimes laughably incomplete readings of bisexual figures like Dionysus).

Despite the very real differences among them, the self-appointed guardians of male spirituality are unanimous in imagining masculinity (as I have noted in chapter 3) as a fragile and vulnerable commodity. And all stress the importance of reconnecting with (mostly absent) fathers and with myths and images of a powerful, effective masculinity. Emphasizing the primacy of process, they argue that a full masculinity must be fought for, that men need "real mentoring" in an age of "discredited ritual and spiritual experience. . . ."[25] Most important, they (much like their cultural feminist sisters) are obsessed with "internalized oppression," questions of self-destruction and violence, and the relationship between masculinity and "the original wound, the scar around which masculine character has traditionally been constructed."[26] Keen perhaps puts it most directly in a question that could stand as the lead-in to each of these books: "Why this connection between masculinity and pain?"[27] Why do men wreak violence both on others and on themselves? For Moore and Gillette, perhaps the greatest crisis confronting men (or at least their so-called Warrior archetype) is linked to masochism and sadism—the one a "self-emascul[ation]" and the other an "impotent rage."[28] They attempt to resolve this crisis in their guide to personal development by asserting that the "fully expressed Warrior" cannot finally purge masochism and sadism. Rather, he "incorporates both the Sadist and the Masochist, but in a fully integrated condition that is cohesive and much more than the sum of its parts."[29] Like Keen, for whom masculinity "requires a wounding of the body," Moore and Gillette insist that pain and destruction are the forces out of which "a new life is born."[30] They fantasize that male subjectivity necessitates a split between masochistic and sadistic "parts" of the self, and they insistently turn the male subject into a kind of reflexive sadomasochist. Yet what can a "fully integrated condition" mean when it is founded on a radical split within the self? Is it the degree or visibility of the split that changes? Is the split more obvious in the "immature" Warrior than in his "mature" brother?[31] Never fully explaining the differences, they emphasize the intractability of the arrangement: "[t]o get out of the sadomasochistic system we may not go around it. We must go *through* it."[32] For them, as for all the new spiritualists, a "fully integrated" masculinity requires a passage through, a surrender to the exigencies of the split psyche, an acquiescence to the "wound" or the "inner feminine" that "works with the male structures to actually support and *enhance* a man's masculinity. . . . "[33] Masculinity, in other words, is founded—yet again—on a submission that is at once painful and pleasurable.

The new male spirituality leaves its mark in countless cultural productions, from *Angels in America* to a bevy of Hollywood films that attempt to capitalize on the allegedly spiritual dimension of everyday life. In order to illuminate how this new masculine spirituality (along with the submission to the "inner feminine") is conceptualized in U.S. culture and the very real cultural work it performs, I want to examine two blockbuster films, Robert Zemeckis's *Forrest Gump* (1994, with a screenplay by Eric Roth) and Jan De Bont's *Twister* (1996, with a screenplay by Michael Crichton and Anne-Marie Martin). Although neither features characters who are explicitly committed to the new spirituality, the narratives of both films are, I believe, deeply impacted by its contours. And despite the fact that the two represent very different genres, both are films of redemption and both feature heroes who must endure a series of trials, or what Keen calls "a pilgrimage into the depths of the self," before achieving what is undisguisedly a form of salvation.[34] Both explicitly engage questions of life and death, and both attempt to read the fate of the nation in relation to various dangers, internal as well as external, that threaten its integrity. Most important, both films are intent on producing white men who are ostensibly kinder and gentler than the action movie heroes of the 1980s.[35] And these new heroes (whose brethren populate a host of other '90s films) accord all too well with the prescriptions for a new masculinity offered by the proponents of the men's spirituality movement. At the same time, these new, more sensitive, heroes by no means eschew the role of victim (nor do they by any means completely displace the reflexive sadomasochists that continue to blast their way through action movies). Rather, by embracing it, they—like so many of their precursors and contemporaries—end up helping to shore up and exonerate the put-upon white male.

STUPID IS AS STUPID DOES

Loosely based on Winston Groom's 1986 novel, and featuring one of Hollywood's most bankable stars, Tom Hanks (fresh from his Oscar-winning performance in Jonathan Demme's *Philadelphia* [1993]), *Forrest Gump* became the "the surprise of the summer movie season," amassing $269.7 million within three months of its release and reaching number five on the list of "all-time box office blockbusters."[36] It then went on to win six Academy Awards, including Best Picture, Best Screenplay Adaptation, and Best Actor for Tom Hanks (his second Oscar in two years). Coproducer Wendy Finerman struggled for nine years to make the film (a crusade dubbed "a Hollywood legend") that, in her words, "does what movies are suppose [*sic*] to do: make you feel alive."[37] Although its initial reviews were generally favorable, all the critics and media pundits agreed that it was Tom Hanks's performance in the title role that made the film a popular success. Janet Maslin opined that Hanks is "the only major American movie star who could have played Forrest without condescension," while Corliss called him "the key ingredient, . . . the one actor whom the mass audience trusts as an exemplar of quality."[38] Moreover, the critics were unanimous in seeing *Forrest Gump* as the film that made Hanks, in David Denby's words, "the central American movie actor."[39] Comparing Hanks to Jimmy Stewart, Henry Fonda, and Gary Cooper, they judged the star a "throwback to old Hollywood." And indeed, it is impossible to understand the film's success without noting Tom Hanks's construction as the sensitive everyman of the 1990s, as both an old-fashioned kind of star, "the extraordinary ordinary man" (like Stewart), and the "nice guy on TV, . . . the genial, comfortable friend you want to invite into your home each week."[40] And an important part of this construction (and of what made *Forrest Gump* seem to some far less reactionary than it demonstrably is) is related to Hanks's liberal credentials, established the year before by his portrayal of a gay man who dies of AIDS in *Philadelphia*, and by his Academy Awards acceptance speech in which he thanked the two gay men whom he deemed responsible for his success (prompting one journalist to note, with Peggy Noonan's blessing, that he "could be the left-wing Ronald Reagan").[41] In addition to celebrating Hanks, the critics also pointed up the different cinematic and literary traditions to which the film is heir, ranging from narratives of the idiot savant (*King of Hearts, Being There, Rain Man*) to satires of innocence (*Candide*), and from portraits of the hero as blank slate (*Zelig*) to "canny, poignant fables of men in domestic crisis" (*Rocky, Kramer vs. Kramer, Rain Man*).[42] Throw in some Frank Capra, a little Industrial Light and Magic, a lot of old rock 'n' roll songs, and you get *Forrest Gump*.

Winston Groom's novel was only a "minor success" when originally pub-

lished (although it topped the best-seller list after the movie's release), and the
film makes radical changes in both the plot and the characterization of the hero
that, I believe, proved decisive for the film's extraordinary popularity.[43] The
novel is a peculiarly vague social satire that uses its idiot savant (much more
savant than the film's hero) to burlesque an array of American iconic figures
and institutions, including NASA, the world of professional wrestling, Hollywood, the military, and Presidents Johnson and Nixon. Like its hero (and unlike the satires of Joseph Heller, Terry Southern, or Kurt Vonnegut), it is strenuously anti-ideological, and it carefully avoids staking out a clear-cut position
on the events it depicts (Johnson and Nixon, for example, are ridiculed for their
personal styles, not their political positions). In the novel, Forrest's idiocy is
patently a pose, a device Grooms uses (as Swift does Gulliver's peregrina-
tions) for the purposes of his rather toothless satire, and the hero, as a result, is
more grotesque and far less empathic than he is in the film.

In Grooms's prose, Forrest is also more stubbornly material and more
highly eroticized, and the book is filled with mildly scatological humor
(Forrest's line "I got to pee" reverberates through its pages).[44] One never forgets his materiality, his small bladder, his physical strength, and his attractive-
ness (the fact that he has "the body of, well, an *Adonis*" [36]). Unlike the film's
hero, he does not shrink from sexual contact with all but Jenny (Robin
Wright), whom he desires for a girlfriend, and his character is structured in part
on running gags concerning his anxieties about "peeing" or having anything
"jam[med] . . . up [his] ass" (17). That Hanks's Forrest, in contrast, is so dematerialized is particularly strange considering the difference between the
two media. Not only is he completely lacking in the physical assertiveness of
his novelistic namesake, but he is also portrayed as being extremely diffident
and modest. When undressing in Jenny's dorm room, he covers himself up
bashfully and appears shocked and horrified (or disgusted?) when she uncov-
ers her breasts. Moreover, unlike Lieutenant Dan (Gary Sinise), who confidently (if not proudly) displays his naked torso when Forrest and Bubba
(Mykelti Williamson) first meet him in Vietnam, Forrest seems always to be
(or to want to be) covered up, even if only with a tank-top shirt. Hanks's
Forrest protests his spectacularization; he does not wish to be made into an
object to be consumed, whether by Jenny or by the spectator. Unlike Grooms's
protagonist, who takes a clear delight in being put on display, Hanks's is constantly abashed, and throughout the film he uses his physical stiffness and
formality as the sign of his chastity, goodness, mental deficiency, and, most
important, his "holiness" (to borrow Maslin's word).[45] He is, in short, a completely spiritualized hero. Averse to being made a spectacle, Hanks's hyper-
sensitive Forrest appears to refuse the kind of aggressive masculinity that is
associated with the film's villains, a.k.a. Forrest's and Jenny's tormenters: the
boys who pummel Forrest with stones, Jenny's abusive father, and the leaders

of SDS and the Black Panthers. I want to argue, however, that this refusal is, in fact, a carefully plotted strategy that the film uses to dissimulate and sanction Forrest's own brutality.

From the very beginning of the film, Forrest, the holy fool, is cast as an accidental victim with an IQ of 75, a casualty of his genes (or a botched delivery, perhaps), of an incompetent orthopedist, and schoolyard bullies. But his idiocy—and brilliance—consist precisely in his disavowal, his (heroic) refusal to embrace the role of victim, or to let himself be savored as an object. And the real genius of the film is that the force of this disavowal is expressed through the relentless displacement of Forrest's victimization. Forrest, in other words, tries almost continually to refuse masochism, to refuse the pleasure of his abasement, preferring to let the characters around him either destroy themselves or be destroyed by forces that the narrative codes as "historical," i.e., beyond their control. For throughout the film, as Corliss points out, almost everyone whom Forrest encounters dies, is injured, or is disgraced: Kennedy, Nixon, George Wallace, Elvis Presley, John Lennon, Bubba, Lieutenant Dan and his other buddies in Vietnam, his mother (Sally Field), and, most important, Jenny.[46] Whenever the TV is on, it seems to be reporting an attempted assassination. Like the feckless hero of a knockabout farce, Forrest has an almost fatal touch and leaves a trail of bodies wherever he goes. And all the victims (whether famous or not), with the exception of Bubba, Jenny, and Forrest's mother, just happen to be white men. For much more distinctly in the film than in the novel, Forrest (like Hanks himself) is constructed as the paradigm of the white male, "the extraordinary ordinary man," and at the same time, the exception, the prodigy—both idiot and savant.

Corliss writes that Forrest miraculously survives the devastation of postwar U.S. history "through his goodness and the miracle of idiot grace."[47] I would like to argue, however, that in fact there is a very different rationale for his survival that is connected at once to his position as victim and to the logic of disavowal and displacement. For like the white male as victim in so many cultural texts, he is able, by an imaginary identification with African Americans and women, to take up the role of victim—vicariously, safely—without suffering what African Americans and women actually have to suffer in the film. From the very beginning, the film assiduously produces Forrest as an ambivalently racialized subject. Cast, like the novel, in the form of a confessional narrative, and using Forrest's voice to provide unity, it posits a listener (or spectator) who, for most of the film, is represented in the frame by the persons who are seated on the bus-stop bench next to Forrest, and who, like the silent spectator, presumably get more and more enrapt in the narrative as it proceeds. Forrest's very first audience is an African-American woman (apparently a nurse) whose "feet hurt" and whose presence immediately foregrounds racial difference (her placement at the bus stop, moreover, is likely to have real resonance for anyone familiar with the history of desegregation in the South). And, as in the novel, the first information he conveys to her is that he is named after a Civil War general, Nathan Bedford Forrest, who he claims was related to his mother. Forrest, it turns out, was not just any general but a Confederate general and, even more important, the man who "started up the Ku Klux Klan" (an identification visualized in the film by the use of a clip from *Birth of a Nation*). So Forrest Gump, is other words, is announced as the descendant and namesake of a champion of white supremacy and perpetrator of genocidal violence.

Forrest's initial construction, however, as a paragon of whiteness (which is to say, racism) is coded as a false identification insofar as the film (much more unequivocally than the novel) appears to be committed to an antiracist project. In one of the several sequences of historical television footage into which Forrest is inserted, he returns a notebook that an African-American woman has dropped as she enters a University of Alabama building during desegregation (much to the chagrin of then-governor Wallace). More important, his friendship with Bubba, who in the film—unlike the novel—is black, is presented as a pivotal moment in his development. For after Jenny (with whom Bubba is identified by his offering Forrest, as she did, a seat on the bus), Bubba is Forrest's only companion ("my best, good friend," Forrest keeps repeating). Bubba gives Forrest the idea of the shrimp business (where he makes his first real money), and the two of them are shown to be "like brothers," in Bubba's words. When they first meet Lieutenant Dan, the latter's racist comment to Bubba about the size of his lips and his snide question, "Are you twins?" are clearly intended to contrast with Forrest's good-natured liberality. Yet what is most curious about Forrest's sense of tolerance is that it appears to be purely instinctual. Despite growing up in Alabama in the '40s and '50s, Forrest never needs to be weaned away from racist beliefs. As if in compensation for his mental deficiencies, he is made intuitively and almost divinely good, the exemplary white liberal, a "saint," in the words of one critic.[48] And while the struggle for desegration is depicted momentarily in the film (unlike the novel), the content of the struggle and issues for which black (and white) people died are never represented or debated.

Yet what is most intriguing about Forrest's relationship with African Americans, and with Bubba, in particular, is the way that desire and identification become so confused. Like Mailer's "white Negro" or Kerouac's Sal Paradise, this white man is not content simply to like or desire or love a black man; he wants to *become* black himself. And after Bubba's death Forrest tries, in essence, to commandeer his life, to become his twin for real (this part of the narrative is entirely the film's invention). All-American entrepreneur that he is, he journeys to Bubba's apparently all- or mostly black Louisiana town, visits his grave, buys a shrimp boat, and starts his own business. In other words, he becomes a (masculinized) entrepreneur by renouncing the (feminized) bourgeois privileges associated with his mother and his mother's social class and taking up residence, as Bubba's surrogate, in an impoverished, working-class community. He becomes a kind of adoptive son to Bubba's mother and sings in the local gospel choir. His lone white face in the choir is both the film's way with a visual joke and the sign of Forrest's taking up a black positionality within the narrative—the sign of his exclusion, his difference, his victimization in relation to white Southern society (this identification is also set up earlier in the film when, as he is being pursued by bullies, the camera zooms in on the Confederate flag license plate on their truck). Like Sal Paradise and so many who came after him, Forrest seems drawn to black culture in part because it represents a sense of community from which he has always felt excluded, and he deliberately fashions himself (and is fashioned by the narrative) as a kind of "white Negro." This means of course that Bubba, his black twin, *had* to have been killed off so that Forrest could take his place.

Lieutenant Dan is another casualty of the narrative. As the most obviously masochistic man in the film, the one who most enjoys living dangerously, he is also the most traditionally masculine and heroic. The product (not unlike Forrest) of a "long, great military tradition," he loses both legs in combat and, for much of the film, is infuriated at Forrest for saving his life in Vietnam ("I should have died out there" is his refrain). When Forrest runs into him in New York, Dan has become a longhaired, self-pitying, self-destructive alcoholic. And even during the first stage of his recovery, when he goes down to Louisiana to help Forrest with his shrimp boat, he lives recklessly, riding out Hurricane Carmen hoisted to the top of the mast, riding the boat (and the hurricane) like a maritime cowboy on a bucking bronco. Yet Dan, unlike Bubba, is clearly constructed as a foil to Forrest. Because, from his first appearance, he is the most spectacularized male in the film, his dismemberment by cinematic trickery (the "single most dazzling special effect" in the film, according to Maslin) is clearly figured as a kind of castration.[49] For when he loses his legs, he loses his sense of masculine self-sufficiency and power and becomes a self-destructive victim whom Forrest then can heal. Dan is castrated, in other words, so that Forrest does not need to be, or rather, so that Forrest's castration can be rendered (nearly) invisible, so that it can, in short, be disavowed. And, tellingly, it is only in Dan's presence that Forrest comes close to being unmanned himself, when one of the whores taunts him for his lack of response to her: "Did you lose your packet in the war or something?" But the film trusts the spectator to understand the irony that it is not Forrest, but Dan, who has lost his "packet" in the war.

Perhaps, however, the most disturbing displacement of Forrest's victimization is onto Jenny. As Corliss points out, Grooms's Forrest is hardly the paragon of virtue, innocence, decorum, and chastity that Zemeckis's is: "he had some sex, did some drugs and missed out on the nuclear family that in the movie Forrest gets to tend." He notes discerningly that in fact Zemeckis and Roth "transferred all of Forrest's flaws" along with those which Corliss dubs "the excesses Americans committed in the '60s and '70s" to Jenny, whose relationship with Forrest is much more important structurally in the film than in the novel.[50] Although described initially as being "like an angel," Jenny, a victim of sexual abuse as a child, does all the wrong things. She poses for *Playboy*, works in a strip joint, takes LSD, cocaine, and heroin, sings folk songs, goes to discos, and flirts repeatedly with suicide. Even more horrifying to the filmmakers than the sex, drugs, and rock 'n' roll, however, is her involvement with radical politics. (Her *nom de striptease*, Bobby Dylan, neatly collapses sexual intemperance into political protest.) Associating with angry, aggressive Black Panthers and being in tow to the irascible head of Berkeley SDS, she is slapped around and abused. The quintessential victim, she epitomizes Freud's feminine masochist, taking a certain perverse pleasure in being hurt and degraded (the film suggests, moreover, that she is compulsively reliving her father's abuse). She is, in Stuart Klawans's piquant phrase, "a walking, talking sponge of bad karma."[51] And (unlike the novel's character) Jenny pays for her multitudinous sins by dying of AIDS, although it is never so named in the film, the most feared and mythologized disease of the age. In what is certainly the most sanitized and romantic death from AIDS in film history (more like *Camille* than *Philadelphia*), Jenny is eliminated, and with her, all those behaviors and qualities that the film—and a large percentage of Americans— find so objectionable. Yet again, a character is sacrificed so that Forrest can retain a purely imaginary integrity.

It is important to emphasize here, however, that Forrest's beneficence and resolve are, in some ways, as deceptive as his antiracist politics. For Forrest is less the saint that most of the critics make him out to be than an expert at manipulation. Unable to take no for an answer, yet refusing to offer his love to Jenny, he attacks her college date, assaults a customer at her strip show, and pummels her SDS boyfriend. Klawans emphasizes that Forrest "keeps himself pure by bullying others: beating up anyone who touches the object of his love, while making the love object feel bad for wanting what Forrest himself won't give." Indeed, he seems attracted to Jenny not in spite but because of her victimization and the violence (sexual and otherwise) with which she is associated and which her presence unleashes in him. For Forrest is drawn compulsively to self-destructive people. Yet none of the critics, except Klawans, found it peculiar that this so-called saint "can find his ideal only in someone who . . . must be made to suffer, again and again."[52] The film, in short, is forced to turn all the characters around Forrest into masochists in order to disguise his own cruelty and violence.

So it is little wonder that *Forrest Gump* has become the iconic movie of the mid-1990s, a film that makes even "grown men cry."[53] For Forrest is the paradigm of the new, sensitive, spiritualized male, the holy fool, the perfect fantasy of the white male as victim, the legitimate descendant of General Nathan Bedford Forrest, the man who discovers an imaginary integrity by abusing and manipulating the people around him all the while believing that it is he who has been the victim, the man who disavows his castration by projecting it onto others, the man who becomes a "white Negro" the better to exploit those whom he both envies and fears, the man who leaves a trail of corpses behind him and wonders what it all means.

RUNNING ON EMPTY

Only in its last half hour or so does *Forrest Gump* explicitly become, as the *New York Times* puts it, "an instant metaphor for the American spirit," and its protagonist, a symbol of the nation.[54] This sequence, which differs radically from the novel and is almost wholly the invention of the screenwriter and director, represents, if not exactly a deepening, then at least an enlargement of the film's themes. It is only then that the film becomes recognizable as what Zemeckis "imagined" it to be: "Norman Rockwell painting the baby boomers."[55] For in its last half hour the nostalgia for small-town America and the romanticization of entrepreneurship on which it is so often based become linked to the construction of the nuclear family and the nation as utopian sites. And at the center of the narrative is the quietly assertive, saintly, powerful, rich, white father who, nonetheless, remains a victim of circumstance. And who runs.

Running is the film's central metaphor, the only activity at which Forrest repeatedly excels and which, in some ways, defines him as a man. And although I am particularly interested in analyzing the film's telescoped representation of his three years of cross-country running, it is important to note how Zemeckis sets up this scene. Forrest has returned home to Alabama to tend his mother during her final illness after having cleaned up in the shrimp business, thanks to the timely intervention of Hurricane Carmen. Newly orphaned and rich, he takes up residence in the family house while cutting grass for free, just to keep himself busy riding the power mower (he does not drive a car). Jenny then unexpectedly returns, and the two are blissfully reunited, "like olden times." Zemeckis invokes virtually all of the cinematic tropes associated with pure, young lovers, and they are depicted walking through the fields together, sitting peacefully at home, and watching the stars. In the climax of this sequence, Forrest and Jenny sit by the lake as fireworks cascade over their heads ("it was the happiest time of my life," Forrest says). There is a cut to a television image of fireworks exploding over the Statue of Liberty (it is presumably July 4, 1976) to solidify the identification between their all-too-chaste relationship and the nation (and, in effect, to align Forrest with Miss Liberty, the other bighearted virgin in the frame). In a moment of erotic and patriotic fervor, Forrest then asks Jenny to marry him, and she refuses. As he lies sleeplessly in bed, however, she comes to him, crawls into bed, and pulls off her nightgown (this time, Forrest doesn't gag). And that is the night, exactly two hundred years after the founding of the republic, when little Forrest (love child of the future, spirit of the rebirth of the nation) is conceived.

The next morning Jenny flees before Forrest awakes, and he spends the day drifting melancholically through the empty rooms. But sitting on the front porch wearing the running shoes that Jenny has given him, he is suddenly inspired: "On that day, for no particular reason, I decided to go for a little run." The following sequence of Forrest jogging coast to coast is perhaps the only one in the film that is more symbolic than literal and therefore calls out for interpretation (one spectator commented quizzically to the *New York Times* that it "was a little weird").[56] The film shows Forrest on the road for three years, rebounding (like Dean Moriarty and Sal Paradise) from one coast to the other. What is perhaps most striking visually about this sequence is that it looks exactly like a TV commercial—with Forrest running through painted deserts and fields of golden grain, along country roads, and in the shadows of the Rocky Mountains. But if it is a commercial, what exactly is being sold? America, of course—the land of beauty, plenty, and diversity—to the accompaniment of the kind of stirring, triumphal, faux–John Williams music (written, in fact, by Alan Silvestri) that is associated with the Steven Spielberg–George Lucas epics set in faraway, exotic places.

But just as important as the American landscape in this extended commercial is the solitary figure at the center of each frame, the man who is unable to provide a motivation for his activity ("I just felt like running") but who knows instinctively that he must. Jogging up hill and down dale (and coincidentally performing the baby boomers' emblematic aerobic exercise), Forrest finally has become his own man, beholden only to the demands of his own body: "When I got tired, I slept; when I got hungry, I ate; when I had to go . . . you know, I went." Nostalgically evoking the assertive and willful masculinity of the pioneer and the self-made man, Forrest suddenly is transformed into a kind of prophet of the new spirituality. Newspapers and TV networks cover the transmigration of this mysterious running figure who, with his long hair and long beard, and his folksy clothes, looks like a cross between Rip Van Winkle and a hippie. "For some reason," he says, "what I was doing seemed to make sense to people." And crowds of runners join him, believing him to be a holy man or New Age guru.[57] "Here's a guy who's got his act together," one man tells Forrest; "here's somebody who's got it all figured out. Here's somebody who has the answer." But what is crucial is that "for some reason," Forrest (much like the angel of history in *Angels in America*) here becomes a conduit for the utopian longings that historically have been identified with the idea of America, the once and future paradise, the promised land of freedom: "Somebody later told me it gave people hope." Yet Forrest's sacred vocation as runner had, in fact, been carefully set up at the beginning of the film. Although imprisoned by the braces on his legs, Forrest, urged on by Jenny, learns how to run in order to escape his tormenters. In this, the only slow-motion sequence of the film (accompanied by a rising diatonic scale that bursts into the same triumphant music that accompanies his jogging), Forrest bursts free of the braces that had confined him. As runner, he is thus figured as the very spirit of transcendence, of a liberated masculinity, of breaking free of one's shackles, and simultaneously as a vehicle for the reconstruction of an independent nation. That is why, perhaps, throughout the film, he has been so dematerialized: the better to turn him into an abstraction.

In this pivotal sequence, while Jenny is carrying and caring for Forrest's son, Forrest becomes a blank screen on which people can project their dearest hopes and deepest, most impossible, desires. Through Forrest's embarking on the equivalent of a medieval pilgrimage (to nowhere), a new savior is constructed who refuses the reckless machismo of a John J. Rambo or Lieutenant Dan in favor of combining, miraculously, the qualities of both premodern and postmodern masculinities. For Forrest represents more than a resurrected medieval saint or exemplum of the entrepreneurial spirit. He also epitomizes the postmodern consumer-as-producer. For despite the enforced poverty of his pilgrimage (he carries nothing but the clothes on his back), this postmodern Saint Jerome manages to invent or, more exactly, to inspire the invention of two of the more egregious emblems of contemporary American culture, the bumper sticker "Shit Happens" and the yellow-and-black "happy face" logo, and consequently to make their marketers wealthy men. This peculiar combination of the premodern and the postmodern, as well as the use of the codes of TV commercials to represent the nation, is symptomatic of the fact that in late capitalist culture even utopia is mediated by the commodity form and that America, as an idea, is now constructed as an object to be consumed by a public greedy for spirituality.

Unlike Jenny, who, according to the taxi driver who picks her up, is "running off," Forrest is not running away but, to borrow a page from Moore and Gillette, running *through*, dedicating himself not to a destination but to a process.[58] And according to the logic of this "Norman Rockwell painting," his running functions as a kind of sacrificial ritual in which he gets rid of what are figured to be the braces on his spirit. Yet insofar as it is sacrificial, Forrest's running is also a trial, an ordeal that he puts himself through in order, as he explains, "to put the past behind [him]." It tacitly confirms Keen's pronouncement that the "path to a manly heart runs through the valley of tears."[59] It gives Forrest the opportunity to purge himself of the violence of his past and of Jenny, whom he says he thought about "most of all" while he was running. Moreover, it turns Forrest, in Corliss's words, into "the ideal guru for the nervous '90s," making him the postmodern equivalent of an ascetic, medieval saint.[60] Yet this sanctification of Forrest also requires his transformation into that which Kaja Silverman dubs the Christian masochist, the one whose self-abnegation functions to turn him into an image "of the suffering Christ, the very picture of earthly divestiture and loss." For although Forrest never articulates it as such, his many admirers discern a vaguely revolutionary motivation behind his running or, more exactly, a heterocosmic impulse, "the desire to remake the world in another image altogether, to forge a different cultural order."[61] Yet quite unlike the cases of Allen Ginsberg and Huey Newton, the other Christian masochists I have examined, this heterocosmic impulse seems decidedly antipolitical—as it does for all the new spiritualists. For the film goes to considerable lengths to deride '60s political radicalism (the Black Panthers and SDS) and to ensure that Forrest's speech at a massive anti–Vietnam War rally remains inaudible, thanks to the timely intervention of an army saboteur. Although in the novel his comments about the Vietnam War consist of one sentence, "It is a bunch of shit," Zemeckis and Roth do not allow their protagonist even that much defiance (83). Rather, as Christian masochist, Forrest becomes a 1990s variation upon the postwar "rebel without a cause," the one who is unable to articulate both what he is for and what he is against, and whose central cultural iconicity is the result precisely of this failure.

One of the most intriguing aspects of Forrest's transformation into a Christian masochist is that his subjectivity thereby comes perilously close to exemplifying the reflexive sadomasochism that, I have argued, has become the hegemonic white masculinity in the United States since the 1970s and the distinctive mark of the white male as victim. For as Silverman emphasizes (drawing on Reik), the Christian masochist, by taking the sins of the world upon himself, "functions both as the victim and as the victimizer, dispensing with the need for an external object."[62] Putting himself through a prolonged expiation, Forrest is also responding to what was in all likelihood the one alloerotic sexual experience of his life. In the deeply puritanical erotics of the film, his sexual intercourse with Jenny functions as a kind of fall into manhood, that is, both as the proof and gratification of his sexual desires and as a contamination. For Jenny, it must be recalled, is hardly the innocent that Forrest apparently is, and as a result, he is, if not exactly violated, at least profaned by a sexual act that is routinely figured in the film as being, Klawans notes, "basically grotesque and tawdry."[63] Forrest's running, in other words, functions, if not exactly to revirginize him, then at least to purge him of the sins of the flesh, magically to restore his supposed innocence, and almost to suggest that Forrest junior represents the result of an immaculate conception. Simultaneously, as an example of Christian masochism, it is the sign of his Oedipalization, of his submission to the Law and to the Father. For Forrest (like Dean Moriarty or Louis Ironson) represents yet another fatherless son, and by running coast to coast he discovers the real identity of his lost father: America. By submitting himself to the nation, he finds his father and his sacred place in the world and, in so doing, finds himself. For it is precisely at this point that Forrest's story ends, which is to say, the flashbacks cease and the film moves into the present, to the bench in Savannah on which he is waiting for a bus to take him to Jenny.

His story told, his sanctification completed, his father recovered, his nation discovered, Forrest is able to move on to the next part of the narrative, which is explicitly about paternity and the denial of castration. For when he visits Jenny in her apartment, Forrest discovers that he is, and has been for some time, the father of little Forrest. And, indeed, the moment of recognition (which Hanks underplays skillfully) represents both the emotional climax of the film and Forrest's mirror stage, as it were. For it signals his entry into the Symbolic, a literal splitting of Forrest into two persons: father and son, senior and junior. The one discovers that he has been a father all along ("He's the most beautiful thing I've ever seen," Forrest senior says); the other finally meets his long-lost sire. Moreover, Forrest junior functions as yet another proof that Forrest senior is not in fact castrated after all, insofar as junior is the proof of senior's sexual and genetic potency (little Forrest turns out to be "one of the smartest in his class"). And because both take up their appointed positions within patriarchy, the nuclear family can be reconstructed as a uto-pian site. Jenny can be, if not exactly redeemed, at least accepted as wife and mother. For Jenny then tells Forrest about the mysterious virus she has contracted (the wages of sin), and she asks Forrest to marry her. In the next scene, the day of the wedding, Jenny appears in a diaphanous white gown, and the rest of the film can be seen to represent her dematerialization, her trans-formation back into the angel she was when Forrest first met her on the school bus many years before. The other crucial arrival at the wedding is that of Lieutenant Dan who, like Forrest, is also miraculously revealed not to have been castrated after all. For he comes in walking on his new, "magic" legs, "custom made," and is accompanied by his fiancée, Susan, who just happens to be Asian-American (suggesting less that Dan, as Forrest puts it, has "made his peace with God" than that he has made peace with a proxy for his former enemy). For like so many fictions that dramatize male masochism, *Forrest Gump* can perform its cultural work of reassuring the anxious white male subject only by magically restoring his imaginary wholeness and integrity, by convincing him that he is not castrated, that he does not love pain, and that he can triumph over his victimization. And more clearly than other con-temporary fictions, *Forrest Gump* demonstrates the linkage between mas-ochism and the new spirituality, that it is precisely by passing humbly and submissively through "the valley of tears" that one stumbles upon one's holiness and one's virility.

THE WOMB OF THE NEW SELF

If *Forrest Gump* represents a reactionary, amnesiac, misogynist, and deceptive example of the new spirituality, then *Twister* can be seen as a relatively salutary counterexample. The first major summer release of 1996, *Twister* was the second most successful film of the year (after *Independence Day*), earning approximately $240 million in its first four months of release.[64] With special effects by Industrial Light and Magic, it tickled and amazed even some usually soured critics, who delighted in seeing such a "magnificently absurd" movie in which cows fly through the air and gas tanker trucks drop from the sky like ripe plums.[65] Generically, *Twister* is something of a hybrid, combining elements of action, romance, occult, and disaster movies. Although it is primarily an action-adventure film (with a *Philadelphia Story*–style romance plot in which a recently separated couple are thrown together and finally realize they are made for each other), De Bont's representation of the tornadoes consistently brings to mind monster movies like *Jaws*, *Alien*, or *The Deep*. For right from the opening credits, the foreboding images of swirling mist accompanied by portentous music and low-pitched growls suggest nothing less than a leviathan on the loose. And the film's choice of Stanley Kubrick's *The Shining* (1981) as the movie to be playing at the ill-fated Galaxy drive-in (as part of a promised "Night of Horrors") in the middle of tornado alley is more than a casual homage. When Jack Nicholson's famously evil leer goes flying off into the skies (along with the movie screen), the film is clearly positioning itself in relation to a history of occult movies.

By drawing on the conventions of the occult, *Twister* is able to pile a number of different (and sometimes contradictory) meanings onto its eponymous destroyer. For Jo (Helen Hunt) and Bill (Bill Paxton) encounter five tornadoes in the course of the film (plus the one that levels Wakita), and the narrative is carefully plotted to save the best—and biggest—till last. But the various tropes used to code the tornadoes constantly suggest the ineffable, the unrepresentable, the sublime. This unique meteorological phenomenon is figured as a prodigy of nature, a brilliantly efficient, stunningly beautiful, and yet unpredictable monster. "You've never seen it miss that house and miss this house and come after you," Jo tells Bill. And throughout the film, De Bont uses an array of contradictory sound effects and music to announce and accompany it: conventional Hollywood creature music, cavernous growls, and (less formulaically) stirring, churning chorales entoned by massed choirs. Much like the radio communication from an alien civilization in Robert Zemeckis's 1997 film *Contact*, the tornado is cast as a utopian figuration, both overpoweringly repellent and attractive, terrifying and luminous. And it is coded explicitly as a sign of the divine. When the crew of tornado chasers chow down at Jo's Aunt Meg's, they explain the Fujita scale of intensity to Melissa (Jami Gertz),

Bill's then fiancée. An F4, Bill says, is "good"; it will "relocate your house fairly efficiently." Melissa then asks, "Is there an F5? What would that be like?" A hush comes over the party as all stop what they are doing. Finally one of the men quietly replies, "The finger of God." For the tornado, alone among natural phenomena, is coded as that which offers the most direct knowledge of God. The tornado *is* God, or rather, the unrepresentable representation of a God of wrath from whom, like the Old Testament God, one must avert one's eyes or perish.

The characterization of the tornado, and the F5 in particular, as the very "finger of God" is crucial to the working out of the film's narrative. For what is perhaps most striking about the behavior of the tornado chasers, especially Jo and Bill, is their unquenchable attraction to danger, their desire to journey into the heart of the storm and survive. Their excuse for this incessant flirtation with death—or with God, take your pick—is science, their plan of setting a device called Dorothy (referencing another rather famous victim of a twister), which contains hundreds of miniature radio transmitters, into the center of the funnel cloud. But in order to do so, they must set it in the tornado's path and beat a hasty retreat. At the end of the film they of course succeed (with an F5, no less) but only at the cost of experiencing firsthand the full fury of the wrath of God. (As the movie proceeds, the theological dimension of the allegory becomes more and more explicit.) For when Jo and Bill sacrifice their truck for Dorothy's sake, they have no choice but to seek cover. But running into a barn, they realize immediately they have entered what Alexander Cockburn calls "the House of Death (. . . replete with the Reaper's scythes)," and they flee. Coming upon a modest shed that houses water pipes reaching deep into the earth, they fasten themselves to the pipes and experience the full force of the F5, which, Cockburn notes, represents a veritable "mime of the Rapture, often described by evangelists as a cyclone carrying the elect to the bosom of you-know-who, while the damned are spun off into perdition."[66] Lifted literally off their feet and swathed in celestial harmonies, Jo and Bill gaze up through the parting clouds into the heavens, into the luminous calm at the center of the storm—into the face of God. When the storm departs, and the water pipes have fortuitously ruptured, they emerge unscathed and reborn, bathed in a now gently flowing baptismal font. For it is clear that Jo and Bill have simultaneously survived their encounter with God, accomplished a scientific mission of no mean importance, and been transfigured: their passionate kiss that ends the film neatly sutures heterosexuality to the divine.

The characterization of the tornado as the life-giving "finger of God" clearly links *Twister* both with the new spirituality of the 1990s and (as Cockburn suggests) with evangelical Christianity. But what interests me more is how the theological sublime figures in the masochistic logic that drives the film's legion of tornado chasers and, in particular, its two heroes. For David Denby is certainly correct to observe that the "heart of the movie is the mad exhilaration of the man and the woman repeatedly hurling themselves at destruction. Bill and Jo are like teenagers drawn to the biggest wave, the highest roller coaster. They *want* to be buffeted and thrown about. They want to test themselves and lose control." For *Twister*'s undeniable frisson comes from the thrill of the chase, as two indefatigable seekers of the ultimate kick climb "the vortex of ecstasy." And the pleasure (which Denby calls "luridly sexual" despite the fact that there is no sex in the movie) is none other than the profoundly masochistic thrill of losing control, of submission, of surrendering one's self completely, of forcing one's self to endure the unendurable.[67] (That *Contact* uses precisely the same formula for pleasure and the same master narrative suggests that the new spirituality may be spawning a new subgenre of occult films.) Both Jo and Bill neatly combine the reflexive sadomasochist with the Christian masochist, the subject whose ego is split between a sadistic half and a masochistic half with the subject who seeks to change the world by remaking "him or herself according to the model of the suffering Christ."[68] The two are classically split, masochistic subjects. Jo is clearly at battle with herself (or at least with the feminine part of herself), while Bill admits that the production of a new self has required a kind of suicide. "There was another Bill, an evil Bill, and I killed him," Bill tries to assure Melissa (in a line that could almost be another reference to *The Shining*). But the film emphasizes that Jo and the "evil" Bill have embarked on a potentially suicidal mission and have produced these doubled selves not only for the erotic thrill but also because of their dedication to a scientific project. Masochistic self-abnegation, in short, is pressed into the service of enlightenment. As is the new spirituality. For unlike many other recent discourses (from new spirituality to poststructuralism) that remain deeply suspicious of Enlightenment epistemologies, *Twister* (like *Contact*) attempts to reconcile the spiritual and the scientific in the persons of dedicated crusaders ready to sacrifice themselves for the betterment of humankind. From the very beginning, *Twister*'s dialogue crackles with meteorological buzzwords—downdrafts, microbursts, Doppler radar—as a sign of the seriousness and expertise of these committed scientists. Moreover, the scientific and the spiritual come together very clearly in Jo's plan to save the project by affixing metal wings to Dorothy's miniature transmitters. For Jo gets the idea from looking at the proliferation of decidedly New Age-y wind chimes scattered outside her Aunt Meg's house. So Dorothy herself comes to unite science and art, rationality with the new sprituality. And if Sam Keen is correct when he observes that "[t]he path to a manly heart runs through the valley of tears," then this conjunction of the scientific and the spiritual also produces the film's two prototypes of the new masculinity who risk their lives for the sake of the community.[69]

What is perhaps most remarkable about *Twister* (like *Contact*) is its success in producing a "now and future" man, a "gentle and earthy" man—in the person of a woman. The film makes it clear that it is not Bill but Jo who has discovered, as Keen would put it, "a new vocational passion," "a peaceful form of virility."[70] She is the one with an unquenchable thirst, with the passion that leads her inexorably into the eye of the F5. Yet Jo's production as the most fully and beneficently masculinized character in *Twister* is by no means a simple process in a genre (whether action or occult) that has depended historically on the fetishization of women. When first discovered in her close-fitting white tank top preparing for the chase, Jo is constructed as an object of desire, as if to reassure the anxious (male) spectator that she will not disrupt the laws of scopophiliac pleasure. But almost immediately she is masculinized by her self-assurance, wit, and cool in the face of both killer storms and Bill's fiancée. Most important, her masculinization is achieved at the expense of the hystericization of Melissa (whose vocation as a reproductive therapist is one of the movie's running gags) and the feminization and domestication of Bill (who is testy and petulant, loses his temper easily, and is about to become what, to the tornado chasers, is the most ineffectual of figures: a TV weatherman). When Jo and Bill are driving to intercept one of the twisters and she notices his cautiously slow driving, she asks, "Have you lost your nerve?" Moreover, she is a Ph.D., clearly the "boss lady" of a group of ragtag slacker-grungers (who also happen to be scientists associated with the University of Oklahoma), themselves indisputably masculinized in relation to their corporatized and feminized opponents, led by Dr. Jonas Miller (Cary Elwes), "a nightcrawler," who is "in it for the money, not the science." Miller, it is explained, "really is in love with himself," and he and his sinister team in their identical black minivans are vaguely homosexualized (after the first tornado chase, one of the slacker-grungers impudently gives Miller's driver an exaggerated kiss on the cheek). Yet at the same time, Jo's masculinization is achieved in part by an almost subliminal association made between her and lesbian culture (and the apparent necessity of that association is a sign of the difficulty of producing a powerful female hero in a misogynist and homophobic culture). For when the camera catches her on her own, she is repeatedly accompanied by (diegetic or nondiegetic) acoustic rock that suspiciously resembles the music of "out" lesbian singers like the Indigo Girls, Melissa Etheridge, and k.d. lang. Although she is clearly heterosexualized by her desire for Bill, an air of deviance clings gently to her and is the sign of her (impossible) occupation of both masculine and feminine positions.[71]

Moreover, as the relentless hystericization of Melissa suggests, the production of a confidently masculinized heroine by no means in itself signals an antimisogynist project. For the villains in this film are routinely feminized—Melissa, Miller, and, more ambivalently, the twister itself. At the beginning of the film, this last clearly suggests a feminized, disorderly, unpredictable threat to social and scientific rationality. And when the tornado chasers encounter double waterspouts, Bill exclaims excitedly, "We got sisters!" But as the film proceeds and becomes increasingly allegorical, the twister also becomes more closely identified with the enigmatic "finger of God." As it does, it becomes a figure of gender undecidability, both masculinized and feminized, a warning of the potentially violent consequences of trying to occupy two positions simultaneously, a frightful version of Jo herself and of the benevolent gender deviance she epitomizes. For when Jo and Bill gaze into the heart of the F5, they see what resembles nothing less (in Stuart Klawans's words) than "a phallus combined with a vaginal canal."[72] And the tornado is fashioned as a figure not only of a kind of monstrous androgyny but also of parthenogenesis, an entity made all the more terrible for its seeming ability to clone itself—the very obverse of Melissa's neurotic clients with their dysfunctional reproductive systems.

More than any other character in *Twister*, Jo (with her masculine name) is constructed as an emblem of the new, spiritualized masculinity. And she is neatly representative of the process that Keen prescribes for the production of the new man. For she (like Ellie in *Contact*) is not afraid of the "dark night of the soul" in which she loses her "old identities" as conqueror and worker.[73] She understands the importance of all those characteristics that Keen enumerates in his "Primer for Now and Future Heroes": communitarianism, wonder, self-sacrifice, empathy, modesty, and humility.[74] Moreover, she is fired by a kind of "moral outrage" at the violation not of the social order but of the order of life and death.[75] For the film's opening sequence sets up Jo's story (much as *Contact* does Ellie's) by presenting the death of her father some twenty-five years before as he works to save his wife and young daughter from the furies of a previous F5. So Jo in effect takes up science and becomes a tornado junkie to avenge his death. As in so many masochistic narratives, a subject's masochistic vocation is directly linked to the presence/absence of the father and the difficult (ir)resolution of the Oedipal crisis. As Keen understands it, the suffering, wounded, masochistic new man must above all grieve for "the aching void of the absent father," and he insists that this is a prerequisite for "the path to vital manhood."[76] And true to form, Jo's masculine identification is to a large extent predicated on her taking up the father's lost cause, even taking his place. "Killing yourself," Bill warns her, "won't bring your dad back." But Jo manages (barely) to evade death and to emerge after the return of the F5 purified, cleansed, and reborn. For the "vaginal canal" of the twister is also a simulacrum of the womb that Keen insists is the site at which transfiguration occurs: "When we arrive at the dark point of despair, we have reached the nadir, the low point in the spiritual journey—the place which is, paradoxically, the womb of the new self."[77]

A STORM IS BLOWING FROM PARADISE

Twister is virtually an all-white movie. With the exception of a lone African-American woman in the National Severe Storm Laboratory at the beginning of the film, all the characters are European-American. And the absence of persons of color is rendered even more noticeable because after the film's prologue, the African-American woman happens to be the first character to come into focus. After crossing the frame, however, she disappears forever as the camera pans to a white man with graying hair. Thenceforth, *Twister* is clearly a film not only about white masculinity (even when it is embodied by a woman) but about whiteness in America. For as constructed in the film, whiteness is revealed as a category that requires the active repression of persons of color. Oklahoma, the setting for the film's action, not only has a tortuous and violent history of racist activism (directed against both blacks and Native Americans) that is nowhere so much as hinted at, but also is the state with the greatest number of Native Americans.[78] Yet after the first five minutes no representatives of these groups appear in the film. Moreover, from the very beginning, the film repeatedly evokes cinematic tropes associated with small-town (i.e., white) America: verdant cornfields, golden fields of grain, expansive skies, rolling hills, small picturesque towns, and nuclear families (usually with shaggy dogs) huddled together for safety against the forces of nature—all accompanied by a quintessentially American, faux–Aaron Copland music.

The allegorical character of the film's antagonist suggests that the threat offered the good citizens of Oklahoma is not only a gendered threat but a racialized one as well. For the gentle white folks, the twister represents a force that sunders nuclear (and extended) families, destroys private property, threatens livelihoods, and imperils the very fabric of society. And it is tempting to see it as an allegorical representation of various racialized others so widely demonized in the media during the mid-1990s: single mothers, drug users, welfare recipients, and legal and illegal immigrants. Moreover, as represented in the press, all these groups (except the last) are fantasized as being, like the twister, indigenous threats, dangers lurking within U.S. society, disasters waiting to happen. And although I believe that this interpretation provides a plausible decoding of *Twister*'s horror—one can never go too far wrong by thinking the worst of U.S. culture—I would prefer to consider the movie in terms of the history of horror films and the genre's relationship to geopolitics. As Fredric Jameson points out, during the 1950s and the height of the Cold War, the Hollywood science fiction film, "with its pod people and brain-eating monsters, testified to a genuine collective paranoia, . . . fantasies of influence and subversion which reinforce the very ideological climate they reproduce." But beginning with *The Exorcist* (1973) and the end of the postwar boom, a "new wave of occult films" began to be produced that "may rather be seen as expressing the nostalgia for a system in which Good and Evil are absolutely black-and-white categories. . . ." For Jameson, *The Shining* (*Twister*'s principal intertext) provides an example precisely of this new convention whereby a "'metaphysical' nostalgia for an absolute Evil" positively and literally haunts the film.[79] I would like to suggest, however, that *Twister* may be analogous less to *The Shining* than to *The Exorcist* in also marking the beginning of a new wave of occult movies in which a new kind of monster is figured, an almost infinitely mobile and unpredictable monster, to be sure, but also a more implicitly utopian and, indeed, almost divine terror.

As I noted in chapter 5, the end of the Cold War marks the demise of a particular polarizing logic between capitalism and communism. With the fall of historical communism, however, a new enemy to U.S. interests was constructed in the form not of an "evil empire" but of a confederation of so-called rogue states that, according to the State Department, sponsor international terrorism: Iran, Iraq, Libya, Syria, and North Korea (with Cuba sometimes thrown in, depending on the urgency of courting Florida's Cuban-American voters). As Michael Klare notes, when the Department of Defense after the Gulf War, "unveiled a long-range defense plan calling for a sustained preparation for a continuing series of Desert Storm–like engagements," it provided a rationale for maintaining military spending at Cold War levels (and thereby justified the continuing slash-and-burn approach to social programs). Armed with this plan, the Bush administration then proposed and was given "a permanent military establishment (or 'Base Force') of about 1.6 million soldiers—enough it is said to fight two Desert Storms simultaneously."[80] This policy has been seconded by the Clinton administration, which, like its predecessor, has used the rogue states doctrine, as Richard Barnet argues, "to legitimize its increasingly unilateral approach to foreign policy by proclaiming the United States the global avenger of terrorism." Because "the criteria" for a rogue state "are vague and . . . capriciously applied," the threat is proving extremely useful in eliciting "[p]ublic fear of unpredictable violence" and building support "for curbing civil liberties." And this fear continues to swell despite even the State Department's reporting that "worldwide deaths due to acts of international terrorism have in recent years declined, from 314 in 1994 to 165 in 1995."[81]

In the discourse of terrorism, the rogue states are constructed, in President Clinton's words, as nations that violate "the rules we have all accepted for civilized behavior."[82] And as national security adviser Anthony Lake observes, they "remain outside the family" of nations, "assault its basic values," and "exhibit a chronic inability to engage constructively with the outside world."[83]

Both the rogue states and the terrorism they allegedly sponsor are thus imagined as being a blow to civilization and to humanity, a kind of international pathology that fails to respect borders, property, and protocol, and assaults "family" "values." And the discourse of terrorism succeeds in large part because of its ability to engender the fear that terrorists may strike anywhere at any time, both at home and abroad. The specters raised by the doctrine of rogue states and the discourse of terrorism are thus startlingly congruent with the fears raised by *Twister* of a new and unpredictable monster that may strike at any moment, destroying property, killing innocent people, and uprooting families. And as with terrorism, the twister is a localized and random threat that (in principle) can never be eradicated. It is always out there, always waiting to strike. The best one can hope for is an early warning system. Unlike *Independence Day*, which, with its invading aliens from outer space, hearkens back nostalgically to the Cold War order, *Twister* announces a new kind of enemy and preys on the fears of those who imagine disaster lurking in every passing cloud and believe that not the world but their community could be annihilated at any moment.

If *Twister*, as I am arguing, allegorizes the specters raised by the discourse of terrorism, then the tornado's figuration as a manifestation of the divine may seem out of character. In fact, however, terrorism is almost always figured as having a religious or quasi-religious motivation. For as Barnet notes, the "evidence supports the view that very few bombers of public places are now in the service of governments—fewer, certainly, than in the cold war years." Rather, terrorism (like so many formerly public institutions during this moment of capitalism's purported triumph) "is being privatized," and bombers are working increasingly "for a political movement, a crime ring or, as more of them are claiming, for God. Practitioners of violence increasingly work for religious sects and political movements (largely ethnic and mostly on the right)."[84] International terrorism, in short, is always linked to a zeal that is religious in its intensity. In U.S. policy, the association of terrorism with Islam in particular is bolstered by the fact that four of the five rogue states are Muslim. And in the popular imagination, the Islamic fundamentalist has become virtually a synonym for terrorist.

But the Clinton administration's position on rogue states grossly misstates the case by ascribing most terrorist acts in the United States to foreign sources. For as Barnet observes, "most of the acts of random violence that victimize Americans are committed not by dark-skinned foreigners in ski masks but by fellow citizens. Over the past ten years bombings and attempted bombings in the United States have nearly tripled, increasing from 1,103 in 1985 to 3,163 in 1994."[85] As the recent slew of attacks on African-American churches and on abortion clinics suggests, the targets of terrorism in the United States are almost always racial or political. Barnet notes that many domestic terrorists belong to militias or other gun-worshiping organizations. These groups have a variety of agendas: They don't like gun control. They don't like the federal government messing with their land, or land they think should be theirs. They don't like paying taxes. They don't like abortions. They hate black people, Jews, gays, foreigners. They are energized by violence. They have a holy mission.[86]

So most homegrown terrorists, "the overwhelming majority of whom are white working-class or lower-middle-class men," are engaged in a kind of holy war.[87] Proclaiming themselves the victims of those whom in fact they have oppressed, they imagine that they are serving God by slaying his enemies. And it is hardly coincidental, I believe, that the locale of *Twister*—Oklahoma—also happens to be the site of the most deadly terrorist act in U.S. history, the 1995 bombing of the Alfred P. Murrah Federal Building in Oklahoma City that claimed 168 lives. As an allegory of terrorism, the film (inadvertently?) exposes the fact that the real source of terrorist violence in the United States is not Iran or Iraq but the paramilitary Right, the self-appointed guardians of white supremacy who dwell among the good citizenry of Oklahoma. Yet all the while revealing the indigenous sources of terrorism, *Twister* also figures white Oklahomans (and, through them, white Americans) as the victims and potential victims of a random violence they can never stem. For read as the allegory it so desperately tries to be, the film proves deeply ambivalent, both unmasking the lie of international terror and yet declaring white men and women—once again—to be the victims of a violence perpetrated against them by inhuman forces over which they have no control.

I would like finally to suggest here that *Twister*'s portentous flirtation with God is linked to more than just the notion of terrorism as a holy war. For the overwhelmingly seductive power of the twister is also indicative of the strange allure of the fantasy of a holy war, even to those who may scorn the values for which it is being fought. For in its sublime undecidability, in its collapse of the divine and the monstrous, the twister—complemented by the scientific project of unraveling its mysteries—finally becomes a profoundly utopian rejoinder to what is surely a uniquely cynical culture. For the allegory of *Twister* strangely suggests that as hated as terrorists may be, they are also envied for believing in something so strongly that they are prepared to die for it. If *Twister* is an accurate cultural barometer, then the new spirituality represents less an achieved state of belief than an overpowering *will to believe*. And in the wake of the Cold War, the spiritual renaissance has become a substitute for a (now lapsed?) faith in democracy and the nation by reconfiguring precisely those utopian hopes that historically have been attached to both these constructions.

And men's spirituality, in particular, understood as a desire to believe, signals both a backlash against and an invidious imitation of the cultural feminism it so despises. For among a profoundly atomized male citizenry, it remains perhaps the only arena (outside of sports stadiums) in which men can congregate and believe—or at least pretend to believe. It represents a substitute, in a profoundly secularized age, for both community and mission, and an attempt to transform reflexive sadomasochism into Christian masochism. Even Moore and Gillette insist that "the Warrior energy" must be "moderated by a higher authority," that a man must be "dedicated to some power beyond his own. . . ."[88] Yet almost inevitably in the men's movement, this dedication is conceptualized in highly personalized and individualized terms, not political ones. For political activism is characteristically regarded as a cheat, and Moore and Gillette reserve as much contempt for "revolutionaries and activists of all kind" (who "fall into the sadistic pole of the Shadow Warrior") as they do for feminists.[89] At the same time, the desire for dedication "to some power beyond [one's] own" betrays the need among the partisans of men's spirituality to submit to "a higher authority," to a moral and epistemological order in which they can believe. If this is the case, then the new spirituality signals less the solution to the problem of masochism than yet another playing out of masochistic fantasy, yet another attempt at transcendence through abjection.

In describing the pilgrimage that men must make to become spiritualized, Keen writes of the importance of submitting to that which one most fears and desires: "that old black magic drawing us down, down into the sweet embrace of flesh, obscure fusion, lost in sensation, out of control."[90] As so particularized, men's spirituality permits its white middle-class constituency to embrace the flesh vicariously because, as *Twister* implies, there is a tremendous erotic thrill in submission, in being "lost" or "out of control." For a pilgrimage "down" allows men to take up a position that not only is marked feminine but that historically has been coded as natural, other, "black." And almost without exception, the newly spiritualized white male needs a savior and guide who is clearly marked as other (preferably African-American, although as *Twister* suggests, female will also do). Forrest Gump needs the good-hearted Bubba so that he can appropriate Bubba's family, church, and corporate instincts. Or in Lawrence Kasdan's *Grand Canyon* (1991), Mack (Kevin Kline) discovers the values of compassion and love only through the timely intervention of the saintly Simon (Danny Glover) who both literally and figuratively saves his life. Or in Mike Nichols's *Regarding Henry* (1991), the barracuda-like lawyer Henry (Harrison Ford), seriously injured in a shooting, learns from his wise African-American physical therapist, Bradley (Bill Nunn), not only how to walk and talk again, but also how to be a kinder, gentler, more loving man. All these films are focused on the process of learning how to adjust to a (post)feminist culture in which men are expected to be both compassionate and virile. And in all these cases, the spiritualized white man discovers his new self in and through the desires of the other. Like "the white Negro" or the gentle man of the counterculture (who are so clearly his forebears), he takes up the position of victim because it leads—fortuitously!— to happiness, love, and prosperity; it reinforces his class status (and the class differences between him and his African-American spiritual adviser) and ensures his continued sovereignty.

It is little wonder that *Forrest Gump*, *Twister*, *Grand Canyon*, and *Regarding Henry* all end with protracted aerial shots, as the camera slowly pulls back and reveals the glory of the American landscape, with its purple mountains' majesty and its infinite, eternally mutable sky. For the content finally of all these shots—and all these films—is the utopian promise that has been linked to the idea of America and to the free, authoritative, white male subject who ostensibly embodies it. At the same time, the aerial shot inevitably dwarfs the white man who is at its center, revealing (perhaps inadvertently) that his dominion is based on submission, in this case on his submission to the land, to the nation, and to the cinematic apparatus to which he is subject and into which he virtually disappears. The necessity of submission suggests that the so-called problem of male masochism, the tightly wound "connection between masculinity and pain" that, I have argued, dates back to the early modern period and is linked inextricably to the development of capitalism, cannot be solved by anyone's wishing it away. The deep-seated cultural logic that defines masculinity as a kind of submission, that discovers a certain pushy and resentful virility precisely in those men who so angrily proclaim themselves victims, cannot be changed by prayer or by a will to believe.

The new spirituality—in its attempted recuperation of the utopian promise of the counterculture—represents an attempt to transform the dross of the '60s into gold. Yet its complete withdrawal from politics and its self-satisfied retreat into the self also mark an incalculable loss. What has happened since that delirious day in 1961 when Allen Ginsberg wrote to Peter Orlovsky, "I think Bill [Burroughs] & [Timothy] Leary at Harvard are going to start a beautiful consciousness alteration of the whole world—actually for real—Leary thinks it's the beginning of a new world"?[91] Or since Herbert Marcuse voiced the hope in his 1969 *Essay on Liberation* that the battle against surplus-repression—and against masochism—would be won, that the individual might soon be able to "satisfy his needs without hurting himself, without reproducing, through his aspirations and satisfactions, his dependence on an exploitative apparatus which, in satisfying his needs, perpetuates his servitude"?[92] Writing when the struggle against that apparatus was at its most intense, Marcuse discerned many forms of "The Great Refusal" and a powerful and "growing opposition to corporate capitalism" in the United States, Europe, and the Third World. Yet Marcuse also keenly understood the power of the "global dominion of corporate capitalism": "its economic and military hold in the four continents, its neocolonial empire, and, most important, its unshaken capacity to subject the majority of the underlying population to its overwhelming productivity and force."[93] Some thirty years later, the picture looks far more bleak: Change four continents to six. Expand the neocolonial empire to the ends of the earth. Multiply capitalism's capacity for subjection tenfold. Factor in the fall of historical communism, the collapse of countless national liberation movements in the Third World, the decline of European social democratic parties, and the synonymy of the Republican and Democratic parties in the United States, and you are left with almost no real opposition.

In moments such as these, one must, arguably, be all the more attentive to those utopian impulses that continue to circulate in culture—like the new spirituality and the kinder, gentler white man who embodies it—despite the fact that they are aimed at such manifestly conservative ends. The task then becomes one of redirecting these impulses through what Marcuse calls "radical enlightenment": "to develop in the exploited, the consciousness (and the unconscious) which would loosen the hold of enslaving needs. . . . " For without "political education in action," he notes, "even the most elemental, the most immediate force of rebellion may be defeated, or become the mass basis of counterrevolution."[94] After a generation of counterrevolution, however, "political education" has been eclipsed by an array of mystifying systems of belief, ranging from bourgeois nationalism to the new spirituality. Yet this eclipse, I believe, is the result not of the failure of the principle of enlightenment but of its slipshod, unequal, and incomplete application. A mere glance at the disparity between the salaries of a CEO and of a data processor in his or her office will reveal that Timothy McVeigh and the other partisans of the Patriot movement—those discomfiting bastard children of the '60s—are not wrong to believe they are oppressed. Their mistake is in presuming that their oppressors are those classes of persons whom they and their forebears have historically subjugated.

NOTES

INTRODUCTION

1. For brief overviews of the Patriot movement, see Chip Berlet and Matthew N. Lyons, "Militia Nation," *Progressive*, June 1995, 22–25, and Scott McLemee, "Public Enemy," *In These Times*, May 15, 1995, 14–19. See also Morris Dees, *Gathering Storm: America's Militia Threat* (New York: HarperPerennial, 1997).

2. Tom Metzgar, leader of the White Aryan Resistance, quoted in Raphael S. Ezekiel, *The Racist Mind: Portraits of American Neo-Nazis and Klansmen* (New York: Viking, 1995), 72.

3. See Peter Schrag, "Backing Off *Bakke*: The New Assault on Affirmative Action," *Nation*, April 22, 1996, 11–14.

4. See Mercedes Lynn de Uriarte, "Baiting Immigrants: Heartbreak for Latinos," *Progressive*, September 1996, 18–20.

5. Norman Mailer, *The White Negro* (San Francisco: City Lights, 1959), 2–3.

6. Ibid., 2.

7. Robert Lindner, quoted in ibid., 7.

8. Mailer, *The White Negro*, 15.

9. Allen Ginsberg, "Howl," in *Collected Poems 1947–1980* (New York: Harper & Row, 1984), 131.

10. Tom Frank, "Hip Is Dead," *Nation*, April 1, 1996, 18.

11. See Mark Crispin Miller, "Free the Media," *Nation*, June 3, 1996, 9–15.

12. Throughout this book, I often append the suffix "-ized" to a number of adjectives to produce words like "racialized," "masculinized," and "heterosexualized." I do so not to be obscurantist but rather to suggest that racial, gendered, and sexual identities are not stable, transparent positions and to indicate that they are always in the *process* of being produced. Moreover, I hope through this terminology to denaturalize these categories in order to point out that what may at first appear to be a natural or biological product is in fact a social and historical construction.

13. Raymond Williams, *Marxism and Literature* (Oxford: Oxford University Press, 1977), 111.

14. Ibid., 110.

15. Eve Kosofsky Sedgwick, " 'Gosh, Boy George, You Must Be Awfully Secure in Your Masculinity!' " in *Constructing Masculinity*, ed. Maurice Berger, Brian Wallis, and Simon Watson (New York: Routledge, 1995), 15–16.

16. Introduction to *Constructing Masculinity*, 2.

17. Sigmund Freud, 1915 footnote to *Three Essays on the Theory of Sexuality*, ed. and trans. James Strachey (New York: Basic Books, 1975), 85.

18. Judith Butler, *Gender Trouble: Feminism and the Subversion of Identity* (New York: Routledge, 1990), 151.

19. See Anne Fausto-Sterling, "How to Build a Man," in *Constructing Masculinity*, 127–34.

20. Judith Butler, "Melancholy Gender / Refused Identification," in *Constructing Masculinity*, 32.

21. Butler, *Gender Trouble*, 25.

22. Ibid., 6.

23. Judith Butler, *Bodies That Matter: On the Discursive Limits of "Sex"* (New York: Routledge, 1993), 1.

24. I find the intentions of speakers and writers particularly problematic in part because they always come before or after the fact and seem predicated on a certain and necessary disavowal. The structure of the unconscious dictates that the author can never know exactly what he or she is doing. Moreover, most writers of fiction are too invested in the power of fictionality and too beholden to the literary marketplace to make trenchant cultural critics. And although I believe that authors' intentions should be listened to insofar as they constitute part of the set of the conditions of performance, they are (with very few exceptions) no more definitive than the judgments of critics.

25. See Kaja Silverman, *Male Subjectivity at the Margins* (New York: Routledge, 1992), 15–19.

26. See, for example, ibid., 26.

27. See ibid., 299–338.

28. See ibid., 55–65.

29. Abigail Solomon-Godeau, "Male Trouble," in *Constructing Masculinity*, 74.

30. Richard von Krafft-Ebing, *Psychopathia Sexualis: A Medico- Forensic Study*, trans. Harry E. Wedeck (New York: G. P. Putnam's Sons, 1965), 127–29.

31. Ibid., 127, 87.

32. Ibid., 127.

33. See especially Theodor Reik, *Masochism in Sex and Society*, trans. Margaret H. Beigel and Gertrud M. Kurth (New York: Grove, 1962).

34. "Pleasure lies in ascertaining guilt, . . . asserting control and subjecting the guilty person through punishment or forgiveness. This sadistic side fits in well with narrative. Sadism demands a story, depends on making something happen, forcing a change in another person, a battle of will and strength, victory/defeat, all occurring in a linear time with a beginning and end." Laura Mulvey, "Visual Pleasure and Narrative Cinema," *Screen* 16, no. 3 (Autumn 1975): 14; see also Teresa De Lauretis, *Alice Doesn't: Feminism, Semiotics, Cinema* (Bloomington: Indiana University Press, 1984), 103–57.

35. English translation (1718) of Johann Heinrich Meibom, *De Flagrorum Usu . . .* , cited in Ian Gibson, *The English Vice: Beating, Sex and Shame in Victorian England and After* (London: Duckworth, 1978), 2–3.

36. See Thomas Laqueur, *Making Sex: Body and Gender from the Greeks to Freud* (Cambridge: Harvard University Press, 1990).

37. Meibom, *De Flagrorum Usu . . .* , quoted in Gibson, *The English Vice*, 4–5.

38. John Lois Delolme, attrib., *The History of the Flagellants, or the Advantages of Discipline; Being a Paraphrase and Commentary on the Historia Flagellantium of the Abbé Boileau, Doctor of the Sorbonne, Cannon of the Holy Chapel, etc., By Somebody who is not a Doctor of the Sorbonne*, translation and adaptation of the Abbé Boileau (London, 1777), 11–13. For a résumé of the Abbé Boileau's *Historia*, see Gibson, *The English Vice*, 6–10.

39. Gibson, *The English Vice*, 23.

40. The classic account of this transformation is Michel Foucault, *The History of Sexuality*, vol. 1, *An Introduction*, trans. Robert Hurley (New York: Vintage, 1980).

41. David Halperin, "One Hundred Years of Homosexuality," in *One Hundred Years of Homosexuality* (New York: Routledge, 1990), 26.

42. See Gibson, *The English Vice*, 27–32.

43. William Acton, *The Functions and Disorders of the Re-Productive Organs* (1857), quoted in Gibson, *The English Vice*, 31–32.

44. Foucault, *The History of Sexuality*, 42 (my emphasis).

45. Jonathan Dollimore, *Sexual Dissidence: Augustine to Wilde, Freud to Foucault* (Oxford: Clarendon Press, 1991), 182.

46. See James Glass Bertram [pseud., Rev. Wm. M. Cooper, B.A.], *A History of the Rod in all Countries from the Earliest Period to the Present Time* (London: William Reeves, 1904?).

47. Ibid., 516.

48. Delolme, *The History of the Flagellants*, 221–22.

49. Ibid., 204.

50. Ibid., 92.

51. Ibid., 327.

52. Ibid., 257.

53. Freud, *Three Essays on the Theory of Sexuality*, 59. By 1919, however, Freud had backed away from this position and maintained that beating fantasies "had already been in existence before" the child was exposed to these "impressions of school life." Freud, "'A Child Is Being Beaten,'" trans. James Strachey, in *Sexuality and the Psychology of Love*, ed. Philip Reiff (New York: Collier, 1963), 108.

54. Lawrence Stone, *The Family, Sex and Marriage in England 1500–1800* (New York: Harper and Row, 1977), 439. For a résumé of the practices of corporal punishment during this period, see 162–71. See also J. H. Plumb, "The New World of Children in Eighteenth-Century England," in *Loving, Parenting and Dying: The Family Cycle in England and America, Past and Present*, ed. Vivian C. Fox and Martin H. Quitt (New York: Psychohistory Press, 1980), 299–312.

55. John Aubrey, *Aubrey's Brief Lives*, ed. Oliver Lawson Dick (London: Secker and Warburg, 1949), xl–xli.

56. Roger Ascham, *The Whole Works of Roger Ascham*, ed. Rev. Dr. Giles (London: John Russell Smith, 1864), 3:81.

57. Aubrey, *Aubrey's Brief Lives*, xciv.

58. For the publication history, see John Locke, *The Educational Writings of John Locke: A Critical Edition with Introduction and Notes*, ed. James L. Axtell (Cambridge: Cambridge University Press, 1968), 13–17, 98–104.

59. Philippe Ariès, *Centuries of Childhood: A Social History of Family Life*, trans. Robert Baldick (New York: Knopf, 1962), 260.

60. For a history of Restoration pornography and descriptions of the content of these three texts, see Roger Thompson, *Unfit for Modest Ears: A Study of Pornographic, Obscene and Bawdy Works Written and Published in England in the Second Half of the Seventeenth Century* (Totowa, NJ: Rowman and Littlefield, 1979).

61. Michel Millot and Jean L'Ange, *The School of Venus*, trans. Donald Thomas (New York: New American Library, 1971), 137.

62. Quoted in Ivan Bloch, *Sexual Life in England* (London: Corgi Books, 1965), 301.

63. Thompson, *Unfit for Modest Ears*, 214–15.

64. Thomas Shadwell, *The Virtuoso*, ed. Marjorie Hope Nicholson and David Stuart Rodes (Lincoln: University of Nebraska Press, 1966), 3.2.60–72.

65. Aubrey, *Aubrey's Brief Lives*, xciv.

66. Thomas Otway, *Venice Preserved*, ed. Malcolm Kelsall (Lincoln: University of Nebraska Press, 1969), 3.1.102–11.

67. Aline Mackenzie Taylor, *Next to Shakespeare: Otway's* Venice Preserv'd *and* The Orphan *and Their History on the London Stage* (Durham: Duke University Press, 1950), 53.

68. Locke, *The Educational Writings of John Locke*, 8.

69. Ibid., 177.

70. Ibid., 149.

71. Ibid., 138, 153.

72. Ibid., 152–54.

73. Charles Taylor, *Sources of the Self: The Making of Modern Identity* (Cambridge: Harvard University Press, 1989), 159.

74. Lynn Hunt, *The Family of the French Revolution* (Berkeley and Los Angeles: University of California Press, 1992), 21.

75. Delolme, *The History of the Flagellants*, 11.

76. Michel Foucault, *Discipline and Punish*, trans. Alan Sheridan (New York: Vintage, 1979), 137.

77. C. Wilson, quoted in Christopher Hill, *The Century of Revolution: 1603–1714* (London: Van Nostrand Reinhold, 1980), 175.

78. Hill, *The Century of Revolution*, 175–82, 227–28.

79. Plumb, "The New World of Children in Eighteenth-Century England," 302.

80. Sigmund Freud, "The Economic Problem in Masochism," in *General Psychological Theory*, ed. Philip Rieff, trans. James Strachey (New York: Collier, 1963), 197–98.

81. Silverman, *Male Subjectivity at the Margins*, 160; Freud, "The Economic Problem in Masochism," 199.

82. Freud, "The Economic Problem in Masochism," 199–200.

83. Ibid., 196. Although Freud's characterization is accepted by most theoreticians of masochism, there are some significant dissents, most notably that of Deleuze, who sees the "weakness of the ego" as a "strategy by which the masochist manipulates the woman into the ideal state for the performance of the role he has assigned to her. If the masochist is lacking in anything, it would be a superego and not an ego at all." Gilles Deleuze, *Coldness and Cruelty* in *Masochism: Coldness and Cruelty, Venus in Furs*, trans. Jean McNeil (New York: Zone Books, 1991), 124.

84. Freud, *Three Essays on the Theory of Sexuality*, 23.

85. Reik, *Masochism in Sex and Society*, 9.

86. Leo Bersani, *The Freudian Body: Psychoanalysis and Art* (New York: Columbia University Press, 1986), 38–39.

87. Silverman, *Male Subjectivity at the Margins*, 192.

88. Taylor, *Sources of the Self*, 162–63.

89. Locke, *The Educational Writings of John Locke*, 149.

90. Stone, *The Family, Sex and Marriage in England 1500–1800*, 223–24. Although Stone's point of view is far more sympathetic to this liberal subject than my own, his chapter "The Growth of Affective Individualism" makes some important and useful historical points about the consolidation of bourgeois subjectivity.

91. Ibid., 253.

92. Ibid., 224.

93. Locke, *The Educational Writings of John Locke*, 143.

94. Ibid., 149.

95. Francis Barker, *The Tremulous Private Body: Essays on Subjection* (London: Methuen, 1984), 45–47.

96. Locke, *The Educational Writings of John Locke*, 117.

97. Stone, *The Family, Sex and Marriage in England 1500–1800*, 325–404.

98. Joan B. Landes, *Women and the Public Sphere in the Age of the French Revolution* (Ithaca: Cornell University Press, 1988), 21.

99. Meibom, quoted in Gibson, *The English Vice*, 3–5.

100. Locke, *The Educational Writings of John Locke*, 147.

101. Freud, "'A Child Is Being Beaten,'" 126.

102. Freud, *Three Essays on the Theory of Sexuality*, 25. In "Instincts and Their Vicissitudes" (1920), Freud theorizes what he calls reflexive sadomasochism, but he does not attempt to explain its ontogenesis.

103. Sigmund Freud, *Beyond the Pleasure Principle*, ed. and trans. James Strachey (New York: Norton, 1961), 44.

104. Freud, "The Economic Problem in Masochism," 194.

105. Silverman, *Male Subjectivity at the Margins*, 58–59.

106. Freud, "The Economic Problem in Masochism," 192–93.

107. Silverman, *Male Subjectivity at the Margins*, 189.

108. Freud, "'A Child Is Being Beaten,'" 192–93.

109. Ibid., 113–19.

110. Ibid.

111. Ibid., 119.

112. Silverman, *Male Subjectivity at the Margins*, 203

113. Freud, "'A Child Is Being Beaten,'" 127. For an astute analysis of the positive and negative Oedipus complexes as elaborated in *The Ego and the Id*, see Silverman, *Male Subjectivity at the Margins*, 360–62.

114. Freud, "'A Child Is Being Beaten,'" 126–27.

115. Freud, "The Economic Problem in Masochism," 199.

116. Freud, "'A Child Is Being Beaten,'" 127–28.

117. Gibson, *The English Vice*, 23.

118. Quoted in ibid., 5–6.

119. Sigmund Freud, "Instincts and Their Vicissitudes," in *The Complete Psychological Works of Sigmund Freud*, ed. James Strachey (London: Hogarth Press, 1957), 14:111–40.

120. Krafft-Ebing, *Psychopathia Sexualis*, 137.

121. Fredric Jameson, *Marxism and Form: Twentieth-Century Dialectical Theories of Literature* (Princeton: Princeton University Press, 1971), 111.

122. Andrew Jamison and Ron Eyerman, *Seeds of the Sixties* (Berkeley and Los Angeles: University of California Press, 1994), 119.

123. Herbert Marcuse, *Eros and Civilization: A Philosophical Inquiry into Freud* (Boston: Beacon, 1966), 48. All further references will be noted in the text.

124. Peter Lind, *Marcuse and Freedom* (New York: St. Martin's Press, 1985), 199.

125. The vast majority of writers I cite in this book (like Marcuse) use the masculine pronoun when denominating both male and female subjects. In several instances, I

point this out in my analyses of their arguments, demonstrating that a putatively ungendered subject is always already masculinized. In other cases, however, I have elected not to call the reader's attention to this usage with a [*sic*], hoping and believing that he or she will already be sensitive to processes of implicit genderization.

126. Paul A. Robinson, *The Freudian Left: Wilhelm Reich, Geza Roheim, Herbert Marcuse* (New York: Harper & Row, 1969), 202.

127. Karl Marx, *Capital: A Critique of Political Economy*, vol. 1, trans. Ben Fowkes (New York: Vintage, 1977), 317.

128. Robinson, *The Freudian Left*, 208.

129. Lind, *Marcuse and Freedom*, 199.

130. See, for example, Catherine Belsey, *Critical Practice* (London: Routledge, 1980); Gilles Deleuze and Félix Guattari, *Anti-Oedipus: Capitalism and Schizophrenia*, trans. Robert Hurley, Mark Seem, and Helen R. Lane (New York: Viking, 1977); and Ernesto Laclau and Chantal Mouffe, *Hegemony and Socialist Strategy: Toward a Radical Democratic Politics* (London: Verso, 1985).

131. Silverman, *Male Subjectivity at the Margins*, 1.

CHAPTER ONE
THE DIVIDED SELF

1. William S. Burroughs, *The Letters of William S. Burroughs, 1945–1959*, ed. Oliver Harris (New York: Penguin, 1993), 88.

2. Quoted in introduction to *The Letters of William S. Burroughs, 1945–1959*, xix.

3. *The Letters of William S. Burroughs, 1945–1959*, 91.

4. Ted Morgan, *Literary Outlaw: The Life and Times of William S. Burroughs* (New York: Avon, 1988), 194.

5. William S. Burroughs, *Queer* (New York: Penguin, 1985), xxii.

6. *The Letters of William S. Burroughs, 1945–1959*, 105. *Junky* was originally published as *Junkie* under the pen name of William Lee.

7. *The Letters of William S. Burroughs, 1945–1959*, 244.

8. Burroughs, *Queer*, xxii.

9. Daniel Odier, *The Job: Interviews with William S. Burroughs* (New York: Penguin, 1989), 97, 114.

10. Ibid., 116.

11. Conrad Knickerbocker, "William Burroughs: An Interview," *Paris Review* 9 (Fall 1965): 39–40.

12. *The Letters of William S. Burroughs, 1945–1959*, 91.

13. Morgan, *Literary Outlaw*, 195–96.

14. Carolyn Cassady, *Off the Road: My Years with Cassady, Kerouac, and Ginsberg* (New York: William Morrow, 1990), 151–52.

15. See *The Letters of William S. Burroughs, 1945–1959*, 135.

16. Ibid., 135.

17. For an analysis of the melancholic introjection of a loved person who has been lost, and its relation to mourning, see Sigmund Freud, "Mourning and Melancholia" (1917), in *Collected Papers*, vol. 4, trans. Joan Riviere (New York: Basic Books, 1949), 152–70.

18. The relationship between and among the beat, hipster, beatnik, and juvenile delinquent is often vague in many '50s texts. The beat and hipster are rarely differentiated in '50s discourses and are understood as being young adults in their twenties and thirties allied with an oppositional subculture. The juvenile delinquent, in contrast, is usually understood as being younger than the others and, as in *Rebel without a Cause* (1955), practicing a mode of rebellion that is identified with a particular stage of life, adolescence, which will presumably pass. The beatnik (whose suffix is derived from the name of the first Soviet Sputnik satellite; see *OED*) is usually understood as a decadent and to some extent commercialized version of the beat. In order to distinguish the Beat writers, as a literary movement, from the wider subculture, I am capitalizing the former.

19. Quoted in Lawrence S. Wittner, *Cold War America: From Hiroshima to Watergate* (New York: Praeger, 1974), 7.

20. See ibid., 30–36.

21. See David Harvey, *The Condition of Postmodernity: An Enquiry into the Origins of Cultural Change* (Cambridge, MA: Blackwell, 1990), 131.

22. See Elaine Tyler May, *Homeward Bound: American Families in the Cold War Era* (New York: Basic Books, 1988), and Gayle S. Rubin, "Thinking Sex: Notes for a Radical Theory of the Politics of Sexuality," in *The Lesbian and Gay Studies Reader*, ed. Henry Abelove, Michèle Aina Barale, and David M. Halperin (New York: Routledge, 1993), 3–44.

23. William H. Chafe, *The Unfinished Journey: America since World War II* (New York: Oxford University Press, 1986), 117–18.

24. Paul Buhle, *Marxism in the United States: Remapping the History of the American Left* (London: Verso, 1991), 195.

25. Morris Zelditch, Jr., "Role Differentiation in the Nuclear Family: A Comparative Study," in *Family, Socialization and Interaction Process*, ed. Talcott Parsons and Robert F. Bales (New York: Free Press, 1955), 339.

26. For an analysis of Cold War domesticity and the construction of gender roles, see May, *Homeward Bound*.

27. Harvey, *The Condition of Postmodernity*, 129, 126.

28. Robert Corber, *Homosexuality in Cold War America: Resistance and the Crisis of Masculinity* (Durham: Duke University Press, 1997), 6.

29. Arthur Schlesinger, Jr., "The Crisis of American Masculinity," in *The Politics of Hope* (Boston: Houghton Mifflin, 1963), 237. But the 1950s did not see the first crisis of gender definition. At the end of the nineteenth century, with the emergence of "The New Woman" in both the United States and Europe, a similar crisis unfolded. See Susan Faludi, *Backlash: The Undeclared War against American Women* (New York: Crown, 1991), 46–55.

30. Graham McCann, *Rebel Males: Clift, Brando and Dean* (New Brunswick, NJ: Rutgers University Press, 1993), 14.

31. John Clellon Holmes, "The Philosophy of the Beat Generation (1958)," in *Nothing Left to Declare* (New York: Dutton, 1967), 123.

32. John Clellon Holmes, "This Is the Beat Generation (1952)," in *Nothing Left to Declare*, 114.

33. Ned Polsky, "The Village Beat Scene: Summer 1960," in *Hustlers, Beats, and Others* (Chicago: Aldine, 1967), 159, 161.

34. Ibid., 160.

35. Ibid., 162.

36. Holmes, "The Philosophy of the Beat Generation (1958)," 123.

37. Ibid., 117.

38. Norman Mailer, *The White Negro* (San Francisco: City Lights, 1959), 2. All further references to *The White Negro* will be noted in the text. Polsky notes that Mailer by no means invented the concept of "the white Negro." Rather, "[a] critic noted in 1930 that white jazzmen of the early 1920s, such as Bix Beiderbecke, 'felt as a reality the spirit of negro blues. Indeed, such bands as the Wolverines were called "white niggers." ' " Polsky, "The Village Beat Scene: Summer 1960," 176.

39. Henry Louis Gates, Jr., *The Signifying Monkey: A Theory of African-American Literary Criticism* (New York: Oxford University Press, 1988), 47, 49.

40. James Baldwin, "The Black Boy Looks at the White Boy," in *Nobody Knows My Name: More Notes of a Native Son* (New York: Delta, 1962), 217.

41. Although Kerouac was very nervous about "The White Negro," Ginsberg characterizes it as "the most intelligent statement [about the beats] I'd seen by any literary-critical person." Quoted in Peter Manso, *Mailer: His Life and Times* (New York: Simon and Schuster, 1985), 260.

42. Baldwin, "The Black Boy Looks at the White Boy," 230. With the development of the Black Power movement, Baldwin's critique of "The White Negro" was itself attacked. Eldridge Cleaver mounted a homophobic assault on Baldwin coupled with a defense of Mailer, which suggests to me the power of heterosexual solidarity, at least during the late 1960s, to assuage racial animosities. See Eldridge Cleaver, *Soul on Ice* (New York: Delta, 1968), 97–111.

43. For an account of these struggles, see Chafe, *The Unfinished Journey*, 146–76.

44. Baldwin, "The Black Boy Looks at the White Boy," 228; Polsky, "The Village Beat Scene: Summer 1960," 181.

45. Dan Georgakas, "The Beats and the New Left," in *Encyclopedia of the American Left*, ed. Mari Jo Buhle, Paul Buhle, and Dan Georgakas (New York: Garland, 1990), 79.

46. Paul S. George and Jerold M. Starr, "Beat Politics: New Left and Hippie Beginnings in the Postwar Counterculture," in *Cultural Politics: Radical Movements in Modern History*, ed. Jerold M. Starr (New York: Praeger, 1985), 194.

47. Ibid., 209.

48. John Tytell, *Naked Angels: The Lives and Literature of the Beat Generation* (New York: McGraw-Hill, 1976), 3.

49. Ibid., 4–5.

50. Andrew Jamison and Ron Eyerman, *Seeds of the Sixties* (Berkeley and Los Angeles: University of California Press, 1994), 154.

51. Georgakas, "The Beats and the New Left," 77.

52. John Tebbel, *A History of Book Publishing in the United States*, vol. 4, *The Great Change, 1940–1980* (New York: R. R. Bowker, 1981), 347.

53. Jamison and Eyerman, *Seeds of the Sixties*, 158.

54. May, *Homeward Bound*, 3, 11.

55. Jennie Skerl, "Ginsberg on Burroughs: An Interview," *Modern Language Studies* 16, no. 3 (Summer 1986): 277.

56. Quoted in *The Portable Jack Kerouac*, ed. Ann Charters (New York: Viking, 1995), 481.

57. George and Starr, "Beat Politics," 203; see Michel Foucault, *The History of Sexuality*, vol. 1, *An Introduction*, trans. Robert Hurley (New York: Vintage, 1978), 101.

58. See, for example, *The Letters of William S. Burroughs, 1945–1959*, and Allen Ginsberg, *Journals Mid-Fifties*, ed. Gordon Ball (New York: HarperCollins, 1995).

59. Skerl, "Ginsberg on Burroughs," 278.

60. Jack Kerouac, "Belief and Technique for Modern Prose," in *The Portable Jack Kerouac*, 483; Peter Bürger, *Theory of the Avant-Garde*, trans. Michael Shaw (Minneapolis: University of Minnesota Press, 1984), 22.

61. Polsky, "The Village Beat Scene: Summer 1960," 179.

62. Raymond Williams, *Marxism and Literature* (Oxford: Oxford University Press, 1977), 113–14.

63. Sacvan Bercovitch, "The Problem of Ideology in American Literary History," *Critical Inquiry* 12, no. 4 (Summer 1986): 644.

64. Williams, *Marxism and Literature*, 114.

65. Gilbert Millstein, "Books of the Times," *New York Times*, September 5, 1957, 27.

66. David Dempsey, "In Pursuit of 'Kicks,'" *New York Times*, September 8, sec. 7, 4.

67. Norman Podhoretz, "The Know-Nothing Bohemians," *Partisan Review*, 25, no. 2 (Spring 1958): 315–16.

68. Leslie A. Fiedler, *Waiting for the End* (New York: Stein and Day, 1964), 164.

69. Kerouac, in particular, was very conservative, or, to take up Bruce Cook's suggestion, libertarian. "Michael McClure," he notes, "recalls that [Kerouac] shocked all his friends in San Francisco in 1956" by his support for Eisenhower. "'It just seemed a weird idea to us then,' he said. 'Not voting we could understand, but *wanting to vote for Eisenhower!*'" (Bruce Cook, *The Beat Generation* [New York: Quill, 1994], 85). Shortly before his death, in the late 1960s, he with great reluctance claimed the hippies as descendants of the Beats and insisted notoriously: "Listen, my politics haven't changed and I haven't changed! I'm solidly behind Bill Buckley, if you want to know. Nothing I wrote in my books—nothing—could be seen as basically in disagreement with this" (Cook, *The Beat Generation*, 88). Despite his angry assertion, the relationship between a writer's beliefs and values and the texts that he or she produces is a good deal more vexed than Kerouac suggests. And while I certainly would not want to claim Kerouac (or Burroughs, for that matter) as a writer of progressive texts, I think it is far more important to examine the historical forces at work on this group of writers than to enumerate their personal beliefs. For ideologically, the most important characteristics of a writer's work are not really within his or her conscious control but are transmitted, as it were, unconsciously through the social, political, economic, and cultural apparatus.

70. Burroughs (1982), quoted in Ann Charters's foreward to *The Beats: Literary Bohemians in Postwar America*, ed. Charters (Detroit: Gale Research Co., 1983), xii–xiii.

71. See May, *Homeward Bound.*

72. Jack Kerouac, *On the Road* (New York: Signet, 1957), 9. All further references will be noted in the text.

73. Cook, *The Beat Generation*, 152.

74. Joan Vollmer, quoted in *The Letters of William S. Burroughs, 1945–1959*, xix; Georgakas, "The Beats and the New Left," 77.

75. Allen Ginsberg interviewed by Allen Young, in *Gay Sunshine Interviews*, vol. 1 (San Francisco: Gay Sunshine Press, 1978), 123.

76. David deLeon, "Anarchism," in *Encyclopedia of the American Left*, 38.

77. G. Ostergaard, "Anarchism," in *A Dictionary of Marxist Thought*, ed. Tom Bottomore (Cambridge: Harvard University Press, 1983), 18.

78. Chafe, *The Unfinished Journey*, 93–94.

79. Wittner, *Cold War America*, 47.

80. Ibid., 114–15.

81. Buhle, *Marxism in the United States*, 197.

82. Cook, *The Beat Generation*, 59–60.

83. DeLeon, "Anarchism," 37.

84. James Baldwin characterizes this passage as "offensive nonsense" (Baldwin, "The Black Boy Looks at the White Boy," 231).

85. Freud, "Mourning and Melancholia," 153.

86. Ibid., 155.

87. Judith Butler, *Gender Trouble: Feminism and the Subversion of Identity* (New York: Routledge, 1990), 57, 61.

88. Jack Kerouac, "Essentials of Spontaneous Prose," in *The Portable Jack Kerouac*, 484–85.

89. Freud, "Mourning and Melancholia," 159.

90. Ibid., 161–62.

91. McCann, *Rebel Males*, 24.

92. Leslie A. Fiedler, "The New Mutants," *Partisan Review* 7 (Fall 1965): 508–10. All further references will be noted in the text. For an important (and related) critique of Fiedler, see Robyn Wiegman, *American Anatomies: Theorizing Race and Gender* (Durham: Duke University Press, 1995), 149–62.

93. For an account of Fiedler's political rehabilitation, see Alexander Bloom, *Prodigal Sons: The New York Intellectuals and Their World* (New York: Oxford University Press, 1986), and Alan M. Wald, *The New York Intellectuals: The Rise and Decline of the Anti-Stalinist Left from the 1930s to the 1980s* (Chapel Hill: University of North Carolina Press, 1987).

94. In fact, in *Dr. Strangelove* the psychotic, paranoid, and suicidal General Jack D. Ripper is terrified about the desecration of his "bodily fluids."

95. Allen Ginsberg, "After All, What Else Is There to Say?" (1949), in *Collected Poems, 1947–1980* (New York: Harper & Row, 1984), 29.

96. M. L. Rosenthal, "Poet of the New Violence," *Nation*, February 23, 1957, 162.

97. Sigmund Freud, "The Economic Problem in Masochism," in *General Psychological Theory*, ed. Philip Rieff, trans. James Strachey (New York: Collier, 1963), 193.

98. Robert M. Lindner, *Rebel without a Cause . . . : The Hypnoanalysis of a Criminal Psychopath* (New York: Grune & Stratton, 1944), 12.

99. Ibid., 2.

100. Ibid., 6; see also Freud, "The Economic Problem in Masochism," 190–201.

101. Lindner, *Rebel without a Cause . . .* , 7; see also Sigmund Freud, "'A Child Is Being Beaten,'" in *Sexuality and the Psychology of Love*, ed. Philip Rieff, trans. James Strachey (New York: Collier, 1963), 107–32.

102. Lindner, *Rebel without a Cause . . .* , 9.

103. Robert Lindner, "The Mutiny of the Young," in *Must You Conform?* (New York: Rinehart, 1956), 23.

104. Ibid., 23.

105. Ibid., 25; for an account of the idea of mass culture as feminine, see Andreas Huyssen, *After the Great Divide: Modernism, Mass Culture, Postmodernism* (Bloomington: Indiana University Press, 1987).

106. Lindner, *Rebel without a Cause . . .* , 6.

107. Quoted in Tytell, *Naked Angels*, 84; for the journal entry, see Allen Ginsberg, *Journals: Early Fifties Early Sixties*, ed. Gordon Ball (New York: Grove, 1977), 83–84.

108. Neal Oxenhandler, "Listening to Burroughs' Voice," in *William S. Burroughs at the Front*, ed. Robin Lydenberg and Jennie Skerl (Carbondale: Southern Illinois University Press, 1991), 135. Burroughs has commented: "There's not that much sadism [in my work]. While I have that reputation, I don't think I dwell very much on torture with a sexual connotation. It certainly is nothing that interests me personally; beating people, being beaten, all that just seems to me to be terribly dull and unpleasant." Odier, *The Job*, 115.

109. Catharine R. Stimpson, "The Beat Generation and the Trials of Homosexual Liberation," *Salmagundi*, nos. 58–59 (Fall 1982, Winter 1983): 377.

110. Ginsberg, *Gay Sunshine Interviews*, 97, 124; Ginsberg, "Many Loves" (1956), in *Collected Poems*, 156.

111. Gerald Nicosia, *Memory Babe: A Critical Biography of Jack Kerouac* (New York: Grove, 1983), 154–55.

112. Ginsberg, *Gay Sunshine Interviews*, 108–9.

113. *The Letters of William S. Burroughs, 1945–1959*, 119; William S. Burroughs, *Junky* (1953) (New York: Penguin, 1977), 72.

114. *The Letters of William S. Burroughs, 1945–1959*, 119; see also Stimpson, "The Beat Generation and the Trials of Homosexual Liberation," 378.

115. Jack Kerouac, *Visions of Cody* (New York: Penguin, 1972), 49, 320, 75. All further references will be noted in the text.

116. Ted Berrigan, "Jack Kerouac," *Paris Review* 43 (Summer 1968): 65.

117. See Eve Kosofsky Sedgwick, *Between Men: Male Homosocial Desire and English Literature* (New York: Columbia University Press, 1985).

118. Nicosia, *Memory Babe*, 362.

119. This erotic triangle is replicated (and its homoerotic content made explicit) with Ginsberg who, while staying with the Cassadys, writes in his journal: "I can sleep with Neal, sleep with Carolyn, sleep with no one, and stay. Or sleep with both and no one alternately amid confusions. Or I can end this mad triangle, all three of us blocked, by leaving." Ginsberg, *Journals: Early Fifties Early Sixties*, 76.

120. Ginsberg, "Many Loves," 156–58.

121. *As Ever: The Collected Correspondence of Allen Ginsberg and Neal Cassady*, ed. Barry Gifford (Berkeley: Creative Arts Book Company, 1977), 28, 38. All further references will be noted in the text.

122. Kaja Silverman, *Male Subjectivity at the Margins* (New York: Routledge, 1992), 191–95.

123. Ginsberg, *Journals: Early Fifties Early Sixties*, 73.

124. Silverman, *Male Subjectivity at the Margins*, 191.

125. Ginsberg, *Collected Poems*, 227.

126. Cassady, *Off the Road*, 29. All further references will be noted in the text.

127. As Silverman emphasizes, however, female masochism is usually more widespread and less conspicuous than male masochism because it is "an accepted—indeed a requisite—element of 'normal' female subjectivity, providing a crucial mechanism for eroticizing lack and subordination." Silverman, *Male Subjectivity at the Margins*, 189.

128. Burroughs, *The Letters of William S. Burroughs*, 37.

129. Paul Breslin, *The Psycho-Political Muse: American Poetry since the Fifties* (Chicago: University of Chicago Press, 1987), 22.

130. Ibid., 24.

131. Thomas Clark, "Allen Ginsberg: An Interview," *Paris Review* 10 (Spring 1966): 23.

132. Breslin, *The Psycho-Political Muse*, 24.

133. Ginsberg, *Collected Poems*, 126. All further references will be noted in the text.

134. Theodor Reik, *Masochism in Sex and Society*, trans. Margaret H. Beigel and Gertrud M. Kurth (New York: Grove, 1962), 72.

135. Breslin, *The Psycho-Political Muse*, 28.

136. Compare Catharine Stimpson: "In his homosexual acts, he masculinizes some male partners—as if they were linked to fathers and brothers—and feminizes himself. In part, he seems less to be acting out the drama of a powerless woman that [*sic*] that of a powerless child who wishes to please himself and men in power. In part, he seems to be taking on a mother's part." "The Beat Generation and the Trials of Homosexual Liberation," 389. And Ginsberg comments that he realized on LSD that "all women and your mother are one. . . ." "Playboy Interview: Allen Ginsberg," *Playboy*, April 1969, 86.

137. For an analysis of "Momism," see May, *Homeward Bound*, 74–75.

138. James E. B. Breslin, *From Modern to Contemporary: American Poetry, 1945–1965* (Chicago: University of Chicago Press, 1984), 104.

139. Ginsberg, *Gay Sunshine Interviews*, 123.

140. Silverman, *Male Subjectivity at the Margins*, 198. It is important to emphasize that although Christian masochism is specifically connected by Silverman to the mythology of Christ, its operation is not dependent on a specifically Christian context or subject. Jews, atheists, and Buddhists may also play the roles of Christian masochists.

141. Breslin, *The Psycho-Political Muse*, 26.

142. Clark, "Allen Ginsberg: An Interview," 31.

143. Silverman, *Male Subjectivity at the Margins*, 206.

144. Clark, "Allen Ginsberg: An Interview," 33–43.

145. See Sri Chinmoy, *Yoga and the Spiritual Life: The Journey of India's Soul* (Jamaica, NY: Agni Press, 1973), and Mircea Eliade, *Yoga: Immortality and Freedom*, trans. Willard Trask (New York: Pantheon, 1958).

146. Clark, "Allen Ginsberg: An Interview," 38.

147. Ibid., 33 (his emphasis).

148. Ibid., 43–44.

149. Ibid., 32.

150. The following abbreviations are used for the remainder of this chapter to indicate the titles of William S. Burroughs's works. *J*: *Junky* (New York: Penguin, 1977); *Q*: *Queer*; *NL*: *Naked Lunch* (New York: Grove Weidenfeld, 1992); *SM*: *The Soft Ma-*

chine (New York: Ballantine, 1973); *TE: The Ticket That Exploded* (New York: Grove, 1987); *NE: Nova Express* (New York: Grove, 1965); *TJ: The Job*; *I: Interzone*, ed. James Grauerholz (New York: Penguin, 1990); *L: The Letters of William S. Burroughs, 1945–1959*; *PR:* Conrad Knickerbocker, "William Burroughs: An Interview," *Paris Review* 9 (Fall 1965): 13–50.

151. See Lydenberg and Skerl, *William S. Burroughs at the Front.*

152. See, for example, Mary McCarthy, "Burroughs' *Naked Lunch*," and David Lodge, "Objections to William Burroughs," in Lydenberg and Skerl, *William S. Burroughs at the Front*, 33–39 and 75–84.

153. See, for example, Robin Lydenberg, *Word Cultures: Radical Theory and Practice in William S. Burroughs' Fiction* (Urbana and Chicago: University of Illinois Press, 1987).

154. Cary Nelson, "The End of the Body: *Radical Space in Burroughs,*" in Lydenberg and Skerl, *William S. Burroughs at the Front*, 122.

155. For an account of the incident, see Morgan, *Literary Outlaw*, 74–75.

156. Quoted in Corber, *Homosexuality in Cold War America*, 27–28.

157. Ibid., 14.

158. Nelson, "The end of the body," 123.

159. Freud, " 'A Child Is Being Beaten,' " 127, 117.

160. Burroughs, quoted in Morgan, *Literary Outlaw*, 51.

161. Silverman, *Male Subjectivity at the Margins*, 205.

162. See Thomas Laqueur, *Making Sex: Body and Gender from the Greeks to Freud* (Cambridge: Harvard University Press, 1990).

163. Oxenhandler, "Listening to Burroughs' Voice," in Lydenberg and Skerl, *William S. Burroughs at the Front*, 145.

164. Morgan, *Literary Outlaw*, 230.

165. See Benedict Anderson, *Imagined Communities: Reflections on the Origin and Spread of Nationalism* (London: Verso, 1991).

166. Truman Loyalty Order, March 22, 1947, in *Documents of American History*, ed. Henry Steele Commager (New York: Appleton-Century-Crofts, 1968), 529–30.

167. Executive Order 10450, April 27, 1953, in *Documents of American History*, 587.

168. Cf. "Contradictory suggestion is the basic formula of the daily press: 'Take drugs everybody is doing it.' 'Drug-taking is WRONG.' Newspapers spread violence, sex, drugs, then come on with the old RIGHT WRONG FAMILY CHURCH AND COUNTRY sound," *TJ*, 45–46.

169. Peter Sloterdijk, *Critique of Cynical Reason*, trans. Michael Eldred (Minneapolis: University of Minnesota Press, 1987), 113–14.

170. In fact, conservative opposition to gun control crystallized in the early 1960s with the attempt, after the John Kennedy assassination, to restrict access to guns.

171. The Employment Act of 1946, in *Documents of American History*, 514–15.

172. Quoted in Chafe, *The Unfinished Journey*, 98.

173. See, for example, Oxenhandler, "Listening to Burroughs' Voice," in Lydenberg and Skerl, *William S. Burroughs at the Front*, 133–47.

174. See Ginsberg, *Gay Sunshine Interviews*, 124.

175. Karl Marx, *Capital*, vol. 1 trans. Ben Fowkes (New York: Vintage, 1977), 126.

176. Ibid., 128.

177. Ibid., 163.

178. Ibid., 165.

179. Clark, "Allen Ginsberg: An Interview," 29.

180. John Tytell, "A Conversation with Allen Ginsberg," *Partisan Review*, 41, no. 2 (1974): 256.

181. Quoted in *The Portable Jack Kerouac*, 482.

182. Kerouac, "Belief and Technique for Modern Prose," in *The Portable Jack Kerouac*, 483.

183. Kerouac, "Essentials of Spontaneous Prose," and "The First Word: Jack Kerouac Takes a Fresh Look at Jack Kerouac," in *The Portable Jack Kerouac*, 485, 487.

184. Kerouac, "About the Beat Generation," in *The Portable Jack Kerouac*, 560.

CHAPTER TWO
REVOLUTION AS PERFORMANCE

1. Seth Cagin and Philip Dray, *Hollywood Films of the Seventies: Sex, Drugs, Violence, Rock 'n' Roll and Politics* (New York: Harper & Row, 1984), 66; Margie Burns, "*Easy Rider* and *Deliverance*, or, the Death of the Sixties," *University of Hartford Studies in Literature*, 22, nos. 2–3 (1990): 45.

2. Harriet R. Polt, "Easy Rider," *Film Quarterly* 23, no. 1 (Fall 1969): 22.

3. Stephen Farber, "End of the Road?" *Film Quarterly*, 23, no. 2 (Winter 1969–70): 7–8.

4. Ibid., 9.

5. See Cagin and Dray, *Hollywood Films of the Seventies*, 64.

6. Timothy Leary, *The Politics of Ecstasy* (London: Paladin, 1970), 103.

7. Ibid., 107.

8. Joseph Roach, *Cities of the Dead: Circum-Atlantic Performance* (New York: Columbia University Press, 1996), 243.

9. "Bourbon on the Rocks," *Newsweek*, July 13, 1970, 58.

10. Ibid., 59.

11. Roach, *Cities of the Dead*, 50.

12. Ibid., 53.

13. Sigmund Freud, "The Economic Problem in Masochism," in *General Psychological Theory*, ed. Philip Reiff (New York: Collier, 1963), 193.

14. Kaja Silverman, *Male Subjectivity at the Margins* (New York: Routledge, 1992), 197.

15. Ibid., 198.

16. Theodore Roszak, *The Making of a Counter Culture: Reflections on the Technocratic Society and Its Youthful Opposition* (Garden City, NY: Doubleday/Anchor, 1969), 56.

17. William H. Chafe, *The Unfinished Journey: America since World War II* (New York: Oxford University Press, 1986), 445.

18. Elaine Tyler May, *Homeward Bound: American Families in the Cold War Era* (New York: Basic Books, 1988), 135.

19. Jerrold M. Starr, "The Peace and Love Generation: Changing Attitudes toward Sex and Violence among College Youth," *Journal of Social Issues*, 30, no. 2 (1974): 80.

20. Jerrold M. Starr, "Cultural Politics in the 1960s," in *Cultural Politics: Radical Movements in Modern History*, ed. Jerrold M. Starr (New York: Praeger, 1985), 242.

21. David Steigerwald, *The Sixties and the End of Modern America* (New York: St. Martin's Press, 1995), 44.

22. See Chafe, *The Unfinished Journey*, 437–39; Lawrence S. Wittner, *Cold War America: From Hiroshima to Watergate* (New York: Praeger, 1974), 237–39; and Steigerwald, *The Sixties and the End of Modern America*, 38–68.

23. James F. Scott, "Brown and Bakke: The Relation between Judicial Decisions and Socioeconomic Conditions," *Phylon*, 41, no. 3 (September 1980): 238.

24. Stanley Aronowitz, "When the New Left Was New," in *The 60s without Apology*, ed. Sohnya Sayres, Anders Stephanson, Stanley Aronowitz, and Fredric Jameson (Minneapolis: University of Minnesota Press, 1984), 20.

25. "The Port Huron Statement," in *The Sixties Papers: Documents of a Rebellious Era*, ed. Judith Clavir Albert and Stewart Edward Albert (New York: Praeger, 1984), 176, 181.

26. Paul Buhle, *Marxism in the United States: Remapping the History of the American Left* (London: Verso, 1991), 231.

27. Ibid., 237.

28. Starr, "Cultural Politics in the 1960s," 261.

29. Ibid., 253.

30. Ibid., 254.

31. Quoted in Wittner, *Cold War America*, 285.

32. Stokely Carmichael, "What We Want," in Albert and Albert, *The Sixties Papers*, 139–40.

33. Robert Blauner, "Internal Colonialism and Ghetto Revolt," *Social Problems* 16, no. 4 (1969): 396. For a critique of Blauner's position, see Michael Omi and Howard Winant, *Racial Formation in the United States: From the 1960s to the 1990s* (New York: Routledge, 1994), 44. See also Stokely Carmichael and Charles V. Hamilton, *Black Power: The Politics of Liberation in America* (New York: Vintage, 1967).

34. Blauner, "Internal Colonialism and Ghetto Revolt," 407–8.

35. Fredric Jameson, "Periodizing the '60s," in *The Ideologies of Theory, Essays 1971–1986*, vol. 2, *The Syntax of History* (Minneapolis: University of Minnesota Press, 1988), 180.

36. Todd Gitlin, *The Sixties: Years of Hope, Days of Rage* (New York: Bantam, 1989), 350.

37. James Weinstein, "The Fortunes of the Old Left Compared to the Fortunes of the New," in *Failure of a Dream? Essays in the History of American Socialism*, ed. John H. M. Laslett and Seymour Martin Lipset (Garden City, NY: Anchor/Doubleday, 1974), 707. A good account of the various splinters of SDS can be found in Aronowitz, "When the New Left Was New," 35–39.

38. Buhle, *Marxism in the United States*, 249.

39. Jameson, "Periodizing the '60s," 181. Marcuse also sees "the new historical Subject of change" as a distinctive characteristic of '60s rebellion. See Herbert Marcuse, *An Essay on Liberation* (Boston: Beacon, 1969), 52–53.

40. Buhle, *Marxism in the United States*, 235–37.

41. Gitlin, *The Sixties*, 28.

42. Leonard Wolf, with Deborah Wolf, *Voices from the Love Generation* (Boston: Little, Brown and Company, 1968), xxi.

43. Peter Berg, in ibid., 250.

44. Starr, "Cultural Politics in the 1960s," 241.

45. Ibid., 241.

46. Patrick Gleeson, in Wolf, *Voices from the Love Generation*, 72.

47. The correspondents of *Time*, *The Hippies* (New York: Time Incorporated, 1967), 21.

48. Daniel Hayes, Jr., quoted in "Trouble in Hippieland," *Newsweek*, October 30, 1967, 87.

49. Warren Hinckle, "A Social History of the Hippies," *Ramparts*, March 1967, 18–19.

50. Paul Kantner, "We Can Be Together," the Jefferson Airplane, *Volunteers*, RCA LSP-4238 (1969). © 1969 Jefferson Airplane. Bowing, doubtlessly, to corporate pressure, the original lyric sheet discreetly substitutes the word "fred" for "fuck."

51. Quoted in Hans Toch, "Last Word on the Hippies," *Nation*, December 4, 1967, 583.

52. Patrick Gleeson, in Wolf, *Voices from the Love Generation*, 66.

53. John Robert Howard, "The Flowering of the Hippie Movement," *Annals of the American Academy of Political and Social Science* 382 (March 1969): 46.

54. Quoted in Martin A. Lee and Bruce Shlain, *Acid Dreams: The CIA, LSD, and the Sixties Rebellion* (New York: Grove, 1985), 166.

55. Gitlin, *The Sixties*, 213.

56. Ibid., 209.

57. Ibid., 213.

58. Free, [Abbie Hoffman], *Revolution for the Hell of It* (New York: Dial Press, 1968), 102.

59. Jameson, "Periodizing the '60s," 188–89.

60. Quoted in Lee and Shlain, *Acid Dreams*, 207.

61. Jameson, "Periodizing the '60s," 189.

62. The correspondents of *Time*, *The Hippies*, 9.

63. Jack Newfield, "One Cheer for the Hippies," *Nation*, June 26, 1967, 809.

64. "The Hippies of Hashberry," *Ebony*, August 1967, 118.

65. Carmichael and Hamilton, *Black Power*, 40.

66. Toch, "Last Word on the Hippies," 585–86.

67. Gwendolyn M. Parker, *Trespassing: My Sojourn in the Halls of Privilege* (Boston: Houghton Mifflin, 1997), 134.

68. "The Hippies of Hashberry," 118.

69. Ron Thelin, in Wolf, *Voices from the Love Generation*, 230.

70. "Trouble in Hippieland," 88; for an account of the racial history of Haight-Ashbury, see Howard, "The Flowering of the Hippie Movement," 44–45.

71. Howard, "The Flowering of the Hippie Movement," 44.

72. "Trouble in Hippieland," 88.

73. Starr, "Cultural Politics in the 1960s," 242.

74. John Lofland, "The New Segregation: A Perspective on Age Categories in America," in *Youth and Sociology*, ed. Peter K. Manning and Marcello Truzzi (Englewood Cliffs, NJ: Prentice-Hall, 1972), 246–47.

75. "Trouble in Hippieland," 88.

76. Lofland, "The New Segregation," 249.

77. The correspondents of *Time*, *The Hippies*, 9.

78. [Hoffman], *Revolution for the Hell of It*, 35.

79. Peter Berg in Wolf, *Voices from the Love Generation*, 259–60.

80. Ibid., 260–61.

81. Ibid., 258.

82. See Numan V. Bartley, *The Rise of Massive Resistance: Race and Politics in the South during the 1950's* (Baton Rouge: Louisiana State University Press, 1969).

83. Charles A. Reich, *The Greening of America* (New York: Bantam, 1971), 270.

84. Ibid., 310–11.

85. Ibid., 268–71.

86. [Hoffman], *Revolution for the Hell of It*, 71.

87. Roszak, *The Making of a Counter Culture*, 74.

88. Wolf, *Voices from the Love Generation*, xlii.

89. Roszak, *The Making of a Counter Culture*, 74.

90. Marc Feigen Fasteau, *The Male Machine* (New York: Delta, 1975), 1.

91. Yvonne Tasker, "Dumb Movies for Dumb People: Masculinity, the Body, and the Voice in Contemporary Action Cinema," in *Screening the Male: Exploring Masculinities in Hollywood Cinema*, ed. Steven Cohan and Ina Rae Hark (London: Routledge, 1993), 234.

92. For a detailed account of this masculinity, see David Savran, *Communists, Cowboys, and Queers: The Politics of Masculinity in the Work of Arthur Miller and Tennessee Williams* (Minneapolis: University of Minnesota Press, 1992), 33–42.

93. George B. Leonard, *The Man and Woman Thing and Other Provocations* (New York: Delacorte, 1970), 147.

94. Reich, *The Greening of America*, 254.

95. Leonard, *The Man and Woman Thing and Other Provocations*, 146.

96. Fasteau, *The Male Machine*, 196.

97. Ibid., 196.

98. See Ellen Willis, "Radical Feminism and Feminist Radicalism," in Sayres, Stephanson, Aronowitz, and Jameson, *The 60s without Apology*, 91–118.

99. Leonard, *The Man and Woman Thing and Other Provocations*, 149.

100. Shalumith Firestone, excerpt from *The Dialectic of Sex*, in Albert and Albert, *The Sixties Papers*, 499.

101. Fasteau, *The Male Machine*, 198.

102. Reich, *The Greening of America*, 253.

103. Nancy Woloch, *Women and the American Experience* (New York: Knopf, 1984), 522.

104. Quoted in Starr, "The Peace and Love Generation," 88.

105. Starr, "The Peace and Love Generation," 74, 84.

106. Ibid., 84.

107. Leonard, *The Man and Woman Thing and Other Provocations*, 145–46.

108. Ibid., 148.

109. Ibid., 148.

110. Ibid., 150.

111. Fasteau, *The Male Machine*, 196.

112. Leslie Halliwell, *The Filmgoer's Companion* (New York: Hill and Wang, 1977), 116.

113. Moira Walsh, "Films: Butch Cassidy and the Sundance Kid," *America*, November 10, 1969, 307.

114. Vincent Canby, "Slapstick and Drama Cross Paths in 'Butch Cassidy,'" *New York Times*, September 25, 1969, 54.

115. Tom Milne, "Butch Cassidy and the Sundance Kid and Tell Them Willie Boy Is Here," *Sight and Sound* 39 (Spring 1970): 102.

116. Ibid., 102.

117. John Luce, "Haight-Ashbury Today: A Case of Terminal Euphoria," *Esquire*, July 1969, 122–24.

118. Quoted in Luce, "Haight-Ashbury Today," 122.

119. Wolf, *Voices from the Love Generation*, 74.

120. Ibid., 75.

121. Leary, *The Politics of Ecstasy*, 106–7.

122. Wolf, *Voices from the Love Generation*, 75.

123. Sigmund Freud, "Instincts and Their Vicissitudes," in *The Complete Psychological Works of Sigmund Freud*, ed. James Strachey (London: Hogarth Press, 1957), 128.

124. Silverman, *Male Subjectivity at the Margins*, 198.

125. Leary, *The Politics of Ecstasy*, 112.

126. Ibid., 110.

127. See John Bryan, *Whatever Happened to Timothy Leary?* (San Francisco: Renaissance Press, 1980).

128. Bernard Wolfe, "The Real-Life Death of Jim Morrison," *Esquire*, June 1972, 110.

129. Joan Didion, "Waiting for Morrison," *Saturday Evening Post*, March 9, 1968, 16.

130. Robert Windeler, "Doors, a Way in and Way Out, Rock on Coast," *New York Times*, November 20, 1967, 61.

131. The *New York Times* and Morrison quoted in Wolfe, "The Real-Life Death of Jim Morrison," 110.

132. Quoted in Wolfe, "The Real-Life Death of Jim Morrison," 110.

133. Sherry, quoted in Wolfe, "The Real-Life Death of Jim Morrison," 110.

134. Ibid., 186.

135. Quoted in Wolf, *Voices from the Love Generation*, 34.

136. Joan Didion, "The Hippie Generation: Slouching Towards Bethlehem," *Saturday Evening Post*, 91.

137. Kate Millett, "Sexual Politics: A Manifesto for Revolution," in Albert and Albert, *The Sixties Papers*, 476–77.

138. Gitlin, *The Sixties*, 108–9, 372.

139. The correspondents of *Time, The Hippies*, 18.

140. Quoted in Wolf, *Voices from the Love Generation*, 34.

141. Ibid., 156.

142. See Jeffrey Weeks, *Sexuality and Its Discontents: Meanings, Myths, and Modern Sexualities* (London: Routledge, 1985).

143. Leary, *The Politics of Ecstasy*, 111.

144. Dan Wakefield, "The War at Home," *Atlantic*, October 1969, 119.

145. See, for example, "Trouble in Hippieland," 87.

146. Ernest Dernburg, cited in Luce, "Haight-Ashbury Today," 122.

147. For an examination of postwar theories of homosexuality, see John D'Emilio, *Sexual Politics, Sexual Communities: The Making of a Homosexual Minority in the United States, 1940–1970* (Chicago: University of Chicago Press, 1983), 140–44, 215–17.

148. This analysis concurs neatly with the "Momism" decried so widely during the domestic revival; see May, *Homeward Bound*, 74–75.

149. Gitlin, *The Sixties*, 108–9.

150. Ibid., 108–9, 371–73.

151. Weinstein, "The Fortunes of the Old Left Compared to the Fortunes of the New," 709.

152. Konstantin Berlandt, "Been Down So Long It Looks Up to Me," in Albert and Albert, *The Sixties Papers*, 450–55. A 1969 SDS statement, although singling out "male supremacy" as an oppressive system, ignores homophobia. "Bring the War Home," in Albert and Albert, *The Sixties Papers*, 247–53.

153. See Cagin and Dray, *Hollywood Films of the Seventies*, 65.

154. The correspondents of *Time*, *The Hippies*, 1, 2.

155. George W. Pierson, *The Moving American* (New York: Knopf, 1973), 4–5.

156. Quoted in Wolf, *Voices from the Love Generation*, 221.

157. Peter Bürger, *Theory of the Avant-Garde*, trans. Michael Shaw (Minneapolis: University of Minnesota Press, 1984), 22.

158. Walter Benjamin, "Surrealism: The Last Snapshot of the European Intelligentsia," in *One-Way Street and Other Writings*, trans. Edmund Jephcott and Kingsley Shorter (London: NLB, 1979), 226.

159. Ibid., 227.

160. Fredric Jameson, *Postmodernism, or, The Cultural Logic of Late Capitalism* (Durham: Duke University Press, 1991), 6.

161. Quoted in Steigerwald, *The Sixties and the End of Modern America*, 156.

162. Reich, *The Greening of America*, 246.

163. Jameson, "Periodizing the '60s," 185.

164. Ibid., 208.

165. Reich, *The Greening of America*, 255, 242.

166. Ibid., 260, 267.

167. Walter Benjamin, "The Work of Art in the Age of Mechanical Reproduction," in *Illuminations*, ed. Hannah Arendt, trans. Harry Zohn (New York: Schocken, 1969), 223–24.

168. Jacques Derrida, *Writing and Difference*, trans. Alan Bass (Chicago: University of Chicago Press, 1978), 234.

169. Quoted in C.W.E. Bigsby, *A Critical Introduction to Twentieth-Century American Drama*, vol. 3, *Beyond Broadway* (Cambridge: Cambridge University Press, 1985), 59.

170. Fredric Jameson, *Marxism and Form: Twentieth-Century Dialectical Theories of Literature* (Princeton: Princeton University Press, 1971), 107.

171. Herbert Marcuse, "Political Preface 1966," in *Eros and Civilization: A Philosophical Inquiry into Freud* (Boston: Beacon Press, 1966), xi. All further references will be noted in the text.

172. Jameson, *Marxism and Form*, 108.

173. Bigsby, *A Critical Introduction to Twentieth-Century American Drama*, 68.

174. Julian Beck, *The Life of the Theatre: The Relation of the Artist to the Struggle of the People* (New York: Limelight, 1991), 52.

175. Julian Beck, "Storming the Barricades," in Kenneth H. Brown, *The Brig* (New York: Hill and Wang, 1965), 13.

176. Ibid., 19, 21.

177. Ibid., 22, 34, 7.

178. Beck, *The Life of the Theatre*, 3.

179. Quoted in Michael Vanden Heuvel, *Performing Drama / Dramatizing Performance: Alternative Theatre and the Dramatic Text* (Ann Arbor: University of Michigan Press, 1991), 43–44.

180. Beck, "Storming the Barricades," 3; Antonin Artaud, *The Theatre and Its Double*, trans. Mary Caroline Richards (New York: Grove, 1958), 54.

181. Beck, "Storming the Barricades," 24, 16.

182. Artaud, *The Theatre and Its Double*, 111. See Derrida, *Writing and Difference*, 232–50.

183. Beck, "Storming the Barricades," 9, 11.

184. Ibid., 11–12.

185. Ibid., 12.

186. John Tytell, *The Living Theatre: Art, Exile, Outrage* (New York: Grove, 1995), xi.

187. Margaret Croyden, *Lunatics, Lovers and Poets: The Contemporary Experimental Theatre* (New York: Delta, 1974), 89.

188. Tytell, *The Living Theatre*, 156.

189. Quoted in ibid., 157.

190. For an account of this tour, see Renfreu Neff, *The Living Theatre: USA* (Indianapolis: Bobbs-Merrill, 1970).

191. See Judith Malina, *The Diaries of Judith Malina 1947–1957* (New York: Grove, 1984). These figures include W. H. Auden, Chester Kallman, John Cage, Merce Cunningham, Frank O'Hara, John Ashbery, Morton Feldman, and many others.

192. Tytell, *The Living Theatre*, 172.

193. Ibid., 189.

194. Ibid., 194.

195. Ibid., 200.

196. Pierre Biner, *The Living Theatre: A History without Myths*, trans. Robert Meister (New York: Avon, 1972), 63.

197. Bigsby, *A Critical Introduction to Twentieth-Century American Drama*, 81; Artaud, *The Theatre and Its Double*, 79.

198. Beck, "Storming the Barricades," 34.

199. Brown, *The Brig*, 47. All further references will be noted in the text.

200. Judith Malina, "Directing *The Brig*," in Brown, *The Brig*, 86. All further references will be noted in the text.

201. Brown, *The Brig*, 43; Biner, *The Living Theatre*, 68.

202. Malina, *The Diaries of Judith Malina*, 256.

203. Biner, *The Living Theatre*, 70.

204. Beck, *The Life of the Theatre*, 14.

205. [Hoffman], *Revolution for the Hell of It*, 68, 39.

206. Judith Malina, *Enormous Despair* (New York: Random House, 1972), 134.

207. [Hoffman], *Revolution for the Hell of It*, 29.

208. Ibid., 64, 59.

209. Ibid., 42.

210. Ibid., 96, 49.

211. Ibid., 13.

212. Beck, *The Life of the Theatre*, 106.

213. Ibid., 162; Jerzy Grotowski, *Towards a Poor Theatre* (New York: Simon and Schuster, 1968), 37.

214. [Hoffman], *Revolution for the Hell of It*, 59.

215. Beck, *The Life of the Theatre*, 1. All further references will be noted in the text.

216. For an analysis of the so-called sex wars inspired in large part by the feminist antipornography activists (including Dworkin and MacKinnon), see *Sex Exposed: Sexuality and the Pornography Debate*, ed. Lynne Segal and Mary McIntosh (New Brunswick, NJ: Rutgers University Press, 1993).

217. See Tytell, *The Living Theatre*, 285–89. For illustrations of Malina's nascent masochism during the 1950s, see Malina, *The Diaries of Judith Malina*, 126, 198, 226, 249, 256.

218. Tytell, *The Living Theatre*, 284.

219. The Living Theatre, *The Legacy of Cain*, written down by Julian Beck and Judith Malina, *Scripts* 1, no. 1 (November 1971): 13.

220. Tytell, *The Living Theatre*, 287.

221. Marcuse, *An Essay on Liberation*, 54.

222. [Hoffman], *Revolution for the Hell of It*, 51.

223. Marcuse, *An Essay on Liberation*, 68–69.

224. Robin Morgan, "Goodbye to All That," in Albert and Albert, *The Sixties Papers*, 511.

225. Ibid., 510, 516.

226. Ibid., 516.

227. Ibid., 512.

228. Silverman, *Male Subjectivity at the Margins*, 197.

229. Vincent Bugliosi with Curt Gentry, *Helter Skelter* (New York: Bantam, 1975), 302; Morgan, "Goodbye to All That," 511.

230. Huey P. Newton, "Revolutionary Suicide: The Way of Liberation," in Albert and Albert, *The Sixties Papers*, 168.

231. Ibid., 169.

232. Ibid., 170.

233. Ibid., 171.

234. Ibid., 170.

235. Ibid., 169.

236. Huey P. Newton, "The Women's Liberation and Gay Liberation Movements: August 15, 1970," in *To Die for the People: The Writings of Huey P. Newton*, ed. Toni Morrison (New York: Writers and Readers, 1973–1995), 152.

237. Ibid., 153.

238. Ibid., 155.

239. Perhaps the most horrifyingly masculinist proposition to be connected with the Panthers is Eldridge Cleaver's defense of rape as "an insurrectionary act." Eldridge Cleaver, *Soul on Ice* (New York: Delta, 1968), 14.

240. Frantz Fanon, *The Wretched of the Earth*, trans. Constance Farrington (New York: Grove, 1968), 316.

CHAPTER THREE

THE SADOMASOCHIST IN THE CLOSET

1. David Ansen with Katrine Ames, "A Movie with All the Right Stuff," *Newsweek*, October 3, 1983, 39–41.

2. David Denby, "Star-Struck," *New York*, October 31, 1983, 78.

3. Pauline Kael, "The Current Cinema: The Sevens," *New Yorker*, October 17, 1983, 178.

4. Ansen with Ames, "A Movie with All the Right Stuff," 39–41.

5. William H. Chafe, *The Unfinished Journey: America since World War II* (New York: Oxford University Press, 1986), 446.

6. Ibid., 446–47.

7. Ibid., 449.

8. Quoted in Neil Lazarus, "Doubting the New World Order: Marxism, Realism, and the Claims of Postmodernist Social Theory," *differences* 3, no. 3 (1991): 105.

9. Michael Rustin, "The Politics of Post-Fordism: or, The Trouble with 'New Times,'" *New Left Review* 175 (1989): 55.

10. Lazarus, "Doubting the New World Order," 113.

11. See Keith Bradsher, "Gap in Wealth in U.S. Called Widest in West," *New York Times*, April 17, 1995, A1+.

12. Fredric Jameson, *Postmodernism, or, The Cultural Logic of Late Capitalism* (Durham: Duke University Press, 1991), x.

13. Ibid., 6.

14. Ibid., 17.

15. Ibid., 20.

16. Ibid., xvi.

17. Timothy Corrigan, *A Cinema without Walls: Movies and Culture after Vietnam* (New Brunswick, NJ: Rutgers University Press, 1991), 12.

18. Margie Burns, "*Easy Rider* and *Deliverance*, or, the Death of the Sixties," *University of Hartford Studies in Literature* 22, nos. 2–3 (1990): 51.

19. Corrigan, *A Cinema without Walls*, 1.

20. Chafe, *The Unfinished Journey*, 436.

21. Christopher Lasch, *The Culture of Narcissism: American Life in an Age of Diminishing Expectations* (New York: Warner Books, 1979), 17. All further references will be noted in the text.

22. Robert Bly, *Iron John: A Book About Men* (Reading, MA: Addison-Wesley, 1990), 8. All further references will be noted in the text.

23. For an account of "masculinity therapy," see R. W. Connell, "Drumming Up the Wrong Tree," *Tikkun* 7, no. 1 (1992): 31–32.

24. David Gelman, "Making It All Feel Better," *Newsweek*, November 26, 1990, 67.

25. Charles Gaines, "Robert Bly, Wild Thing," *Esquire*, October 1991, 126–27.

26. See Lance Morrow, "The Child Is Father of the Man," *Time*, August 19, 1991, 53; and Don Shewey, "Wild in the Suites," *Village Voice*, November 5, 1991, 43.

27. Gerri Hirshey, "White Guys with Drums," *Gentleman's Quarterly*, December 1991, 89.

28. For an excellent critique of *Iron John* and its many errors, see Connell, "Drumming Up the Wrong Tree," 31–36.

29. For an analysis of "Momism," see Elaine Tyler May, *Homeward Bound: American Families in the Cold War Era* (New York: Basic Books, 1988), 74–75.

30. The most detailed descriptions (and devastating critiques) of the weekend retreats are Doug Stanton's "Inward, Ho!" *Esquire*, October 1991, 113–22, and Jon Tevlin's "Of Hawks and Men: A Weekend Retreat in the Male Wilderness," *Utne Reader*, November/December 1989, 50–59.

31. Robert Moore and Douglas Gillette, *King, Warrior, Magician, Lover: Rediscovering the Archetypes of the Mature Masculine* (New York: HarperCollins, 1990), 93.

32. Jack Thomas, "Following the Beat of a Different Drum," *Boston Globe*, August 21, 1991, 46.

33. Don Shewey, *In Defense of the Men's Movement* (St. Paul: Ally Press, 1992), 15–16.

34. Susan Faludi, *Backlash: The Undeclared War against American Women* (New York: Crown, 1991), 310.

35. Gordon and Katz quoted in Jack Thomas, "The New Man: Finding Another Way to be Male," *Boston Globe*, August 21, 1991, 46.

36. Carol Bly, "The Danger in Men's Groups," *Utne Reader*, November/December 1989, 59.

37. Trip Gabriel, "Call of the Wildmen," *New York Times Magazine*, October 14, 1990, 39; Morrow, "The Child Is Father of the Man," 53.

38. One of Bly's followers is more explicit about the homophobic innuendo in Bly's assertion and maintains that "the women's movement" is "largely driven by lesbians." Chris Harding, quoted in Thomas, "The New Man: Finding Another Way to be Male," 46.

39. Warren Farrell, excerpt from *The Liberated Man*, in *The Forty-Nine Percent Majority*, ed. Deborah S. David and Robert Brannon (Reading, MA: Addison-Wesley, 1976), 51–55.

40. Connell, "Drumming Up the Wrong Tree," 32.

41. See Faludi, *Backlash*, 283–90.

42. George F. Gilder, *Sexual Suicide* (New York: Quadrangle/New York Times Book Co., 1973), 3. All further references will be noted in the text.

43. Fred Pfeil, *White Guys: Studies in Postmodern Domination and Difference* (London: Verso, 1995), 173.

44. For a fine analysis of gender politics during the height of the Cold War, see May, *Homeward Bound*, especially 68–75.

45. For an account of the economic discrimination against women during this period, see Mary P. Ryan, *Womanhood in America: From Colonial Times to the Present*, 2d ed. (New York: New View Points, 1979), 227–35.

46. Pfeil, *White Guys*, 174.

47. Ansen with Ames, "A Movie with All the Right Stuff," 39–41; Jack Kroll with Constance Guthrie and Janet Huck, "Who's That Tall, Dark Stranger?" *Newsweek*, November 11, 1985, 68; Richard Gilman, introduction to Sam Shepard, *Seven Plays* (New York: Bantam, 1984), xi; Robert Mazzocco, quoted in William Kleb, "Sam Shepard," in *American Playwrights since 1945: A Guide to Scholarship, Criticism and Performance*, ed. Philip C. Kolin (New York: Greenwood, 1989), 387.

48. Kleb, "Sam Shepard," 392.

49. See, for example, Kenneth Chubb and the Editors of *Theatre Quarterly*, "Metaphors, Mad Dogs and Old Time Cowboys," in *American Dreams: The Imagination of Sam Shepard*, ed. Bonnie Marranca (New York: Performing Arts Journal Publications, 1981), 187–209.

50. Don Shewey, *Sam Shepard* (New York: Dell, 1985), 43.

51. Kroll with Guthrie and Huck, "Who's That Tall, Dark Stranger?" 68.

52. Kevin Sessums, "Sam Shepard: Geography of a Horse Dreamer," *Interview*, September 1988, 71; and Blanche McCrary Boyd, in *Cosmopolitan*, quoted in Lynda Hart, "Sam Shepard's Pornographic Visions," *Studies in the Literary Imagination*, 21, no. 2 (Fall 1988): 73.

53. Carol Rosen, "Silent Tongues: Sam Shepard's Explorations of Emotional Territory," *Village Voice*, August 4, 1992, 35.

54. Michiko Kakutani, "Myths, Dreams, Realities—Sam Shepard's America," *New York Times*, January 29, 1984, sec. 2, 26.

55. Rosen, "Silent Tongues," 35–36.

56. Sam Shepard, *Mad Dog Blues*, in Shepard, *The Unseen Hand and Other Plays* (New York: Bantam, 1986), 257.

57. Mel Gussow, "Shepard's 'Suicide in B Flat' Presented by Yale Repertory," *New York Times*, October 25, 1976, 42; Martin Tucker, *Sam Shepard* (New York: Continuum, 1992), 108; Shewey, *Sam Shepard*, 111.

58. See especially, Tucker, *Sam Shepard*, 108–11.

59. Gussow, "Shepard's 'Suicide in B Flat,'" 42; Jack Kroll, "High-Pressure Jazz," *Newsweek*, November 8, 1976, 109.

60. Sam Shepard, *Suicide in B-Flat*, in Shepard, *Fool for Love and Other Plays* (New York: Bantam, 1984), 216. All further references will be noted in the text.

61. Sigmund Freud, *Beyond the Pleasure Principle*, ed. and trans. James Strachey (New York: Norton, 1961), 35.

62. J. Laplanche and J.-B. Pontalis, *The Language of Psychoanalysis*, trans. Donald Nicholson-Smith (New York: Norton, 1973), 97, 102. For an important elaboration of Freud's theory of the death instinct, see Jean Laplanche, *Life and Death in Psychoanalysis*, trans. Jeffrey Mehlman (Baltimore: Johns Hopkins University Press, 1976), 103–24.

63. Sigmund Freud, *Three Essays on the Theory of Sexuality*, ed. and trans. James Strachey (New York: Basic Books, 1962), 25.

64. Sigmund Freud, "The Economic Problem in Masochism" (1924), in *General Psychological Theory*, ed. Philip Rieff, trans. James Strachey (New York: Collier, 1963), 194.

65. Laura Mulvey, "Visual Pleasure and Narrative Cinema," *Screen* 16, no. 3 (Autumn 1975): 14.

66. Theodor Reik, *Masochism in Sex and Society*, trans. Margaret H. Beigel and Gertrud M. Kurth (New York: Grove, 1962), 49.

67. Ibid., 50.

68. Ibid., 77.

69. Ibid., 80.

70. Ibid., 78.

71. Ibid., 59.

72. Freud, "The Economic Problem in Masochism," 198–99.

73. Ibid., 193.

74. Kaja Silverman, *Male Subjectivity at the Margins* (New York: Routledge, 1992), 189.

75. Freud, *Three Essays on the Theory of Sexuality*, 25.

76. See, for example, the case histories in Reik, *Masochism in Sex and Society*, 50–51, 80.

77. Ibid., 49.

78. Shooter's self-contained narrative (based on a Sufi fable) of the moth and the candle in *Action* is merely a mystical revision of this master narrative. See Sam Shepard, *Action*, in *Fool for Love and Other Plays*, 185.

79. Judith Butler, *Subjects of Desire* (New York: Columbia University Press, 1987), 48.

80. Bonnie Marranca, "Alphabetical Shepard: The Play of Words," in *American Dreams: The Imagination of Sam Shepard*, 30. See also Florence Falk, "Men without Women: The Shepard Landscape," in *American Dreams*, 90–103; and Hart, "Sam Shepard's Pornographic Visions," 69–82.

81. Kakutani, "Myths, Dreams, Realities—Sam Shepard's America," 26.

82. Falk, "Men without Women," 97; Alan Shepard, "The Ominous 'Bulgarian' Threat in Sam Shepard's Plays," *Theatre Journal* 44, no. 1 (March 1992): 60.

83. Eve Kosofsky Sedgwick, *Between Men: English Literature and Male Homosocial Desire* (New York: Columbia University Press, 1985), 3.

84. Ibid., 86.

85. Ibid., 21.

86. Ibid., 21.

87. For a demonstration of homophobia in Shepard's writing, see Shepard, "The Ominous 'Bulgarian' Threat in Sam Shepard's Plays"; for an examination of the homophobic attitudes of the counterculture, see chapter 2.

88. Sam Shepard, *The Tooth of Crime*, in *Seven Plays*, 241, 236.

89. Rosen, "Silent Tongues," 36.

90. Sigmund Freud, "Instincts and Their Vicissitudes," in *The Complete Psychological Works of Sigmund Freud*, ed. James Strachey (London: Hogarth Press, 1957), 14:127–28.

91. Silverman, *Male Subjectivity at the Margins*, 327.

92. Laplanche and Pontalis, *The Language of Psychoanalysis*, 317.

93. Shepard, *Action*, in *Fool for Love and Other Plays*, 182, 190.

94. Shepard, *The Tooth of Crime* in *Seven Plays*, 247.

95. Reich, *Masochism in Sex and Society*, 177.

96. Silverman, *Male Subjectivity at the Margins*, 326.

97. Ryan, *Womanhood in America*, 227.

98. Ibid., 228.

99. "Statement by Chicago Women's Liberation" (February 1969), in *Sisterhood Is Powerful: An Anthology of Writings from the Women's Liberation Movement*, ed. Robin Morgan (New York: Vintage, 1970), 531.

100. Chafe, *The Unfinished Journey*, 434–36.

101. Faludi, *Backlash*, xvii; see also Ryan, *Womanhood in America*, 235.

102. Allan Nevins and Henry Steele Commager, *A Pocket History of the United States*, 9th ed. (New York: Pocket Books, 1992), 569.

103. Chafe, *The Unfinished Journey*, 447–49.

104. Ibid., 438.

105. Ibid.

106. Lawrence S. Wittner, *Cold War America: From Hiroshima to Watergate* (New York: Praeger, 1974), 314.

107. See James F. Scott, "Brown and Bakke: The Relation between Judicial Decisions and Socioeconomic Conditions," *Phylon* 41, no. 3 (1980): 240–46.

108. "How the Justices Disagreed," *Time*, July 10, 1978, 10.

109. Quoted in "Bakke Wins, Quotas Lose," *Time*, July 10, 1978, 15.

110. Robert L. Allen, "The Bakke Case and Affirmative Action," *Black Scholar*, September 1977, 9.

111. Kevin P. Phillips, Letter to the *Atlantic*, January 1979, 77.

112. Allen, "The Bakke Case and Affirmative Action," 11.

113. For an analysis of this change, see Fredric Jameson, "Periodizing the '60s," in *The Ideologies of Theory: Essays 1971–1986*, vol. 2, *The Syntax of History* (Minneapolis: University of Minnesota Press, 1988), 178–208.

114. Ibid., 185.

115. Jerrold M. Starr, "The Peace and Love Generation: Changing Attitudes toward Sex and Violence among College Youth," *Journal of Social Issues* 30, no. 2 (1974): 80.

116. Tom Wolfe, *The Right Stuff* (New York: Farrar, Straus, Giroux, 1979), 24, 28.

117. Connell, "Drumming Up the Wrong Tree," 32.

118. The word "homosexual" is, of course, an invention of the late nineteenth century. And it is impossible to gauge how "gay" men might have been understood before that time since the category did not exist. Sodomites, however, were by no means simply a benign part of "the large community of men." See David M. Halperin, "One Hundred Years of Homosexuality," in *One Hundred Years of Homosexuality and Other Essays on Greek Love* (New York: Routledge, 1990), 15–40; and *Reclaiming Sodom*, ed. Jonathan Goldberg (New York: Routledge, 1994).

119. See Teresa de Lauretis, *Alice Doesn't: Feminism, Semiotics, Cinema* (Bloomington: Indiana University Press, 1984), 103–57.

120. Don Shewey, "Stepbrothers: Gays and the Men's Movement," *Sun*, May 1993, 5, 7.

121. Judith Butler, *Bodies That Matter: On the Discursive Limits of "Sex"* (New York: Routledge, 1993), 3.

122. Shewey, "Stepbrothers," 7.

123. See Don Shewey, "Building Bridges at Buffalo Gap," *Common Boundary*, September/October 1992, 23–31.

124. "We don't like what is going on now, and we do know we don't have any

future. As social power decreases faster and faster, state power increases faster and faster. And we see ourselves, if you will pardon the expression, as the new niggers." Quoted in Raphael S. Ezekiel, *The Racist Mind: Portraits of American Neo-Nazis and Klansmen* (New York: Viking, 1995), 72.

125. Richard Zoglin, "An Outbreak of Rambomania," *Time*, June 24, 1985, 72–73.

126. Yvonne Tasker, "Dumb Movies for Dumb People: Masculinity, the Body, and the Voice in Contemporary Action Cinema," in *Screening the Male: Exploring Masculinities in Hollywood Cinema*, ed. Steven Cohan and Ina Rae Hark (London: Routledge, 1993), 234.

127. Susan Jeffords, *Hard Bodies: Hollywood Masculinity in the Reagan Era* (New Brunswick, NJ: Rutgers University Press, 1994), 27.

128. Susan Jeffords, *The Remasculinization of America: Gender and the Vietnam War* (Bloomington: Indiana University Press, 1989), 129.

129. Ibid., 130. For an account of the differences, see 127–30.

130. David Denby, "Blood Simple," *New York*, June 3, 1985, 72; Jacques Lacan, "The Meaning of the Phallus," quoted in Chris Holmlund, "Masculinity as Multiple Masquerade: The 'Mature' Stallone and the Stallone Clone," in Cohan and Hark, *Screening the Male*, 217, 222.

131. Mulvey, "Visual Pleasure and Narrative Cinema," 9.

132. Ibid., 14.

133. Barbara Creed, "From Here to Modernity: Feminism and Postmodernism," *Screen* 28, no. 2 (Spring 1987): 65.

134. Jeffords, "Can Masculinity Be Terminated?" 245.

135. According to Stallone, "Men . . . go out of their way sometimes to create catastrophe just to prove their mettle." Susan Faludi, "The Masculine Mystique," *Esquire*, December 1996, 91.

136. Pauline Kael, Review of *Rambo*, *New Yorker*, June 17, 1985, 117.

137. Charles Leerhsen, "Blood, Sweat and Cheers," *Newsweek*, June 3, 1985, 62.

138. Silverman, *Male Subjectivity at the Margins*, 326.

139. Leerhsen, "Blood, Sweat and Cheers," 62.

140. For an example of neoconservative support, see the appreciative review of *First Blood* in *Commentary* (Richard Grenier, "All Turkish, No Delight," *Commentary* 75, no. 1 [January 1983]: 62–63).

141. Kael, Review of *Rambo*, 117

142. Jeffords, *The Remasculinization of America*, 13; see also Steve Neale, "Masculinity as Spectacle: Reflections on Men and Mainstream Cinema," in Cohan and Hark, *Screening the Male*, 14. I would amend Jeffords, however, by suggesting that sadomasochism represents not a displacement of eroticism but the working out of an underlying structure of desire. For Jeffords's position differs from Mulvey's (and mine) by seeming to regard sadomasochism as a displacement of desire rather than as a libidinal logic in its own right. Mulvey, on the other hand, argues that the masculinized gaze is by definition both sadistic and desiring.

143. See Janet Bergstrom, "Enunciation and Sexual Difference (Part One)," *Camera Obscura*, nos. 3–4 (Summer 1979): 58.

144. It is hard to believe that David Morrell, in naming his protagonist, was completely unaware of the patterns of desire and abjection produced in Rimbaud's poetry.

For an examination of Rimbaud's sadomasochistic predispositions (as well as his homosexual relationship with Verlaine), see Paul Schmidt, "Visions of Violence: Rimbaud and Verlaine," in *Homosexualities and French Literature*, ed. George Stambolian and Elaine Marks (Ithaca: Cornell University Press, 1979), 228–42.

145. Michael Rogin, " 'Make My Day!': Spectacle as Amnesia in Imperial Politics," *Representations* 29 (Winter 1990): 114.

146. Just as the new, white masculinity that emerged during the 1970s represents a reactionary development of the more feminine countercultural masculinities of the 1960s, so does poststructuralism to some extent represent a retrenchment on the part of the Left in the wake of the collapse of mass-movement politics and the anticolonialist struggles for national liberation. Accordingly, I agree with Aijaz Ahmad that "dominant strands within . . . 'theory,' as it has unfolded *after* the movements of the 1960s were essentially over, have been mobilized to domesticate, in institutional ways, the very forms of political dissent which those movements had sought to foreground, to displace an activist culture with a textual culture, . . . and to reformulate in a postmodernist direction questions which had previously been associated with a broadly Marxist politics" (Aijaz Ahmad, *In Theory: Classes, Nations, Literatures* [London: Verso, 1992], 1). As examples of these "dominant strands," see Catherine Belsey, *Critical Practice* (London: Routledge, 1980); Gilles Deleuze and Félix Guattari, *Anti-Oedipus: Capitalism and Schizophrenia*, trans. Robert Hurley, Mark Seem, and Helen R. Lane (New York: Viking, 1977); Jill Dolan, *The Feminist Spectator as Critic* (Ann Arbor: University of Michigan Press, 1990); and Ernesto Laclau and Chantal Mouffe, *Hegemony and Socialist Strategy: Toward a Radical Democratic Politics* (London: Verso, 1985).

147. Silverman, *Male Subjectivity at the Margins*, 328, 1.

148. Leo Bersani, *The Freudian Body: Psychoanalysis and Art* (New York: Columbia University Press, 1986), 38–39. See also Leo Bersani, *Homos* (Cambridge: Harvard University Press, 1995).

149. Robert D. Stolorow, "The Narcissistic Function of Masochism (and Sadism)," *International Journal of Psycho-Analysis* 56 (1975): 441–46.

150. Freud, *Three Essays on the Theory of Sexuality*, 25.

151. Reik, *Masochism in Sex and Society*, 156.

152. Liz Kotz, "The Body You Want: Liz Kotz Interviews Judith Butler," *Artforum*, November 1992, 88.

153. Paul Smith, "Eastwood Bound," in *Constructing Masculinity*, ed. Maurice Berger, Brian Wallis, and Simon Watson (New York: Routledge, 1995), 91.

154. Ellis Cose, "To the Victors, Few Spoils," *Newsweek*, March 29, 1993, 54.

155. Quoted in David Gates, "White Male Paranoia," *Newsweek*, March 29, 1993, 51.

156. Quoted in ibid., 50.

157. Gates, "White Male Paranoia," 49.

158. Cose, "To the Victors, Few Spoils," 54.

159. See, for example, John Kifner, "Bomb Suspect Felt at Home Riding the Gun-Show Circuit," *New York Times*, July 5, 1995, A1+.

160. Faludi, *Backlash*, 65–70.

161. Ibid., 65.

162. Bradsher, "Gap in Wealth in U.S. Called Widest in West," A1, D4.

163. Chip Berlet and Matthew N. Lyons, "Militia Nation," *Progressive*, June 1995, 24.

164. J. Hoberman, "Victim Victorious: Well-Fed Yuppie Michael Douglas Leads the Charge for Resentful White Men," *Village Voice*, March 7, 1995, 32–33.

165. Pfeil, *White Guys*, 239.

166. For a fine close reading of this scene, see ibid., 240–41.

167. Ibid., 241.

168. My thanks to Kerry Quinn for her insights into *Falling Down*'s relationship to commodity culture.

169. Kifner, "Bomb Suspect Felt at Home Riding the Gun-Show Circuit," A18–19.

170. Patrick J. Buchanan, *Right from the Beginning* (Washington: Regnery Gateway, 1990), 25, 75.

CHAPTER FOUR
QUEER MASCULINITIES

1. David Ansen, "Hell Bent for Leather," *Newsweek*, February 18, 1980, 92.

2. Arthur Bell, "Bell Tells," *Village Voice*, July 30, 1979, 36.

3. Vito Russo, " 'Cruising': The Controversy Continues," *New York*, August 13–20, 1979, 46.

4. "Protesters Call the Film 'Cruising' Antihomosexual," *New York Times*, July 26, 1979, B7; Les Ledbetter, "1,000 in 'Village' Renew Protest against Movie on Homosexuals," *New York Times*, July 27, 1979, B2.

5. Ansen, "Hell Bent for Leather," 92.

6. Martin P. Levine, "The Life and Death of Gay Clones," in *Gay Culture in America*, ed. Gilbert Herdt (Boston: Beacon, 1992), 69–70.

7. The disclaimer: "This film is not intended as an indictment of the homosexual world. It is set in one small segment of that world which is not meant to be representative of the whole."

8. Leo Bersani, *The Freudian Body: Psychoanalysis and Art* (New York: Columbia University Press, 1986), 39.

9. John Stoltenberg in "Forum on Sadomasochism," in *Lavender Culture*, ed. Karla Jay and Allen Young (New York: Jove/Harcourt Brace Jovanovitch, 1978), 92.

10. Sally Roesch Wagner, "Pornography and the Sexual Revolution: The Backlash of Sadomasochism," in *Against Sadomasochism: A Radical Feminist Analysis*, ed. Robin Ruth Linden, Darlene R. Pagano, Diana E. H. Russell, and Susan Leigh Star (San Francisco: Frog in the Well, 1982), 30.

11. See, for example, Robin Morgan, "The Politics of Sado-Masochistic Fantasies," and Sarah Lucia Hoagland, "Sadism, Masochism, and Lesbian-Feminism," both in Linden et al., *Against Sadomasochism*, 112, 160.

12. See, for example Vivienne Walker-Crawford, "The Saga of Sadie O. Massey," in Linden et al., *Against Sadomasochism*, 147–51.

13. For an excellent critique of anti-S/M feminism, see Gayle Rubin, "The Leather Menace: Comments on Politics and S/M," in *Coming to Power: Writings and Graphics on Lesbian S/M*, ed. SAMOIS (Boston: Alyson, 1981; rev. ed. 1987), 194–229.

14. See *Sex Exposed: Sexuality and the Pornography Debate*, ed. Lynne Segal and Mary McIntosh (New Brunswick, NJ: Rutgers University Press), 1993.

15. See Rubin, "The Leather Menace," 194–210.

16. Ibid., 222. This is confirmed by Dennis Altman, who writes that S/M became linked "symbolically . . . with male homosexuality in the eighties as firmly as effeminacy . . . was in the sixties and early seventies." Dennis Altman, *The Homosexualization of America* (Boston: Beacon Press, 1983), 191.

17. Roger Angell, "The Current Cinema," *New Yorker*, February 18, 1980, 126; Robert Hatch, "Films," *Nation*, February 23, 1980, 218; *Progressive*, May 1980, 54.

18. Seymour Kleinberg, "Where Have All the Sissies Gone?" *Christopher Street* 2, no. 9 (March 1978): 6–7.

19. Jeffrey Weeks, *Sexuality and Its Discontents: Meanings, Myths and Modern Sexualities* (London: Routledge, 1985), 236–37; Altman, *The Homosexualization of America*, 190.

20. Altman, *The Homosexualization of America*, 192.

21. Wickie Stamps, "S&M Girls: Ungagging Dyke Sex," *Outweek*, March 31, 1991, 41.

22. Tina Portillo, "I Get Real: Celebrating My Sadomasochistic Soul," and Pat Califia, "The Limits of the S/M Relationship, or Mr. Benson Doesn't Live Here Anymore," in *Leatherfolk: Radical Sex, People, Politics, and Practice*, ed. Mark Thompson (Boston: Alyson, 1991), 55, 230.

23. Scott Tucker, "The Hanged Man," in *Leatherfolk*, 12.

24. Mark Thompson, introduction, and Michael Bronski, "A Dream Is a Wish Your Heart Makes: Notes on the Materialization of Sexual Fantasy," both in *Leatherfolk*, xvi, 64.

25. John Preston, "What Happened?" in *Leatherfolk*, 214–15.

26. Michael Bronski, "The Mainstreaming of S&M: From Leather to Lifestyle, from Fetish to Fashion," *Outweek*, March 13, 1991, 37.

27. Preston, "What Happened?" 211.

28. David Stein, "S/M's Copernican Revolution: From a Closed World to the Infinite Universe," in *Leatherfolk*, 153.

29. Ibid., 154; Bronski, "The Mainstreaming of S&M," 37. The emphasis is Bronski's.

30. John Preston, in *Flesh and the Word: An Anthology of Erotic Writing*, ed. John Preston (New York: Plume, 1992), 59.

31. Aaron Travis, "Blue Light," in *The Flesh Fables* (Norwalk: Fire Island Press, 1990), 14. All further references will be noted in the text. The story is also available in Preston, *Flesh and the Word*, 125–57.

32. Theodor Reik, *Masochism in Sex and Society*, trans. Margaret H. Beigel and Gertrud M. Kurth (New York: Grove, 1962), 77.

33. Pat Califia, *Sensual Magic* (New York: Masquerade Books, 1993), 151.

34. Sigmund Freud, "The Economic Problem in Masochism," in *General Psychological Theory*, ed. Philip Rieff (New York: Collier, 1963), 193.

35. Reik, *Masochism in Sex and Society*, 59.

36. Kaja Silverman, *Male Subjectivity at the Margins* (New York: Routledge, 1992), 206.

37. Liz Kotz, "The Body You Want: Liz Kotz Interviews Judith Butler," *Artforum*, November 1992, 88; Silverman, *Male Subjectivity at the Margins*, 190.

38. Kotz, "The Body You Want," 88.

39. Leo Bersani, *Homos* (Cambridge: Harvard University Press, 1995), 103.

40. Larry Townsend, *The Leatherman's Handbook II*, 3d ed. (New York: Carlyle Communications, 1993), 87.

41. Sigmund Freud, "Fetishism," in *Collected Papers*, ed. James Strachey (London: Hogarth Press, 1950), 5:199–200.

42. Kaja Silverman, "The Lacanian Phallus," *differences* 4, no. 1 (1992): 89.

43. Ibid., 89; Jacques Lacan, "The Subversion of the Subject and the Dialectic of Desire in the Freudian Unconscious," in *Ecrits: A Selection*, trans. Alan Sheridan (New York: Norton, 1977), 319.

44. Elizabeth Grosz, *Jacques Lacan: A Feminist Introduction* (London: Routledge, 1990), 119.

45. Silverman, "The Lacanian Phallus," 92–93.

46. Freud, "Fetishism," 199; Elizabeth Grosz, "Lesbian Fetishism?" in *Fetishism as Cultural Discourse*, ed. Emily Apter and William Pietz (Ithaca: Cornell University Press, 1993), 105.

47. Judith Butler, "The Lesbian Phallus and the Morphological Imaginary," in *Bodies That Matter: On the Discursive Limits of "Sex"* (New York: Routledge, 1993), 83–84.

48. Lacan, "The Subversion of the Subject and the Dialectic of Desire," 320.

49. Sigmund Freud, *Three Essays on the Theory of Sexuality*, ed. and trans. James Strachey (New York: Basic Books, 1962), 25. In fact, if one accepts Deleuze's critique of the complementarity of sadism and masochism, what Freud seems to be describing here is more the emblematic masochistic scene in which the so-called sadist is in fact acceding to the fantasies of the masochist. Thus Deleuze distinguishes between the sadist of sadism and the sadist of masochism: "The woman torturer of masochism cannot be sadistic precisely because she is in the masochistic situation, she is an integral part of it, a realization of the masochistic fantasy." Gilles Deleuze, *Coldness and Cruelty* in *Masochism: Coldness and Cruelty, Venus in Furs*, trans. Jean McNeil (New York: Zone Books, 1991), 41. Deleuze argues that sadism and masochism are not complementary since the masochistic sadist (unlike the true sadist) does not really want to destroy the bottom. This distinction between the two kinds of sadist seems to me to be particularly useful for analyzing what usually is called S/M.

50. Townsend, *The Leatherman's Handbook II*, 15.

51. Pat Califia writes that "[w]hen a strong connection exists between top and bottom, the top undergoes an ecstatic experience that is partly made up of a vicarious version of the bottom's trip and is partly the top's independent experience." "The Limits of the S/M Relationship," 225.

52. Robert D. Stolorow, "The Narcissistic Function of Masochism (and Sadism)," *International Journal of Psycho-Analysis* 56 (1975): 441–43.

53. Bronski, "A Dream Is a Wish Your Heart Makes"; Robert H. Hopcke, "S/M and the Psychology of Gay Male Initiation: An Archetypal Perspective," in *Leatherfolk*, 61, 71.

54. Tucker, "The Hanged Man," 7.

55. Califia, "The Limits of the S/M Relationship," 231.

56. "A Masochist," in George Stambolian, *Male Fantasies / Gay Realities: Interviews with Ten Men* (New York: The SeaHorse Press, 1984), 8.

57. Townsend, *The Leatherman's Handbook II*, 76.

58. See Gayle Rubin, "Thinking Sex," in *The Lesbian and Gay Studies Reader*, ed. Henry Abelove, Michèle Aina Barale, and David M. Halperin (New York: Routledge, 1993), 3–44.

59. Wickie Stamps distinguishes among three different groups of S/M lesbians: lesbian separatists; those involved with the gay male S/M community; and "members of co-gender clubs" who "have a lot of contact with heterosexual men." See Stamps, "S&M Girls," 39.

60. Juicy Lucy, "If I Ask You to Tie Me Up, Will You Still Want to Love Me?" in *Coming to Power*, 38.

61. Susan Farr, "The Art of Discipline: Creating Erotic Dramas of Play and Power," and Kitt, "Taking the Sting Out of S/M," both in *Coming to Power*, 183, 62.

62. Butler, "The Lesbian Phallus," 84.

63. See Rubin, "The Leather Menace," 216–18; Butler, "The Lesbian Phallus," 85.

64. Butler, "The Lesbian Phallus," 85–86.

65. Ibid., 88–89.

66. Stamps, "S&M Girls," 40; Juicy Lucy, "If I Ask You to Tie Me Up," 30.

67. Butler, "The Lesbian Phallus," 86.

68. Pat Califia, "The Calyx of Isis," in *Macho Sluts* (Boston: Alyson, 1988), 86.

69. Ibid., 120.

70. Ibid., 120, 129.

71. Ibid., 123, 95, 122.

72. Pat Califia, "Daddy," in *Melting Point* (Boston: Alyson, 1993), 76.

73. Donna Minkowitz, "Daddy Is a Dyke," *Village Voice*, June 28, 1994, 31.

74. See Sigmund Freud, "'A Child Is Being Beaten,'" in *Sexuality and the Psychology of Love*, ed. Philip Rieff, trans. James Strachey (New York: Collier, 1963), 107–32.

75. Dyke Daddy Jo Leroux, quoted in Minkowitz, "Daddy Is a Dyke," 31.

76. "And here it should be clear that the lesbian phallus crosses the orders of *having* and *being*; it both wields the threat of castration (which is in that sense a mode of 'being' the phallus, as women 'are') and suffers from castration anxiety (and so is said 'to have' the phallus, and to fear its loss)." Butler, "The Lesbian Phallus," 84.

77. Preston, "What Happened?" 220.

78. Mark Thompson, "Black Leather Wings," in *Leatherfolk*, 158.

79. Ibid., 162; Preston, "What Happened?" 218.

80. Samuel M. Steward, "Dr. Kinsey Takes a Peek at S/M: A Reminiscence," in *Leatherfolk*, 84.

81. Preston, "What Happened?" 217.

82. Thompson, introduction, to *Leatherfolk*, xv. See also Elaine Tyler May, *Homeward Bound: American Families in the Cold War Era* (New York: Basic Books, 1988).

83. Bronski, "A Dream Is a Wish Your Heart Makes," 58.

84. See Vito Russo, *The Celluloid Closet: Homosexuality in the Movies* (New York: Harper & Row, 1981), 238.

85. Bronski, "A Dream Is a Wish Your Heart Makes," 62.

86. *Gay and Lesbian Stats: A Pocket Guide of Facts and Figures*, ed. Bennett L. Singer and David Deschamps (New York: The New Press, 1994), 32.

87. Townsend, *The Leatherman's Handbook II*, 346.

88. "Crown of Thorns" is in Travis, *The Flesh Fables*, 102–36.

89. For a psychological study of this process, see Roy F. Baumeister, "Masochism as Escape from Self," *Journal of Sex Research* 25, no. 1 (February 1988): 28–59.

90. Townsend, *The Leatherman's Handbook II*, 351.

91. Preston, "What Happened?" 212–13.

92. For an assessment of the queer politics of the early '90s, see Lisa Duggan, "Making It Perfectly Queer," *Socialist Review*, Spring 1992, 11–31. For a provocative analysis of Queer Nation specifically, see Lauren Berlant and Elizabeth Freeman, "Queer Nationality," in *Fear of a Queer Planet: Queer Politics and Social Theory*, ed. Michael Warner (Minneapolis: University of Minnesota Press, 1993), 193–229.

93. Abbie Hoffman, from *Revolution for the Hell of It*, in *The Sixties Papers: Documents of a Rebellious Decade*, ed. Judith Clavir Albert and Stewart Edward Albert (New York: Praeger, 1984), 421.

94. See Stein, "S/M's Copernican Revolution," 142–56.

95. Tucker, "The Hanged Man," 11.

96. See Michelangelo Signorile, "Clone Wars," *Outweek*, November 28, 1990, 39–45.

97. See, for example, Jonathan Dollimore's concept of transgressive reinscription, *Sexual Dissidence: Augustine to Wilde, Freud to Foucault* (Oxford: Clarendon Press, 1991), or Kobena Mercer's rereading of Mapplethorpe's photographs of black men as "a subversive recoding." Mercer, *Welcome to the Jungle: New Positions in Black Cultural Studies* (New York: 1994), 199.

98. Bersani, *Homos*, 51.

99. Bronski, "A Dream Is a Wish Your Heart Makes," 62.

CHAPTER FIVE
MAN AND NATION

1. "Transcript of President Bush's Address on the State of the Union," *New York Times*, January 29, 1992, A17.

2. See Michael T. Klare, *Rogue States and Nuclear Outlaws: America's Search for a New Foreign Policy* (New York: Hill and Wang, 1995).

3. Deutch quoted in Brian Knowlton, "CIA Chief Predicts Surge in Terrorism," *International Herald Tribune*, December 20, 1995, 1.

4. Paul Piccone, "The Crisis of Liberalism and the Emergence of Federal Populism," *Telos* 89 (Fall 1991): 9.

5. "Transcript of President Bush's Address on the State of the Union," *New York Times*, January 29, 1992, A17.

6. Ibid., A16.

7. "Transcript of Bush's State of the Union Message to the Nation," *New York Times*, February 1, 1990, D22; "Transcript of Bush's State of the Union Message to the Nation," *New York Times*, January 30, 1991, A12; "Transcript of President Bush's Address on the State of the Union," *New York Times*, January 29, 1992, A16.

8. "Transcript of Bush's State of the Union Message to the Nation," *New York Times*, January 30, 1991, A12.

9. Tony Kushner, *Angels in America: A Gay Fantasia on National Themes. Part Two: Perestroika* (New York: Theatre Communications Group, 1994), 49. All further references will be cited in the text by part (2) and page number.

10. Joseph Roach has suggested to me that the closest analogue to *Angels* on the American stage is, in fact, *Uncle Tom's Cabin*, with its tremendous popularity before the Civil War, its epic length, and its skill in addressing the most controversial issues of the time in deeply equivocal ways.

11. John Lahr, "The Theatre: Earth Angels," *New Yorker*, December 13, 1993, 133.

12. Jack Kroll, "Heaven and Earth on Broadway," *Newsweek*, December 6, 1993, 83.

13. Robert Brustein, "Robert Brustein on Theatre: *Angels in America*," *New Republic*, May 24, 1993, 29.

14. John E. Harris, "Miracle on 48th Street," *Christopher Street*, March 1994, 6.

15. Frank Rich, "Critic's Notebook: The Reaganite Ethos, with Roy Cohn as a Dark Metaphor," *New York Times*, March 5, 1992, C15.

16. John Clum, *Acting Gay: Male Homosexuality in Modern Drama* (New York: Columbia University Press, 1994), 324.

17. Tony Kushner, *Angels in America: A Gay Fantasia on National Themes. Part One: Millennium Approaches* (New York: Theatre Communications Group, 1993), 95. All further references will be cited in the text by part (1) and page number.

18. Frank Rich, "Following an Angel for a Healing Vision of Heaven and Earth," *New York Times*, November 24, 1993, C11.

19. Clum, *Acting Gay*, 314.

20. See, for example, Andrea Stevens, "Finding a Devil Within to Portray Roy Cohn," *New York Times*, April 18, 1993, sec. 2, 1–28.

21. Raymond Williams, *Modern Tragedy* (Stanford: Stanford University Press, 1966), 87. For my analysis of the persistence of this form in modern drama, especially in the work of Arthur Miller, see *Communists, Cowboys and Queers: The Politics of Masculinity in the Work of Arthur Miller and Tennessee Williams* (Minneapolis: University of Minnesota Press, 1992), 29–33.

22. Williams, *Modern Tragedy*, 98. In most versions of liberal tragedy, the hero is male or, in the case of *Hedda Gabler*, masculinized. Yet there are exceptions to this formula, even in Ibsen (most notably Nora). And although liberal tragedy has also served as the structural formula for allegedy feminist plays (like *The Heidi Chronicles*), it has been connected historically to male subjectivities.

23. David Savran, interview with Tony Kushner, in *Speaking on Stage: Interviews with Contemporary American Playwrights*, ed. Philip C. Kolin and Colby H. Kullman (Tuscaloosa: University of Alabama Press, 1996), 307.

24. Sigmund Freud, "The Economic Problem in Masochism," in *General Psychological Theory*, ed. Philip Rieff (New York: Collier, 1963), 193.

25. Tony Kushner, *Angels in America: Part Two: Perestroika*, manuscript dated May 7, 1991, 44–45.

26. Savran, interview with Tony Kushner, 308.

27. Freud, "The Economic Problem in Masochism," 199.

28. Savran, interview with Tony Kushner, 307.

29. "A hush fell over the audience; you could hear yourself breathing. Then, in a loud, phlegmy voice a man behind us said: 'I've never seen *that* before.' He started to say it again, for emphasis, but his wife must have muffled it with her scarf. . . ." Harris, "Miracle on 48th Street," 7.

30. Lahr, "The Theatre: Earth Angels," 132.

31. David Román, "November 1, 1992: AIDS/*Angels in America*," in *Acts of Intervention: Gay Men, U.S. Performance, AIDS* (forthcoming from Indiana University Press), 45–47 n. 33.

32. Savran, interview with Tony Kushner, 308.

33. Terry Eagleton, *Walter Benjamin, or Towards a Revolutionary Criticism* (London: Verso, 1981), 177.

34. Walter Benjamin, "Theses on the Philosophy of History," in *Illuminations*, ed. Hannah Arendt, trans. Harry Zohn (New York: Schocken Books, 1969), 253. All further references will be noted in the text.

35. Tony Kushner explains: "I've written about my friend Kimberly [Flynn] who is a profound influence on me. And she and I were talking about this utopian thing that we share—she's the person who introduced me to that side of Walter Benjamin. . . . She said jokingly that at times she felt such an extraordinary kinship with him that she thought she was Walter Benjamin reincarnated. And so at one point in the conversation, when I was coming up with names for my characters, I said, 'I had to look up something in Benjamin—not you, but the prior Walter.' That's where the name came from. I had been looking for one of those WASP names that nobody gets called anymore." Savran, interview with Tony Kushner, 305.

36. Jacques Lacan, "The Signification of the Phallus," in *Ecrits: A Selection*, trans. Alan Sheridan (New York: Norton, 1977), 286.

37. Elizabeth Grosz, *Jacques Lacan: A Feminist Introduction* (London: Routledge, 1990), 74, 67.

38. Benjamin maintained a far less condemnatory attitude toward the increasing technologization of culture than many other Western Marxists. In "The Work of Art in the Age of Mechanical Reproduction," for example, he writes of his qualified approval of the destruction of the aura associated with modern technologies. He explains that because "mechanical reproduction emancipates the work of art from its parasitical dependence on ritual, . . . the total function of art" can "be based on another practice—politics," which for him is clearly preferable. Benjamin, "The Work of Art in the Age of Mechanical Reproduction," in *Illuminations*, 224.

39. Although one could cite a myriad of sources, this quotation is extracted from Milton Friedman, "Once Again: Why Socialism Won't Work," *New York Times*, August 13, 1994, 21.

40. Krishan Kumar, "The End of Socialism? The End of Utopia? The End of History?" in *Utopias and the Millennium*, ed. Krishan Kumar and Stephen Bann (London: Reaktion Books, 1993), 61; Francis Fukuyama, *The End of History and the Last Man*, quoted in Kumar, "The End of Socialism?" 78.

41. Friedman, "Once Again: Why Socialism Won't Work," 21.

42. Aijaz Ahmad, *In Theory: Classes, Nations, Literatures* (London: Verso, 1992), 69. Ahmad is summarizing this position as part of his critique of poststructuralism.

43. David Richards, "'Angels' Finds a Poignant Note of Hope," *New York Times*, November 28, 1993, sec. 2, 1.

44. See Eve Kosofsky Sedgwick, *Epistemology of the Closet* (Berkeley and Los Angeles: University of California Press, 1990), 48–59.

45. It is not the people who constitute a bona fide suspect class (like African Americans) that are suspect, but rather the forces of oppression that produce the class. For an important analysis of the legal issues around equal protection, see Janet Halley, "The

Politics of the Closet: Towards Equal Protection for Gay, Lesbian, and Bisexual Identity," *UCLA Law Review* 36, no. 5 (June 1989): 915–76.

46. Major L. Wilson, *Space, Time and Freedom: The Quest for Nationality and the Irrepressible Conflict, 1815–1861* (Westport, CT: Greenwood Press, 1974), 4.

47. J. Hector St. John Crèvecoeur, *Letters from an American Farmer* (Garden City, NY: Dolphin Books, n.d.), 46.

48. Ralph Waldo Emerson, "The Young Americans," in *Manifest Destiny*, ed. Norman A. Graebner (Indianapolis: Bobbs-Merrill, 1968), 8.

49. Benedict Anderson, *Imagined Communities: Reflections on the Origin and Spread of Nationalism* (London: Verso, 1991), 6.

50. See Lawrence Kohl, *The Politics of Individualism: Parties and the American Character in the Jacksonian Era* (New York: Oxford University Press, 1989).

51. Frantz Fanon, *The Wretched of the Earth*, trans. Constance Farrington (New York: Grove Weidenfeld, 1968), 200.

52. Lauren Berlant, *The Anatomy of National Fantasy: Hawthorne, Utopia, and Everyday Life* (Chicago: University of Chicago Press, 1991), 20, 29.

53. Quoted in F. O. Matthiessen, *American Renaissance: Art and Expression in the Age of Emerson and Whitman* (London: Oxford University Press, 1941), 6.

54. Thomas Jefferson, quoted in Albert K. Weinberg, *Manifest Destiny: A Study of Nationalist Expansionism in American History* (Baltimore: Johns Hopkins University Press, 1935), 40.

55. Klaus J. Hansen, *Mormonism and the American Experience* (Chicago: University of Chicago Press, 1981), 46–47. Unlike the score of apologetic texts written by Mormons, Hansen's volume is the most rigorously historicized—and thus the most trustworthy—of all the accounts of Mormonism. It is the only one to look carefully at the development of the religion in terms of the ideologies of the National Period.

56. Myra Jehlen, *American Incarnation: The Individual, the Nation, and the Continent* (Cambridge: Harvard University Press, 1986), 13.

57. Anderson, *Imagined Communities*, 77.

58. Hansen, *Mormonism and the American Experience*, 49–50.

59. See Ernest R. Sandeen, *The Roots of Fundamentalism: British and American Millenarianism 1800–1930* (Chicago: University of Chicago Press, 1970), 42–58.

60. Hansen, *Mormonism and the American Experience*, 52.

61. *The Book of Mormon: An Account Written by the Hand of Mormon upon Plates Taken from the Earth*, trans. Joseph Smith (Salt Lake City: The Church of Jesus Christ of Latter-day Saints, 1977), n.p.

62. Fawn M. Brodie, *No Man Knows My History: The Life of Joseph Smith, the Mormon Prophet* (New York: Knopf, 1945).

63. Hansen, *Mormonism and the American Experience*, 55.

64. See Frederick Merk, *History of the Westward Movement* (New York: Knopf, 1978), 332.

65. *The Book of Mormon*, 1 Nephi, 12:23.

66. Hansen, *Mormonism and the American Experience*, 9.

67. Twain is cited in ibid., 10.

68. Thomas Hart Benton, "Speech on the Oregon Question: Delivered to the Senate of the United States May 22, 25, and 28, 1846," in *Manifest Destiny and the Imperialism Question*, ed. Charles L. Sanford (New York: John Wiley & Sons, 1974), 45.

69. Joseph Smith, quoted in Hansen, *Mormonism and the American Experience*, 72.

70. See Richard L. Bushman, *Joseph Smith and the Beginnings of Mormonism* (Urbana: University of Illinois Press, 1984), 170.

71. Hansen, *Mormonism and the American Experience*, 117–19.

72. For a catalog of this violence, see Jan Shipps, *Mormonism: The Story of a New Religious Tradition* (Urbana: University of Illinois Press, 1985), 155–61.

73. Hansen, *Mormonism and the American Experience*, 124–26.

74. Ibid., 27, 66.

75. Anderson, *Imagined Communities*, 10–11.

76. Timothy Brennan, "The National Longing for Form," in *Nation and Narration*, ed. Homi K. Bhabha (London: Routledge, 1990), 50.

77. Anderson, *Imagined Communities*, 10–11.

78. Hans Kohn, *Nationalism: Its Meaning and History* (Princeton: Van Nostrand, 1965), 11.

79. Sacvan Bercovitch, "The Problem of Ideology in American Literary History," *Critical Inquiry* 12 (Summer 1986): 642–43, 645.

80. John L. O'Sullivan, "The Great Nation of Futurity" (1839), in Graebner, *Manifest Destiny*, 17.

81. Leonard J. Arrington and Davis Bitton, *The Mormon Experience: A History of the Latter-day Saints* (New York: Knopf, 1979), 110.

82. Ibid., 96.

83. Shipps, *Mormonism*, 61.

84. John L. O'Sullivan, "Manifest Destiny," in Sanford, *Manifest Destiny and the Imperial Question*, 27. William Clayton, quoted in Arrington and Bitton, *The Mormon Experience*, 102.

85. Hazel Carby, "The Multicultural Wars," in *Black Popular Culture, a project by Michele Wallace*, ed. Gina Dent (Seattle: Bay Press, 1992), 197.

86. Bercovitch, "The Problem of Ideology in American Literary History," 649.

87. *The Book of Mormon*, 2 Nephi 2:11.

88. Berlant, *The Anatomy of National Fantasy*, 31.

89. Jehlen, *American Incarnation*, 82–83.

90. Barry Brummett, *Contemporary Apocalyptic Rhetoric* (New York: Praeger, 1991), 37–38.

91. This is corroborated by Kushner's own statements: "The strain in the American character that I feel the most affection for and that I feel has the most potential for growth is American liberalism, which is incredibly short of what it needs to be and incredibly limited and exclusionary and predicated on all sorts of racist, sexist, homophobic and classist prerogatives. And yet, as Louis asks, why has democracy succeeded in America? And why does it have this potential, as I believe it does? I really believe that there is the potential for radical democracy in this country, one of the few places on earth where I see it as a strong possibility. It doesn't seem to be happening in Russia. There is a tradition of liberalism, of a kind of social justice, fair play and tolerance—and each of these things is problematic and can certainly be played upon in the most horrid ways. Reagan kept the most hair-raising anarchist aspects of his agenda hidden and presented himself as a good old-fashioned liberal who kept invoking FDR. It may just be sentimentalism on my part because I am the child of liberal-pinko parents, but I do believe in it—as much as I often find it despicable. It's sort of like the Democratic

National Convention every four years: it's horrendous and you can feel it sucking all the energy from progressive movements in this country, with everybody pinning their hopes on this sleazy bunch of guys. But you do have Jesse Jackson getting up and calling the Virgin Mary a single mother, and on an emotional level, and I hope also on a more practical level, I do believe that these are the people in whom to have hope." Savran, interview with Tony Kushner, 305–6.

92. See Tony Kushner, "A Socialism of the Skin," *Nation*, July 4, 1994, 9–14.

93. Berlant, *The Anatomy of National Fantasy*, 32.

94. Bercovitch, "The Problem of Ideology in American Literary History," 644.

95. Hansen, *Mormonism and the American Experience*, 126.

96. Amy Kaplan, " 'Left Alone with America': The Absence of Empire in the Study of American Culture," in *Cultures of United States Imperialism*, ed. Amy Kaplan and Donald E. Pease (Durham: Duke University Press, 1993), 16.

97. Sedgwick used this phrase during the question period that followed a lecture at Brown University, October 1992.

98. Barbara Janowitz, "Theatre Facts 93," insert in *American Theatre*, April 1994, 4–5.

99. Pierre Bourdieu, "The Field of Cultural Production, or: The Economic World Reversed," in *The Field of Cultural Production: Essays on Art and Literature*, ed. Randal Johnson (New York: Columbia University Press, 1993), 37–38.

100. Editor's introduction to Bourdieu, *The Field of Cultural Production: Essays on Art and Literature*, 15.

101. *Gay and Lesbian Stats: A Pocket Guide of Facts and Figures*, ed. Bennett L. Singer and David Deschamps (New York: The New Press, 1994), 32.

102. Bourdieu, "The Production of Belief: Contribution to an Economy of Symbolic Goods," in *The Field of Cultural Production: Essays on Art and Literature*, 83–84.

103. Bercovitch, "The Problem of Ideology in American Literary History," 645.

104. Donald E. Pease, "New Americanists: Revisionist Interventions into the Canon," *boundary 2* 17, no. 1 (1990): 23. This essay provides an important critique of Bercovitch.

105. Michel Foucault, *The History of Sexuality*, vol. 1, *An Introduction*, trans. Robert Hurley (New York: Vintage, 1980), 96.

106. Guy Trebay, "In Your Face!" *Village Voice*, August 14, 1990, 34.

107. For a résumé of the characteristics of the new social movements, see Joshua Gamson, "Silence, Death, and the Invisible Enemy: AIDS Activism and Social Movement 'Newness,' " in *Ethnography Unbound: Power and Resistance in the Modern Metropolis* (Berkeley and Los Angeles: University of California Press, 1991), 37–38.

108. Peggy Sue, in "Queer," interviews by Steve Cosson, *Out/look*, no. 11 (Winter 1991): 20.

109. Henry Abelove, "From Thoreau to Queer Politics," *Yale Journal of Criticism* 6, no. 2 (1993): 25.

110. Allan Bérubé and Jeffrey Escoffier, "Queer/Nation," *Out/look*, no. 11 (Winter 1991): 12–14.

111. Lauren Berlant and Elizabeth Freeman, "Queer Nationality," in *Fear of a Queer Planet: Queer Politics and Social Theory*, ed. Michael Warner (Minneapolis: University of Minnesota Press, 1993), 196.

112. Esther Kaplan, "A Queer Manifesto," in Trebay, "In Your Face!" 36.

113. Bérubé and Escoffier, "Queer/Nation," 12.

114. See Henry Abelove, "The Queering of Lesbian/Gay History," *Radical History Review* 62 (1995): 44–57, and Rosemary Hennessy, "Queer Visibility in Commodity Culture," *Cultural Critique* 29 (Winter 1994–95): 31–76.

115. Eve Kosofsky Sedgwick, *Tendencies* (Durham: Duke University Press, 1993), 8.

116. See in particular, Maria Maggenti, "Women as Queer Nationals," *Out/look*, no. 11 (Winter 1991): 20–23 and Trebay, "In Your Face!" 37–39.

117. Berlant and Freeman, "Queer Nationality," 197.

118. See Bourdieu, "The Field of Cultural Production, or: The Economic World Reversed," 29–73.

119. Neil Lazarus, "Disavowing Decolonization: Fanon, Nationalism, and the Problematic of Representation in Current Theories of Colonial Discourse," *Research in African Literatures* 24, no. 4 (Winter 1993): 69.

120. Anderson, *Imagined Communities*, 2.

121. Ahmad, *In Theory*, 32.

122. See Lazarus, "Disavowing Decolonization" and Brennan, "The National Longing for Form."

123. Ahmad, *In Theory*, 38.

124. See Fanon, *The Wretched of the Earth*, 213–14.

125. Ibid., 36.

126. Ibid., 197.

127. Frantz Fanon, *Black Skin, White Masks*, trans. Charles Lam Markmann (New York: Grove, 1967), 197.

128. Brennan, "The National Longing for Form," 52.

129. Jason Bishop, in "Queer," interviews by Steve Cosson, 16.

130. Stokely Carmichael and Charles V. Hamilton, *Black Power: The Politics of Liberation in America* (New York: Vintage, 1967), 5–6.

131. Kobena Mercer, "Skin Head Sex Thing: Racial Difference and the Homoerotic Imaginary," in *How Do I Look? Queer Film and Video*, ed. Bad Object-Choices (Seattle: Bay Press, 1991), 201.

132. Jehlen, *American Incarnation*, 9.

133. Oscar Wilde, "The Soul of Man under Socialism," in *Intentions and Other Writings* (Garden City, NY: Dolphin Books, n.d.), 207.

134. Fanon, *The Wretched of the Earth*, 210.

135. Monique Wittig, "The Point of View: Universal or Particular?" in *The Straight Mind and Other Essays* (Boston: Beacon Press, 1992), 61–62.

136. Fanon, *The Wretched of the Earth*, 247–48 (emphasis added).

137. Gayatri Chakravorty Spivak, "Subaltern Studies: Deconstructing Historiography," in *In Other Worlds: Essays in Cultural Politics* (New York: Routledge, 1988), 207.

138. Wendy Brown, "Wounded Attachments: Late Modern Oppositional Political Formations," in *The Identity in Question*, ed. John Rajchman (New York: Routledge, 1995), 202.

139. Ibid., 206–7.

140. Elisa Glick, "Genderfuck and Other Fashionable Utopias: Challenging the Politics of Pro-Sexuality" (unpublished manuscript, 1994), 13.

141. Keith Bradsher, "Gap in Wealth in U.S. Called Widest in West," *New York Times*, April 17, 1995, 1.

142. Hennessy, "Queer Visibility in Commodity Culture," 58.

143. Ahmad, *In Theory*, 316–18.

144. Mikhail Gorbachev, *Perestroika: New Thinking for Our Country and the World* (New York: Harper & Row, 1987), 37.

145. Ibid., 17–18.

146. Lazarus, "Disavowing Decolonization," 93.

147. Ahmad, *In Theory*, 327 n. 36.

148. Fanon, *The Wretched of the Earth*, 314.

CHAPTER SIX
THE WILL TO BELIEVE

1. Tom Harpur, quoted in Marci McDonald, "The New Spirituality," *Maclean's*, October 10, 1994, 45. McDonald estimates that North Americans spent $35 billion (U.S.) in 1993 on what she calls "self-development" (46).

2. Eugene Taylor, "Desperately Seeking Spirituality," *Psychology Today*, November/December 1994, 56.

3. Mary C. Hickey and Lynn Langway, "Supertrends," *Ladies Home Journal*, November 1995, 204.

4. McDonald, "The New Spirituality," 45; Taylor, "Desperately Seeking Spirituality," 56.

5. William Irwin Thompson, quoted in McDonald, "The New Spirituality," 46.

6. See, for example, Taylor, "Desperately Seeking Spirituality," 57.

7. Ibid., 68.

8. Ibid., 58.

9. See, for example, Bob McCullough, "The New Spin Is Spirituality," *Publishers Weekly*, May 16, 1994, 40.

10. Denise, who teaches yoga to cancer patients, quoted in McDonald, "The New Spirituality," 45.

11. McDonald, "The New Spirituality," 46.

12. See Taylor, "Desperately Seeking Spirituality," 57–58.

13. Ibid., 62–66.

14. McDonald, "The New Spirituality," 46.

15. Quoted in Taylor, "Desperately Seeking Spirituality," 68.

16. Quoted in ibid., 57.

17. McDonald, "The New Spirituality," 46–47.

18. Sam Keen, *Fire in the Belly: On Being a Man* (New York: Bantam, 1991), 47.

19. For corroboration of the racial and class-based nature of this constituency, see McDonald, "The New Spirituality," and Taylor, "Desperately Seeking Spirituality."

20. Fred Pfeil, *White Guys: Studies in Postmodern Domination and Difference* (London: Verso, 1995), 209.

21. Taylor, "Desperately Seeking Spirituality," 62. For an analysis of the false universality produced by capitalism as opposed to a true internationalism founded in the socialist movement, see Neil Lazarus, Steven Evans, Anthony Arnove, and Anne Menke, "The Necessity of Universalism," *differences* 7, no. 1 (1995): 75–145.

22. Keen, *Fire in the Belly*, 88.

23. Bob Summer, "Male Spirituality on the Move," *Publishers Weekly*, March 11, 1996. For an evaluation of the mainstream figures, in particular their responses to feminism, see Pfeil, *White Guys*, 167–85.

24. Robert Moore and Douglas Gillette, *The Warrior Within: Accessing the Knight in the Male Psyche* (New York: Avon, 1992), 148; Keen, *Fire in the Belly*, 89.

25. Moore and Gillette, *The Warrior Within*, 159–60.

26. Keen, *Fire in the Belly*, 30.

27. Ibid., 29.

28. Moore and Gillette, *The Warrior Within*, 121.

29. Ibid., 122.

30. Keen, *Fire in the Belly*, 31; Moore and Gillette, *The Warrior Within*, 153.

31. See Moore and Gillette, *The Warrior Within*, 121–31.

32. Ibid., 131.

33. Ibid., 156.

34. Keen, *Fire in the Belly*, 127.

35. For an excellent analysis of these new sensitive men, see Pfeil, *White Guys*, 37–70.

36. Sarah Lyall, "It's 'Forrest Gump' vs. Harrumph," *New York Times*, July 31, 1994, sec. 4, 2; Stuart Elliott, "'Gump' Sells, to Viacom's Surprise," *New York Times*, October 7, 1994, D1.

37. Richard Corliss, "The World According to Gump," *Time*, August 1, 1994, 53.

38. Janet Maslin, "Tom Hanks as an Interloper in History," *New York Times*, July 6, 1994, C9; Corliss, "The World According to Gump," 53.

39. David Denby, "Stupid Fresh," *New York*, July 18, 1994, 50.

40. Richard Corliss, "Hollywood's Last Decent Man," *Time*, July 11, 1994, 58.

41. Kevin Sessums, "Tom Terrific," *Vanity Fair*, June 1994, 148.

42. Corliss, "The World According to Gump," 54.

43. Jerry Adler, "'Tis a Gift to Be Simple," *Newsweek*, August 1, 1994, 58.

44. Winston Groom, *Forrest Gump* (New York: Pocket Books, 1994), 21. All further references will be noted in the text.

45. Maslin, "Tom Hanks as an Interloper in History," C14.

46. Corliss, "The World According to Gump," 53.

47. Ibid., 53.

48. Denby, "Stupid Fresh," 51.

49. Maslin, "Tom Hanks as an Interloper in History," C9.

50. Corliss, "The World According to Gump," 54.

51. Stuart Klawans, "Films," *Nation*, September 5/12, 1994, 250.

52. Ibid., 250.

53. Corliss, "The World According to Gump," 54.

54. Lyall, "It's 'Forrest Gump' vs. Harrumph," 2.

55. Quoted in Corliss, "The World According to Gump," 54.

56. Quoted in Lyall, "It's 'Forrest Gump' vs. Harrumph," 2.

57. As Denby points out, the running sequence contradictorily evokes the "Pied Piper religious whimsy of the hippie era that the rest of the movie is putting down." Denby, "Stupid Fresh," 51.

58. See, for example, Moore and Gillette, *The Warrior Within*, 131.

59. Keen, *Fire in the Belly*, 135.

60. Corliss, "The World According to Gump," 54.

61. Kaja Silverman, *Male Subjectivity at the Margins* (New York: Routledge, 1992), 198.

62. Ibid., 196.

63. Klawans, "Films," 250.

64. Bernard Weinraub, "Summer's Big Bangs Yield to Thoughts of Oscar," *New York Times*, September 10, 1996, C14.

65. Anthony Lane, "Master Blaster," *New Yorker*, May 20, 1996, 101.

66. Alexander Cockburn, "Beat the Devil: Bill's Tricks, Bill's Anchor Chain," *Nation*, June 17, 1996, 10.

67. David Denby, "Scenes from a Marriage," *New York*, May 27, 1996, 76.

68. Silverman, *Male Subjectivity at the Margins*, 198.

69. Keen, *Fire in the Belly*, 135.

70. Ibid., 121.

71. The film *Contact* also masculinizes its heroine, Ellie (Jodie Foster), by means of her intense dedication to science and rationality. Yet it is able pointedly to heterosexualize her (and resist associating her with lesbian cultural artifacts) in part because of the many rumors that Foster herself is lesbian. These rumors, then, effortlessly provide the subliminal lesbian associations that *Twister* must work actively to produce for Helen Hunt as Jo.

72. Stuart Klawans, "Barnum and Bill," *Nation*, June 10, 1996, 36.

73. Keen, *Fire in the Belly*, 148.

74. See ibid., 125–85.

75. Ibid., 165.

76. Ibid., 137.

77. Ibid., 147.

78. In 1990, Oklahoma had 252,400 Native Americans. *State and Metropolitan Area Data Book 1991* (Washington: U.S. Department of Commerce, 1991), Alabama–Wyoming 15. For a history of race relations in Oklahoma, see H. Wayne Morgan and Anne Hodges Morgan, *Oklahoma: A Bicentennial History* (New York: Norton, 1977).

79. Fredric Jameson, "Historicism in *The Shining*," in *Signatures of the Visible* (New York: Routledge, 1992), 96–97.

80. Michael T. Klare, "The New 'Rogue State' Doctrine," *Nation*, May 8, 1995, 625. See also Klare, *Rogue States and Nuclear Outlaws: America's Search for a New Foreign Policy* (New York: Hill and Wang, 1995).

81. Richard T. Barnet, "The Terrorism Trap," *Nation*, December 2, 1996, 18–19.

82. Quoted in ibid., 18.

83. Quoted in Klare, "The New 'Rogue State' Doctrine," 625.

84. Barnet, "The Terrorism Trap," 19.

85. Ibid., 19–20.

86. Ibid., 20.

87. Scott McLemee, "Public Enemy," *In These Times*, May 15, 1995, 16.

88. Moore and Gillette, *The Warrior Within*, 154.

89. Robert Moore and Douglas Gillette, *King, Warrior, Magician, Lover: Rediscovering the Archetypes of the Mature Masculine* (New York: HarperCollins, 1990), 93.

90. Keen, *Fire in the Belly*, 141.

91. Allen Ginsberg and Peter Orlovsky, *Straight Hearts' Delight: Love Poems and Selected Letters, 1947–1980*, ed. Winston Leyland (San Francisco: Gay Sunshine Press, 1980), 207.

92. Herbert Marcuse, *An Essay on Liberation* (Boston: Beacon, 1969), 4.

93. Ibid., vii.

94. Ibid., 57. Jürgen Habermas, the foremost contemporary proponent of enlightenment and of the necessity of completing the modernist project, emphasizes that one crucial aspect of "enlightenment is the irreversibility of learning processes, which is based on the fact that insights cannot be forgotten at will; they can only be repressed or corrected by better insights." Thus he militates—despite the contrary claims of men's spirituality or poststructuralist orthodoxies—in support of an "enlightenment [that] can only make good its deficits by radicalized enlightenment. . . ." Jürgen Habermas, *The Philosophical Discourse of Modernity: Twelve Lectures*, trans. Frederick Lawrence (Cambridge: MIT Press, 1987), 84.

INDEX

Abelard, Pierre, 16
Abelove, Henry, 281
Academy Awards, 161, 298
ACT UP (organization), 237, 280
Action (S. Shepard), 179, 185, 189–90, 345n.78
Acton, William, 14
Adorno, Theodor, 140
Afghanistan, 197, 198, 199, 201
Africa, 112, 194, 196–97
African Americans: caretaker role of, 251; cultural nationalism of, 284, 285–86, 288, 294; diasporic character of, 287; domestic terrorists and, 316, 317; economic status of, 192, 207; enslaved, 263, 271, 286; executive positions of, 206; female, 134, 135, 300–301; Fiedler on, 41, 65, 66; in *Forrest Gump*, 300–302; hippies and, 118–22; imaginary identification with, 300; legal status of, 193, 355n.45; Mailer on, 50–51, 52, 120; in masochistic fantasies, 33; men's movement and, 170, 196; music of, 122, 290, 328n.38; in *Oklahoma*, 314; in *On the Road*, 61–62, 188; performance penchant of, 252; photographs of, 353n.97; in Reconstruction Era, 156; sexual symbolism of, 215–16; spiritualized whites and, 318, 319; *Suicide in B-Flat* and, 180; suicides by, 157. *See also* Black Power movement; civil rights movement; "white Negro" concept
Ahmad, Aijaz: on Marxism, 258, 291–92; on nationalism, 283, 284; on poststructuralism, 348n.146; on socialism, 290
AIDS (disease): in *Angels in America*, 243, 252, 255–56; in *Forrest Gump*, 303; Fraser on, 294; indifference to, 236; in mass media, 233; in *Philadelphia*, 298. *See also* HIV infection
Alabama, 301, 304
Albee, Edward, 66, 259, 261, 288
Alfred P. Murrah Federal Building bombing (1995), 3, 5, 206, 209, 317
Algeria, 284, 285
Alien (film), 309
Allen, Karen, 215
Allen, Robert, 193
Allied Powers, 47

Althusser, Louis, 117
Altman, Dennis, 219, 350n.16
American Civil War, 263, 264
American Graffiti (film), 165
American Indians. *See* Native Americans
American Nazi Party, 121
American Renaissance, 264, 268, 269, 275
American Revolution, 262, 265, 266
Ames, Katrine, 161
Anderson, Benedict, 93, 263, 265, 268, 283
Anderson, Jack, 87
Andros, Phil, 234
Angels in America (Kushner), 241–62, 288, 297; capital amassed by, 279; on citizenship, 240, 259, 285; dissensus in, 273–74; economic systems and, 290; feminized positionality in, 32; *Forrest Gump* and, 305; historical order and, 272–73; humanism and, 291, 292; on migration, 286–87; Mormonism and, 265–70, 277; national vision and, 264; Queer Nation and, 243, 281–82, 283, 284; utopianism of, 275–76
"Angelus Novus" (Klee), 254
Ann Arbor, 120
Ansen, David, 161, 213
Antarctica, 294
Antigone (Sophocles/Hölderlin/Brecht), 143
Arab nationalism, 284
Arab states, 273
Aretino, Pietro, 19
Ariès, Philippe, 19
Aronowitz, Stanley, 111
Artaud, Antonin, 53; Beck and, 141–42, 150; Hoffman and, 148; Living Theatre and, 143, 144; Malina and, 146; performance theater and, 139
Ascham, Roger, 18
Asian religions: Beat writers and, 64; counterculture and, 114, 119, 128, 137; Ginsberg and, 83; new spirituality and, 294. *See also* Buddhism; Hinduism
Aubrey, John, 18
Austen, Jane, 26

Back to the Future (film), 165
Bakhtin, Mikhail, 107
Bakke, Allan, 5, 97, 192–93